THE ILLUSTRATED TRIP

THE ILLUSTRATED TRIP

with contributions from

Blair Jackson, Dennis McNally, Stephen Peters, and Chuck Wills

Penguin
Random
House

Managing Art Editor Louise Dick
Senior Designers Mabel Chan, Phil Gamble
Design Victoria Clark, Anita Ruddell, Jerry Udall, Emily Wilkinson
Additional Design Blue Island, Cooling Brown, Howells Design
DTP/Design Dean Scholey
Design Assistant Caroline Quiroga
DK India Aparna Sharma, Kavita Dutta, Shefali Upadhyay, Pallavi Narain

Managing Editor Jake Woodward
Senior Editors Victoria Heyworth-Dunne, Phil Hunt, David Lloyd
Editorial Assistant Michelle Crane
Editorial Consultants Kingsley Abbott, Ihor W. Slabicky

Picture Research Maria Gibbs
Production Manager Sarah Coltman
Production Controller Wendy Penn
Jacket Design Bob Warner
Jacket Editor Beth Apple
Background Art Mark Preston
Indexer Margaret McCormack

Editorial Direction Andrew Heritage
Art Direction Bryn Walls

First American Edition, 2003
This edition published in the United States in 2015 by
DK Publishing
345 Hudson Street
New York, New York 10014

Grateful Dead lyrics © Copyright Ice Nine Publishing Company, Inc.
Used with permission.
All Grateful Dead logos, official Grateful Dead artworks, and Grateful Dead
merchandise reproduced courtesy of Grateful Dead Productions.
Cover Art by Stanley Mouse © 2003 Mouse Studios, Inc.

Copyright © 2003, 2015 Dorling Kindersley Limited
A Penguin Random House Company

15 16 17 18 19 10 9 8 7 6 5 4 3 2 1
001—285067—June/2015

All rights reserved.
Without limiting the rights under the copyright reserved above, no part of this
publication may be reproduced, stored in or introduced into a retrieval system, or
transmitted, in any form, or by any means (electronic, mechanical, photocopying,
recording, or otherwise), without the prior written permission of the copyright owner.

Published in Great Britain by Dorling Kindersley Limited.

A catalog record for this book is available from the Library of Congress.

ISBN 978-1-4654-4008-2

DK books are available at special discounts when purchased
in bulk for sales promotions, premiums, fund-raising, or
educational use. For details, contact: DK Publishing Special
Markets, 345 Hudson Street, New York, New York 10014
SpecialSales@dk.com

Printed and bound in China

A WORLD OF IDEAS:
SEE ALL THERE IS TO KNOW

www.dk.com

Contents

PUBLISHER'S NOTE

The first task of anyone creating a book about the Grateful Dead is to humbly acknowledge those that came before. Online and in print, tireless scholars have toiled for years to chronicle the music, history, and subculture that grew up around the band; the Dead have been the subject of more insightful analysis and just plain good writing than any other rock group or performer. And the sole motivation, for most, is love of the Grateful Dead and the desire to preserve their legacy. Without these labors, the book you're holding would have been an impossible undertaking.

The backbone of the book is the Timeline, an encyclopedic entity that snakes throughout these pages and from which all entries and features hang. Every one of the band's 30 years together is covered page by page, month by month. And it continues until Summer 2003—the first project to bring the story completely up to date. In a work of this ambition, inevitably, there must be a disclaimer.

First, despite expert fact-checking and extensive research and cross-referencing, the freewheelin' nature of the subject and haziness around certain dates means that there may be some mistakes in this book. For any such errors, we apologize and encourage feedback for later editions.

Second, in the world of the Grateful Dead, there's no such thing as consensus. Wherever two Deadheads are gathered, there's likely to be three opinions on anything. Thus, the views expressed in this book about the relative merits of albums, shows, etc., are those of the contributors, and as the saying goes, your mileage may vary.

So, who did what? The project has been split between four extremely talented writers. Blair Jackson has superbly crafted many of the book's Biography boxes, some Scene boxes, and the picture captions. Dennis McNally has done a wonderfully thorough read-through and been the resident expert fact-checker. Between them, Blair and Dennis have also concocted the introductory essays to each section. Stephen Peters has provided fantastic insight into the albums of the Grateful Dead and also individual numbers—60-plus of these have been written up as Song features, a selection that is sure to cause endless debate. Chuck Wills has exhaustively researched and expertly written all of the Timeline entries, many of the Scene boxes, and a portion of Biography and Album boxes … and then some.

Ihor Slabicky—proto-taper, Dead scholar, and author of *The Compleat Grateful Dead Discography* (tcgdd.freeyellow.com)—has also done a superb job selecting over 220 Classic Shows "…based primarily on great music (long extended jams) and uniqueness, and secondly, or maybe even thirdly, on historical value." He expands, "Sometimes, I pared a whole run of shows down to one, really terrific, show; other choices are simply personal favorites. Perhaps my choices were very haphazard and irrational, but sometimes you have to be that way!" Ihor's selection is indicated throughout the book with a ★ next to the gig entry.

It would be unjust not to acknowledge the enormous support we have received from members past and present of the Dead's extended family, from photographers, and from Deadheads around the world. This book is a testimony to the enduring spirit of the Dead ethos.

On with the show. Welcome to *Grateful Dead: The Illustrated Trip*, a project that isn't meant to be a substitute for *DeadBase*, the *Taping Compendiums*, Deadlists.com, Deaddiscs.com *et al.*, but rather a celebration in pictures and words of a peerless group of musicians who have, quite simply, made a lot of people smile and dance.

"Let there be songs to fill the air..."

FOREWORD

When Ram Rod's house burned down, destroying the world's largest collection of firsthand Grateful Dead memorabilia, I silently congratulated myself on making the decision not to become a collector of our stuff. "Sic transit gloria mundi," I avowed. In the conflagration, every Grateful Dead poster ever struck got smoked if not crisped, along with annotated autograph working copies of songs he collected in the wake of our recording sessions. Enough T-shirts to outfit a festival.

Above: Robert Hunter, January 1991

Even so, I couldn't avoid accumulating a certain amount of stuff that came my way; stuff that molders in my basement. All I truly prize are the unknown number of cassette tapes, low-quality hand-held recorder variety, of composition sessions with Garcia. The joking and repartee of our working hours, the first hints of what were to become melodic motifs of the songs, the tap of the typewriter against a background of chords. The "Try this and see how it fits," and the "Yeah, that'll do, gimme some more of that." Funny thing I noticed: after a work session with Jerry playing my guitar, it tended to stay tuned for days.

If there's anything I wish I'd taken more trouble to save, it's the handwritten drafts of the songs, but their fate was often unkind and peremptory. They got cut up, verses sliced out and taped together toward the making of a complete copy. There were no word processors in those days to perform plebeian cut and paste routines. Once there was a word processor, the multiple handwritten drafts stopped; there was no need for them or the often remarkable doodles on the margins, the cigarette burns and wine stains, bits of meals long consumed, phone numbers, lists of possible rhyming words. Maybe there's a bit of the collector in me after all; lately I've been writing a few first drafts by hand again before transferring to word processor.

In the olden days, relics of saints, their very bones, were prized above all other collectibles; above their teachings, no doubt. Relics of the true cross abound, sufficient to crucify a small army of saviors. Could be that the urge to collect was part of the urge to become one, or as close as possible, to the spirit of the originator of the artifacts. The mania of collectors is a well-known phenomenon. In modern times, A.J. Weberman's dedicated rifling of Dylan's trash has become the stuff of legend. And God alone knows who possesses the originals of masterpieces such as the Mona Lisa. Counterfeits are well known to adorn the walls of the world's museums. It's pretty certain that La Gioconda in the Louvre is not the original of Leonardo's masterpiece, in fact not even the second or third counterfeit but possibly the sixth. I have a famous Picasso litho bought at a junk sale for fifty bucks that fooled the experts until someone at Sotheby's discovered that it was 1/32 of an inch too small around the borders. They said it was a sophisticated laser reproduction, replete with aged paper, watermarks, penciled signature, and signs of appropriate age. It still makes a fine thing to hang in the living room and I'm not yet a hundred percent convinced it's a fake. It just might have shrunk due to some odd geophysical phenomenon. Nor were the experts unanimous in the judgment. One said it was most probably counterfeit but such a good one he offered me five grand for it. Not my Picasso, pal. I love it as much as if it were genuine. I had a cheap copy of it on my wall for years, now I have a better one. So what makes an artifact "real"? Its undoubted authenticity or the pleasure it gives? The truth is, the intangible outweighs the tangible in the mind of the true collector.

So in dealing with memorabilia, we're dealing with intangibles in tangible dress. The wind of the West flutters our tie-dyed banners and wends its way, scented with patchouli and other herbal essence, through the darkness of the dominion, whispering ancient messages of hope and deliverance to receptive souls. A breath of it may turn the pages of this very book, left open on the mythic coffee table for which it was designed. What is like the wind? It bloweth where it listeth and none so broad as can contain it, or raise it by an act of will alone upon the scorched and barren land.

I wouldn't assert that the Grateful Dead sports the largest collection of rock memorabilia on the face of the planet. The Beatles probably outstrip us. But I'd say that more of it is arguably art than many can lay claim to. And it's probably unique in embodying varying aspects of a recognizable art movement, San Francisco psychedelia, specifically through the auspices of its chief architects: Kelley, Mouse, and Griffin in particular. The Grateful Dead and San Francisco '60s art are well-nigh indistinguishable, even when not specifically Dead related. Lithographs, being easily reproducible, are more amenable to distribution than bulkier artifacts such as Fab Four plastic figurines with spring-loaded heads, fuzzy Rolling Stones dice, or inflatable Madonna dolls.

Never heir to the profits of merchandising, cast into the outer darkness of subsistence on songwriting royalties (pass the biscuits, baby), I've taken an understandably jaundiced view toward the subject. This intro is my atonement. I've come to understand that the art movement that accompanied the rise of the Dead is as much a part of what we became in the public eye as the songs and the playing of them. Our twin logos (the "Bones & Bolts," a lightning bolt in a grinning skull, more popularly known as a "Stealie," that appeared as the album cover of *Steal Your Face*—"steal your money is more like it!" one critic said about that album—and the Skeleton & Roses logo) are far more familiar to the world at large than are the musical offerings. Bachelard, citing Roupnel, asks: "...what remains of the historical past, what lasts from it? Only that which has reasons for beginning again." Not allowing our tattered banners fall seems as good a reason as any.

And what if some of those banners are counterfeit? The accumulated stains and grime of time, gathered in the places they embellished, argues for authenticity in a larger sense. This book details not only the faces of the artifacts themselves, but the times and places in which the significant soil was accumulated.

If there had been no Grateful Dead, it would have been necessary to invent one. If this particular band of misfits had not happened to become the Grateful Dead, somebody else would've had to do it. Those kindred folk of the late sixties had their favorite bands, but they were the Grateful Dead. So, in one way or another, it had to be in that time, with a set of common attitudes, and maybe even the same name. The dictionary might have fallen open to "grateful dead" set off in a mystic light for some other group of nameseekers. Then they would have had to live and die these roles. And they would have needed to have resembled us: ill-shorn, perplexed, pissed off at the government, the record companies, military mindset, and bad TV. More inclined to try to change the world from outside than from within, we allied with no movement but our own and hence became one. Movement, that is. The detailed proof is contained in the record in your hands.

The spirit of the Grateful Dead is decidedly noncommercial, whereas merchandising is really nothing but, with however fine a shine. "It was the best butter, you know," said the Mad Hatter consulting the pocket watch which he'd lubricated with butter and which he declared to be right two times a day. The anti-commerciality of the Dead lent its artifacts paradoxical luster. We stood for something that was arguably a noble attitude, as far as those things go and as far as it went.

In the parking lot and fringes of gigs, an artisan culture sprouted up naturally, and just as naturally alerted the business world at large of the profits to be gained from rock tie-ins. In light of this annoying knowledge, our lawyers decided to shut down the artisans en toto because of the influx of true counterfeiters, merchandise companies who dumped great quantities of bad tie-dyes in our lot, due to our laissez-faire non-policy. The counterfeiters were overcome and the artisans responded by continuing to create the forms sans logo, or else using the trademarks surreptitiously. But the commercial dogs were unleashed. They're hard to train and don't differentiate. Trying to stop corporate commercialism resulted in the evolution of new product by artisans that was reminiscent of the feel if not the logocentricity of what was already in creation. Generic. That particular bad decision didn't stymie the growth of the art, only its Grateful Dead specificity. Without apology, that's how it went down. You see how it is. Conclusions to which we were led by the very system we tried to cut loose from.

Come hear Uncle John's Band
And buy a souvenir
That's how we afford the gas
To get our crazy asses here

Looking through this book, you'll find evidence of an authentic and diverse native culture, all the baggage of a self-defined cultural substratum requiring admittance to the larger sphere of agreement known as civilization. We have flags, a code of ethics, professorial dissertations aplenty attesting to our credibility—

Above: *The Grateful Dead shot by Herb Greene in 1967*

and a music both unique and universal in the familiar American roots we incorporated, or that, more accurately, incorporated us. Touched by rock, blues, folk, Miles, Coltrane, bluegrass, Beethoven, bop, and Berio (me by Eliot, Joyce, the Stanley Brothers, and Bobby Burns), we did what only we could do. Had there been a different Grateful Dead than us, the music and words would have been different, if to the same necessary effect. But what we were was the one it was, perhaps is; the prototype from which subsequent counterfeits are to be struck. And, as I argued above, who is to say at what point counterfeit becomes authentic? Just try to avoid our errors. Lay off the hard stuff.

The function of this presentation, cobbled of snapshots, dates, trivia, and artifacts, lies in its pointing to a precise ineffable toward which, in our better moments, we collectively aspire; to serve to remind us lest we forget. To evoke the happy land and its cheerful compatriots— a land of freedom, self-sufficiency, and trips into the unknown to see what music lies there. I suggest putting on an ancient bootleg tape of one of the '60s shows, hissing like the winds of space, while thumbing through it.

Robert Hunter

MAYBE IT'S BECAUSE SAN FRANCISCO is 3,000 miles from New England, with its judgmental Puritan associations; maybe it's a legacy of San Francisco's freewheeling first years as an American city, when the sleepy Mexican port town was transformed by hordes of raffish Yankee gold-seekers and the whores, thieves, traders, and gamblers that followed them; maybe it's down to the environment—the nearby redwood-clad hills, the beautiful bay, and the Mediterranean climate... Whatever the reasons, San Francisco has long had a reputation as a hospitable place for the unconventional.

As far back as 1859, one Joshua Norton arrived there and proclaimed himself "Norton I, Emperor of the United States and Protector of Mexico." Norton was a familiar sight on the streets for decades, wearing an elaborate uniform and paying for drinks and meals with his own "currency."

From the gold-rush onward San Francisco's easygoing intellectual atmosphere drew writers, artists, and musicians, many of them determinedly "Bohemian." There was writer Samuel Clemens, better known as "Mark Twain"; Bret Harte, with his tales of the mining camps; poet Joaquin Miller, the "Bard of the Sierras"; and Ambrose Bierce, pioneer of "psychological" fiction and compiler of *The Devil's Dictionary*. In the early 1900s came novelist Jack London, and Ina Coolbrith, California's first great woman writer.

San Francisco's literary bohemia centered on the Bohemian Club, founded in the early 1870s, and on the "Montgomery Block" at Montgomery and Columbus, which attracted writers, artists, and intellectuals. In 1959, the latter was razed to make way for that icon of contemporary San Francisco, the Transamerica Corporation's pyramidal skyscraper. In another irony, the Bohemian Club, with its famous "summer encampment" on the Russian River, has evolved into a bastion of the establishment—the writers and artists now replaced by industrialists and politicians.

> **"My visit to San Francisco is gradually drawing to a close, and it seems like going back to prison...after living in this Paradise."**
>
> LETTER FROM MARK TWAIN DURING HIS FIRST TRIP TO SAN FRANCISCO IN 1863

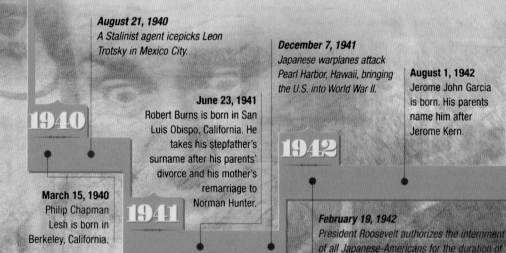

August 21, 1940
A Stalinist agent icepicks Leon Trotsky in Mexico City.

1940

March 15, 1940
Philip Chapman Lesh is born in Berkeley, California.

1941

June 23, 1941
Robert Burns is born in San Luis Obispo, California. He takes his stepfather's surname after his parents' divorce and his mother's remarriage to Norman Hunter.

December 7, 1941
Japanese warplanes attack Pearl Harbor, Hawaii, bringing the U.S. into World War II.

1942

August 1, 1942
Jerome John Garcia is born. His parents name him after Jerome Kern.

February 19, 1942
President Roosevelt authorizes the internment of all Japanese-Americans for the duration of the war—including more than 5,000 San Francisco residents—to prevent "sabotage."

1943

September 11, 1943
Mickey Hart is born in Brooklyn, New York.

Four-year-old Phil Lesh undergoes a musical epiphany during spring 1944 when he hears the opening bars of Brahms' First Symphony during a New York Philharmonic radio broadcast.

1944

March 19, 1944
Tom Constanten is born in Long Branch, New Jersey.

June 6, 1944
D-Day: Allied Forces land in Normandy, France.

April 30, 1945
Adolf Hitler commits suicide in his Berlin bunker as Soviet troops close in.

1945

February 14, 1945
Dresden, Germany, is destroyed in a firestorm caused by Allied bombing, an event Kurt Vonnegut (who witnessed the attack as a POW) will later memorialize in Slaughterhouse Five.

April 15, 1945
President Franklin Roosevelt dies of a stroke; Harry Truman becomes the new U.S. president.

Harry Bridges and the General Strike of 1934

The Bay Area attracted not only intellectuals and artists but also political and social activists, and the passions were not mutually exclusive. Author Jack London, for example, was an ardent socialist, while "muckraking" journalist and novelist Upton Sinclair ran for governor of California in 1934 with a socialistic program called EPIC (End Poverty in California).

The same year also saw one of the bitterest labor struggles in U.S. history played out in San Francisco. In May 1934 the fiery Harry Bridges led San Francisco's dockworkers out on strike to win recognition for the International Longshoremen's Association (ILA) and, in doing so, provoked a short-lived but violent general strike. Clashes between strikers and police, troops, "citizen's deputies," and other vigilantes took place daily. The ILA strike continued until both sides accepted arbitration, ultimately leading to recognition for the ILA, which later became the International Longshoremen's and Warehousemen's Union. In a neat piece of historical tidiness, Longshoremen's Hall, near Fisherman's Wharf, was built as the union's "hiring hall" and was a venue the Grateful Dead would play eight times in the '60s.

Tales of the infamous strike were still a staple at Joe Garcia's, the bar Jerry Garcia's mother ran at 1st and Harrison streets, from the late 1940s onward. No doubt Jerry also grew up hearing stories of the city's radical past from his maternal grandmother, Tillie Clifford, a union stalwart.

Right: The atomic bomb explodes over Hiroshima, signaling the end of World War II

The Founding of KPFA

Among the many events that lead to the establishment of the Bay Area Beat scene was the founding of KPFA, the first radio station of the Pacifica Foundation. The station went live on April 15, 1949, broadcasting from Berkeley on the then little-used FM band. Pacifica was conceived by Lewis Hill during World War II while he was confined in a camp for conscientious objectors. Lewis envisioned Pacifica as a radio community where all viewpoints could be freely espoused; to that end, Pacifica was (and is) completely noncommercial, supported by grants and by listeners themselves.

In its early years, KPFA programs included debates on the Korean War and anti-marijuana laws and poetry readings by Lawrence Ferlinghetti, Kenneth Rexroth, and others, occasionally running afoul of the FCC, the House Un-American Activities Committee, and similar bodies. The station quickly established itself as a forum for dissent and for broadening human understanding through the arts.

In the early '60s, Gert Chiarito's Saturday-night folk program, *The Midnight Special*, was a focal point for the Bay Area folk community, including Jerry Garcia, who appeared on the show *(see page 24)* in a hookup arranged by Phil Lesh, who volunteered as an engineer at the station.

Kenneth Rexroth

A key link in San Francisco's Bohemian-to-Beat-to Hippie chain, Indiana-born Kenneth Rexroth moved to San Francisco in 1927, and he remained in the Bay Area until his death in 1982. Rexroth's first love was painting but it was as a poet that he made his name in the '40s and '50s, with sensual, accessible verse that stood at the opposite end of the poetical spectrum from the academic dryness of T.S. Eliot and the obscurity of Ezra Pound. Philosophically, Rexroth both looked back to Whitman and the Transcendentalists and ahead to the Beats, promoting the transformative power of nature (he often camped in the Sierras), Asian religion and literature (he studied Buddhism and Taoism and translated Japanese and Chinese poetry), and constructive engagement with the world (a self-described enthusiast for "sex, mysticism, and revolution," he was involved in "radical" causes all his life, from the IWW to the anti–Vietnam War movement).

In the spring of 1947, Jerry loses most of the middle finger of his right hand in an accident while helping his brother Clifford ("Tiff") chop wood at the family's vacation cabin.

October 16, 1947
Bob Weir is born. Adopted as an infant, he is raised in Atherton, California.

October 1, 1949
Mao Zedong proclaims the People's Republic of China.

1947

1949

August 6, 1945
Hiroshima, Japan, is destroyed by a U.S. atomic bomb. Eight days later World War II is over when Japan surrenders.

August 22, 1945
Donna Jean Thatcher, the future Donna Jean Godchaux, is born in Muscle Shoals, Alabama.

1946

May 7, 1947
William Kreutzmann is born in Palo Alto, California.

August 25, 1947
Joe Garcia drowns in a fishing accident on the Trinity River in northern California. Jerry later claims that he witnessed his father's death, which is unlikely.

October 3, 1947
John Perry Barlow is born in Jackson Hole, Wyoming.

1948

July 19, 1948
Keith Godchaux is born in Concord, California.

May 7, 1945
Victory in Europe (VE) Day: Germany surrenders to the Allies.

September 8, 1945
Ronald McKernan is born in San Bruno, California.

January 30, 1948
A Hindu extremist assassinates Mahatma Gandhi.

May 14, 1948
The state of Israel is born.

Early Blues

The blues is defined by "blue" or "bent" notes that don't fit easily into the Western chromatic scale. It is a tradition rooted in the rural Southern African-American experience, so it's the music of the downtrodden—laments for lost freedom, for lost love, and a world where only hardship was guaranteed. Earliest direct ancestors of the blues were "field hollers"—rhythmic call-and-response chants—and the form evolved into a secular counterpart, especially in the deeply impoverished Mississippi cottonlands. After the Civil War the 12-bar-structure developed. The guitar overtook the banjo as chief blues instrument around the turn of the 20th century. W. C. Handy was the self-proclaimed "Father of the Blues" before World War I, while Bessie Smith and Ma Rainey sold many thousands of records on "race" labels like Vocalion in the 1920s.

In the South in the '20s and '30s bluesmen rambled from juke joint to juke joint playing on a Saturday night for a taste of bootleg whiskey and some folding cash, including legends like Lightnin' Hopkins, Charley Patton, Blind Lemon Jefferson, and Robert Johnson.

Meanwhile, hundreds and thousands of African Americans migrated north, especially to Chicago and Detroit. Acoustic guitars were inaudible in raucous nightclubs, so in the '40s bluesmen like Elmore James, Muddy Waters, and Howlin' Wolf began using amplified instruments and a rhythm section of bass and drums. The electrification of the blues was to inspire a generation of musicians, including the Dead, some 20 years later.

Below: The "deep blues" of Muddy Waters influenced a generation.

City Lights Bookstore

Many young poets relocated to San Francisco in the early 1950s. In '53, SF State professor Peter Martin started publishing a literary magazine, *City Lights* (the name was inspired by the great Charlie Chaplin film) from an office at Broadway and Columbus in the city's North Beach section. The same year, New York-born, Sorbonne-educated poet Lawrence Ferlinghetti joined Martin in opening a bookstore, City Lights, in the storefront. Originally an all-paperback bookstore—the first in the U.S.—City Lights quickly became the epicenter of the Beat Scene in the Bay Area. In '55, Ferlinghetti expanded City Lights' operations into book publishing with the *Pocket Poets* series; one of the first volumes in the series, Allen Ginsberg's *Howl and Other Poems*, resulted in a trial on obscenity charges, which Ferlinghetti won, in a major victory for freedom of expression. Ferlinghetti himself published his best-known verse collection, *A Coney Island of the Mind*, in 1958.

As of this writing, City Lights remains open in its original location—a still-vital literary landmark. Ferlinghetti was named poet laureate of San Francisco in 1998.

Above: Outside City Lights Bookstore: Neal Cassady, Allen Ginsberg, painter Robert LaVigne, and Lawrence Ferlinghetti. **Right:** Lawrence Ferlinghetti at City Lights.

August 14, 1951
William Randolph Hearst, the nation's most powerful newspaper publisher, dies.

1950

1951

June 25, 1950
North Korea invades South Korea; U.S. forces aid South Korea under the United Nations flag.

February 21, 1951
Vince Welnick is born in Phoenix, Arizona.

After a short-lived second marriage, Ruth Garcia marries a third time, to Wally Matusiewicz, and the family moves to suburban Menlo Park.

March 5, 1953
Josef Stalin, dictator of the Soviet Union for 25 years, dies.

June, 1953
The City Lights bookstore opens in San Francisco.

1952

July 27, 1953
An armistice ends the Korean War.

October 21, 1952
Brent Mydland is born in West Germany, where his serviceman father is stationed.

1953

January 20, 1953
Dwight D. Eisenhower begins his first term as president.

1950 - 1955

12

Laird Grant

When Jerry Garcia and his family moved from San Francisco to the more suburban environs of Menlo Park, the first buddy he made turned out to be a friend for life—Laird Grant. Together, they goofed through middle school, discovered the joys of pot and other substances, and shared many adventures. Grant was the band's first equipment manager/roadie, hauling gear from gig to gig (for no pay at first) and, once Owsley was on the scene as sound man, learning the ropes of an increasingly complicated sonic set-up. He accompanied the band on their first East Coast jaunt in the spring of 1967, but quit his job after the Monterey Pop Festival in June. Later, he was the stage manager at the Carousel Ballroom, and for most of the next decades he would be on the periphery of the Dead scene, doing odd jobs, such as carpentry for the Dead's office in San Rafael, helping Garcia build a small recording studio in his Stinson Beach house, etc. For Grant's thirtieth birthday, Garcia bought his buddy a piece of land in Mendocino County, where he still lives.

Right: Marlon Brando stars in the 1953 biker movie The Wild One, giving postwar pop culture its first great antihero.

Allen Ginsberg and Howl

"I saw the best minds of my generation destroyed by madness, starving hysterical naked, dragging themselves through the negro streets at dawn looking for an angry fix, angelheaded hipsters burning for the ancient heavenly connection to the starry dynamo in the machinery of night…" The opening of Allen Ginsberg's ecstatically harrowing long poem *Howl* sounded the tocsin for the Beat Generation; along with the publication of Jack Kerouac's *On The Road*, *Howl* transformed what had been a fringe literary and artistic movement into a phenomenon that would revolutionise

Hold back the edges of your gowns, ladies, we are going through hell.

—WILLIAM CARLOS WILLIAMS IN HIS
INTRODUCTION TO *HOWL AND OTHER POEMS*.

American culture and, indeed, create the countercultural soil from which the Grateful Dead would rise.

Born in New Jersey in 1926, Ginsberg became friends with the Beat "core group"—Jack Kerouac, Neal Cassady, William S. Burroughs, and associates—while attending Columbia University in the '40s. After a succession of odd jobs Ginsberg wound up in San Francisco, where he first unleashed *Howl* at the Six Gallery—a small space over a garage at 3119 Fillmore Street—on October 6, 1955. Organized and MC'd by Kenneth Rexroth, the first Six Gallery event included readings by Ginsberg, Gary Snyder, Michael McClure, and Philip Whalen, plus Philip Lamantia reading the work of the recently deceased John Hoffman. Subsequently enshrined in Beat legend, Ginsberg's emotive declamation of *Howl* stole the show: the intense young poet delivered the lines like a demented cantor, while Jack Kerouac sat at the edge of the stage, banging a jug of cheap wine on the floor and shouting, "Go! Go!"

Howl appeared in book form in March 1956 in *Howl and Other Poems* and the publisher, City Lights Press, was soon slapped with obscenity charges thanks to the poems' explicit sexual (and homoerotic) imagery. After a major trial, Judge Clayton Horn declared *Howl* not obscene, giving the poem and the poet massive publicity. Ginsberg's real offense to straight society, of course, was to laud dope fiends, lefties, homos, radicals, and other societal rejects in the era of Eisenhower and Joe McCarthy.

Ginsberg became not only perhaps America's most famous post-World War II poet but also the Grand Old Man of several iterations of American counterculture. He died in New York in April 1997.

November 25, 1954
Bruce Hornsby is born in Williamsburg, Virginia.

1954

1955

May 21, 1955
Chuck Berry records "Ida Red"; as "Maybellene," it's the first popular rock 'n' roll song.

May 12, 1954
Bill Haley and the Comets record "Rock Around the Clock."

July 18, 1955
Disneyland opens outside Los Angeles, California.

October 6, 1955
Six Gallery Reading.

October 1955
Another great antihero emerges in the form of James Dean as *Rebel Without a Cause* debuts.

1950 - 1955

13

The Flowering of Rock 'n' Roll

In May '55, "Rock Around the Clock" by Bill Haley and the Comets hit number one on the U.S. charts. The song had actually been released the previous year but went nowhere until it was included on the soundtrack of the juvenile-delinquent movie *Blackboard Jungle*. So 1955 is as good a year as any to designate as year zero for rock 'n' roll.

Like most genres of American popular music, rock 'n' roll emerged from a stew of influences, but the main ingredient was electrified urban blues, which by the late '40s had become—thanks to an expanded instrumental lineup and a pronounced backbeat—rhythm & blues. (The term "rock 'n' roll" comes from R&B slang for what a later generation would call "getting it on.") "Rock Around the Clock" may have announced the arrival of rock 'n' roll to mainstream (i.e., white) radio stations and record stores, but Louis Jordan, Joe Turner (the latter's "Shake Rattle and Roll" especially), and other artists had laid down the basic grooves by 1950.

Racial cross-pollination, too, in the form of country elements, led to the full mid-'50s flowering of rock 'n' roll. Chuck Berry melded bright, uptempo country guitar with the drive of R&B—and his original lyrics conjured up a world where rock 'n' roll spelled lighthearted teenage kicks. Also in 1955, Elvis Presley emerged from Memphis' Sun Studios to conquer America, and then the world. (It should be remembered that some of the King's early hits, including "Hound Dog," were covers of established R&B tunes.)

December 1, 1955
Rosa Parks refuses to move to the back of a segregated bus in Montgomery, Alabama, sparking a boycott of the city's public transport led by a young minister, Rev. Martin Luther King, Jr.

Left: The "brown-eyed handsome man": Chuck Berry.

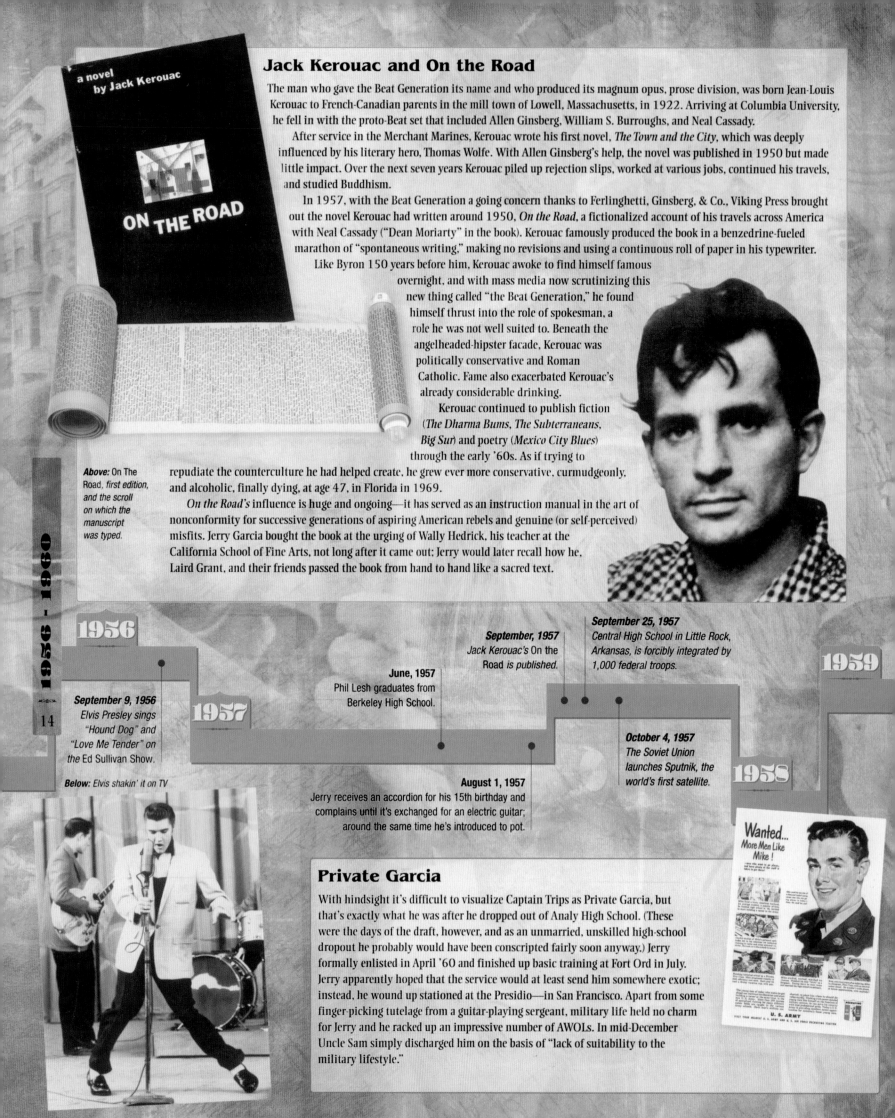

Jack Kerouac and On the Road

The man who gave the Beat Generation its name and who produced its magnum opus, prose division, was born Jean-Louis Kerouac to French-Canadian parents in the mill town of Lowell, Massachusetts, in 1922. Arriving at Columbia University, he fell in with the proto-Beat set that included Allen Ginsberg, William S. Burroughs, and Neal Cassady.

After service in the Merchant Marines, Kerouac wrote his first novel, *The Town and the City*, which was deeply influenced by his literary hero, Thomas Wolfe. With Allen Ginsberg's help, the novel was published in 1950 but made little impact. Over the next seven years Kerouac piled up rejection slips, worked at various jobs, continued his travels, and studied Buddhism.

In 1957, with the Beat Generation a going concern thanks to Ferlinghetti, Ginsberg, & Co., Viking Press brought out the novel Kerouac had written around 1950, *On the Road*, a fictionalized account of his travels across America with Neal Cassady ("Dean Moriarty" in the book). Kerouac famously produced the book in a benzedrine-fueled marathon of "spontaneous writing," making no revisions and using a continuous roll of paper in his typewriter. Like Byron 150 years before him, Kerouac awoke to find himself famous overnight, and with mass media now scrutinizing this new thing called "the Beat Generation," he found himself thrust into the role of spokesman, a role he was not well suited to. Beneath the angelheaded-hipster facade, Kerouac was politically conservative and Roman Catholic. Fame also exacerbated Kerouac's already considerable drinking.

Kerouac continued to publish fiction (*The Dharma Bums*, *The Subterraneans*, *Big Sur*) and poetry (*Mexico City Blues*) through the early '60s. As if trying to repudiate the counterculture he had helped create, he grew ever more conservative, curmudgeonly, and alcoholic, finally dying, at age 47, in Florida in 1969.

On the Road's influence is huge and ongoing—it has served as an instruction manual in the art of nonconformity for successive generations of aspiring American rebels and genuine (or self-perceived) misfits. Jerry Garcia bought the book at the urging of Wally Hedrick, his teacher at the California School of Fine Arts, not long after it came out; Jerry would later recall how he, Laird Grant, and their friends passed the book from hand to hand like a sacred text.

Above: On The Road, *first edition, and the scroll on which the manuscript was typed.*

1956

September 9, 1956
Elvis Presley sings "Hound Dog" and "Love Me Tender" on the Ed Sullivan Show.

Below: Elvis shakin' it on TV

1957

June, 1957
Phil Lesh graduates from Berkeley High School.

September, 1957
Jack Kerouac's On the Road *is published.*

September 25, 1957
Central High School in Little Rock, Arkansas, is forcibly integrated by 1,000 federal troops.

1959

October 4, 1957
The Soviet Union launches Sputnik, the world's first satellite.

1958

August 1, 1957
Jerry receives an accordion for his 15th birthday and complains until it's exchanged for an electric guitar; around the same time he's introduced to pot.

Private Garcia

With hindsight it's difficult to visualize Captain Trips as Private Garcia, but that's exactly what he was after he dropped out of Analy High School. (These were the days of the draft, however, and as an unmarried, unskilled high-school dropout he probably would have been conscripted fairly soon anyway.) Jerry formally enlisted in April '60 and finished up basic training at Fort Ord in July. Jerry apparently hoped that the service would at least send him somewhere exotic; instead, he wound up stationed at the Presidio—in San Francisco. Apart from some finger-picking tutelage from a guitar-playing sergeant, military life held no charm for Jerry and he racked up an impressive number of AWOLs. In mid-December Uncle Sam simply discharged him on the basis of "lack of suitability to the military lifestyle."

Wanted... More Men Like Mike!

Alan Trist

Fleeing the army for Palo Alto, Jerry Garcia met his lifelong friend, Alan Trist (born 1942), whose English father, a distinguished academic and head of the Tavistock Institute, was at Stanford. At the cool Palo Alto bookstore, Kepler's, Alan found Jerry playing his guitar at a table in the back, and they became instant "fixtures," Alan charmed by the "most gentlemanly bum" he'd ever met.

Alan was tweedy, enthusiastic and, for the literature-hungry Jerry, a resource, with his knowledge of Rimbaud, Dylan Thomas, and the Beats. For his part, Alan was inspired by the upbeat spirit of this scene in a generally despairing United States. Joined by Hunter, the friends circulated—Grace Cathedral to hear the Vatican organist play the complete Bach for organ, bizarre foreign films at the Cento Cedar, and coffeehouses.

Alan and Jerry were also injured in the spectacular car crash in February '61 that killed their friend Paul Speegle.

Rock 'n' Roll's Rocky Ride

Rock 'n' roll's cataclysmic period was between March '58 (when Private Presley was inducted into the army) and February '59 (when the plane carrying Buddy Holly, Richie Valens, and J.D. "The Big Bopper" Richardson crashed). In about the same timeframe, Jerry Lee Lewis lost many followers when he married his teenage cousin, while Little Richard left rock 'n' roll for the ministry. A car crash claimed Eddie Cochran (and maimed Gene Vincent) in '60, and two years later Chuck Berry got sent to the Big House on a morals charge. This Dark Age would end in '64 when the Beatles landed.

But many rockers graduated to other genres, like folk, which promised greater authenticity than commercial pop: in the '60s Jerry Garcia and friends dropped electrics for acoustics and began absorbing the country blues and ballads of the *Harry Smith Anthology (see page 23.)*

Right: "You ain't nothin' but a pri-vate!"

Right: Kennedy's election heralded a more optimistic time in America.

15

1960

May 1960
Phil Lesh's composition "Finnegan's Awake" is performed by the College of San Mateo's Jazz Band at the annual "Expressions in Jazz" concert.

June 1960
Phil Lesh graduates from College of San Mateo.

June 30, 1960
Alfred Hitchcock's chiller *Psycho opens.*

November 9, 1960
John F. Kennedy defeats Richard Nixon to win the presidency.

Below: The "Beatnik look" was widely mocked by mainstream America.

Grant Avenue: Tourist Trap

The fate of the Beats foreshadowed what would happen to the Hippies a decade later: a small, close-knit group who shied away from self-labeling, and who were more interested in self-expression than in changing the world, were inflated into a media phenomenon and, in the eternal American way, marginalized through commercialization. By the late '50s the stereotype was well-established in Mr. and Mrs. Straight America's mind: the beatnik wore a black turtleneck sweater, beret, and goatee, avoided gainful employment, and frequented dim basement clubs where he drank espresso and listened to poets free-associate to the accompaniment of bongo drums. Soon, sightseeing buses carried straights past the Beat landmarks of North Beach—the same way they would trundle tourists through Haight Ashbury in '67 *(see page 70).*

Eventually the Beatsploitation cooled. The true values of the original Beats—the importance of self-expression, the need for expansion of consciousness, rejection of conformity—would be absorbed by the generation born in the '40s and '50s, the Baby Boomers. And the boomers, as Hippies, would inculcate these values into American society as a whole.

In truth, the distinction between the Beats and the Hippies was simply a few years and a few points of style. So it's fitting that the two eldest members of the preeminent hippie band, the Grateful Dead, spent their formative years at the height of the Beat phenomenon in San Francisco—"picking up basic beatnik chops," as Jerry Garcia later put it.

THE GOLDEN ROAD

January 1961 – October 1965

Switching from the anarchic acoustic folk and blues of Mother McCree's Uptown Jug Champions to start an electric band in the middle of 1965 "was Pigpen's idea," Garcia said. "He'd been pestering me for a while—he wanted me to start up an electric blues band. That was his trip…" Pigpen had been listening to both acoustic and electric blues since boyhood, but in 1964 there was a contemporary influence at work. The Beatles—clean-cut, charming, and pop—had been followed in the British Invasion by a new band, which was none of those things. The Rolling Stones looked and sounded rawer and much more blues-based, and their first album had deeply impressed Pigpen, who told Garcia, "We can do

---

The Warlocks clown around for photographer Herb Greene near Ocean Beach in San Francisco, 1965. "Beatle boots" were all the rage, but the future Dead always had more Rolling Stones than Beatles in them.

this!" His rap worked. Garcia continued, "[So] theoretically it's a blues band, but the minute we get electric instruments it's a rock 'n' roll band because, wow, playin' rock 'n' roll is fun! Pigpen, because he could play some blues piano and stuff like that, we put him on organ immediately, and the harmonica was a natural, and he was doing most of the lead vocals at the time."

It's not quite accurate to say that the Warlocks and the first incarnation of the Grateful Dead were "Pigpen's band" exactly, but there's no question that he was a primary focal point for the group, especially during their first couple of years, when so much of their repertoire was R&B and blues cover tunes. As Garcia noted, "He was the guy who really sold the band, not me or Weir… Pigpen is what made the band work."

To say the least, shy and homely Ron McKernan was an unlikely rock star. But he was born into the blues, you might say. In the late '40s and early '50s his father, Phil, was a disc jockey known as "Cool Breeze" on the most popular blues and R&B radio station in the Bay Area, and when Ron was growing up, their Palo Alto home was filled with records his dad brought home. Ron never liked school and didn't fit in socially with the mostly white student populace—he was more comfortable hanging out with black friends from across the freeway in East Palo Alto. By his early teenage years he was drinking cheap screw-top wines, in part to emulate his blues heroes.

Dave McQueen, who was one of the East Palo Alto crowd that befriended Pigpen, tells a typical story about the teenage Ron McKernan: "I had an 'in' with the owner of the Choo-Choo Inn, a black honky-tonk on the tracks in San Mateo, through Lester Hellum, who would sit in with the house band. T-Bone Walker was going to play there and Ron heard about it from one of the corner kids. Ron was spending more time in East P.A. than he was at home at that point. Anyway, he came to me like any normal rotten teenager when he really wants something he can't scheme on alone, so I talked to the owner and got him a table right up front. T-Bone stood there and played right in front of him the whole night. Ron was in heaven! At the end he said to T-Bone, 'See you in 20 years, Mr. Walker!' He talked about it for weeks."

Garcia and McKernan were the first of the future Grateful Dead to hook up, probably in 1961—Garcia was fresh out of the army, jobless, and living hand-to-mouth in Palo Alto. Ron was 16, dropping out of high school. "I was the only person who played any blues on the guitar, so he hung out with me," Garcia remembered. "And he picked it up, just by watching and listening to me, the basic Lightnin' Hopkins stuff. Then he took up the harmonica and everyone called him Blue Ron'—the black people anyway... All the black people loved Pigpen. They loved that he played the blues. He wasn't like a white boy trying to be black." Or as their mutual friend Laird Grant said, "He wasn't white. He had no color."

Ron's unkempt appearance earned him the Pigpen nickname (after a character in the "Peanuts" comic strip), and though he didn't care for it at first, the name stuck—according to Garcia, even Ron's mother called him

"He'd get encouragement from the band and from the audience and then there was no holdin' back, because it fed on itself; he started to create his own style. Here's Pig, down and dirty, talkin' about the basics: gettin' laid."

BOB MATTHEWS TO BLAIR JACKSON, *1993*

Pigpen at times. Garcia and Pigpen were both part of the same burgeoning (but modest) folk music scene on the Peninsula in the early '60s; occasionally they even shared the stage together, Garcia backing up Pig while he sang the blues. Their social circles also overlapped; both were drawn to bohemian types— artists, jazz and folk musicians, people who were living outside of, or on the fringes of, "straight" society. And though Garcia spent most of 1962 to early '64 diving seriously into various white acoustic music styles, playing in a succession of short-lived old-time and bluegrass groups, he stayed friendly with Pigpen and occasionally even played some blues and rock 'n' roll with him as pickup members of an electric group called The Zodiacs, who gigged at local parties. Then, when a young acquaintance of Garcia's named Bob Weir approached Jerry about joining a jug band he and some high school classmates were forming, Garcia brought Pigpen along to the first rehearsal. Mother McCree's Uptown Jug Champions played irregularly around the Bay Area for about a year beginning in late January 1964, with the front line of Garcia, Weir and Pigpen augmented by an ever-shifting cast of whoever-was-around-for-the-gig—founding member Bob Matthews (later the Dead's sound engineer) estimated 20 different people played with the band at one time or another. The repertoire was gloriously eclectic—country blues and urban blues, jug band tunes, R&B, novelty songs, some rock 'n' roll; almost anything was fair game.

But when Pigpen convinced Garcia to start an electric band, that was a different kind of commitment, and it called for some new players. Weir was into the change, and signed on as rhythm guitarist and vocalist. For drums they recruited a hot young player who'd been teaching at the same music store where Jerry worked, Bill Kreutzmann. The bass slot went to the son of the music store owner, Dana Morgan, Jr., though he would quickly be replaced by musical brainiac but novice bassist Phil Lesh, a friend of Garcia's. This was the Warlocks: "We were kind of patterned after the Rolling Stones," Garcia said. "This was during the British Invasion... [and] me and Pigpen both had that background in the old Chess records stuff—Chicago Blues like Howlin' Wolf and Muddy Waters, and people like

Jimmy Reed, Chuck Berry. It was real natural for us, and we even did those kinds of tunes in the jug band. So it was an easy step to make it into a sort of proto–blues band… Pigpen was the perfect front-man, except that he hated it; getting him to do it was really a bitch."

Nevertheless, Pigpen took naturally to the spotlight, and even behind his shrill Vox Continental organ—and later, the warmer Hammond B-3 favored by one of his idols, Jimmy Smith—he was a completely commanding presence on stage, digging into the deep blues of songs like Slim Harpo's "King Bee" and Elmore James' "It Hurts Me Too," and whipping the crowd into a frenzy with his remarkable vocal improvisations on Wilson Pickett's "Midnight Hour" and one of the band's first great original songs, "Caution." He could switch roles at the drop of a hat—testifyin' preacher second, lecherous back door man the next; he sold each equally well. From time to time, too, Pig would leave his keyboard and go out to center stage and lay down a rap in front of the band: "He had great stage presence," Garcia said. "Out in front of the crowd he could work the band, and he'd really get the audience going. He always had more nerve than I could believe. He'd get the audience on his side, and he'd pick somebody out—like a heckler—and get on them. He'd crack us up. Sometimes he'd just kill me!"

"I think a lot of it came from listening to contemporary music and creating his own licks out of it," said Bob Matthews of Pigpen's amazing extemporaneous rambles. "Wilson Pickett, James Brown—all these guys had their little raps, and while they didn't go on as long as Pigpen's, if you went to their shows you'd find out they went a lot longer than the four bars on the record. With Pigpen it started with 'Midnight Hour,' I guess. He saw [other singers do it], and then the Grateful Dead gave him the opportunity to try it: what better vehicle could you get for stretching out? Pig wants to stretch out? Great! You'd find the rest of them right there giving him every opportunity and encouragement. He'd get encouragement from the band and from the audience and then there was no holdin' back, because it fed on itself; he started to create his own style. Here's Pig, down and dirty, talkin' about the basics: gettin' laid."

Grateful Dead manager Danny Rifkin thought of Pigpen as "the most dynamic-appearing character of the whole group. I remember one of those early gigs, we had these big Voice of the Theater speakers and I hurt my back carrying them. I remember standing in front of Pigpen at

this gig and he blew my mind—he kind of made me dance and got my back healed; it was that kind of experience. He had an almost shamanic quality; kind of a revival tent meeting type of thing. I liked those grooves— 'Midnight Hour,' 'Good Morning Little Schoolgirl,' 'Love Light'—kind of tribal, primal, great to dance to. Pigpen had a nice round voice and he played the crowd like a preacher."

Of course, after the Warlocks became the Grateful Dead at the dawn of the Acid Tests in the fall of 1965, the group took on a new and different personality, gathered from such disparate sources as the expansive jazz of John Coltrane and Miles Davis, Indian classical music. More dramatically, the band's own experimentation with psychedelics began to exert more influence on their music. Pigpen never cared for psychedelics (or pot, for that matter)—he was always a juicer; in that way he was similar to Big Brother singer Janis Joplin, with whom he had a brief but torrid affair in the summer of '66. "I think his self-perception was the blues life," said Danny Rifkin. "He kind of spoke black English vernacular, had a black girlfriend [Veronica Barnard], played the blues, drank wine. He was definitely of a different consciousness than the rest of us."

As Garcia, Lesh, and Weir started to write more original material in 1967, stretching the conventional pop song form as if it were Day-Glo elastic, Pigpen increasingly found it difficult to keep up with the complex rhythm and tempo shifts of the band's new music. Although a rudimentary organist, Pigpen didn't really work at his craft, and the band's long, stoned rehearsals frankly left him cold. The changes in the Dead's music during this period really happened in spite of Pigpen, not with him. Amazingly enough, though, the other players didn't really expect Pigpen to come along on their acid-fueled interstellar flights. They liked him just fine the way he was, (which doesn't mean that they didn't try to dose him from time to time), and appreciated what he brought to the band and its sound.

According to the Dead's other manager during that era, Rock Scully, "No matter how screwed up on LSD and how crazy it got for us, you could always look to Pigpen to bring you down to Earth and be there for you. Even musically, when the band was going way, way out in 'Dark Star,' they knew they could listen to Pig and have some sense of where they were. So he was reliable in that way. You knew he wasn't seeing snakes. When Garcia's guitar turned into a snake, Pigpen saw it as a guitar, and Jerry could rely on him to do that."

"He was our anchor," Garcia agreed. "We'd be out of our minds—just ZOWWWGOINNNNNGG!—and we'd be tethered to Pigpen. You could rely on Pigpen for a reality check: 'Hey man, is it too weird, or what?' And he'd say, 'No, man, it's cool.' Everybody used him on that level. He was like gravity. Hells Angels would be sitting around a room fucked up on acid and Pigpen would be taking care of them! It was so great. Pigpen was like a warm, cozy fire."

The Dead's rapidly growing fan base never seemed concerned about whether Pigpen was fitting in with the group's new direction, either. They knew that in the midst of all that weirdness and abstraction and dissonance, Pigpen would suddenly appear, all macho bravado and swagger, grab the reins, and suddenly the band would settle into the groove of Howlin Wolf's "Smokestack Lightning," or Junior Parker's "Next Time You See Me," or the song that became Pigpen's big showstopper in the late '60s, Bobby "Blue" Bland's "Turn On Your Love Light." A Dead show could've gone in a hundred different directions over the course of a night, but usually it wasn't truly over until Pigpen said it was, raising the roof with "Love Light" or "Midnight Hour" or, if they were taking the spacey route, his own masterful contribution to the early Dead canon, "Alligator" into the locomotive craziness of "Caution," which often ended in a cacophonous wash of ear-splitting feedback.

In the Haight-Ashbury district, where the band moved in the fall of 1966, Pigpen was a beloved local celebrity. He was depicted on the first Grateful Dead t-shirt—his greasy, benevolent biker image worked neatly with the group's puzzling moniker—and he could occasionally be found holding court on the front steps of the band's pad at 710 Ashbury Street. Jon McIntire, who would later help manage the Dead, recalled, "Pigpen was real open and friendly. There was

"He was the guy who really sold the band, not me or Weir... Pigpen is what made the band work." JERRY GARCIA TO BLAIR JACKSON, *1993*

already enough 'star' vibe around Garcia and a glamour vibe around Bobby, and he was kind of spaced because he was a macrobiotic type, and Phil was not living at 710. But Pig was real open and available and a lot more immediately warm, to me anyway, than the other guys were. I think that was a relatively common reaction for folks who weren't already friends with all of them."

Pigpen had his own set of friends, too, and he entertained them endlessly at 710, sitting around telling funny stories or playing blues on an acoustic guitar in the kitchen or in his room, which Weir described as "a dark little cave." "It was The Pigpen Show," Bob Matthews joked. "He'd be the host."

Garcia recalled, "You'd go in there and there might be half a dozen hippies and some black people hanging out, drinking wine and listening to Pigpen doing whatever he was doing...People would be hanging on his every word. He was so clever. He'd be making up songs with these hilarious words he'd make up on the spot!"

Pigpen played a somewhat cheesy-sounding Vox Continental organ (above) *for a couple of years; then he switched to the warmer tones of the Hammond B-3, an instrument favored by his idol Jimmy Smith.*

By the fall of 1968, the original quintet was a septet, with the addition of second drummer Mickey Hart and keyboardist Tom Constanten, a friend of Phil's who was brought in to navigate the band's more challenging original music. Pigpen's musical role was diminished considerably, especially on albums, but he continued to be a major force in the band's shows.

In the early '90s, Garcia defended Pigpen's position on the way the Dead were going: "It seemed like we were heading some [musical] place and Pigpen just wasn't open to it. It's not that he couldn't have cut it; he actually could have dealt with it. He had the musicality to deal with it. He was a real musical guy; he was innately musical. But you know, the other thing is we were sort of off on a false note, you know what I mean? We were doing something that was forced; it wasn't really natural.

We were doing music that was self-consciously weird. If we had paid more attention to Pigpen, it probably would have saved us a couple of years of fucking around."

There are many Deadheads who would certainly not agree with that bit of revisionism from Mr. Garcia, but the fact is there was something magnificently earthy, soulful, and real about what Pigpen brought to the band, from his first days in the jug band to the last notes he would sing with the group in mid-1972. The band would scale unbelievable heights without Pigpen, who died on March 8, 1973, but there's no doubt Garcia was being completely sincere when he said, in 1988, "Really, it hasn't felt quite right since Pigpen's been gone. But on the other hand, he's always been around a little. He hasn't been entirely gone."

Friday January 20
President John F. Kennedy takes the oath of office as the nation's 35th (and second-youngest) president, with an inaugural address that calls on Americans to "Ask not what your country can do for you—ask what you can do for your country."

Sunday February 19
Leaving a party at the Chateau, Jerry Garcia, Alan Trist, artist Paul Speegle, Jr., and Chateau "manager" Lee Adams go for a drive in Adams' Studebaker. Adams takes a curve too fast and the car somersaults into a field. Speegle is killed instantly; Adams and Trist are seriously hurt; Jerry goes through the windshield but escapes with a broken collarbone and bruises. The accident has a profound effect on Garcia.

Robert Hunter takes in a performance of *Damn Yankees* at Palo Alto's Commedia Dell'Arte Theatre and meets one of the show's lighting techs—Jerry Garcia. Garcia introduces Hunter to Trist a few days later. The trio's first adventure was a jaunt to Berkeley in an unsuccessful attempt to find a theater showing the animated movie version of George Orwell's *Animal Farm*.

Wednesday March 1
President Kennedy launches the Peace Corps, in which Americans (mostly idealistic young ones) will go to "undeveloped" countries to provide educational, technical, and other assistance.

For a time Jerry Garcia and Robert Hunter live in their cars, surviving on canned pineapple swiped by Hunter from army stores during his National Guard service, and trading guitar licks.

Monday April 17
A U.S.-backed force of Cuban exiles lands at the Bahia de Cochinos (Bay of Pigs) on the coast of Cuba in an effort to overthrow the rule of the island nation's communist leader, Fidel Castro. The invasion proves a humiliating failure.

Thursday May 4
Civil-rights activists dubbed "Freedom Riders" leave Washington, D.C. for New Orleans in a campaign to integrate racially segregated interstate facilities in the South. The ride ends in Alabama with firebombings and beatings from irate whites.

Friday May 5
Billed as "Bob & Jerry," Jerry Garcia and Robert Hunter play their first paying gig—for $5.00—at the eighth-grade graduation festivities for Menlo Park's Peninsula School. Later in the month the short-lived duo performs its second, and final, gig, a student party at the Arroyo Room at Stanford.

Above: Another fortuitous meeting at Kepler's: Rodney Albin asks Garcia to perform at his newly opened coffeehouse, the Boar's Head. Garcia leaves to spend some time in San Francisco with his girlfriend, Barbara Meier, but takes up Albin's offer on his return.

"A guy who was part of our social scene then, Paul Spiegel [sic], who was a painter—and really the most talented person in our scene—got killed in this accident... I had this feeling that my life had been spared to do something... I felt that whatever, it's important not to take any bullshit, to either go the whole hog or not at all."
JERRY GARCIA IN DAVID GANS'S *CONVERSATIONS WITH THE DEAD*.

Palo Alto

If any community can claim pride of place in the birth of the Dead, it's Palo Alto. Home to about 50,000 people in 1960, Palo Alto was both a bedroom community (in this case, for San Francisco, about 40 miles to the north) and a well-heeled city in its own right, with ample cultural amenities and urban sophistication, the latter qualities greatly enhanced by the presence of prestigious Stanford University. (And, as with all university towns, Palo Alto had a long-standing bohemian scene.) The city's population grew by about 20 percent in the Baby-Boom 1950s, most of the newcomers being professional families attracted by the city's beautiful setting, excellent schools, and general light-washed northern California ambiance. As with many American cities, Palo Alto is twinned with a less affluent (and largely African-American) community, East Palo Alto. Major stops on the Grateful Dead Historical Trail would include:

Kepler's Book Store

Actually located in neighboring Menlo Park, Kepler's was owned by Roy Kepler, a social activist and pacifist who had helped set up both the nearby Peninsula Peace Center and the Berkeley public-radio station KPFA. Kepler's was the kind of place where Beat poets like Lawrence Ferlinghetti did readings, the shelves held mostly well-thumbed paperbacks, and students, musicians, and other indigent intellectual types could just hang out all day. Jerry Garcia met several people at Kepler's who would be key to the formation and continuation of the Grateful Dead, including Willy Legate, probably the first person in Garcia's social circle to take LSD, and Alan Trist, an Englishman who would later run Ice Nine,

the band's publishing operation. Jerry also picked up some money by working around the store.

"Kepler's had a back room. If I recall correctly, the room was divided. One half had books about halfway up the wall. Then it had this area that had tables, chairs, and a coffee machine. It wasn't a coffeehouse. It was just a reading area but some people like Garcia had taken it over and started bringing their instruments and playing."
PETER ALBIN IN ROBERT GREENFIELD'S *DARK STAR: AN ORAL BIOGRAPHY OF JERRY GARCIA*

St. Michael's Alley

The coffee house of choice for the Kepler's crowd was St. Michael's Alley on Palo Alto's University Avenue. "St. Mike's" was already something of a musical landmark in '61, since the newly crowned queen of folk music, Joan Baez, had performed there regularly as a high-school student.

The Chateau

The third pole of the Palo Alto area hipster scene in '61 was a rooming house known as the Chateau, which, like Kepler's, was actually in Menlo Park, just off Sand Hill Road. A sprawling three-story manse, the Chateau was owned by an artist, Frank Serratoni, who rented out rooms to a young coterie of students, artists, and uncategorizable eccentrics of the type later labeled as "hippie." Besides serving as a refugee camp for dropouts from the crew-cut, clean-cut America of the New Frontier era, it was the scene of frequent parties that attracted kindred souls from the Peninsula and beyond.

The Boar's Head

Run by Rodney Albin and George Howell, the Boar's Head was another link in the chain of Bay Area coffeehouses that incubated the Grateful Dead and many other Bay Area bands. The Boar's Head was located in a loft above the San Carlos Book Stall, another hip bookstore just outside of Menlo Park.

"The Boar's Head was no bigger than fifteen by twenty [feet]. People would gather on Friday and Saturday nights. We had a little stage with maybe a foot-high riser tucked in the corner. The place could hold no more than twenty-five people, but it was packed… It was an open-mike scene: two, three songs, pass the hat."
Peter Albin in Robert Greenfield's Dark Star: An Oral Biography of Jerry Garcia.

Bobby Petersen

One of Phil's closest friends during his pre-Warlocks days on the Peninsula, Bobby Petersen (born 1936) was an unusual character—a diminutive, gnomelike bohemian who lived hard and fast, rarely had two dimes to scrape together, but had the soul (and skills) of a poet. "He was a mad beatnik poet," Phil said, "a road character and a storyteller; a road pirate, actually." Lesh credited Petersen for turning him on to pot when they lived together in the early '60s, and later Petersen supplied the lyrics for three of Lesh's recorded Grateful Dead songs: "New Potato Caboose" (1967), "Pride of Cucamonga" (1974) and, greatest of all, "Unbroken Chain" (1974). A fourth song, 1986's "Revolutionary Hamstrung Blues" was performed once by the Dead but never recorded. A book of Petersen's poetry, *Alleys of the Heart*, was published in 1988.

A former schoolmate of Jerry Garcia's, Marshall Leicester, arrives home for summer vacation from Yale and encounters Jerry holding court at Kepler's. A talented banjo and guitar player, Leicester helps Garcia develop his fingerpicking style and broadens his knowledge of the folk and bluegrass canon.

Phil Lesh graduates from the College of San Mateo and shortly thereafter meets Tom "T.C." Constanten. The two bond immediately when Lesh overhears T.C. pontificating that "Music stopped being created in 1750, but it started again in 1950." Lesh and T.C. move in together and both enroll at UC Berkeley, the latter to study astronomy.

Saturday November 18
A tape made at the Chateau during a party dubbed the "Groovy Conclave" includes Garcia performing "Matty Groves," the mournful murder ballad "The Long Black Veil," and Hoyt Axton and Ken Ramsey's "Greenback Dollar"—a chart hit for the Kingston Trio in 1963. Among the other groovers are Phil Lesh and Tom Constanten.

DECEMBER '61

NOVEMBER '61

18

JUNE '61

Throughout the summer of '61, Garcia, Hunter on bass and mandolin, and Marshall Leicester (on banjo and autoharp) play at the Boar's Head. At least one tape from the period exists, probably made by Rodney Albin; the set includes the Carter Family's "Wildwood Flower" and another hootenanny standby, "Darling Corey."

During this period, Rodney Albin and his brother Peter, Ellen Cavanagh, and Ron McKernan perform as the Second-Story Men. Not yet dubbed "Pigpen", McKernan goes by the handle "Blue Ron."

Alan Trist returns to England and Marshall Leicester goes back to Yale. Around the same time, Jerry Garcia meets Phil Lesh, though the exact where-and-when of the meeting is, like so many events of this period, subject to varying accounts.

Roger Maris of the New York Yankees hits 61 home runs in a single season, breaking the record Babe Ruth set in 1927. Jerry Garcia moves into the Chateau—or rather into a car on the grounds. Eventually he takes residence in a dirt-floored space that was once a root cellar. The house's denizens now also include Robert Hunter, who is working on a novel he plans to title *The Silver Snarling Trumpet*; Jerry's old friend Laird Grant is camped out (literally) nearby.

OCTOBER '61

SEPTEMBER '61

29

JULY '61

21

AUGUST '61

Friday July 21
Astronaut Alan Shepard becomes the first American in space with a 15-minute sub-orbital flight from Cape Canaveral, Florida.

Below: Jerry Garcia and Robert Hunter played a handful of local gigs as "Bob and Jerry."

Friday September 29
The career of Bob Dylan (born Robert Zimmerman in Hibbing, Minnesota) is kickstarted by Robert Shelton's New York Times review of his run at Gerde's Folk City in Greenwich Village.

The Harry Smith Anthology

One of the primary sources for Marshall Leicester, Garcia, and Hunter—and for every aspiring folk musician of the time—was the *Anthology of American Music*, known as the "Harry Smith Anthology" after its "editor." Smith, an original Beat scenester, collected 84 78-rpm records, recorded and released between 1927 and 1932 but largely forgotten, put them onto six newfangled "long-playing" records, and brought out the *Anthology* on Folkways Records in 1952.

In a sense, the collection was a bootleg—probably the most important bootleg in the history of American music. The songs included everything from Cajun dances to Gospel shouts, and from Delta blues to Appalachian ballads; the performers ranged from the Carter Family and Blind Lemon Jefferson to Hoyt Ming and his Pep Steppers and the Alabama Sacred Harp Singers.

The *Anthology* quickly became, in critic Greil Marcus's phrase, "the founding document of the American folk revival," studied in dorms and suburban basements from Boston to Berkeley. (Garcia and Hunter, too poor to buy a copy, made do with a friends'; Jerry reportedly played the songs at 16 rpm to work out the fingering.) Many *Anthology* songs became staples for the most famous folk revivalists; Joan Baez recorded no fewer than nine, and if anyone you know has doubts about the *Anthology*'s influence on Bob Dylan, play them the Bently Boys' "Down on Penny's Farm," then put on "Maggie's Farm" from *Bringing it All Back Home*.

The *Anthology* was commercially unavailable for many years, but in 1997 Smithsonian Folkways reissued it on CD as the *Smithsonian Anthology of American Folk Music* to a rapturous reception—six years after Harry Smith died, broke.

As his interest in bluegrass deepens, Jerry Garcia and others in his musical circle frequently travel to the Ash Grove, an L.A. club that attracts a lot of touring folk and bluegrass acts. At the Ash Grove he meets a local bluegrass band, the Country Boys, who subsequently change their name to the Kentucky Colonels. Jerry later credits the Colonels' guitarist, Clarence White, as a major influence on his style.

Having dropped out of Berkeley, Lesh and T.C. manage to get themselves into a composition course being taught by Luciano Berio at Mills College in Oakland.

Garcia meets aspiring fiddler Ken Frankel at Lundberg's Fretted Instruments in Berkeley. Frankel, Garcia, Hunter (mandolin), and Joe Edmiston (banjo) coalesce as the Thunder Mountain Tub Thumpers, supplemented occasionally by Jim Edmisten (bass), Marshall Leicester, and other members of the Bay Area folk scene.

JANUARY '62

Luciano Berio

Born in Oneglia, Italy, in 1925, Berio was deeply influenced in the 1950s by serialism and the pioneering electronic music of Karlheinz Stockhausen, but his own early compositions went beyond the confines of academic "avant-garde" music to include settings of folk songs and works based around the writings of James Joyce and e.e. cummings. During his time at Mills, Berio mentored a remarkable group of Bay Area artists, including Steve Reich, later famous for brilliant "minimalist" works like 1988's *Different Trains*. Berio's eclectic and adventurous approach to music had a profound impact on Phil Lesh and Tom Constanten and so, in turn, on the music of the Grateful Dead, especially on *Anthem of the Sun*.

Renaming themselves the Hart Valley Drifters, Garcia, Hunter, Frankel, and the Edmistons play a political rally for Hugh Bagley, candidate for Monterey County sheriff.

JUNE '62

Although they'd met before, Phil Lesh and Jerry Garcia connect seriously at a party in early 1962. Lesh persuades Garcia to record a demo tape, which he gives to Gert Chiarito, host of the popular Midnight Special folk show on KPFA, the Berkeley public-radio station where Lesh volunteers as an engineer. Chiarito is impressed enough to book Garcia for a special edition of the show, broadcast as "The Long Black Veil," after the mournful ballad Garcia performs.

One Flew Over The Cuckoo's Nest by Ken Kesey is published. The grim satire, set in a mental hospital, is later made into an Oscar-winning film starring Jack Nicholson.

FEBRUARY '62

Tuesday February 20
Mercury astronaut John Glenn rockets into space aboard the Friendship 7, becoming the first American to orbit the earth.

20

11

Monday June 11
With the addition of Marshall Leicester and Dick Arnold on fiddle, the Hart Valley Drifters become the Sleepy Hollow Hog Stompers. They gig regularly at the "new" Boar's Head, the club having relocated to San Carlos's Jewish Community Center. Jerry is now sharing banjo duties with Marshall, and a tape of a June 11 performance shows how Garcia & Co. were moving away from "conventional" folk into more technically challenging bluegrass territory.

"Thank you so much. If you're wonderin' why in an old-timey band you can't understand the words very well, it's because that we don't know 'em. And we can't figure 'em out off the record so we make up our own as we go along."
JERRY GARCIA TO THE BOAR'S HEAD AUDIENCE.

MAY '62

11

APRIL '62

Friday May 11
As the Thunder Mountain Tub Thumpers, Garcia, Hunter, Frankel, and the Edmistons open the Stanford University Folk Festival.

MARCH '62

Neal Cassady

Neal Cassady was a Beat legend. He was the Dean Moriarty character in Kerouac's *On the Road*, Cody Pomeray in *Visions of Cody* and *The Dharma Bums*, and the subject of poems by Allen Ginsberg and writings by William Burroughs. Cassady connected to the Dead through Ken Kesey (they were both veterans of the Perry Lane days of '62 and '63), who enlisted him to help drive the Pranksters' psychedelic bus on its epic cross-country journey in the summer of 1964; the Dead befriended him during the Acid Tests the following year. (All of this is recounted in Tom Wolfe's *The Electric Kool-Aid Acid Test*.)

Cassady had a huge impact on the nascent Grateful Dead, and not just because of his uncanny ability to carry on five conversations at once, or his mesmerizing death-defying high-speed driving, or his knack for endlessly juggling a large hammer. "He was the first person I met who he himself was the art," Garcia marveled. "Most people I know didn't understand him at all." Bob Weir noted that the Dead gleaned some of their improvisational approach to music and life from hanging with Cassady, whom he termed "one of our teachers, as well as a playmate." Cassady was immortalized in Weir's song "The Other One": "There was Cowboy Neal at the wheel on the bus to never-ever land…"

Below: Garcia and Hunter practice before a 1962 show at Stanford University.

Students for a Democratic Society (SDS) issues the "Port Huron Statement" — a call to action that serves as the tocsin for a decade of social activism and political radicalism on America's college campuses.

JULY '62

10

Tuesday July 10
Telstar, the world's first commercial communications satellite, is launched into orbit—an advance celebrated in a groovy instrumental number by the Ventures.

The Wildwood Boys

With Marshall Leicester back at Yale in the fall, the Sleepy Hollow Hog Stompers become the Wildwood Boys, with a straight-up bluegrass repertoire and a lineup including Garcia, Hunter, and two newcomers—David Nelson (guitar) and Norm Van Maastricht (bass).

SEPTEMBER '62

AUGUST '62

5

Sunday August 5
Actress Marilyn Monroe is found dead in her Hollywood home.

Bob Weir enrolls at the Fountain Valley School in Colorado Springs, where he bonds with fellow troublemaker John Perry Barlow.

Sunday October 28
After a week when the world teeters on the brink of nuclear war, the Cuban Missile Crisis ends when the Soviet Union agrees to withdraw the nuclear missiles it has stationed on the island nation.

OCTOBER '62

1   **28**

Monday October 1
Protected by a federal marshal and troops, James Meredith becomes the first African-American to enroll at the formerly segregated University of Mississippi.

Jorma Kaukonen

One of the most highly regarded musicians on the Peninsula folk scene was guitarist Jorma (then known as "Jerry") Kaukonen. Born in Washington, D.C., Kaukonen's guitar influences were blues greats like Howlin' Wolf, Sonny Boy Williamson, and, especially, The Rev. Gary Davis.

A regular at the Tangent (see page 26), Kaukonen was, like Jerry Garcia, sought after as a teacher as well as a performer; Bob Weir later said that he and his fellow aspiring guitar heroes traded tapes of his solos "like baseball cards." After graduating from Santa Clara University in 1965, Kaukonen's pal Paul Kantner tapped him for lead guitar for the Jefferson Airplane. In 1969 Kaukonen joined Airplane bassist Jack Casady to form Hot Tuna, a band that survived the Airplane's breakup and continues today.

Kaukonen has had an active and varied career outside Jefferson Airplane, both with Hot Tuna and on his own. (Among his projects was a 1995 album with Tom Constanten, which consisted of eleven versions of "Embryonic Journey," Kaukonen's acoustic number from the Airplane's *Surrealistic Pillow* album). He also runs a music camp in southeastern Ohio.

December 1962

25

Bluegrass

Although it derives from the uptempo, fiddle-driven "hillbilly" music of the upper South, bluegrass didn't emerge as a distinct genre until just before World War II, when Bill Monroe and his Blue Grass Boys took Nashville's Grand Ole Opry by storm.

Monroe, an irascible perfectionist, more or less single-handedly established bluegrass on the country scene; veterans of his band include guitarist Lester Flatt and banjo picker Earl Scruggs, who went on to launch the Foggy Mountain Boys, and Carter Stanley, who also performed with his brother Ralph as the Stanley Brothers.

Typically based around a lineup of guitar, five-string banjo, mandolin, fiddle, and standup bass, bluegrass has been likened to "acoustic rock 'n' roll," but comparisons to jazz are equally apt. Just as jazz uses pop tunes and standards as a springboard for improvisation, bluegrass kicks traditional songs into high gear, with every non-rhythm instrument taking solos in turn—a process known as "passing the break."

Complex and speedy, bluegrass held great appeal for folk musicians looking for something more challenging than the conventional strummin' and pluckin' folk styles of the early '60s. "Bluegrass had a kind of shock value, like rock 'n' roll had shock value in a way," recalled Neil Rosenberg, who played banjo with the Redwood Canyon Ramblers, probably the first bluegrass band to form in the Bay Area, around 1960. "Electric instruments were considered outré by all of us. So if you wanted to do something that really set people's teeth on edge and kind of kicked butt, bluegrass was it."

Bluegrass continues to be one of country's most dynamic genres: mandolinist Ricky Skaggs headed up the "Newgrass" revival in the 1980s, while fiddler Alison Krauss brought the music to a wider audience in the 1990s; and in 2000 the soundtrack to the Coen Brothers' film *O Brother Where Art Thou?* (with Ralph Stanley among the contributors) took the "high lonesome sound" into a new millennium.

Right: Bill Monroe

Wednesday November 7
South Africa sends African National Congress official and anti-apartheid activist Nelson Mandela to prison, where he will remain for 28 years.

NOVEMBER '62

7   **10**

Saturday November 10
Although the lineup and band name is the subject of some debate (various sources say it was the Hart Valley Drifters, others the Liberty Hill Aristocrats), it is certain that Jerry Garcia and others, including Robert Hunter and David Nelson, played two gigs in one day on this date—the first at SF State University and the second at the College of San Mateo Folk festival in the evening. Jerry Garcia also does a less-than-well-received solo set at the CSM festival.

DECEMBER '62

"It was the first time I'd seen Garcia play… It was funny, because he didn't go over too well. At the time he was sort of exploring the roots of American music and playing a lot of old-timey stuff … Most of the audience was fairly clean-cut cut college kids into the Kingston Trio and the slicker kinds of sounds, and this sort of authentic old-timey stuff was a little strange to most of them." DAVID PARKER, CSM AUDIENCE MEMBER TO BLAIR JACKSON

David Nelson

Wildwood Boys guitarist David Nelson was a friend of the Albin brothers and something of a prodigy—he'd learned pedal-steel guitar at an age when many of his peers still struggled on their six-strings. Nelson remained part of the Grateful Dead's musical circle for more than three decades, most notably as a member of the New Riders of the Purple Sage, and he played and sang on tracks from *Workingman's Dead* and *American Beauty*. (Nelson also performed on *Aoxomoxoa*, but details of his contribution are sketchy.)

Nelson played in one of Jerry Garcia's acoustic outfits in the mid-1980s, including the famous 1987 run at the Lunt-Fontanne Theater. Like Garcia, he periodically returned to his musical roots, most notably as part of the Good Old Boys in the mid-'70s, in which Nelson joined with several of the first-generation bluegrass musicians who had inspired him in the early '60s.

Since 1994, Nelson has performed and recorded with the David Nelson Band, whose lineup includes NRPS and Kingfish alum Bill Laymon, Kingfish vets Mookie Siegel and Barry Sless, and drummer Charlie Crane. In 1999, Nelson, Siegel, and Sless joined Phil Lesh & Friends for two shows; Phil returned the favor by joining the DNB for a SEVA Foundation benefit later that year.

Above: Young Billy Kreutzmann with sister Marcia and two unknown friends, early '60s. Notice the Fats Domino and Buddy Rich–Max Roach album covers.

January 1963

26

Saturday May 4
The newlyweds appear at the Tangent billed as Jerry and Sara, performing eight songs including "Deep Elem Blues," "Long Black Veil," and (ironically, given the circumstances) "The Man Who Wrote 'Home Sweet Home' (Never Was a Married Man)." Garcia also plays fiddle on "Keno the Rent Man"—a tape from this show captures his only known public outing on the instrument.

MAY '63

JUNE '63

17

Monday June 17
John Profumo, secretary of state for war in the cabinet of British Prime Minister Harold MacMillan, resigns following revelations that he shared a mistress with a Soviet naval officer who may have been a spy.

4   18

Saturday May 18
As the Hart Valley Drifters, Garcia, Hunter, Frankel, and Nelson play the Monterey Folk Festival (Peter, Paul, and Mary are the headliners). The band wins Best Amateur Group and Garcia is named Best Banjo Player.

Saturday April 27
Jerry Garcia and Sara Lee Ruppenthal (who is pregnant) marry at the Palo Alto Unitarian Church. David Nelson is best man, and the Wildwood Boys entertain at the reception. Phil Lesh arrives just in time for the wedding, from Las Vegas, where he'd been working at the post office while writing "Foci for Four Orchestra," a piece modestly scored for 125 musicians.

APRIL '63

27

Having broken up with Barbara Meier the preceding Christmas, Jerry Garcia becomes involved with Sara Lee Ruppenthal, daughter of a Stanford professor and a serious folkie (Joan Baez is a friend). They meet—where else?—at Kepler's.

FEBRUARY '63

The Tangent, a coffeehouse above a delicatessen in Palo Alto, opens. Run by two Stanford Hospital doctors, Stu Goldstein and David Schoenstadt, the Tangent (occasionally known as the Top of the Tangent) quickly becomes a focus of the Bay Area folk scene.

JANUARY '63

23

Saturday February 23
The Wildwood Boys (Garcia, Hunter, and David Nelson), play the Tangent for the first time. "Blue Ron" McKernan also gigs at the Tangent around this time as part of the Second-Story Men.

MARCH '63

John Perry Barlow

A native of Wyoming, John Perry Barlow (b.1947) met Bob Weir at Fountain Valley School in Colorado Springs; Weir, a notorious academic underachiever, had been sent there by his parents. It wasn't until the early '70s that they began a fruitful songwriting relationship. This produced such Dead classics as "Cassidy," "Let It Grow," "Estimated Prophet," "Throwing Stones," "Lost Sailor," "Saint of Circumstance," and "Hell in a Bucket." Barlow supplied lyrics for Weir's solo ventures and for most of Brent Mydland's songs. In 1990 Barlow co-founded the Electronic Freedom Foundation, an organization "which promotes freedom of expression in digital media," and he has become known all over the world as an articulate speaker and thoughtful writer on issues relating to cyberspace, individual liberties, and much more.

Bob Weir spends the summer driving a tractor on John Perry Barlow's family ranch in Cora, Wyoming. When Fountain Valley School authorities decide that only one of the two can return, Weir goes back to California, enrolls in Pacific High School in Los Altos Hills, and buys a Harmony Sovereign guitar.

The Chateau scene ends when the house is sold, sending David Nelson and Robert Hunter to new digs on Hamilton Street in Palo Alto, while Jerry Garcia, who has already moved to Mountain View with Sara, takes a job teaching guitar at Dana Morgan's Music Store. The Wildwood Boys continue to gig at the Tangent and occasionally at the Coffee Gallery in San Francisco.

The summer also sees Jerry Garcia's return (briefly) to rock 'n' roll when Dana Morgan's manager, Troy Weidenheimer, recruits him into his East Bay party band, the Zodiacs. Having mastered guitar and banjo and made forays into the mandolin and fiddle, Jerry now picks up the electric bass and lays down bottom for the Zodiacs at Stanford frat frolics.

JULY '63

Above: Nelson, Garcia, and Hunter as the Wildwood Boys.

Bob Weir learns guitar by hanging around the folk-club circuit, and at least once takes the stage at the Tangent with Debbie Peckham, Rachel Garbet, and Michael Wanger as The Uncalled Four.

OCTOBER '63

The Black Mountain Boys sign up for what would have been their first true tour, an outing up the Pacific coast with the folk duo Michaela and future Quicksilver Messenger David Freiberg. The "Bay City Minstrels" tour is canceled when the promoter absconds with the advance money.

NOVEMBER '63

Friday November 22
President John F. Kennedy is felled by an assassin's bullets in Dallas, Texas, plunging the nation—and the world—into mourning. Two days later, the alleged assassin, Lee Harvey Oswald, is himself shot to death at Dallas police headquarters.

DECEMBER '63

Sunday December 22
Jerry Garcia gets the ultimate gig for a bluegrass picker—opening for Bill Monroe, in this case at the Ash Grove in Los Angeles. Playing as the Bad Water Valley Boys, the lineup includes Robert Hunter (who is now living in L.A.), Ken Frankel, and Marshall Leicester.

8 **22** **31**

December 1963 | 27

AUGUST '63

28

Wednesday August 28
Civil Rights leader Dr. Martin Luther King, Jr. leads more than 200,000 marchers through the streets of Washington, D.C., to the Lincoln Memorial, where he delivers his stirring "I have a dream" speech.

22

Friday November 22
On the same day that JFK is assassinated, Aldous Huxley, author of Brave New World and an early advocate of psychedelic drugs (The Doors of Perception) dies in Los Angeles.

Sunday December 8
Sara Garcia gives birth to a daughter, Heather. Robert Hunter is the godfather.

Tuesday December 31
On the afternoon of New Year's Eve, Bob Weir, Bob Matthews, and Rich McCauley hear some amazing banjo picking coming out of Dana Morgan's. Investigating, they encounter Jerry Garcia, who—oblivious to anything but music, as usual—is wondering why none of his students have shown up. Garcia hands Weir a guitar, and the two jam their way into 1964.

Robert Hunter's picking chops haven't progressed at the same rate as his literary skills and he is eased out of the Wildwood Boys and replaced by Eric Thompson. The new lineup plays as the Black Mountain Boys.

SEPTEMBER '63

The Zodiacs

If the various folk and bluegrass groups in which Jerry Garcia, Robert Hunter, et al. played stand as the first major strand in the evolution of the Grateful Dead, and the avant-garde efforts of Phil Lesh and Tom Constanten are the second, then the Zodiacs—whose lineup also included Bill Kreutzmann and Ron McKernan—is the third. The Zodiacs, however, are the least-known and least-documented of the proto-Dead bands, since no recordings of them are known to exist. Nevertheless, Jerry Garcia's stint in the band, brief and intermittent as it was, reawakened him to the possibilities of electric instruments. In particular, Troy Weidenheimer turned Jerry on to the guitar work of the great R&B guitarist Freddy King. Also, the experience of playing in a hard-working rock 'n' roll/rhythm & blues band, so different from performing on the more rarefied coffeehouse/hootenanny circuit, gave Jerry a valuable lesson in how to get an audience in the groove.

"Troy taught me the principle of 'hey—stomp your foot and get on with it.' He was a great one for instant arrangements… He had a wide-open style of playing that was very, very loose, like when we went to play gigs at the Stanford parties, we didn't have songs or anything, and he would just say play B-flat… and we'd just play along and he'd jam on top of it, so a lot of my conceptions of the freedom available to your playing really came from him." JERRY GARCIA TO DENNIS MCNALLY.

Jug Band Music

A subset of the folk revival of the '50s and '60s, the jug band craze was inspired by African-American dance music of the '20s, the chief sources being the Memphis Jug Band and Gus Cannon's Jug Stompers. Jug band music was good-timey, old-timey music to dance and drink to, often featuring rowdy, foot-tapping tunes with funny and/or salacious lyrics. The Jim Kweskin band was pretty much solely responsible for the genre's revival. Kweskin was the nominal leader, but Geoff Muldaur did most of the lead vocal and guitar work; the band's lineup also included Maria D'Amato, the future Maria Muldaur. The group spawned countless imitators after its first album, *The Jug Band*, in 1963. The DIY simplicity of jug-band instrumentation—kazoo, washboard, washtub bass, guitar, banjo, and, of course, a jug to blow into—fueled its popularity. Like the skiffle craze in Britain, with which it has some parallels, the jug band craze was widespread but brief; by 1966 most jug band musicians had moved back to other folk genres or ahead into rock 'n' roll.

6

Monday March 16
Proclaiming a "War on Poverty," President Lyndon Johnson asks Congress for $700 million in funding for social programs.

Friday March 6
Garcia and Hunter (who has been studying Scientology and miscellaneous esoterica in L.A.) return to bluegrass as the Black Mountain Boys for a show at the Tangent. Jorma Kaukonen opens.

"We're the Black Mountain Boys, otherwise known as the Black Mountain String Band, the greatest string band since King Solomon's Mines..."
JERRY GARCIA TO THE TANGENT AUDIENCE

Tapes made at the Tangent during this period include Pigpen backed, on separate gigs, by Peter Albin ("John Henry," "Hoochie Coochie Man") and Jorma Kaukonen ("Diamond Rag Blues").

Jim Kweskin and the Jug Band arrive from Cambridge, Massachusetts, for a week's residence at the Cabale in Berkeley. Garcia, McKernan, & Co. take in the shows and decide to form a jug band at the suggestion of Bob Matthews, who is taking banjo lessons from Garcia.

Tuesday February 25
Twenty-two-year-old boxer Cassius Clay blitzes Sonny Liston to become the World Heavyweight Champion.

Thursday February 27
At the opposite end of the musical spectrum from the jug-band scene, Phil Lesh and Tom Constanten are active in Bay Area avant-garde classical music circles. Lesh and Steve Reich perform a semi-improvisational piece for Event III (Coffee Break), a multimedia event featuring the San Francisco Mime Troupe.

Saturday January 25
The Tangent, Palo Alto, California

Mother McCree's Uptown Jug Champions plays their first gig at the Tangent, which remains home base for the increasingly popular ensemble.

David Grisman

Performer, producer, and a true giant of American acoustic music, David Grisman was born in 1945. He took up the mandolin in part because, he later said, "no one played it" at the time. In a bit of serendipity, one of his high-school teachers was a relative of Ralph Rinzler, mandolin player for the Greenbriar Boys, so that David was able to study with a master.

After a stint playing in the Even Dozen Jug Band, Grisman formed his own group, the New York Ramblers. He met Jerry Garcia at a bluegrass festival in 1964, and a year later visited the Bay Area just in time to give the Warlocks their first national write-up, a mention in the prestigious folk music magazine *Sing Out*.

After dabbling with rock 'n' roll (on sax) in Earth Orchestra, Grisman again went west and hooked back up with Garcia, who brought him into the *American Beauty* sessions to play mandolin on two tracks, and in 1973 was at the center of Garcia's bluegrass group, Old and in the Way. Influenced by Django Reinhardt, Grisman by this time had developed a style that was lighter, more melodic, and jazzier than the traditional bluegrass attack, which came to be known as "Dawg music." In the 1990s, he resumed his close association with Garcia, the two of them recording a number of albums for Grisman's Acoustic Disc label.

Mother McCree's Uptown Jug Champions

By mid-January the basic lineup of a new band had formed around Jerry Garcia, Bob Weir (washtub bass and jug), Ron McKernan (harp and vocals), Tom Stone (banjo), and Dave Parker (washboard)—although, as usual, other friends dropped in and out, including Bob Matthews, who was fired after failing to master the intricacies of the kazoo. The presence of Pigpen (as Blue Ron was now known) was key to the new band's sound, adding a blues element to the basic jug band equation. At Robert Hunter's suggestion, the band decided to perform as Mother McCree's, to which David Nelson appended "Uptown Jug Champions." The group never spelled its name the same way twice.

"We did some Jesse Fuller tunes—'Beat It on Down the Line' is a Jesse Fuller tune. 'The Monkey and the Engineer,' another Jesse Fuller tune. We did 'Stealin''... 'New Minglewood Blues,' in the original form that we did it... was a jug band song." BOB WEIR IN DAVID GANS'S *CONVERSATIONS WITH THE DEAD*.

The Brits Invade

On February 7, 1964, Pan Am Flight 101 deposited four young Liverpudlians on the tarmac at New York's John F. Kennedy Airport. The screams of 3,000 fans drowned out the jet engines. Two days later, the Beatles (*below*) appeared on Ed Sullivan's Sunday-night variety TV show; 73 million people tuned in. The British Invasion had begun. "Invasion," though, is a misnomer. The Beatles and the bands that followed in their wake—the Rolling Stones, the Kinks, Herman's Hermits, the Animals, Gerry and the Pacemakers, the Dave Clark Five, and, later, the Yardbirds, the Who, and Cream—may have started life in Britain, but their musical influences were all-American. John Lennon, Paul McCartney, Keith Richards, Mick Jagger, Eric Clapton, and hundreds of other young Brits had grown up listening to, and then playing, 1950s rock 'n' roll (and in the case of Clapton and various Stones, blues and R&B), finding in American music a sense of freedom and fun conspicuously absent from their post–World War II homeland, with its rationing, rain, and unemployment lines.

Most purist American folkies dismissed the Brit bands as purveyors of simplistic yeah-yeah tunes for hormone-stoked teenagers, but the more perceptive saw beyond the hype and realized that the "invaders" had revitalized rock 'n' roll. The Beatles won more converts after *A Hard Day's Night* hit the big screen later in the year; Richard Lester's movie made the Beatles seem witty, slightly subversive, and, well, hip.

Sandy Rothman

Sandy Rothman was a multi-instrumental whiz (guitar, dobro, banjo, and mandolin) who got into bluegrass after hearing the Redwood Canyon Ramblers, the pioneering Bay Area bluegrass outfit, while in junior high school in Berkeley. Rothman had already spent the summer of '63 at Bean Blossom, and a couple of years later he got the dream gig—playing in Bill Monroe's Bluegrass Boys, which he did (on guitar) from the mid-'60s to the early '70s, before joining Earl Taylor's Stoney Mountain Boys on banjo. By the time he hooked back up with Jerry Garcia in 1986, Rothman's career was in the doldrums, but a reversal of fortune came when Rothman, Garcia, and David Nelson began playing the old stuff again. The three formed the nucleus of the acclaimed 1987 Jerry Garcia Acoustic Band, with Rothman also producing the band's *Almost Acoustic* album. In the 1990s he released *Bluegrass Guitar Duets* (with Steve Pottier) and his first solo album, *The Old Road to Home*.

Jerry Garcia and Sandy Rothman begin a cross-country trip (in Jerry's '61 Corvair) to Bill Monroe's Brown County Jamboree in Bean Blossom, Indiana, visiting friends and fellow bluegrass enthusiasts along the way.

The Black Mountain Boys play the San Francisco State College Folk Festival at the Top of the Tangent, Palo Alto, California.

Thursday May 21
Phil Lesh's work "6⅞" for Bernardo Moreno is a featured composition at a series of Music Now "Koncerts" from May 21–30 at a music center on Capp Street in San Francisco. Lesh doesn't perform, but the six-piece ensemble includes Tom Constanten on prepared piano. Pioneered by John Cage, "prepared piano" involves modifying an ordinary piano—for example, inserting metal objects between the strings—to produce unconventional sounds. The 24-minute "6 7/8" for Bernardo Moreno foreshadowed both the freewheeling experimentalism that Lesh and T.C. brought to the recording studio for *Anthem of the Sun* and the "Space" element of Grateful Dead shows.

21 24

Sunday May 24
Garcia and Rothman arrive at Bean Blossom and worship at the shrine of bluegrass master Bill Monroe. Jerry can't bring himself to approach Monroe.

Stopping at another bluegrass event in Sunset Park, Pennsylvania, Jerry Garcia meets and jams with David Grisman, beginning a musical association that will last more than 30 years. Jerry and Sandy go on to visit friends in New England (including Marshall Leicester) before Jerry returns to California.

The San Francisco Mime Troupe

A group whose history intersected with the Grateful Dead's at several times and on several levels, the San Francisco Mime Troupe was founded by R.G. "Ronnie" Davis in 1959. Mime, in the SFMT's version, most definitely did not mean actors in berets and white makeup tugging imaginary ropes. The SFMT's style was not traditional "pantomime" but rather a highly politicized adaptation of Commedia Dell'Arte, the "street theater" of the Italian Renaissance. Performing in parks and wherever else they could find space and an audience, the SFMT sought—as it still does—to make people "laugh at the absurdities of contemporary life and at the same time, see their causes."

The SFMT grew out of an acting workshop, but its early-'60s members included, as one later recalled, "dockworkers, college students, socialist organizers, market analysts, musicians, opera singers, vegetarians, drug addicts, ballet dancers, criminals, and bona fide eccentrics," among them Peter Coyote (then Peter Cohon, and now a celebrated actor) and Emmett Grogan. Coyote and Grogan would, in 1966, help startup the Digger collective (see page 59). Bill Graham was the Troupe's business manager for a time. By the spring of 1964, the SFMT's events had gone multimedia, with light shows, "projections," "movements," and experimental music.

The SFMT pushed the envelope of civic tolerance even in sophisticated San Francisco, and in 1962, the city's parks department refused the Troupe a permit for a park performance. The ensuing court case, which the SMFT won the following year, established the right of artists to perform in the city's public spaces, a ruling that would foster the development of the Bay Area music scene.

On the Bus

A literal and figurative cross-country trip, the Pranksters' 1964 bus odyssey was conceived as a run to New York timed to coincide with the World's Fair and the publication of Ken Kesey's second novel, *Sometimes a Great Notion*. Kesey originally planned to take a small group in a station wagon or flatbed truck, but Ken Babbs found a 1939 International Harvester school bus that had been fitted out with bunks and other amenities by its Menlo Park owner. Intrepid Trips, Inc. bought the bus for $1,500. After various modifications, including installing a sound system designed to maximize mind-warp, Kesey & Co. gave the bus a psychedelic paint job and changed the destination sign to "Furthur." (The warning sign on the back read "Caution: Weird Load.")

After a shakedown cruise up the coast, *Furthur* left Kesey's home at La Honda in early July with 14 people on board, a benzedrine-fueled Neal Cassady at the wheel, a jug of LSD-laced orange juice in the cooler, and some 16mm cameras and tape recorders—the idea was to record the Pranksters' interactions with the citizenry for a movie. (Though the Pranksters shot hundreds of hours of film during the trip, the movie never materialized, but footage made its way onto video in the late '90s).

Furthur rolled across the Southwest to New Orleans (where the group unintentionally integrated a segregated beach on Lake Ponchartrain) and swung north from Florida, hitting Manhattan in mid-July. They took a side trip up to Millbrook, the upstate mansion where Timothy Leary played high priest in his League of Spiritual Discovery, but the meeting was a bust—the Pranksters' Wild-West psychedelic style didn't jibe with the more formal, cerebral East Coast approach. The bus returned to California (minus a few of those who had started out) by way of the upper Midwest, landing back at La Honda in late August. *Furthur* had further adventures, though it never went so far afield again; eventually the bus came to rest in Kesey's Oregon cattle pasture, where it remains today.

"You're either on the bus or off the bus." PRANKSTER SAYING.

It was a party, all right. But in July of 1964 not even the hip world in New York was quite ready for the phenomenon of a bunch of people roaring across the continental U.S.A. in a bus covered with swirling Day-Glo mandalas aiming movie cameras and microphones at every freaking thing in this whole freaking country… TOM WOLFE, THE ELECTRIC KOOL-AID ACID TEST.

The Merry Pranksters

Who were the Merry Pranksters, that band of intrepid travelers of both inner space and the Great American Road? The core group—the capital-P Pranksters—included old friends of Kesey (like Ken Babbs, a Vietnam vet), relatives, and various people who had heard that something special was happening at Kesey's place in La Honda and wanted in. This last group included Neal Cassady *(see page 24)*, Page Browning (an alum of the Chateau in Palo Alto), Sandy Lehman-Haupt (a young audio engineer), Ron Bevirt (a military vet like Babbs), and others including Paula Sundsten, George Walker, Jane Burton, and Mike Hagen. Most became better known by Prankster nicknames; Neal Cassady, for example, became Sir Speed Limit.

The Pranksters shared the conviction that altering individual consciousness was the first step in breaking down the barriers that trapped people in the outdated modes of conventional existence. LSD was a key element, its effects enhanced by electronics, music, lights, props, and costumes. The Prankster circle expanded to include future luminaries like Steward Brand, Hugh Romney, Mountain Girl, the Grateful Dead, and lots of small p-pranksters who got on the metaphorical bus. Many are still riding today.

AUGUST '64

7

Right and above: Neal Cassady at work (driving) and play on the Pranksters bus.

President Lyndon Johnson signs the Civil Rights Act into law. The act outlaws discrimination on the basis of race in jobs, housing, and public accommodations.

JULY '64

Friday August 7
Following reports of North Vietnamese attacks on U.S. warships, Congress passes the Gulf of Tonkin Resolution, giving President Johnson the authority to "take all necessary measures… to prevent further aggression" by North Vietnam.

Getting Stoned

"We can do that!" Pigpen enthusiastically announced to Jerry Garcia upon hearing the first album by the Rolling Stones, *England's Newest Hitmakers*. With songs by Buddy Holly, Slim Harpo, Willie Dixon, Chuck Berry, Holland-Dozier-Holland, and others, the record had deep roots in American blues and R&B. The Beatles' film, *A Hard Day's Night*, had made being in a band seem like unsurpassable fun, but the Stones 1964 offering provided a model that was possibly attainable; after hearing the Stones, Pigpen was just itching to start an electric band.

"Way back early we developed a whole lot of our blues chops from listening to the Rolling Stones." BOB WEIR TO BLAIR JACKSON, *1992*

Above and left: Every few months—or whenever the mood struck—the Merry Pranksters would repaint the bus, or portions of it, while high on LSD. Needless to say, America had never before seen anything quite like it.

SEPTEMBER '64

29

Tuesday September 29
The Warren Commission, set up by President Johnson to investigate the assassination of President John F. Kennedy, reaches the conclusion (later much disputed) that Lee Harvey Oswald acted alone in the crime.

Arizona Senator Barry Goldwater wins the Republican nomination for president at the party's convention in San Francisco. Students at the University of California organize a 32-hour sit-in—it is the birth of the Free Speech Movement.

OCTOBER '64

NOVEMBER '64

3

Tuesday November 3
President Johnson is reelected in a landslide victory over his Republican challenger, Barry Goldwater.

December 1964

31

"There were 12 or so Pranksters, and we all had to take on Prankster identities— that's where 'Mountain Girl' came from, and it's just kinda stuck! Kesey, a.k.a. 'Chief,' was the definite uncontested leader—it was his bus and his gas card!"
MOUNTAIN GIRL, *2003*

Carolyn "Mountain Girl" Adams

Born in 1946 in the Hudson River Valley, Carolyn Adams was expelled from school for what she called "lots of stunts" just before graduation. She lit out for California and landed a job as a lab technician at Stanford, where unauthorized psychedelic research got her fired. She fell into the Palo Alto scene, met Neal Cassady at St. Michael's coffeeshop, and joined up with the Pranksters shortly after the 1964 transcontinental trip. (Cassady nicknamed her "Mountain Girl," soon shortened to "M.G.," after she set up housekeeping in a tent at La Honda.) Kesey was especially taken with M.G.'s combination of beauty, brains, and adventurousness, and the two had a daughter, Sunshine, born in Mexico in 1966.

Through the Pranksters, M.G. became friends with Jerry Garcia (according to one account, they met while sweeping up after an Acid Test), a friendship that became romance in the fall of 1966. Two daughters followed, Annabelle in 1970 and Theresa ("Trixie") in 1974. By Trixie's birth, though, Jerry and M.G. were drifting apart as Jerry became involved with Deborah Koons. M.G. and the girls moved to Oregon, where she wrote a highly regarded treatise on marijuana cultivation. In the mid-'80s, she joined with other Grateful Dead family members to launch the Hulogosi Press publishing collective.

Jerry and M.G. married backstage at the Dead's 1981 New Year's Eve show, though the couple did not cohabit again until after Jerry's collapse in 1986. They divorced in 1993. Following Jerry's death M.G. became embroiled in an ugly legal dispute with Deborah Koons, Jerry's wife at the time of the death, over the financial terms of Jerry and M.G.'s divorce agreement. In 1997 a court ruled in M.G.'s favor. Koons appealed and the following year M.G. agreed to a settlement with the Garcia Estate. Today, M.G. lives in San Francisco, where she writes and paints.

[Mountain Girl] was one big loud charge of vitality. Here comes Mountain Girl—it was a thing that made you pick up, as soon as you saw her mouth broaden into a grin and her big brown eyes open, open, open, until they practically exploded like sunspots in front of your eyes...
TOM WOLFE, *THE ELECTRIC KOOL-AID ACID TEST.*

Jerry Garcia plays the Offstage with a lineup that includes various local players—probably his last purely bluegrass show for many years.

DECEMBER '64

10

Thursday December 10
Martin Luther King, Jr. receives the Nobel Peace Prize.

By the start of 1965 the collective, centered around Garcia, Weir, and Pigpen, was already making the jump from acoustic jug band to electric band—the amplified instruments coming from Dana Morgan's Music Shop, the group's headquarters for after-hours rehearsals and jams. Dana Morgan, Jr. took up bass duties, Pigpen (now working as a janitor at Morgan's) began supplementing his harp with the electric organ, and local bar band vet Bill Kreutzmann, a.k.a. Bill the Drummer, joined on skins.

Mother McCree's Uptown Jug Champions played their last gig at the College of San Mateo folk festival in January. At some point in early 1965 the new band named themselves the Warlocks. The title was inspired by J.R.R. Tolkien's *Lord of the Rings* trilogy, which Bob Weir (along with hundreds of thousands of other hipsters) was deeply absorbed in at the time.

"[At first] we didn't consider ourselves a blues band, we thought of ourselves more or less as a bug-eyed rock and roll band. We did a lot of blues because Pigpen at that time was heavily into the blues… [We also] performed a lot of Bob Dylan and Rolling Stones material, but we didn't record that."

BOB WEIR, IN *NEW MUSICAL EXPRESS*, 1972

Progressive Jazz

Among the many musical influences in the mix in 1965 was progressive jazz. Jerry Garcia was a longtime fan of Miles Davis and John Coltrane, but it was Phil Lesh who, in 1965–66, introduced Bill Kreutzmann to the work of Elvin Jones (Coltrane's drummer in the early '60s), and turned all of his new bandmates on to the "free jazz" of alto saxophonist Ornette Coleman *(below)*.

In 1959, Coleman and his quartet arrived at the Five Spot in New York City and started a firestorm of controversy in the jazz world. Coleman left traditional chords and keys behind in favor of collective, spontaneous improvisation, and he promoted bass and drums from rhythm into melodic instruments in their own right. Coleman called the new approach "harmelodics" or "free jazz," and he put it down on vinyl in two albums, *Free Jazz* and *The Shape of Jazz to Come*.

Jazz conservatives charged that by overturning established conventions of rhythm, harmony, and melody, Coleman was creating mere noise—an accusation confirmed, to some, by the fact that Coleman and his sidemen often played on toy instruments. Free jazz, however, challenged many jazz (and, later, rock) musicians to new heights of improvisation.

It would take some time for Coleman's influence to be felt directly in the Grateful Dead's music, but "there could have been no 'Dark Star' without *Free Jazz*" (Oliver Trager.) Coleman played with the Grateful Dead twice *(see pages 411 and 421)* and Jerry Garcia played on three tracks on *Virgin Beauty* (1988) with Coleman's Prime Time ensemble.

JANUARY '65

| 1 ~ 11 | 12 | 13 ~ 23 | 24 | 25 ~ 31 |

Tuesday January 12
The first show in the U.S. to devote itself to pop music airs on national TV. NBC's *Hullabaloo!* premieres with famous folksters the New Christy Minstrels and British invaders the Zombies and Gerry and the Pacemakers.

Sunday January 24
British statesman Winston Churchill dies at age 90.

Saturday February 13
President Lyndon Johnson orders "Rolling Thunder," a massive bombing campaign against North Vietnam; shortly afterward, U.S. combat troops land in South Vietnam.

FEBRUARY '65

| 1 ~ 12 | 13 | 14 ~ 20 | 21 | 21 ~ 28 |

Sunday February 21
African-American activist Malcolm X is assassinated in Harlem's Audubon Ballroom.

MARCH '65

| 1 | 2 | 3 | 4 | 5 | 6 | 7 | 8 ~ 31 |

Sunday March 7
Alabama State Troopers attack civil-rights marchers led by Martin Luther King, Jr., on their way to the state capital at Selma.

Ken Kesey

While Jerry Garcia was settling into the Palo Alto folk music scene, a young writer named Ken Kesey was creating a scene of his own just across town.

Kesey was born in Colorado in 1935. Kesey's family moved to rural Oregon in 1936, and he grew into a true All-American boy, equally excellent on the wrestling mat, the drama-club stage, and in the classroom. Kesey graduated from the University of Oregon in 1957, got a writing fellowship to Stanford, and headed to Palo Alto with his wife, the former Faye Haxby.

Kesey's cottage on Perry Lane quickly became clubhouse to a freewheeling circle of young writers and intellectuals, several of them—Robert Stone, Larry McMurtry, and Ed McClanahan—also destined for fame down the line. Around 1960, Kesey decided to make some money by signing up as a test subject for a federally funded pharmaceutical research program at the Veterans' Hospital in Menlo Park, where he worked as a janitor. There, in a fluorescent-white clinical setting, government docs dosed Kesey with a variety of psychoactive substances, including LSD. In short order, Uncle Sam's LSD was finding its way out of the hospital and into the venison chili at Kesey's Perry Lane parties.

The psychedelicized Kesey abandoned his work-in-progress novel, *Zoo*, and shifted literary gears into *One Flew over the Cuckoo's Nest*, a huge critical and popular success when it hit the stores in February 1962. The following year Kesey moved to a cabin up in the redwood-clad hills of La Honda, where an eclectic assortment of malcontents and visionaries, including Neal Cassady *(see page 24)* of *On the Road* fame, assembled around him. In 1964, after finishing his second novel, *Sometimes a Great Notion*, Kesey & Co., now self-dubbed the Merry Pranksters, piled into a converted school bus and headed cross-country and into history.

Returning to California, Kesey proselytized the Psychedelic Gospel in the Acid, fathered a daughter by Carolyn "Mountain Girl" Adams *(see page 31)*, and fled to Mexico in 1966 following a pot bust. He eventually did a short stint on a California work farm before returning to Oregon to run his family's dairy.

In keeping with his creed— "I'd rather be a lightning rod than a seismograph"—Kesey remained intimately involved with the "counterculture" he had done so much to create, and for the next 35 years he worked on a variety of literary and multimedia projects, often in collaboration with family members or with Prankster vets like Ken Babbs and Stewart Brand. Another novel, *Sailor Song*, hit print in 1992. Ken Kesey died of liver cancer in 2001.

A new and critical element is added to the mix when a friend supplies Jerry Garcia with two hits of LSD.

The Byrds (with veteran Bay Area folkie David Crosby on guitar and vocals) release their version of Bob Dylan's "Mr. Tambourine Man." (Dylan, in fact, did not release his own version until June, by which time the Byrds' single had hit #1.)

Friday April 23
Federal narcotics agents raid the Kesey home at La Honda, apparently under the impression that the Pranksters are doing something heavier than the still-legal LSD. Kesey and 12 Pranksters get run in on pot and "morals" charges, all eventually dropped or reduced. The government agents are undeterred by a hastily scribbled sign at the gates of the La Honda compound—it reads "No Admittance Five-Day Countdown In Progress."

| 1 | 2 | 3 | 4 | 5 | 6 | 7 | 8 | 9 | 10 | 11 | 12 | 13 | 14 | 15 | 16 | 17 | 18 | 19 | 20 | 21 | 22 | **23** | 24 | 25 | 26 | 27 | 28 | 29 | 30 |

"Yeah, this is what I've been looking for... I've been a seeker all along, and this is at least part of what I was looking for and maybe even more." JERRY GARCIA ON HIS FIRST LSD TRIP.

LSD

One April morning in 1943, Swiss chemist Albert Hoffman *(below)* brushed his hand against his mouth and accidentally absorbed a minute dose of a chemical compound he had synthesized while researching blood stimulants. His lab notes tell the rest of the story:

I was seized by a peculiar restlessness associated with a sensation of mild dizziness... I lay down and sank into a kind of drunkenness which was not unpleasant and which was characterized by extreme activity of imagination. As I lay in a dazed condition with my eyes closed... there surged upon me an uninterrupted stream of fantastic images of extraordinary plasticity and vividness and accompanied by an intense, kaleidoscope-like play of colors.

Correctly deducing that his condition had been caused by the compound he'd been working with—Lysergic Acid Diethylamide-25—Hoffman deliberately took a larger dose several days later, with correspondingly longer and more intense effects. Hoffman's unintentional and intentional adventures were the first acid trips.

For thousands of years, of course, people in many cultures have ingested plants and fungi to achieve visions, prophecy, and connection with the divine. LSD's effects are in fact very similar to those of naturally occurring substances like peyote and psilocybin mushrooms; the advent of LSD, though, meant that these mystical experiences were now available in a convenient synthetic form, via a drug so potent that its dosage is measured in thousandths of a gram.

After Hoffman's discovery, research into 'psychedelics' (coined by English scientist Humphrey Osmond in the mid-'50s) proceeded along two strands. First, psychiatrists and other behavioral professionals used LSD and similar drugs to help treat conditions ranging from alcoholism to depression—often with very encouraging results. LSD was perfectly legal then (Sandoz Ltd., Hoffman's employer, being the main source) and there was no real stigma attached to its use—individuals such as actor Cary Grant and journalist Clare Booth Luce were enthusiastic trippers, while *Brave New World* author Aldous Huxley sang the praises of LSD and mescaline (the active alkaloid of the peyote cactus) in 1957's *The Doors of Perception*.

At the same time, the U.S. military and the CIA conducted semi-clandestine programs to research substances which could prove useful in the Cold War effort; substances which might disorient the communist hordes, or achieve some form of "mind control" over them. In the process, thousands of test subjects were dosed with LSD and other drugs—some unwittingly.

The government also funded studies at hospitals and universities— programs that used paid volunteer test subjects, which is how Ken Kesey, Robert Hunter, and others were introduced to psychedelics.

But few Americans were aware of LSD until Timothy Leary and Richard Alpert, two Harvard professors, were fired by the university in 1963 after it was decided that their psychedelic research had gotten out of hand. The charismatic Leary— half mystical guru, half snake-oil salesman—quickly became LSD's most prominent public advocate, especially after he claimed aphrodisiac properties for the drug in an interview with *Playboy* magazine.

The Powers That Be began to get nervous as more people "turned on" to LSD. Lurid urban legends circulated about people who went on trips and never came back mentally, or who leapt off buildings while tripping as they thought they could fly, or went blind from staring at the sun in acid-induced fascination... California bowed to public and political pressure and outlawed LSD in October 1966; a federal ban followed in 1967.

Sue Swanson and Connie Bonner

Joining the Warlocks in the back room at Dana Morgan's were Sue Swanson and Connie Bonner, two high-school juniors who would become Grateful Dead lifers—indeed, if anyone can claim to be the original Deadheads, it's these two.

Sue Swanson, a friend of Bob Weir's sister Wendy, got to know Bob Weir at (public) Menlo-Atherton High School in 1964, where Bob wound up after getting the boot from (private) Pacific High School. Sue and her friend Connie Bonner became "musical assistants" of a sort to the nascent Warlocks; one of their jobs was flipping the records the boys played along to as they worked up their electric chops. Connie and Sue also rounded up kids from Menlo-Atherton for the band's first public gig *(see page 34)*.

After the Warlocks evolved into the Grateful Dead, Sue organized the band's first fan club, the *Golden Road to Unlimited Devotion*, and together with Bob Matthews, Sue and Connie also published the first Grateful Dead "zine," *The Olompali Sunday Times*, in 1967.

Both Sue and Connie continued to be deeply involved in the band's operations and the lives of its members. (Sue, for example, stood in for Jerry Garcia at the births of his daughters Annabelle and Trixie). When the digital era arrived, Sue took on the role of technical guru for the band's office and merchandising operations, and she serves today as information systems manager.

In 2001, Connie (now Connie Bonner Mosley) contributed to the liner notes of *The Golden Road* (1965–1973), Rhino Records' acclaimed boxed reissue of the band's Warner Brothers–era recordings.

The Warlocks

When Garcia, Pigpen, and Weir formed an electric rock 'n' roll band in early '65, they modeled the group on the Rolling Stones and Muddy Waters' five-piece band. The Warlocks played many songs (covers and originals) from the first two Stones records, plus tunes by Jimmy Reed, Howlin' Wolf, and Lightnin' Hopkins, and old country and folk songs that made the transition from the acoustic Mother McCree's to the electric group. With Bill Kreutzmann on drums and Dana Morgan, Jr. initially handling the bass (replaced by Phil Lesh in June '65), The Warlocks competed on the Peninsula with dozens of other similar bands.

Phil Lesh joins the Warlocks

Everyone from Garcia, to Jerry's friends and former folk music partners Eric Thompson and David Nelson, to future New Riders leader John Dawson, claims to have helped Phil Lesh learn the rudiments of playing electric bass after he agreed to join The Warlocks. Mostly, though, Lesh taught himself, basing his approach on what he knew from having played the violin when he was younger and on his own innate musicality. As Garcia later noted, "Phil doesn't listen to any bass players; he listens to his mind."

"Garcia takes me aside and puts a beer in my hand and says 'Listen, man, you're gonna play bass in my band.' 'But… I… er… who, me? Well, that might be possible.' Actually, it excited the shit out of me because it was something to do. And the flash was, 'Oh shit, you mean I can get paid for having fun?'." PHIL LESH IN ZIG ZAG MAGAZINE, 1974.

Lesh's first gig came just three weeks after he accepted Garcia's challenge, at Frenchy's nightclub in Hayward.

Wednesday May 5
Magoo's Pizza Parlor, Menlo Park, California

The newly electrified group makes its first public performance as the Warlocks at Magoo's Pizza Parlor, a Menlo Park teen hangout.

"The Warlocks were a sight for sore eyes to be sure—boots, tight jeans, striped T-shirts. This band of ex-folk and bluegrass musicians didn't wear the hairstyles of the day. Their hair was longer than the Beatles'!" CONNIE BONNER MOSLEY, 2001.

1	2	3	4	5

Wednesday May 12
Magoo's Pizza Parlor
Menlo Park, California

Word having spread, the Warlocks play to a full house at their second gig at Magoo's. Phil Lesh—who now enjoys the Rolling Stones and Bob Dylan as well as John Cage and Karlheinz Stockhausen—misses the show but joins the after-party.

"Danny Rifkin [future GD manager] led the Haight community dancing through the aisles. This was before any of the flower shit."

PHIL LESH ON THE MAY 14 STONES GIG IN DAVID GANS'S *CONVERSATIONS WITH THE DEAD*

6 ~ 11	12	13	14	15	16	17	18	19	20	21	22	23	24	25	26	27	28	29	30	31

Friday May 14
The Stones roll in: In another event that galvanizes the nascent Bay Area music scene, the Rolling Stones, the Byrds, and several other groups play San Francisco's Civic Auditorium. Phil Lesh is in the audience, along with many other future practitioners of the "San Francisco sound."

Thursday May 27
Magoo's Pizza Parlor, Menlo Park, California

Phil Lesh, having already been introduced to LSD (he and Tom Constanten spent their first trip listening to Mahler symphonies), drops acid with friends Hank Harrison and Bobby Petersen and catches the Warlocks at Magoo's. Jerry is seized with inspiration at the sight of his friend. Dana Morgan, Jr. isn't working out on bass; Jerry knows Phil is interested in taking up an electric instrument; Q.E.D.

Roots of the Bay Area Music Scene

The British Invasion, Bob Dylan's new directions, electric instruments, LSD—in the first half of '65 there was a buzz around San Francisco Bay. The hip vanguard of the area's Baby Boomers were now in their teens and twenties and, having absorbed the ethos of their Beat forebears, eagerly called for, to paraphrase a poet, "stronger wine and madder music." Northern California became the nexus of the new in politics, in social mores, and in the lively arts—with music the liveliest.

The May 14 multi-band show at San Francisco's Civic Auditorium, sponsored by radio station KYA, had a galvanizing effect on the emerging scene. So did the opening of a new club, the Matrix, three months later; Jefferson Airplane *(below)* played the opening night. The Airplane were perhaps the most promising group at the time, marrying the folk and pop sensibilities of leaders Marty Balin and Paul Kantner with the vocal talents of a dynamic female singer—Signe Anderson. Their trademark soaring harmonies were backed by one of the area's top guitarists, blues specialist Jorma Kaukonen, and a thundering bassist, Jack Casady. The Airplane were the first major S.F. band to be signed, but didn't really hit their stride until Grace Slick replaced Anderson.

In other news that spring and summer, George Hunter and Mike Wilhelm formed the Charlatans, a band whose look (cowboy psychedelic with Edwardian overtones) was at first more highly cultivated than the music, but which had

a big influence on the scene anyway. Their psychedelic sojourn in rural Virginia City, Nevada, became the stuff of rock legend, but once they returned to the Haight they never quite jelled the way the other top bands did.

Hoping to emulate the rock 'n' roll success of their former-folkie friends Roger McGuinn and David Crosby of The Byrds, Dino Valenti and guitarist John Cipollina formed the nucleus of what would become Quicksilver Messenger Service *(above)*, though the band's development was arrested (literally) when Valenti was busted for pot and speed. Quicksilver carried on without him, establishing a tough two-guitar attack with the addition of Gary Duncan.

Meanwhile, Rodney Albin, late of the Palo Alto scene, was holding regular jam sessions in the basement of his uncle's house at 1090 Page Street in Haight-Ashbury, out of which Big Brother & The Holding Company emerged; they debuted at the Trips Festival in January '66. When an unknown Texas-born blues belter named Janis Joplin joined the band in June '66, the group immediately became a top local draw.

Across the bay in Berkeley, Country Joe & the Fish cooked up a potent mixture of psychedelic rock and politically charged tunes that would eventually make them one of the biggest bands of the era. And all the while, the Merry Pranksters and the magic bus were rolling toward the Acid Tests…

Janis Joplin

Janis Joplin was a most unlikely superstar. A homely girl from Port Arthur, Texas (b. 1943), she left home at 17 to sing folk and blues songs in clubs and cafes in Austin and Houston; by 1965, she'd moved to California, spending time in both Venice (near L.A.) and the Bay Area, impressing many with her rough-hewn vocal style and deep appreciation of the blues. She moved back to Texas briefly in early 1966, but returned to San Francisco a few months later at the urging of fellow Texan Chet Helms (of the Family Dog collective) to join the psychedelic rock and blues band Big Brother & the Holding Company. Word spread quickly about the group's remarkable singer, and the Grateful Dead got to know Joplin well when the two groups lived near each other in rural Marin County during part of the summer of '66. The hard-drinking Joplin found a soulmate (and, for a time, a lover) in Pigpen.

It wasn't until Big Brother brought down the house at the Monterey Pop Festival in June 1967 that people outside California took much notice of Joplin. The following year, the band's second album, *Cheap Thrills*, became a huge hit and established Janis as a bona fide rock goddess. Joplin, with guitarist Sam Andrew in tow, left Big Brother in 1969 and formed the tighter, more R&B-oriented Kozmic Blues Band. During this period, Joplin lived in the Marin County town of Larkspur, a few blocks from the house shared by Garcia, Mountain Girl, and Robert Hunter. In early 1970 she formed the Full Tilt Boogie Band and in late June she joined the Dead, The Band, the New Riders, and a number of other bands on the famous Festival Express train tour across Canada.

Unfortunately, Joplin battled drug and alcohol dependence for most of her professional life, and on October 4, 1970, she OD'd on heroin in a Hollywood hotel room at age 27. Her posthumous album, *Pearl*, shot to Number One shortly after its release in January 1971, and yielded the singer's smash version of Kris Kristofferson's "Me & Bobby McGee," which the Dead also covered around that time. Robert Hunter dedicated "Bird Song," introduced by the Dead in February 1971, to Joplin.

Wielding a Gibson bass "with a neck like a telephone pole," Phil Lesh plays his inaugural show with the Warlocks. The Frenchy's gig is supposed be for two nights, but the "teen club's" manager un-invites them for the second night and stiffs them on their fee.

JUNE '65

| 1 – 11 | 12 | 13 | 14 | 15 | 16 | 17 | 18 | 19 | 20 |

| 21 | 22 | 23 | 24 | 25 | 26 | 27 | 28 | 29 | 30 |

35

Tuesday June 29
The Red Dog Saloon opens in Nevada.

The Red Dog Saloon

One of the key places in the evolution of the San Francisco "scene" was located not on the shores of the Bay but high up in the Sierras in Virginia City, Nevada, an old mining town popular with tourists looking for a remnant of the Old West. Chandler "Chan" Laughlin and two friends, Mark Unobsky and Don Works, decided that what Virginia City needed was an even wilder Wild West experience. They bought an old hotel, the Comstock Lodge, and turned it into a Hollywood-fantasy version of a rip-roarin' western watering hole, but with good music and food. The Red Dog Saloon opened for business on June 29 and soon began drawing tourists from California and Nevada—along with a stream of Bay Area hipsters who mixed old-fashioned cowboy style with new-fashioned chemical experimentation. Among them were the Charlatans, who established themselves as the house band. (They were billed—on what's considered the first "psychedelic poster"—as being "direct from San Francisco" although by some accounts they had never played together before.)

Unfortunately, the Charlatans' followers included the police, and after one of the band members got busted for pot at the beginning of September, they all got fired. Shortly thereafter the Red Dog shut down—much to the disappointment of Ken Kesey, who had come up with some Pranksters to party just then.

Short-lived as it was, the Red Dog interlude cast a shadow as long as a gunfighter at high noon. The Charlatans set a pattern and a path that would soon be followed by Jefferson Airplane, the Grateful Dead, Quicksilver Messenger Service, and other bands, while the young Bay Area hipsters who'd had so much fun in the mountains wasted no time in re-creating a localized scene back home.

"Everything was bizarre in those days. Society had no recognition of what we represented or that we were a problem. Nobody will ever be allowed to have as much fun as we had." CHAN LAUGHLIN IN THE *LAS VEGAS REVIEW-JOURNAL*, DECEMBER 2002.

The Garcias move into a Palo Alto home shared with, among others, David Nelson and Robert Hunter.

The Warlocks play several gigs at the start of August, although precise dates are unclear. Their first club gig takes place at the Fireside Club, San Mateo, California, where they possibly perform three nights. Gigs in Redwood City follow, at Big Al's Gas House, and Cinnamon A-Go-Go.

Wednesday August 4
The Lovin' Spoonful—a New York-based group with jug-band roots similar to the Warlocks'—plays Mother's in San Francisco, and the Warlocks and friends catch the show. Mother's is the first local venue to promote itself as a "psychedelic nightclub."

Saturday August 7
An amazing and unlikely association begins when about 40 Hell's Angels roar into La Honda for a two-day party. (Kesey connected with the Angels while hanging out with journalist Hunter S. Thompson, who is researching a book on the "outlaw bikers.") Cop cars hover outside and neighbors cower in their basements, but the two renegade groups have a great time.

The Pranksters had what looked like about a million doses of the Angels' favorite drug—beer—and LSD for all who wanted to try it. The beer made the Angels very happy and the LSD made them strangely peaceful and sometimes catatonic…
TOM WOLFE, THE ELECTRIC KOOL-AID ACID TEST.

AUGUST '65

| 1 | 2 | 3 | 4 | 5 | 6 | 7 | 8 | 9 |

JULY '65

| 1 ~ 24 | 25 | 26 ~ 31 |

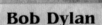

Sunday August 1
Jerry Garcia, Phil Lesh, Bob Weir, and friends mark Jerry's 23rd birthday with an acid trip (Weir's first).

Friday August 6
President Johnson signs the Voting Rights Act of 1965 into law. The act outlaws various practices used by Southern states to keep African-Americans from the polls.

Saturday August 7
The Mime Troupe's performance of Il Candelaio is stopped half way through by the SFPD on the grounds of obscenity. Director RG Davis is arrested, and Bill Graham, the Mime Troupe's new manager, announces he will host a benefit on November 6th for Davis's defense fund.

Sunday July 25
After an acoustic set at the Newport Folk Festival the previous day, Bob Dylan returns to the festival stage with an electric guitar, backed by a band that includes Mike Bloomfield on guitar and Al Kooper on organ, and launches into "Maggie's Farm," followed by "Like a Rolling Stone," and "Phantom Engineer." Contrary to popular belief, Dylan is not booed offstage by folkie purists infuriated that their god has sold out to the philistine forces of rock 'n' roll. There are plenty of pissed-off people in the audience and backstage (Pete Seeger reportedly went looking for a fire ax to cut the electrical cables) but Dylan's set is only cut short due to technical problems and the fact that he's only rehearsed three songs with his band, and he returns with his acoustic for "It's All Over Now, Baby Blue." Nevertheless, Dylan's "electric set" at Newport '65 has gone down in rock history as the day that American popular music changed.

Ralph J. Gleason

Born in New York City in 1917, Gleason worked briefly in radio before moving to San Francisco. By his own account, he wasn't much interested in music until, temporarily bedridden by measles, he had little to do but listen to the radio. In 1940 Gleason helped found a magazine, *Jazz Directions*, and in 1950 he began writing a jazz and pop column, "The Lively Arts," for the *San Francisco Chronicle*. The column became widely syndicated and, with his writing for *Down Beat* and other publications, it made him one of the country's most influential music critics.

Gleason, an early supporter of Lenny Bruce and Bob Dylan, among others, was the first established music writer to pick up on the Bay Area scene in 1965–66, and his writings on the Jefferson Airplane, the Dead, and other bands served as an elder statesman's imprimatur for all involved. In 1967 he joined Jann Wenner to launch *Rolling Stone* magazine. A year later he published *The Jefferson Airplane and the San Francisco Sound*, probably the first book-length appraisal of the subject. He continued as an editor of and contributor to *Rolling Stone* until his death in 1975.

Bob Dylan

Arguably the most important figure in postwar pop music, Bob Dylan was born Robert Zimmerman in Duluth, Minnesota, in 1941. He came to New York City and, with a drawling delivery patterned after idol, Woody Guthrie, a new name, and a carefully contrived persona, he became the boy wonder of the coffeehouse scene and, for a time, the consort of folk queen Joan Baez. On his second album, *The Freewheelin' Bob Dylan* (1963), he came into his own as a songwriter, and his profile got a boost when Peter, Paul, & Mary had a hit with his "Blowin' in the Wind." Dylan infuriated folk purists with 1965's *Bringing It All Back Home*, seven of its eleven tracks featured Dylan backed by a rock 'n' roll band. When he appeared onstage with an electric guitar at the 1965 Newport Folk Festival, his apostasy was complete. Dylan soon conquered the pop world. His single "Like a Rolling Stone" climbed to No. 2 on the charts—the first tune to crack Top 40 radio's three-minute song-length barrier. Brilliant albums followed, notably *Highway 61 Revisited* (1965), *Blonde on Blonde* (1966), *John Wesley Harding* (1967), *Nashville Skyline* (1969), and *Blood on the Tracks* (1975). After a near-fatal heart infection in 1997, the master came back to form with *Time Out of Mind*, followed up in 2001 with *Love and Theft*.

Bill Graham

Born Wolfgang Grajonza in Berlin in 1931, the future Bill Graham made it into America just before the Holocaust; some of his relatives weren't so lucky. Adopted by a family in the Bronx, he changed his name, studied at City College, served on the front line in Korea with distinction, and worked as a singing waiter at Grossinger's, the famous Catskills resort, before moving to L.A. in the early '50s. Graham's first love was acting, but casting directors found his looks "too ethnic," i.e., Jewish. (He would later appear in several movies, including Francis Ford Coppola's *Apocalypse Now*.) Graham moved to San Francisco, getting a good salary in the corporate world, but like so many people in the city in the early '60s, he was looking for more out of life.

Graham became business manager for the San Francisco Mime Troupe in '65. While hosting SFMT events he discovered his true metier as a concert promoter, and first met the just-named Grateful Dead—beginning 25 years of symbiosis between the band and "Uncle Bobo." Graham combined New York *chutzpah* with San Francisco idealism. His organizational skills were phenomenal, as was his attention to detail. Graham moved rock into the arena era and oversaw charitable events like Live Aid, the Arms tour, and the Amnesty International tour.

Graham died in a helicopter crash in October 1991. The Dead headlined the November 3 "Laughter, Love, and Music" tribute in Golden Gate Park and further honored Graham with a special Rex Foundation Award, presented annually since 1996.

| 17 | 18 ~ 30 | 31 |

Tuesday August 31
The Beatles play San Francisco's Cow Palace. Hoping to lure the Fab Four to La Honda, Kesey & Co. ride Furthur into town bearing a banner that reads "The Merry Pranksters Welcome the Beatles." The Pranksters have to make a run for the bus when the audience rushes the stage and the show ends in a stampede for the exits.

Wednesday August 11
Racial tensions explode into rioting in the Watts section of Los Angeles; 34 people are killed and at least a thousand injured over the next five days.

| 13 | 14 | 15 | 16 |

Friday August 13
The Matrix coffeeshop opens at 3138 Fillmore Street in San Francisco. Jefferson Airplane are the opening-night act, and band members including Paul Kantner and Marty Balin, are part-owners of the club. San Francisco Chronicle music critic Ralph J. Gleason is in attendance, and his article "Jefferson Airplane—Sound and Style" marks the first mention of the emerging "San Francisco sound" in the "mainstream" media.

| 10 | 11 | 12 |

The Hell's Angels

The "Outlaw Biker" story really begins in July 1947, when the Pissed Off Bastards gang tore up Hollister, a small northern California town. Condemned by the American Motorcycle Association as outlaws, by the late 1950s the Hell's Angels Motorcycle Club had evolved out of various California groups. The Angels' numbers were small but their reputation was fearsome, especially after accusations of rape were leveled against several members in 1964. The Angels were mainly young, white, working-class men united by total devotion to their Harley-Davidson "choppers," utter contempt for the mores of "straight" America, and a willingness to beat the crap out of rival gang members and anyone else who pissed them off.

The Hell's Angels, incredibly, formed a mutual admiration society with the pacifistic Pranksters, and by 1965 the Angels had countercultural cred—they were, after all, rejecting the values of conventional society in their own way. But the Angels' politics—conservative, to put it mildly—proved problematic, more so after Oakland Angels tangled with anti–Vietnam War protesters (see October 16, 1965). Friendships between individual Angels and members of the Pranksters/Dead survived, but the honeymoon was over. And then, in 1969, came Altamont (see page 105).

Today, the Angels claim a membership of several thousand in about 36 chapters. Contemporary Angels say that it's all about the bikes, though they've never shaken their reputation for violence and the outlaw mentality.

Sunday September 5
San Francisco Examiner
"Hippie" article.

"Lady, what this little séance needs is *us*."

PHIL LESH TO LURIA CASTELL OF THE FAMILY DOG.

Saturday October 16

In Berkeley, some 14,000 demonstrators protest the escalating Vietnam War; they are serenaded by the Instant Action Jug Band featuring "Country Joe" McDonald and Barry "The Fish" Melton. Together with the first Family Dog show that night, the demonstration marks the quickening of the Bay Area as a socio-politico-musico community.

The day also sees a challenge to the dalliance between the hip community and the Hell's Angels when Oakland chapter president Sonny Barger leads a phalanx of Angels in blocking the demonstrators' route through Oakland.

Saturday October 30

The second Family Dog–produced dance is promoted as "A Tribute to Sparkle Plenty," keeping the comic-book character motif going. The (non-performing) Warlocks & friends arrive at Longshoremen's Hall after a sunshine daydream of a day tripping in outer Marin County, and immediately understand that they've found their *milieu*.

Friday October 15

The Coffee Gallery in San Francisco hosts the debut performance of another new band, the Great Society. The lineup includes brothers Darby and Jerry Slick and Darby's wife, Grace Slick.

Saturday October 16

The first Family Dog dance, billed as "A Tribute to Dr. Strange" in psyche-dada tribute to the Marvel Comics character, is held at the Longshoremen's Hall, San Francisco. The Charlatans and Jefferson Airplane play while Bill Ham's light show helps trippers trip the light fantastic.

Nobody was quite prepared for it. The people who weren't stoned on acid looked stoned... There were all these... crazy... people... wearing Haight-Ashbury Victorian clothes, cowboy and Indian costumes, slinky antique gowns, paisley prints, spacesuits, with paint on their faces and feathers in their hair, dancing, dancing.
CHARLES PERRY, ROLLING STONE, FEBRUARY 1976

Another historical "what if?": A couple of Family Dog members had gone to the In Room to check out the Warlocks as a possible band for their first show, but they decided the boys didn't have enough original songs to make the cut.

The H Word

The *San Francisco Chronicle's* competitor, the *San Francisco Examiner*, noted that the city's Haight-Ashbury section was attracting artists, musicians, political activists, and other eccentric/bohemian types. Low rents were behind the migration. Much of the area had been earmarked for demolition in order to build a freeway, which would have been a bonanza for local property owners. When the freeway plan was canceled, landlords let the area's beautiful, many-roomed Victorian houses go to seed to such an extent that soon they could be rented on the cheap, leading to an influx of students and the aforementioned bohemians. The article referred to the Haight's new denizens as "hippies"—a neologism derived from "hipster," the old synonym for "beatnik"—the first use of the term in print, at least in the context of San Francisco.

The Family Dog

Encapsulating the mix of art, entertainment, and altruistic entrepreneurialism that produced the San Francisco scene, the "collective" began in the Dog House, a Pine Street boarding house that sheltered Jack Towle, Ellen Harmon, Luria Castell, and artist Alton Kelley, the latter three veterans of the Red Dog. In the best let's-put-on-a-show tradition, the foursome decided, in the fall of '65, to produce and promote a dance at San Francisco's Longshoremen's Hall, tapping the abundant local talent pool for music. They dubbed their venture the Family Dog. (There are several versions of how they came up with the name: it might have memorialized Ellen Harmon's recently deceased pooch, or derived from the name of the house they shared, or possibly it was a reference to a facetious scheme to operate a pet cemetery.) The first Family Dog-produced dance (see October 16) and the two that followed were key events in the evolution of the nascent "hippie" community. In 1966, after Luria Castell relocated to Mexico, Chet Helms (see page 56) took over the name and began producing regular shows at the Avalon Ballroom and, later, at the Great Highway.

John Cipollina

Born in Berkeley, California, on August 24, 1943, John Cipollina spent his early boyhood in Latin America—where, perhaps, he first absorbed the sound of the flamenco guitar, one of the musical strands he wove into his own distinctive idiom. In the Bay Area he played in bands with styles ranging from folk to rock 'n' roll. After an early collaboration with folk singer Dino Valenti was cut short, Cipollina met drummer Greg Elmore and fellow guitarist Gary Duncan at the first Family Dog show at Longshoremen's Hall. Cipollina already knew David Freiberg, a bass player, from the Sausalito folk circuit, and Jim Murray was enlisted on rhythm guitar—the initial lineup of Quicksilver Messenger Service was set, and the band played its first gig at the Fillmore Auditorium, on February 12, 1966.

To many scenesters, Quicksilver was the San Francisco band, with a hard-edged bluesy sound propelled by Cipollina and Duncan's guitars. Like the Dead, QMS lived together for a period on a ranch. Locals soon came to resent their new neighbors when Cipollina's pet timber wolf started preying on local livestock.

Throughout the late '60s QMS and the Grateful Dead appeared on the same bills and the band members became good friends. Cipollina remained a fixture on the Bay Area scene in the '70s and '80s, playing in at least a dozen bands, including the Dinosaurs; he also jammed with the Dead 13 times in the late '70s and early '80s, including six New Year's Eve shows. A respiratory ailment claimed his life in 1989.

Louder and Weirder: The In Room

In September the Warlocks truly came together as a band when they landed a six-week engagement at the In Room, a cocktail lounge in Belmont, California. Like the Beatles' famous stint at Hamburg's Star Club, the In Room gig was rock 'n' roll boot camp for the Warlocks: they played five nights a week, five 50-minute sets a night, doing hard-driving rock 'n' roll and rhythm & blues, sometimes backing up visiting acts like the Coasters, sometimes sharing the bill with other local bands, including the Misfits, an early incarnation of Moby Grape.

It was a tough room—a dark dive frequented by serious boozers and pickup artists, the kind of place where bouncers had to protect the waitresses from over-ardent customers. But it was at the In Room where the individual band members—with their widely differing musical influences and levels of experience—learned each other's idiosyncrasies and figured out how to meld them into a powerful collective sound.

And as the Warlocks' confidence and cohesion grew, they began to play, as Jerry Garcia later recalled, "louder and weirder"—the weirdness stoked by joints smoked in the parking lot between sets, and, when they could get it, by LSD (although not yet while playing). Pigpen, with his true bluesman's devotion to the bottle, begged off. By the end of the six weeks the loudness and weirdness proved too much for the club's management; the regulars were staying away, and although the Warlocks were now attracting a following of their own, they weren't invited back.

Right: Some of the mere handful of photos that exist of the Warlocks. Note that although Pigpen is behind his Vox organ, he also uses a hand-held microphone at points, befitting his role as sometime lead singer.

LISTENING FOR THE SECRET

November 1965 – December 1969

Each of the five original members of the Grateful Dead brought something unique to the band's chemistry. Garcia came to the electric guitar after intensive stints playing bluegrass and old-time music on the acoustic guitar and banjo. Pigpen was steeped in blues and R&B. Weir's style had been informed by strum folk music and fingerpicking country blues. Drummer Bill Kreutzmann was playing rock 'n' roll and R&B but listening to jazz. As for Phil Lesh—well, when he replaced Dan Morgan, Jr. as bassist in the Warlocks, he'd never played a note on the instrument before. Yet he quickly became perhaps the most interesting and unusual player in the group, and he developed into one of the true titans of the electric bass.

The band on the steps of 710 Ashbury, early 1967. Not exactly the sort of group one expected to find on a golf course. The hat behind Phil was apt, however—he had played in school bands.

For Lesh, The Bus came by in May 1965. He'd known Garcia for several years; indeed, working as a volunteer engineer for the noncommercial radio station KPFA back in the winter of 1962. Phil had helped Jerry, then an earnest aspiring folkie, get on the prestigious *Midnight Special* program hosted by Gert Chiarito. Three years later, following the Warlocks' second-ever gig (which he had missed) Phil found himself at a party with the band and a bunch of their friends—many of whom he knew from traveling in the same Boho circles on the Peninsula. During the party, Lesh and Garcia went off to a friend's car to smoke some pot that one of Weir's friends had bought from the already legendary Neal Cassady, and, as Phil remembered it years later, "At some point during this party I mentioned that I might like to get into playing some electric instrument. I said, 'maybe bass guitar,' something like that. It was a stoned moment and I didn't think any more about it."

About two weeks later, well-lubricated on LSD, Lesh and some friends went to see the Warlocks play at Magoo's pizza parlor: "We came bopping in there and it was really happening. Pigpen ate my mind with the harp, singing the blues. They wouldn't let you dance but I did anyway—we were so fuckin' stoned! During the set break, Jerry took me off to a table and said 'How'd you like to play bass in this band? Our bass player is not a musician, and we have to tell him what notes to play.' I said, 'By God, I'll give it a try!'" In another interview he recalled of that night, "I knew something great was happening, something bigger than everybody, bigger than me for sure."

His fate secure, Lesh got a loaner bass from a local instrument shop called Guitars Unlimited, then his girlfriend bought him a funky single pick-up Gibson "with a neck like a telephone pole." He recalled, "When I first played an electric instrument, I played it for seven hours straight and I couldn't sleep that night. It got me so high that I knew something had to be happening—something extremely different from acoustic [playing]. Then, of course, you start taking acid and the phenomenon magnifies further."

Garcia and various others showed him the rudiments of bass, but from the very beginning Phil approached the instrument in his own way. "What I did was come to the bass as a musician, period," he said. "It was obvious there were certain fundamentals that had to be observed—deal with the bass drum, play the root of certain chords—but after six months of that it was obvious to me as a musician that a whole bunch of that could be disposed of."

Phil's own musical background was completely different from that of the other band members. Growing up across the bay in El Cerrito and Berkeley, his first instrument was the violin; he loved classical music. Later, he took up the trumpet and played in his high school marching band and concert band, then in the jazz band at the College of San Mateo, where he also started to get into writing music. Increasingly, though, he was drawn to more radical styles of music: the adventurous jazz of John Coltrane, Miles Davis, Charles Mingus, and others; modern "classical" composers like Arnold Schoenberg and Charles Ives; and electronic music pioneers such as Karlheinz Stockhausen, Morton Subotnick, and Luciano Berio (with whom he studied briefly at Mills College).

Lesh took to writing extremely complex (some might say unperformable) pieces, but gradually drifted away from both the academic world and from composing. By 1965, he was just another seemingly goal-less, disaffected young adult—trapped in a post office job he hated, growing his hair long, smoking weed and taking speed, then discovering acid, and, on that fateful May night, having his true destiny revealed to him.

It didn't matter that Phil had never played bass before he joined the Warlocks. They were all pretty much amateurs when they started. As Phil later noted, "We all learned how to play together, and that's why we play well together." He never studied (or copied) the great bass players of the era such as Bill Wyman, Paul McCartney, or Motown ace James Jamerson. Instead, he fashioned his own style of playing based on the complicated musical notions that swirled constantly in his head—everything from Bach and Palestrina to acoustic jazz bassists.

"Phil was a very high dude in those days," Rock Scully noted. "Now he's considered a genius, but in those days he was just this weird ex-postal worker who'd just taken up the bass but had some really neat ideas musically. He was willing to push that envelope."

Phil might have been a fairly conventional player during the first few months after he joined the band, but by the time the group became the Grateful Dead, just before the Acid Tests began, he was already transforming into a highly idiosyncratic musician. Rather than accepting the established notion that the bass is essentially just a low-end time-keeper, always serving the chordal roots of a given song, Lesh understood that there is both beauty and power in constructing imaginative melodic lines, while still retaining the instrument's important rhythmic function. From the outset, too, Phil and Garcia had a special musical relationship based on a shared love of melodic and rhythmic exploration and of intense chaos. Sometimes clashing, other times dancing beautifully together, their sympathetic union was at the heart of the Dead's sonic maelstrom for 30 years.

"Instead of figures or patterns or connective tissue like regular bass players do," Garcia marveled in the '90s, "he [might play] a line that's actually the length of the song. It's like a beautiful melody when you hear it back at twice the speed. You hear all kinds of lovely syncopations and all these incredible things in it… When the time comes to do what the bass has to do, like hit the root on a key chord of whatever, Phil is usually there for the important stuff. There's the required stuff and the elective stuff. For Phil, the required stuff is about one percent of what he plays. You have to forget what you think you know about the bass in order to get next to it, because it drives regular people crazy. Ask the drummers.

"You have to have faith in what Phil is playing," Garcia continued. "That's the key. He plays the bass as though he invented the instrument and nobody had ever played it before him."

"He's about as angular as a bass player could be and then some," added Weir. "It's his own little specialty. And after nearly thirty years of playing with him, you learn not to intuit what he's going to do, because

"When I first played an electric instrument, I played it for seven hours straight and I couldn't sleep that night. It got me so high that I knew something had to be happening."

PHIL LESH TO HANK HARRISON, *THE DEAD BOOK*, 1972

that's not possible. He can intuit your intuition and not be there. He can hear you thinking and make sure he's not supplying what you're expecting. So you learn to live with that. If you have any sort of neurosis, you're in the wrong band."

Phil was the perfect bass player for the Grateful Dead during their most adventurous and psychedelic period, from the fall of 1967 through the summer of 1969. It was during this era that the band started developing complex and expansive songs and jams that reflected the players' increased skill and dexterity, and demonstrated their truly telepathic ability to breathe as one musical organism—what Mickey Hart, who joined the group in September 1967, calls "entrainment." Phil was right in the thick of the swirl—always eager to steer the music to bold new spaces, and also strongly involved in the group's original material: he helped write "Alligator" with Pigpen and Robert Hunter; he penned "New Potato Caboose" (which was sung by Weir) with his good friend Bobby Petersen, the mad poet who had originally turned him on to pot; he and Garcia wrote "St. Stephen" to Hunter's words; he was the musical architect of "The Eleven," that marvelously intricate, rotating jam in 11/4 time; and of course he was intimately involved with the group's greatest foray into space, "Dark Star."

"'Dark Star' has always had the potential to go absolutely anywhere," Phil commented in one interview. "We designed it that way in the first place, and it turned out to be a very appropriate vehicle for trying a whole lot of different things through the years. That was the one we sort of tacitly agreed upon where anything was okay."

"The way we approach music is a different road than almost anybody else—that improvisational attitude," Lesh noted in another interview. "It's one thing we all agreed on at the beginning—subconsciously, because we didn't really talk about it until much later. Once we had the experience that we could do it, then we started trying to rationalize formal connections so we could extend even further."

Even in the Dead's many shorter songs, the challenge from day one was to improvise creatively within the fixed structures, to keep the tunes constantly mutable and evolving. "I just try to do something different all the time," Lesh explained, "because most of the songs we do are strophic—in other words, sections repeat—so I just try to develop what I'm playing through those many repetitions to the greatest extent I can. In other words, it might start out simple and then take off from there. Literally, I cannot play the same thing for every verse; it's not in me."

Phil has often said that the period encompassing *Anthem of the Sun*, *Aoxomoxoa*, and *Live/Dead* was his favorite era of Dead music because it was so fresh, free, and unpredictable. It was a time when the band was rehearsing for several hours every day, stretching out as musicians, investigating unusual time signatures, deliberately going "outside" and throwing caution to the wind; as he and other band members said through the years, letting "the music play the band."

"The basic idea," he explained of his approach to playing, "is always to be part of the flow of the eternal current of music always going on in some dimension. So when our group mind is tuned properly, we can open a door or pipeline to that dimension, and that music comes through us. We don't make up that music; it is dictated, in a sense. Everybody gets a different piece of it, but it all fits together, so the idea is to surf that flow or stream like a solar wind or an ocean current and take people through many different twists and turns and realms of activity."

That "current" never stops, either. Asked in 2003 whether playing an open-ended song like "Dark Star" in the post-Garcia Dead feels like a continuation of earlier versions of the song, Lesh had this characteristically cosmic answer: "'Dark Star' today is an extension of the 'Dark Star' that has drifted through all of us since 1967. 'Dark Star' is always playing somewhere, all we do is tap into it. I'm serious. There are several other Grateful Dead tunes that are like that; 'Dark Star' is the classic. It's always playing and we just pick up on what's happening in the moment. We just open the door and walk into it and bring it back."

The audience, too, has always been part of the equation: "At the very beginning I used to think of there being a carrier wave that was stringing us all together, the audience and the band," Lesh said. "For the first three or four years of the Grateful Dead it seemed as if there was information being transmitted back and forth on that carrier wave. Then in the early '70s it seemed to change, in that energy and the link was still there, but what was transmitted back and forth was just energy; there wasn't information of any kind."

In another interview he stated, "I've always felt, from the very beginning—even before the Acid Tests—that we could do something that was, not necessarily extra-musical,

Though Phil hung out at 710 Ashbury, home to most of the Dead in the late '60s, he and his girlfriend Florence Nathan (later known as Rosie McGee) lived on nearby Belvedere Street.

Phil is that he was also very seriously irreverent and he really did not have any patience for pomposity or pretension. He loved to goad people. If they couldn't take it, he'd do it even more. It wasn't meant to be mean or malicious, but it was definitely there, and if you got him going he wouldn't stop. Hassinger was fair game, definitely. Anybody who was terminally straight, it was all over for them."

Lesh, Garcia, and soundman Dan Healy effectively took over the completion of that album—together they conceived of the idea of combining live and studio tracks into a trippy collage, which they also mixed, six hands

"You have to have faith in what Phil is playing. That's the key. He plays the bass as though he invented the instrument and nobody had ever played it before him."

JERRY GARCIA TO JON SIEVERT, *GUITAR PLAYER*, SPECIAL GRATEFUL DEAD ISSUE, 1993

but something where music would only be the first step. Something maybe even close to religion—not in the sense of 'The Beatles are more popular than Jesus,' but in the sense of the actual communing. We used to say that every place we play is church."

Both perfectionist and taskmaster, Lesh pushed the other band members hard in the late '60s, both onstage and in the studio. He could also be hostile to and dismissive of "outsiders" who didn't share his values or his cosmic musical vision. Just ask poor Dave Hassinger, who bailed out of the production of *Anthem of the Sun* in late 1967 in part because Phil was so difficult to deal with. "He's very, very opinionated," Hassinger complained years later. "He would be worrying about the sound of his bass to the point where it got almost ridiculous, I thought."

"Phil always has really strong ideas about what's right and how he wants something to be or how he wants it to happen," commented Rosie McGee, Lesh's girlfriend at the time of the *Anthem* sessions. "Sometimes, if he knows what he wants but he doesn't know how to get there, to him it's not unreasonable if it's going to take 300 hours… The other thing about

operating the console. And whether it actually achieved Phil's stated goal of sounding like "a thousand-petal lotus flowering from nothing," the album stands as one of his greatest contributions to the Dead canon, a deeply weird picture of a strange and exciting time and headspace. Add to that a live document from the period—say, *Two from the Vault*, recorded in August '68, or *Live/Dead*, from February '69—and you have a portrait of a restless and fearless searcher, capable of astounding feats of musical and metaphysical magic.

Lesh would enjoy many other peak periods with the band—for instance, there are many who believe his work between '72 and '74 was unsurpassed in its power, imagination, and stylistic diversity. And there's no doubt that he has continued to mature and develop as a player through years, even into his sixties. But as much as anyone, Phil has carried the torch for the Dead's psychedelic roots and for the spirit of '60s music up to the present day. It turns out that what Garcia stated years ago has always been true: "If Phil is happening, the band is happening."

During his brief spell as manager, Hank Harrison books the Warlocks into Pierre's—a distinguished jazz club fallen on hard times. The boys play 20-minute sets in between the topless dance acts. The exact length of the engagement isn't known, but it was probably no more than three nights.

1 2 3 4 5 6 7 8

Saturday November 6
One night and two big events. The third Family Dog dance takes place at Longshoremen's Hall featuring the Charlatans and L.A. imports Frank Zappa and the Mothers of Invention (see page 53). At the Calliope Ballroom on Howard Street, Bill Graham's first foray into rock 'n' roll is a benefit for the San Francisco Mime Troupe's defense fund, following their bust for performing a bawdy Commedia Dell'Arte in a park. Jefferson Airplane play along with New York rockers the Fugs, while Lawrence Ferlinghetti and Allen Ginsberg read.

Wednesday November 3
The "Emergency Crew" demo.

Monday November 1
The Warlocks get their first write-up in a national publication—folk magazine *Sing Out!*: "David Grisman found the Warlocks to be the best rock-and-roll group he heard in California. He especially liked a song written by their lead guitarist, Jerry Garcia, titled 'Bending Your Mind' [sic]."

Monday November 8
A power-grid overload shuts off electricity for two days in seven northeastern U.S. states and part of Canada.

Right: Photographer Herb Greene togs out the band in borrowed clothes and snaps them in various Beatles-esque poses; their first photo shoot.

Owsley Stanley, a.k.a. "Bear"

Owsley Stanley, nicknamed Bear for his hairy chest, was born in 1935 in Kentucky and developed his gift for engineering and electronics in the Air Force. After leaving military service, he was turned on to LSD by a friend. He'd always been a spiritual seeker, inspired by alchemy, and the drug promised the alchemical transformation of the human spirit. He learned to produce high-quality LSD, especially the legendary "Orange Sunshine." Despite manufacturing a million trips in the mid-'60s, he gave a lot away and was never the "LSD Millionaire" of tabloid legend.

Hooking up with the Pranksters led Bear to the Muir Beach Acid Test—and the Grateful Dead. By early '66, he had become both bankroll and soundman to the band. Focusing his technical skills on their audio gear, in 1969 he helped launch Alembic, which was a quantum leap in sound quality for the band, and a big influence on performance audio in general.

Inevitably Owsley ran afoul of the law and, after the Bourbon Street bust *(see page 112)*, he served two years in federal lockups. In 1973 he produced *The History of the Grateful Dead, Vol.1* and, from 1974, continued to contribute his sound skills part-time. Owsley moved to Australia and took up jewelry-making, and a bizarre high-protein diet. He died in an auto accident in 2011.

The Emergency Crew Session

The Warlocks' only foray into a recording studio was an audition for Autumn Records, a small label whose acts included Bobby Freeman and the Beau Brummells.

The band went into the tiny Golden State Studio in San Francisco in the throes of an identity crisis *(see right)* and decided to record the demo as the Emergency Crew. The session produced six tracks, including two covers—the traditional "I Know You Rider" and a rocked-up version of Gordon Lightfoot's "Early Morning Rain."

Of the four originals, "Caution (Do Not Stop On Tracks)" was the only number to find its way into the Grateful Dead repertoire. "I Can't Come Down" had derivatively Dylanesque lyrics from Jerry Garcia ("With secret smiles like a Cheshire Cat/And leather wings like a vampire bat…") but "Mindbender" (a.k.a. "Confusion's Prince") and "The Only Time is Now" did contain discernible flashes of what the future held.

The Emergency Crew didn't land a contract but the session tape was later widely bootlegged before its eventual release in 2001 as part of *The Golden Road* box set. It is also available separately, with other early live and studio material, on 2003's *Birth of the Dead*.

The Naming

During November it was decided to rename the band after Phil Lesh spotted a record by another group calling themselves the Warlocks (the future Velvet Underground or the Texas band that evolved into ZZ Top?). Jerry Garcia spotted "grateful dead" while flipping through a dictionary—a 1955 *Funk and Wagnalls New Practical Standard Dictionary*, to be precise—at Phil Lesh's apartment. The other band members weren't overly enthusiastic, but the name stuck—no surprise given the alternatives, which, according to David Shenk and Steve Silberman's *Skeleton Key*, included the Hobbits, Vanilla Plumbago, and Mythical Ethical Icicle Tricycle.

Despite parental suspicions, the term "grateful dead" does not have occult or satanic connotations. Nor does it have any connection to *The Egyptian Book of the Dead*. The definition, according to the same 1955 *Funk & Wagnalls New Practical Standard Dictionary of the English Language*, is "The motif of a cycle of folk tales which begin with the hero's coming upon a group of people ill-treating or refusing to bury the corpse of a man who had died without paying his debts. He gives his last penny, either to pay the man's debts or to give him a decent burial. Within a few hours he meets with a traveling companion who aids him in some impossible task, gets him a fortune, saves his life, etc. The story ends with the companion's disclosing himself as the man whose corpse the other had befriended." Such tales appear in a number of different cultures and Bob Franzosa collated thirteen variations in his 1989 study *Grateful Dead Folktales*. In the same year Hulogosi Press published Alan Trist's *Water of Life: A Tale of the Grateful Dead*, a "children's book for all ages" inspired by the archetype.

Saturday November 27
First Acid Test, "The Spread," Soquel, California.

25

27 28 29 30

The Acid Tests

The fruit of the mind-expanding madness first cultivated at La Honda, the Acid Tests were circuses with an infinite number of rings, and in which there was no distinction between the audience and the performers. It's probably impossible to describe the Acid Tests in mere words, although Tom Wolfe's New Journalism classic, *The Electric Kool-Aid Acid Test* (1968), came very close.

The dozen or so Tests were held around the Bay Area, L.A., and Oregon between December 1965 and October 1966. Admission was a dollar, which got you a paper cup to dip into the celebrated Kool-Aid, and the party typically went on until dawn. Neal Cassady often served as a ringmaster of sorts, while the Kens, Kesey and Babbs, overlaid their own cosmic rap. Pranksters "played" the Thunder Machine, an ever-evolving percussive sculpture, and no Acid Test was complete without movie projectors, microphones, tape recorders, and various sound-manipulating devices feeding into and out of the PA. Various Tests also included Roy Seburn's light show, vats of Day-Glo paint to smear everywhere (and on everyone), rolls of toilet paper to tear up and throw under the strobe lights… And, of course, there was the music of the Grateful Dead to get the synapses sizzling even faster.

However, the Dead were only one part of the scene, no different than any of the other participants except that they wielded musical instruments. Sometimes they played for hours on end and sometimes they played only a few minutes; sometimes they didn't play at all.

Kesey's legal troubles, the criminalization of LSD, and public complaints about hundreds of young people behaving strangely led to the demise of the Tests . The final event, the Acid Test Graduation Ceremony, took place on October 31, 1966.

"The Acid Test was the prototype for our whole basic trip . . . It was something more incredible than just rock 'n' roll and a light show . . . "
JERRY GARCIA IN ROLLING STONE, 1970.

Most scholars of psychedelia agree the first Acid Test took place on November 27, 1965, at Ken Babbs's place, "the Spread," in Soquel, near Santa Cruz. Numbers were small, but among those present were Jerry Garcia, Phil Lesh, and Bob Weir. Although various members of the Dead had intersected with Kesey & Co. in the past—back in the Perry Lane days in Palo Alto *(see page 32)*—the evening marked the beginning of the "formal" Prankster–Grateful Dead alliance, with Lesh and Weir agreeing to help plan the next Test the following Saturday, December 4, in San Jose.

The venue was the domicile of a local scenester known unto history only as "Big Nig." The house was too small for the 400 or so people who showed up, and although the wiring eventually proved too fragile for all the sound and light gear, the event probably qualifies as the Grateful Dead's first gig under the new name. The Rolling Stones were also playing in San Jose that night, so a Prankster posse including Sue Swanson, Connie Bonner, and Neal Cassady was dispatched to bring them in. Alas, they returned from the Civic Auditorium empty-handed.

The following Saturday, December 11, the Acid Test moved to a log cabin in Muir Beach, near San Francisco. Present that night were Florence Nathan, who would begin a long relationship with Phil Lesh, and Owsley Stanley, already famous in the Bay Area for his LSD. It was the latter's first Grateful Dead experience and he responded to the music by repeatedly scraping a chair across the floor; later he drove his car into a tree while fleeing imaginary police…

"The music was scary. Pushing me to the edge. The sound of Garcia's guitar was like the claws of a tiger… I thought to myself, 'These guys are going to be greater than the Beatles someday.'" OWSLEY STANLEY IN DAVID GANS'S CONVERSATIONS WITH THE DEAD.

December 18, and for the fourth Saturday running a Test took place—this time in Palo Alto. During the evening Jerry Garcia earned his nickname, "Captain Trips," after he was seen tipping his hat to a policeman in the club's parking lot—"tips" immediately became "trips" in Pranksterspeak. Among the newer Pranksters present was one Hugh Romney.

Eternal scenester, New Yorker, and one-time roommate of Bob Dylan, Hugh Romney (later Wavy Gravy), moved to California in 1962 and soon got drawn into Prankster circles. A co-founder of the Hog Farm—one of the first communes, and to this day a socially minded cooperative— Romney and friends also famously provided frontline security at Woodstock in 1969 … and at the Texas Pop Festival two weeks later, where B.B. King christened Romney with his famous handle.

Friday December 10
Fillmore Auditorium, San Francisco, California

Another benefit for the San Francisco Mime Troupe, Appeal II is produced by Bill Graham and features, among others, the Grateful Dead, Jefferson Airplane, and the Great Society. It is one of Graham's first encounters with the band. The event takes place at the Fillmore—formerly a ballroom, latterly a jazz and R&B venue, and soon to be the mothership of the burgeoning San Francisco sound.

"It was incredible because of the formlessness… Everybody was creating. Everybody was doing everything." JERRY GARCIA, TO JANN WENNER, 1972

December 4
"Big Nig's," San Jose, California
Acid Test.

11 12 13 14 15 16 17 **18** 19 20 21 22 23 24 25 26 27 28 29 30 **31**

1 2 3 4 5 6 7 8 9 **10**

Saturday December 11
Muir Beach, California
Acid Test.

Saturday December 18
Big Beat Club, Palo Alto
California. Acid Test.

Friday December 31
As 1965 ends, there are over 180,000 U.S. troops in Vietnam; the number of U.S. deaths tops 1,500.

TRIPS FESTIVAL

LONGSHOREMEN'S HALL
(400 NORTH POINT)
JANUARY 21-22-23
8 TO 12 PM
(SEE OTHER SIDE)

1966

Trips Festival

The idea of a sort of super–Acid Test taking place over a couple of days originated not with the Pranksters, but with Ramon Sender of the Tape Music Center and Stewart Brand.

Brand was an early psychedelic explorer and friend of the Pranksters who later edited *The Whole Earth Catalog* and then started The Well, one of the first popular on-line conferences. Together with Sender he conceived of a "crazy ceremonial" in which the entire hip community would take part. At the end of December 1965 they hooked up with the Pranksters, and planning for the event, which was to bring together all the disparate strands of the Bay Area psychedelic renaissance, began. The Trips Festival proved a major success, with more than 10,000 people participating over three days (January 21–23, 1966). Stewart Brand talked the event up as an "Acid Test without the acid." As if; there were few straight people in the room.

Saturday night was Prankster night, and that meant the Dead, though Big Brother played as well. Jerry was tripping so heavily when the time came for the band to start that he barely noticed the bridge of his guitar had collapsed. He looked down to see "this guy with the little sweater and clipboard" trying to find bits of the broken bridge. It was Jerry's first face-to-face encounter with Bill Graham. "I've always loved him for that," Jerry said much later. One memorable element of the Dead's performance came when champion gymnast Dan Millman leapt off the balcony onto a trampoline under a barrage of strobe lights—no one could be quite sure if it was real or an illusion.

"It was over three nights and it was the first really big collaborative effort in S.F. It was in the Longshoremen's Hall, which was the perfect place. It was an architectural gem—tall, narrow and with mezzanines in various places. There were a mass of different things: filmmakers, light shows, and all aspects of the experimental community. It was well publicized and organized, and a guy had been hired to be the organizer. He had a clipboard and a whistle and at first he wouldn't let us in. It was Bill Graham, and we said to him 'you can't not let us in—we're the band.' But we weren't on his list, so we had to lie eventually to get in! We did one night out of the three and it was wild. Ken [Kesey] had set up an overhead projector pointing up to the ceiling, and he was writing onto it. There was live music being mixed with things like Stockhausen. We were doing a sort of live mixing with commentaries. We even added our Prankster music, which of course nobody liked!"
MOUNTAIN GIRL 2003

NEVER TRUST A PRANKSTER!

Left and Right: *Freaking freely at the Trips Festival.*

"Anyone who thinks they're God, go onstage." PROJECTED BY KESEY

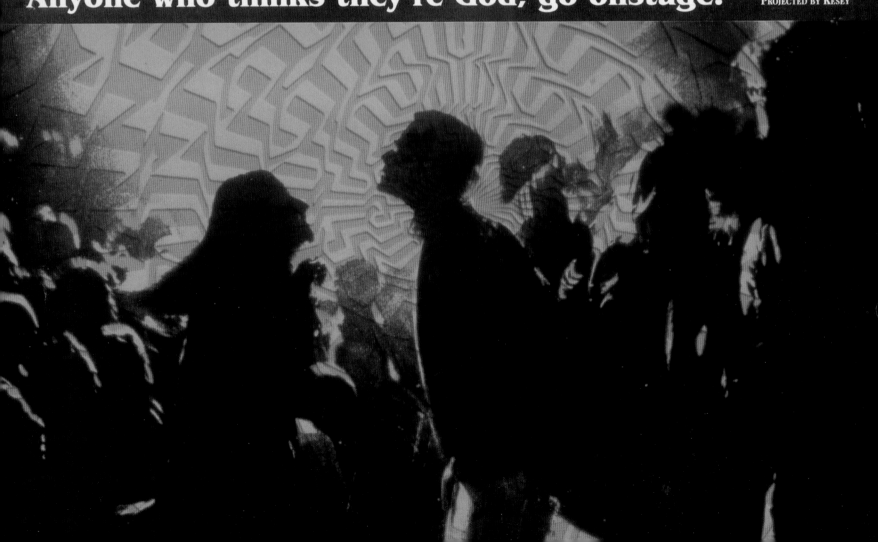

Monday January 3
The Psychedelic Shop opens on Haight Street and quickly becomes one of the focal points of the emerging scene.

Saturday January 1
Beaver Hall, Portland, Oregon

Portland Acid Test.

Saturday January 8
Fillmore Auditorium
San Francisco, California

Fillmore Acid Test.

Friday January 7
The Matrix, San Francisco, California

The night's set list is typical of the band's repertoire at this time—a mix of R&B ("In the Midnight Hour"), country blues ("Parchman Farm," "Death Don't Have No Mercy"), and "modern" folk ("Early Morning Rain" and two Dylan numbers, including "It's All Over Now, Baby Blue").

| **8** | 9 ~ 12 | **13** | **14** |

Friday January 14
Fillmore Auditorium, San Francisco, California

Appeal III—Another Mime Troupe Benefit—at the Fillmore Auditorium sees the Great Society headline, with the Dead appearing between the Mystery Trend and Sam Thomas & the Gentlemen's Band. The event marks the end of Bill Graham's business association with the SFMT.

Thursday January 13
The Matrix, San Francisco, California

The band plays at least a couple of shows at the Matrix between January 13–20. Among the songs performed is Lieber & Stoller's "I'm a Hog for You," a hit for the Coasters in 1959, and the perfect vehicle for Mr. McKernan's sweaty, funky delivery.

| **15** | 16 | 17 | **18** | **19** |

Saturday January 15
Sunday January 16
The Matrix, San Francisco, California

Wednesday January 19
Just three days after receiving a six-month prison-farm sentence for marijuana possession, Kesey, out on bail, gets busted for pot again, this time with Mountain Girl. With his legal problems multiplying, Kesey hatches a plan to prank his own suicide and take it on the lam to Mexico.

Left, right, and below: In the groove at the Trips Festival. That's Kesey in the space suit.

Rock Scully & Danny Rifkin

On January 8, 1966, San Francisco State student Rock Scully was managing the Charlatans and putting on a Family Dog dance with that band at California Hall in S.F. when he stumbled into the Fillmore Acid Test and had his mind blown by the Grateful Dead. Shortly after that night, the Dead's soundman, Owsley Stanley, invited Scully to become the Dead's manager. He agreed, but only if he could bring along his friend, Danny Rifkin, a college dropout who was building manager at 710 Ashbury Street, which became the Dead's house later in 1966. Together, Scully and Rifkin navigated the treacherous waters of the "straight" music business for the band, landing them their first contract with Warner Bros. Records in the fall of 1966.

The soulful and spiritual Rifkin was part of the Dead's management only sporadically through the years. He took several sabbaticals, but always seemed to find his way back in some capacity. Scully brought energy and promotional ability and grew into his role with the band. His ongoing drug dependency led to his ouster from the organization in the mid-'80s.

With co-writer David Dalton, Scully penned the alternately amusing and harrowing memoir, *Living With The Dead*, published in 1996 *(see page 452)*.

Tuesday January 18
As part of the pre-event hype surrounding the Trips Festival, a piece in the *San Francisco Chronicle* makes one of the first direct references to the psychedelic scene.

| 22 | 23 |

Saturday January 22
Sunday January 23
Longshoremen's Hall, San Francisco, California

Trips festival *(see pages 48-49)*.

Friday January 28
The Matrix, San Francisco, California

Big Brother & the Holding Company and the Loading Zone also appear.

| 24 | 25 | 26 | 27 | **28** | **29** |

Saturday January 29
The Matrix, San Francisco, California
Sound City Recording Studios, San Francisco, California

Sound City Acid Test. A double-header for the band and Garcia's vocal cords as the evening begins with a set at the Matrix.

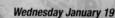

Acid Tests '66

In the new year the multimedia mindblowers now known as the Acid Tests went into high gear—literally and figuratively. "The Acid Test[s] started expanding at an incredible rate," Jerry Garcia recalled. "They had virtually no advertising or anything. You sort of had to be a detective to find out where they were gonna be. But even so they got to be immensely popular."

The first Acid Test of 1966 took place—probably!—on New Year's Day, in Oregon—Kesey's home turf—at Portland's Beaver Hall. The journey north was more intense than the actual event; *Furthur* broke down, everyone crammed into the back of a rental truck, which Neal Cassady piloted over ice-slicked roads and through a raging blizzard—a feat only the *fastestmanalive* could have pulled off.

Next stop was the Fillmore on January 8, the same night the Charlatans and the Jefferson Airplane played a Family Dog show at California Hall. In true communal spirit, Rock Scully, the Charlatans' manager, and Ken Kesey agreed that tickets for one event would be valid at the other. The Test ended on the early side with the police shutting down the power around 2:00 a.m., but not before Phil Lesh and Bob Weir had sung a wildly dissonant "Star-Spangled Banner" in imitation of a TV station ending its broadcast day. The night also led to another contretemps between the Grateful Dead and the "guy with the clipboard," Bill Graham, who had subleased the venue using Bill Kreutzmann as liaison. The Pranksters had painted the Fillmore's bathrooms in Day-Glo paint, and it seems the leaseholder, Charles Sullivan, was less than amused.

The last Acid Test before Kesey left for Mexico took place on January 29 in a small recording studio in the South of Market area. The event was low-key and mainly noteworthy for the recruitment of Bear, by Phil Lesh, as the Grateful Dead's soundman. According to Ken Babbs, Sound City was more of an attempt to record the sounds of a Test than a Test in its own right—and an LP was released, in small numbers, later in the year. The highlight of the record is an "interview" of Kesey and Babbs by someone variously identified as "Frank Frey" or "Jim the Host," who served as a "straight man" for Kesey:

Kesey: "… The first Prankster rule is that nothing lasts. And if you start there, and really believe that nothing lasts, you try to achieve nothing at all times."
Interviewer: "Well, if you're trying to achieve nothing, then why do you put so much effort into achieving nothing?"
Babbs: "We have nothing else to do."

As the Pranksters and the Dead had temporarily relocated to L.A., the next Test took place in the City of Angels on February 6—a day after the band's arrival. The Northridge Acid Test (promoted as a "happening") got underway in a Unitarian church in Northridge in the Valley—"A marvelous modern building shaped like a huge Bermuda onion," in Tom Wolfe's description.

February 12 witnessed the last of the major Tests and perhaps the most legendary, the Watts Acid Test. In fact, the event took place in a job-training center in Compton, not Watts. Less than six months earlier, Watts had exploded in one of the worst race riots in U.S. history, and there was still a lot of nervous tension in the air. About 200 people showed up, and many of them weren't hip as to what was in the Kool-Aid. Despite Hugh Romney's efforts to keep the uninitiated away from the punchbowl, it was a hot night and people threw back cup after cup. Unfortunately, a dosage miscalculation meant that the contents of the punchbowl were much stronger than usual. "The rest of the evening," Prankster Lee Quarnstrom observed, "was as weird as you might expect."

The potent Kool-Aid freaked a number of people out and, as so often the case, it fell to the non-tripping Pigpen to calm things down. The worst casualty was a young lady who'd just had a fight with her boyfriend and began repeatedly screeching "Who cares? Who cares?" Her discomfort started to freak out other people until Pigpen launched into a soothing rap: "I want to tell ya a little story now… Everything's gonna be all right now… I wanna tell everybody in the house right now, there's many things that you gotta do one more time. You got to think about your neighbors—You got to think about your friends—You got to think about your brothers… You got to think about everybody that means something…"

Although Pigpen got people's heads straight, the presence of the LAPD was a bummer. By morning the building was surrounded by L.A.'s finest, but LSD was still legal and the Pranksters had the proper permits, so all the police could do was arrest a few individuals on the usual flimsy charges.

To the City of Angels

During a rehearsal session at the "Questing Beast" in Berkeley on February 5, the Grateful Dead decided to depart the Bay Area for L.A. The band reasoned it would be easier to get "noticed" in L.A.—the center of the West Coast music business. The Pranksters were also heading to L.A. where they planned to host a couple of Acid Tests. Bear would join the band there later, along with the new "management team"— Rock Scully and Danny Rifkin. The Dead's sudden departure led to the cancellation of two scheduled shows (February 10 at the Cabale and February 11 at the Fillmore Auditorium).

FEBRUARY '66

1 2 3 4 5 **6** 7 8 9 10 11 **12** 13 14 15 16 17 18 19 20 21 22 **23** 24 **25**

Sunday February 6
Northridge Unitarian Church, Los Angeles, California

Northridge Acid Test.

Saturday February 12
Youth Opportunities Center, Compton, California

Watts Acid Test.

Wednesday February 23
Friday February 25
The band may have played two gigs—one at an unknown venue, one possibly at L.A.'s Ivar Theater—on these dates, but little documentation exists, and tapes circulating that purport to be from these shows may include material from later shows.

Saturday March 12
Danish Center, Los Angeles, California

Pico Acid Test
The Dead are known to have played "Viola Lee Blues," "You See a Broken Heart," and "In the Midnight Hour."

Saturday March 19
Carthay Studios, Los Angeles, California

Carthay Acid Test
The Pranksters and the Dead had planned an Acid Test at UCLA, but lurid publicity about the Watts Test meant it was shifted to Carthay Studios at the last minute. It was the final L.A. Acid Test and, indeed, by this time Kesey's "first Prankster rule" that "nothing lasts" had come true. Ken Babbs' heavy-handed approach alienated some of the group, while Bear and the Pranksters had an uneasy relationship, to say the least. Soon after, the entire scene split—some Pranksters returned to San Francisco, the rest took *Furthur* into Mexico to find Kesey; the band and Bear decided to stay in L.A. and pursue their hope of "making it in the record business." Jerry and Sara Garcia also began to drift apart during this period.

The Pink House

Deadquarters during the L.A. sojourn was an old Spanish-style dwelling on the fringes of Watts, which the band dubbed the Pink House. Owsley took over the top floor and the band members and their girlfriends crashed on the floors of the basically unfurnished pad.

"It turned out [the Pink House] was right next door to a whorehouse, and the whorehouse patrons would throw pot seeds out the window, so there were little pot plants growing all around—that's all we needed, since we were bringing the cops there almost every day because of the noise." BEAR TO BLAIR JACKSON

Meat me in L.A.
Years before Dr. Atkins became famous, Bear was an ardent proponent of an all-meat diet. And as Bear was paying the rent and bankrolling the band, what Bear ate, the band ate. The refrigerator was stocked with nothing but milk, eggs, and huge hunks of prime beef: the usual bill of fare was steak and eggs for breakfast, steak sandwiches (with smuggled bread) for lunch, and for dinner... steak. Once a week Owsley grudgingly allowed the band a meal at Canter's Deli, where he regarded their orders of fruit and vegetables as a personal affront.

March 1966

Above: *March 25, Troupers Hall, L.A., one of the few "regular" gigs the Dead played on their L.A. trip.*

Friday March 25
Troupers Hall
Los Angeles, California

The band's last gig of the Spring '66 L.A. expedition takes place in a retired actor's club. They net $75, most of which gets spent afterward at a late-night feast at Canter's.

Vietnam

Events in Vietnam would cast a shadow over the '60s throughout the world and particularly in the United States. After evicting its French colonial overlords in the 1950s, Vietnam split into communist North Vietnam, ruled by the dictator Ho Chi Minh, with aid from Russia and China, and South Vietnam, nominally democratic but ruled, in fact, by a succession of weak, corrupt dictators who were propped up by the U.S.

Around 1960 a communist guerrilla movement, the Vietcong, began a guerrilla war—with Northern support. The U.S. sent equipment and "advisers" to the South Vietnamese military and then, from March 1965, bombers and increasing numbers of U.S. troops, all this on the theory—"the domino theory"—that if South Vietnam fell to communism, so would the rest of East Asia.

There'd been demos in the Bay Area against U.S. involvement in Vietnam as early as 1965 but support for the war was still pretty widespread in much of America in '66, except in the Haight. As for the Grateful Dead, they were happy to play fundraisers for antiwar organizations, but they collectively refused to identify themselves with this or any "cause." It was a policy the band upheld consistently for its entire career. Bob Weir later said of the band's attitude toward Vietnam, "We were realistic enough to realize that there was nothing we could do that was going to change anything [but] in our hearts we were against it."

L.A. Blues

In April, with money running low, Bear (who usually gives away more acid than he sells) converted his aerie in the Pink House into a lab and brewed up one of his best-known vintages of LSD—Blue Cheer. Myth has it that powder from the attic lab soon coated most of the surfaces in the house, so everyone was tripping to one extent or another all the time, which, needless to say, made sleep difficult and made the side of beef in the fridge look even less appetizing. Myth or not, it's a cheery tale!

DRESS the way YOU are

Trips

THE GRATEFUL DEAD
THE LOADING ZONE
CELEBRITY DROP IN'S
TRIPS REGULARS

BEACH and MASON on FISHERMAN'S WHARF

APRIL FRI. 22nd, SAT. 23rd, SUN. 24th 9 p.m. to 1 a.m.

LONGSHOREMEN'S HALL SAN FRANCISCO

1966?

PRE-SALE $2.00

The Store - Berkeley, 2491 Telegraph Ave.; Sherman Clay - Oakland, 2101 Broadway;
City Lights - San Francisco, 261 Columbus and Downtown Center Box Office, 325 Mason

AT THE DOOR $2.50

🎸 **Friday April 22**
🎸 **Saturday April 23**
Sunday April 24

Longshoremen's Hall, San Francisco, California

After six weeks in L.A. the Grateful Dead are no closer to getting "the big break" than they'd been in San Francisco. And they're homesick, and keenly aware that big things are doing around the Bay while they sit in the Pink House in a cloud of acid dust and meat grease. When Rock Scully books them into Longshoremen's Hall for three nights (for $375) they leave L.A. almost as quickly as they left San Francisco, arriving with just a few hours to spare before the first show.

The band shares the bill with the Loading Zone for all three nights. The shows are promoted *(left)* as the "196? Trips Festival: Dress the Way You Are" and some of the performers from the original event *(see pages 48-49)* reprise their roles.

Rancho Olompali

The band had nowhere to stay on their return to San Francisco, and for a week everyone couch-surfed. Then, as often happened in those years, the women—in this case, Bear's girlfriend Melissa Cargill and Phil Lesh's girlfriend Florence Nathan—were the ones to get it in gear. Melissa and Florence managed to find a 26-room adobe manse, Rancho Olompali, on a beautiful spread of land (complete with swimming pool) near Novato in Marin County. ("Olompali," in the language of the Miwok Indians, meant something like "place of the southern people.") All this for $1,100 for six weeks.

Olompali was a mellow place—even though, while tripping, some of its new denizens picked up angry vibes from the spirits of the expropriated Miwoks. The Dead and their growing circle of friends and associates held a couple of legendary parties in those six weeks, attended by anybody who was anybody in the San Francisco rock scene—Jorma Kaukonen, Jack Casady, Grace Slick (who, like Pigpen, preferred booze to acid), Janis Joplin, Neal Cassady, George Hunter...

"*[Olompali] was completely comfortable, wide open, high as you wanted to get, run around naked if you wanted to, fall in the pool, completely open scenes ... Everything was just super-groovy. It was a model of how things could be really good...*" JERRY GARCIA, *1971*

April 1966

53

The L.A. Scene

San Franciscans look down on L.A. as a crass and phony wasteland. So when the Dead, Owsley, and the Merry Pranksters took the Acid Test to Los Angeles in early '66 it wasn't because they were determined to turn on and enlighten Hollywood starlets and surf bums. The Pranksters were edging closer to their exiled leader Ken Kesey, then hiding out in Mexico. The Dead were along for the ride, while perhaps dipping a toe in record industry waters. Neither group created much of a stir there.

The most popular group in L.A. in '66 was, in fact, a TV creation—The Monkees, whose onscreen antics and catchy pop tunes captivated millions of Americans every week. But there *were* real bands in L.A. The Beach Boys made what many consider their greatest album, *Pet Sounds*, in 1966. The Mamas and the Papas hailed from New York but came to epitomize a certain breezy, commercial Southern California sound with a string of hits. By 1966, too, The Byrds had notched up several best-selling singles with their pleasing blend of Beatles harmonies, jangly guitars, and Dylan's strong influence. Country-rock pioneers Buffalo Springfield always seemed to be falling apart, but with a talented front line of singers and guitarists that included Stephen Stills, Neil Young, and Richie Furay (later of Poco), they gained a large following and made a couple of albums now regarded as classics.

Much darker were a pair of bands who regularly filled Hollywood's Sunset Strip nightclubs. Love, led by singer/guitarist Arthur Lee, were snapped up by Elektra Records and quickly snared a hit with the single "My Little Red Book" from their eponymous 1966 LP. It was Lee who convinced the label to sign The Doors, with lead singer/poet/shaman Jim Morrison. Their exceptional first two albums would come out in 1967 and catapult the band from a residency at the Whisky A-Go-Go to national stardom.

Another Southland group making waves was the electric blues 'n' boogie band Canned Heat, with the gritty guitar of Al Wilson and the vocals of Bob "Big Bear" Hite. And finally, the incomparable Mothers of Invention, whose leader, Frank Zappa, was already in top form—mixing rock, jazz, avant-garde, and more as they pilloried and parodied American culture on their *Freak Out!* album. Hard to believe, but Zappa was just warming up...

"The only good thing about L.A. is they've got about a thousand TV stations." PIGPEN, *1967*

This page and opposite: *The Dead's parties at Rancho Olompali, during* March *and April 1966, were legendary.*

In the months after their return from L.A. the Grateful Dead are known to have gigged fairly frequently, perhaps as often as five nights a week, as evinced by dates on posters and handbills and the recollections of people on the scene. And in that casual, collegiate scene, nobody was particularly scrupulous about keeping records, so the dates and venues of the band's shows in this period aren't precisely documented. The shows listed here are ones for which there is some sort of documentary evidence, although they probably represent only a few of the Grateful Dead's performances in the Spring and Summer of '66.

MAY '66

1	2	3	4	5	6	7

Saturday May 7
Harmon Gym, University of California, Berkeley, California

The Dead play Peace Rock 3, third in a series of benefits for the Vietnam Peace Day Committee, together with the Charlatans, the Great Society, and the Billy Moses Blues Band. It's also Bill Kreutzmann's 20th birthday.

56

May 1966

Scorpio Rising

At some point in June or July the Grateful Dead had their first recording session for commercial release. The band's photographer friend Herb Greene hooked them up with Gene Estribou. He was apparently something of an amateur, but the Dead wanted to make records, so up the stairs they went.

The result was the Grateful Dead's first "official" record release, a 45 of "Don't Ease Me In" backed with "Stealin'," both old-time numbers (the former a country blues popularized by Henry Thomas, the latter a jug-band number first recorded by the Memphis Jug Band.) Both songs dated back to the Warlocks days, and "Don't Ease Me In" went back even further, to Mother McCree's repertoire. Interestingly, at a time when a lot of scenesters viewed the Grateful Dead as (more or less) Pigpen's backup band, Jerry Garcia sang lead on both songs, although "Stealin'" featured Pigpen's Hammond organ more heavily than Garcia's lead guitar.

The single was "released" in very small numbers during the summer. Jerry Garcia later recalled that perhaps 150 records were pressed, sold only in local scene spots like the Psychedelic Shop. The band certainly didn't think much of their first single: in an interview for *Mojo Navigator* (an early Haight music 'zine) in August, Bob Weir advised the interviewer to burn the record.

Saturday May 14
Veterans Memorial Hall, Berkeley, California

14	15	16	17	18	19	20 – 24	25	26	27

Sunday May 15
Thousands of antiwar protesters surround the White House in one of the first major demonstrations aimed at ending U.S. involvement in Vietnam.

Thursday May 19
Avalon Ballroom, San Francisco, California

A benefit evening for the old Straight Theater and the campaign to turn it into a dance hall. The boys line up with the Wildflower and the Outfit, and the evening sees the first performance of "Good Lovin'." Also appearing is Beat poet Michael McClure.

Dan Healy

"I was always a tinkerer," says Dan Healy, the Dead's live sound mixer, equipment guru and occasional studio engineer from late 1967 until 1994 (with a sabbatical during 1970). "While other kids were playing cowboys and Indians, I was learning how to use a soldering iron." Healy grew up in the redwoods north of San Francisco, but moved to the Bay Area to work in the tech end of radio and recording in the early '60s. A friendship with John Cipollina of Quicksilver Messenger Service led him to the Grateful Dead, who were struggling with primitive P.A. systems as they played the ballrooms and clubs around town in '66 and '67. Healy was instrumental in nurturing the group's obsession with obtaining the best possible live and studio equipment, cost-be-damned. Along with Owsley Stanley and others, Healy developed the infamous Wall of Sound in 1974, and he was part of all the other sonic innovations the group adapted through the years, into the early '90s. Healy tacitly encouraged bootleg taping of Dead shows, which eventually led to the first authorized taping section by any band, in the fall of 1984.

Saturday May 28
Avalon Ballroom, San Francisco, California

The Grateful Dead return to the Avalon for its first Family Dog show (as performers at least), billed as the "Hayfever Dance" because the other acts are the Leaves and the Grassroots.

> "[The Dead] wasn't just more rock 'n' roll but a whole new kind of music. A new approach. A new philosophy...something new and rewarding."
>
> DAN HEALY, RECALLING HIS FIRST GRATEFUL DEAD GIG, TO JYM FAHEY, *1992*

Chet Helms

Texan Chet Helms gravitated to San Francisco in the mid-'60s and became one of the leaders of the underground scene through his link with the Family Dog—first dealing pot to the group then joining the "family's" greater circle and adopting their name for a series of dances he put on beginning in '66. A patron of the early San Francisco poster artists, Helms was a sort of anti-Bill Graham—promoting dances and benefit concerts with the best local bands at San Francisco's Avalon Ballroom and, later, at the Family Dog on the Great Highway, profits be damned. Not surprisingly, Graham the capitalist eventually succeeded in putting Helms' humble operation out of business, but Helms' legacy as a caring curator of S.F.'s early scene has survived, and he can still be counted on to turn up at important hippie events around town.

Friday June 3
Saturday June 4
Fillmore Auditorium, San Francisco, California

The boys play both shows with Quicksilver Messenger Service and a visiting band from L.A., the Mothers of Invention. In the audience is Dan Healy, a friend of John Cipollina.

In June or early July, the Dead appear, and probably perform, at a conference on LSD at the University of California Medical Center in San Francisco.

JUNE '66

28	29	30	31	1	2	3	4

Sunday May 29
California Hall, San Francisco, California

Along with the Charlatans, the Grateful Dead play a benefit—"Aid in the End of Marijuana Prohibition"—for LEMAR (Legalize Marijuana), a coalition of pro-pot activists that includes Chet Helms. LEMAR's unofficial headquarters is the Blue Unicorn Coffee Shop, another stop on the Haight-Ashbury Historical Trail. The efforts of LEMAR are particularly courageous given the laws of the time: legendary San Francisco cop Art Gerrans, whose beat in '66 included the Haight, later told *Rolling Stone* journalist Charles Perry: "In those days, if you got someone with four or five marijuana cigarettes, they were convicted of a felony."

Friday June 10
Saturday June 11

Avalon Ballroom, San Francisco, California

These two Avalon shows are with Quicksilver Messenger Service, so the shows are billed as (what else?) "The Quick and the Dead." Wordplay aside, the Grateful Dead are now one of the established bands on the scene and no longer just "Kesey's house band." The New Tweedy Brothers also appear.

Monday June 13
The Supreme Court rules, in Miranda vs. Arizona, that police must inform suspects of their Constitutional rights when they are placed under arrest.

Friday June 17
Saturday June 18

Veterans Memorial Hall, San Jose, California

With the Jaywalkers both nights.

Below: Jerry looking groovy while Bobby and Pig get in on the vibes at Lagunitas scout camp, Marin County.
Below left: Jerry Garcia at Lagunitas

"GOOD LOVIN'"
CLARK/RESNICK

Unlike other reworkings of more obscure material, "Good Lovin'" had already been a recent hit for both The Olympics and The Rascals and appeared on albums by The Kingsmen and the Dave Clark Five when the Grateful Dead added it to their setlist in 1966 (first performed on May 19.) Written by Arthur Resnick and Rudy Clark, the song served as one of Pigpen's signature tunes in over 100 recorded performances between 1966 and 1972, with an all-time classic from Princeton, New Jersey, on April 17, 1971 ranking high with fans. After Pigpen's death in '73 the band shelved "Good Lovin'" for a while, test-driving the song just three times before Weir decided it was ripe for return in '77. The radio-friendly version that went out over the air with the release of *Shakedown Street* (1978) was tame compared to the live performances, and with Weir at the helm the Dead played the song almost 300 more times. The Other Ones continued to share the love from 1998 to 2002.

June 1966

57

California Cowboys & Indians

The lease on Rancho Olompali ran out at the end of June, but before the 30 of the month the Grateful Dead found less palatial but equally agreeable digs deeper into Marin County: a decommissioned scout camp in Lagunitas, with various outbuildings and lodges. Over the summer that corner of the county was colonized by psychedelic settlers; QMS were in nearby Olema, and Big Brother were just down the road from the Dead's spread. Soon, Big Brother's new vocalist, Janis Joplin, hooked up with Pigpen—a fellow devotee of the bottle and the blues—for some noisy summer lovin'.

The Quicksilver boys affected the same kind of cowboy look as the Charlatans, so the Dead naturally took on the role of Indians and planned an ambush. Appropriating paint and feathers from the old camp's craft

lodge and bows and arrows from the archery range, they charged the Quicksilver bunkhouse in a frenzy of firecrackers and war whoops, quickly overwhelming the "cowboys." In July, the Quicksilver Cowboys planned some very public revenge. With Bill Graham's connivance, they decided to storm the stage of the Fillmore while the Dead were playing, tie them up, and appropriate their instruments for a rendition of Hank Williams's "Kaw-Liga was a Wooden Indian."

Unfortunately there had recently been a small race riot in the mostly African-American Fillmore neighborhood, and the cops rolled up quickly. The Quicksilvers were carrying toy pistols but very real and very illegal pot, and they got busted.

Mr. Smith Goes to San Francisco

In the audience at one of the San Francisco shows was a dapper Yalie named Joe Smith, president of Warner Bros. Records. He'd been invited by his friend Tom Donahue *(see page 70)*, who was on his way to becoming one of the country's most influential rock DJs and who appreciated the Grateful Dead.

Warner Bros. had only been in existence for eight years and had no rock 'n' roll acts on its artist roster (unless you count the Everly Brothers), but Smith (no Mr. Jones) quickly grasped that something was going on here. Smith, in fact, tried to persuade his higher-ups to let him sign *every* unsigned Bay Area band, but there wasn't the budget for that. So Smith began courting the Grateful Dead.

In 1966 Warner Bros. was far from the powerhouse it would become, and the Grateful Dead were having too much fun doing what they were doing to care overmuch about landing a recording contract… on the other hand, why not? The band prevailed on Brian Rohan *(see page 71)* to represent them in negotiating a contract with the label, reasoning that if he could keep Kesey from doing serious jail time, he'd certainly be able to look out for their interests *(see September 30, 1966)*.

Soul/R&B Music Scene

From the outset, the Grateful Dead mostly played black music—vintage and modern blues and R&B (or "soul" as it became known in the '60s). A typical Dead set in 1966 might include then-current tunes like "Dancing in the Streets" by Martha & the Vandellas, "Midnight Hour" by Wilson Pickett, and "Pain in My Heart" by Otis Redding; in this way the Dead were like many other "cover" bands (albeit a hip one that also played obscure jug band tunes). The three artists cited above represented three of the dominant strains of soul music in the mid-'60s.

Martha & the Vandellas *(below)* came from Motown Records, which churned out dozens of hits. Backed by a strong core of talented songwriters and an incredible group of (uncredited) musicians, the Motown/Tamla/Gordy artists served up a bright, infectious soul sound loaded with memorable hooks and plenty of personality. For years, the pop and R&B charts were filled with destined-to-be-classic tunes by The Supremes, The Marvelettes, Marvin Gaye, Little Stevie Wonder, The Temptations, the Four Tops, The Miracles, and many others.

Wilson Pickett was emblematic of Atlantic Records' soul artists. Based in New York and run by Turkish immigrants Ahmet and Nesuhi Ertegun and producers/engineers Jerry Wexler and Tom Dowd, Atlantic became one of the top jazz and R&B labels of the '50s and '60s, signing everyone from John Coltrane and Charles Mingus to The Coasters and Ray Charles. Atlantic's soul records were often characterized by punchy horn arrangements and a sound that emphasized the instruments rather than echo and reverb. Other top Atlantic groups included The Drifters, Ben E. King, Aretha Franklin, and Otis Redding.

Before signing with Atlantic, the prodigiously talented Redding was a mainstay of Memphis-based Stax/Volt Records, a regional label famous for its gritty soul records that mixed R&B, blues, and gospel, and often featured one of the best house bands ever assembled—Booker T. & the MGs. Other top acts for the company included Rufus Thomas, his daughter Carla Thomas, Sam & Dave, and blues guitar great Albert King.

Friday July 8
Saturday July 9
Santa Venetia Armory,
San Rafael, California

JULY '66

1 2 3 4 5 6 7 8 9 10 ~ 13 14 15 16 17

Sunday July 3
Fillmore Auditorium,
San Francisco, California

Billed as the "Independence Ball." Also on the bill are the L.A. band Love and Group B.

Thursday July 14
Friday July 15
★ **Saturday July 16**
Sunday July 17
Fillmore Auditorium, San Francisco, California

Billed as "A Pleasure Dome," from the Samuel Taylor Coleridge's opium-inspired 1816 poem "Kubla Khan" ("In Xanadu did Kubla Khan/A stately pleasure dome decree…"), the opening night's show teams the band with the Hindustani Jazz Quartet and Big Brother & the Holding Company. The other three shows are all with the Jefferson Airplane—the Grateful Dead are now on the same bill as San Francisco's rock royalty. Saturday's show sees the first special guests, Joan Baez, Mimi Farina, and Marty Balin, share vocals with Pigpen on "In the Midnight Hour," the band's showstopper. The fourth gig of the run is a matinee show, starting at 2:00 p.m.

Friday July 29
Saturday July 30
Sunday July 31
Pacific National Exhibition, Vancouver, British Columbia, Canada

The PNE Garden Auditorium is probably the largest venue played by the band thus far, with a stage so elevated that the band worries about falling off the edge.

18 19 20 21 22 23 24 25 26 27 28 29 30 31

The First Tour

At the end of July the band left California (and the U.S.) for the first time for five shows in British Columbia, three at the rather grand Pacific National Exhibition Garden Auditorium and two in a small Vancouver club. It was not a particularly gratifying introduction to life on the road: their roadie, Laird Grant, got turned away by officious border functionaries, the band's one car died, and (in an ongoing problem) they frequently took the stage late because of the perfectionist Bear's habit of tinkering with the amps or other equipment until the last possible moment.

Above: At the Avalon and other venues, the Dead would often play into the wee hours.

🎸 **Friday August 19**
🎸 **Saturday August 20**
Avalon Ballroom,
San Francisco, California

Both gigs with
Sopwith Camel.

Saturday August 27 🎸
Sunday August 28 🎸
IDES Hall, Pescadero, California

With QMS and Colossal Pomegranate. The band heads
south to Pescadero as part of the entertainment for
the Tour Del Mar, a three-day coastal bicycle race.
The pre-race publicity sees the Dead riding around San
Francisco's Civic Center in a cavalcade of convertibles.

Bearwell

Shortly after returning from Canada, Bear and the band came to a parting of the ways. Bear's bankroll (which he had largely emptied in the band's service) had kept the band going in the lean months of early '66, but the Grateful Dead were now an established act, if hardly a profitable one; more importantly, from the band's perspective, Bear's inveterate experimentation with the sound system was getting in the way of gigs. So Bear went back to applying his other great talent—making LSD—after buying the band new gear and selling the system he'd built them to Bill Graham for the Fillmore.

The Diggers

August brought the formation of a group with whom the Grateful Dead were to have an ongoing, if not always easy relationship throughout the Haight-Ashbury era: The Diggers. The Diggers were not a rock band but a group of young activists who took the political street theater of the San Francisco Mime Troupe and the Artist's Liberation Front to another level, and added an element of direct action on top of that.

The group got their name from the rural radicals of 17th-century England, who wanted the common lands planted with crops for the poor instead of serving as grazing lands for the flocks of the wealthy. In that spirit, The Diggers fed the hungry of the Haight and elsewhere, distributing soup and their famous "Digger bread" in Golden Gate Park and making other goods available *gratis* in their Free Store at 1762 Page Street.

The Diggers were not motivated by conventional spiritual or political thinking. Freedom from the constraints of contemporary society was what they were about—they liked to call themselves "life actors"—and since money was the chief form of control in American society, they sought to create a small corner of the world where the profit motive didn't apply. "It's free because it's yours." was one of their sayings.

The Diggers' leaders included Emmett Grogan, a life-long schemer who became a social revolutionary in the late '60s and died in 1978. Another founder of the collective was Peter Coyote. Now a well-known actor, Coyote was a member of the radical San Francisco Mime Troupe in the mid-'60s before joining The Diggers, and his memoir, *Sleeping Where I Fall*, is one of the more colorful accounts of the '60s counterculture. Other leaders included **Peter Berg**, **Peter Cohon**, **Ken Minault**, **Paul Jacobs**, and **Billy Murcott**—although they all rejected the concept of leadership, naturally.

🎸 **Friday August 5**
🎸 **Saturday August 6**
Afterthought,
Vancouver, British Columbia, Canada

🎸 **Friday August 12**
🎸 **Saturday August 13**
Fillmore Auditorium,
San Francisco, California

Both gigs with
Jefferson Airplane.

Sunday September 11
Fillmore Auditorium, San Francisco, California

Bill Graham's "A Gigantic All-Night Jazz/Rock Dance-Concert" brings together the best of the Bay Area's jazz and blues acts (the Joe Henderson Quartet, Jon Hendricks, Elvin Jones, Big Mama Thornton, and the Danny Zeitlin Trio) with some of the new rock 'n' roll groups (the Great Society, the Jefferson Airplane, Wildflower, and the Grateful Dead) to raise funds for the Both/And jazz club.

| 2 | | 4 | 5 | 6 | 7 | 8 | 9 | 10 | 11 |

Sunday September 4
Fillmore Auditorium, San Francisco, California

With Quicksilver and the Great Society—but the Grateful Dead head the bill, a Fillmore first.

Friday September 2
La Dolphine, Hillsborough, California

The band play a private "debutante" party in upscale Hillsborough.

Friday September 16
Saturday September 17
Avalon Ballroom, San Francisco, California

Both shows with the Oxford Circle. The poster for the shows, by Stanley Mouse and Alton Kelley, marks the appearance of the first great image in Grateful Dead iconography—the skeleton wreathed with roses.

Friday September 23
Saturday September 24
Pioneer Ballroom, Suisun City, California

Both gigs with the 13 Experience and a light show from the Diogenes Lantern Company.

| 13 | 14 | 15 | 16 | 17 | 18 | 19 | 20 | 21 | 22 | 23 | 24 |

Kelley & Mouse

Artists Alton Kelley and Stanley Mouse created some of the most memorable posters and album covers to emerge from San Francisco's eclectic underground in the '60s and '70s. Kelley was an art school dropout from Maine who moved west in the late '50s and by 1965 had become part of The Charlatans' bohemian scene and a founding member of the Family Dog collective. Stanley Mouse was a trained artist from Detroit who specialized in hot rod art until he hooked up with the Family Dog and started doing posters (both alone and with Kelley) for their dances. An early piece, the famous skeleton with roses, was an adaptation of a 19th-century work by E.J. Sullivan that illustrated an edition of The Rubaiyat of Omar Khayyam. Separately or together they were responsible for a number of Dead album covers including *Workingman's Dead*, *American Beauty*, *Skull & Roses*, *Europe '72*, *Mars Hotel*, and *Terrapin Station*.

Friday September 30

The recording contract with Warner Bros. is dated September 30, 1966, although the band would not physically scrawl their names until December. In the contract, no budget limits are set on studio time, but costs are to be deducted from royalties, set at 8 percent. It is a fairly standard recording contract for the period except that the band retained its publishing rights.

| 25 | 26 | 27 | 28 | 29 | 30 | 1 | 2 |

Friday September 30
Saturday October 1
Sunday October 2
Commons, San Francisco State College, San Francisco, California

The band perform at an Acid Test put on by Stewart Brand as the "Whatever It Is Festival." The event includes the Committee, the Congress of Wonders, Bill Ham's Light Show, Ann Halprin's Dance Workshop, Mimi Farina, and the Only Alternative. The band's performance is sub-par because Pigpen is finally dosed, and freaks out.

710 Ashbury

Toward the end of September the Grateful Dead decamped from Lagunitas and settled into what would become both the band's communal home and the "living room" for the Haight-Ashbury scene: 710 Ashbury (*left*).

Built around 1910, the 13-room house had lately served as a rooming house, managed by Danny Rifkin, who lived in 710A—the basement. The entire band bedded down at 710 for a few weeks, until Phil Lesh and Florence Nathan and Bill and Brenda Kreutzmann found a house to share on nearby Belvedere Street. That left Jerry Garcia (joined by Mountain Girl in early '67), Pigpen (ensconced in a room behind the kitchen, later shared with his girlfriend, Veronica "Vee" Barnard), Bob Weir (who slept upstairs), and Rock and his girlfriend Tangerine as the permanent residents (the living room also served as Danny and Rock Scully's "office"), plus a constant stream of visitors and guests who "crashed" for a night, or a few months.

It was a fun, messy, stimulating, nurturing, enlightening, occasionally infuriating environment. And it was truly communal: everyone pooled their money to cover rent and food. However, the distribution of household chores was not exactly equitable. It was the women—the "chicks" or "old ladies," in the parlance of the time—who wound up doing the cooking, cleaning, and laundry.

Seven-ten was the focal point of a scene that was growing, but which was still small and localized. Everybody knew everybody, and everybody passed through the stained-glass-framed front door of 710 Ashbury at one point or another. The denizens of 710 would have been incredulous, in late 1966, if a visitor from the future had informed them that by the end of the following year 710 would be a stop on a tourist-bus route through the heart of hippiedom.

Alice D. Millionaire

On October 5, the San Francisco *Chronicle* ran a banner headline: "Strange Success Story of the LSD Millionaire." The accompanying front-page story began with an account of one Augustus Stanley Owsley roaring up to an L.A. bank on a motorcycle, "clad in boots, black leather jacket, and a white crash helmet," and changing fistfuls of small bills into hundreds.

The article also reported "For a while he took a rock 'n' roll group under his wing and allowed them to practice at his cottage behind a dilapidated apartment house on Berkeley Way in Berkeley. But the neighbors complained and he stopped."

Needless to say, the Grateful Dead loved it, and collectively penned this punning song tribute to Bear, performed it at the Love Pageant Rally and only a few times afterword. A studio version is among the previously unreleased tracks on 2001's *The Golden Road* box set, and Phil Lesh & Friends revived the song in 2002.

Below, right, and bottom:
Thursday October 6. The Dead play the "Love Pageant Rally" in Golden Gate Park on the day when LSD becomes illegal in California.

Saturday October 8
Ken Kesey is arrested after being spotted by some off-duty FBI agents on the Bayshore Freeway. His lawyers work out a plea deal that includes the promise that Kesey will organize some kind of event in which he will urge his "followers," and the youth of America, to forgo LSD. Thus the "Acid Test Graduation" is conceived.

Friday October 14
TMU Deck,
Stanford University,
Palo Alto, California

Saturday October 15
The Heliport, Sausalito, California

The heliport is also the band's chief rehearsal space at this point.

Friday October 21
Saturday October 22
Fillmore Auditorium, San Francisco, California

One of Bill Graham's famous double bills pairs the Grateful Dead with the legendary Texas bluesman Lightnin' Hopkins. The Chocolate Watch band and/or the Loading Zone also play both nights. These shows mark the debut of the first bit of Grateful Dead merchandising: a t-shirt bearing the image of Pigpen. Today they're the Holy Grail of GD memorabilia.

Sunday October 23
Las Lomas High School, Walnut Creek, California

Originally scheduled for the town's public library, the band have to shift to the high school for this afternoon show.

| 8 | 9 | 10 – 13 | 14 | 15 | 16 | 17 | 18 | 19 | 20 | 21 | 22 |

Saturday October 8
Mount Tamalpais Amphitheatre, Marin County, California

The band plays the Mount Tamalpais Peace Festival, along with QMS and Brazilian guitarist Bola Sete.

Saturday October 8
Sunday October 9
Fillmore Auditorium, San Francisco, California

After an afternoon at Mount Tam, another night with the Paul Butterfield Blues Band and Jefferson Airplane. The lineup is the same for the Sunday afternoon show.

Sunday October 16
Golden Gate Park, San Francisco, California

A "free festival" organized by the Artist's Liberation Front, founded by the SFMT's Ronnie Davis. It's also Bob Weir's 19th birthday. In the America of 1966, he's still too young to vote or drink.

Wednesday October 26
The North Face Ski Shop, Berkeley, California

The Grateful Dead play the opening of North Face, now a multimillion-dollar sporting-goods empire.

Friday October 7
Fillmore Auditorium, San Francisco, California

The Dead and Jefferson Airplane support the Paul Butterfield Blues Band.

| 3 | 4 | 5 | 6 | 7 |

| 23 | 24 | 25 | 26 | 27 | 28 | 29 | 30 | 31 |

Thursday October 6
Golden Gate Park, San Francisco, California

New York has already made the manufacture, sale, and possession of LSD illegal by the fall of 1966, and California follows with a law that goes into effect today. Hundreds of people gather in the Panhandle section of Golden Gate Park for a protest rally, variously known as the "Love Pageant Rally" or the "Lunatic Protest Demonstration." The Grateful Dead and Big Brother provide the music.

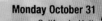

Monday October 31
California Hall, San Francisco, California

The first of the Grateful Dead's 14 Halloween shows, this one is billed as the "Dance of Death Costume Ball." QMS and Mimi Farina also play. More significant than this show is the event they don't play at—the so-called Acid Test Graduation. It is attended by only 50 people and takes place in a warehouse in South of Market. It is the last Acid Test and, effectively, the swan song of the Pranksters.

"BERTHA"

GARCIA/HUNTER

Considering the Dead's reputation for dabbling in everything from folklore to other-worldly experiences, it's ironic that "Bertha," which made its official bow on the band's eponymously-titled 1971 double live disc, was initially inspired by an electric fan the Dead had in their offices. "It would hop along the ground," Garcia recalled the year of the song's debut. "The fan was a little off-kilter and it would bounce around and bang up and down, and it would blow this tremendous gale wind." But that merely served as the origin point for another classic tale about a troublesome and clearly obsessive lover, one that prompts the harried protagonist of the story to beg, "I am on my bended knees, Bertha, don't you come around here anymore." "Bertha" was an instant fan favorite and often served as a rousing set opener, with performances in over 300 concerts between its debut during a 1971 run at the Capitol Theater and the last performance with Garcia in June of 1995. It made a welcome return with The Other Ones in 2002.

Friday November 4
Saturday November 5
Avalon Ballroom, San Francisco, California
With the Oxford Circle.

Wednesday November 9
Fillmore Auditorium, San Francisco, California

Saturday November 12
The Old Cheese Factory, San Francisco, California
With Andrew Staples.

| 1 | 2 | 3 | 4 | 5 | 6 | 7 | 8 | 9 | 10 | 11 | 12 | 13 |

November 1966

62

Sunday November 13
Avalon Ballroom, San Francisco, California

The Grateful Dead join forces with QMS and Big Brother for a "Zenefit" to raise funds for the San Francisco Zen Center's mountain retreat, Tassajara, in the Ventana wilderness near Big Sur.

Friday November 18
Saturday November 19 ★
Sunday November 20
Fillmore Auditorium, San Francisco, California

All shows feature James Cotton and his blues band (see June 25, 1992, and September 22, 1993), plus Lothar & the Hand People. Saturday marks the first multi-beat intro to "Beat it On Down the Line"; tonight, it's 11 beats. The last show is a benefit for the SNCC (Student Non-Violent Coordinating Committee). Jon Hendricks MC's and Johnny Talbot & De Thangs also play.

| 14 | 15 | 16 | 17 | 18 | 19 | 20 |

Getting the Airplane off the Ground

At the end of October the Jefferson Airplane (now including Grace Slick from the Great Society) were in L.A. struggling to record their second album for RCA. A couple of days later Jerry Garcia flew down to help them out. Garcia played lead on four songs, and more importantly, punched up "Somebody to Love," a fairly simple song in its original livery, into a full-on Wagnerian arrangement that perfectly suited Slick's vocal delivery. Jerry even contributed the album title when he said one of the songs was as "surrealistic as a pillow."

Released in February 1967, *Surrealistic Pillow* hit No. 3 on the charts and generated two top-ten singles. The album broke the San Francisco sound nationwide, and though the Airplane credited Jerry as "Musical and Spiritual Adviser" on the jacket, RCA downplayed his contribution for many years.

Fire in the City

Around this time the band were in the studio again, for an unusual one-off project: backing up the great jazz vocalist Jon Hendricks (late of Lambert, Hendricks, and Ross) on "Fire in the City," a song for the soundtrack of *Sons and Daughters*, a film chronicling anti-Vietnam demonstrations at UC Berkeley. Lambert hit it off especially well with Pigpen. As with the band's first single, "Fire in the City" was out of (legitimate) circulation until 2001's *The Golden Road* box set.

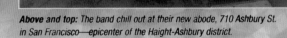

Above and top: The band chill out at their new abode, 710 Ashbury St. in San Francisco—epicenter of the Haight-Ashbury district.

| 21 | 22 | 23 | 24 | 25 | 26 | 27 |

Thursday November 24
The band host a Thanksgiving Dinner for fifty or so of their closest friends at 710, complete with pot-stuffed turkey.

Sunday November 27
Fillmore Auditorium, San Francisco, California

Bill Graham hosts a private Thanksgiving dinner at the Fillmore for various musicians and scenesters, capped by a set from the Grateful Dead.

"These are the good old days."

PHIL LESH'S THANKSGIVING TOAST

Monday November 28
Tuesday November 29
Wednesday November 30
Thursday December 1
The Matrix, San Francisco, California

With Jerry Pond.

Friday December 9
Saturday December 10
Sunday December 11
Fillmore Auditorium, San Francisco, California

Three gigs at the Fillmore with Big Mama Mae Thornton and Tim Rose. Sunday's show is a matinee.

DECEMBER '66

28	29	30	1	2	3 ~ 7	8	9	10	11	12 ~ 18	19

Friday December 2
Pauley Ballroom,
University of California,
Berkeley, California

Billed as a "Dance Macabre." With Country Joe & the Fish.

Monday December 19
The band gets their first mention in a wide-circulation national magazine—and a very nice one at that—in a *Newsweek* article, "The Nitty Gritty Sound," reporting that the band are second in "popularity" only to the Jefferson Airplane: "[The Grateful Dead are] blues oriented, and so far unrecorded. Their hard, hoarse, screeching sound is pure San Francisco…"

Above and right: Onstage, early December, at the Fillmore Auditorium, San Francisco, California.

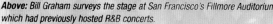
Above: Bill Graham surveys the stage at San Francisco's Fillmore Auditorium, which had previously hosted R&B concerts.

The First New Year's Eve Show

The band capped off an amazing year with their first New Year's Eve show for Bill Graham, beginning a tradition that would continue for a quarter-century ('69, '73, '74, and '75 excepted) until Graham's death in 1991. Stage Manager Jim Haynie played the role of New Year's Baby, complete with diaper. Jefferson Airplane and QMS also played, and Country Joe & the Fish, who headlined the Avalon's New Year's Eve festivities, headed to the Fillmore to jam into the early hours of '67—a year in which this small, localized scene would take on new and astonishing dimensions.

December 1966

63

"ME AND MY UNCLE"
PHILLIPS

Written in a classic country vein worthy of Johnny Cash or Merle Haggard, one of the most surprising things about this perennial Weir cover may be the fact that it was written by the band's contemporary John Phillips, better known as the purveyor of such pop pearls as "California Dreamin'" and "Monday, Monday" with the Mamas and the Papas. Though Phillips' version wasn't released until after his death in 2001, a live take had already appeared on The Judy Collins Concert (1964) before the Dead appropriated it from 1966 (first played December 1, '66 at The Matrix) as part of Weir's ongoing fascination with what would later be dubbed "rockabilly." First released on *Grateful Dead* (1971), this tale of betrayal and a card game gone wrong was often found preceding either Johnny Cash's "Big River" or Weir and Barlow's "Mexicali Blues" from 1978 on, but was also used as a lead-in to "Maggie's Farm" in the 1990s. It would eventually become the most-played song in the band's repertoire, with almost 600 recorded performances between 1966 and 1995. The Other Ones "tried to wash off some of that dust and dirt" again during their 2000 tour, and the song is still common in shows by Weir's band Ratdog.

Wednesday December 21
Continental Ballroom,
Santa Clara, California

Wednesday December 28
Governor's Hall,
Sacramento, California

The "Beaux Arts Ball" with QMS.

Thursday December 29
Santa Venetia Armory,
San Rafael,
California

With Moby Grape and Morning Glory.

20	21	22

23	24	25	26	27	28	29	30	31

Tuesday December 20
Fillmore Auditorium,
San Francisco, California

The band opens for Otis Redding. Redding won't achieve huge pop success until after his sizzling appearance at Monterey in 1967 *(see page 72)*, but to those in the musical know, he's the man, and Bill Graham books him for three nights at the insistence of various Fillmoreans, including the Dead and Janis Joplin.

Friday December 23
Saturday December 24
Avalon Ballroom,
San Francisco, California

With the Steve Miller Blues Band and Moby Grape.

Friday December 30
Saturday December 31
Fillmore Auditorium,
San Francisco, California

A triple bill of QMS, Jefferson Airplane, and the Grateful Dead for these shows, the second of which is the band's first New Year's Eve show for Bill Graham.

"MORNING DEW"
DOBSON

"Morning Dew" was a textbook example of how the politically-charged folk songs of the early 1960s helped prompt the late '60s counterculture to find its own voice. Written by Canadian singer/songwriter Bonnie Dobson after she was inspired by a viewing of the 1959 film *On The Beach* and a subsequent discussion on the perils of the Atomic Age, this early statement against nuclear war portrayed a post-apocalyptic Adam and Eve asking, "Where have all the people gone today?" The song took on even more weight when the Dead electrified it starting in 1967, and over the course of 28 years and nearly 250 performances the band's version evolved from a healthy clip into a slower, more deliberately reflective pace. Garcia's high, squealing guitar solo during the song's thunderous break helped punctuate the melancholy bleakness found in Dobson's baneful wasteland, leading to a blowout finale over which Garcia cried, "I guess it doesn't matter anyway!" Among the best recordings of "Dew" are a November 11, 1967, take in L.A.; a version played during the classic Harpur College show in Binghamton, New York, on May 2, 1970; and one from the equally lauded May 8, 1977, show at Barton Hall in Ithaca, New York.

"The Be-In was a defining moment in the whole counterculture hippie scene" STEVE BROWN, *2003*

January 1967

64

The Human Be-In

While watching the Love Pageant Rally (*see page 61*), Richard Alpert (Timothy Leary's associate and the future Baba Ram Dass) had remarked "It's a human be-in." The success of that event led the Haight scenesters to plan a really big gathering of all the tribes now grouped under the term "hippie." Allen Cohen, editor of the *Oracle*, the Haight's underground journal of record, and artist/activist Michael Bowen headed up the planning, and posters by Rick Griffin and Mouse went up announcing "A Gathering of the Tribes for a Human Be-In."

On the unusually sunny morning of January 14, the tribes began to fill Golden Gate Park's Polo Field. They came from the Haight, from Berkeley, from Big Sur, from the East Bay, from the Peninsula, from the northern counties… 10,000 people, maybe even 20,000. Many of those present remember thinking something along the lines of, who knew there were so many of us?

The entertainment began in the afternoon and alternated between poetry from the Beat elder statesmen (Gary Snyder, Michael McClure, Lawrence Ferlinghetti, the ubiquitous Allen Ginsberg) and speeches from various luminaries with music from "all the S.F. bands": specifically, the Airplane, Country Joe & the Fish, Quicksilver, the Charlatans, and the Grateful Dead. The Dead began with "Morning Dew," continued with "Good Mornin' Little Schoolgirl," with jazzman Charles Lloyd joining in on flute rather than his usual sax, and finished with "Viola Lee Blues." Ralph Gleason (*see page 36*) wrote in the San Francisco *Chronicle*: "[The Dead's] set was remarkably exciting, causing people to rise up wherever they were and begin dancing. Dizzy Gillespie… asked who the Dead were and commented on how they were swinging." There could be no higher praise.

A hippie–Hells Angels rapprochement meant the bikers guarded the electrical cables (a mysterious power cut had interrupted Quicksilver's set) and even reunited lost children with their parents. The Diggers handed out turkey sandwiches, some of them seasoned with White Lightning, a special batch of acid brewed by Bear. At the other end of the Polo Grounds, the *haut-monde* San Francisco Olympic Club—studiously ignoring the thousands of dancing, tripping, ecstatic hippies—played a rugby match.

The overall mellowness masked some tensions on the grandstand. The Berkeley radicals, Jerry Rubin foremost among them, had insisted on a piece of the Be-In, and Rubin's strident political spiel didn't go down well with the largely apolitical hippies; their goal was to create a life off the grid, not to take over the grid. Timothy Leary's speech wasn't well received, either; despite his cred as a psychedelic pioneer, Leary seemed to want to establish a Church of LSD, with himself as Pope, in contrast to the anticlerical impulses of the West Coast crowd.

The music, the sun, the inner and outer glow was what mattered, and these would be forever imprinted in the memory of those who were there. As the shadows lengthened, Ralph Gleason wrote, "[Allen Ginsberg's] voice came over the sound system, asking everyone to run towards the sun and watch the sunset. Later, he asked everyone to help clean up the debris and they did. And so it ended; the first of the great gatherings… This is truly something new and not the least of it is that it is an asking for a new dimension to peace… for the reality of love and a great nest for all humans."

The Be-In also saw the participation of many Beat Generation luminaries, passing the torch to the new counterculture. Finally, it was the start of national media hype about those crazies in San Francisco—which was to accelerate, with a lot of unhappy consequences.

The phantom parachutist

Toward the end of Dead set a parachutist landed. Legend is confused—Gay-Glo colors? Paisley? Was he naked? An alien? Whatever, the descent added a touch of extra magic to an afternoon where magic, by all accounts, abounded.

Opposite Page: The Dead onstage, Alan Ginsberg, Timothy Leary and the crowd at the Human Be-In.

JANUARY '67

| 1 | 2 | 3 | 4 | 5 | 6 | 7 | 8 | 9 | 10 | 11 | 12 | 13 |

| 14 | 15 | 16 | 17 | 18 | 19 | 20 | 21 | 22 | 23 | 24 | 25 | 26 | 27 | 28 | 29 | 30 | 31 |

Friday January 6
Freeborn Hall, University of California, Davis, California

With Big Mama Mae Thornton.

Friday January 13
Fillmore Auditorium, San Francisco, California

The Grateful Dead headlines, followed by the Junior Wells Chicago Blues Band and the Doors, in from L.A. The Doors had just released their first album and had lip-synched "Break on Through" on the *Shebang* TV show, but they were pretty much an unknown quantity in San Francisco. Although both bands are informed by some of the same influences (the Beats, psychedelics), the Dead don't think much of the histrionic Lizard King and his minstrels. Too L.A., too flashy.

Saturday January 14
Sunday January 15
Fillmore Auditorium, San Francisco, California

Be-In or no Be-In, it's a gig night for this hard-working band, and they're back at the Fillmore for two shows with Junior Wells and the Doors. Sunday's show is a matinee.

Friday January 27
Saturday January 28
Sunday January 29
Avalon Ballroom, San Francisco, California

With Moby Grape and Big Brother for "Mantra-Rock." Sunday's show is a benefit for the International Society of Krishna Consciousness's just-opened Rada-Krishna Temple in the Haight. The Hare Krishnas enjoy the imprimatur of Allen Ginsberg, and dabbling in "Eastern" spiritual traditions is an established countercultural pastime. Hare Krishna, transcendental meditation, and other offshoots and appurtenances of Hinduism will be for hippies what Zen Buddhism was for the Beats.

Sunday January 1
Panhandle, Golden Gate Park, San Francisco, California

Along with Big Brother, the Dead play the "New Year's Day Wail," a party for the Diggers (*see page 59*) thrown by the Hells Angels. (The Diggers had helped bail an Angel out of jail in December.)

Friday January 13
Berkeley Community Theatre, Berkeley, California

At Bill Graham's request, the band subs for Jose Feliciano, who is scheduled to open for the Mamas & the Papas and who's stuck In traffic somewhere. It's the first of 22 Grateful Dead appearances at this venue. Feliciano arrives in time to open the late show, allowing the Dead to head to the Fillmore.

Saturday January 14
Polo Field, Golden Gate Park, San Francisco, California

The Human Be-In. First "Morning Dew."

Friday January 20
Santa Monica Civic Auditorium, Santa Monica, California

The band plays prior to a lecture by Timothy Leary, enhanced with a slide show by Ralph Metzner.

Friday January 27
Apollo astronauts Roger Chaffee, Gus Grissom, and Edward White are killed during an accident during training at Cape Canaveral, Florida.

Friday February 10
Santa Venetia Armory,
San Rafael, California

Right: The band hang out in Garcia's bedroom at 710 Ashbury.

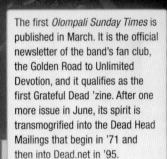

Sunday February 12
Fillmore Auditorium,
San Francisco, California

A Lincoln's Birthday benefit for the Council for Civic Unity, with Moby Grape, Sly and the Family Stone (featuring Sylvester Stewart), the New Salvation Army Banned, and Notes from the Underground.

Friday February 24
Saturday February 25
Sunday February 26
Fillmore Auditorium,
San Francisco, California

With Otis Rush and his Chicago Blues Band and Canned Heat. Sunday's show is a matinee.

The Flowering of the West Coast Music Scene

In a scene that was changing week by week as young people from all over the country streamed into San Francisco, just a few months separated the "first generation" S.F. bands (GD, Quicksilver, Airplane, et al.) and the "second generation" that sprang up in late 1966 and early 1967. The rock ballrooms were in full swing at the Fillmore Auditorium, the Avalon Ballroom, and at the much larger Winterland; the Haight echoed with the sounds of hundreds of great and terrible new groups rehearsing in garages and flats in Victorian houses; psychedelics and pot were plentiful and cheap; and record company scouts descended on the city hoping to sign the next hit-makers.

The nucleus of Moby Grape moved to the Bay Area from Los Angeles and immediately made waves around town with their strong harmonies and energetic live show. They were snapped up by Columbia Records and in 1967 recorded one of the strongest debut albums to come out of the San Francisco scene. Unfortunately, they were over-hyped by their label, various internal and management problems dogged them, and they never quite fulfilled their potential. Like the gritty Butterfield Blues Band, Steve Miller came from Chicago (though he was originally from Texas) and was steeped in the blues and R&B of that milieu. In 1966 he moved to S.F. and formed The Steve Miller Blues Band, combining his authentic Southside guitar sound with strong original rock material. This group also introduced San Francisco to a future favorite son, Texan Boz Scaggs.

Among the diverse acts rising from the Bay Area during this period was Sopwith Camel, who scored a surprise Top 40 hit but never had much local credibility; the Santana Blues Band, led by Mexican guitar phenom Carlos Santana and keyboardist Gregg Rolie (with their moniker trimmed to Santana, they would begin to take off following their Fillmore West debut in early '68); the hard, heavy, and not particularly good Blue Cheer; the Sons of Champlin, who expertly blended blue-eyed soul with jazz and rock jam sensibilities; and perhaps greatest of all, the multiracial soul-rock band Sly & the Family Stone, who became one of the most influential groups to emerge in the late '60s.

The music scene would go through many more permutations following Monterey in June of 1967 and the incredible deluge that overwhelmed the Haight during the fabled Summer of Love that followed. Bands such as It's a Beautiful Day (led by violinist David LaFlamme), Berkeley's swampy Creedence Clearwater Revival, and the fine rock/R&B band the Electric Flag—led by Michael Bloomfield—all attracted strong local followings. But Monterey also established San Francisco as a favorite destination for top out-of-town acts, too, including Cream, Jimi Hendrix, and The Who.

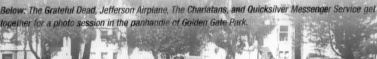

Below: The Grateful Dead, Jefferson Airplane, The Charlatans, and Quicksilver Messenger Service get together for a photo session in the panhandle of Golden Gate Park.

The first *Olompali Sunday Times* is published in March. It is the official newsletter of the band's fan club, the Golden Road to Unlimited Devotion, and it qualifies as the first Grateful Dead 'zine. After one more issue in June, its spirit is transmogrified into the Dead Head Mailings that begin in '71 and then into Dead.net in '95.

Friday March 3
Winterland Arena,
San Francisco, California

Billed as "The First Anniversary Love Circus."

Friday March 10
Saturday March 11
Sunday March 12
Monday March 13
Tuesday March 14
Wednesday March 15
Thursday March 16
Whisky-A-Go-Go,
San Francisco, California

"GOLDEN ROAD (TO UNLIMITED DEVOTION)"
MCGANNAHAN SKJELLYFETTI

The Grateful Dead had already played their share of other artists' party songs before working up this early entry of their own, the first track on the band's debut album *Grateful Dead* (1967) and one of the few that was credited to the entire group. In truth, the song was credited to McGannahan Skjellyfetti, the collective pseudonym the guys had cribbed from a character in Kenneth Patchen's novel *Memoirs of a Shy Pornographer*. But it's most notable not for its credits but its content, serving as an early and frenetic sampling of the celebratory atmosphere the Dead would continue to foment throughout their career. Though it was major label Warner Bros.' choice for the album's only single, the live fate of "Golden Road" was sealed quickly, with only a handful of '67 performances documented. "That was sort of a group writing experience before Hunter was with us," Garcia explained nearly 25 years later. "We kept it simple. But you know, what could you say, really? 'We took a bunch of acid and had a lot of fun?'" Nevertheless, as a pop prototype of what was yet to come, the recorded version of this one is an indispensable and utterly enjoyable artifact.

GRATEFUL DEAD
Grateful Dead

Released by Warner Bros. (WS-1689) on March 17, 1967

Side One

1. **The Golden Road (To Unlimited Devotion)**
   (McGannahan Skjellyfetti)
2. **Beat It On Down The Line**
   (Fuller)
3. **Good Morning, Little School Girl**
   (Demarais)
4. **Cold Rain And Snow**
   (McGannahan Skjellyfetti)
5. **Sittin' On Top Of The World**
   (Jacobs/Carter)
6. **Cream Puff War**
   (Garcia)

Side Two

1. **Morning Dew**
   (Dobson/Rose)
2. **New, New Minglewood Blues**
   (McGannahan Skjellyfetti)
3. **Viola Lee Blues**
   (Lewis)

Personnel

Jerry Garcia – guitar, vocals
Bill Kreutzmann – drums
Phil Lesh – bass
Pigpen (Ron McKernan) – keyboards, harmonica, vocals
Bob Weir – guitar

Produced by Dave Hassinger

In the tradition of the age-old "chicken vs. the egg" conundrum, the Dead's self-titled 1967 debut for Warner Bros. begged the question of whether the Grateful Dead weren't ready for the studio or the studio weren't ready for the Grateful Dead. Warner certainly wasn't ready—the label was throwing its hat into the rock ring for the first time, unknowingly giving birth to one of the weirdest relationships a corporation and an artist would ever know. Ironically, the band's first attempt at capturing their version of the "San Francisco sound" for a full-length record was recorded at RCA's Studio A in Hollywood.

The band had picked producer Dave Hassinger, whom they admired for his previous work on the Rolling Stones' "(I Can't Get No) Satisfaction" and the Jefferson Airplane's *Surrealistic Pillow* LP. But unlike those discs, *Grateful Dead* didn't even crack the Top 100. Hassinger, whom Carolyn Garcia would later describe as a "typical L.A. guy, with jowls, heavy tan," and "long, slicked-back hair," had his hands full with the band, who'd decided to pump up the proceedings with the amphetamine Dexamyl during the four-day recording session.

The album was a mix of covers ("Good Morning Little Schoolgirl," "Viola Lee Blues") and originals ("The Golden Road [To Unlimited Devotion]," released as a single backed by another original, "Cream Puff War") that featured in the band's set lists of the time, but the demands of major label conventionality went against the Dead's free-form ideals, so four lengthy tracks were cut short. Mouse and Kelly designed the cover, with some band input—the lettering became less readable because (as Garcia said later) they worried that the content of the lettering might be seen as "pretentious."

Friday March 17
Release of *Grateful Dead* album.

Sunday March 19
Fillmore Auditorium, San Francisco, California

Matinee with Chuck Berry and Johnny Talbot & De Thangs.

| 28 | 29 | 30 | 31 |

| 17 | 18 | 19 | 20 | 21 | 22 | 23 | 24 | 25 | 26 | 27 |

Tuesday March 28
Wednesday March 29
Thursday March 30
Friday March 31
Rock Garden, San Francisco, California

Friday March 17
Saturday March 18
Winterland Arena
San Francisco, California

Chuck Berry headlines. Johnny Talbot & De Thangs also on the bill.

Monday March 20
Warner Bros. throws the band an album release party at Fugazi Hall, a North Beach club. Suits and hippies mingle (or not). Joe Smith tells everyone how proud he is that Warner Bros. is introducing the Grateful Dead to the world.

Friday March 24
Saturday March 25
Sunday March 26
Avalon Ballroom, San Francisco, California

With Johnny Hammond & his Screaming Nighthawks and Robert Baker.

Also appearing is Charles Lloyd, the sax man who'd guested (on flute) at the Human Be-In, and his stellar quartet. Jerry's mother comes to see the band—the first time she'd seen her son performing since the coffeehouse days.

All pictures: The band rehearsing at the Sausalito Heliport in Spring 1967.

FM Rising

At 6:00 p.m. on April 7, 1967, Tom "Big Daddy" Donahue eased his 300-plus-pound bulk behind the control console of radio station KMPX-FM and changed rock music forever. In Europe, pirate radio stations disseminated new and challenging rock music, but AM-dominated, chart-driven America lacked an equivalent medium—until Donahue took over a nearly bankrupt San Francisco Spanish-language FM station, KPMX, and began an overnight rock show with a stack of records borrowed from friends.

Donahue chose the playlist on the basis of what he and others on the scene considered good or at least interesting, without reference to a record's current or potential chart position, and he spun album cuts, not just singles. He played records in thematic "sets" and sometimes—heresy on AM—he might even play an entire LP. Donahue also mixed up genres, so that Miles Davis might follow Bob Dylan who in turn would be followed by, say, the Grateful Dead. No screaming DJs; no jingles; no silly promotions or contests, just thoughtful analysis and news of genuine interest to the listening community.

Thus was "progressive" or "free-form" FM broadcasting born. Rock now had a home. KPMX was soon broadcasting rock 24 hours a day. Donahue later exported the format to L.A. and it was quickly taken up around the country.

Sunday April 9
Panhandle, Golden Gate Park, San Francisco, California

The band start jamming at 710 and winds up in the park in the afternoon. This is just one of several spontaneous (more or less), free performances in the area.

Sunday April 9
Longshoremen's Hall, San Francisco, California

The show is part of a "Week of Angry Arts" in support of the Spring Mobilization to End the War. Other bands include Quicksilver, Big Brother, Country Joe & the Fish, and the Sopwith Camel—however, the Camel goes on late because the Dead's set runs over and their set is cut short when the hall cuts the power.

Wednesday April 12
Fillmore Auditorium, San Francisco, California

Another benefit for the legally challenged Mime Troupe; with the Airplane, Quicksilver, Moby Grape, Andrew Staples, and the Loading Zone.

Monday April 17
Banana Grove, Ambassador Hotel, Los Angeles, California

Wednesday April 5
A tour-bus line begins offering the "Hippie Hop," an excursion through the Haight advertised as "The only foreign tour within the limits of the continental United States." Seven-ten is one of the stops.

Friday April 7
The dawn of KPMX-FM.

The band makes its Hollywood debut in *Petulia*, directed by Richard Lester, who was also responsible for *A Hard Day's Night*. The film is released the following year.

APRIL '67

1   2   3   4   5   6   7   8

Saturday April 1
Sunday April 2
Rock Garden, San Francisco, California

With the Charles Lloyd Quartet and the Mystery Trend.

9   10   11

12   13   14   15   16   17   18 – 27

Friday April 14
Saturday April 15
Sunday April 16
Kaleidoscope, Hollywood, California

With Jefferson Airplane and Canned Heat.

April 1967

70

Below and right: The band rehearse in April 1967.

Friday April 28
Stockton
Ballroom, Stockton,
California

Sunday April 30
Boxing authorities strip Muhammad Ali (the former Cassius Clay, who changed his name after joining the Nation of Islam movement) of his heavyweight title when the boxer resists the military draft.

28   29   30

Saturday April 29
Earl Warren
Showgrounds, Santa
Barbara, California

With the Doors, UFO,
and Captain Speed. The
uneasy relationship
between the Dead and
the Doors continues, as
Pigpen rejects Ray
Manzarek's suggestion
that they share the
same Vox organ.

Sunday April 30
The Cheetah,
Santa Monica,
California

Two shows today:
afternoon and
evening.

The band goes to a Russian River
retreat for a working vacation.
The period is covered by
"experimental" filmmaker Robert
Nelson, whose seven-minute film
entitled *Grateful Dead* later wins
an award in Europe.

MAY '67

1

Monday May 1
Rendezvous Inn
San Francisco
California

During May the
band have a weekly
Monday night gig at
the Rendezvous
Inn, a gay bar on
Geary Street.

Love and Haight

Media coverage of the Be-In and side events like the hit song "San Francisco (Be Sure To Wear Flowers in Your Hair)," a single written by John Phillips and sung by his friend Scott MacKenzie to promote the Monterey Pop Festival, brought tens of thousands of young Americans to San Francisco in the spring-summer of 1967. Most were in their teens and 20s, the apex of the Baby-Boom bulge on the demographic curve, and all were determined to be a part of what came to be known as the "Summer of Love." Some saw, sampled, and split back to school or the hometown or continued the journey elsewhere in the best *On the Road* tradition. Many chose to stay indefinitely. Unfortunately, there too many pilgrims. The city's social services, even augmented by grassroots groups like the Diggers, were hard-pressed to provide food and medical care for the hippie influx.

Then there was the matter of drugs. As demand rose, dealing, a semi-philanthropic enterprise among the early hippies, became a big business, with the concomitant rise in violence, and the types of drugs changed from pot and acid to speed and heroin, with a predictably horrific downturn in "vibe." And along with thousands of "gentle people" came parasites and predators.

Negative focus

What those young seekers came for was a joyous scene centered on rock and roll and other arts that affirmed respect for the earth and all its people, and of the spiritual and spontaneous over the material and preprogrammed. The old-timers of the Haight sought to live life on their own terms and have some fun. Unfortunately, their success meant that the number of seekers escalated beyond what the environment could sustain.

In April, a mimeographed street newsletter called ComCo reported on a rape: "Pretty little 16 yr old middle-class chick comes to the Haight... gets picked up by a street dealer who spends all day shooting her full of speed... feeds her 3000 mikes (micrograms of LSD, about 15 times the usual dose) & raffles off her temporarily unemployed body... Rape is as common as bullshit on Haight Street."

The focus was shifting to the negative. It would only get worse over the summer, as the local and then the national and then the global media homed in on the squalor and the drugs and the human casualties and ignored the very real but less sensational achievements of the scene, in the arts—music and graphics— and in social thinking; much of the origins of feminism, gay rights, and environmental thinking can be traced to the Haight.

Ironically, something very similar would happen to the Dead's own scene in the late '80s and '90s, as too many seekers arrived to overload a very fragile ecosystem.

Left: By the summer of '67, Haight Street was packed with hippies and young runaways 24 hours a day, and attracting gawking tourists as well.

Friday May 5
Saturday May 6
Fillmore Auditorium,
San Francisco,
California

With the Paupers
and Collage.

Thursday May 18
Awalt High School,
Mountain View, California

The band play a high-school
assembly at the behest of
Randy Groenke, Jerry Garcia's
one-time banjo student.

Saturday May 20
Continental
Ballroom, Santa Clara,
California

Monday May 29
Napa County
Fairgrounds, Vallejo,
California

With Project Hope.

2 | 3 | 4 | 5 | 6 | 7 – 10 | 11 | 12 – 17 | 18 | 19 | 20 | 21 – 28 | 29 | 30

Brian Rohan

Brian Rohan, soon to be considered *the* rock 'n' roll attorney in San Francisco, represented the Dead in negotiations for the first contract with Warner Bros. in the fall of 1966. At the time he had zero knowledge of or connection to rock 'n' roll, but his hip pedigree was already in place—he had worked for left-leaning S.F. attorney Vincent Hallinan and had successfully kept Ken Kesey out of jail following a pot arrest. With another attorney, Michael Stepanian, he founded the Haight Ashbury Legal Organization (HALO), which had its offices downstairs in the Dead's pad at 710 Ashbury Street at the time of their October 1967 pot bust. He continued to give legal advice to the Dead (and many other Bay Area bands) for many years.

Thursday May 11
Marigold
Ballroom, Fresno,
California

Tuesday May 30
Winterland Arena, San Francisco, California

The "big five" San Francisco Bands—the
Dead, the Airplane, Quicksilver, Big Brother,
and the Charlatans—share the stage
(probably for the first and only time) in a
benefit for the Haight-Ashbury Legal
Organization (HALO), founded by Brian Rohan
and his partner Michael Stepanian to help
the ever-increasing number of hippies
running afoul of the law. The concert raises
more than $12,000.

31

Wednesday May 31
The band fly to New
York on a Warner Bros.–
sponsored trip. It is the
first time any of the band,
save Jerry, briefly, have
been to the Big Apple.

New York Music Scene

When the Dead arrived in New York for the first time in June 1967, there was already a slight buzz about the group in the city's burgeoning hippie community. New York had enjoyed its own Be-Ins, "happenings," and counterculture events, so it was not unusual that the Dead would devote two days of their two-week New York stay to free outdoor concerts.

New York didn't have the same kind of community of bands as San Francisco, nor the venues or promoters to forge an equivalent of the Bay Area's ballroom scene, but it had always attracted musicians of every stripe. A number of fine bands emerged from the city in the mid- and late '60s, including the Lovin' Spoonful, who, like the Dead, had roots in the early '60s jug band revival, and the popular and influential Blues Project, who also had members with strong jazz influences. Two other artists who successfully straddled the folk and rock worlds were Johnny Rivers and Richie Havens.

In a purer rock vein, the Young Rascals were white suburban kids who played a soulful strain of rock and roll, and on the heavier side was Vanilla Fudge, who had a smash hit in 1967 with "You Keep Me Hangin' On." However, the rockin' rulers of Manhattan during the spring of '67 were unquestionably the Velvet Underground (*left*)—a hippie-hating anti-Dead led by Lou Reed and managed for a time by artist Andy Warhol. They were raw, aggressive, and considerably darker than most of what was coming out of San Francisco—as much a reflection of their own environment as the San Francisco bands were of theirs.

Monday June 12
The Cheetah, New York, New York

With the Group Image.

Sunday June 18
Monterey Pop Festival

The Dead appear on the third day of the festival.

12	13	14	15	16	17	18	19	20

Saturday June 3
Gymnasium, SUNY, Stony Brook, New York

The band ventures out to Long Island to play a show. The campus (appropriately named, given its rep as a "party school") is home to Grateful Dead early adopter Howie Klein and two *Crawdaddy!* editors, Sandy Pearlman and Richard Meltzer. This confluence of Dead-friendly, rock-savvy personalities helps establish Long Island as major Deadhead territory.

Thursday June 8
Bandshell on the Mall, Central Park, New York, New York

The band tries to recreate some of that Golden Gate Park ambience in the midst of Central Park's 800 acres, with middling success. Among those who take in the free show is jazz great Charles Mingus, who arrives in a chauffeur-driven Cadillac with a flask of martinis.

Thursday June 15
Straight Theater,
San Francisco, California

Although it won't officially open for a few more weeks, the band plays the "Christening" of the Straight Theater.

Friday June 16
The first International Monterey Pop Festival begins: About 7,500 inside the seating area (and maybe up to 35,000 outside), 1,000 "journalists" (most, in fact, celebrity guests and other hangers-on), 100,000 fresh orchids from Hawaii, 32 bands and performers, and the inevitable special batch from Bear (this one dubbed "Monterey Purple") are in the mix. It lasts for three days.

JUNE '67

1	2	3	4	5	6	7	8	9	10	11

Thursday June 1
Tompkins Square Park, New York, New York

After an opening set by Richie Havens, the Dead play their first East Coast show. It goes reasonably well, though the dynamic between band and audience isn't quite what it is back home—especially when someone tosses a framed lithograph of Jesus into the drum kit.

Tuesday June 6
Wednesday June 7
Thursday June 8
Friday June 9
Saturday June 10
Sunday June 11
Café au Go-Go, Greenwich Village, New York, New York

Luke & the Apostles play all six gigs. Eric Andersen is also on the bill for the last four shows. Frank Zappa and the Mothers of Invention are also playing this week, upstairs (the Dead are downstairs.) The opening night sees the first "documented" version of "Alligator." The lyrics come from Robert Hunter, Garcia's old friend. Garcia wrote to tell him that he'd like Hunter to come to San Francisco. Thus began one of the most significant words-and-music partnerships in rock history.

Monterey Pop

The Monterey Pop Festival would be not only one of the major musical events of the '60s, but the template for virtually every other rock festival from Bickershaw to Bonnaroo. You couldn't have a rock festival just two-and-a-half hours' drive from the Haight in 1967 without the San Francisco groups, of course. They, however, were collectively wary of what looked like a scheme on the part of the L.A. types (the show was being organized by L.A. producer Lou Adler) to capitalize on their determinedly noncommercial scene. Even after the bands decided to play, the issue of being included (or not) in a documentary film to be shot by the distinguished D.A. Pennebaker remained a sticking point, and the Dead never did agree to take part.

Over Friday and Saturday, Jefferson Airplane, Janis Joplin, and especially Otis Redding take their part in music history with fantastic sets. After a Sunday afternoon dream-out with Ravi Shankar, the Dead are ready to play on Sunday night. They are preceded by a generally unknown British band, The Who. Musically, their set wasn't outstanding, but it ended with the band's trademark guitar-smashing, smoke-bomb-exploding, drum-kit-dynamiting feedback-frenzy following "My Generation." The audience roared while the Dead stood backstage, open-mouthed, wondering how they were going to follow *that*.

By doing what they did best, of course: by getting people up and dancing. "Foldin' chairs are for foldin' up and dancin' on," Bob advised the crowd, and the band launched into "Viola Lee Blues." It was, in the opinion of many, a pretty good little set, but few would remember.

The band relinquished the stage to Brian Jones of the Rolling Stones, who introduced the Jimi Hendrix Experience. The group's first album, *Are You Experienced?*, had generated sufficient buzz to win them the top billing at the festival, but few in the U.S. had seen them perform. The Experience set the place on fire, literally and figuratively, with Jimi coaxing sounds as yet unheard from his Strat, playing it in ways as yet unimagined, and finally immolating it in a Dionysian "sacrifice."

Left, far left and top left: Sunday 18 June, the band plays the last day of the First International Monterey Pop Festival.
Below: *The Dead play for free in Golden Gate Park.*

Sunday July 23
Straight Theater, San Francisco, California

The band joins Big Brother, Phoenix, and the Wildflower for the official "opening" of the Straight Theater (which was 'christened on 6/15). The highlight of the Dead's set is Neal Cassady rapping over the Dead jamming, some of which later finds its way into Deadhead hands on an acetate insert to Hank Harrison's *The Dead Book*.

Wednesday June 21
Polo Field, Golden Gate Park, San Francisco, California

The band return to the site of the Human Be-In to play the Summer Solstice Festival, the "official" kickoff to the Summer of Love. The sound is greatly enhanced by new amps and other equipment that somehow accompanied the band back from Monterey. The Dead later return the gear to its rightful owner on Karmic principles.

Sunday July 16
Eagles Auditorium, Seattle, Washington

With the Daily Flash and Magic Fern.

Tuesday July 18
Masonic Temple, Portland, Oregon

With Poverty's People, U.S. Cadenza, and the Nigells.

Friday July 21
Saturday July 22
Continental Ballroom, Santa Clara, California

With Sons of Champlin and the Congress of Wonders.

JULY '67

| 1 – 12 | 13 | 14 | 15 | 16 | 17 | 18 | 19 | 20 | 21 | 22 | 23 | 24 | 25 | 26 |

Thursday July 13
PNE Agradome, Vancouver, British Columbia, Canada

With Daily Flash and the Love-Ins.

Sunday July 16
Golden Gardens Beach, Seattle, Washington

Afternoon show.

| 21 | 22 | 23 | 24 | 25 | 26 | 27 | 28 | 29 | 30 |

Wednesday June 28
Oakland Auditorium Arena, Oakland, California

Thursday July 27
Detroit erupts into race rioting after police raid a social club on the city's mostly African-American West Side. Three days of violence leaves 38 people dead.

| 27 | 28 | 29 | 30 | 31 |

Monday July 31
O'Keefe Centre, Toronto, Ontario, Canada

With the Jefferson Airplane and Luke & the Apostles. As a good-will gesture, the band (at Bill Graham's behest) plays a post-show set for the Centre's staff. It's also Jerry Garcia's 25th birthday.

"TURN ON YOUR LOVE LIGHT"
MALONE/SCOTT

This classic cover from Dead co-founder Ron "Pigpen" McKernan's stable found the frontman swaggering with the kind of rough-hewn charisma that reflected what rock at its raunchiest was all about. Written by Deadric Malone and Joseph Scott, and first performed by the Dead on August 5, 1967, "Turn On Your Love Light" had marked the first U.S. hit for bluesman Bobby Bland, who reached #28 with it on January 20, 1962. The extended Dead version provided an early showcase for the band's live prowess on the 1969 double disc *Live/Dead*, but for Pigpen it was also another chance to play macho matchmaker. "I know that all you fellas… might want to get yourself a little female company," he teases in a memorable 1971 show at Princeton University. "You—do you have any particular young lady in your sights this evening?" The Dead fired this one up over 300 times between 1967 and 1995, with performances led by Weir from 1981 on. Among the best versions are one from June 7, 1969 at the Fillmore in San Francisco featuring Janis Joplin, two more from a February 1970 run at the Fillmore East in New York, and a latter-day take from Nassau Coliseum on March 29, 1990 with contemporary jazz great Branford Marsalis on saxophone.

Sunday August 20
Non performance! The band arrives to play a mini-festival at Mount Tamalpais, but no one has bothered to make sure there'd be any electricity.

Friday August 25
Saturday August 26
King's Beach Bowl, Lake Tahoe, California

With the Creators.

19 20 21 22 23 24 25 26 27 28 29 – 31

Wednesday August 23
The Hippie Temptation: The Dead's first national TV appearance.

Monday August 28
Lindley Meadows, Golden Gate Park, San Francisco, California

The band plays at a memorial party for Hells Angel Chocolate George, a good friend of the band, who had been killed in a car accident days before.

Sunday August 13
West Park, Ann Arbor, Michigan

The band plays at least one free outdoor show in this university town.

Saturday August 19
American Legion Hall, Lake Tahoe, California

Thursday August 10
Chelsea Hotel Roof, New York, New York

13 14 15 16 17 18

The band heads down to the Big Apple to entertain at a party on the roof of the Chelsea Hotel—the famous 23rd Street hostelry that has sheltered writers and artists including William S. Burroughs, Tennessee Williams, and Virgil Thomson, and where Sid Vicious would stab Nancy Spungen (allegedly) eleven years later. The event is a fundraiser—the "Trip Without a Ticket"—in which the Diggers, now established in New York, seek to score some donations from the city's liberal and artistic elite.

Tuesday August 15
On this serendipitous night, one of Bill Graham's great double bills—Count Basie and Chuck Berry—plays the Fillmore. In the audience is Mickey Hart, working, at that time, with his father Lenny at Hart Music in San Carlos. At some point a complete stranger points out Bill Kreutzmann and suggests that Mickey introduce himself to "the Grateful Dead's drummer." Mickey never again met the stranger, but he took his advice. Bill and Mickey go to the Matrix to see some of Big Brother's show, then drive around the streets for hours in Bill's Mustang, bonding over their passion for percussion and occasionally pausing to jump out and work up a rhythm on the car hood, a garbage can lid, or whatever. Bill subsequently invites Mickey to come by and sit in any time *(see page 76)*.

Sunday August 6
Place Ville Marie, Montreal, Quebec, Canada

From a tiny street stage, the band play a free show for a crowd of about 25,000.

10 11 12

Friday August 11
Saturday August 12
Grande Ballroom, Detroit, Michigan

AUGUST '67

1 2 3 4 5 6 7 8 9

Tuesday August 1
Wednesday August 2
Thursday August 3
Friday August 4
Saturday August 5
O'Keefe Centre, Toronto, Ontario, Canada

With the Jefferson Airplane and Luke & the Apostles. The Toronto *Globe and Mail*'s music critic would have this to say about the Dead's performance: "Simian… not volume, not intensity, but noise… like a jet taking off in your inner ear, while the mad scientist was perversely scraping your nerves to shreds." Saturday's show sees the first performance of "Turn On Your Love Light."

Sunday August 6
Youth Pavilion, Expo 67, Montreal, Quebec, Canada

From the Place Ville Marie, the band move to the grounds of Expo 67, a "World's Fair"-type exhibition with a futuristic theme, mid-60s style—lots of geodesic domes and monorails. After Montreal the band cut loose from the Airplane and head south of the (Canadian) border for a few days of rock 'n' roll rest 'n' relaxation at the Hitchcock family-owned Millbrook estate, where Timothy Leary et al conducted their psychedelic "research." The invite comes from Ron Rakow *(see page 82)*, who, providentially, is romantically involved with Peggy Hitchcock.

Opposite page: Summer at 710 Ashbury. *Far left:* Garcia at the O'Keefe Center, Toronto, August 1–5. *Left:* Pigpen gives a photographer the Evil Eye.

The Hippie Temptation

The title pretty much says it all: CBS News sent Harry Reasoner (squareness personified) to the Haight, and, *quelle surprise*, Mr. Reasoner (and various psychiatrists, law-enforcement officials, and other talking heads from the straight world) was not enthusiastic about what he found. The show included a brief interview with the band and included footage of them playing "Dancin' in the Streets." It's the Dead's first national TV appearance (if that's the right term).

Jerry Garcia: What we're thinking about is a peaceful planet. We're not thinking of anything else. We're not thinking about any kind of power, we're not thinking about any of those kinds of struggles. We're not thinking about revolution or war or any of that. That's not what we want. Nobody wants to get hurt. Nobody wants to hurt anybody. We would all like to live an uncluttered life, a simple life, a good life, you know, and think about moving the whole human race ahead a step, or a few steps . . .
Phil Lesh: Or half a step . . .
Jerry Garcia: Yeah or half a step or anything.
Harry Reasoner: Well, there are the hippies. They make you uncomfortable, because there is obviously something wrong with the world they never made, if it leads to these grotesqueries. At their best they are trying for a kind of group sainthood, and saints running in groups are likely to be ludicrous. They depend on hallucination for their philosophy. And finally, they offer a spurious attraction of the young, a corruption of the idea of innocence.
FROM *THE HIPPIE TEMPTATION*

Friday September 8 🎸
Saturday September 9 🎸
Eagle's Auditorium, Seattle, Washington

With Fat Jack and Magic Fern both nights. It's also Pigpen's 22nd birthday on the Friday.

Unlike in May, when the band escaped to a friend's property at Rio Nido, in early September they stay closer to Dance Hall.

Following the departure of original roadie Laird Grant in the summer, Bob Richards takes over and a new driver is recruited: Larry Shurtliff, a.k.a. Ram Rod.

SEPTEMBER '67

| 1 | 2 | **3** | 4 | 5 | 6 | 7 |

Sunday September 3 ★
Monday September 4 ★
Dance Hall, Rio Nido, California

The band play a local club for a couple of nights (or possibly just one), including an amazing 30-plus-minute workout on "In the Midnight Hour," which appears on *Fallout from the Phil Zone* 30 years later, and rehearsed what would become THE Grateful Dead song, "Dark Star."

9

8

Saturday September 9 🎸
Volunteer Park, Seattle, Washington

After the Seattle gigs, the band fly to Los Angeles, where Dave Hassinger awaits them at RCA Studios. Though the band were determined not to rush through the recording of their second album for Warner Bros., Jerry recalled that they accomplished "absolutely nothing" in their first sessions.

| 10 | 11 | 12 | 13 | 14 | **15** |

Friday September 15 🎸
Hollywood Bowl, Hollywood, California

Together with the Jefferson Airplane and Big Brother, the band play the Hollywood Bowl—at 18,000 seats, by far the biggest venue they've yet performed in—for a show billed as "Bill Graham presents The San Francisco Scene in Los Angeles."

"DARK STAR"
GRATEFUL DEAD/ROBERT HUNTER

The most legendary entry in the Dead's arte intera, "Dark Star" has spawned more fan appreciation, scholarly deconstruction, and interstellar recreation than any other song. A Hunter/Garcia track first appearing in its purest state as a live offering on the band's double-disc 1969 set *Live/Dead* (a relatively staid studio version had come out in 1968 as a single-only release and reappeared on a later greatest hits package), "Dark Star" provided an early canvas upon which the band could stretch its improvisational skills, resulting in a sonic cataclysm in which "the forces tear loose from the axis." "It's our music at one of its really good moments," Garcia said in 1971. "'Dark Star' has meant, while I'm playing it, almost as many things as I can sit here and imagine." The first documented performance of the song took place at a Shrine Exhibition Hall show in Los Angeles on December 13, 1967, though an embryonic version that inspired Hunter to write the song's first few lines of lyrics was played during a rehearsal in September '67 at a dance hall in Rio Nido, California. The lengthiest version (at over 48 minutes) took place on May 11, 1972, in Rotterdam, Netherlands. But the fans' most popular choice for the best "Dark Star" was played during a show from the Fillmore East in New York on February 13, 1970, a long-time taper's favorite. Bassist Phil Lesh once explained the magic of the tune, saying it had "always had the potential to go absolutely anywhere. We designed it that way in the first place… that was the one we tacitly agreed upon where anything was okay." The song was more than okay for the Other Ones, who took it to the next level with a constant change-up that incorporates "Dark Star" jams and reprises mixed in with other Dead classics.

Friday September 29 🎸
Saturday September 30 🎸
Straight Theater, San Francisco, California

Denied a dance permit, the theater gets around this by becoming a dance school. On Friday a dance leader intones, "What I would like everyone to do is close your eyes and relax, and note how your heart is pumping," upon which the Dead begin playing "Dancing in the Streets." Sons of Champlin also play.

| 26 | 27 | 28 | **29** | **30** |

Ram Rod 1947–2006

The heart and soul of the Dead's equipment crew from the summer of 1967 until the end of the line in 1995, Ram Rod (known to only a few by his given name Larry Shurtliff) may well be the most famous roadie ever. Raised in eastern Oregon, Larry came into the Dead's orbit through Ken Kesey's Merry Pranksters. His *nom de prank* originated from a stay in Mexico with Kesey & Co. during the summer of '66—Kesey called for a volunteer to cram a bunch of people into a VW and Larry volunteered for the job, joking that he was "Ramon Rodriguez, famous Mexican guide," and the name stuck. According to Garcia, Ram Rod "was just suddenly there, working [in the fall of '67]," and never left. He became crew chief and at various times Garcia's guitar roadie and tech for the always-demanding Mickey Hart.

Into the Jetstream

Having taken up Bill Kreutzmann's invitation to stop by, Mickey Hart was at the September 30 Straight Theater show. Bill and Mickey went out and found a second drum kit, and the band launched into "Caution." Hart felt like he was "whipped into a jet stream," but when the set was over, in Dennis McNally's words, "the band included six people." Bob Weir and Pigpen were somewhat wary of the newcomer, and Bob, at least, felt he was "outvoted" when the others invited Mickey to join the band. As for Mickey, he went back to San Carlos only long enough to toss his set of store keys onto the sidewalk in front of Hart Music before moving in with Bill and Phil Lesh.

| 16 ~ 21 | **22** | **23** | **24** |

Friday September 22 🎸
Saturday September 23 🎸
Family Dog, Denver, Colorado

The band travel to the Mile-High City to help the Family Dog open their new ballroom. Mother Earth are also on the bill.

Sunday September 24 🎸
City Park, Denver, Colorado

Right: That's Airplane bassist Jack Casady in the Captain Trips hat.

76

Friday October 6
The Summer of Love having turned into an autumn of discontent, the Diggers organize a "Death of Hippie" ceremony to put to rest the semi-imaginary construct responsible for it all. After a procession through the Haight (right), the Diggers burn a coffin full of beads, flowers, and other hippie regalia in the Panhandle. It is a year to the day after the Love Pageant Rally.

Thursday October 5
In response to the bust, the Dead hold a press conference *(above)*.

| 1 | 2 | 3 | 4 | 5 |

Monday October 16
A San Francisco Grand Jury indicts the 11 people arrested at 710 for various possession charges.

Monday October 2
The infamous 710 Bust: SFPD raids Deadquarters.

| 6 | 7 - 13 | 14 | 15 | 16 |

Sunday October 1
🎸 Greek Theatre, University of California, Berkeley, California

With Charles Lloyd and Bola Sete, the band play "A Benefit for the Economic Opportunity Program."

Saturday October 14
Continental Ballroom, Santa Clara, California

"THE OTHER ONE"
WEIR

The Dead's first genuine magnum opus and the centerpiece of *Anthem of the Sun* (1968), "That's It For The Other One" usually filled an area that was roughly the dimensions of all space and time. From its earliest days as part of a longer piece that began with a funereal prologue titled "Cryptical Envelopment," the song that was eventually referred to simply as "The Other One" provided a blast of heavy psychedelia at its purest, with exploding roses and a bus driven by "Cowboy Neal" Cassady of Beat Generation fame among its many vivid images. For the Dead it opened up wider vistas that would soon be filled with other expansive classics such as "Dark Star" and "Terrapin Station." "The thing about 'The Other One' that was so thrilling was that it had all these climaxes at this incredible rate," drummer Mickey Hart said in 1984. "Kreutzmann and I started to do this phasing trip, where we'd split the band... we called it 'going out.'" Donning a new guise inspired by the song's title, The Other Ones continued to play "The Other One," adding to the over 550 versions the Dead had logged from 1967 to 1995. Among the best of the bunch are a pair of real smokers from February 13, 1970, and May 2, 1970.

The Bust at 710

Given the Grateful Dead's identification with weed and acid, a bust was probably inevitable, and at 3:30 p.m. on October 2, Norbert "the Nark" Currie led the SFPD Narcotics Squad into 710 Ashbury. This being a high-profile bust, Currie had state officials and a press contingent in tow. (The evidence for the raid—for which no warrant was sworn—reportedly came from a friend of Ken Kesey who was facing child-molestation charges, and who ratted in return for leniency.)

Jerry Garcia and M.G. were out, so the bust netted Pigpen (who didn't smoke pot), Bob Weir (who'd sworn off all drugs earlier in '67), Florence Nathan, Vee Barnard, Toni Kaufman, Sue Swanson, Rock Scully, Danny Rifkin, Bob Matthews, and Christine Bennett. At the Hall of Justice the arrestees found lots of friends: four other group houses in the Haight had also been raided. The cops had 710 staked out in an effort to nab Jerry and M.G. but their quick-thinking friend and neighbor, Marilyn Harris, tipped the couple off. A search of 710 had turned up about a pound of pot and hash. With Brian Rohan in full effect they were all bailed out within six hours, except for Swanson and Bennet, who were under 21 and thus minors in the eyes of the law. The bust was front-page news on the next day's *Chronicle*.

Above: Out on bail after the bust.

| 22 | 23 | 24 | 25 | 26 | 27 | 28 | 29 | 30 | 31 |

Sunday October 22 ★
🎸 Winterland Arena, San Francisco, California

A benefit for the Marijuana Defense Fund. Quicksilver and Big Brother also play. It's the first "documented" performance of "The Other One" *(left)* and the first "Cryptical Envelopment."

Tuesday October 31
🎸 Winterland Arena, San Francisco, California

This Halloween show, also with Quicksilver and Big Brother, is billed as "Trip or Freak!"

All pictures: *Life at 710 Ashbury.*

No Moss?

On November 9 the first issue of a new biweekly magazine, edited out of offices in a dilapidated South of Market building, hit the stands: *Rolling Stone*. The magazine was the brainchild of 21-year-old editor/entrepreneur Jann Wenner (*below*), who'd been on the fringes of the Prankster/band scene while at Berkeley, where he wrote a column under the *nom de plume* "Mr. Jones" for the *Daily Cal*. The money for the startup came from his wife, Jane Schindelheim Wenner, and Ralph Gleason (*see page 36*), eminent pop and jazz critic lately of the San Francisco *Chronicle*, supplied moral authority and street cred.

There were already rock-oriented journals in existence—most notably *Crawdaddy!*—but they tended to focus solely on fine points of musicology. *Rolling Stone* differed in a couple of respects. First, it was, as Wenner himself said, "an industry paper," the industry being rock music. Second, *Rolling Stone* encompassed not only the music but everything else of interest to the Baby Boomers who listened to it. The first issue, for example, featured a muckraking piece by Michael Lydon on what actually happened to the money from the Monterey festival, a photo feature on the 710 Ashbury bust, and, on the cover, a photo of John Lennon as he appeared in Richard Lester's movie *How I Won the War*.

Wenner has been accused of many sins—a tendency toward sycophancy and a chronically disorganized management style among them—but in the mag's early years he had a terrific gift for finding talented writers and photographers (Lydon, Hunter S. Thompson, Jon Landau, Dave Marsh, Annie Leibovitz, Ben Fong-Torres, Lester Bangs, and a host of others) and letting them rip.

Rolling Stone quickly established itself as rock's journal of record, and it's still published today, albeit with somewhat diminished authority. By the 1990s Wenner's empire had grown to include *US* and *Men's Journal*.

Thursday November 9
The first issue of *Rolling Stone* magazine is published, featuring The Grateful Dead's pot bust.

Sunday November 12
Winterland Arena,
San Francisco, California

A "Benefit for the Bands."

Tuesday November 14
American Studios,
North Hollywood,
California

9 10 11 12 13 14 15~30

Friday November 10
Saturday November 11 ★
Shrine Exhibition Hall,
Los Angeles, California

The band plays this 6,000-seat venue for the first time in two shows billed as "The Amazing Electric Wonders" with Buffalo Springfield and Blue Cheer (a proto–heavy metal "power trio" whose name is said to derive from one of Bear's legendary brews.)

NOVEMBER '67

1 2 3-8

Right and opposite page: Bill Graham's stage manager, Jim Haney, brings in the New Year at Winterland.

Back to L.A.

From mid-November to mid-December the band was essentially based in L.A., living in a rather gothic mansion that belonged to the Hitchcock family and rehearsing and recording at American Studios in North Hollywood. Tapes from these sessions include versions of "Alice D. Millionaire," "Dark Star," "The Other One," and a new song from Bob Weir, "Born Cross-Eyed."

Wednesday December 13
Shrine Exhibition Hall,
Los Angeles, California

First documented public performance of "Dark Star."

Right: Jefferson Airplane at the Dead's New Year's Eve show, Winterland Arena.

Friday December 22
Saturday December 23
Sunday December 24
Palm Gardens, New York, New York

As their equipment goes to New York in a caravan consisting of a Dodge van and an International Harvester truck, the band flies to the city to play shows there and to continue work on the new album. The band's East Coast base is the home of a friend of Bob Weir's in Englewood, New Jersey, just across the Hudson River from Manhattan. The Palm Gardens gigs are with Group Image.

| 22 | 23 | 24 |

Left: Bill Graham (pointing) enjoying the midnight moment. Later, he would do the midnight entrances.

Dave Hassinger

For years, engineer/producer Dave Hassinger has been mocked in Grateful Dead circles for being the guy who was nearly driven crazy by the antics and demands of the Dead during sessions for *Anthem of the Sun* in the fall of 1967. He left in a huff and complained bitterly to Warner Bros. boss Joe Smith, who had signed the group in late 1966. Smith in turn fired off a letter to Dead manager Danny Rifkin complaining about the Dead's "lack of professionalism" and noting that *Anthem* was "the most unreasonable project with which we have ever involved ourselves." The Dead finished the record themselves in early 1968. That said, it should be noted that Hassinger is one of the most revered engineers in the history of rock, with credits that include the Stones' "Satisfaction," "Paint It Black" (and others), Jefferson Airplane's *Surrealistic Pillow* and albums by everyone from Sam Cooke to Linda Ronstadt to the Dead (the first album).

| 25 | 26 | 27 | 28 |

Tuesday December 26
Wednesday December 27
Village Theater, New York, New York

Located at 6th Street and Second Avenue, the Village Theater would very soon be transformed into the Fillmore East and become the East Coast's premiere rock venue, but at the end of '67 it is a decrepit pile with a massive hole in the roof. At one point it actually snows on the band as they play. Take Five also plays both shows.

Friday December 29
Saturday December 30
Psychedelic Supermarket, Boston, Massachusetts

The Grateful Dead's first Beantown gigs take place in an underground club—literally; the Psychedelic Supermarket is located next to a subterranean parking lot, giving it acoustics similar to a giant cinder block.

| 29 | 30 | 31 |

Hassinger Hassled

The band came to New York in the main to work at Olmstead Studios on 48th Street and Century Studios on 52nd Street, which were reputed to have the best eight-track systems in the business. The band treated their studio time as a learning experience; they were eager to explore the technological possibilities the studio offered to add depth and richness to their music, just as they sought new ways of creative interplay through improvisation onstage. Warner Bros, however, wanted an album. His patience worn thin, Hassinger snapped when Bob Weir said he wanted to reproduce the sound of "thick air" on "Born Cross-Eyed." "He wants what?" said Hassinger before decamping. Hassinger, for his part, said that the real breaking point was the band's refusal to sing collectively to cover their individual vocal weaknesses—that and Phil Lesh, with whom Hassinger had a major personality conflict. In any event, Joe Smith was enough of a realist to understand that neither carrot nor stick was going to work with this particular band. He allowed the Dead to finish the album themselves, with the band's soundman Dan Healy replacing Hassinger at the controls, but not before upbraiding the band in the famous letter of December 23—which the band sent back with Smith's spelling and grammatical errors corrected.

Sunday December 31
The band (minus Bill Kreutzmann, who is driving the gear back with Ram Rod and Bob Matthews) fly home to San Francisco on New Year's Eve. Bob Weir and Mickey Hart go to Winterland. Jerry and Phil go home—which, for Jerry, now meant an apartment shared with Mountain Girl in the Richmond neighborhood. Seven-ten Ashbury would remain the band's headquarters (and home to a few people) for a few more months, but the tribe it had sheltered through the high times and low times of 1967 was moving on.

| 1–16 | 17 | 18 | 19 |

The Carousel Venture

At the start of '68, Bill Graham's Fillmore and the Family Dog's (i.e., Chet Helms') Avalon venues were the two poles around which the musical scene revolved, with Winterland, also run by Bill Graham Productions, for the bigger events. Graham and Helms could be difficult to deal with, so there was a growing desire among the San Francisco bands (the Dead in particular) for, essentially, a ballroom of their own. Once known as the El Patio, the Carousel, at Market Street and Van Ness Avenue, could accommodate 2,000 people. Given its size and location, it seemed ideal for an experiment in musical collectivism. Early in 1968, the Airplane (the most popular band in the country at this point), the Dead, and Quicksilver entered into a somewhat ambiguous collective, the "Triad," in which each agreed to play the Carousel gratis in return for a percentage of the gate. The arrangement was brokered by Ron Rakow, who also leased the venue from its owner.

Ron Rakow

"Cadillac Ron" Rakow was a financial wizard and hustler who befriended the Dead in the Haight, ran the Carousel Ballroom (unsuccessfully) for the band in 1968, and helped them start their own record label. However, in 1976, he wrote himself checks for $275,000, effectively bankrupting the record company.

Kidd Candelario

Bill "Kidd" Candelario (*left*), went from doing odd jobs at the Carousel Ballroom to becoming an integral member of the Grateful Dead's road crew until Garcia's death. Big, sarcastic, and sometimes mean, he was a perfect fit: "He could be one of the most ornery guys in the whole wide world," said Garcia.

Wednesday January 17
Carousel Ballroom, San Francisco, California

A celebration of "Benjamin Franklin's Birthday," with Quicksilver and Jerry Abrams Head Lights, including the first public performances of two new songs with lyrics by Robert Hunter, "The Eleven" (*see page 87*) and "China Cat Sunflower" (*see page 100*). The show also sees the first documented "Feedback" segment in a show. The precursor to "Space," "Feedback" was pure electronic improvisation, without even a theme to jam around—just Jerry, Bob, and Phil feeding back their guitar output into their amps to create snarling, buzzing, wailing dissonance.

Wednesday January 31
Taking advantage of a cease-fire for the Tet (New Year's) holiday, Vietcong and North Vietnamese forces launch attacks throughout South Vietnam. The Tet Offensive ends with heavy losses for the communists, but it turns public opinion in the U.S. against the war.

| 20 | 21 | 22 | 23 | 24 | 25 | 26 | 27 | 28 | 29 | 30 | 31 |

Saturday January 20
Eureka Municipal Auditorium, Eureka, California

The first "Spanish Jam," loosely based on a theme from Miles Davis's *Sketches of Spain*, as well as another jazz-influenced jamming platform, "Clementine."

Monday January 22 ★
Friday January 26
Saturday January 27
Eagles Auditorium, Seattle, Washington

With Quicksilver: "The Quick and the Dead" according to the billing.

Monday January 29
College Center Ballroom, Portland State College, Portland, Oregon

With QMS and the PH Phactor Jug band.

Tuesday January 30
EMU Ballroom, University of Oregon, Eugene, Oregon

Tour of the Great Northwest

The Dead's nine-show outing through northern California, Washington, and Oregon was the first tour mapped out by the band itself (or more precisely by a troika of Rock Scully, Brian Rohan, and Ron Rakow) without the customary recourse to local promoters. Quicksilver came along for most of the shows, leading those dates to be billed, inevitably, as "The Quick and the Dead." The two bands also revived their running game of Cowboys and Indians.

Musically, the tour reflected the new directions the band's music was taking. Songs now began to flow into each other, rather than having distinct "beginnings" and "endings"—a typical set became more like a linked suite than a mere collection of songs, and the songs themselves became vehicles for ever more incandescent jamming. A lot of the old rock 'n' roll and R&B material got left behind as the band scaled the heights of psychedelic improvisation, but tunes like the spare, haunting "Death Don't Have No Mercy" and Pigpen's no-holds-barred, rip-snorting "Turn On Your Love Light" translated well into the new style.

Below: Yes, kids, in the '60s even hip people sometimes wore hideous plaid pants. Nice paisley on Garcia, though.

Neal Cassady 1926–1968

Four days before what would have been his 42nd birthday, the seemingly indestructible Neal Cassady died in San Miguel de Allende, Mexico, from a combination of exposure, tequila, and amphetamines. The previous night in Portland, Bob Weir (the band member who, in the end, became closest to Neal) had added new lyrics to "The Other One":

The bus came by and I got on
That's when it all began
There was cowboy Neal at the wheel
Of the bus to never-ever land
Comin,' comin', comin,' around
Comin' around in a circle.

It's difficult to briefly summarize Neal Cassady's impact on two generations of American counterculture. Raised on Denver's skid row and constantly in motion from youngest boyhood to premature death, he was a force of nature who could seem possessed of supernatural force. He never wrote more than some unfinished fragments; his life was his art, and he lived that life with a roman-candle-like intensity that set the Beat generation afire (Neal was the "Dean Morality" of Jack Kerouac's *On the Road* and the "secret hero" of Allen Ginsberg's *Howl*). Then Cassady went from on the road to On the Bus with Kesey and the Pranksters, becoming, in effect, the living bridge between the Beats and the hippies. He was a true American original, a hammer-juggling Huck Finn whose Mississippi was the American highway; like Walt Whitman, he contained multitudes.

"There's no experience in my life yet that equals riding with Cassady in, like, a '56 Plymouth or a Cadillac through San Francisco or from San Jose to Santa Rosa. He was the ultimate something—the person as art." JERRY GARCIA

Bob Matthews

A one-time high school classmate of Bob Weir's in Palo Alto, Bob Matthews was a founding member of Mother McCree's Uptown Jug Champions (for whom he played washboard and kazoo until Garcia fired him) and one of the original supporters of the Warlocks and then the Grateful Dead—he helped start their fan club and his '55 Plymouth was the group's first equipment car. He went on to be one of the Dead's early crew chiefs but later graduated to doing studio and live recording work for the band, as well as doing live engineering at the Carousel Ballroom for a time. With partner Betty Cantor, he engineered and/or co-produced many of the Dead's classic albums, including *Aoxomoxoa*, *Live/Dead*, *Workingman's Dead*, "Skull & Roses," *Europe '72*, and others, as well as Garcia's and Weir's first solo ventures.

Wednesday February 14 ★
Carousel Ballroom, San Francisco, California

Country Joe & the Fish help the Dead "officially" open the collectively operated Carousel Ballroom in a Valentine's Day concert broadcast live on both KMPX and Berkeley's KPFA public-radio station—the first live "simulcast" in rock history. The band dedicated the second set to the memory of Neal Cassady.

14 15 16 **17** 18 19 20 21 **22 23 24** 25 26 27 28 29

Saturday February 17
Selland Arena,
Fresno, California

With Country Joe & the Fish.

Thursday February 22
Friday February 23
Saturday February 24
King's Beach Bowl,
Lake Tahoe, California

With Morning Glory. The band's shows are billed as "Trip and Ski." Selections from these gigs were released as *Dick's Picks Volume 22* in 2001.

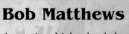

FEBRUARY '68

1 **2 3 4** 5 6 7 8 9 10 11 12

Sunday February 4
Gym, South Oregon College, Ashland, Oregon

With Quicksilver.

Sunday February 4
Neal Cassady dies.

Friday February 2
Saturday February 3
Crystal Ballroom, Portland, Oregon

"Clementine" from Saturday's show is included on 1999's *So Many Roads* box set.

Betty Cantor-Jackson

In a world that was (and still is) completely dominated by men, Betty Cantor was one of the first successful female recording engineers. Not bad for a one-time member of the Family Dog collective who was selling hot dogs at the Carousel Ballroom when she was taken on as an apprentice by Bob Matthews. Together Bob and Betty (as they were known) recorded all the Dead's late '60s and early '70s albums (with the exception of *American Beauty*, which was cut by Steve Barncard), and Cantor was involved to varying degrees with most of the group's (and Garcia's) records through the early '80s. She later gained notoriety in bootleg Taper circles for being the source of the famous "Betty Boards"—exquisite live soundboard tapes of the Dead that got into trading circulation when the contents of her storage locker were auctioned off in the late '80s.

No Left Turn Unstoned

Throughout the first months of '68 the band continued work on the next album, mostly at San Francisco's Columbus Recording Studio. It would ultimately be called *Anthem of the Sun* but the working title was an old Prankster saying, "No Left Turn Unstoned." When he could get away from his Air Force duties, Phil Lesh's friend and fellow *avant-gardista* Tom Constanten came by to add *musik concrete* touches to the keyboard parts, including inserting coins and other objects between piano strings. When Dave Hassinger was still overseeing the album, T.C. dropped a gyroscope into his piano, creating a sound he described as "not unlike a chain saw"; Hassinger "cleared his seat by a full four and a half feet when he heard it." Constanten's approach was especially evident on "That's It For The Other One," which expanded "The Other One" into a four-part suite.

The post-Hassinger studio work was largely accomplished by Jerry Garcia, Phil Lesh, and Dan Healy. It was Phil who came up with the idea of overlaying tapes of live shows (most from the Great Northwest Tour) over the studio tracks. At the mixing board, Healy proved more than equal to the task, even though he sometimes had to manipulate the tape decks by hand to sync music from different performances.

"I always felt that it was hard to do real constructive work with musicians on acid, but I guess there were some great records made that way."
DAVE HASSINGER TO BLAIR JACKSON, *1967*

Below: All three pictures are Sunday March 3, the Haight Street Free Concert, San Francisco

Monday March 11
Sacramento Memorial Auditorium, Sacramento, California

The band opens for Cream, the new UK "supergroup" with Eric Clapton on guitar, Jack Bruce on bass, and Ginger Baker on drums. Like the Dead, Cream plays what can be described as a heavily psychedelicized blues; like the Dead, they play LOUD—so loud, in fact, that the Brits fry their amps and have to play their set using the Dead's gear.

Thursday March 7
San Quentin State Prison, San Quentin, California

Unlike Johnny Cash, who would record a stunning live album here in 1969, the Dead don't play inside the Big House, but outside it, from a flatbed truck as they'd done in the Haight four days earlier. The show is at the behest of the Diggers.

7 | 8 | 9 | 10

March 1968

84

Sunday March 3
Haight Street, San Francisco, California

MARCH '68

1   2   3

Friday March 1
Saturday March 2
The Looking Glass, Walnut Creek, California

The Haight Street Free Concert

The Grateful Dead played a lot of "free," often spontaneous, concerts in the Haight-Ashbury years—though the term "free" seems somehow inappropriate given the band's ethos and the general zeitgeist of the time and place. This show is remembered most fondly of all, largely because it has come to be regarded as the band's goodbye to the Haight, and because, after the ravages of the Summer of Love, magic could still happen.

The concert came about after a nasty dust-up between hippies and cops about two weeks earlier. Hoping to ease tensions, the city proclaimed a "street festival" for March 3, with the streets of the Haight closed to traffic.

It was an opportunity the band wasn't about to pass up. Playing atop a flatbed truck with power tapped from the Straight Theater, the boys kicked off with "Viola Lee Blues," and as the first notes crackled, people began to gather until the streets (and stoops, and rooftops) were packed. "Viola" was followed by "Smokestack Lightning," "Turn on Your Love Light," "It Hurts Me Too," and—naturally—"Dancin' in the Street."

Friday March 15
Saturday March 16
Sunday March 17
Carousel Ballroom, San Francisco, California

Three gigs with the Jefferson Airplane. The Airplane is now flying high and they're usually out of town, so their involvement in the Carousel "Triad" is minimal; Ron Rakow is essentially running the operation. Friday is also Phil Lesh's 28th birthday. The band ends Saturday's show with an a capella rendering of a traditional tune from the Caribbean, "And We Bid You Goodnight," the first outing for this gentle closer.

15 | 16 | 17

Monday March 18
Green Street, San Francisco, California

The staff of KMPX FM, Tom "Big Daddy" Donahue's pioneering rock station, walk out on strike around 3:00 am on Monday morning. When the Carousel show ends, the Dead, members of the Airplane, and Steve Winwood head over to Green Street to entertain the picket line—aboard the usual flatbed truck. Two days later the band plays a benefit for the strikers—many of whom would give up on KPMX and go on to form KSAN.

Wednesday March 20
Avalon Ballroom, San Francisco, California

KMPX benefit concert.

Friday March 22
Saturday March 23
State Fair Coliseum, Detroit, Michigan

With Eric Burdon & The Animals.

18 | 19 | 20 | 21 | 22 | 23 | 24 | 25

Sunday March 24
The band's brief jaunt to Michigan was to have included a benefit in Grand Rapids today, but a blizzard keeps the band in Detroit and the show is canceled.

Tuesday March 26
Melodyland Theatre, Anaheim, California

With Jefferson Airplane.

26 | 27 | 28 | 29 | 30 | 31

Friday March 29
Saturday March 30
Sunday March 31
Carousel Ballroom, San Francisco, California

With Chuck Berry and Curly Cook's Hurdy Gurdy Band.

Sunday March 31
President Lyndon B. Johnson surprises the nation by announcing he will not seek the Democratic nomination in the upcoming presidential election.

Inaction Reaction

To "go where the music takes you" can take a lot of psychological courage, and the band's commitment to experimentation and improvisation led them up peaks of heavenly intensity and down into valleys of devilish disorder that tested everyone's nerves at times—even that of an intrepid musical explorer like Phil Lesh. At one point in one of these shows Phil was so overcome that he took his hands off his instrument and simply stopped playing for a time. On the way to the dressing room after the set, he was confronted by an angry Jerry Garcia, who said "You play, motherfucker!" and shoved the bassist. Both were taken aback by what had happened. Later, listening to the tapes, they would like the show so much that parts of it were multitracked onto *Anthem of the Sun*. The dust-up proved to the band, however, the truth of Nietzsche's saying that if you stare long enough into the abyss, it will start to stare back.

"It was like the music itself was escalating. Everything became a vehicle to go 'out' with, and the jamming was so focused but still totally on the edge of being out of control. I remember thinking, 'This music is way, way unusual'… I remember being scared sometimes. I mean, there were times when Phil was making the bass notes so big that I thought I was going to explode…" DICK LATVALA TO BLAIR JACKSON, 1996

"You play, motherfucker!"

JERRY GARCIA, TO PHIL LESH BACKSTAGE

Friday April 26
Saturday April 27
Sunday April 28
Electric Factory, Philadelphia, Pennsylvania

The band's first Philly shows.

19 | 20 | 21 | 22 | 23 | 24 | 25 | 26 | 27 | 28   **29 | 30**

Thursday April 4
Dr. Martin Luther King, Jr. is assassinated in Memphis. Anger over King's murder fuels riots in 124 U.S. cities.

APRIL '68

1 | 2 | 3 | 4 | 5 – 18

Friday April 19
Saturday April 20
Sunday April 21
Thee Image, Miami, Florida

The band's first shows in Florida, and the boys also spend some time working on the album at Criteria Studios in Miami. All three nights with Blues Image, the Kollektions, and the Bangles (*not* the same Bangles who opened for the band at Keifer Arena on October 10, 1988).

Wednesday April 3
Winterland Arena, San Francisco, California

Another benefit for the KPMX strikers, with the Electric Flag (featuring ex-Butterfield Blues Band guitarslinger Mike Bloomfield), It's a Beautiful Day, Moby Grape, Mother Earth, and the Youngbloods.

April 1968

85

A Beautiful Day in the Neighborhood

One of the more interesting of the late-period purveyors of the San Francisco Sound was It's a Beautiful Day, which coalesced around David LaFlamme (who at one time played violin in the Utah Symphony Orchestra) and his keyboardist wife, Linda. Their eponymous first album—"A startling amalgam of folk and psychedelia," in the words of a later reviewer—came out in 1969 and generated an FM hit, "White Bird." The LaFlammes split up personally and professionally not long afterward. They had gotten to know the Dead when they lived in the Haight, and Jerry Garcia played on two tracks—pedal steel on "It Comes Right Down to You," and banjo on "Hoedown"—on the group's second album, *Marrying Maiden*, released in 1970. At the time, banjo and pedal steel were strictly private pursuits for Jerry. The group broke up for good a couple of years later, though various former members surface from time to time to perform under the original name.

Sunday May 5
Central Park, New York, New York

A free afternoon show with the Jefferson Airplane and the Paul Butterfield Blues Band. The concert is promoted as a kind of "San Francisco in New York" event, and Bob Weir kicks off the Dead's set by telling the crowd "Welcome to San Francisco!" (Of course, the Butterfield Band was "Born in Chicago," as the title of their signature song proudly proclaims.)

"No tricks, just music, hard, lyric, joyous—pure and together, dense and warm as a dark country summer night. There's the Dead and then there's everybody else..."
DON MCNEIL IN THE *VILLAGE VOICE*

Friday May 10
U.S. and North Vietnamese representatives meet in Paris to begin peace talks aimed at ending the war in Vietnam.

Left and above: Sunday May 5, Central Park, New York City. Garcia's playing a Gibson Les Paul guitar.

Saturday May 11
The Dome,
Virginia Beach, Virginia

1	2	3	4	5	6	7	8	9	10	11

Friday May 3
Low Library Plaza, Columbia University, New York, New York

Saturday May 4
Gymnasium, SUNY, Stony Brook, New York

With the Incredible String Band.

Tuesday May 7
Wednesday May 8
Thursday May 9
Electric Circus, New York, New York

Six shows spread over three days—the first pair on Bill Kreutzmann's 22nd birthday. After the last Electric Circus show Mickey Hart visits Electric Lady Studios and jams with Jimi Hendrix, Jack Casady, and Steve Winwood.

Saturday May 18
Santa Clara County Fairgrounds, Santa Clara, California

The Northern California Folk-Rock Festival, with Eric Burdon and the Animals, Big Brother, Country Joe & the Fish, the Electric Flag, the Jefferson Airplane, Kaleidoscope, and Taj Mahal.

12 – 16	17	18	19 – 23	24	25

Friday May 17
Saturday May 18
Shrine Exhibition Hall, Los Angeles, California

With the Steve Miller Band and Taj Mahal.

Friday May 24
Saturday May 25
National Guard Armory, St. Louis, Missouri

The band's first shows in Missouri, with Iron Butterfly. This show also marks the first public appearance of "St. Stephen," twinned with "The Eleven."

Below: Phil Lesh on his way to the Central Park free concert, Sunday May 5.

The Great Columbia Caper

The band arrived in New York City in the aftermath of a student strike at Columbia University. For a week, 5,000 students had occupied five buildings on the Morningside Heights campus, protesting the university's ties to the "military-industrial complex" and its plans to build a gym in Morningside Park, a public park in the predominantly African-American neighborhood, adjacent to the campus. Police had ejected the strikers from the buildings they occupied on April 30, but the university remained tense and in a state of virtual "lockdown," with police and security guards controlling all access to the campus. Which gave Rock Scully an idea; he got in touch with the strike's organizers and offered up the band for a free gig on campus, which meant they'd have to be smuggled in. Think of the publicity—San Francisco's Grateful Dead flummoxing the fuzz to play for New York student radicals. The band members, true to form, didn't care much about the political element, but they were still Pranksters at heart, and this was an irresistible opportunity.

The band and equipment made it through the security checkpoint hunkered down in the back of a bread delivery truck, and they were set up and playing on the steps of Low Library before security or the administration could react. And they immediately got pissed off at the leading radicals, who—though the band had made it clear beforehand that their PA system was for music only—tried to commandeer the mics for speechifying. At one point, Bob Weir had to kick one of them in the ass when the Ivy-League Lenin blocked his view of Phil and Jerry. A film about the strike made by student filmmakers contains footage of the band playing two songs.

"ST. STEPHEN/THE ELEVEN"
GARCIA/LESH/HUNTER & LESH/HUNTER

Although you won't find him in your copy of *The Picture Book of Saints*, "St. Stephen" was one of the most beloved if not elusive characters in the Grateful Dead gallery. Bearing little resemblance to his namesakes, whether the Christian martyr who died in A.D. 34 or the Hungarian king who reigned from 997 to 1038, the Dead's Stephen was another Hunter concoction whose spiritual path seemed marred with misunderstanding and rejection, evidenced in lines like "Wherever he goes the people all complain." "I had been working on this a long time before I gave it to the Grateful Dead," Hunter said in 1986. "I don't know what to say about this song, except that it was very important to me... It's still one of my favorites." Written with Garcia and Lesh, by the time it appeared on *Aoxomoxoa* (1969) the song was being linked live with "The Eleven," a complex Hunter/Lesh number whose odd time signature (11/8) had been employed to help the band develop their chops. (The first twinning of these songs came in St. Louis on May 24, 1968.) "When we started working on 'The Eleven' back in the late '60s, we'd spend hours and hours and hours every day just playing groups of 11," Garcia would say later. "You can't play confidently and fluidly in those times without really knowing what you're doing." The pairing would turn up on *Live/Dead* (1969), though "The Eleven" had left the band's live rotation by mid-'70 and "St. Stephen" made an exit on October 31, 1983 after having been intermittently retired since 1971. Fans were astonished when The Other Ones reintroduced it with their first show on June 4, 1998.

Thursday May 30
Friday May 31
Saturday June 1
Carousel Ballroom,
San Francisco, California

With harpist Charlie Musselwhite
and Petrus.

JUNE
'68

| 26 ~ 29 | 30 | 31 | 1 | 2 | 3 |

Friday June 7
Saturday June 8
Sunday June 9
Carousel Ballroom, San Francisco, California

With Jefferson Airplane and Fleetwood Mac. Fleetwood Mac would go on to pop mega-super-stardom in the '70s and '80s but in their original lineup they were a hard-driving Brit blues band based around the guitar of Peter Green, who wrote "Black Magic Woman," later a hit for Santana in a *muy caliente* rendition.

| 4 | 5 | 6 | 7 | 8 | 9 | 10 | 11 | 12 | 13 |

Thursday June 6
The Airplane and the Dead attempt an impromptu memorial concert for the slain Robert Kennedy in Golden Gate Park, but the city government refuses to grant a permit.

Tuesday June 4
Senator Robert F. Kennedy, brother of slain president John F. Kennedy and frontrunner for the Democratic presidential nomination, is fatally shot in L.A.

Wednesday June 19
Carousel Ballroom, San Francisco, California

A benefit for the Black Man's Free Store. With Richie Havens. By late spring of '68 the Carousel Ballroom *(see page 82)* is floundering. The business end of the venture was probably doomed from the start, especially because of the lease, which guaranteed the (absentee) landlord not only rent but a percentage of receipts. There were booking problems, legal problems, and so on. But it was fun while it lasted: the Carousel was indeed a place where the affiliated musicians and their associates could do their own thing, and they did it with a vengeance; it was as much a clubhouse and community center as it was a performance venue. By now, though, it just isn't bringing in enough money to keep the dream going, and despite meetings and schemes, no one involved seems to be able to form a coherent plan.

| 14 | 15 | 16 | 17 | 18 | 19 | 20 | 21 | 22 | 23 | 24 | 25 | 26 | 27 ~ 30 |

Friday June 14 ★
Saturday June 15
Fillmore East, New York, New York

The band play four gigs over two days with the Jeff Beck Group and the Seventh Sons. The Jeff Beck Group's singer (making his U.S. debut) is Rod Stewart. This is the first time they play at this venue: formerly the old, ramshackle Village Theater, where the Dead had nearly gotten frostbite the preceding December, it had been acquired by Bill Graham and was becoming the place for live rock on the East Coast, if not the whole country. Unlike the Carousel, the Avalon, and the Fillmore Auditorium in San Francisco, the Fillmore East had been built as a theater, not a ballroom, and Graham spared no expense in turning it into a 2,600-seat space that was both functional and elegant.

Monday June 24
The law hands down sentences related to the bust at 710 Ashbury. In spite of (or perhaps because of) all the hype surrounding the episode, the long arm of the law comes down lightly, given the drug laws of the day: Rock Scully and Bob Matthews are slapped with $200 fines; Pigpen and Bob Weir (again, a rich irony, since they were the two 710 denizens who didn't smoke pot) $100 apiece.

Below: The Dead traveling to New York for their gigs on June 14–15.

June 1968

87

Studio Star

Around this time Warner Bros. released a single—studio versions of "Dark Star" and "Born Cross-Eyed"—in anticipation of the July release of *Anthem of the Sun*. A beast like "Dark Star" could hardly be contained on a seven-inch 45, so this version, while interesting as a period piece, bears little resemblance to its live form. (Maybe the most interesting part is the fadeout over a banjo, presumably played by Jerry.) This version was probably recorded (or assembled) during the November '67 recording session in L.A.. The B-side, "Born Cross-Eyed," is somewhat different from the version that wound up on *Anthem of the Sun*. The single failed to make the slightest dent in the charts or attract much attention—and in any event, Warner Bros only pressed about 2,000 copies. The single surfaced again on Warner Bros' 1977 *What a Long Strange Trip It's Been* compilation and on 2001's *The Golden Road* box set.

ANTHEM OF THE SUN

Grateful Dead

Released by Warner Bros. (WS-1749) on July 18, 1968

Side One

1. **That's It For The Other One**
   I. Cryptical Envelopment
   (Garcia)
   II. Quadlibet For Tender Feet
   (Weir)
   III. The Faster We Go, The Rounder We Get
   (The Grateful Dead)
   IV. We Leave The Castle
   (The Grateful Dead)
2. **New Potato Caboose**
   (Lesh/Petersen)
3. **Born Cross-Eyed**
   (Weir)

Side Two

1. **Alligator**
   (Lesh/McKernan/Hunter)
2. **Caution (Do Not Stop On Tracks)**
   (McKernan)

Personnel

Tom Constanten – prepared piano, piano, electronic tape
Jerry Garcia – lead guitar, acoustic guitar, kazoo, vibraslap, vocals
Mickey Hart, Bill Kreutzmann – drums, orchestra bells, gong, chimes, crotales, prepared piano, finger cymbals
Phil Lesh – bass, trumpet, harpsichord, guiro kazoo, piano, timpani, vocals
Pigpen (Ron McKernan) – organ, celesta claves, vocals
Bob Weir – rhythm guitar, 12-string guitar, acoustic guitar, kazoo, vocals

Produced by the Grateful Dead

NOTORIOUSLY REFERRED TO AT THE TIME by Warner Bros. president Joe Smith as "the most unreasonable project with which we have ever involved ourselves," *Anthem of the Sun* left the Dead unsupervised in the studio to create what is still one of the most innovative albums ever made.

Having inadvertently prompted producer Dave Hassinger to jump ship after Weir's request to manifest the sound of "thick air" in the studio, the band proceeded to rewrite the still-young rules of rock recording with some truly bizarre results that were hinted at by the album's cover, a depiction of the band members in a surreal mandala of masked incarnations, inspired by a hallucinogen-fired vision of artist and band friend Bill Walker.

Though early reports that the album would be a double LP and feature such disparate elements as a marching band and Simon and Garfunkel proved to be untrue, what the band did present—original songs that combined live and studio recordings culled from over half a dozen different settings in a loose attempt to honor the mythical piece of music from Mu that inspired the album's title—took things to a heretofore unexplored plateau. As Garcia told David Gans, "There's parts of it that sound dated, but parts of it are far out, even too far out... we weren't making a record in the normal sense; we were making a collage."

While this particular piece of artwork ended up putting the Dead even further into debt with their label, it seems the band still had the last laugh, once again shaking up the straights as they utilized to full advantage an ill-conceived part of their pact with the corporate world. As Garcia would later say, "They were foolish enough to let us execute a contract in which we had no limit as to studio time."

"It's so completely unlike anything you ever heard before that it's practically a new concept in music."

NEW MUSICAL EXPRESS

Thursday July 4
July 4, 1968, is not an independence day for the Dead and the other partners, staff, and hangers-on at the Carousel. Bill Graham has done a deal with the Carousel's owner and so, in the words of Carousel concessions manager Jon McIntire, "Four months of the greatest, loosest thing that ever, to my knowledge, happened anywhere" comes to an end. Bill shuts the doors of the Fillmore Auditorium (henceforth known as the "Old Fillmore") and on July 5 the Carousel reopens as the Fillmore West (though it is called the Carousel-Fillmore for a while). For the Dead, the short, happy life of the ballroom would have an ongoing legacy in human form: Bill "Kidd" Candelario, Betty Cantor (later Cantor-Jackson), Bert Kanegson, Jon McIntire, and Jonathan Riester join the Dead family through the Carousel Connection.

Thursday July 11
Shrine Exhibition Hall, Los Angeles, California

With Blue Cheer.

Friday July 12
Saturday July 13
King's Beach Bowl, Lake Tahoe, California

With Working Class.

Thursday July 18
Anthem of the Sun is released.

Rex Jackson

Today, former Grateful Dead road crew member Donald "Rex" Jackson is most remembered for the philanthropic organization that bears his name—the Rex Foundation, founded in the early '80s to allow the Grateful Dead (and some of their friends) to quietly donate money to various charities and non-profit groups. But Rex the roadie, a rough-and-tumble free spirit from Oregon, first came onto the Dead scene in 1968, a time when the band was beginning to travel a lot outside of California and amassing more and more gear.

Jackson was a key member of the equipment crew until his death in an automobile accident in September 1976, an event that inspired Donna Godchaux's song "Sunrise" (from *Terrapin Station*). Jackson had one son, Cole, by GD sound engineer Betty Cantor (who also took on Rex's last name), and a daughter by Eileen Law of the Dead office—Cassidy, whose birth was immortalized in the Bob Weir–John Barlow song of the same name.

Haight to Marin

By summer '68 most of the Dead had fled the Haight for beautiful Marin County. There were other changes, too, in the band's management and staff. Dan Healy had gone out with Quicksilver, so Bear (awaiting sentencing on an LSD bust) came back as soundman. Danny Rifkin was in Europe, so Jonathan Riester (as road manager) and Jon McIntire (as business manager-in-training) from the Carousel crowd came to help Rock. Burt Kanegson also helped, quickly finding a Marin County replacement for their Potrero Hill rehearsal hall: a warehouse just outside the gates of Hamilton Air Force Base (Air Force vets Mickey and T.C. must have been amused) in Novato. The managers worked out of an office on Union Street in the city, and Mickey soon took over the rent on a property owned by the town of Novato, "the Ranch," which would become an alternate clubhouse. In another business development, the band formally did business with Bill Graham for the first time, signing on to his Millard Booking Agency—in part-payment for a loan to the ever-pecunious band.

Wednesday August 28
Avalon Ballroom,
San Francisco, California

| 25 | 26 | 27 | 28 | 29 | 30 | 31 |

Friday August 30
Saturday August 31
Fillmore West,
San Francisco, California

With New Orleans'
Preservation Hall Jazz Band
and the Sons of Champlin.

Thursday August 26
Police and demonstrators clash during the Democrat Party's Chicago convention (August 26–29), and at least 700 people are injured.

Tuesday August 20
Wednesday August 21
Thursday August 22
Fillmore West, San Francisco, California

The band's first show (of 44 between '68 and '71) in the "new" venue, formerly the Carousel Ballroom, with Kaleidescope and Texas blues-guitar great Albert "the Iceberg" Collins.

Friday August 23
Saturday August 24
Shrine Exhibition Hall,
Los Angeles, California

| 20 | 21 | 22 | 23 | 24 |

Clockwise from left: Bill Kreutzmann, Grace Slick, Phil Lesh, Phil Lesh again, Ken Kesey. All pictures are from the First Annual Newport Pop Festival, Orange County Fairgrounds, Costa Mesa, California, Sunday August 4.

Sunday August 4
Orange County Fairgrounds, Costa Mesa, California

First Annual Newport Pop Festival. One of several "pop" festivals spawned by Monterey *(see pages 72–73)*, this one includes a lot of big acts (the Airplane, Eric Burdon & the Animals, the Byrds, Canned Heat, Country Joe, the Electric Flag, Iron Butterfly, Quicksilver, Charles Lloyd, and others) but doesn't measure up in terms of ambience and performance. The Dead and the Airplane relieve the pressures of the day with a cream-pie fight.

AUGUST '68

| | 2 | 3 | 4 | 5 – 19 |

Friday August 2
Saturday August 3
The Hippodrome, San Diego, California

The band's first San Diego shows, with Curly Cook's Hurdy-Gurdy Band and Maya.

Sunday September 1
Palace of Fine Arts,
San Francisco, California

Afternoon concert—Haight-Ashbury
Medical Clinic Benefit.

Fillmore West, San Francisco,
California

With New Orleans' Preservation Hall
Jazz Band and the Sons of Champlin.

Monday September 2 ★
Betty Nelson's Organic Raspberry Farm, Sultan, Washington

The Sky River Festival. More or less on the spur of the
moment, the band decides to play this relatively small
(20,000 people) festival on an organic farm in Washington
State, near the Skykomish River. Big Mama Mae Thornton
and James Cotton jam with various combinations of band
members on the closing day of the festival.

Friday September 20
Berkeley Community Theatre,
Berkeley, California

At this show, during "Alligator," Mickey Hart's
tabla tutor, Shankar Ghosh, and Vince Delgado,
another of Ghosh's pupils who specialized in the
Middle Eastern doumbek, join Mickey and Bill for
a four-way rhythmic journey to the East.

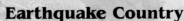

20 21 22 23 24 25 26 27 28 29 30

Sunday September 22
Del Mar Fairgrounds, Del Mar, California

With the Ace of Cups, Quicksilver, the Buddy
Miles Express, Mother Earth, Sons of Champlin,
Phoenix, and Curly Cook's Hurdy-Gurdy Band.

Earthquake Country

After returning from the Sky River Festival at Betty Nelson's Raspberry Farm,
the band began recording its third album, tentatively titled *Earthquake
Country*, at Pacific Recording Studios in San Mateo. Having been educated in
the ways of the studio on *Anthem of the Sun*, the recording went fast, and by
the end of the year most of the album was "in the can"—at which point,
however, Bob Matthews convinced Pacific Recording to take delivery of one
of the first sixteen-track recorders in the world, and the band ditched the
eight-track masters and started over.

One of the outtakes from the *Earthquake Country* sessions was "Barbed
Wire Whipping Party," (lyrics by the band) which has not yet made its
way onto any "official" Grateful Dead release (Robert Hunter personally
blocked its inclusion on the *Golden Road* box set). "Whipping Party" was a
Pranksterish exercise in sound manipulation, with multiple mics and tape
delays, and a tank of nitrous oxide on hand; stoked up on the happy gas,
the boys recited acid-Dadaist lines like "The barbed wire whipping party
set out into the razor-blade forest…" "Meat, meat, gimme my meat…"
"Push it and pull it…"

*Above and right: Monday
September 2, Betty Nelson's
Organic Raspberry Farm, Sultan,
Washington. The Sky River Festival.
It was around this time that the
band started to link "Dark Star,"
"St. Stephen," and "The Eleven."*

Clockwise from left: Bob Weir with Ram Rod; Phil Lesh with girlfriend Florence Nathan (later known as Rosie McGee); Jerry Garcia. All pictures from Monday September 2. Betty Nelson's Organic Raspberry Farm, Sultan, Washington: the Sky River Festival.

OCTOBER '68

1 2 3 4 **5**

Saturday October 5
Sacramento Memorial Auditorium, Sacramento, California

Tuesday October 8
Wednesday October 9
Thursday October 10
The first "Mickey and the Hartbeats" show takes place at The Matrix in San Francisco. Jack Casady of the Airplane and ex-Butterfield Blues Band guitar man Elvin Bishop jam with the band, on and off, throughout the show.

6 7 **8** 9 **10**

Friday October 11
Saturday October 12 ★
Sunday October 13
Avalon Ballroom, San Francisco, California

With Linn County, Lee Michaels, and Mance Lipscomb. Born around 1895 in Texas, Lipscomb was a living link to some of the band's roots; a "songster" in the tradition of Leadbelly, Lipscomb didn't begin recording until he was "discovered" by folkies in 1960. Sunday's show is broadcast on Berkeley's KPFA.

11 **12 13** 14-17

Friday October 18
The Bank, Torrance, California

With the Cleveland Wrecking Company.

Sunday October 20
Greek Theatre, University of California, Berkeley, California

Monday October 21
Jerry Garcia and Mickey Hart jam with Jack Casady, Jorma Kaukonen, and Spencer Dryden at the Jefferson Airplane's ornate manse at 2400 Fulton Street.

Thursday October 31
President Johnson temporarily halts bombing of North Vietnam.

18 19 **20** 21 22-28 **29** 30 31

Tuesday October 29
Wednesday October 30
Thursday October 31
Mickey and the Hartbeats at The Matrix, once again joined by Jack Casady and Elvin Bishop.

Introducing Mickey and the Hartbeats

In the summer of 1968 internal tensions in the Grateful Dead came to a head—well, sort of. Jerry Garcia, Phil Lesh, Bill Kreutzmann, and Mickey Hart were at odds, musically, with Bob Weir and Pigpen. Bob (not yet 21 years old, it should be remembered), was unfocused and not up to speed, literally and figuratively, in his playing. Pigpen had been the frontman and spirit of the group for its first couple of years, but he remained rooted in the blues and R&B tradition while the group was going forward in the new direction mapped out in *Anthem of the Sun*. Meetings were held, much talking was done, and in the end the majority prevailed: Bob and Pig were out. However, given the band's fervent anti-hierarchicalism and dislike of confrontation, no one had the heart to enforce the decision, and indeed the two firees didn't seem to understand that they'd been fired. The band continued to gig as the full six-man band.

In the fall, however, there seemed to be a way out of the impasse. The Grateful Dead became two bands: the six-man Grateful Dead, and Mickey and the Hartbeats, a progressive, improvisational, group composed of Jerry, Phil, Bill, Mickey, and guest performers.

The new ensemble played only seven shows, all of them at The Matrix, between October and December. In the end, the erstwhile Hartbeats decided that whatever their musical flaws, Bob and Pigpen were still part of what made the Good Old Grateful Dead good, and the two returned—though, of course, they'd never really left. A very Grateful Dead kind of situation.

"Oh yeah, for a few months. We were the junior musicians in the band and Jerry and Phil in particular thought that we were sort of holding things back. The music wasn't able to get as free because it was hog-tied by our playing abilities, which was kind of true."

BOB WEIR ON BEING FIRED FROM THE BAND, TO BLAIR JACKSON

Friday November 1
Silver Dollar Fairgrounds, Chico, California

Monday November 4
Longshoremen's Hall, San Francisco, California

Tuesday November 5
Republican Richard M. Nixon narrowly defeats Democrat Hubert H. Humphrey to become the 37th president of the United States.

Sunday November 17
Eagles Auditorium, Seattle, Washington
A benefit for Native American causes.

Thursday November 7
Friday November 8
Saturday November 9
Sunday November 10
Fillmore West, San Francisco, California
With Quicksilver and Linn County.

Friday November 22
Veterans Memorial Auditorium, Columbus, Ohio

Saturday November 23
Memorial Auditorium, Ohio University, Athens, Ohio
An unscheduled show (T.C.'s first) on the university's campus, in gratitude for Ohio University students making up most of the (small) audience at the preceding night's show.

1 2 3 **4** **5** 6 **7** 8 9 **10** 11 - 16 **17** 18 - 21 **22** **23**

Underground Press, Poster Art, Comix, and Art

The mid-'60s explosion in creativity that took place in California, New York, and ultimately across the country found expression not only in music, but in other arts as well.

In San Francisco, for example, the artists who created the posters that advertised shows at the Avalon, the Fillmore, the Carousel, and other venues were as celebrated as the musicians themselves. The "Big Five" poster artists, as they became known, were the team of Stanley "Mouse" Miller and Alton Kelley, who adapted the "Skeleton and Roses" motif for the Grateful Dead; surfer dude Rick Griffin, already well-known as creator of the cartoon character "Murphy" before he got psychedelicized at the Watts Acid Test; Wes Wilson, whose lettering style was an acid-influenced adaptation of avant-garde European typography; and Victor Moscoso, master of color, who had studied under Josef Albers at Yale. As well as the poster boys, there were also the other masters of visual psychedelia, the light-show artists, the most famous of them being Bill Ham and Glenn McKay in San Francisco and Joshua White in New York.

Just as drugs and social commentary deconstructed rock 'n' roll and reconstructed it into rock, the same influences were at work on another American populist art form—the comic book. In the late '60s underground comics (or "comix," to differentiate them from child-friendly fare) thrived, with artists like R. Crumb ("Mr. Natural" et al.), Gilbert Shelton ("The Fabulous Furry Freak Brothers"), and a host of others taking on religion, sex, dope, politics, and anything else worth sending up. Zap Comix began publishing in 1967 and a year later Gary Arlington opened the San Francisco Comic Book Store, the movement's West Coast HQ.

Underground journalism flourished as well, "underground" being defined as any publication that deemed itself free of the influence of the "mainstream" media, which were seen as being hopelessly "co-opted" by the government and business interests. Underground publications ranged from newssheets run off in dorm rooms using mimeograph machines "borrowed" from the dean's office, to widely distributed journals like New York City's *Village Voice*. In the Bay Area, the best-known underground papers were the *Berkeley Barb* and the *Oracle*, published from September 1967 in the Haight by Allen Cohen, who declared that the paper would strive to have a "direct effect on consciousness."

Right: Poster artists of the mid-60s, including Stanley "Mouse" Miller, Alton Kelley, and Victor Moscoso.
Below: The offices of the Oracle, based in a disused laundromat.

Taking on T.C.

In late November the (full) band left for a short tour of the Midwest (with a run to the Spectrum in Philly, to put in an appearance at the "Quaker City Rock Festival"). They would return to California with a new member—Tom Constanten. He'd worked with them in the studio on *Anthem of the Sun*, but starting at the University of Ohio, Athens, show on November 23, T.C. was in as a full-time keyboardist. As with the "firing" of Pigpen and Weir, the recruitment of T.C. was somewhat vague and muddled. Phil Lesh, T.C.'s friend and the band member with the closest musical affinity to him, was the prime mover in bringing him on board, apparently with Jerry Garcia's support, and the rest of the band had to accept the *fait accompli*. The acquisition of T.C. as a second keyboardist further marginalized Pigpen who, at some shows, wound up doing little more than banging a set of conga drums.

Sunday November 24
Hyde Park Teen Center, Cincinnati, Ohio

24 25 26 **27** **28** 29 30

Wednesday November 27
Thursday November 28
Kinetic Playground, Chicago, Illinois
With Procol Harum.

"MOUNTAINS OF THE MOON"
GARCIA/HUNTER

This beautiful, harpsichord-laden fable was written during the creative throes that would result in the rich spring of songs found on *Aoxomoxoa* (1969). But unlike the rest of that album, most of which was recorded using a 16-track deck, "Mountains of the Moon" captures a unique intimacy brought about by a live-in-the-studio feel. "Jerry, Bob, Phil, and I recorded the basic tracks in the same room at the same time," keyboard player Tom Constanten remembered later. "Phil was wrestling with an upright bass." For its live incarnation in December '68 and during a small handful of shows in 1969, Garcia donned an acoustic guitar. "I had an acoustic setting in mind from the get-go, and it turned out pretty much how I envisioned it," he once told Dead scribe Blair Jackson. "I don't know what made me think I could do a song like that, but something at the time made me think I could do it. I like the tune a lot." It also featured in an early Dead TV appearance on *Playboy After Dark* in July of 1969 and in a reworked form by Hunter starting in 1997, but mostly remained a lunar casualty until Lesh dusted it off for Phil & Friends and then The Other Ones in the late '90s.

"DIRE WOLF"
GARCIA/HUNTER

Like those mythical animals that appear in everything from Native American folktales to more modern legends like Bigfoot and the Loch Ness Monster, "Dire Wolf," a song from the album *Workingman's Dead* (1970) that first appeared live on June 7, 1969, finds Hunter's imagination running free in a frozen forest where an evil four-legged predator resides. The song's true origins are less ominous, coming in fact from a horror movie Garcia and Hunter had caught while living together in Larkspur in 1969. "The song... was inspired, at least in name, by watching *The Hound of The Baskervilles* on TV," Hunter shared in 1996. "We were speculating on what the ghostly hound might turn out to be, and somehow the idea that maybe it was a dire wolf came up." During a 1984 interview, Garcia said that the song's chorus of "Don't murder me" had reminded him of how he felt in the Bay Area while the serial murderer known as the Zodiac Killer was wreaking havoc there (the killings started in 1968). "The refrain got to be so real to me," he said. "'Please don't murder me!'" The song was played by the Dead over 200 times between 1969 and 1995, and reappeared in two The Other Ones shows featuring guest Susan Tedeschi in November of 2002.

Above: *Selling the Oracle on Haight Street. The underground magazine was founded by Allen Cohen in September 1967.*

Friday December 6
The Spectrum, Philadelphia, Pennsylvania

Quaker City Rock Festival.

DECEMBER '69

Friday December 13
Saturday December 14
The Bank, Torrance, California

With Magic Sam and the Turnquist Remedy.

| 1 | 2 – 5 | 6 | 7 | 8 – 12 | 13 | 14 | 15 | 16 |

Sunday December 1
Grande Ballroom, Detroit, Michigan

With Popcorn Blizzard.

Saturday December 7 ★
Bellarmine College, Louisville, Kentucky

Monday December 16
A jam-heavy "Mickey and the Hartbeats" extravaganza at The Matrix: the Airplane's Jack Casady and Spencer Dryden, Big Brother drummer David Getz, guitar whiz Harvey Mandel, and George Chambers of the Chambers Brothers join at various times.

Tom Constanten

Erudite and eccentric, keyboardist Tom Constanten (b. 1944) hooked into the Dead scene through Phil Lesh, who met the Las Vegas native when both enrolled at the University of California at Berkeley in 1961, Lesh in the music program, Constanten in astrophysics, of all subjects. At the time, they shared a love of avant-garde music and Beat literature (among other things), and Constanten went on to be mentored by *moderne* music titans such as Luciano Berio and Karlheinz Stockhausen. He enlisted in the U.S. Air Force in the mid-'60s to avoid being drafted into the Marines and sent to fight in Vietnam, but he managed to keep up his friendship with Lesh during the Dead's formative years, and even got involved with the early psychedelic scene in Nevada and San Francisco.

His first collaboration with the Dead was a section of taped electronic music and avant-garde piano for the closing section of "That's It For The Other One" on *Anthem of the Sun* in 1968. In November of that year he was discharged from the Air Force and joined the Dead as keyboardist, a post he held until the beginning of 1970. He is most famously heard on *Aoxomoxoa* and *Live/Dead*. He continues to play and teach piano and make occasional recordings.

Friday December 20
Saturday December 21
Shrine Exhibition Hall, Los Angeles, California

With Country Joe, Mint Tattoo, Pulse, and the Sir Douglas Quintet. Friday's show sees the first "Mountains of the Moon."

Saturday December 28
The Catacombs, Houston, Texas

With Quicksilver (probably; show details are sketchy).

Sunday December 29
Gulfstream Park Race Track, Hallandale, Florida

The Miami Pop Festival.

| 20 | 21 | 22 – 27 | 28 | 29 | 30 | 31 |

Tuesday December 31
Winterland Arena, San Francisco, California

Billed by Bill Graham as "the Fillmore Scene at Winterland," the New Year's Eve show runs from 9:00 pm on December 31 to 9:00 am on January 1, ending in breakfast for all the survivors. Other acts include Quicksilver, It's a Beautiful Day, and Santana. The Dead opened with "In the Midnight Hour" before the "Dark Star">"St. Stephen">"The Eleven">"Turn on Your Love Light" sequence that's now at the heart of their performances.

PLAYBOY

HUGH M. HEFNER
Editor-Publisher

February 12, 1969

The Grateful Dead
c/o Jonathan Reister
2195 Union Street
San Francisco, California

Dear Jerry, Ron, Phil, Bob, Bill
Micky and Tom:

Thank you for your really great performance on "Playboy
After Dark". Your participation played an important
part in the success of this particular show.

I've had an opportunity to see the film of the show and
enjoyed it so much I wanted to share it with you. As an
expression of my appreciation, I have had the filmed segment
of your performance mailed to you. I hope you'll enjoy
it as much as I did.

Again, thanks for appearing -- and for having made the
taping session as enjoyable to do as I think it will be
to watch.

All best,

Hef

Hugh M. Hefner
Editor-Publisher
PLAYBOY Magazine

Hangin' with Hef

One of the oddest stops on the Grateful Dead's long strange trip was L.A.'s Television City, where, on January 18, the boys were performing guests on *Playboy After Dark*, Hugh Hefner's syndicated late-night exercise in midcentury-modern-style hedonism. The taping was a beautifully incongruous episode. Tom Constanten recalled that the studio, set up to look like Hef's platonic ideal of a swingin' bachelor pad, featured shelves full of "mindless books not even worth stealing" and noted that the hi-tech hi-fi system was actually a fake. A gaggle of pretend partygoers—actors and models—milled around the set. There was genuine weirdness in the air, as some of the Dead's crew had dosed the cast's coffee urn and even, it is said, Hef's omnipresent Pepsi.

The band's bit began with "St. Stephen," following which Hef bantered for a few minutes with Jerry Garcia, who was draped in a colorful Mexican serape. Hef had certainly done his homework: he referenced the "Death of Hippie" ceremony *(see page 77).* "Yeah," Jerry replied, "We're all big people now." The music continued with a fine "Mountains of the Moon" and later some "Love Light" over the closing credits. The episode aired on July 10, 1969.

17	18 – 23	24	25	26	27 – 30

Friday January 17
Unknown Venue,
Santa Barbara,
California

Friday January 24
Saturday January 25
Sunday January 26
Avalon Ballroom, San Francisco, California

With Initial Shock and Sons of Champlin. Friday's show sees the first "Dupree's Diamond Blues" and "Doin' that Rag." The band retires "Clementine Jam" following Sunday's show—"The Eleven">"Turn on Your Love Light" from this show appears on *Live/Dead (see page 104)*. Recorded on the Ampex tape recorder borrowed from Pacific Recording, they are the first live sixteen-track recordings ever made.

1	2	3	4	5	6 – 16

Thursday January 2
Friday January 3
Saturday January 4
Sunday January 5
Fillmore West, San Francisco, California

With Blood, Sweat & Tears and Spirit.

All pictures: On the plane to Santa Barbara for their gig on Friday January 17 at an unknown venue. Jerry and Mickey Hart (left); Ram Rod, Pigpen, and Rock Scully (above); Garcia and Phil Lesh (below).

"DUPREE'S DIAMOND BLUES"

GARCIA/HUNTER

Inspired by the true story of Frank Dupree, a criminal from South Carolina who was sentenced to hang after a jewelry store robbery and whose pursuit led to the deaths of three people, "Dupree's Diamond Blues" from *Aoxomoxoa* (see page 99) marks the first time lyricist Robert Hunter was inspired by the wealth of folk songs and ballads from the past—the second came a few months later in the form of "Casey Jones" (see page 412). The Dead's version shares at least one reference with an early gem called "Dupree" in its mention of Dupree's love-interest Betty's "jelly roll," an early blues slang term for sex, and the band had also performed the traditional "Betty and Dupree" at one point. Musically, the group took Garcia's quirky melody and layered it with some suitable touches that blended perfectly with the song's psychedelic ragtime feel. "It reminds me of a little cartoon strip with cartoon characters," Garcia said in 1971. A single version of the song flopped, and the group only played it a handful of times after its first appearance on January 24, 1969, before retiring it for nearly a decade. After a brief reprise in '77 and '78, "Dupree's" made over four dozen more Dead appearances between 1982 and 1994 and was later worked into shows by Phil & Friends.

At the end of January the band sets out on a tour of the Midwest and Northeast. At this point the band's following is bicoastal; they haven't made much impact in the big square states, outside of college towns, and this tour will see arguments between the band and promoters who want "regular songs," not long stretches of improvisation. The traveling Dead are fast acquiring a reputation as mad, bad, and dangerous to know among airport staff, cabin attendants, and hotel employees (their style runs to firecrackers in the bathtub.)

FEBRUARY '69

31	1	2	3	4	5	6

Sunday February 2
Labor Temple, Minneapolis, Minnesota

Wednesday February 5
The Music Box, Omaha, Nebraska

Thursday February 6
Kiel Auditorium, St. Louis, Missouri

Friday January 31
Saturday February 1
Kinetic Playground, Chicago, Illinois

With the Grassroots. While in Chicago, Bear gets pulled over for driving erratically and winds up a guest of some representatives of the Illinois law enforcement community, at which point they discover that they have the "LSD Millionaire" in their midst. A late-night gratuity to an accommodating city official springs Bear within hours. Chicago—the city that works.

Friday February 7
Stanley Theatre, Pittsburgh, Pennsylvania

Two shows—an early and a late—at which the Dead share the bill with the Velvet Underground and that other quintessential New York group, the Fugs, a literary-satirical-musical troupe based around Ed Sanders, Tuli Kupferberg, and Ken Weaver.

7	8	9	10	11	12	13	14	15	16 ~ 18	19

Sunday February 9
The Lyric Theater, Baltimore, Maryland

The First Baltimore Rock Festival (early show), with the Chambers Brothers, who also play with the Dead in a late show.

Tuesday February 11
Wednesday February 12
Fillmore East, New York, New York

At Tuesday's early show the band opens for Janis Joplin—who has now left Big Brother & the Holding Company—and covers the Beatles' "Hey Jude" (Pigpen on lead vocal) for the first (of three) times, although in the '80s the song's "Na Na Na" finale frequently appears as a coda to Traffic's "Dear Mr. Fantasy," sung by Brent Mydland. Tuesday's late show and both shows on Wednesday are also with Janis Joplin.

Friday February 14
Saturday February 15 ★
Electric Factory, Philadelphia, Pennsylvania

Wednesday February 19
Fillmore West, San Francisco, California

A show billed as the "Frontiers of Science Celestial Synapse." With the Golden Toad.

Wednesday February 26
The Matrix, San Francisco, California

"Mickey and the Hartbeats" gig.

20	21	22	23 ~ 25	26	27	28

Friday February 21 ★
Saturday February 22 ★
Dream Bowl, Vallejo, California

★ Thursday February 27
Friday February 28
Fillmore West, San Francisco, California

With Pentangle and the Sir Douglas Quintet. Thursday's "Dark Star" and "St. Stephen" appear on *Live/Dead*.

Trouble All Around

By the spring of '69 the band was in serious financial trouble. They owed about $200,000 to Warner Bros., and when Rock Scully and Brian Rohan approached Joe Smith about getting another advance, he literally chased them out of the office. Not long afterward Bill Graham ceased to take an active role in the band's management after an argument with Bear. And so to lead them out of the valley of insolvency, they chose… Lenny Hart, Mickey's off-again, on-again father, who had lately become a self-ordained Fundamentalist preacher. One of Lenny's first acts was to try to convince the band to accept an offer to appear in a "Rock 'n' Roll Western" movie, *Zachariah*, but as they had with *The President's Analyst*, they decided to steer clear —even though the movie was written by their spiritual confreres, the Firesign Theatre (the band was replaced by Country Joe & the Fish). Lenny also alienated Jonathan Riester, who quit, so Jon McIntire moved into the road manager slot. Later in the year, Lenny extended their contract with Warner Bros. without the band's knowledge—even though Columbia Records was interested in signing them.

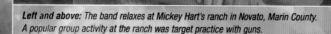

Left and above: The band relaxes at Mickey Hart's ranch in Novato, Marin County. A popular group activity at the ranch was target practice with guns.

Friday April 4
Saturday April 5
Sunday April 6
Avalon Ballroom, San Francisco, California

Aum and the Flying Burrito Brothers play all three shows. Sunday's performance is broadcast on KPFA Berkeley.

APRIL '69

30 31 1 2 3 **4** 5 6 7 8 9 10 **11**

Friday March 21
Saturday March 22
Rose Palace, Pasadena, California

The Paul Butterfield Blues Band and Brit import Jethro Tull, featuring a blues flutist named Ian Anderson, play both shows.

Saturday March 29
Ice Palace, Las Vegas, Nevada

Friday April 11
University Auditorium, University of Arizona, Tucson, Arizona

A benefit for the University's Student Peace Association.

Below: Pigpen plays with a dog at Mickey Hart's ranch in Novato, Marin County.

Wednesday March 12
Fillmore West, San Francisco, California

A benefit for striking students at San Francisco State College. The strike began in November '68 and lasted four bitter months.

16 17 18 19 20 **21 22** 23 24 25 26 **27 28 29**

Thursday March 27
Unknown Venue, Merced, California

Friday March 28
Student Center, Modesto Junior College, Modesto, California

1 2 3 4 5 - 11 **12** 13 14 **15**

Saturday March 1 ★
Sunday March 2
Fillmore West, San Francisco, California

Pentangle and the Sir Douglas Quintet play the first two nights. "Death Don't Have No Mercy," "Feedback," and "And We Bid You Goodnight" from Sunday's show appear on *Live/Dead*.

Saturday March 15
Hilton Hotel, San Francisco, California

The band plays at the Black and White Ball, a fundraising event for the San Francisco Symphony Orchestra. They go on late, play for an hour, and then leave. It's also Phil Lesh's 29th birthday. The Dead's set tonight also includes the breakout of "Hard to Handle" by the late, great Otis Redding. "Handle" would remain in the rotation through the end of the Pigpen era, and the song became, along with "Love Light," one of Pig's star turns.

The Music Scene in '69

By the middle of 1969, most of the successful San Francisco bands had fled the city for the more genteel environs of Marin County to the north. Having toured almost nonstop since 1966, the first wave of groups had built substantial followings nationwide and were peaking as live acts, as the 1969 concert LPs *Live/Dead*, Quicksilver's *Happy Trails*, and Jefferson Airplane's *Bless Its Pointed Little Head* demonstrate. Of San Francisco's original Big Four, only Big Brother & the Holding Company was in disarray—Janis Joplin had left the band to go solo. Elsewhere in the Bay Area, Creedence Clearwater hit the Top Ten with their *Bayou Country* LP and the indelible hit "Proud Mary," and Sly & the Family Stone scored with *Stand!*

In 1969, the Beatles and the Rolling Stones were still the reigning kings of rock; each released a masterpiece that year—*Abbey Road* and *Let It Bleed* respectively. This was the year that The Who broke through to a mass American audience with *Tommy*, and a number of other British acts were bubbling under the surface in America, including The Moody Blues, Jethro Tull, Pink Floyd, Led Zeppelin, Jeff Beck and, by the year's end, prog rock progenitors King Crimson.

Back in the States, the influence of country music became pervasive. Bob Dylan morphed into a honey-voiced country crooner and appeared on Johnny Cash's TV show. His former backup group, The Band, put out a pair of albums (*Music From Big Pink*, released the previous July, and *The Band*) that blended rock 'n' roll with ageless American roots. The Flying Burrito Brothers, led by Gram Parsons, put out their seminal debut, *The Gilded Palace of Sin*, as did Poco, a group featuring two former members of Buffalo Springfield. Another Springfield alumnus, Neil Young, released the country-tinged *The Loner* and his first album with Crazy Horse, *Everybody Knows This is Nowhere*. Meanwhile the Springfield's Stephen Stills turned up in Crosby, Stills & Nash: their debut album was one of the most influential of the era.

In Georgia, the Allman Brothers Band were starting to make noise with their unique fusion of psychedelic rock, R&B, and deep blues. In New York, Miles Davis was turning jazz on its head with the rock-influenced *In A Silent Way* and the revolutionary sessions for *Bitches Brew*. Jimi Hendrix was a top draw in U.S. arenas, riding the success of *Electric Ladyland*. The Doors were forced off the road after Jim Morrison allegedly exposed himself in Miami.

And then that summer came Woodstock…

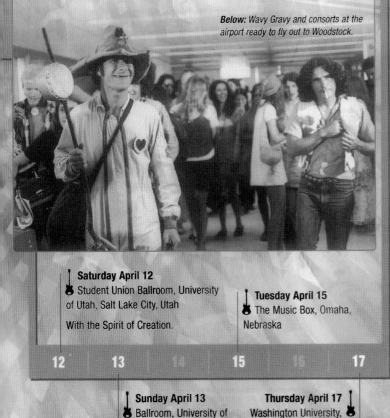

Below: *Wavy Gravy and consorts at the airport ready to fly out to Woodstock.*

GRATEFUL DEAD AND GEORGE STAVIS FRI APR 18 8-11 PM PURDUE MEMORIAL UNION BALLROOMS

TICKETS $2.50 ADVANCE $3.00 AT DOOR

MAIL CHECKS TO: PURDUE PEACE UNION BOX 656 PMC PURDUE UNIVERSITY LAFAYETTE, IND.

Friday April 18
Memorial Union Ballroom, Purdue University, Lafayette, Indiana

With George Stavis, purveyor of "occult Improvisational compositions for 5-string banjo and percussion."

Sunday April 20
Clark University, Worcester, Massachusetts

With Roland Kirk (later Rahsaan Roland Kirk), the jazzman famous for his inventive work on unusual and/or archaic instruments (this show may have taken place on April 19). In a piece of synchronicity, Professor Robert Goddard taught at Clark University in the 1910s and 1920s, when he developed the solid-fuel rocket, ancestor of the vehicles that allowed humankind to explore… space.

18 19 20

21 22 23 24

Monday April 21 ★
Tuesday April 22 ★
Wednesday April 23 ★
The Ark, Boston, Massachusetts

On the first night the band opens the second set with a one-off jam on "Foxy Lady" from the Jimi Hendrix Experience's *Are you Experienced?* (1967).

Friday April 25
Saturday April 26 ★
Electric Theater, Chicago, Illinois

The Saturday show's "Viola Lee Blues" appears on 1997's *Fallout from the Phil Zone*. Setlists for this show often include "What's Become of the Baby?"; there's some debate over whether the band actually played the song or whether a taped studio version (*Aoxomoxoa* had not yet been released) was played over the PA during "Feedback" (if the former, it would be "Baby's" sole live performance).

25 26 27 28 29 30

Sunday April 27 ★
Labor Temple, Minneapolis, Minnesota

With jazz keyboardist Bobby Lyle and his quintet.

Lenny Hart

Mickey Hart's father Lenny was a drummer himself, but he'd abandoned the family during Mickey's youth and didn't reappear in Mickey's life until he was about 20. Later he became a preacher and convinced the band that he'd be doing good works for the Lord by helping the Dead to do well. But he was still an odd choice to manage the band's business affairs when the group found itself in dire financial trouble. Yet Lenny talked a good game and so the Dead trusted him. This was not a wise move. The elder Hart ended up ripping off the band for more than $150,000, which essentially left the group penniless. The treachery so wounded Mickey that he left the band for over four years beginning in 1971.

Saturday April 12
Student Union Ballroom, University of Utah, Salt Lake City, Utah

With the Spirit of Creation.

Tuesday April 15
The Music Box, Omaha, Nebraska

12 13 14 15 16 17

Sunday April 13
Ballroom, University of Colorado, Boulder, Colorado

Thursday April 17
Washington University, St. Louis, Missouri

MAY '69

| 1 | 2 | 3 | 4 | 5 | 6 |

Saturday May 3
Sierra College, Rocklin, California

The Dead play an afternoon show.

Friday May 2
Saturday May 3
Winterland Arena, San Francisco, California

With Jefferson Airplane and Mongo Santamaria.

Sunday May 11
Aztec Bowl, SD State University, San Diego, California

With Canned Heat, Lee Michaels, Santana, and Tarantula. Carlos Santana and his percussionists sit in for part of the Dead's set.

Friday May 9
Hall of Flowers, County Fairgrounds, San Mateo, California

Friday May 23
Saturday May 24
Seminole Indian Village, West Hollywood, Florida

A festival with a vaguely Native American theme: The Big Rock Pow Wow. Also appearing are Aum, the Echo, Jane & the Electric Jive, Timothy Leary, Nervous System, NRBQ, Joe South, Sweetwater, Johnny Winter, and the Youngbloods.

| 7 | 8 | 9 | 10 | 11 | 12 | 13 | 14 | 15 | 16 | 17 ~ 22 | 23 | 24 | 25 ~ 27 |

Wednesday May 7
Polo Field, Golden Gate Park, San Francisco, California

With the Jefferson Airplane.

Saturday May 10
Rose Palace, Pasadena, California

Thursday May 8
Unknown venue, California

Friday May 16
Campolindo High School, Moraga, California

With Frumious Bandersnatch—who take their name from Lewis Carroll's poem, "The Jabberwocky"—and the Velvet Hammer.

Thursday May 29
Robertson Gym, UCSB, Santa Barbara, California

A "Memorial Day Ball," with Lee Michaels and the Youngbloods.

| 28 | 29 |

Saturday May 31
MacArthur Court, University of Oregon, Eugene, Oregon

The first "Long Black Limousine."

Wednesday May 28
Winterland Arena, San Francisco, California

The "People's Park Bail Ball," held as a benefit for protesters arrested earlier in May after demonstrating at the closure of a "People's Park" in Berkeley. With the Airplane, Santana, Elvin Bishop, the Bangor Flying Circus, and C.C. Revival.

| 30 | 31 |

Friday May 30
Springer's Inn, Portland, Oregon

Below: Onstage on Saturday June 21, at Fillmore East, New York.

May 1969

98

Rick Griffin

Artist extraordinaire Rick Griffin came from California's surf culture, where in the early '60s, as a staff artist for *Surfer* magazine, he popularized his cartoon creation, Murphy. By 1966, he'd seen The Charlatans perform, had attended an L.A. Acid Test, and been intrigued by the work of Kelley & Mouse, Wes Wilson, Victor Moscoso, and others. He moved to San Francisco and immediately found work drawing posters for the Family Dog. He was an early contributor to the Zap Comix and his first foray into working with the Dead produced the sublime psychedelisexual cover for the Dead's third album, *Aoxomoxoa*. He later went on make covers for *Wake of the Flood* and *Without A Net*, and he designed the band's 20th anniversary "minuteman" logo in 1985. Griffin died in a motorcycle accident in 1991.

Bill's ding-dong

Bill Graham was always wary of what he ate or drank—with good reason— around the band and its associates, but at one of his shows someone managed to get some liquid LSD on his soda can. A blissed-out Bill joined the Dead on stage, and he joyfully banged on cowbells and gongs for the whole performance. "One of the dozen greatest nights of my life," Bill later said. Mickey Hart gave him a gilded cowbell as a souvenir.

Wednesday June 11
California Hall, San Francisco, California

Bob Weir performs with Garcia, Lesh, Constanten, Hart, John "Marmaduke" Dawson, David Nelson, and Peter Grant as "Bobby Ace and the Cards from the Bottom of the Deck." The evening marks the beginnings of the band which would become The New Riders of the Purple Sage.

JUNE '69

| 1 ~ 4 | 5 | 6 | 7 | 8 | 9 | 10 | 11 | 12 | 13 | 14 |

Thursday June 5
Friday June 6
Saturday June 7
Sunday June 8
Fillmore West, San Francisco, California

With Junior Walker & the All-Stars and the Glass Family. On Friday Elvin Bishop jams on the only "Checkin' Up On My Baby." The band also breaks out "The Green, Green Grass of Home." Saturday marks the first "Dire Wolf" and Janis Joplin adds vocals to "Turn on Your Love Light." Sunday sees the only "The Things I Used to Do" and "Who's Lovin' You Now."

Friday June 13
Fresno Convention Center, Fresno, California

The rockabilly legend Ronnie Hawkins joins in on "Good Morning Little Schoolgirl" and the "Love Light" closer.

Saturday June 14
Monterey Peninsula College, Monterey, California

With Aum.

Friday June 20
Saturday June 21
Fillmore East, New York, New York
Four shows (early/late) with Buddy Miles Express and Savoy Brown.

Sunday June 22
Central Park, New York, New York
The band's third show in the park.

Sunday June 29
The Barn, Rio Nido, California
Same bill as June 27 and 28.

15 16 17 18 19 **20 21 22** 23 24 25 26 **27 28 29** 30

Friday June 20
Release of *Aoxomoxoa*.

Friday June 27
Saturday June 28
Veterans Auditorium, Santa Rosa, California
With Hot Tuna, Joey Covington, and the Cleanliness & Godliness Skiffle Band.

AOXOMOXOA
Grateful Dead
Released by Warner Bros. (WS-1790) on June 20, 1969

Side One
1. **St. Stephen**
   (Garcia/Lesh/Hunter)
2. **Dupree's Diamond Blues**
   (Garcia/Hunter)
3. **Rosemary**
   (Garcia/Hunter)
4. **Doin' That Rag**
   (Garcia/Hunter)
5. **Mountains Of The Moon**
   (Garcia/Hunter)

Side Two
1. **China Cat Sunflower**
   (Garcia/Hunter)
2. **What's Become Of The Baby**
   (Garcia/Hunter)
3. **Cosmic Charlie**
   (Garcia/Hunter)

Personnel

Tom Constanten – keyboards
Jerry Garcia – guitar, vocals
Mickey Hart – percussion
Bill Kreutzmann – percussion
Phil Lesh – basses, vocals
Pigpen (Ron McKernan) – vocals, keyboards, harmonica
Bob Weir – guitars, vocals

Produced by the Grateful Dead

THOUGH THE DEAD WEREN'T ABLE TO BROADEN their recording horizons enough to match the breadth of their ever-evolving live trip by 1969, having a chance to make the first-ever sixteen-track rock album helped. Recorded at Pacific Recording Studios in San Mateo, California, and Pacific High Recording, San Francisco, between September 1968 and March 1969, the band's first completely self-produced effort was also their most ambitious and costly to date. The title *Aoxomoxoa* was a palindrome (a word that spells the same forward and backward) believed to have been invented over 2,000 years ago by Sotades the Obscene. The trippy cover art by local concert poster hero Rick Griffin surely would have made old Sot proud, a suggestive eruption of electric surreality adorned with subterranean fetal creatures and cosmic spermatozoa clinging to a blazing yellow orb.

The album's eight songs covered a wide swath of experimental terrain, from smart rock ("St. Stephen") to delicate medieval balladry ("Mountains Of The Moon"), and even abstract, self-serving sonic soundscapes ("What's Become Of The Baby"). It was at once creatively unique and commercially inaccessible, leaving even the Dead finding it hard to get their heads around.

"A lot of the *Aoxomoxoa* songs are overwritten and cumbersome to perform," Garcia told Blair Jackson over a decade later. "But at the time, I wasn't writing songs for the band to play—I was writing songs to be writing songs." On that level, the disc marked the start of what Garcia called a "really serious collaboration" with lyricist Robert Hunter, and though *Aoxomoxoa* would put the band a reported $180,000 in the hole with its label Warner Bros., well, you can't put a price on magic. Cooed a *Rolling Stone* reviewer at the time: "No other music sustains a lifestyle so delicate and loving and lifelike." Or Dead-like, as it were.

I Know You Riders

A self-styled "country bar band" and one of the Grateful Dead's longest-lived and best-loved "spinoffs," the New Riders of the Purple Sage began to come together in the spring of '69, when Jerry Garcia began playing pedal-steel behind the guitar and voice of John "Marmaduke" Dawson, an old friend and fellow folkie from the Palo Alto days. Besides Dawson's fine original songs, the duo covered country classics at a regular Wednesday-night gig at a Palo Alto coffeehouse, the Underground. Jerry and "McDuke," as he was usually called, began woodshedding at Mickey Hart's Novato ranch with David Nelson, another old friend from Palo Alto, on electric guitar, and Mickey and Phil Lesh were soon playing along.

The group soon took the name New Riders of the Purple Sage, from Zane Grey's classic early-1900s western tale. They first performed under the new name in Seattle (August 20 or 21, 1969) and at the Family Dog at the Great Highway the following week. The Riders would go on to be the Dead's opening act from 1970 until 1971, when Garcia would turn over the pedal steel chair to Buddy Cage and the Riders would go out on their own. NRPS was a manifestation of a fusion of rock and country that had been going on for a couple of years, most visibly with albums like Bob Dylan's *Nashville Skyline*, the Band's *Music from Big Pink*, the Byrds' *Sweetheart of the Rodeo*. The transition reflected a late-'60s sense, as earlier utopian hopes faded amid war, assassinations, and unrest, that music, like the scene in general, had gotten maybe a little too far out and weird. The musicians reached out for the warmth, simplicity, and tradition that country offered, not as comfort music, but as a return to their own roots. And it felt good.

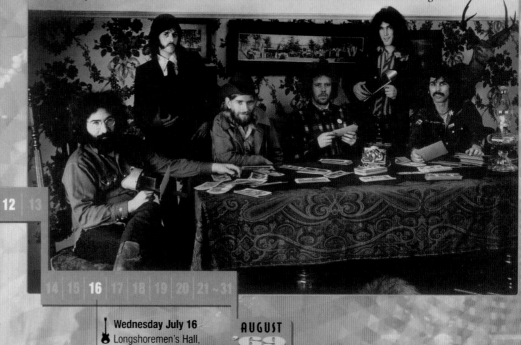

Several shows in July and August have to be canceled for various reasons, including another concert in New York's Central Park (scheduled for July 12); a three-show run in Hawaii (scheduled for July 25–27); and three shows at the Fillmore West in early August, for which posters are actually printed and distributed.

JULY '69

1 | 2 | **3** | **4** | **5** | 6 | **7**

Monday July 7
Piedmont Park, Atlanta, Georgia

A free afternoon concert.

Thursday July 3
Reed's Ranch, Colorado Springs, Colorado

With Zephyr, Holden Caulfield, and Devon Michaels.

Friday July 4
Saturday July 5
Electric Theater, Chicago, Illinois

The Independence Day show includes the band's only known performance of Porter Wagoner's prison lament known as "Let Me In."

Tuesday July 8
Rock Pile, Toronto, Ontario, Canada

Two shows.

8 | 9 | **10**

Thursday July 10
Gallagher Estate, Norwalk, Connecticut

The band entertains at a Hells Angels party

The Dead episode of *Playboy After Dark* airs. Sales of serapes go through the roof the following day.

11 | **12** | 13

Friday July 11
Saturday July 12
NY State Pavilion, Flushing Meadow Park, New York, New York

The band play at the site of the 1964 World's Fair in Queens. Working as a security guard is a local guy named Steve Parish, who later becomes one of the Dead's hardcore roadies. Last performance of "Mountains of the Moon."

14 | 15 | **16** | 17 | 18 | 19 | 20 | 21~31

Wednesday July 16
Longshoremen's Hall, San Francisco, California

AUGUST '69

1 | **2** | **3** | 4~15 | **16**

Saturday August 2
Sunday August 3
Family Dog at the Great Highway, San Francisco, California

Both shows with Ballet Afro-Haiti and blues great Albert Collins, "the Master of the Telecaster." Saturday sees the first performance of "Seasons." Having been forced to shut down the Avalon Ballroom, Chet Helms has managed to resurrect the Family Dog at this San Francisco venue, named the Great Highway for its location on the beach.

Saturday August 16
Woodstock Music & Art Fair, Max Yasgur's Farm, Bethel, New York

"CHINA CAT SUNFLOWER"/"I KNOW YOU RIDER"
HUNTER/GARCIA & TRADITIONAL

With a playful absurdity worthy of the senseless verse of Lewis Carroll or the silly prose of John Lennon, "China Cat Sunflower" represents the Dead at an early creative high point. The song, which appeared on the band's *Aoxomoxoa* LP (1969), was one of the first fruits of what would become a long-time collaboration between guitarist Jerry Garcia and lyricist Robert Hunter. Hunter attributed the inspiration for the track to poet Dame Edith Sitwell, and part of a line from Sitwell's poem "Trio For Two Cats And A Trombone" appears in the wordsmith's mention of the "palace of the Queen Chinee," while Carroll's famous Cheshire Cat gets a wink and a nod in the song's "one-eyed Cheshire." "I think the germ of it came in Mexico," Hunter said in 1978. "I had a cat sitting on my belly, and was in a rather hypersensitive state, and I followed this cat out to, I believe it was Neptune... I wrote part of it in Mexico and part of it on Neptune." Though the studio version of the song served as a delightful psychedelic jig all its own, the band soon began pairing it with the traditional "I Know You Rider," a popular song on the folk circuit in the mid-1960s and a favorite of Dead contemporaries like Joan Baez, Janis Joplin, and Hot Tuna (the first pairing came on July 5, 1969, at Chicago's Electric Theater). The transition from the trippy stylings of "China Cat" to the Dead's souped-up version of "Rider" provided for one of the band's most-consistently solid jams, a perfect synthesis of psychedelia and folk that proved to be such an ideal fit that the group coupled the songs all but two times over the course of over 500 performances between the fall of 1969 and the summer of 1995. The Other Ones continued the tradition, playing what fans have come to know as "China Rider" over a dozen times between 1998 and 2002.

Down on Yasgur's Farm

For all the clichés and legends ascribed to it over the years, Woodstock was truly an epochal event, in both its scale and its impact on the collective consciousness. Four hundred thousand people, more or less, made it to the festival; at least a million more tried to get there. The lineup was a collection of rock royalty that exceeded even Monterey, including the Who, Jimi Hendrix, Joan Baez, the Airplane, and on and on. An amazing event, and of course the Dead—human, not showmen—blew it; or at least so they said.

Blowing it at Bethel

Dead scholar Christian Crumlish uses the marvelous phrase "reverse mystique" to describe how the band's fans turned the Grateful Dead's foibles into fables. Witness Deadheads' custom of cheering blown or flubbed lyrics at shows. The Dead's performance at Woodstock is the best example of this reverse-mythologizing; although they weren't great, they probably weren't as bad as they later claimed, but they almost bragged about their "failure."

The circumstances certainly weren't optimum. They were late, both because Bear had insisted on fixing the electrical ground on the stage and because their heavy equipment had squashed the turntable set up for quick stage changeovers. A monsoon was raging, their amps were picking up random radio signals, and the stage was still not properly grounded, so that Jerry recalled seeing "blue balls of electricity bouncing across the stage and into my guitar when I touched the strings."

The boys opened with "St. Stephen," which didn't finish but somehow went into "Mama Tried" (quite a stylistic segue). "High Time" petered out as they tried to sort out the gear problems. After finishing "High Time," it was "Dark Star">"Lovelight" and then in out of the rain.

Off the stage, they had a ball. In Jerry's words: "The thing about Woodstock was that you could feel the presence of time travelers from the future who had come back to see it. You could sense the significance of the event as it was happening. There was a kind of swollen historicity—a truly pregnant moment. You definitely knew that it was a milestone; it was in the air."

Given their low opinion of their performance, the Dead would never have allowed the makers of the Woodstock movie to use their footage. With appropriate irony, this became a decision they never had to make. When Dead fan and future film genius (and cameraman at Woodstock) Martin Scorsese came to edit their performance, he discovered that the light levels while they were onstage were so low that the film was completely unusable. Eighteen years before they made the album, they were in the dark. The film hit the cutting room floor, and the Dead would realize, as Jerry told manager Jon McIntire as he left the stage, that "it's nice to know that you can blow the most important gig of your career and it really doesn't matter." And it didn't.

WOODSTOCK MUSIC & ART FAIR presents AN AQUARIAN EXPOSITION in WHITE LAKE, N.Y.

3 DAYS of PEACE MUSIC

AUGUST 15, 16, 17.

101

Above top and middle: Garcia plays and Pigpen sings at Woodstock. Above bottom: Billy and Mickey at Woodstock. Left: The Groovy Way at Woodstock.

Thursday August 21 ★
Aqua Theater, Seattle, Washington

With NRPS. This show may have taken place on August 20. Whichever, it includes the breakout of "Easy Wind," an homage to Robert Johnson written for Pigpen by Robert Hunter. Charles Lloyd added his flute to "New Minglewood Blues" and "China Cat Sunflower."

Thursday August 28
Friday August 29
Saturday August 30
Family Dog at the Great Highway, San Francisco, California

The first show is with NRPS, and all three with Phoenix, and Commander Cody. Thursday's show may qualify as a Mickey and the Hartbeats gig, since the personnel would appear to be Jerry Garcia, Phil Lesh, Mickey Hart, Bill Kreutzmann, and future Jerry Garcia collaborator Howard Wales (see page 115) on keyboards. It's the last performance of Jimmy Reed's "It's a Sin," (though the song is the takeoff point for a jam on June 18, 1974). The show also includes the first "The Eleven Jam."

Saturday August 23
Pelletier Farm, St. Helens, Oregon

The band play the Bullfrog Festival, which was originally to be held at the Columbia County Fairgrounds but has to move to private property after a local judge voids the promoters' contract. Many local bands perform.

Sunday August 24
Paradise Valley Resort, Squamish, British Columbia, Canada

A Vancouver Pop Festival set. Also appearing are the Chambers Brothers, the Byrds, Chrome Syrcus, Guess Who, the Rascals, the Rotary Connection, and Merrilee Rush. On the bill, too, is proto-shock rocker Alice Cooper (nee Vincent Furnier), a Phoenix, Arizona, homeboy of future Dead keyboardist Vince Welnick.

Alchemists of Sound

When Bear returned as the Dead's soundman, he catalyzed a loose collective, Alembic, to find ways to improve live sound, recording technology, and instrumentation. (In alchemy, an alembic is a vessel in which base metals are transmuted into precious ones.) Besides Bear, the group included Bob Matthews, Betty Cantor-Jackson, Dan Healy, a former Ampex engineer, Ron Wickersham, and instrument-maker Rick Turner. (Another great luthier, Doug Irwin, joined a couple of years later, as did taping tech Dennis "Wizard" Leonard.) The group originally worked out of a shed in the back of the band's rehearsal space at Hamilton Air Force Base, but moved to San Francisco in 1970.

The Alembic crew was exploring unknown sonic territory. The PA and other gear used by rock bands at the time produced a sound that ranged from barely acceptable to awful. Alembic would change that, and not only for the Grateful Dead: Alembic's combined workshop/studio/research lab became, in Doug Irwin's phrase, "a one-stop shop for rock 'n' roll," serving bands including the Who, the Airplane, and Emerson, Lake & Palmer. Alembic is still in business today, now specializing in building custom guitars and pickups, in Santa Rosa, California.

"[Our goal was] to take the sound that the musicians produced on stage, like when they played it together in a room, amplify it without changing it, and put it out to the audience. Phil and I often discussed this idea of mine. We called the stage environment the 'microcosm,' the audience area was called the 'macrocosm.' It followed a statement in Alchemy: as above, so below." BEAR, 2003

Saturday September 6
Sunday September 7
Family Dog at the Great Highway, San Francisco, California

Saturday is a night of old-time rock 'n' roll with Jefferson Airplane. Jorma Kaukonen sings lead on the opener, "Peggy Sue," followed by Jerry Garcia singing lead on "That'll Be the Day" (the band's only performances of both Buddy Holly classics) and "Baby What You Want," while Hot Tuna drummer Joey Covington takes lead vocal duties on "Louie Louie," "Twist & Shout" (in its only GD performance), and "Blue Moon." It's also first time out for "Johnny B. Goode," "It's All Over Now," and "Big Railroad Blues."

3   4   5   6   7

SEPTEMBER '69

1   2

Monday September 1
Baton Rouge International Speedway, Prairieville, Louisiana

The New Orleans Pop Festival, with Janis Joplin, the Who, and many others.

Below: *The Dead rarely posed for group photos during Tom Constanten's tenure with the group, but a shot from this session, taken in Novato, Marin County, was used on the inner gatefold of Live/Dead and was also used for promotion.*

September 1969

102

Left and far left: Phil Lesh chills at home in September. Lesh has often said that '68 and '69 were his favorite years of Dead music, though he played well during every era.

Sam Cutler

As road manager for the Rolling Stones' American tour in the fall of 1969, Sam Cutler encountered the Grateful Dead when the two bands decided they would throw a free concert in the Bay Area at the end of the Stones' tour—this, of course, became the debacle known as Altamont, and Cutler was involved in every aspect of the planning, including hiring the Hells Angels for "security." Despite that disaster, the brash Englishman shortly thereafter became the Dead's road manager, a position he held until the beginning of 1974, encompassing their greatest growth period.

Friday September 26
Saturday September 27
Fillmore East, New York, New York

Country Joe & the Fish and Sha Na Na play at the early and late shows on both days. At Saturday's early show the band tunes up to "Take Me Out to the Ballgame." A tribute, perhaps, to the amazin' '69 Mets, who had just won the National League East Championship...? Although the band have yet to break out "Uncle John's Band" in public, the early show closes with the first "Uncle John's Jam."

OCTOBER '69

26	27	28	29	30	1	2	3	4

Thursday October 2
Friday October 3
Saturday October 4
Boston Tea Party, Boston, Massachusetts

Monday September 29
Tuesday September 30
Wednesday October 1
Café au Go-Go, New York, New York

The band play early and late shows on all three days.

Sunday October 5
The band are advertised as playing on a bill at the Houston Coliseum, Houston, Texas, with the Airplane, Hot Tuna, and Sons of Champlin, but does not perform at this show.

5	6	7 - 15

Monday October 6
Family Dog at the Great Highway, San Francisco, California

JEFFERSON AIRPLANE
GRATEFUL DEAD
SONS OF CHAMPLIN
LIGHTS: GLENN McKAY'S HEADLIGHTS

2 DAYS ONLY - FRI • SAT 2
OCT. 24 + 25
WINTERLAND
POST AND STEINER STREETS

The Road to Altamont

The chain of events that led to Altamont, the worst disaster to befall the Grateful Dead, began in early September when Rock Scully flew to London to lay the groundwork for a proposed free concert in Hyde Park by the San Francisco bands. Rock got caught with a few hits of acid. Busted and far from home, he contacted Chesley Millikin, a friend from San Francisco then working in London. In the course of getting Rock out on bail, Millikin hooked up Rock with the Rolling Stones' road manager, Sam Cutler. The rock 'n' roll freebooters bonded quickly, and Rock floated the idea of capping the Stones' upcoming Stateside tour by playing a free festival (then at the conceptual stage of planning) in the Bay Area. After all, the West Coast deserved a Woodstock of its own. In October, when the Stones arrived in L.A. to prepare for the tour, Rock, Danny Rifkin, and other scenesters met with Mick Jagger and Sam Cutler. Momentum started to build.

Friday October 17
Unknown Venue, San Jose, California

17	18 - 23	24	25	26

27 - 29	30	31

Friday October 31
San Jose State University, San Jose, California

Friday October 24
Saturday October 25
Sunday October 26
Winterland, San Francisco, California

Hot Tuna, Jefferson Airplane, and Sons of Champlin play all three nights. On Saturday Stephen Stills may have played on "Turn On Your Lovelight." Sunday marks the last "Doin' that Rag."

"We may be a little prejudiced but let's get one thing said—on any given night, the very greatest rock and roll band in the world, The Grateful Dead."
BILL GRAHAM TO THE SATURDAY SHOW AUDIENCE

LIVE/DEAD
Grateful Dead

Released by Warner Bros. (2WS-1830) on November 10, 1969

Side One
1. **Dark Star**
(Hunter/Garcia/Lesh/McKernan/Weir/Hart/Kreutzmann)

Side Two
1. **St. Stephen**
(Hunter/Garcia/Lesh)
2. **The Eleven**
(Hunter/Lesh)

Side Three
1. **Turn On Your Love Light**
(Scott/Malone)

Side Four
1. **Death Don't Have No Mercy**
(Rev. Gary Davis)
2. **Feedback**
(McGannahan Skjellyfetti)
3. **And We Bid You Goodnight**
(Traditional)

Personnel

Jerry Garcia – guitar, vocals
Phil Lesh – bass, vocals
Bob Weir – guitar, vocals
Mickey Hart – percussion
Bill Kreutzmann – percussion
Tom Constanten – keyboard
Pigpen (Ron McKernan) – vocals, congas, organ on "Death Don't Have No Mercy"

Produced by the Grateful Dead, Bob Matthews, and Betty Cantor

WITH THEIR PENCHANT FOR LIVE MAGIC already firmly established by the end of the 1960s, it's a wonder the Dead hadn't released a concert album before this. Though they had already experimented with live passages in the earlier *Anthem of the Sun* release, *Live/Dead* was the first, authentic sampling of a pure dose of good ol' Grateful Dead. Recorded with a 16-track mobile studio in San Francisco during a handful of early 1969 shows, the album featured a 23-minute-long "Dark Star," crackling versions of "St. Stephen" and its adopted companion piece "The Eleven," and reworked Dead power covers like "Love Light" and "Death Don't Have No Mercy."

The cover art by R.D. Thomas captured the era's feel, featuring a vision of feminine wonder that one imagines might be the muse of music, Polyhymnia, overseeing a Dead show, rising from a symbol-covered coffin with a thin black staff in one hand and a golden ball of healing chrism in the other.

The album did wonders for the Dead's financial situation with its label. "This was about the time we were finishing up work on the *Aoxomoxoa* project and Warner Bros. was pointing out that they had sunk $100,000-plus into it and hadn't seen a product yet," keyboardist Tom Constanten told Sandy Troy. "So someone had the idea that if we sent them a double live album, three discs for the price of one wouldn't be such a bad deal, and they went for it." Released on November 10, it was as fitting an adieu to the decade that had spawned them as the band could hope to offer. "We'd only recorded a few gigs to get that album," Garcia later told *Rolling Stone*. "If you take *Live/Dead* and *Aoxomoxoa* together, you have a picture of what we were doing at that time."

Live/Dead would set a precedent for a string of live albums that would eventually outnumber the band's studio output, from the triple-disc travelogue *Europe '72* to the ongoing *Dick's Picks* series.

NOVEMBER '69

1	2	3	4	5	6	7	8	9

Monday November 10
Release of *Live/Dead*.

Saturday November 15
Across the nation, demonstrators march in opposition to the war in Vietnam: 250,000 people gather at the Washington Monument; a slightly smaller number gather in Golden Gate Park in San Francisco.

Saturday November 1
Sunday November 2
Family Dog at the Great Highway, San Francisco, California

With Danny Cox and Golden Toad.

Friday November 7
★ Saturday November 8
Fillmore Auditorium, San Francisco, California

Alligator and the South Bay Experimental Flash play both shows. Saturday sees the first "Cumberland Blues"; the show is released as *Dick's Picks Volume 16*.

10	11	12	13	14	15	16	17	18	19	20	21	22 - 30

Saturday November 15
Lanai Theater, Crockett, California

A benefit for the Vietnam Moratorium Day.

Friday November 21
Building A, Cal Expo, Sacramento, California

Thursday December 4
Friday December 5
Sunday December 7
Fillmore West, San Francisco, California

The Flock and Humble Pie, the latter featuring Steve Marriott and a 19-year-old guitarist named Peter Frampton, play all three shows. Thursday is breakout night for "Uncle John's Band" and "Black Peter."

Saturday December 13
Swing Auditorium,
San Bernardino,
California

Friday December 26
McFarlin Auditorium,
SMU, Dallas, Texas

Another acoustic opening set (this time *sans* Kreutzmann). Stills also introduces one of his own songs, "Black Queen," with the Dead backing him (see April 16, 1983). As far as can be determined it's the band's only performance of "Gathering Flowers for The Master's Bouquet."

Monday December 29
★ **Tuesday December 30**
Wednesday December 31
Boston Tea Party,
Boston, Massachusetts

The band's only New Year's Eve show outside California includes the last "Slewfoot."

Saturday December 6
Altamont

Wednesday December 10
Thursday December 11
Friday December 12
Thelma Theater,
Los Angeles, California

On Wednesday Stephen Stills guests on "Casey Jones," "Good Mornin' Little Schoolgirl," and "Morning Dew."

Friday December 19
Saturday December 20
Sunday December 21
Fillmore Auditorium, San Francisco, California

Osceola and the Rhythm Dukes play all three shows. Friday night begins with an acoustic set (*sans* Phil Lesh), with first performances of "Monkey And The Engineer," "I've Been All Around This World," and "Little Sadie." The electric set opens with the breakout of "Mason's Children," which wasn't on an "official" release until *Dick's Picks Volume 4* (1996). Robert Hunter later noted that the song dealt "obliquely with Altamont." Saturday marks the first performance of another Altamont commentary, Hunter/Garcia's "New Speedway Boogie" (see page 387).

Sunday December 28
International Speedway, Hollywood, Florida

The Hollywood Pop Festival.

Above: *The crowd at Altamont.*
Below: *Hells Angels at Altamont.*

Altamont

Planning for Altamont went on through November, with Rock Scully and Sam Cutler in the forefront. At one meeting the issue of the Hells Angels came up. What actually happened is still hotly debated. It was later widely reported that the decision was made to hire the Hells Angels to provide "security" for an emolument of $500 worth of beer. Others, including Sam Cutler, deny any such "formal" arrangement. According to this camp, everyone involved knew the Angels would be there anyway, so it seemed sensible to let them hang out around the stage and make themselves useful.

So the concert was on, and during the last stages of the Stones' tour in November, Mick Jagger announced that the band would play a free show on December 6 in Golden Gate Park. Because of Jagger's announcement, the free show with the Stones almost fell through at the last minute, as San Francisco's city hall refused to provide a permit for Golden Gate Park, so that was out. The location was then shifted to Sears Point Raceway, about 35 miles north of San Francisco.

But, with less than two days to the show date, Filmways, the company that owned the raceway, suddenly decided they needed more money, which the Stones refused to pay. With things looking bleak, a call came in from one Dick Carter, who owned an auto-racing track, Altamont Raceway, in Livermore, off Interstate 580, about 40 miles east of the city. Carter had heard about the trouble at Sears Point and decided that having a big rock show at his track would be good for publicity, and would the organizers consider holding the concert there?

They most certainly would. Altamont was the place where what could go wrong, did. Because the site was moved at the last second, the stage was too low, placing a bad choice in security guards, the Hells Angels, in a risky position at an ugly facility—a demolition derby racetrack.

Also, the Stones' brilliant current material, "Sympathy for the Devil" and "Midnight Rambler," evoked less-than-mellow vibes, especially from the (generally) massively drugged audience members who insisted on pushing to the front. The Angels responded in kind, and as the day went on, the violence they directed against crazies in the audience extended to musicians like Marty Balin and Stephen Stills.

After sets from Santana, the Flying Burrito Brothers, Jefferson Airplane, and Crosby, Stills, and Nash, everyone got to sit for two hours and wait for the Stones, the Dead having taken a good look at the chaos careening on and in front of the stage and saying "no, thanks." The madness only increased when Mick & Co. took the stage, and during "Under My Thumb," a young man named Meredith Hunter pulled out a pistol and waved it around. A nearby Angel slashed Hunter several times with a knife before a knot of Angels kicked him to the ground and into a lifeless pulp (the Angel with the knife was later acquitted of murder on the grounds of self-defense). The Stones continued, but they were, in Dennis McNally's words, "playing for their lives." Like Macbeth, the Dead & Co. had supp'd full of horrors. They choppered out, and on the short flight back to the city they tried to make out the constellations in the night sky—anything to take their minds off an event that had turned into a debacle—a debacle that, with the best of intentions, they'd helped to bring about. The band was supposed to play the Fillmore that night, but they were too depressed and bailed out of the show.

SEEKING ALL THAT'S STILL UNSUNG

January 1970 – April 1976

To a stranger's eye, the Grateful Dead in early 1970 appeared to have considerable problems. Altamont was still a vivid, nightmarish memory. Late in January most of the Dead were busted for drugs in New Orleans. The band also shrank by one during the visit, as Tom Constanten left; even though the decision was mutual, it suggested stress. Then, in March, they discovered that their manager (and their percussionist's father), Lenny Hart, had been systematically stealing from them. He vanished and they were flat broke, just as the debt to Warner Bros. generated by their endless studio costs for *Anthem of the Sun* and *Aoxomoxoa* peaked at close to a quarter-million dollars.

The band in 1976, after Mickey Hart had once again been brought back from exile and into the fold, with new members Keith and Donna Godchaux. Maybe Phil Lesh should have been the tie designer.

But inside the Dead, as they settled down to recording in March 1970, things seemed only normally chaotic, and these people were extremely comfortable with chaos. What was important was the music, and the songs Garcia and Hunter had been writing for the past year were fine indeed. Pigpen had been the front man for a blues band, and Lesh had been of inestimable sway in the most recent experimental phase of the Dead. But during 1969, as the Dead launched themselves on nightly interstellar expeditions on the rocket ship "Dark Star," something else was also happening to their music.

The change had begun around January, when Robert Hunter and his lover Christie Bourne had moved in with Garcia and his wife Carolyn. Hunter and Garcia had been pals and sometime musical collaborators since 1961. As the Dead began to write original material in late 1966 and into 1967, Garcia realized that he desperately needed a lyricist. "I'm really a jive

"I think basically the Grateful Dead is not for cranking out rock and roll, it's not for going out and doing concerts... I think it's to get high... To get really high is to forget yourself. And to forget yourself is to see everything else." JERRY GARCIA TO JANN WENNER AND CHARLES REICH, *ROLLING STONE*, 1971

lyricist," he said later. "My lyrics come from right now—put pencil on paper, and what comes out, if it fits, it fits. I didn't think about them, I just made the first, obvious choices and never rewrote. It took me a long time to sing them out, because they embarrassed me." Hunter had written some lyrics for Pigpen's "Alligator," and then around Labor Day he dropped in on the band, which was rehearsing a new, unnamed tune. He listened a while, scratched out some words, and at a break handed Garcia the first verse of a song called "Dark Star." The band also used Hunter lyrics for "St. Stephen" and "China Cat Sunflower," but it was only when Hunter moved in to Garcia's home that they truly began to be songwriting partners.

One night after Hunter had been there a couple of days, every one else went out, and he got a bit tipsy—"that explains," he said, "(the song's) good-time feel"—and sat down with a tape recorder to retell the story of an outlaw named Frank Dupree. "Dupree's Diamond Blues" was the first of a string of Hunter/Garcia compositions early in the year, including the exquisitely beautiful "Mountains of the Moon" and "Doin' That Rag." In April, Garcia acquired a pedal steel guitar, and the musical atmosphere at the Larkspur turned country-western. Month by month, songs that sounded almost traditional if one didn't study the lyrics too closely crept into the band's repertoire—"Dire Wolf," "Casey Jones," "High Time," "Cumberland Blues," and the anthemic "Uncle John's Band," among others. All the while, they were working on the highly psychedelic album Aoxomoxoa. Mickey Hart later reflected that they were exceptionally stoned during the making of the album because "we were trying to camouflage the transition. It was instinct. I don't think it was an intellectual choice, but I think that there was a gray area that we were passing through. We were groping at finding the form."

In early 1970 they looked up and realized that the new Hunter/Garcia material was clearly, as Lesh put it, their "strong suit," and though the soaring jams weren't suddenly dropped, the band was now capable of more. What they would record in March (along with the essentially companion album recorded in September) would redefine the group as a fully rounded American song band, capable of moving from blues to psychedelia to country ballad in the same set. Though Garcia's lead guitar had been at the center of the Dead as either blues or psychedelic band, his vocals and roots in bluegrass would put him in the center of the Dead's development over the next several years. His influence was not only musical, but also social—his charismatic personality combined with his own (and the band's) utter antiauthoritarianism made him a leader who wouldn't lead. Characteristically, he told one reporter, "We don't have any plans. We'll do anything that we like. There's no reason to restrict yourself. A plan is only something to deviate from and none of us have the kind of minds that are capable of planning, anyway." Instead, he set an example—he just plain loved to play.

Their debt to Warner Bros. and post-Lenny poverty dictated a stripped-down semi-acoustic country-western approach to recording, which was entirely appropriate for the new material. One song they were covering around that time was Merle Haggard's "Workingman's Blues"; one night Garcia murmured to Hunter as they drove home from the session that this album was turning into the *Workingman's Dead* version of the band— and so it was. A year later, he would say of the album that they were "out of our pretentious thing... not an experimental music group but... a good old band"—in other words, a band that very much resembled the bands that he had first organized in Palo Alto in 1961.

Thanks to Hunter's postmodern lyrics, the songs they were now recording—the miner's lament "Cumberland Blues," the pedal-steel romance of "High Time," and the stark old-timey death songs "Dire Wolf" and "Black Peter"—were not at all traditional. But Garcia's playing and singing connected them deeply to the American song tradition he and Hunter had trained in a decade before. If Hunter had not been steeped in that material, he would hardly have been able to transcend and create something timeless of his own, something that, because of their closeness, Garcia could sing as his own. And Garcia's voice, while limited in range and power, could communicate emotion as well as any singer alive. The great Dead ballads, either original or covers (such as "Morning Dew") became transcendent moments.

Their audience began to grow dramatically, primarily because the muse was very, very kind to them in 1970. As the year passed, Hunter and the band worked out the greatest of road songs, "Truckin'," for Weir, and then Bobby presented him with the changes to what he thought of as a sweet country ditty, but which became a ripping show-closer, "Sugar Magnolia." Lesh produced what became a tribute to his dying father, "Box of Rain." Garcia didn't do too badly, either—the extraordinary "Attics of My Life," a lovely romantic farewell, "Brokedown Palace," and a truly great country outlaw tune, "Friend of the Devil." And, finally, a prayer/hymn that became one of the greatest of all Dead songs, "Ripple."

Serendipity was always one of the Dead's strengths. They'd scheduled time to be part of a film project sponsored by Warner Bros., the *Medicine Ball Caravan*, which would take several bands and friends across the country in a mobile Woodstock, stopping to put on concerts at various sites. At the last possible second, an unusually sensible member of Dead management decided that there were band members who didn't want to sleep in tepees, and pulled the plug on their participation. This had the happy consequence of giving the band, minus their sound company and regular recording engineers, who stayed with the Caravan, some free time. The band dropped into the Wally Heider studios, met a superb engineer named Steve Barncard, and ended up recording what was probably the best-sounding and definitely the most popular and accessible Dead album ever, *American Beauty*.

By mid-1971, the band had almost recovered from the depredations of Lenny Hart, to the point that they actually started having a few gaps in their calendar. But Jerry's craving for music—pretty much a daily need—demanded more. Garcia recorded a solo (really solo—he played all the instruments except drums) album, *Garcia*, an eclectic mix of music from electronica ("Eep Hour") to a beautiful gospel tune called "The Wheel." Also that summer, although he'd

been appearing on friends' albums already ("Déjà Vu," "Blows Against the Empire," "Songs for Beginners"), Garcia now he began a conscious side career, joining a Monday night jam at the tiny club called The Matrix, led by the very out-there keyboardist Howard Wales, which also included bassist John Kahn, who would be one of Garcia's primary musical life partners. Eventually the quartet began to draw, Wales decided to exit, and they brought in the keyboardist Merl Saunders.

It was at one of these quartet gigs that Garcia was approached by a beautiful woman named Donna Jean Godchaux, who told him, "Well [my husband] Keith is [the Dead's new] piano player, so I'm gonna need your home number so we can keep in touch." Interestingly, the Godchaux couple didn't even know that Pigpen was ill and that the Dead were looking for a pianist—it was merely the sort of convenient cosmic coincidence that was a part of life with the Dead.

On the more serious level, while the band continued to be a bunch of firecracker-loving, music-playing, good-time pirates, they began to create institutions that made them a self-contained behemoth. The most important of these projects was the Grateful Dead Record Company, which came about primarily through Garcia's influence. Though Warner Bros. had treated them well on the whole, it was time, as always, for an adventure, for something… risky. To Garcia, a truly independent record company was "the most exciting option to me just in terms of 'What are

we gonna do now that we're enjoying this amazing success?' The nice thing would be not to sell out at this point and instead come up with something far out and different which would be sort of traditional with us."

The idea was delayed while the band absorbed Keith as a player. One main result was that a logical third album (after *Workingman's Dead* and *American Beauty*) full of tunes like "Tennessee Jed," "Jack Straw," and "He's Gone" became part of a live triple album that documented their monumental jaunt to Europe early in 1972. Once they returned, the idea of a record company became a priority, and as 1973 passed, it became their grail. Their friend Ron Rakow had envisioned a truly independent record company, and proposed that the band not only go it alone but pretty much leave conventional methods entirely behind, at one point suggesting that they sell records from converted ice cream trucks. In the end, the plan was a little more modest; they raised money by selling the international distribution rights to Atlantic, and by the spring of 1973, the Grateful Dead Record Company (GDRC) was a going concern.

As the year passed, Pigpen died from the damage caused by the drinking that he'd finally given up, but the band pressed on. They didn't talk about it much, but it was clear that they hadn't forgotten Pig; you could hear it in *Wake of the Flood*, their next album, the first from GDRC. Tunes like "Eyes of the World" and "Weather Report Suite" touched what one critic called "mythic journeys, the cycle of the seasons, death and rebirth, a good hard look into the dark unknown" but with an "indomitably light heart." Garcia had almost wanted to end the band when they lost Pig, but music so filled his life—the Dead, the side band with Merl and Kahn, and a bluegrass outfit called Old & In the Way—that he recovered his drive.

Along with the independent record company, the band had

committed to a technological vision—a campaign to make a truly great sound system. By 1974, the campaign had been won—and the Dead had also lost. They had created the "Wall of Sound," the most remarkable, beautiful- sounding, awesome-looking piece of electronics ever created—641 speakers behind the band rising the width of the stage and 40 feet high in a solid wall. It was a triumph of design, but so costly that they could not support it. By the summer, as they were putting out the second GDRC album, *Mars Hotel*, they were beginning to mull the process of stopping the train. In October 1974, they played five shows at their home base, Winterland in San Francisco, and the Grateful Dead came to a rest as a touring band.

Although the band couldn't tour, they could still make music. Garcia, of course, was gigging with Kahn and Saunders five days after the "final" Dead concert. But in January the Dead (the whole Dead; Mickey Hart had returned to stay from his self-imposed exile on the last night at Winterland) began to hang out, for the first time going into a studio with no material in hand. Manager Rock Scully later speculated that this period represented an attempt by Garcia to stop his and Hunter's domination of the songwriting process in the band, Weir and Lesh being much less prolific. Perhaps if they started from scratch, Garcia could step back. It didn't work that way—the bulk of the songs were still listed as Hunter/Garcia—but it was still fun. They started simply by noodling without pressure. Notes drifted out of their group subconscious and became chords. Rhythms became beats and then more beats. Hunter joined them, writing lyrics that had a very different feel from the tall tales of a few years before. It was as though they were meditating together, and it was a fascinating collection. The centerpiece was an atonal masterpiece called (as was the album) "Blues for Allah" that took all of side two; yet in years to come, Deadheads would dance like crazy to such bouncy tunes as Garcia and Hunter's "Franklin's Tower."

The Grateful Dead at the Orpheum Theater in San Francisco during their 1976 "comeback" tour. The band introduced a number of new songs and arrangements.

A thousand other things filled their time during what they called their hiatus. These included *The Grateful Dead Movie*, shot during the last run at Winterland, which obsessed Garcia. It cost so much money that—along with other factors—the Grateful Dead Record Company finally went down the tubes in the spring of 1976, shortly after they announced that "vacationing is too exhausting to continue, meaning the Grateful Dead has decided to get back into touring."

But the important thing that happened in that time was, at least to Garcia, that the Dead had passed through the fire and were not consumed. "The survival of the Grateful Dead, I think that's my main trip now… Well, I feel like I've had both trips (the Dead, and an individual one)… And, really, I'm not that taken with my own ideas. I don't really have that much to say, and I'm more interested in being involved in something that's larger than me. And I really can't talk to anybody else either," he said, laughing.

"I just see us as a lot of good-time pirates. I'd like to apologize in advance to anybody who believes we're something really serious."

JERRY GARCIA TO FRANK FEDELE, *ORGAN MAGAZINE, NOVEMBER 1970*

Saturday January 10
Golden Hall, Community Concourse, San Diego, California

With Savoy Brown and Aum.

Friday January 16 ★
Springer's Inn, Portland, Oregon

With River.

Saturday January 17
Oregon State University, Corvallis, Oregon

Sunday January 18
Springer's Inn, Portland, Oregon

JANUARY '70

1 | 2 | 3 | 4 – 9 | 10 | 11 – 15 | 16 | 17

Friday January 2
Saturday January 3
Fillmore East, New York, New York

Early and late shows on both dates with Lighthouse and Cold Blood. Friday's early-show opener, "Mason's Children," appears on 1997's *Fallout from the Phil Zone*. Taking a leaf from Elvis in Vegas, perhaps, the band take the stage at both Friday shows to the stirring strains of Richard Strauss's "Also Sprach Zarathustra," popularly known as "Theme from *2001: A Space Odyssey*."

18 | 19 | 20 | 21 | 22 | 23 | 24 | 25 | 26

Thursday January 22
Friday January 23
Saturday January 24
Sunday January 25
Monday January 26
Honolulu Civic Auditorium, Honolulu, Hawaii

With Jefferson Airplane. The band's five-night run in Honolulu and two shows later in the year *(see page 119)* were the Grateful Dead's only Hawaiian appearances, but the band loved the islands and Hawaii became a popular vacation destination, especially for Jerry Garcia and Bill Kreutzmann; the latter moved to the islands more or less permanently in the mid-1990s. Shortly after returning to the mainland, Tom Constanten decided to leave the band. It was an amicable parting. The Dead's new country-influenced direction wasn't T.C.'s forte, and he had accepted an offer to work on a new musical, Tarot.

"TRUCKIN'"

GARCIA/HUNTER/LESH/WEIR

One of the best songs ever written about the touring experience, "Truckin'," from *American Beauty* (1970), was also the Dead's biggest "hit" for much of the band's three decades together, crawling its way to No. 68 in 1971 before "Touch of Grey" thrust them into the Top Ten almost 17 years later. The ultimate autobiographical account of life with the Dead circa 1970, "Truckin'" detailed the rigors of the road as well as a controversial storm that had been brewing around the band and its merry group of followers at the time, culminating in a well-publicized drug bust in New Orleans *(see above)*. "Busted down on Bourbon Street," Hunter wrote in the song's lyric. "Set up like a bowling pin, knocked down, it gets to wearing thin; they just won't let you be."

Garcia remembered the song as marking a transformation in Hunter's development as a lyricist. "The early stuff he wrote that we tried to set to music was stiff because it wasn't really meant to be sung," he told *Rolling Stone* in 1972. "After he got further and further into it, his craft improved, and then he started going out on the road with us...'Truckin'' is the result of that sort of thing." The version that managed to chart was a hastily-constructed radio edit that was nothing like the extended takes that the Dead would play more than 500 times over the next 25 years, including a November 6, 1977 set-ender from Rochester, New York that many consider the band's best. Recognized by the United States' Library of Congress as a National Treasure in 1997, "Truckin'" also yielded the band's unofficial motto with the line, "Lately it occurs to me, what a long strange trip it's been." The journey moved on with The Other Ones, who continued to play the song starting in 1998.

Busted down on Bourbon Street

The Dead probably shouldn't have taken it so easy in the Big Easy. Members of the Airplane had been busted there recently, and a hotel security guard had tipped off Pigpen that a bust might be imminent. After the first night's show, however, Bill Kreutzmann, Mickey Hart, Bob Weir, and various others gathered in Bob's room for the usual herbal refreshments. The NOPD Narc Squad entered forthwith; like the 710 Ashbury bust *(see page 77)*, this was a PR event, so there seemed to be a battalion of cops present; unlike the 710 bust, these cops had a warrant. Jerry had been out on the town and walked in on the bust; he turned on his heel and almost made it to the elevator before being collared. The cops ransacked the band's rooms (they may have searched the rooms previously, during the show) finding only the room shared by non-druggers T.C. and Pigpen to be clean. And so nineteen people—including Bear, whom the New Orleans *Times-Picayune* declared "the 'King' of Acid," and all the Dead except Pigpen and T.C.—went off to jail. They were bailed out eight hours later by Lenny Hart, who used the proceeds from the night's show.

This was serious; Louisiana's drug laws were particularly draconian. Warner Bros. came to the rescue in the form of Joe Smith, who contacted New Orleans District Attorney Jim Garrison. Smith told Garrison that Warner Bros. intended to make a major contribution to Garrison's upcoming reelection campaign, with the tacit understanding that prosecutors would go easy on those arrested and that the band would avoid the Crescent City. And indeed, the Grateful Dead would not return to Louisiana for seven years *(see page 211)* or to New Orleans for a decade *(see page 255)*. Bear suffered most, since he'd been busted for LSD in '67, and restrictions on his travel would make it increasingly difficult for him to continue as soundman.

Friday January 30
Saturday January 31
The Warehouse, New Orleans, Louisiana

With Fleetwood Mac and the Flock. Most of the band is busted in their hotel after Friday's show. On Saturday, equipment problems led to an acoustic second set, with first performances of "Sawmill," "Old Old House" (often called "Bowed in Memories" or "Bound in Memories"), and "Katie Mae."

"Pigpen and I felt like kids again, wandering through the antique gun shops on Royal Street the afternoon before our first show."
TOM CONSTANTEN,
BETWEEN ROCK & HARD PLACES: A MUSICAL AUTOBIODYSSEY

FILLMORE WEST
38

Thursday February 5
Friday February 6
Saturday February 7
Sunday February 8
Fillmore West, San Francisco, California

With Taj Mahal and Bigfoot for all four shows. Saturday's show, with NRPS also, sees the last performances of "The Green Green Grass of Home" and "Seasons" *(see page 100)*.

FEBRUARY '70

27 | 28 | 29 | 30 | 31 | 1 | 2 | 3 | 4 | 5 | 6 | 7 | 8

Sunday February 1
The Warehouse, New Orleans, Louisiana

The band plays a benefit for itself to defray the legal costs of the bust, with Mick Fleetwood and Peter Green of Fleetwood Mac jamming on "Turn On Your Love Light." Annabelle, daughter of Jerry Garcia and Mountain Girl, is born.

"I called the hotel on Bourbon Street, and the receptionist said 'Sorry, honey, but they're all in jail. The police took them away in the morning!'" MOUNTAIN GIRL, 2003

"Being the Dead, [the band] invited the police who'd arrested them to come to the benefit, and being from New Orleans, the cops had taken them up on the offer."
DENNIS MCNALLY

Wednesday February 4
Family Dog at the Great Highway, San Francisco, California

"Hard to Handle" and "China Cat Sunflower" >"I Know You Rider" from this show are taped by KQED, the Bay Area's public television station, and broadcast on December 13, 1970.

Monday February 2
Fox Theatre, St. Louis, Missouri

The band had been scheduled to play here the previous day, too, but canceled to stay at the Warehouse for the "bust benefit."

February '70 Fillmore Run

The Grateful Dead's six-show run (three nights, two shows a night) at the Fillmore East in February '70 is the stuff of Deadhead legend, with the late, three-set show on February 13 considered by some to be the Night of Nights—perhaps the greatest of the band's 3,200-odd shows.

What made the run so special? For one thing, early '70 found the band at a moment of creative convergence, capable of moving between its newer, more lyrical songs and take-no-prisoners, roof-raising jams. Then there was the ambience of a great venue (including the renowned Joshua Light Show), the special brand of "tough love" for which New York audiences were already renowned, and the energizing and empathetic presence of a true band of brothers, the Allman Brothers. But there was more to this run than any single combination of variables. Deadheads use the term "X Factor" to describe the intangible element that elevates mere performance into something higher; on February 13, 1970, the X Factor was at its highest.

The Show of Shows

It was sometime between 1:00 and 2:00 am by the time Love and the Allmans finished. After the Dead plugged in, a packing-case "coffin" appeared on stage, and out stepped Zacherle, the "Cool Ghoul," a late-night DJ for WNEW, New York's progressive rock FM station. He succinctly introduced the main attraction: "Ladies and Gentlemen, the Grateful Goddamn Dead!" After an electric set, the band played an acoustic set (highlighted by the first performance of the Everly Brothers classic "Wake Up Little Susie"), and then the opening notes of "Dark Star" began the final electric set, "[A] seamless hour of music that launched a million trips: one of the most coherent, fluid, subtle, and adventurous passages of twentieth-century music, in any idiom," in the words of Steve Silberman. Fifteen minutes of solid

applause followed the closer, "Love Light," before the band returned for a soothing "We Bid You Goodnight," and when the doors opened the pale light of a New York winter morning flooded in.

Capturing the Magic

The legendary quality of the February '70 Fillmore East shows was reinforced by the fact that tapes of the shows were among the first to be widely circulated among Deadheads. John Chester, the Fillmore East's sound engineer, surreptitiously patched into the soundboard, and the resulting tapes—the famous "Chester Reels"—were then dubbed by Alan Mande, one of Chester's assistants. Some time later Mande gifted pioneer Taper Bob Menke with copies.

Several songs (mostly from the acoustic sets) from the February 13 and 14 late shows were selected by Bear for *History of the Grateful Dead, Volume 1 (Bear's Choice)*, but it was 26 years before the great second sets made it into "official" release. The result was 1996's *Dick's Picks Volume 4*, with material from both 12/13 and 12/14—because there were gaps in Bear's original 7-inch tapes, bits of the 15-inch Chester tapes were spliced in to fill them.

"The run… provided the quintessential snapshot of the Grateful Dead at their finest. There are several defining strands in Grateful Dead history, but none is as notorious as this, and none is more deserving of the attention, providing showcase versions of almost all the Dead's important songs." JOHN W. SCOTT DEADBASE EDITOR

★ **Wednesday February 11**
Fillmore East, New York, New York

Two shows with Love and the Allman Brothers. At the 11:30 pm show Duane and Gregg Allman and Fleetwood Mac's Peter Green join in for one of the greatest "guest appearances" ever—jamming through "Dark Star" illuminated into the first "Spanish Jam" in nearly two years, into a "Love Light" featuring some of Pigpen's most inspired rapping.

Friday February 13 ★
Saturday February 14 ★
Fillmore East, New York, New York

Two shows on each day, with Love and the Allman Brothers. A three-set extravaganza, the acoustic set of the February 14 late show includes the first performance of the plaintive traditional "Dark Hollow," which, along with "Hard to Handle" and "I've Been All Around This World," appears on 1973's *History of the Grateful Dead, Volume 1 (Bear's Choice)*; the opener, "Casey Jones," and the entire second set appears on 1996's *Dick's Picks Volume 4*.

11 | 12 | 13 | 14 | 15 ~ 19

Thursday February 12
Ungano's Night Club, New York, New York

Little is known about this show, played at a small club frequented by musicians and music-industry "insiders."

Friday February 20
Panther Hall, Fort Worth, Texas

With Quicksilver Messenger Service.

Saturday February 21
San Antonio Civic Center Arena, San Antonio, Texas

20 | 21 | 22 | 23

Monday February 23
Austin Municipal Auditorium, Austin, Texas

Sunday February 22
Sam Houston Coliseum, Houston, Texas

With Lovelight.

Left: Family Dog at the Great Highway, San Francisco, California, Wednesday February 4.

24 | 25 | 26 | 27 | 28

Friday February 27
Saturday February 28
Family Dog at the Great Highway, San Francisco, California

With Commander Cody and the Lost Planet Airmen. Saturday's show features the final performance of "Mason's Children."

"FRIEND OF THE DEVIL"
DAWSON/GARCIA/HUNTER

The only song on which Hunter and Garcia share a credit with New Riders of the Purple Sage member and long-time Dead crony John Dawson almost had a different fate than its place on the band's album *American Beauty* (1970). Says Dawson: "'Friend of the Devil' was written when Bob Hunter was still a prospective member of New Riders… He came up with the opening theme of that song, and he had all the words written out, but he didn't have any music for that particular part." Enter Garcia, who heard a tape of the song while visiting the Riders and, according to Hunter, "snapped it up, much to the New Riders' dismay." The song's original, upbeat tempo was slowed down considerably after Garcia heard a version that Kenny Loggins had worked up as a ballad. "*American Beauty* was the first and most impacting Dead album for me," Loggins explained in 1999. "My rendition came out of my own style and an afternoon of singing songs with pals over lunch." In addition to over 300 live performances by the Dead (the first at Port Chester's Capitol Theater on March 20, 1969) and over 100 more during Garcia's solo shows, other recorded versions of the song appeared on albums by Hunter, the New Riders, and Garcia and David Grisman.

114

During March, Jerry Garcia plays pedal steel on the Crosby, Stills, Nash & Young classic, "Teach Your Children." Given the huge sales and widespread airplay enjoyed by the single and the *Déjà Vu* LP on which it appears, a strong case can probably be made that this is the widest penetration of the public's ear by Jerry, or the Grateful Dead, or any of its members.

MARCH '70

| 1 | 2 | 3 | 4 | 5 | 6 |

Sunday March 1
Family Dog at the Great Highway, San Francisco, California

With Commander Cody and the Lost Planet Airmen.

Saturday March 7
Star Theatre, Phoenix, Arizona

| 7 | 8 | 9 ~ 16 |

Sunday March 8
Santa Monica Civic Auditorium, Santa Monica, California

With Cold Blood. This show may actually have taken place on March 7.

Tuesday March 17
Kleinhans Music Hall, Buffalo, New York

The band plays a benefit for the Buffalo Philharmonic Orchestra; the BPO's musical director is Lukas Foss, a colleague of Luciano Berio *(see page 24)*, mentor to Phil Lesh and Tom Constanten. Members of the orchestra, including percussionist Lynn Harbord, sit in for "Drums."

| 17 | 18 | 19 | 20 | 21 | 22 | 23 |

Friday March 20
Saturday March 21
Capitol Theater, Port Chester, New York

Four shows over two days. Friday's opener is the first of 16 shows in 1970–71 at this venue. The late shows each night feature the same electric-acoustic-electric set format pioneered the previous month at the Fillmore East. Friday's show sees the revival of some **old favorites**—the first "Deep Elem Blues" **since December 1, 1966**, and the first "Don't Ease Me In" since June 6, 1967—and the breakout of a new original credited to Jerry Garcia, Robert Hunter, and John Dawson: "Friend of the Devil." On Saturday the band retires "He Was a Friend of Mine" and "The Seven" (a polyrhythmic jam similar to "The Eleven") and performs Rufus Thomas's "Walking the Dog" for the first time.

Tuesday March 24
Pirate's World, Dania, Florida

| 24 | 25 ~ 31 |

Besides his gigs with the Dead and NRPS, studio work (with Jefferson Airplane/ Starship, Crosby, Stills, Nash & Young, Brewer & Shipley), and the odd movie soundtrack (*Zabriskie Point*), Jerry Garcia somehow found time, in the spring and summer of 1970, to gig regularly at The Matrix with Howard Wales and some friends of his.

APRIL '70

| 1 | 2 | 3 | 4 ~ 8 |

Friday April 3
Field House, University of Cincinnati, Cincinnati, Ohio

With the Lemon Pipers, the one-hit wonders responsible for "Green Tambourine." Ken Kesey was also in attendance. It's also the breakout of "Candyman," a saucy, old-time-sounding Hunter/Garcia original that would stay in the rotation through 277 shows.

Left: The band in one of their typically cooperative moods for a photographer. This is their idea of "holding still." Below: Garcia in a much more relaxed pose.

Larcenous Lenny

In early '70 Lenny Hart was negotiating to take over management of Chet Helms' Family Dog, and it soon became clear to Chet and his associates that Rev. Hart's business methods were unorthodox. When confronted about the disposition of a check that Jerry Garcia was supposed to have received for his soundtrack work on the film *Zabriskie Point* and an ultimatum from Ram Rod of the it's-him-or-me variety, Lenny took off for Mexico with his girlfriend, a bank teller who'd helped cover the tracks of his financial malfeasance.

It became plain that Lenny had been stealing outright, diverting revenue into a Nevada bank account to the tune of at least $150,000. In effect, he'd nearly bankrupted the band. The personal toll on Mickey Hart was immeasurable; he'd been burned by his father in the past, but the revelation of Lenny's treachery plunged him into a depression which was almost suicidal, and which would be a leading factor in his decision, a year later, to take a sabbatical.

In the wake of Lenny's escape the band's management structure and support staff shifted. Rock Scully left off active management for a promotional role, something for which he was more suited. Sam Cutler became road manager. Jon McIntire moved up to overall band management, while the husband–wife team of Dave and Bonnie Parker (Dave had played washboard with Mother McCree's) tackled the books.

Parker soon found them a house in San Rafael, known thereafter as "Fifth and Lincoln," to serve as the band's office. The band also rented a post office box with a number—1073—that would become imprinted in the memories of a couple of generations of Deadheads.

Miles to go

Miles Davis and his acclaimed *Bitches Brew* band opened all four nights of the band's April '70 Fillmore West run, and Miles, to put it mildly, was a hard act to follow. Although the master of cool was mating rock with jazz to create what would be called "fusion," he was a notoriously prickly character and did not suffer rock musicians—most of whom he considered stylistically ignorant and technically weak—gladly. Following Miles was nerve-wracking, but they acquitted themselves well, though there was no interband jamming (one can only dream about what might have been). Miles and Jerry Garcia hit it off personally, while Mickey was awed by percussionist Airto Moreira. Miles/Dead remains one of the most brilliant of Bill Graham's eclectic double bills. The Dead played the electric-acoustic-electric three-set format.

Jerry Garcia and David Grisman later put the Dawg treatment on several Miles tunes, collected on the fourth Garcia/Grisman album, 1998's *So What* (Acoustic Disc ACD-33).

Friday April 24
Saturday April 25
Mammoth Gardens, Denver, Colorado

24	25	26	27	28	29	30

Sunday April 26
York Farm, Poynette, Wisconsin
The "Sound Storm Festival."

"HE'S GONE"
GARCIA/HUNTER

One of the most personal songs in the Dead's catalog, "He's Gone" was written as an unflattering tribute to Lenny Hart, the father of drummer Mickey Hart and the man who served as the group's manager long enough to embezzle a large sum from them (*see left*). The incident caused a rift that would result in the younger Hart leaving the band for over three years. First performed at the Tivoli Gardens in Denmark on April 17, 1972, "He's Gone" was released on the triple album documenting that year's European tour and has appeared on nearly a dozen of the *Dick's Picks* volumes. In later years, the song and its refrain of "Like a steam locomotive rolling down the track, he's gone and nothing's gonna bring him back" served as an apropos eulogy for friends and members of the Dead's extended family who had passed away. Played by the Grateful Dead over 300 times between 1972 and 1995, the song took on new poignancy when The Other Ones started playing it in August 2000.

Howard Wales

Organist Howard Wales had credentials in both the rock and jazz worlds when he and Garcia, bassist John Kahn, and drummer Bill Vitt started jamming informally at The Matrix on Mondays. After toiling in relative anonymity for years, the low-key gig with Garcia significantly elevated Wales' profile. The group cut an instrumental album called *Hooteroll?* for the Douglas label in 1971, and Garcia was "special guest" on a short tour to promote the record. The best showcase of their jazzy, freeform side is on *Side Trips, Volume One*, a live CD released in 1998.

Friday April 17
Saturday April 18
Sunday April 19
Family Dog at the Great Highway, San Francisco, California

With NRPS and Charlie Musselwhite. Friday's show includes the second—and last—performance of the Everly Brothers' "Cathy's Clown." Saturday's show includes the first performances of "Roberta," a traditional tune recorded by Leadbelly, and Lightnin' Hopkins' "The Rub" (a.k.a. "Ain't it Crazy"), and the only known performances of "The Flood" and "Walk Down the Street." Sunday sees the second and last outing for "Roberta" and the third and last for "Sawmill," as well as the breakout of another Lightnin' Hopkins number, "She's Mine." The band may also have played (for the only time) something called "Big Breasa," but this is another "mystery song."

Wednesday April 15
Winterland Arena, San Francisco, California

9	10	11	12	13	14	15

Thursday April 9
Friday April 10
Saturday April 11
Sunday April 12
Fillmore West, San Francisco, California

With Miles Davis, Stone the Crows, and the Clouds. Coming out of a reprise of "Good Lovin'" on Sunday, the band launches into a one-off exercise in western-swing-psychedelia usually rendered as "Cowboy Song" on tape labels. The band also breaks out James Brown's "It's a Man's World" with Pigpen in full effect.

EMENT **STARTS ON PAGE 22**

DEBUT DEAD

San Francisco band booked for Hollywood Fest

THE Grateful Dead, one of the original San Francisco bands, will make their British debut on May 24, at the Hollywood Music Festival. But Captain Beefheart and Steppenwolf, previously announced as appearing at the festival, will not be playing.

Organisers

"Beefheart's manager told me that he couldn't get a band together," said Ellis Elias of the Red Bus Company, organisers of the festival, which will be held near Newcastle-under-Lyme. "Steppenwolf's tour has been cancelled, so we can't have them either."

The Dead, who feature influential guitarist Jerry Garcia, were in at the beginning of the West Coast acid-rock scene, and like the Jefferson Airplane, they have played free at many benefits and open air concerts in San Francisco, as well as being regulars at the Fillmore West and the Avalon Ballroom.

Rumoured

16	17	18	19	20	21	22	23

Hollywood Fest, not just one concert, at the Hollywood Festival, but may tape a television appearance.

Friday April 17
Apollo 13 and its three-man crew, previously bound for the Moon, splashes down safely in the Pacific, four days after a ruptured oxygen tank crippled the spacecraft.

HOLLYWOOD '70

Hollywood, UK

The Grateful Dead had made sketchy arrangements for a European tour in '68, which fell through, and later there were planning meetings (as David Nelson recalled to Blair Jackson) with a view to a European expedition by all the big San Francisco bands; but this was also aborted. So the band's first overseas show would be a one-off—an appearance at the giant Hollywood Festival at Newcastle-under-Lyme in the Midlands of England. (A planned second UK date, in London, fell through.)

Arriving in London and traveling northward by "coach" (bus), the band joined a bill encompassing acts from Mungo Jerry to Black Sabbath to Traffic. Musically, the Dead were pretty much an unknown quantity, but as usual their reputation as the most "hippie" of "hippie bands" preceded them, so they drew a good crowd for their set, performed on an outdoor stage at the Lower Finney Green Farm, in stereotypically damp and cool English weather.

By most accounts it was one of those ragged-but-right performances. Problems with the PA plagued the first part of the set, but as "Dark Star" began, one of those magic moments happened and the X-factor kicked in, as reported below by journalist Dick Lawson in *Frendz*:

"During 'Dark Star,' we lost reality and soared. Above the canopy over the stage, at an exact ninety degrees to the scaffolding and at a height of 30 thousand feet, a silver dart crossed the sky, blazing a double vapour trail. It split the air in two, cracked the sphere. The brilliant blue crumbled. Nothing. Empty. Void. It was as if Captain Trips had been waiting for that moment, expecting it to happen. He picked up the pieces and carefully reassembled them the way he wanted, each note a truer, whiter, blacker high. They moved into the thunderous crashing, bouncing earthquake of 'St. Stephen' and softly into 'Turn on Your Lovelight.'"

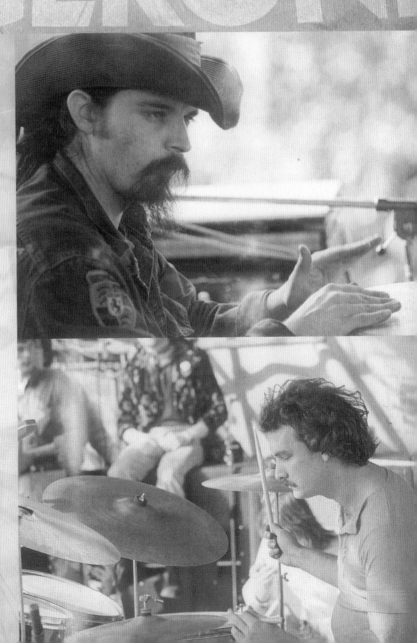

An American Poet in London

In the spring of '70 Robert Hunter became, in effect, a full member of the band, although, equating relative anonymity with artistic autonomy, he would later deliberately lower his profile. But at this point he was on the payroll and he traveled with the group to England, camping in the London flat of Alan Trist *(see page 15)*. A wordsmith like Hunter could not help but feel inspired at being in the land of Shakespeare, Milton, and Blake, and he was further inspired by the case of Greek wine Trist had left in the flat as a welcoming gift. There, in a single day, Hunter wrote the lyrics that became three of the Dead's best-loved songs: "To Lay Me Down," "Ripple" *(see page 358)*, and "Attics of My Life" *(see page 370).*

Right: David Nelson and Garcia in a studio session for the first New Riders album.

May 1970

118

MAY '70

Sunday May 3
Field House, Wesleyan University, Middletown, Connecticut

With NRPS. A free show. The campus is beset by "radicals" in emulation of the near-takeover of Yale.

★ Wednesday May 6
Kresge Plaza, Massachusetts Institute of Technology, Cambridge, Massachusetts

With NRPS. Another free show, this one for striking M.I.T. students. The band meets up with Ned Lagin *(see page 182),* a musician and fan.

Thursday May 7
Dupont Gymnasium, MIT, Cambridge, Massachusetts

With NRPS. The band jams around the Youngbloods' "Darkness, Darkness" during the "Lovelight" closer. It's Bill Kreutzmann's 24th birthday.

Friday May 8
Farrell Hall, SUNY, Delhi, New York

With NRPS.

Saturday May 9
Worcester Polytechnic Institute, Worcester, Massachusetts

With NRPS.

Sunday May 10
Atlanta Sports Arena, Atlanta, Georgia

With the Allman Brothers Band and the Hampton Grease Band, purveyors of "suckrock." The Allmans join the Dead for the band's only performance of "Will the Circle Be Unbroken."

Thursday May 14
Merramec Community College, Kirkwood, Missouri

With NRPS, who join the Dead for the acoustic encore, "Cold Jordan." "Attics of My Life" debuts.

★ Friday May 15
Fillmore East, New York, New York

Two shows. With NRPS, the Guess Who, Cold Blood, and Buddy Miles. The early show's "Easy Wind" appears on *Fallout from the Phil Zone*. The late show marks the first (traditional) "The Ballad of Casey Jones" and "A Voice from on High" (a.k.a. "I Hear a Voice Callin'"). Dave Nelson joins in on the "Cold Jordan" encore.

Saturday May 16
Temple University, Philadelphia, Pennsylvania

With Cactus, the Steve Miller Band, and Jimi Hendrix.

Sunday May 17
Fairfield University, Fairfield, Connecticut

Tuesday May 19
Washington University, St. Louis, Missouri

With NRPS.

Sunday May 24
Hollywood Festival, Lower Finney Green Farm, Newcastle-Under-Lyme, England

Friday May 1
Alfred College, Alfred, New York

Saturday May 2 ★
Harpur College, SUNY, Binghamton, New York

Harpur College in upstate Binghamton, part of New York's state university system, is a highly progressive little school. Camille Paglia, intellectual firebrand author of *Sexual Personae*, was a Harpur undergrad in the late '60s and later recalled how the campus was "seething with raw creative energy. People called it Berkeley East." Perhaps for this reason, the band feels at home; but for whatever reason, this is another "primal" show, one which many Deadheads would rate as among the band's best, period. The show, in Dennis McNally's words, "was simply staggering, a concert with so much quality in so many styles that it became deservedly legendary."

"You folks should all follow the fine example of the fellow over here who got it on with his girlfriend. And we're gonna take a short break, and I want you all to feel each other for ten minutes while we do. But we'll come back and play some more. Honest we will."

PHIL LESH TO THE AUDIENCE BEFORE INTERMISSION

All Aboard

While *Workingman's Dead* hit the stores, the band embarked on one of its most remarkable adventures, the "Trans-Continental Pop Festival." The idea was to load a private train with rock acts and travel from Toronto to Vancouver, playing shows along the way. As a movable rock festival, it wasn't particularly successful, but as a rolling party and jam session, it passed into rock 'n' roll legend.

On board with the Dead and NRPS were Eric Anderson, Delaney and Bonnie, The Band, Ian and Sylvia and their band, the Flying Burrito Brothers, the Great Speckled Bird, Buddy Guy, Tom Rush, and Janis Joplin. For five days the Express crossed prairie, forest, and mountain, while the 140 or so musicians, crew, and friends jammed, sang, took in the scenery, made love, and drank. (Alcohol was the default drug because people were paranoid about the border crossings; even the normally teetotal Jerry Garcia got tanked on tequila.) Several of the songs the band heard played (including "Me and Bobby McGee," by Kris Kristofferson by way of Janis Joplin, and Woody Guthrie's "Goin' Down the Road Feeling Bad," by way of Delaney Bramlett) became part of the Dead's rotation.

In 1997 almost a hundred hours of film from the trip surfaced. In 2003 a fine film, *Festival Express*, that includes the Dead playing "Candyman" and Garcia playing (on the train) "Cold Jordan," is nearing completion with an expected 2004 release.

"I had flown out to join them. Every time the train stopped they got out to buy more liquor! It was an enormous party that went on and on. No kids, just a very raunchy party! There were gigs along the way, and radio spots to do. The Canadian DJs were very straight, and not at all thrilled with the long hair and everything else." MOUNTAIN GIRL, 2003

1 | 2

3 | 4 | 5 | 6 | 7

8 | 9 | 10 | 11 | 12 | 13 | 14 | 15 | 16 | 17

18 | 19 | 20 | 21 | 22

23 | 24 | 25 ~ 31

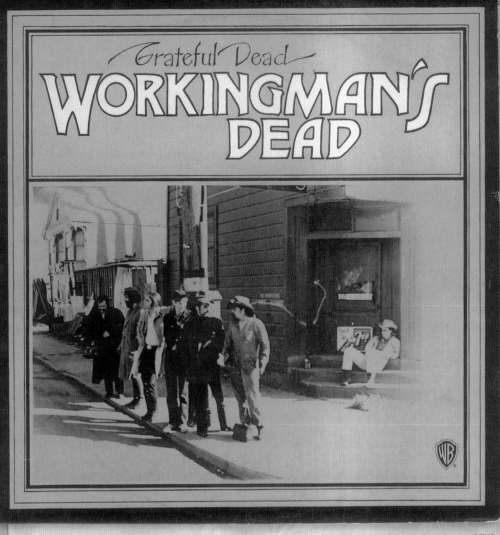

Grateful Dead

WORKINGMAN'S DEAD

WORKINGMAN'S DEAD

Grateful Dead

Released by Warner Bros. (WS-1869) on June 26, 1970

Side One

1. **Uncle John's Band**
   (Garcia/Hunter)
2. **High Time**
   (Garcia/Hunter)
3. **Dire Wolf**
   (Garcia/Hunter)
4. **New Speedway Boogie**
   (Garcia/Hunter)

Side Two

1. **Cumberland Blues**
   (Garcia/Hunter/Lesh)
2. **Black Peter**
   (Garcia/Hunter)
3. **Easy Wind**
   (Hunter)
4. **Casey Jones**
   (Garcia/Hunter)

Personnel

Jerry Garcia – lead guitar, pedal steel guitar, vocals
Bob Weir – guitar, vocals
Phil Lesh – bass, vocals
Pigpen (Ron McKernan) – keyboards, vocals
Bill Kreutzmann – drums
Mickey Hart – drums

Produced by Bob Matthews and Betty Cantor in association with the Grateful Dead

Below: *The album's back cover features Mouse Studios' drawings of the band members.*

As ROUGH-HEWN AND WARM-HUED as the Stanley Mouse cover photo of our heroes on a desolate street corner (the guy standing next to Garcia is Robert Hunter), *Workingman's Dead* marked a major turning point for the Dead and their music. With earlier, fuzzy logic psychedelic forays now giving way to a clearer down-home sensibility in songwriting that had its roots firmly in the soil of the American folk and country idioms rather than some unmapped region of the cosmos, the band decided it was time to get their vocal act together. For inspiration they looked to friends and consummate three-part harmonizers Crosby, Stills and Nash, and while the strains of Garcia, Weir, and Lesh working their way through new vocal challenges like "Uncle John's Band," "High Time,"

and "Cumberland Blues" weren't quite in CSN's league, they marked a quantum leap forward for a group who had spent much of their first few years letting the music do the talking.

"Hearing those guys sing and how nice they sounded together, we thought, 'We can try that. Let's work on it a little,'" Garcia said. "I'd worked in the studio with them and we'd spent some time hanging out. So it was like an inspiration." Another inspiration was to record the album on the cheap. Unlike previous studio excursions with seemingly no end in sight, *Workingman's Dead* was recorded and mixed in just nine days, all at a time when financial and personal pressures were swirling around the band in the form of a falling-out with manager Lenny Hart and the recent bust in New Orleans.

JUNE '70

1 – 3 | 4 | 5 | 6 | 7

Thursday June 4
Friday June 5
Saturday June 6
Sunday June 7
Fillmore West, San Francisco, California

With NRPS and Southern Comfort. Thursday's "Swing Low, Sweet Chariot" is the first, as is Saturday's "Frozen Logger," and "Sugar Magnolia" *(see page 394)* on Sunday, when "The Eleven" is retired and the band plays their only jam on "Louie Louie."

8 | 9 | 10 | 11 | 12 | 13 | 14 – 18

Friday June 12
Saturday June 13
Honolulu Civic Auditorium, Honolulu, Hawaii

With NRPS and Quicksilver both nights plus the Steve Miller Band on Saturday.

19 | 20 | 21

Friday June 19
Mid-South Coliseum, Memphis, Tennessee

With Country Joe & the Fish and Illusion. The South is still not a place to let go—the band are warned that power will be cut if the audience dances.

22 | 23 | 24 | 25

Sunday June 21
Pauley Ballroom, University of California, Berkeley, California

A benefit for American Indian causes.

★ **Wednesday June 24**
Capitol Theater, Port Chester, New York

Two shows with NRPS. With the earlier run at the Capitol *(see March 20–21)*, these gigs are ranked highly by the cognoscenti, and are noted for some of the first high-quality tapes.

26 | 27 | 28 | 29 | 30

Sunday June 28
Coronation Park, Toronto, Canada

A free gig after Garcia concedes to pressure from the local radical "collective."

Saturday June 27
Canadian National Exhibition Hall, Toronto, Canada

Friday June 26
Workingman's Dead is released.

Working up the Charts

June's *Workingman's Dead* was the band's first commercial success. To the utter joy of Joe Smith, the album hit a high of No. 27 on the charts and was certified gold. (It is said that when Joe first heard "Uncle John's Band," it was so different that he suspected he was being pranked.) But as usual there were complications. Warner Bros. released "Uncle John's Band" as a single (with "New Speedway Boogie") in May, but it got little airplay—it was overlong (at about four minutes, thirty seconds) for AM and the lyrics included the *verboten* expletive "Goddamn." Jerry Garcia worked with WB engineers on an "edited" version, which, he later said, wound up an "atrocity" when the engineers ignored his instructions. The single ultimately reached a fairly respectable No. 69.

"Casey Jones," with its cocaine reference, was also problematic in terms of airplay—although the "cocaine song" was an established trope in folk and blues music from the late 19th century on. (Incidentally, cocaine was still a relative novelty, and the band was sniffing it only sporadically as a "stimulant," although they would shortly—with the rest of the rock world—enter a blizzard that would last for a decade.)

There was also concern that the band's fans might not be willing to go down the country road. "We realized we'd done something different [with *Workingman's Dead*]," Bob Weir told an interviewer in 2002, "But we still didn't know if people would like it." They did; of course there were some disappointed that the band had (in the studio at least) moved away from psychedelicized improvisation, but the record's accessibility brought them legions of new fans. The cherry on the critical sundae came at the end of the year when a *Rolling Stone* readers' poll voted *Workingman's Dead* the best rock record of 1970. The runners-up included CSN's *Déjà Vu* and Van Morrison's *Moondance*.

JULY 1970

1   2

🎸 **Wednesday July 1**
Winnipeg Fairgrounds, Winnipeg, Manitoba, Canada

With NRPS.

July 1970

120

🎸 **Friday July 3**
McMahon Stadium, Calgary, Alberta, Canada

With NRPS. Final show of the "Trans-Continental Pop Festival."

🎸 **Wednesday July 8**
Mississippi River Festival, Edwardsville, Illinois

3   4   5   6   7   8

🎸 **Thursday July 9**
🎸 **Friday July 10**
Saturday July 11
Sunday July 12 ★
Fillmore East, New York, New York

Four midnight shows with NRPS. Thursday marks the final performance of "Silver Threads Among the Gold." Saturday's acoustic set includes the only performance of "So Sad (To Watch Good Love Go Bad)" and the breakout of the bluegrass standard "Rosalie McFall." Two acoustic breakouts on Sunday: the traditional "Cocaine Blues" (a.k.a. "Cocaine Habit Blues") and Leroy Carr's "How Long Blues." The show also sees the retirement of "She's Mine" and the band's only performance of "Bring Me My Shotgun."

Below: Mountain Girl, Jerry and friends have a rousing good time backstage at an early-'70s outdoor concert. Note the tie-dye on Garcia. The famous black t-shirts come later.

9   10   11   12   13

🎸 **Tuesday July 14**
🎸 **Thursday July 16**
Euphoria Ballroom, San Rafael, California

With NRPS, David Crosby, and the Rubber Duck Company. Tom Constanten returns as a guest on Tuesday, and David Crosby plays on two songs. It's also the first performance of "El Paso," with Bob Weir, naturally, on lead. On Thursday, a drunk and raucous Janis Joplin guests on "Turn on Your Lovelight."

14   15   16   17 ~ 29   30   31

Thursday July 30 🎸
The Matrix, San Francisco, California

With NRPS. A purely acoustic show, highlighted by the breakout of "To Lay Me Down," a Hunter/Garcia lament to lost love.

"EL PASO"

ROBBINS

Richly evocative of the Old West and perhaps the strongest example of the Dead's enduring passion for cowboy song covers, "El Paso" became a live staple for the band after its first performance on July 14, 1970, and continued as part of their repertoire until July 5, 1995; it is featured on the live album *Steal Your Face* (1976). Country star Marty Robbins wrote the song in 1959, when it charted at No.1, becoming a million-seller and the first country song to be awarded a Grammy. Robbins' career spanned over 30 years, and he continued to write and tour until his death in 1982. A confirmed Old West enthusiast (his grandfather was a Texas Ranger), Robbins penned many Western songs but also recorded everything from country pop to Hawaiian music. "El Paso" was one of many classics that appeared on the legendary album *Gunfighter Ballads and Trail Songs* (1959). The song remains one of the best examples of a peculiar genre that relies on narration by a dead person, and is an early example of the type of "Outlaw Country" later developed by Willie Nelson. Another Robbins song, "Big Iron," was covered by Bob Weir and Kingfish on their debut album.

Above: *The office staff in San Rafael, early '70s (left to right): Dale Franklin, David Parker, Jon McIntire, Sam Cutler (standing), Alan Trist, Bonnie Parker, Annette Flowers, unidentified.*

In the summer of '70, Tom "Big Daddy" Donahue convinced Warner Bros. to underwrite the "Medicine Ball Caravan" that would crisscross the country doing concerts. Who better to star than the Grateful Dead? Donahue lined up Delaney and Bonnie, Alice Cooper, the Youngbloods, and Nik Kershaw, but the band members weren't thrilled with the prospect of living in teepees for two weeks, not to mention the potential such a tour presented for getting busted again. The Dead pulled out but there was indeed a tour, an album, and a movie.

Around this time Bob Weir lived at a ranch on Nicasio Valley Road. Among the people on the scene was Eileen Law, heavily pregnant with the child of roadie Rex Jackson. As Cassidy Law entered the world, Bob worked on a song *(see page 167)* that would be forever linked to the event—and to another Cass[a]dy.

AUGUST '70

| 1 | 2 | 3 | 4 | **5** | 6 ~ 16 |

Wednesday August 5
Golden Hall, Community Concourse, San Diego, California

With NRPS. The Dead's performance is entirely acoustic (as far as can be determined) with two sets, including the final performances of "A Voice from On High" and "The Ballad of Casey Jones," and the band's only known performance of Carl Perkins' barroom ballad "Drink Up and Go Home."

| 17 | **18** | **19** | 20 | 21 | 22 | 23 |

Monday August 17
Tuesday August 18
Wednesday August 19
Fillmore West, San Francisco, California

With NRPS. Tuesday is a big night for breakouts, with three new originals, two of them soon to be certified Dead classics: "Box of Rain," "Truckin" *(see page 112)*, and "Operator," the latter one of only four Pigpen originals recorded by the band. The band retires three acoustic numbers on Wednesday: "Cocaine Blues," "Swing Low, Sweet Chariot," and "Cold Jordan."

| 24 | 25 | 26 | 27 | **28** | **29** | **30** | 31 |

Friday August 28
Saturday August 29
The Club, Los Angeles, California

With NRPS.

Sunday August 30
KQED Studios, San Francisco, California

The band plays "Easy Wind," "Casey Jones," "Candyman," "Brokedown Palace," and "Uncle John's Band" for KQED's Calibration show, which is also broadcast on radio.

"BOX OF RAIN"
HUNTER/LESH

Easily one of the most personal songs in the entire Dead canon, "Box of Rain" is also one of the most popular of bassist Phil Lesh's contributions to the group, as well as the track the band chose to kick off their classic LP *American Beauty* (November 1970). Written in August 1970 with lyricist Robert Hunter, who once commented that he had scribbled the tune's words "as fast as the pen would pull," "Box of Rain" served as a tribute to Lesh's sick father and is packed with symbolic imagery, from the "walk into splintered sunlight" that echoes common reports of near-death experiences to the cleansing rain that promises to "ease the pain." "Phil Lesh wanted a song to sing to his dying father and had composed a piece complete with every vocal nuance but the words," Hunter wrote in the compendium of lyrics he named after the song. "If ever a lyric 'wrote itself,' this did." "I sort of identified that song with my dad and his approaching death," Lesh said in filmmaker Jeremy Marre's documentary *Classic Albums: Anthem to Beauty*. "The lyrics that (Hunter) produced were so apt, so perfect. It was very moving, very moving for me to experience that during the period of my dad's passing." So personal was the track that unlike the rest of the songs from *American Beauty*, "Box of Rain" didn't appear in the Dead's live set until late in 1972, and even then only sporadically. When it was reintroduced in 1986 after a 13-year absence, it often appeared as the band's response to an increasingly common Lesh fan chant of "Let Phil sing." After serving as the very last song the Dead would ever play live with Jerry Garcia, "Box of Rain" routinely appeared in sets by Lesh's side project, Phil and Friends, as well as in sets by The Other Ones.

Thursday September 17
Friday September 18
★ Saturday September 19
★ Sunday September 20
Fillmore East, New York, New York

With NRPS. The second show features the last performance of "It's A Man's World" and the first performance of Hunter/Garcia's "Till the Morning Comes," which the band only played live five times, and never after the end of this year. On Saturday Pigpen sings "Good Mornin' Little Schoolgirl" for the last time. On the final night David Grisman and David Nelson guested on mandolin during the Dead's acoustic set. The band introduces the "Goin' Down That Road Feeling Bad Jam" in "Not Fade Away."

SEPTEMBER '70

1 – 7	8	9	10	11	12	13	14	15	16	**17**	**18**	**19**	**20**

Friday September 18
Death of Jimi Hendrix.

Tuesday September 8
Jerry Garcia's mother Ruth (now Ruth Matusiewicz) is severely injured in a freak car accident on September 8—she fails to set her parking brake while trying to free her dog from between the gas pedal and the brake, where it had somehow become caught. She finally passed away three weeks later. Within the same timeframe, Phil Lesh's father Frank died of cancer. Intimations of mortality would be plainly evident in the band's upcoming songs.

Richard Loren

During September's Fillmore East run, Jerry Garcia caught up with David Grisman *(see page 28)*, who was then managing a promising new act, the Rowan Brothers, with a partner, Richard Loren. Jerry and Richard hit it off and after Loren, Grisman, and the Rowans lit out for the West Coast later in the year, Loren began managing Jerry's burgeoning solo career. Eventually he took on a management role (including acting as a booking agent) for the Dead.

122

VINTAGE DEAD
Grateful Dead

Released by Sunflower (SUN-5001) in October 1970

Side One
1. **I Know You Rider**
   (Traditional arr. Grateful Dead)
2. **It Hurts Me Too**
   (James)
3. **It's All Over Now, Baby Blue**
   (Dylan)
4. **Dancin' In The Streets**
   (Stevenson/Gaye/Hunter)

Side Two
1. **In The Midnight Hour**
   (Cropper/Pickett)

Personnel

Jerry Garcia – lead guitar, vocals
Bob Weir – rhythm guitar
Pigpen (Ron McKernan) – organ, vocals
Bill Kreutzmann – drums
Phil Lesh – bass

Produced by Robert Cohen

VINTAGE, PERHAPS, BUT THIS MAJOR LABEL live release and its companion disc *Historic Dead* serve as prime examples of why the Dead were wary of record labels to begin with. Culled from recordings made at the Avalon Ballroom in San Francisco in September of 1966, the material from *Vintage Dead*—basically versions of five of the group's favorite cover songs, including "I Know You Rider" and "Midnight Hour"—was originally envisioned as part of a suite of live albums that was also to include discs by Jefferson Airplane and the Charlatans, all recorded by Avalon co-partner Robert Cohen. When MGM bought the tapes behind his back and released the discs on their Sunflower label, Cohen's knee-jerk reaction was to erase the recordings he had made of the other groups, drawing the ire of music historians for decades to come. Though the circumstances surrounding its release were dubious, *Vintage Dead*, with its John Pierce cover artwork, provided a rare 40-minute glimpse of the group's magic in an era before their tapes became more widely circulated.

> "Here it is, in its liveness, pressed on acetate for those who were not there when the Avalon was."
>
> ROBERT COHEN, ALBUM LINER NOTES

Saturday September 26
Terrace Ballroom,
Salt Lake City, Utah

Sunday October 4
Death of Janis Joplin.

21	22	23	24	**25**	**26**	27 – 30

Saturday October 10
Colden Auditorium,
Queens College,
Queens, New York

With NRPS. The first full "Feeling Bad."

Friday September 25
Pasadena Civic Auditorium, Pasadena, California

OCTOBER '70

1	2	3	**4**	5	6 – 9	**10**	**11**

Jimi Hendrix 1942 – 1970

The usually ebullient Fillmore East crowd was subdued by the news that Jimi Hendrix had died in London the previous night—September 18. Born in Seattle, James Marshall Hendrix served in the 101st Airborne before working as a sideman for R&B acts like the Isley Brothers and Ike Turner. Eventually, he moved to England and put together his band the Jimi Hendrix Experience. Their first album (*Are You Experienced?*, 1967) and legendary performance at Monterey *(see page 73)* finally brought him great honor in his own land. In the mere three years that remained of his life, he produced only two (though extraordinarily fine) studio albums—*Axis: Bold as Love* and *Electric Ladyland*—and a torrent of later-released jams, yet few musicians have had such an astonishing influence in such a brief period of fame.

Sunday October 4
Monday October 5
Winterland Arena, San Francisco, California

With NRPS, Quicksilver, the Airplane and Hot Tuna. Another simulcast on KQED TV and FM radio—state-of-the art quadraphonic stereo, the first in history, actually, with KSAN and KQED joining forces to provide four channels of sound. The second Winterland show is the last at which the Dead share a stage with old friends and friendly rivals Quicksilver.

Sunday October 11
Marion Shea Auditorium,
Patterson State College,
Wayne, New Jersey

Above right: With Pigpen leading the charge (and some help from the light show operator) the Dead get the crowd going with a version of "Turn On Your Lovelight."
Right: The Airplane's Paul Kantner and Grace Slick confer with Bill Graham, as Garcia looks on.

Saturday October 17
Cleveland Music Hall, Cleveland, Ohio
With NRPS.

Saturday October 24
Kiel Opera House,
St. Louis, Missouri

25 | 26 | 27 | 28 | 29 | 30 | 31

Friday October 30
Saturday October 31
Gymnasium, SUNY, Stony Brook, New York

12 - 15 | 16 | 17 | 18 | 19 | 20 | 21 | 22 | 23 | 24

Friday October 16
Irvine Auditorium, University of
Pennsylvania, Philadelphia, Pennsylvania
With NRPS. It's Bob Weir's 23rd birthday.

Sunday October 18
Tyrone Guthrie Theater,
Minneapolis, Minnesota
Early and late shows, with NRPS.

Friday October 23
McDonough Arena, Georgetown
University, Washington, D.C.
With NRPS.

Four shows in two days with NRPS. Saturday's late show
is Halloween night, and "Viola Lee Blues" goes to the
grave after 32 documented performances since early '66
(Given "Viola's" heavy rotation in the band's early days,
this is probably a significant undercount.)

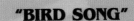

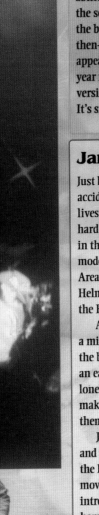

"BIRD SONG"
GARCIA/HUNTER

One of the gentlest and most melodic entries in the Dead oeuvre, "Bird Song" appeared on Jerry Garcia's debut solo disc *Garcia* (1972) before being adopted by the Dead to become one of their most compelling ballads ever. "All I know is, something like a bird within her sang," Garcia murmurs, taking us on a journey with a songbird who eventually takes flight. The transformation of the track from a studio cut to a live offering could at times test the limits of the band's singing abilities, though when delivered flawlessly, the high note appearing at the end of the song's bridge section was arguably the most transcendent vocal moment in the band's entire catalog. Hunter later revealed that the song was inspired by the then-recently-deceased Janis Joplin with an inscription reading "For Janis" that appeared with the lyrics of the song in his book *A Box of Rain*. After a seven-year retirement during the '70s, the song reappeared in a bare new acoustic version in 1980 and remained in the group's electric repertoire through 1995. It's since been resurrected by the Other Ones.

Janis Joplin 1943 – 1970

Just before the October 4 show the band heard of another death: Janis Joplin had accidentally overdosed on heroin at a Hollywood motel. Having shared their lives since Palo Alto, Janis was like family to the Dead, so her death hit them hard. Born in Texas, Joplin was the quintessential kid who couldn't fit in, and in the blues of Ma Rainey and Bessie Smith she found a means of expression, a model for living, and a shield for her vulnerability. After moving to the Bay Area, then going back to Texas, she returned again to San Francisco—at Chet Helms' instigation—and joined her awesome vocal talents to Big Brother and the Holding Company's instrumental power.

As with Hendrix, Monterey made Joplin a true star—she shot to the top in a milieu that was generally something of a boys' club. But she could be one of the boys, drinking, drugging, and screwing *con mucho gusto*. All this made Joplin an early feminist icon, but the whiskey and dope did little to ease her fundamental loneliness. She once famously described her life as making love to thousands of people onstage and then going home alone.

Joplin left Big Brother toward the end of 1968 and the next year released a fine album backed by the Kozmic Blues Band. By late 1969 she was moving away from blues into gentler, more introspective material. She also seemed happy and in control, making her death seem that much more tragic. *Pearl*, her final album, was released posthumously and yielded a massive hit, "Me and Bobby McGee," which would be performed by the Grateful Dead more than 100 times. Pearl was Joplin's nickname, and a fitting one: she made something sublime and eternal from the grit of her everyday life.

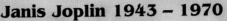

THE GRATEFUL DEAD

AMERICAN BEAUTY
Grateful Dead
*Released by Warner Bros. (WS-1893)
in November 1970*

Side One
1. **Box Of Rain**
   (Hunter/Lesh)
2. **Friend Of The Devil**
   (Garcia/Hunter/Dawson)
3. **Sugar Magnolia**
   (Hunter/Weir)
4. **Operator**
   (McKernan)
5. **Candyman**
   (Garcia/Hunter)

Side Two
6. **Ripple**
   (Garcia/Hunter)
7. **Brokedown Palace**
   (Garcia/Hunter)
8. **Till The Morning Comes**
   (Garcia/Hunter)
9. **Attics Of My Life**
   (Garcia/Hunter)
10. **Truckin'**
    (Garcia/Hunter/Lesh/Weir)

Personnel
Jerry Garcia – guitar, pedal steel, piano, vocals
Phil Lesh – bass, guitar, piano, vocals
Bob Weir – guitar, vocals
Pigpen (Ron McKernan) – harmonica, vocals
Mickey Hart – percussion
Bill Kreutzmann – drums
Dave Torbert – bass on "Box Of Rain"
Dave Nelson – electric guitar on "Box Of Rain"

124

IN CONTRAST TO THEIR EXTENDED studio frolicking of the 1960s, *American Beauty* was more music to the ears of the Dead's record label—a collection of countrified rock songs and folksy ballads that would mark the band's closest pass at a masterpiece and their last studio effort for Warner Bros.

The cover of *American Beauty* featured a Mouse and Kelley rendering of a dark red rose surrounded by the title in shiny, ornate letters that can also be seen to read "American Reality," a Zen-like twist that managed to capture the odd duality of being the Dead. Featuring some of the group's most personal work, the album's songs of reflection ("Box of Rain"), frivolity ("Sugar Magnolia"), and reality ("Truckin'") were inspired by events of the time. "My mother died while we were making *American Beauty*," Garcia said. "And Phil's father died. It was raining down hard on us while that record was going on. They're good tunes, though."

Having just learned the joys of economy with *Workingman's Dead*, the band had entered Wally Heider Recording Studios in San Francisco as a mean, lean playing machine. With a few close friends along for the ride (the New Riders, David Grisman, Howard Wales, and Ned Lagin all appear on the album), they proceeded to lay down a true classic. "*American Beauty* shows the Grateful Dead's playing, singing and songwriting skills in full stride," Hunter wrote in the 1994 Dead dictionary *Skeleton Key*.

The album's title was suggested by Christine Bourne, friend of Robert Hunter; she nominated *Big Full Fat American Beauty Rose*, which was pruned down to *American Beauty*.

> ## "They said they had an album coming out and immediately the rose came to me."
> ALTON KELLY TO BLAIR JACKSON

NOVEMBER
'70

| 1 – 4 | 5 | 6 | 7 | 8 | 9 | 10 | 11 |

Monday November 9
Tuesday November 10
Action House, Island Park, New York
With NRPS.

Monday November 16
Fillmore East, New York, New York
With NRPS and Hot Tuna.

Saturday November 21
Sargent Gym, Boston University, Boston, Massachusetts
With NRPS. New friend Ned Lagin guests on keyboards.

Sunday November 22
Middlesex County Community College, Edison, New Jersey

Friday November 27
The Syndrome, Chicago, Illinois

| 17 ~ 19 | 20 | 21 | 22 | 23 | 24 – 26 | 27 |

Thursday November 5
Friday November 6
Saturday November 7
Sunday November 8 ★
Capitol Theater, Port Chester, New York
With NRPS. Early and late shows on Friday.

Wednesday November 11
Thursday November 12
Friday November 13
Saturday November 14
46th St. Rock Palace, Brooklyn, New York
With NRPS.

| 12 | 13 | 14 | 15 | 16 |

Friday November 20
The Palestra, University of Rochester, Rochester, New York
With NRPS.

Saturday November 21
A live radio show at WBCN Studios, Boston, featuring Duane and Gregg Allman, Garcia, and Weir.

Monday November 23
Anderson Theater, New York, New York
A benefit for the New York chapter of the Hells Angels.

Right: Garcia at Wally Heider Recording Studio, San Francisco, December 1970.

An excerpt from the *Live/Dead* version of "Dark Star" and an original instrumental piece, "Love Scene," by Jerry Garcia were included on *Zabriskie Point*, released this year, an instant art-house classic by Michelangelo Antonioni of *Blow-Up* fame.

DECEMBER '70

| 28 | **29** | 30 | 1 - 11 | **12** | **13** | 14 | **15** | 16 | **17** | 18 | 19 | **20** |

Sunday November 29
Club Agora, Columbus, Ohio

With NRPS. The first performance (of 118) of "Me and Bobby McGee."

Saturday December 12
Santa Rosa Fairgrounds, Santa Rosa, California

With NRPS.

Tuesday December 15
Wednesday December 16
Thursday December 17
Another short-term Grateful Dead spinoff forms for a few shows at The Matrix, San Francisco. This time it's Jerry Garcia, Phil Lesh, Mickey Hart, and David Crosby, playing as" Jerry Garcia & Friends" or "Acoustic Grateful Dead."

Cool Publishing

The Grateful Dead was unusual for its time in retaining publishing rights to its music *(see page 60)*, but the band needed someone to manage its publishing. Toward the end of 1970 Jon McIntire and the band invited Alan Trist *(see page 15)*, then working for the Tavistock Institute, a prestigious progressive think-tank, to run the band's nascent publishing operation, Ice Nine, which would handle all the rights for the band's original songs, deal with licensing, publish songbooks, and the like. Trist accepted and began working out of the San Rafael office.

Monday December 21
The same Crosby/Garcia/Lesh/Hart lineup as the preceding Matrix shows, although the Pepperland, San Rafael gig is billed as "Acoustic Grateful Dead."

Wednesday December 23
Winterland Arena, San Francisco, California.

"Acoustic Grateful Dead" with NRPS, Hot Tuna, and Lizard. A dual benefit concert, for a Montessori School, and for Bear's ongoing legal battles.

125

December 1970

BLOWS AGAINST THE EMPIRE

Paul Kantner/Jefferson Starship

Released by RCA (LSP 4448) (SF 8163) in November 1970

Side One
1. **Mau Mau (Amerikon)**
   (Covington/Kantner/Slick)
2. **The Baby Tree**
   (Sorrels)
3. **Let's Go Together**
   (Kantner)
4. **Child Is Coming**
   (Crosby/Kantner/Slick)

Side Two
5. **Sunrise**
   (Slick)
6. **Hijack**
   (Balin/Blackman/Kantner/Slick)
7. **Home**
   (Kantner/Nash/Sawyer)
8. **Have You Seen the Stars Tonite**
   (Crosby/Kantner)
9. **XM**
   (Garcia/Hart/Kantner/Sawyer)
10. **Starship**
   (Balin/Blackman/Kantner/Slick)

Personnel
Paul Kantner — guitar, vocals, banjo, bass machine
Grace Slick — piano, vocals
Harvey Brooks — bass
Jack Casady — bass
Joey Covington — drums, congas
David Crosby — guitar, vocals
David Freiberg — vocals
Jerry Garcia — guitar, banjo, pedal steel
Mickey Hart — percussion
Peter Kaukonen — guitar
Bill Kreutzmann — drums
Graham Nash — congas, vocals

THE SCIENCE-FICTION CONCEPT ALBUM was conceived by the Airplane's Paul Kantner and executed by the "Planet Earth Rock 'n' Roll Orchestra," an informal ensemble of players from all the Bay Area bands (and some from beyond the Bay) with its headquarters at Wally Heider's Studio.

Blows Against the Empire (which also marked the point the Airplane became the Starship) was certainly P.E.R.R.O.'s most ambitious undertaking. Taking a (loose) leaf from Robert Heinlein's *Stranger in a Strange Land*, the album envisioned an outer-space utopia founded by rockers aboard a hijacked spacecraft. (Kantner once suggested that if Bear was supplied with a private island, the proper tools, and $50 million, he could build a starcruiser himself.) Whether the concept is pretentious or progressive, the album contains some delightful music, much of it courtesy of various members of the Dead. Retrospectively, *Blows* seems like the last great flowering of the musical idealism and collaborative spirit that had taken root in and around San Francisco half a decade earlier.

| **21** | **22** | **23** | 24 | 25 |

Tuesday December 22
Sacramento Memorial Auditorium, Sacramento, CA

With NRPS.

Saturday December 26
Sunday December 27
Monday December 28
Legion Stadium, El Monte, California

Saturday's show sees the final "Till the Morning Comes." NRPS joins the band for Sunday and Monday's gigs.

Sunday December 27
Jerry Garcia and Bob Weir do a radio interview at KPPC Studios, Pasadena, and harmonize with John "Marmaduke" Dawson and David Nelson on some Sunday night music, including "Swing Low, Sweet Chariot," "Sunday Quartet," and "Cold Jordan."

| **26** | **27** | **28** |

| 29 | 30 | **31** |

Thursday December 31
Winterland Arena, San Francisco, California

Back in the Bay Area for New Year's Eve, the Dead played Winterland with NRPS, Hot Tuna and Stoneground, part of which was televised on KQED and broadcast on KSAN FM. Each one of the balloons that drop at midnight has a hit of Orange Sunshine attached.

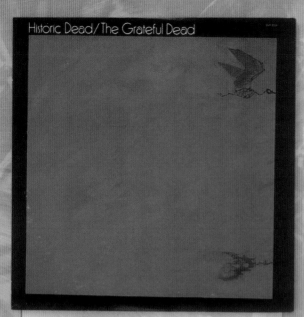

Historic Dead / The Grateful Dead

"DEAL"

GARCIA/HUNTER

Lyricist Robert Hunter's penchant for songs about gambling makes an early appearance in "Deal," a cautionary tale of playing the odds both in cards and in life that served as the lead track on Jerry Garcia's debut solo release *Garcia* (1972) but had been part of the Dead's musical corpus since the year before. The song's refrain echoes the title of the traditional folk song "Don't Let Your Deal Go Down" almost word for word, though the admonitions that appear throughout its verses are pure Hunter. "Goes to show you don't ever know," he advises at the end of each of the track's three verses. "Watch each card you play and play it slow. Don't you let that deal go down." "In songs like 'Deal,' there are almost definite instructions being given on how to approach things," the lyricist acknowledged in 1986. In addition to over 400 performances with the Dead that spanned 24 years between 1971 and 1995, during which the song evolved into one of the most explosive in the band's arsenal, Garcia played his classic rocker in almost 300 solo gigs. The Other Ones brought it back in August 2000.

HISTORIC DEAD
Grateful Dead

HOT ON THE HEELS of its previous live release *Vintage Dead (see page 122)*, MGM released this second disc of Grateful Dead concert tapes circa 1966 on its Sunflower imprint, much to the consternation of the band's "official" major label Warner Bros. Recorded at the Avalon Ballroom and The Matrix in San Francisco as part of an abandoned slice-of-history multi-disc project that was to chronicle the San Francisco rock scene, the disc included just four songs timing out at a paltry 28 minutes, though rare covers of "Lindy" and "Stealin'" alone were worth the price of the vinyl and the album stood as one of the best-quality recordings of the era for decades until the Dead themselves began mining their own extensive vault of early classics in the 1990s.

Released by Sunflower (SNF-5004) in 1971

Side One
1. **Good Morning Little Schoolgirl**
   (Williamson)
2. **Lindy**
   (Traditional arr. Grateful Dead)

Side Two
1. **Stealin'**
   (Cannon/Traditional)
2. **The Same Thing**
   (Dixon)

Personnel

Jerry Garcia – guitar, vocals
Bill Kreutzmann – drums
Phil Lesh – bass
Pigpen (Ron McKernan) – keyboards, harmonica, vocals
Bob Weir – guitar, vocals

Produced by Robert Cohen (Side 1) and Peter Abram (Side 2)

In early 1971 Jerry Garcia (and occasionally Mickey Hart and Bill Kreutzmann) continued to visit Wally Heider's studio to work on Planet Earth Rock 'n' Roll Orchestra projects. At the same time, the full band rehearsed a number of new originals, several of which would debut during February's Capitol Theater run.

JANUARY '71

1 ~ 20   21

Thursday January 21
Freeborn Hall,
University of California,
Davis, California

With NRPS. Mickey Hart sits out this show.

Friday January 22
Lane Community College, Eugene, Oregon

With NRPS. Ken Babbs introduces the band.

22   23   24   **25**   26

Monday January 25
Seattle Center Arena, Seattle, Washington

With NRPS.

Left: Garcia in January 1971, a month before the Dead introduced a slew of great new tunes (see next page).

FEBRUARY '71

1 ~ 16

A Big Week at the Capitol

The band's six-night run with NRPS at the Capitol (the last shows at this venue) was one of the most eventful weeks in their history: in Dennis McNally's words, "In the course of a week's residence, the Dead helped with a scientific experiment, lost a drummer, added a lyricist, and introduced eight new songs, seven of them original."

Five new originals were broken out on the first night, all of them significant additions to the Dead's canon: "Bertha" *(see page 62)*, "Greatest Story Ever Told," "Loser," "Playing' In The Band" *(see page 429)*, and "Wharf Rat" *(see page 384)*. "Greatest" first hit vinyl on Bob's '72 solo album *Ace* and appeared again a few months later on Mickey's *Rolling Thunder* LP, under its working title, "Pump Song." The band would perform "Greatest" 271 times, although it wasn't on any official release until 1981's *Reckoning*. "Loser" is a brilliant Hunter/Garcia portrait of the degenerate gambler, glorying in denial of reality as he draws to fill that inside straight—and yet being somehow affirmed, even transfigured in that moment when the card leaves the deck: "Put your gold money where your love is, baby…." "Loser" would be dealt into 345 shows and appear on '81's *Dead Set*. "Bird Song" *(see page 123)* and "Deal" were broken out on Friday.

ESP experiments at shows

Dr. Stanley Krippner, a leading researcher into Extra Sensory Perception (ESP), enlisted the Grateful Dead's help in an experiment to establish whether or not, in his words, "sleeping subjects are able to incorporate aspects of randomly selected target stimuli into their dreams." In other words, could a group of people mentally transmit an image into the subconscious of someone fast asleep—and would the sleeper remember the image upon awakening? What if the "transmitter" group had their own consciousness modified through music and/or psychedelics—like the audience at a Dead show? Krippner connected with the Dead through Mickey Hart, who met him at a party for one of the drummer's musical mentors, Ustad Allarakha. The doctor had already performed a pilot experiment using another group, the Holy Modal Rounders, best-remembered today for contributing "If You Want to Be a Bird" to the *Easy Rider* soundtrack (Richie Havens was one of the "sleep subjects"). Finding the results "statistically significant," Krippner and his associates—via a suggestion from Jerry—decided on a large-scale, six-night experiment based around the Dead's Capitol run.

And so, at precisely 11:30 p.m. on each night of this run—when the band would be well into the second set—the following sequence of slides was

Above: The Capitol, February 1971.

projected above the stage: 1. You are about to participate in an ESP experiment; 2. In a few seconds you will see a picture; 3. Try using your ESP to "send" this picture to Malcolm Bessent; 4. He will try to dream about the picture. Try to "send" it to him; 5. Malcolm Bessent is now at the Maimonides Dream Laboratory in Brooklyn. (Bessent was the great nephew of the great mystic and activist Annie Besant (1847–1933), founder of the Theosophical movement and an early supporter of independence for India. Wheels within wheels… .) Next, one of Krippner's assistants opened a randomly selected envelope containing a slide of some figurative piece of artwork—Magritte's *Castle of the Pyrenees*, for example. Then the audience was supposed to mentally beam the image to Bessent, who was about 50 miles to the south.

Krippner and his colleagues Charles Honorton and Montague Ullman reported their findings in "ESP and the Dream phase of sleep explored with The Grateful Dead," published in the *Journal of the American Society of Psychosomatic Dentistry and Medicine*. The researchers concluded that, compared to those of a "control" sleeper, Bessent's results were, as with the earlier experiment, "statistically significant," though they noted that "future work is needed to explore this intriguing possibility." It certainly was an intriguing sideline for the band, even if some audience members treated the experiment with bemused indifference.

Mickey leaves the band

The first Capitol gig would be Mickey's last before going on indefinite hiatus. The band and its family held him blameless regarding his father's thievery *(see page 115)* and indeed everyone was supportive, but Lenny Hart's shenanigans took a deep psychic toll that manifested itself in depression, sleep problems, and finally a stress-related mental and physical near-breakdown. "Confused, unbalanced, I wanted to flee and hide, bury my head and cry," he later said. He stayed on the band's payroll and, with a three-album solo contract from Warner Bros., settled down in the Barn at his Novato ranch. Mickey didn't exactly rusticate: he built a 16-track studio at the Barn, recorded *Rolling Thunder* (1972—see page 148) and *Diga* (1976—see page 185), played on solo albums by Robert Hunter and Ned Lagin, and continued his lifelong exploration of percussion and rhythm, and their role in human society. Mickey also rejoined the band, de facto, on 10/20/74 for the Winterland show, "the Last One" *(see page 175)*, after which the rest of the band took a breather of their own. He was a significant contributor to "Blues for Allah," and when regular performances began in June '76, the four-armed attack of the Rhythm Devils was back in effect.

★ **Thursday February 18**
ESP Experiment Show,
Capitol Theater, Port Chester,
New York

Friday February 19
ESP Experiment Show,
Capitol Theater, Port
Chester, New York

Saturday February 20
ESP Experiment Show, Capitol
Theater, Port Chester, New York

Sunday February 21
ESP Experiment
Show, Capitol Theater,
Port Chester, New York

Tuesday February 23
ESP Experiment Show, Capitol
Theater, Port Chester, New York

Wednesday February 24
ESP Experiment Show, Capitol Theater,
Port Chester, New York

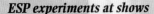

17 18 19 20 21 22 23 24 25 26 27 28

Steve Parish

Big, loud, and aggressive, Steve Parish epitomized the tough, biker side of the Grateful Dead road crew, a dedicated but crazy group Garcia once said was "merciless; they'll just gnaw you like a dog." Originally from New York, he befriended GD crew members Ram Rod and Rex Jackson during some New York-area shows in 1969 and within two years had moved to the San Francisco Bay Area and become part of the crew. He would stay with the Dead for the rest of their history and enjoyed a particularly close relationship with Garcia, humping equipment for the guitarist's many solo bands beginning in the early '70s, and acting as guitar tech and, later, road manager for the Jerry Garcia Band. Most recently Parish managed Bill Kreutzmann's group The Trichromes.

With the departure of TC and Mickey Hart the band returned to being a quintet. There were also changes that reflected the Dead's established status as a touring act; for the April college tour they used buses. As the band now owned Alembic *(see page 102)* outright, Bob Matthews toured with a sound crew including Bill "Kidd" Candelario *(see page 82)*, Steve Parish *(above)* and Sparky Raizene, with Joe Winslow driving the truck. The Dead/NRPS stage crew included Ram Rod, Rex Jackson, and Sonny Heard.

March 1971

MARCH '71

1 | 2 | 3 | 4 | 5

Wednesday March 3
Fillmore West, San Francisco, California

The "Airwaves Benefit," with Gestalt Fool Theatre Family, the American Indian Dancers, the New Generation Singers, and Shades of Joy. The last group featured sax man Martin Fierro, who later contributed to *Wake of the Flood (see page 161)*, played eight shows with the Dead in 1973, and was also a member of the Legion of Mary *(see page 173)*.

"MAMA TRIED"
HAGGARD

Another of the many country songs that guitarist Bob Weir brought into the Dead cover catalog, "Mama Tried" ended up in the band's shows almost as quickly as country icon Merle Haggard released it, with the first 1969 versions following close on the heels of Haggard's album *Mama Tried* (1968). The song's story of a "railroad child" who sets out for adventure on the tracks and ends up sentenced to "life without parole" almost seems like a precursor to some of those that would be told by Garcia and Hunter's coming flood of loser-heroes. "Mama tried to raise me better, but her pleading I denied," the narrator explains in the chorus. "That leaves only me to blame, 'cause Mama tried." A live version by the Dead is included on October '71's *Grateful Dead (see page 137)*, as well as numerous volumes of the *Dick's Picks* series. Often paired with Weir and Barlow's similarly flavored "Mexicali Blues" starting in 1978, the Dead had played "Mama Tried" almost 300 times by 1995. They weren't the only group to see the song's crossover potential—versions were also made by Joan Baez, the Everly Brothers, and Percy Sledge.

Friday March 19
The Syndrome, Chicago, Illinois
With NRPS.

Wednesday March 17
Thursday March 18
Fox Theatre, St. Louis, Missouri
With NRPS. Wednesday sees the last-ever "Feedback."

Saturday March 13
Jenison Field House, Michigan State University, East Lansing, Michigan
With NRPS.

17 | 18 | 19 | 20 | 21 | 22 | 23

Sunday March 21
Exposition Center, Milwaukee, Wisconsin

Saturday March 20
Fieldhouse, University of Iowa, Iowa City, Iowa
With NRPS.

Wednesday March 24
Sufi Benefit, Winterland Arena, San Francisco, California

A benefit for the Sufi Choir of San Francisco; Ice Nine Publishing's Phil Davenport is a member. "Johnny B. Goode" from this show appears on *Skullfuck*.

APRIL '71

24 | 25 ~ 31 | 1 | 2 | 3 | 4 | 5 | 6

Sunday April 4
Monday April 5
Tuesday April 6
Manhattan Center, New York, New York

The band's only gigs at this venue. Billed (with NRPS) as "Dance Marathons," dancing is impossible—the place is too packed every night. Sunday sees the final "Easy Wind," while Monday marks the debut of "Sing Me Back Home." Tonight's "Big Railroad Blues" appears on *Skullfuck*. On Tuesday, Pigpen revives "I'm a Hog for You Baby" for the first time since '66—and for the last time—and Buddy Holly's "Oh Boy" debuts.

6 ~ 10 | 11 | 12 | 13 | 14 | 15 | 16

Thursday March 11
University Centre Ballroom, Northern Illinois University, DeKalb, Illinois

There's very little documentation for this show—and in fact it may not have taken place.

Sunday March 14
Camp Randall Field House, University of Wisconsin, Madison, Wisconsin

Friday March 5
Oakland Auditorium, Oakland, California

A benefit for the Oakland Black Panthers' Free School Breakfast. As always, the band is wary of association with political causes, but also as always, personal relationships trump such concerns—the band had met Panther leader Huey Newton while flying to a show, and hit it off over martinis.

128

Wednesday April 7
Thursday April 8
Boston Music Hall, Boston, Massachusetts

With NRPS. Thursday sees the breakout of the silky '67 Smokey Robinson and the Miracles classic "I Second That Emotion."

Tuesday April 13
Scranton Catholic Youth Center, Scranton, Pennsylvania

With NRPS.

| 7 | 8 | 9 | 10 | 11 | 12 | 13 |

Saturday April 10
East Hall, Franklin and Marshall College, Lancaster, Pennsylvania

Monday April 12
Pittsburgh Civic Arena, Pittsburgh, Pennsylvania

With NRPS.

Below: Wednesday March 3, Fillmore West, San Francisco. That's the famous Heavy Water light show behind the boys.

Wednesday April 14
Bucknell University, Lewisburg, Pennsylvania

With NRPS.

Thursday April 15
Allegheny College, Meadville, Pennsylvania

With NRPS.

| 14 | 15 | 16 | 17 | 18 | 19 |

Saturday April 17 ★
Dillon Gym, Princeton University, Princeton, New Jersey

The band's only ever Princeton show sparked (pun intended) a legend among succeeding generations of Princetonian Deadheads. A security guard was supposed to have hassled Jerry Garcia about smoking a joint, at which Jerry reputedly hurled the J at the campus cop's feet and proclaimed that the band would never play here again. Legends aside, this show—with NRPS—is renowned for what is perhaps Pigpen's most brilliant "Lovelight" rap.

Sunday April 18
Lusk Field House, SUNY, Cortland, New York

With NRPS.

Sunday April 25
Monday April 26
Tuesday April 27
Wednesday April 28 ★
Thursday April 29 ★
Fillmore East, New York, New York

NRPS plays all five nights. On Monday Duane Allman plays on three songs. "Big Boss Man" and "Wharf Rat" from this show (and "The Other One" from Wednesday and "Me and My Uncle" from Thursday) appear on *Skullfuck*. The Beach Boys guest for Tuesday's second set and the Dead play their only version of Merle Haggard's "Okie from Muskogee" as well as the more standard Haggard cover "Mama Tried" *(see opposite)*. On Wednesday Pigpen gets dosed and Tom Constanten subs on keys. The final Fillmore East show sees the last "I Second That Emotion" and "Alligator."

| 24 | 25 | 26 | 27 | 28 | 29 | 30 |

Tuesday April 20
The Supreme Court rules that students may be bused to different districts to racially integrate public schools.

Thursday April 22
Bangor Municipal Auditorium, Bangor, Maine

With NRPS. The band's first and only ever show at this venue.

Saturday April 24
Wallace Wade Stadium, Duke University, Durham, North Carolina

The band's first show in North Carolina. With NRPS, the Beach Boys, and the Paul Butterfield Blues Band. For various reasons this event—billed as "Joe College Weekend"—fills fewer than 10,000 of this football stadium's 50,000 seats. This probably counts as the largest non-festival venue played by the band thus far.

| 20 | 21 | 22 | 23 |

Thursday April 29
An L.A. judge sentences Charles Manson and three of his female followers to death for their '70 murder spree. (The sentences will later be changed to life imprisonment when California outlaws the death penalty.)

Wednesday April 21
Rhode Island Auditorium, Providence, Rhode Island

With NRPS. The band's first show in Rhode Island.

"NEW NEW MINGLEWOOD BLUES"

LEWIS

Relating the evolution of this long-time Dead cover's title might sound like a comedy bit from "Spinal Tap." Also known at various times as "Minglewood Blues," "New Minglewood Blues" and "All New Minglewood Blues," one thing is certain—the original version was written by Memphis blues granddaddy Noah Lewis (1895–1961), who was also responsible for the early Dead favorite "Viola Lee Blues," and refers to a factory north of Memphis, Tennessee, called Minglewood where Lewis had worked. "I was born in a desert, raised in a lion's den," the song begins, setting an assertive tone that the band would later emulate on originals like "Jack Straw" and "I Need a Miracle." "My number one occupation is stealing women from their men." First appearing on a 1928 single by Lewis's group Cannon's Jug Stompers, "Minglewood" was part of the Dead's terrain from early on, featuring in setlists from 1966 and in studio form on *Grateful Dead* (1967), where "New, New Minglewood Blues" was credited to the group's collective songwriting moniker of McGannahan Skjellyfetti. It was last performed on April 29, 1971 before being retired until July 1976. Through the years, Weir took creative license to adapt the song's reference to local women to over 50 locales in the U.S. and Europe, including "Deutsche fillies," "Pittsburgh girls," and "Southern belles," and continued to play the song during solo shows and sets by The Other Ones.

Merl Saunders

Organist Merl Saunders was a number of years Garcia's senior and had already had a successful career as a jazz and R&B keyboardist by the time he hooked up with the guitarist in 1971. Saunders replaced Howard Wales at The Matrix jam sessions in San Francisco and then moved on, with bassist John Kahn and drummer Bill Vitt, to a residency at the Keystone Korner jazz club and the New Monk (later the Keystone Berkeley). A master of the Hammond B-3 organ, Saunders had performed with the likes of Lionel Hampton, Miles Davis, B.B. King, Paul Butterfield, and others. Garcia credited Saunders with opening him up to the world of jazz and pop standards. They played together from 1972–1975 (which yielded the 1974 *Live At Keystone* album and a pair of Saunders "solo" discs), then again in the jazzy group Reconstruction in 1979. Their last collaboration was on Saunders' *Blues From the Rainforest* "new age" CD in 1988.

Right: Monday June 21, Château d'Hérouville, France. The band's tie-dyed amp covers were made by their friend Courtney Pollock.

Saturday May 29
Sunday May 30
Winterland Arena, San Francisco, California

With NRPS, R.J. Fox, and James and the Good Brothers. The first night of this Memorial Day weekend run is remembered as the "Acid Punch Night," thanks to a heavily dosed beverage that sent a number of people on some very bad trips; 30 of them wound up in the emergency room. The attendant publicity (and an unjustified rebuke of Bill Graham by the SFPD) led Graham to announce that the Fillmore West, too, would soon close its doors. Saturday's show also sees the first "Promised Land."

| 22 | 23 | 24 | 25 | 26 | 27 | 28 | 29 | 30 |

Left: To save money, BGP stamped the back of older tickets with current show dates. This reused ticket was valid for a (non-Dead) show at the Fillmore on the 18th May and for the Dead show at the Winterland on the 29th.

VALID ONLY
SAT. MAY 29
GRATEFUL DEAD
WINTERLAND $2.00

Valid Friday Only $3.00

May 1971

The band take most of May '71 off, but the ever-active Jerry Garcia continues with his several solo and side projects, including regular gigs at Berkeley's Keystone club, where he works up his jazz/funk/R&B chops with Merl Saunders, who will become, after John Kahn *(see page 156)*, perhaps his most frequent collaborator. Jerry also brought Saunders into the studio to do some organ overdubs on the "live" *Skullfuck* album.

130

MAY '71

| 1 | 2 | 3 | 4 | 5 | 6 | 7 | 8 |

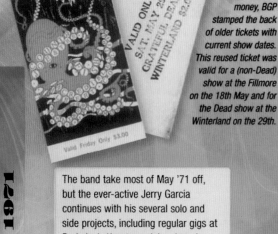

Parlez-Vous Dead?

June brought a weird, wonderful, one-off gig on the manicured grounds of a 16th-century chateau at Auvers, outside Paris. The impetus for the band's second overseas jaunt was a free festival—"Free Freedom Three Days"—sponsored by a French fashion designer, Jean Bouquin, who owned a boutique that catered to the Parisian *jeunesse dorée*. Bouquin's motivations in setting up the fête were either to impress his *haut-monde* friends, to use it as a springboard into politics by scoring points with the youth of France (this was just a couple of years after student radicals had nearly fomented another French Revolution), or to drum up business for the recording studio his friend, composer Michel Magne, had installed in his chateau. Whatever the reason, Bouquin decided it would be good to have this American hippie band in the lineup. The band accepted readily, because Bouquin agreed to fly over not only the musicians and crew but also many of the band's ever-growing family of girlfriends, friends, and staffers. Who could say *non* to such a junket? The party set down in *La Belle France* only to discover the festival was a literal washout thanks to the worst rains in years. So they camped out in the Château d'Hérouville, not doing any recording but taking full advantage (when the lousy weather permitted) of the swimming pool, the tennis courts, and the magnificent wine cellar (Pigpen preferred duty-free bourbon, until he was laid low by some kind of illness—a harbinger of sad events to come). Phil Lesh was delighted to learn that Frederic Chopin had once been a guest at the chateau. And there was a day trip to the City of Lights, where some visiting American hippies were amazed and delighted to run into the Grateful Dead at the Eiffel Tower.

But the band had come to play, and play they did, throwing a free Summer Solstice show (complete with Bill Ham's light show projected against the chateau) for 200 or so bemused villagers of Auvers. A TV crew came out from Paris to record the event, which was later broadcast on French TV and radio. After the band closed with "Johnny B. Goode," there was a rollicking party that ended with most of the revelers, including the local *Chef des Gendarmes*, in the pool. After the tortuous process of checking the equipment through the notorious French customs bureaucracy, the band & co. flew back to San Francisco, arriving exactly a week after the trip had first been proposed.

Above: *Monday June 21. The wine was flowing at Château d'Hérouville, in Auvers, France.*

| 1 | 2 | 3 | 4 | 5 | 6 – 20 | 21 | 22 |

| 24 | 25 | 26 | 27 |

Sunday June 27

The Fillmore East closes. It is a sad turn of events: the band's shows at this venue had played an important part in developing an East Coast following, and they played some of their finest performances here. All together, the Dead played the Fillmore East 42 times, plus two times when it was the old Village Theater (see page 81).

Monday June 21
Château d'Hérouville,
Hérouville, France

Last performance of "Long Black Limousine."

"PROMISED LAND"

BERRY

It may not have been the region of milk and honey referenced in Moses' time, but Chuck Berry's "Promised Land" was a place the Dead visited often after debuting their version at Winterland Arena in San Francisco on May 29, 1971. Released on Berry's album *St. Louis to Liverpool* (1964) and written while he was serving time in Missouri for interstate transportation of an underage female for "immoral purposes," the song's geographical details posed a peculiar problem for the rocker. "I remember having extreme difficulty... in trying to secure a road atlas of the United States to verify the routing of the Po' Boy from Norfolk, Virginia to Los Angeles," Berry wrote in his autobiography. "The penal institutions then were not so generous as to give a map of any kind, for fear of providing the route for an escape." Covers of Berry's "Around and Around" or "Johnny B. Goode" had turned up at over twenty Dead gigs before the arrival of "Promised Land," and by the last show of 1995 the band had played the three songs a total of just over 1,000 times.

'60s SF Clubs: End of an Era

By mid-'71 the "psychedelic ballrooms" that had incubated the Dead, the Airplane, Quicksilver, Big Brother, and all the other makers of the San Francisco sound had passed into rock history. The Avalon—the prototype and locus of the scene in its first couple of years—had shut its doors in late '68. In a way it was remarkable it lasted that long; the Family Dog collective *(see page 38)* ran it more as an "environmental theater" (Dennis McNally) than a business, meaning lots of people got in free. In the end, though, it was noise complaints (probably contrived), not red ink, that shuttered the legendary ballroom. The Family Dog (which, by then, meant Chet Helms) moved to a new location, the Great Highway, but that closed down in the summer of '70. In the end, Bill Graham, as usual, saw the future a little more clearly than others: whether or not the fans (and the musicians) liked it, rock was now a business and bands at the Dead's level had simply outgrown the old, beloved venues. Henceforth Winterland-size (and bigger) venues would be the norm for established bands.

The San Francisco ballrooms—with their elegant old fixtures, swirling light shows, sprung dance floors, and anything-goes vibe—have come to represent a time when performers and the audiences enjoyed an unmatched rapport, and when the confluence of consciousness expansion, music, and art opened up new realms of human experience. Over the next quarter-century it would devolve mainly on the Dead to carry that spirit forward.

"At the Fillmore Auditorium you had to climb up the stairs to the lobby… God help you if Bill caught you sneaking in! He'd scream at you and throw you out onto the sidewalk on your ass. When shows started to get bigger, Graham moved across the street to Winterland Arena. Winterland became the Grateful Dead's home venue for many memorable years." STEVE BROWN, 2003.

With a tale of love's woes in the best of the Hunter/Garcia tradition and a gentle, ambling rhythmic line leading to an ascending Garcia jam that routinely reached dizzying heights, "Sugaree" broke loose in almost 500 combined solo and Grateful Dead shows, yet another of the numerous windfalls that both Jerry and the band reaped from the *Garcia* (1972) album. The song was that album's only single, as well as one of the few Dead solo efforts to ever get decent airplay on American radio. But compared to that three-minute version, the song's first official appearance on the live album *Steal Your Face* (1976) clocked in at 7:30, and some renditions topped out at 12 minutes or more. The refrain's coaxings to "Shake it, shake it Sugaree" directly echoed the title of blues and folk legend Elizabeth Cotten's song and album "Shake Sugaree," but Hunter passages like "I'll meet you at the Jubilee; and if that Jubilee don't come, maybe I'll meet you on the run" bore no resemblance. First played on July 31, 1971, "Sugaree" carried on into the new millennium, making the Other Ones rotation from 1998 before becoming part of the new Dead's 2003 set list.

Saturday July 31 ★
Yale Bowl, New Haven, Connecticut

Another Ivy League show—for an audience of 10,000, big numbers for the day—highlighted by the breakout of two Hunter/Garcia originals: "Sugaree" and "Mr. Charlie," a bluesy Pigpen/Hunter collaboration. Deadheads have long speculated as to who or what "Mr. Charlie" was or is. The name is a trope in the blues idiom, used as a euphemism for plantation overseers, chain-gang guards, or the exploitative white man in general, though some have speculated that "Mr. Charlie" represents heroin or cocaine. Tonight also sees the last (of four) "Darkness Jams."

Thursday August 5
Friday August 6 ★
Hollywood Palladium, Hollywood, California

With NRPS (and a lunar eclipse on Friday). "Hard to Handle" from Friday's show appears on 1997's *Fallout from the Phil Zone.*

Sunday July 25
President Nixon formally certifies a ratification of the 26th Amendment to the Constitution, which gives 18-year-olds full voting rights.

AUGUST '71

25 | 26 | 27 | 28 | 29 | 30 | **31** | 1 | 2 | 3 | **4** | 5 | 6

Sunday July 4
Fillmore West closes. The Dead played the Fillmore West 44 times, plus 15 shows when it was the Carousel Ballroom *(see page 82).*

JULY '71

1 | **2** | 3 | 4 | 5 | 6 | 7 | 8 | 9 | 10 ~ 24

Monday July 26
Having slipped back across the border, Lenny Hart is spotted in San Diego and arrested. The band doesn't press criminal charges but files a civil suit to get their money back. Lenny eventually coughs up perhaps a third of the money he'd embezzled. He is prosecuted by the D.A. on criminal charges anyway.

Wednesday August 4
Terminal Island Correctional Facility, San Pedro, California

The band reportedly plays a benefit for Bear while he is doing time at this location, but details are sketchy.

Friday July 2
Fillmore West, San Francisco, California

With NRPS and the Rowans, with Jerry Garcia sitting in on the latter's set. The Dead dedicate "The Other One" to Bear—then serving time at the Terminal Island Correctional Facility in L.A.—and close out its Fillmore West career with "Not Fade Away">"Goin' Down The Road Feeling Bad">"Not Fade Away." As with the last show at the Fillmore East, the audience applauds for 10 minutes until the boys return with a "Johnny B. Goode" encore.

The show is broadcast on radio stations KSAN and KFSX and filmed (with other final-week performances at the Fillmore West) for a documentary. *Fillmore: The Last Days* was released in 1972, and the band can be seen playing "Casey Jones" and "Johnny B. Goode."

FILLMORE WEST

Above: The Dead became a quintet again for much of 1971, before Keith Godchaux was hired.

Saturday August 7
Golden Hall, Community Concourse, San Diego, California

With NRPS.

7   8   9   10   11   12

"BROWN-EYED WOMEN"
GARCIA/HUNTER

Dramatic images of a bootlegging family in the throes of the Prohibition and the Great Depression add up to make Garcia and Hunter's "Brown-Eyed Women" one of the Dead's most fully realized home-spun folk tales, a chronicle of hard times set at a pivotal crossroads of American history. "Delilah Jones was the mother of twins, two times over and the rest was sins," Garcia sings. "Raised eight boys, only I turned bad; didn't get the lickings that the other ones had." Never recorded in a studio setting, the song made its first appearance on the band's *Europe '72* disc after a live debut in Chicago on August 23, 1971. It remained a concert standard for the rest of the group's 30 years together, with almost 350 performances between 1971 and 1995, and reemerged as part of the Other Ones' setlist in the fall of 2002. Though *Europe '72* and the "Grateful Dead Anthology" songbook originally cited a singular woman in the title, Hunter later set the record straight, identifying the song as "Brown-Eyed Women" in his book *A Box of Rain*. Tape archivist Willy Legate confirmed the anomaly in *DeadBase VIII*. "Robert Hunter actually wrote and intended it to be 'Brown-Eyed Women,' the way Jerry Garcia really sings it. This is a classic case of a typographical error."

3302

Good Only
FRI. 7:00 P.M.
JULY **30**
1971
GAELIC PARK
GENERAL ADMISSION $4.00

14   15   16 ~ 22

Saturday August 14
Sunday August 15
Berkeley Community Theatre, Berkeley, California

With NRPS. David Crosby lends his voice to the closing sequence on Saturday: "Johnny B. Goode" and "Uncle John's Band."

AUDITORIUM

Thursday August 26
Gaelic Park, Bronx, New York

The band's only show at this venue, and Pigpen's last show for three months. Shortly after the summer '71 tour, Pigpen more or less collapses physically and in mid-September he is in the hospital with an ulcer and liver, kidney, and spleen degeneration. With Pigpen sidelined at least temporarily, the band has to scramble to find a keyboardist before the next tour. The problem solves itself when Donna Jean Godchaux *(see page 142)* encounters Jerry Garcia at the Keystone and tells him her husband Keith will be the Dead's next piano man. And he is.

23   24   25   26   27 ~ 31

Monday August 23
Tuesday August 24
Auditorium Theatre, Chicago, Illinois

The band's first show at this venue sees the breakout of "Brown-Eyed Women." Tuesday and two days later in New York mark the band's only performances of a "phantom song" that acquired the title "Empty Pages." Sung by Pigpen, it was probably written by him.

NEW RIDERS OF THE PURPLE SAGE
New Riders of the Purple Sage
Released by Columbia (C-30888) in August 1971

Side One
1. **I Don't Know You**
(Dawson)
2. **Whatcha Gonna Do**
(Dawson)
3. **Portland Woman**
(Dawson)
4. **Henry**
(Dawson)
5. **Dirty Business**
(Dawson)

Side Two
1. **Glendale Train**
(Dawson)
2. **Garden of Eden**
(Dawson)
3. **All I Ever Wanted**
(Dawson)
4. **Last Lonely Eagle**
(Dawson)
5. **Louisiana Lady)**
(Dawson)

Personnel
Mickey Hart – percussion, drums
Jerry Garcia – banjo, guitar, guitar (steel)
Commander Cody – piano
John Dawson – guitar, vocals
John Desautels – drums
Spencer Dryden – percussion, drums, vocals
David Nelson – guitar, mandolin, guitar (electric), vocals
Dave Torbert – bass, guitar, vocals

Produced by New Riders Of The Purple Sage

CONSIDERING THE DEAD'S folk and bluegrass origins, it made perfect sense that the band would spawn a country-rock alter ego like the New Riders of the Purple Sage. The original lineup consisted of old jamming buddies John "Marmaduke" Dawson (who wrote all ten of the songs on this eponymous debut) and David Nelson alongside Garcia, Hart, and Lesh. The players had changed slightly by the time the NRPS headed into the studio for this Columbia release, with Garcia still appearing as a full-fledged member, while Lesh's role was filled by Dave Torbert and Hart turned the sticks over to the Jefferson Airplane's Spencer Dryden on all but two tracks. (Commander Cody also contributed piano to two songs, while Lesh would be credited as executive producer.) It was a solid band playing wonderful material, and the result was a classic that took its rightful place among the Flying Burrito Brothers and the countrified Byrds to help define a unique period in American roots rock. The album hit a respectable No. 39 on the *Billboard* charts in its original incarnation.

Keith Godchaux

Pianist Keith Godchaux had played in a succession of unmemorable rock and jazz groups in the San Francisco Bay Area when his wife Donna approached Jerry Garcia at one of the guitarist's club gigs in September 1971 and convinced him to let Keith audition for the Dead, their favorite band. The timing was perfect—Pigpen was missing gigs because of a debilitating liver condition and Garcia was looking to bring a new keyboardist into the Dead's mix. A few days later Godchaux found himself rehearsing with Garcia, who was sufficiently impressed by the pianist's range that he brought Bill Kreutzmann down to the studio to play with him, too. He was basically hired on the spot and first went on the road with the band during their 1971 fall tour.

Godchaux brought much to the group's live sound, particularly from '72 to '74, and his recorded work with the group peaked with the *Mars Hotel* album in 1974. Though drug problems made him a less effective player later, he also enjoyed a successful tenure with the Jerry Garcia Band from 1976 through 1978. By mutual agreement he and Donna left the Dead in the spring of 1979. He was killed in an auto accident a year later.

Monday September 13
A force of more than 1,500 New York state police storm Attica Prison in upstate New York, which prisoners had taken over. The assault frees 28 hostages but leaves 31 prisoners and 9 hostages dead.

The fall tour (which went on until mid-December) saw Keith Godchaux integrate into the band quite quickly, musically and personally. The New Riders were still with the Dead, but in November Jerry Garcia relinquished pedal steel duties to Buddy Cage.

Saturday October 23
Sunday October 24
Easttown Theatre, Detroit, Michigan

With NRPS.

Thursday October 21
Friday October 22
Auditorium Theatre, Chicago, Illinois

With NRPS. "Frozen Logger" goes into permanent deep freeze after Thursday's show.

SEPTEMBER '71

OCTOBER '71

| 1 ~ 12 | 13 | 14 ~ 23 | 24 | 25 | 26 | 27 | 28 | 29 | 30 | 1 | 2 ~ 18 | 19 | 20 | 21 | 22 | 23 | 24 | 25 |

Friday September 24
Grateful Dead (Skull & Roses), a.k.a. *Skullfuck*, is released.

Tuesday October 19
Northrup Auditorium, Minneapolis, Minnesota

The band's first show with Keith Godchaux on board sees the debut of six originals: "Tennessee Jed," "Jack Straw" *(see page 143)*, "Mexicali Blues," "Comes a Time," "One More Saturday Night *(see page 438)*, and "Ramble on Rose." "Tennessee Jed," a Hunter/Garcia number, is a countrified catalog of comical calamities suffered by the title character. "Mexicali," the first Bob Weir/John Perry Barlow collaboration to be performed by the Dead, is inspired by a tequila-fueled road trip through southern Mexico taken by Weir, Barlow, and Jon McIntire in early '71. "Comes a Time," a gentle Hunter/Garcia ballad, is an audience favorite performed at more than 60 shows. Frankenstein and his creator, Mary Shelley, 1920s evangelist Billy Sunday, and nursery-school favorites Jack and Jill are just a few of the characters name-checked in "Ramble on Rose," performed some 316 times.

"...And when you're just standing there on the stage boogying away and you can see 5,000 people going up and down in a wave like an ocean, it tends to give you a feeling like you're doing something right." PHIL LESH

Tuesday October 26	Wednesday October 27	Friday October 29	Saturday October 30	Sunday October 31
The Palestra, University of Rochester, Rochester, New York With NRPS.	Onondaga County War Memorial, Syracuse, New York With NRPS.	Allan Theatre, Cleveland, Ohio With NRPS. "Beat It on Down the Line gets an 11-beat intro.	Taft Auditorium, Cincinnati, Ohio With NRPS.	Ohio Theatre, Columbus, Ohio With NRPS. The show's second set appears on 1995's *Dick's Picks Volume 2*.
26	**27**	**28**	**29**	**30**	**31**

GRATEFUL DEAD

Grateful Dead

Released by Warner Bros. (2WS-1935) in September 1971

Side One

1. **Bertha)**
   (Garcia/Hunter)
2. **Mama Tried**
   (Haggard)
3. **Big Railroad Blues**
   (Lewis arr. Grateful Dead)
4. **Playing In The Band**
   (Weir/Hunter)

Side Two

1. **The Other One**
   (Kreutzmann/Weir)

Side Three

1. **Me and My Uncle**
   (Phillips)
2. **Big Boss Man**
   (Smith/Dixon)
3. **Me and Bobby McGee**
   (Kristofferson/Foster)
4. **Johnny B. Goode**
   (Berry)

Side Four

1. **Wharf Rat**
   (Garcia/Hunter)
2. **Not Fade Away**
   (Petty/Hardin)
3. **Goin' Down The Road Feeling Bad**
   (Traditional arr. Grateful Dead)

Personnel

Jerry Garcia – guitar, vocals
Bill Kreutzmann – drums
Phil Lesh – bass, vocals
Pigpen (Ron McKernan) – organ, harmonica, vocals
Bob Weir – guitar, vocals
Merl Saunders – organ on "Bertha," "Playing In The Band," "Wharf Rat" (overdubbed in studio)

Produced by the Grateful Dead

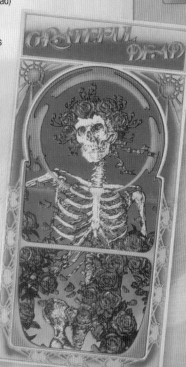

THE DEAD FIRST STRUCK GOLD—sales of 500,000 units—with their next live release, *Grateful Dead*, a.k.a. *Skull & Roses*, a.k.a. *Skullfuck*, a monster double album that found the band introducing three originals ("Bertha," "Playing In The Band" and "Wharf Rat") with a generous sampling of the country ("Mama Tried," "Me and My Uncle"), blues ("Big Boss Man"), and rock ("Johnny B. Goode," "Not Fade Away") covers that typically rounded out set lists at the time. Its cover art opened into a new gatefold of the famous Kelley and Mouse rendering of a 19th-century E.J. Sullivan illustration for the *Rubaiyat* of Omar Khayyam, first seen in the duo's earlier Avalon concert poster.

Having delivered two solid studio albums the preceding year, while steadily building its reputation as a live act, the Dead were in Warner Bros.' good graces. So, naturally, the band judged that it was time to yank the corporate chain once more, in this instance by insisting that the new live album be titled *Skullfuck*. A hand-wringing Joe Smith brokered a summit meeting between the band and Warner Bros. and patiently explained that Sears and J.C. Penney would never carry an album with such a title—as if that was going to cut any ice with the band. Eventually, the boys "relented" after promises of a huge PR budget. In fact, while the Dead were certainly intrigued by the idea of putting out an album called *Skullfuck*, it was really, as Jerry Garcia said later, "more a joke on our part." In the end, Warner Bros. chose to call the album *Grateful Dead*, a title so close to that of the band's first effort (*The Grateful Dead*) that it caused confusion for years and eventually prompted the long-time nickname of "Skull and Roses" to be added as a parenthetical addendum in catalog listings. The inside cover's invitation for fans to unite and send in their name and address to get information would mark the first appearance of the term "Deadheads," a tag that would, to put it mildly, stick.

Thursday November 11
Atlanta Municipal
Auditorium, Atlanta, Georgia

With NRPS.

Friday November 12
San Antonio Civic Auditorium,
San Antonio, Texas

With NRPS.

Sunday November 14
Texas Christian University, Fort Worth, Texas

With NRPS. A 25-beat intro to "Beat It on Down the Line" and the first performance of Hank Williams' "You Win Again."

Monday November 15
Austin Municipal
Auditorium, Austin, Texas

With NRPS.

Wednesday November 17
Albuquerque Civic Auditorium,
Albuquerque, New Mexico

With NRPS.

Saturday November 20
Pauley Pavilion, University of
California, Los Angeles, California

With NRPS.

NOVEMBER '71

1 ~ 5	6	7	8	9	10	11	12	13	14	15	16	17	18	19	20

Saturday November 6
Sunday November 7
Harding Theater,
San Francisco, California

With NRPS. First performance on Sunday of the 1961 blues instrumental "Hide Away," by Freddie King, one of Jerry Garcia's guitar heroes. The band will perform "Hide Away" just once more, 18 years later *(see 6/21/89)*. Someone born the year the band first played it would be old enough to vote by the time it came around again.

Below: The Dead Heads newsletter often featured doodles by Garcia, poetry and absurdities from the pen of Robert Hunter, and artwork and letters sent in by fans.

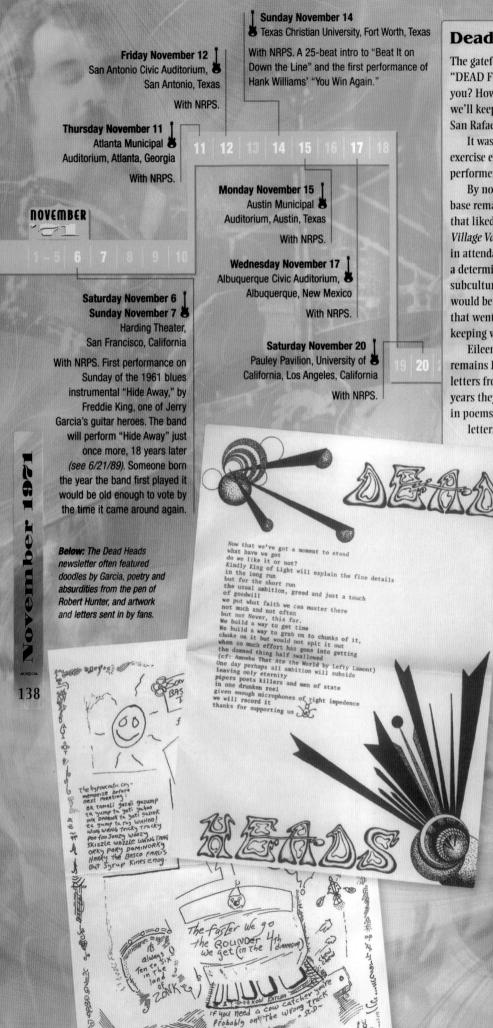

Dead Freaks Unite

The gatefold sleeve of *Skullfuck* bore a message: "DEAD FREAKS UNITE; Who are you? Where are you? How are you? Send us your name and address and we'll keep you informed. Dead Heads, P.O. Box 1065, San Rafael, California 94901."

It was the start of probably the most remarkable exercise ever in community-building between a group of performers and their fans, and one that continues today.

By now it was lost on no one that while the Dead's fan base remained small, at least in comparison to, say, Creedence or the Stones, people that liked the Dead liked the Dead *a lot*. In his review of the '70 Felt Forum run, *Village Voice* critic Robert Christgau had noted how many "regulars" seemed to be in attendance, and how, from the way they compared notes, they'd obviously made a determined effort to see as many shows as possible. The Deadhead community, or subculture, or whatever, was coalescing, and the "Dead Freaks Unite!" campaign would be a major catalyst in the process. And as a "small-scale, grass-roots" campaign that went around established channels to make a direct connection, it was perfectly in keeping with the band's amorphous yet consistent philosophy.

Eileen Law *(see page 140)* was soon put in charge of the mailing list, and she remains Den Mother to the Deadheads to this day. By the end of '71 about 350 letters from 'Heads (or Freaks) had arrived at the band's office; within a couple of years they'd received something like 40,000. In a two-way channel, Deadheads sent in poems, rants, dreams, prophecies, treatises, appreciations, and artworks; the letters and envelopes themselves were often works of art. In return, Deadheads received (at irregular intervals) communiqués about the state of the band (even when the news was not good), upcoming tours and recordings, and anything else relating to the Grateful Dead experience. There were 25 mailings between October '71 and February '80, after which the Grateful Dead Almanac and ultimately Dead.net replaced them.

The Dead Head mailings were not mere newsletters. The band occasionally included record samplers and many mailings featured artwork from Jerry Garcia and whimsically profound (or is it profoundly whimsical?) writing and artwork from Robert Hunter.

DEAD HEADS
P.O. BOX 1065
SAN RAFAEL, CA
94901

Above: Address of the Deadheads' official fan club.

Wednesday December 1
Thursday December 2
Boston Music Hall, Boston, Massachusetts

With NRPS. Wednesday's show marks the return of Pigpen, so the Dead are back to being a two-keyboard band for the first time since Tom Constanten's departure *(see page 112)*. Pig, however, is still weak and his musical presence is muted.

DECEMBER '71

1	2	3

"BIG RIVER"
CASH

Yet another in the extended list of country covers the Dead enjoyed trotting out, this Johnny Cash cornerstone was introduced on *Johnny Cash Sings The Songs That Made Him Famous* (1959) before the Man in Black left Sun Records for a more permanent home at Columbia. Debuted by the Dead during the 1971 New Year's Eve show in San Francisco (*right*), the song was released on *Steal Your Face* (1976) and ended up on 14 of the first 28 *Dick's Picks* CDs. It proved a worthy complement for the band's cross-country travels, with references to a number of cities that dot the path of the Mississippi River providing a background for a thwarted lover who "taught that weepin' willow how to cry" and vows to flood the Mighty Mississip' with his own tears. Played almost 400 times, this popular cover's last showing took place on July 6, 1995, at Maryland Heights, Missouri, less than 20 miles from the locale of St. Louis mentioned in the song.

Saturday December 4
Sunday December 5 ★
Monday December 6
Tuesday December 7
Felt Forum, New York, New York

The Felt Forum is the old name for the Theatre at Madison Square Garden, not to be confused with MSG's main arena, which the Dead will play 52 times between '79 and '94 (the Felt Forum/Theatre's capacity is about 5,000; the arena can hold 18,000).

All shows are with NRPS. Saturday's first set includes Chuck Berry's classic holiday novelty, "Run Rudolph Run." The second night sees the first "Dark Star Jam" in more than three years and the only known GD performance of another country chestnut, "I Washed My Hands in Muddy Water."

Tuesday December 14
Wednesday December 15
Hill Auditorium, Ann Arbor, Michigan

With NRPS. The last performance on Wednesday of "Run Rudolph Run" and the debut of Bo Diddley's much-covered boast, "Mannish Boy."

4 | 5 | 6 | 7 | 8 | 9 | 10 | 11 | 12 | 13 | **14** | **15** | 16 ~ 20

Thursday December 9
Friday December 10
Fox Theatre, St. Louis, Missouri

With NRPS. Last-ever "China Cat Jam" on Friday.

139

HOOTEROLL?

Howard Wales and Jerry Garcia

Released by Douglas #5 (manufactured and distributed by Columbia – KZ 30859) in December 1971

Side One

1. **South Side Strut**
   (Fierro/Wales)
2. **A Trip To What Next**
   (Wales)
3. **Up From The Desert**
   (Wales)

Side Two

1. **DC-502**
   (Wales)
2. **One A.M. Approach**
   (Wales)
3. **Uncle Martin's**
   (Wales)
4. **Da Birg Song**
   (Wales)

Personnel

Howard Wales – piano, organ
Jerry Garcia – guitar
John Kahn – bass
Curly Cook – rhythm guitar
Bill Vitt – drums
Michael Marinelli – drums
Ken Balzall – trumpet
Martin Fierro – saxophone, flute

Produced by Alan Douglas and Doris Dynamite

RECORDED AT A TIME when Garcia's jamming wanderlust had started to lead to numerous side projects, *Hooteroll?* was a worthwhile if slightly uneven instrumental gem recorded with Howard Wales, the keyboardist and Garcia jam-mate who had played on the Dead's *American Beauty*. Marking the first release bearing his name as a solo artist, the album was an early sampling of what Garcia was capable of outside of the context of the Dead, whether in the brassy funk of "South Side Strut," the warm acoustic runs and slide flourishes of "Da Birg Song," or the neo-fusion of "Morning In Marin," a track added for the album's re-release that touted a style of free form jazz similar to one Garcia would explore 17 years later with Ornette Coleman.

Though Wales and Garcia continued to play together in 1972, an intended follow-up to *Hooteroll?* never materialized, thanks in part to Dead envy, according to Wales. "The only person I was friends with was Jerry," he said in '97. "In fact, [the rest of the band] were very jealous over the fact that we did *Hooteroll?* together." A second album eventually appeared in the form of 1988's *Side Trips*, a live CD culled from 1970 jam sessions at The Matrix.

"I never got along with the rest of those guys [in the Grateful Dead]. There was a lot of jealousy." HOWARD WALES

Friday December 31
Winterland Arena, San Francisco, California

With NRPS and Yogi Phlegm—the latter a Sons of Champlin offshoot including Bill Vitt, a frequent musical collaborator of Jerry Garcia's, on drums. Bill Graham so hated the name ("inspired" by a nonexistent Indian guru) that he added "Sons of Champlin" in parentheses on the poster—shades of the first Grateful Dead show at the Fillmore Auditorium, which billed the band as "formerly the Warlocks." Donna Jean Godchaux lends her voice to "One More Saturday Night," though she will not be an "official" band member for another three months. The end of the year is the beginning for Johnny Cash's "Big River" and the Pigpen original "Chinatown Shuffle."

21 | 22 | 23 | 24 | 25 | 26 | 27 | 28 | 29 | 30 | **31**

1 | 2 | 3 | 4 | 5 | 6 | 7 | 8 | 9 | 10 | 11 | 12 | 13 | 14

Sunday January 2
🎸 Winterland Arena, San Francisco, California

With NRPS and Yogi Phlegm. The band's first show of the year (and their last show for two months) includes a "phantom song" in the first set. Noted in setlists as "Your Love at Home," this is the only performance of the song.

"If you stop to think how many groups could get any of us out on January 2nd, there would be very few of them. There's only one that would do it for me, and I hope they do it for you—the Grateful Dead."
BILL GRAHAM'S INTRODUCTION TO THE SHOW

Below: *Jerry Garcia in early 1972, which would be one of the Dead's strongest years ever.*

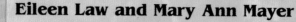

Eileen Law and Mary Ann Mayer

The Grateful Dead built their organization in the '60s and early '70s primarily from the ranks of their friends. Two of them, Mary Ann Mayer and Eileen Law, had been in and around the Bay Area music scene for a number of years when they were hired on to work at the San Rafael (Marin County) house that became the Dead's headquarters for nearly 25 years. Mayer came on board around the time the Dead printed an appeal/invitation on the sleeve of the *Skull & Roses* album for "Dead Freaks" to write to them. She became the designated mail gatherer for what became known as Dead Heads—their fan club/mailing list.

In 1972, Eileen Law took over when Mayer went on the road with the band to Europe as their official photographer. Mayer and Law put together the charming and informative Dead Heads newsletter that went out to everyone on their growing mailing list in the mid-'70s. Eileen continued to shepherd the mailing list, collect press clippings about the group, and act as *de facto* liaison between the band and their fans for the rest of their history. In fact, she still works in that capacity.

"The Dead found that when they did the last newsletter mailout at a cost of $18,000 they had more than 10,000 address changes."
EILEEN LAW TO BLAIR JACKSON

The Greening of Garcia

In January '72 *Rolling Stone* published a lengthy interview with Jerry Garcia and Mountain Girl (the magazine's first interview with Garcia, incidentally, despite the close early ties between the Dead and *Rolling Stone*). Jann Wenner *(see page 80)* had conducted the interview the preceding summer at the Garcias' new home in Stinson Beach, at the instigation of and in collaboration with Charles Reich.

Reich, a Yale law professor, had published *The Greening of America* in 1970. A work of pop philosophy that postulated that the "new generation" was transforming society by achieving a higher level of consciousness, rising above the materialism of previous generations in the process, the book caught the zeitgeist of the era perfectly and became a bestseller.

Jerry—an eclectic reader and serious thinker—fascinated Reich. Here was a new kind of rock star—neither showman (i.e., Jagger), shaman (i.e., Morrison), or satyr (i.e., Page and Plant) but instead, a seer and a sage. Reich returned to Stinson Beach for another conversation, aided by good weed. (This interview was published under the title "A Stoned Sunday Rap.")

The interviews appeared in book form in 1972, as *Garcia: A Signpost to New Space*, published by (ironically named) Straight Arrow Books. While the interviews are a fascinating glimpse into the mind of Jerry, the book had the side effect of adding to Jerry's reputation as some sort of guru, when all he really wanted to be was a guitarist.
"Reich: How do you manage to be so optimistic?
Garcia: Music is something that has optimism built into it. Optimism is another way of saying 'space.' Music has infinite space. You can go as far into music as you can fill millions of lifetimes. Music is an infinite cylinder, it's open-ended, it's space. The form of music has infinite space as a part of it, and that, in itself, means its momentum is essentially in that open place."
FROM *GARCIA: A SIGNPOST TO NEW SPACE* BY JERRY GARCIA, JANN WENNER, AND CHARLES REICH

GARCIA

Jerry Garcia

*Released by Warner Bros. (BS -2582)
in January 1972*

Side One

1. **Deal**
   (Garcia/Hunter)
2. **Bird Song**
   (Garcia/Hunter)
3. **Sugaree**
   (Garcia/Hunter)
4. **Loser**
   (Garcia/Hunter)

Side Two

1. **Late For Supper**
   (Garcia)
2. **Spidergawd**
   (Garcia/Kreutzmann/Hunter)
3. **Eep Hour**
   (Garcia/Kreutzmann)
4. **To Lay Me Down**
   (Garcia/Hunter)
5. **An Odd Little Place**
   (Garcia/Kreutzmann)
6. **The Wheel**
   (Garcia/Hunter/Kreutzmann)

Personnel

Jerry Garcia – acoustic guitar, electric guitar, pedal steel guitar, bass, piano, organ, samples, vocals
Bill Kreutzmann – drums
Robert Hunter – lyrics

Produced by Bob Matthews, Betty Cantor with Ramrod, and Bill Kreutzmann

Left: Since there was no title on the album cover itself—a collage by Bob Seidemann—a sticker with Garcia's name was slapped on the front—usually over the pubic hair.
Below: The offending pubes (and breast) even led to this censored version, designed for the South African market.

Wɪᴛʜ Gᴀʀᴄɪᴀ ᴛʜᴇ ʀᴇʟᴜᴄᴛᴀɴᴛ musical guru continuing to draw cultural interest outside of the Dead, it wasn't surprising that he was the first to ink a solo deal with the band's label, Warner Bros. "Jerry had a very high profile at that point," said Bob Matthews, who co-produced the resulting album with Betty Cantor, Ram Rod, and Bill Kreutzmann. "He was very active in his solo career, as well as highly-recognized publicly as an individual... so Warner was very interested." Garcia decided to take advantage of the opportunity to the fullest, stretching his wings on everything from soon-to-be classics such as "Deal" and "Bird Song" to weird electronic experiments with equally peculiar titles like "Spidergawd" and "Eep Hour." "I'm doing it to be completely self-indulgent, musically," he said just before the album was released. "I'm just going on a trip. I have a curiosity to see what I can do and I've a desire to get into 16-track and go on trips which are too weird for me to want to put anybody else I know through."

Recorded over a three-week period in the summer of 1971 at Wally Heider Studios in San Francisco (to dissuade visits from the curious, a sign was reportedly posted outside that read "Closed Session—Anita Bryant"), Garcia played all of the instruments except drums. It also included what Hunter would later consider to be some of his most direct lyrical contributions. "There was a point, I think, really high on that *Garcia* album, where all those songs occur, where the message was being laid out in no uncertain terms," he told David Gans in 1978. Though *Garcia* was hardly a chart-topper, it outsold albums by T. Rex and America released at the time, and its six conventional songs would find their way into the Dead's set lists for decades.

At the start of '72 the band took an honest-to-God vacation for the first time in years, with no shows between January 2 and March 5. (A couple of shows were scheduled for the Marin County Veterans Auditorium mid-February, but these had to be canceled.) For Bob Weir, it was a working vacation in several ways. He spent a couple of weeks with John Perry Barlow in an isolated cabin on the Barlows' Bar Cross ranch in Wyoming. Days, they struggled to get hay to snowbound cattle; nights, they worked on songs, stimulated by 101-proof Wild Turkey and the presence of a ghost. Returning to San Francisco, Weir began recording his first solo album, *Ace* (see page 144), with help from the rest of the band. Truly a busman's holiday for all.

Monday February 21
President Richard Nixon stuns the world by making a surprise visit to the People's Republic of China, which has been essentially ignored by the U.S. since the communist takeover of that nation in 1949.

1 2 3 4 5 6 7 8 9 10 11 12 13 14 15 16 17 18 19 20 **21** 22 23 24 25 26 27 28 29

| 1 | 2 | 3 | 4 | 5 | 6 – 20 |

🎸 Tuesday March 21
🎸 Wednesday March 22
Academy of Music, New York, New York

🎸 Thursday March 23 ★
🎸 Saturday March 25
Academy of Music, New York, New York

| 21 | 22 | 23 | 24 | 25 |

🎸 Sunday March 26
🎸 Monday March 27
Tuesday March 28
Academy of Music, New York, New York

🎸 **Sunday March 5**
🎸 Winterland Arena,
San Francisco, California

This American Indian Benefit is with NRPS and Yogi Phlegm. (Jerry Garcia and Phil Lesh sit in with the latter when a couple of YP members get stuck in traffic.) The show sees the breakout of "Black-Throated Wind."

The Academy Run

The first night of the seven-show run saw the breakouts of "Looks Like Rain" and "Two Souls in Communion." Saturday was a benefit/party for the New York City chapter of the Hells Angels, and was Donna Jean Godchaux's first "official" appearance as a band member.

Also on Saturday, Bo Diddley stopped by to do an opening set backed by the boys, including the only GD performances of Bo's "Take It All Off" and "Pollution," Bert Berns' "Are You Lonely for Me Baby?" and the Holland/Dozier/Holland classic "How Sweet It Is (To be Loved by You)," the first performance of "Hey Bo Diddley," and the second and final take on "Mannish Boy."

Born in McComb, Mississippi in 1928 as Ellas Otha Bates McDaniels, Bo Diddley introduced the propulsive "shave-and-a-haircut, two-bits" riff that became, in the mid-'50s, one of the

Right: Bobby and Pigpen, Academy of Music, New York

fundamental building-blocks of rock 'n' roll. Musically, Diddley straddled the line between the electric blues of Muddy Waters and the rock 'n' roll of Chuck Berry. As a performer, Bo at the height of his fame was a true original—who else, in 1958, would dare to name a song after *himself?*—wielding a square guitar, backed by a band including a woman guitarist ("the Duchess") and a maracas player (Jerome Green). He also proved adept at adopting his style to the pop flavor-of-the-month on albums like 1963's *Bo Diddley is a Twister* and 1963's *Surfin' with Bo Diddley*. As of mid-2003 he's still out there laying down the big beat.

The last night of the run's encore is a special treat for the locals—the only-ever performance of "The Sidewalks of New York" (instrumental only) into "One More Saturday Night" (even though it's Tuesday).

This eventful run was the Grateful Dead's only visit to this venue under its original name; the Academy later became the Palladium, where the band played a five-show run (April 29 through May 4, 1977).

Below: Academy of Music, New York. These shows marked the formal introduction of Donna Godchaux as a band member.

Below and bottom: Academy of Music, New York. Billy (below) and Phil and Keith (bottom).

142

Donna Godchaux

As a teenager growing up in Muscle Shoals, Alabama, Donna Jean Thatcher (born in 1945) gravitated toward the dynamic R&B recording scene in her hometown, becoming a backup singer of some note and working with the likes of Percy Sledge, Aretha Franklin, Ray Stevens, Sam Cooke, Boz Scaggs, Elvis Presley, and many others. Restless in Alabama, Donna moved to the San Francisco Bay Area, where she met and married pianist Keith Godchaux. When Keith joined the Dead in the fall of '71, it was fairly natural that she, too, would get involved with the group.

After contributing to Bob Weir's solo album, *Ace*, she joined the band as a backup singer in the spring of 1972, and stayed until the winter of 1979. She and Keith recorded one solo album (*Keith & Donna*, 1975) during their tenure with the Dead, and the two also spent a couple of years in the Jerry Garcia Band. After Keith's death in 1980, she had a Christian conversion and eventually married a gospel musician named David MacKay. Today, the MacKays live in Alabama and still perform and record occasionally. Donna has also made sporadic appearances with former Grateful Dead members since Garcia's death.

Over There

On April Fool's Day the band flew out of New York, arriving in London on Easter Sunday to begin the band's first—and long-postponed—European Tour. A couple of years earlier there'd been a scheme to bring the Dead and the other big San Francisco bands to the continent by ocean liner, but that had fallen through, as had a more recent idea for the Dead to tour Germany and the Low Countries via canal.

It had taken years for the band to reach a level of fiscal and logistical stability that made a full-scale overseas tour feasible. Neither the band nor Warner Bros. thought the tour would be particularly profitable, although, as it happened, ticket sales for most of the 20 shows were pretty good. (The band played 22 shows in all, plus a free show in Lille and a radio appearance.) The real impetus for the tour was to expand the group's European fan base and to come home with material for a new live album.

The boys weren't traveling light. In the best if-the-band-goes-everybody-goes tradition, in all 43 people departed for the continent—not just the musicians, crew and support staff (which now included Candace Brightman, the new lighting designer) but office staff, wives, girlfriends, kids, and friends. And they brought with them about seven tons of PA and other gear—much of it custom-designed Alembic stuff that would thoroughly baffle customs officials, hall technicians, and fire-code inspectors in five countries. The 16-track recorder alone was so big it required its own truck.

Candace Brightman

Lighting designer Candace Brightman worked at many top New York rock venues before joining the Dead's staff for the Europe '72 tour. Her imaginative artistry—like the Dead's music, completely improvised—was an important part of the band's shows, and to this day she works with The Dead (and with others).

Wednesday April 26
Jahrhundert Halle, Frankfurt, West Germany

The Jahrhundert Halle is a giant plastic dome built during the Nazi era, but the acoustics are quite good, and most of this show appears on the 1995 Vault release *Hundred Year Hall*.

Monday April 24
Rheinhalle, Dusseldorf, West Germany

25 **26** 27 28 **29** 30

19 20 **21** 22 23 **24**

Saturday April 29
Musikhalle, Hamburg, West Germany

Friday April 21
Beat Club, Bremen, West Germany

The band had been delighted at seeing their Danish audiences openly smoking hashish, but the Germans were a bit more uptight about these things, so the convoy approached the border in a cloud of smoke as everyone consumed their stashes. As it turned out, there would be (relatively) few hassles with border officials.

Monday April 17
Tivoli Concert Hall, Copenhagen, Denmark

A three-set show, with the first and second sets televised on the "TV from the Tivoli" show. It's also the breakout show for "He's Gone" *(see page 115)*—the only song to have its debut on the tour.

16 **17** 18

★ **Friday April 14**
Tivoli Concert Hall, Copenhagen, Denmark

"Brown-Eyed Women" from this show appears on *Europe '72*.

Sunday April 16
Aarhus University, Aarhus, Denmark

1 **2** 3 4 5 6 **7** 8

Sunday April 2
The band arrives in London to start the European Tour.

★ **Friday April 7**
★ **Saturday April 8**
Wembley Empire Pool, London, England

The chilly, drafty Empire Pool in suburban Wembley wasn't supposed to be the tour's first venue; the band was booked into North London's Rainbow Theatre, but the Rainbow went out of business while the Dead were in New York. Rock Scully managed to switch the gigs to the Empire, though the band had to share the house with a badminton tournament. On Friday, remembering 3/25, no doubt, the boys soundcheck to "Hey Bo Diddley." "Cumberland Blues" from Saturday's show appears on *Europe '72*.

9 10 **11** 12 13 **14** 15

"JACK STRAW"

WEIR/HUNTER

"We can share the women, we can share the wine..." So begins (and ends) one of the best outlaw tales the Dead had to offer. The song was written by Hunter and Garcia and debuted in Minneapolis, Minnesota, on October 19, 1971 before officially appearing on *Europe '72* (1972). The title character bore little resemblance to either the historical British figure who helped incite the Great Revolt of 1381 or the modern British foreign secretary who share his name; rather, the Dead's Jack is a murdering drifter who takes his chances in gambling and in life, although Hunter was quick to point out that he was just a fiction—especially the "share the women" line. "I think that people often believe that the character... is expressing my personal sentiments, which is not the case," he insisted in 1988. "I heard from a lot of feminist groups about that one when it first came out." Giving Weir a chance to flex some real rhythm guitar muscle, "Jack Straw" appeared mostly at the beginning of Dead shows from 1977 on, with over 450 versions between 1971 and 1995. It was also the first song played by The Other Ones during their debut in San Francisco on June 4, 1998.

Tuesday April 11
Newcastle City Hall, Newcastle-upon-Tyne, England

Bob Weir would recall this show as having "the coldest, stiffest audience I've ever played for." Tonight sees the first UK outing for "Jack Straw" *(see left)*.

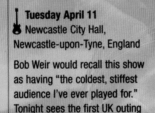

Right: Europe '72. Many years after the fact, Phil commented that on the Europe '72 tour, Bill Kreutzmann played "like a young god."

143

On the Bus(es)

The Band & Co. barnstormed across Europe aboard two buses: The Bozo bus and the Bolo bus. As Willy Legate described the vehicles in his liner notes to *Europe '72*, "The subtle difference in character and import and atmosphere between the two omnibuses was so profoundly hidden and enigmatic that you could never understand it." In fact, the Bolo/Bozo bus factionalism was rather pronounced. The Bozo bus was the party wagon, equipped with gag-shop masks and props, and it got its name from the Firesign Theatre comedy troupe's album *I Think We're All Bozos on this Bus*. The Bolo bus was mostly occupied by the crew and those (like Phil Lesh) who preferred to catch as many Z's as possible between shows.

Friday May 5
The band are forced to cancel a gig at the Lille Opera House, Lille, at the last moment and are literally run out of town *(see below)*.

1 | 2 | 3 | 4 | 5 | 6

🎸 **Wednesday May 3**
🎸 **Thursday May 4**
Olympia Theatre, Paris, France

The band's arrival in Paris marks the halfway point of the tour, so Warner Bros. underwrites a big dinner at La Grande Cascade in the Bois de Boulogne. The waiters wind up stoned. "China">"Rider," "Tennessee Jed," and "Jack Straw" from Wednesday's show appear on *Europe '72*, as does Thursday's "Sugar Magnolia."

No Night at the Opera

After the May 4, Olympia, show a student radical type harangued the band. Rex Jackson administered some tough love (a well-aimed ice-cream!), after which the young man tampered with the band's equipment truck in some fashion, making it completely unroadworthy for the next day's drive. So, while the band's buses made it to the next night's gig in Lille, the gear didn't. The word "refund" didn't appear in the promoter's vocabulary in any language, so the audience was enraged at the cancellation. Phil Lesh and Bob Weir tried to explain and apologize but were practically run off the stage. The refugees holed up in a dressing room while the angry mob pounded on the door. The only way out was through a window and down a drainpipe, onto the roof of a truck, and then a sprint for the bus. Weir was the last out and he hit the roof of the truck just as the dressing-room door gave way.

Management scrambled to find a replacement equipment truck. There followed a flat-out race for the ferry to England and thence to Wigan, Greater Manchester, for the Bickershaw Festival. They just made it; at least one car that got in their way didn't.

144

THE NAME ON THE SPINE may have read Bob Weir, but the music inside was by none other than the good ol' Grateful Dead. Though the eight songs on Weir's "solo" debut had all been written by the guitarist—two with Robert Hunter and five others with childhood friend John Barlow—many had already appeared in the band's live sets, and two were inspired by ideas that appeared in different form on drummer-in-absentia Mickey Hart's solo effort *Rolling Thunder*. Weir readily acknowledged his cohorts' contributions on what *Rolling Stone* had outright called "the best Grateful Dead album to appear since *Live/Dead*." "It was all me singing, all my songwriting. I started by using a couple of different musicians, and it just settled in to being a Grateful Dead record right quick," he told David Gans nearly a decade later.

The album also marked a particularly prolific period for Weir and his new composing cohort Barlow. Though one critic's declaration at the time that Weir was "the leader the Dead might need for self-renewal" was debatable, all but one of *Ace*'s selections proved to have staying power, remaining in the Dead's repertoire through to the 1990s.

ACE
Bob Weir
Released by Warner Bros. (BS-2627) in May 1972

Side One
1. **Greatest Story Ever Told**
(Weir/Hunter)
2. **Black Throated Wind**
(Weir/Barlow)
3. **Walk In The Sunshine**
(Weir/Barlow)
4. **Playing In The Band**
(Weir/Hunter)

Side Two
5. **Looks Like Rain**
(Weir/Barlow)
6. **Mexicali Blues**
(Weir/Barlow)
7. **One More Saturday Night**
(Weir)
8. **Cassidy**
(Weir/Barlow)

Personnel

Bob Weir – guitar, vocals
Jerry Garcia – guitar, pedal steel
Donna Godchaux – vocals
Keith Godchaux – piano
Bill Kreutzmann – drums
Phil Lesh – bass, vocals
Dave Torbert – bass

Produced by everybody involved
Cover art by Kelley/Mouse studios

Wednesday May 10
Concertgebouw, Amsterdam, Netherlands 🎸

Tonight's "He's Gone" appears on *Europe '72*.

🎸 **Thursday May 11 ★**
Rotterdam Civic Hall, Rotterdam, Netherlands

Final outings for "Who Do You Love" and "Caution (Do Not Stop on Tracks)."

13 | 14

🎸 **Saturday May 13**
Lille Fairgrounds, Lille, France

The Dead make good their promise to do a free show in Lille, reportedly reducing the promoter to tears.

7 | 8 | 9 | 10

11 | 12

Below: Not content to try cricket, the Dead play a game of baseball on the Europe tour.

🎸 **Sunday May 7**
Bickershaw Festival, Wigan, Greater Manchester, England

With NRPS (who are touring Europe on their own). The band performs before about 8,000 people in cold, rainy, and windy conditions.

"The Dead made the sun shine, took us into the Cosmos by way of a Southern California roadhouse and put us all back together again… Golden Gate Park had girdled the Earth and landed in Wigan."
JERRY UDALL, BICKERSHAW VETERAN

Right: Europe '72

No. 000362
£2.25

No. 016647
£2.25

Above, top right and right: Europe '72.

1 ~ 16	17	18 ~ 30

Thursday May 18
Kongressaal Deutsches Museum,
Munich, West Germany

According to Rock Scully in *Living with the Dead*, the band kills pre-show time at the museum and Jerry is in awe of the world's largest crystal of cocaine hydrochloride.

Monday May 15
A gunman shoots George Wallace, Alabama governor and independent presidential candidate, paralyzing him for life.

17	18	19 ~ 22
23	24	25	26	27 ~ 31

15	16

Tuesday May 16
Radio Luxembourg,
Luxembourg

The band plays live on
Radio Luxembourg.

Tuesday May 23
Wednesday May 24
Thursday May 25
Friday May 26 ★
Strand Lyceum, London, England

With NRPS. Tuesday sees the first "Rockin' Pneumonia and the Boogie Woogie Flu" and Wednesday marks the final "It Hurts Me Too," and the last "Turn on Your Love Light" with Pigpen. "It Hurts Me Too" and "You Win Again" from this show—and "Truckin'" and "Morning Dew" from the last—appear on *Europe '72*. "Sittin' on Top of the World" is retired on Thursday, and it's the last "Good Lovin'" with Pigpen on lead. Friday sees the last "Chinatown Shuffle," "Mr. Charlie," "Next Time," and "Two Souls in Communion/The Stranger."

Saturday June 17
Hollywood Bowl,
Hollywood, California

With NRPS. It's Pigpen's final show. Breakout of "Stella Blue" *(see page 379).*

STEVE
Hollywood Bowl

145

Pigpen's Last Show

June 17 at the Hollywood Bowl marked the end of the road for Pigpen. He had quit drinking completely after his serious illness in the fall of '71—"My only vices now are smoking cigarettes and pestering the wenches," he told an interviewer—but the damage to his organs had already been done. The European Tour (on which he'd gone against doctors' orders) had further taxed his weakened constitution, even though he'd largely forsaken his trademark rave-ups. The once-burly bluesman, now pale and thin, needed time off to try to recover. On tour that fall, Bob Weir would always tell audiences that Pigpen was sick and needed their best wishes.

Living alone in an apartment in Corte Madera, Pigpen worked on his planned solo album, but he grew physically weaker and mentally depressed. At one point toward the end of the year, he refused to see his girlfriend, Vee Barnard, telling her, "I don't want you around when I die."

"When they came back from Europe, the rest of the band would go on tours, Keith went out and Pig stayed home. Pig would call the office—it was just a skeleton crew—and he was really having a hard time with the band on the road and him being out of that. He would call and just want to talk. We all felt really bad for him because here was this person that I once thought was a Hells Angel, and now he was just this little thin person. It was like seeing someone get cancer and then just deteriorate. He had this thin, thin face, but he'd still have his little hat on."
Eileen Law (quoted in *The Golden Road*)

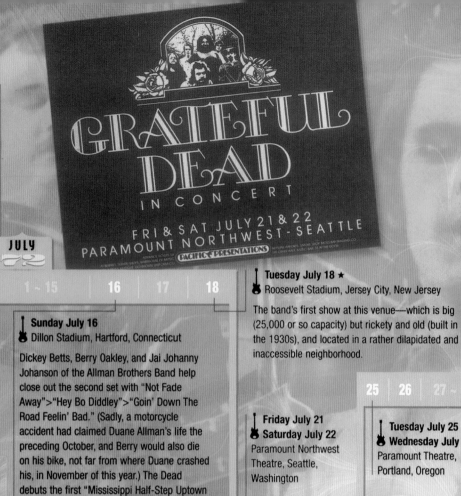

GRATEFUL DEAD
IN CONCERT

FRI & SAT JULY 21 & 22
PARAMOUNT NORTHWEST - SEATTLE

PACIFIC PRESENTATIONS

Below: In the early '70s, the visual experience at indoor shows was augmented by a trippy version of the group's name in lights and by the ubiquitous spinning mirror ball, a favorite since their SF ballroom days.

🎸 Sunday July 16
🎤 Dillon Stadium, Hartford, Connecticut

Dickey Betts, Berry Oakley, and Jai Johanny Johanson of the Allman Brothers Band help close out the second set with "Not Fade Away">"Hey Bo Diddley">"Goin' Down The Road Feelin' Bad." (Sadly, a motorcycle accident had claimed Duane Allman's life the preceding October, and Berry would also die on his bike, not far from where Duane crashed his, in November of this year.) The Dead debuts the first "Mississippi Half-Step Uptown Toodleoo," a jaunty Hunter/Garcia number that sprawls across several musical styles.

🎺 Tuesday July 18 ★
🎤 Roosevelt Stadium, Jersey City, New Jersey

The band's first show at this venue—which is big (25,000 or so capacity) but rickety and old (built in the 1930s), and located in a rather dilapidated and inaccessible neighborhood.

🎺 Friday July 21
🎤 Saturday July 22
Paramount Northwest Theatre, Seattle, Washington

🎸 Tuesday July 25
🎸 Wednesday July 26 ★
Paramount Theatre, Portland, Oregon

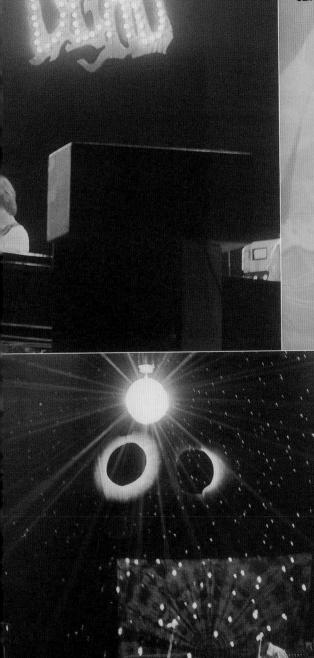

The Field Trip

Known variously as the Field Trip, the Springfield Creamery Show, and the Kesey Creamery Benefit, 8/27/72 at Veneta remains among the handful of legendary Dead shows, an event in which set and setting produced a performance that many Deadheads feel attained a truly supernatural level. Jerry Garcia sometimes spoke of times when "the music played the band," and this was certainly one of them.

The road to Veneta started when the small dairy operation run by Ken Kesey's brother Chuck and Chuck's wife Sue, the Springfield Creamery, ran into financial trouble. According to the Prankster History Project, one of the creamery's biggest customers, a local school district, canceled their contract out of fear that associates of Chuck's brother would dose the kiddies' milk. Ken Kesey asked the Dead to come up to the Eugene area (now home not only to the Pranksters but to many back-to-the-land hippie types) to do a benefit, and they readily agreed. Having missed the Acid Test Graduation (*see page 61*), the band would now play the Acid Test Homecoming, so to speak.

The Keseys rented the Old Renaissance Faire Grounds—a lovely expanse of hills and meadows, carpeted at this time of year with wildflowers. Tickets were printed on labels for the creamery's yogurt, with "Acidophilus" where the promoter's name would usually be (geddit?).

August 27 was hot. Really hot. It was reportedly the hottest day in the history of Oregon and the temperature hit a high of (depending on who you talk to) between 100°F and 108°F. Miraculously (or due to the timely arrival of a water truck), there don't seem to have been any serious casualties from the heat—and much of the crowd decamped to the treeline in search of shade. There was no escape for the band, however; in another triumph of planning, the stage faced west into the full force of the afternoon sun. "We're changing our name to 'the Sun-Stroked Serenaders,'" Bob Weir joked at one point. The heat and sun meant the instruments were pretty much out of tune through the show, but as the boys got deeper into the music, and vice-versa, conventionalities like tuning seemed irrelevant.

The band played three sublime sets, the highlight for most being the monstrous "Dark Star" that kicked off the final set. A "One More Saturday Night" encore (it was Sunday) ended the party as the sunlight shaded into dusk.

Sunshine Daydream

Filmmaker Phil DeGuere (*see page 314*) and members of the Pranksters' own movie crew, Far West Action Picture Service, set up seven cameras to record the show. (Jerry Garcia reportedly wondered why anyone would want to see a movie of a Grateful Dead performance, since "we just stand there.") The band didn't like either the rough cut or a later version that alternated shots of the show with "archival" Prankster footage, so the movie, *Sunshine Daydream*, went into bootleg purgatory, although there were reports of an official release in 2003.

"That old sun is making our instruments get mighty strange."

BOB WEIR TO THE AUDIENCE

---

11 | 12 | 13 | 14 | 15

Wednesday August 16
The Summer Olympics begin in Munich, Germany. The games are marred by the terrorist murder of 11 Israeli athletes.

Saturday August 12
Sacramento Memorial Auditorium, Sacramento, California

16 | 17 | 18 | 19 | 20

Sunday August 20
San Jose Civic Auditorium, San Jose, California

21 | 22 | 23 | 24 | 25 | 26

Monday August 21
Tuesday August 22
Thursday August 24
Friday August 25
Berkeley Community Theatre, Berkeley, California

NRPS join the band for Thursday's gig. Following the Berkeley Community Theatre shows, Bear returns to the band's circle. He'd done two years of federal time at Terminal Island and then Lompoc, where he acquired his metalworking and jewelry-making skills. There's a lot of friction between Bear and the crew, however, and he finds his diminished role frustrating.

Nancy's Honey Yogurt Acidophilus Grade A
PRESENTS
THE GRATEFUL DEAD
AUGUST 27th
Springfield Creamery
Springfield, Oregon

Sunday August 27 ★
Old Renaissance Faire Grounds, Veneta, Oregon

With NRPS.

27 | 28 | 29 | 30 | 31

ROLLING THUNDER

Mickey Hart

Released by Warner Bros. (BS-2635) in September 1972

Side One

1. **Rolling Thunder (Shoshone Invocation)**
   (Rolling Thunder)
2. **The Main Ten (Playing In The Band)**
   (Hart/Hunter/Weir)
3. **Fletcher Carnaby**
   (Hart/Hunter)
4. **The Chase (Progress)**
   (Hart)
5. **Blind John**
   (Monk/Stetson)

Side Two

1. **Young Man**
   (Hart/Monk)
2. **Deep, Wide and Frequent**
   (Hart)
3. **Pump Song**
   (Hart/Hunter/Weir)
4. **Gran'ma's Cookies**
   (Hart)
5. **Hangin' On**
   (Monk/Stetson/Hart)

Personnel

Mike Hinton – marimbas
Nancy Hinton – marimbas
Alla Rahka – rain
Zakir Hussain – rain, table
John Cipollina – guitar
Bob Weir – guitar, vocals
Tower of Power Horns
Stephen Stills – bass
Mickey Hart – drums, field drums, tympani, percussion
Carmelo Garcia – percussion
Sam Andrews – guitar
Robbie Stokes – guitar, bass
David Freiberg – guitar, bass, piano, vocals, water pump, viola; **Steven Schuster** – flute; **Jerry Garcia** – guitar, insect fear; **Grace Slick** – piano, vocals; **Greg Errico** – drums; **Barry Melton** – guitar, vocals; **Paul Kantner** – vocals; **Phil Lesh** – vocals, bass; **Carmelo Garcia** – timbales, congas; **Terry Haggerty** – guitar; **Bill Champlin** – organ

MICKEY HART ASSEMBLED an impressive cast for his first solo effort, including Grace Slick, Stephen Stills, and John Cipollina, along with his former (and future) Dead buddies Garcia, Lesh, and Weir. Though the album was less high-profile than debut solo bids by Garcia and Weir released the same year by Warner Bros, it served as one of the earliest mainstream forays into what would become known as world music. The album included two songs, "The Main Ten" and "Pump Song," that had already been fleshed out by the Dead as "Playin' In The Band" and "Greatest Story Ever Told," respectively. Despite his temporary departure from the band—from 1971 to 1974—they supported the effort, even including mention of it in their third newsletter to Dead fans, enthusing that the record featured "Mickey as well as at least thirty of the heaviest musicians around these days… really a fine album!" The disc's only single, "Blind John," was one of three not credited to Hart. (The flip side, "Pump Song," was said to have taken its rhythmic pattern from that of a pump located on Hart's California ranch.) But *Rolling Thunder* was pure Mickey, giving fans an early taste of what was to come in the years ahead from the percussionist who never met a genre he didn't like.

"Every now and then we get the feeling you'd like to hear us do something nice and straight. Well, we never ever do anything nice and straight. Well, we're going to do the beginning of this song and we're going to start out nice and straight. And then we're going to take the end of the song and we're going to finish it up real weird." BOB WEIR, CHANNELING TINA TURNER BEFORE THE SEPTEMBER 3 SHOW'S "EL PASO"

Thursday September 21
The Spectrum, Philadelphia, Pennsylvania

The band's first show (on their own—see *12/06/68*) at this 18,000-seat venue.

Saturday September 23
Sunday September 24
Palace Theatre, Waterbury, Connecticut

The "Cryptical Envelopment" segment of "The Other One" goes into a 13-year hibernation after Saturday (see *6/16/85*). On Sunday Donna Jean Godchaux and Jerry Garcia are on lead vocals for the breakout of Dolly Parton and Porter Wagoner's duet "Tomorrow is Forever," which will appear at nine more shows in '72 and once more in the penultimate pre-hiatus Winterland show (see *10/19/74*).

19	20	21	22	23	24	25	26	27	28

Tuesday September 19
Roosevelt Stadium, Jersey City, New Jersey

Tuesday September 26
★ **Wednesday September 27**
Thursday September 28
Stanley Theatre, Jersey City, New Jersey

Tuesday sees the last performance of "You Win Again."

"CRYPTICAL ENVELOPMENT"
GARCIA

First appearing on the Dead's experimental second album *Anthem of the Sun* (1968) as the opening segment of a multi-part, 12 minute-plus suite of music called "That's It For The Other One" (*see page 77*), "Cryptical Envelopment" sets a somber scene in which an unidentified martyr faces his inevitable fate. "The other day they waited," the song begins. "The sky was dark and faded; solemnly they stated, 'He has to die.'" Garcia explained the passage in 1991. "That's an extension of my own personal symbology for 'The Man of Constant Sorrow,' the old folk song," he said, "which I always thought of as being a sort of Christ parable." The song, often along with its reprise, was documented in nearly 100 shows before Garcia abandoned it in the fall of 1972. "It wasn't happening for me emotionally," he explained. "Certain songs stop being viable because they are not graceful enough to keep performing in a natural way." That didn't stop the guitarist from bringing "Cryptical" back into the fold for five shows in 1985, while The Other Ones later treated newer fans to this rare piece of their Dead past by including the section in five more concerts in 2002.

Sunday September 3
Folsom Field, University of Colorado, Boulder, Colorado

The "Meteorological Synchronicity" mythos is further established when the heavy rains cease during the show.

Saturday September 9
Sunday September 10
Hollywood Palladium, Hollywood, California

On Sunday David Crosby guests on "Dark Star," "Jack Straw," "Sing Me Back Home," and "Sugar Magnolia."

Sunday September 17
Baltimore Civic Center, Baltimore, Maryland

15	16	17

Friday September 15
Saturday September 16
Boston Music Hall, Boston, Massachusetts

1	2	3	4 – 8	9	10	11 ~ 14

Dead Dynamics

Despite the departure of Pigpen and Mickey Hart, the sextet that set out on tour in September '72 was a band at the top of its game. In the opinion of many Deadheads, this tour may have been the band's best, at least in terms of consistently excellent shows.

Bob Weir essentially inherited the role of frontman from Pigpen, and he had fun with it. With his jazz orientation and bright, full sound, Keith Godchaux was working out perfectly. The presence of Donna Godchaux, the first really superb vocalist in the group, vastly upgraded their harmonies. Phil Lesh continued to boldly go where no bassist had gone before, and on the skins, Bill Kreutzmann was "just kickin' our butts every which way," as Phil noted in an interview around this time. As for Jerry, his solos now built to peaks of fluid intensity that Deadheads dubbed "Jerry's Tigers" or "the Tiger's Roar." Jerry now mostly played "the Wolf," an ax custom-made for him by Doug Irwin.

In terms of improvisation, the band pulled back from the psychedelic precipice in favor of a more jazzlike approach—a stylistic development which, again, was underpinned by the addition of Keith Godchaux. The Dead had now established a performance pattern that saw the more "discrete" songs in the first set, with extended jamming in the second set.

Monday October 23
Tuesday October 24
Performing Arts Center, Milwaukee, Wisconsin

The band wind up in the same hotel as Senator George McGovern, the Democratic presidential candidate. McGovern's Secret Service detachment has their nerves frayed by the band and crew's habit of ambushing one another with firecrackers. It is in Milwaukee, too, that tour rage compels Bob Weir and Bill Kreutzmann to get into a fight about the relative freezing temperatures of cement or metal. Ram Rod, thankfully, is on hand to break it up.

Monday October 30
Ford Auditorium, Detroit, Michigan

Saturday October 28 ★
Cleveland Public Hall, Cleveland, Ohio

Friday October 27
Veterans Memorial Auditorium, Columbus, Ohio

Thursday October 26
Music Hall, Cincinnati, Ohio

Saturday October 21
Vanderbilt University, Nashville, Tennessee

Tuesday October 17
Wednesday October 18 ★
Thursday October 19
Fox Theatre, St. Louis, Missouri

OCTOBER '72

Monday October 9
Winterland Arena, San Francisco, California

Grace Slick performs some scat-style vocal stylings over a second-set-opening jam. The show also marks the first live performance of "Box of Rain."

Monday October 2
Springfield Civic Center Arena, Springfield, Massachusetts

The last "Uncle John's Jam," as a sandwich between "Drums" and "Morning Dew."

Saturday September 30
Soccer Field, American University, Washington, D.C.

Below left, below, and right:
October 17–19, Fox Theatre, St. Louis, Missouri: Jerry backstage; the Fox Theatre marquee; and Phil Lesh.

FOX THEATER
527 No. GRAND, ST. LOUIS, MO.
KSHE-FM PRESENTS
GRATEFUL DEAD
PRODUCED BY PACIFIC PRESENTATIONS & SKY HIGH ASSOC.
TUESDAY EVE. 8:00 P.M.
OCT.
17
1972
GENERAL ADMISSION $4.50
NO REFUND — NO EXCHANGE

October 1972

149

Name: Tony Dwyer

GRATEFUL DEAD
IN CONCERT
STAGE PASS

TONITE GRATEFUL DEAD TONITE

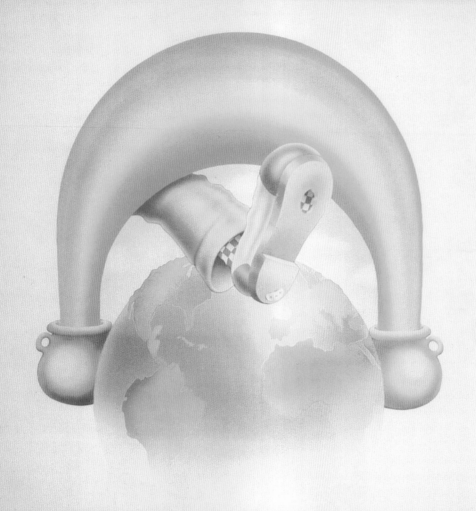

EUROPE '72
Grateful Dead

Released by Warner Bros. (3WS-2668) in November 1972

Side One
1. **Cumberland Blues**
   (Garcia/Lesh/Hunter)
2. **He's Gone**
   (Garcia/Hunter)
3. **One More Saturday Night**
   (Weir)

Side Two
1. **Jack Straw**
   (Weir/Hunter)
2. **You Win Again**
   (Williams)
3. **China Cat Sunflower**
   (Garcia/Hunter)
4. **I Know You Rider**
   (Traditional)

Side Three
1. **Brown Eyed Woman**
   (Garcia/Hunter)
2. **Hurts Me Too**
   (James/Sehorn)
3. **Ramble On Rose**
   (Garcia/Hunter)

Side Four
1. **Sugar Magnolia**
   (Weir/Hunter)
2. **Mr. Charlie**
   (McKernan/Hunter)
3. **Tennessee Jed**
   (Garcia/Hunter)

Side Five
1. **Truckin'**
   (Garcia/Lesh/Weir/Hunter)
2. **Epilogue**
   (Grateful Dead)

Side Six
1. **Prelude**
   (Grateful Dead)
2. **Morning Dew**
   (Rose/Dobson)

Personnel

Jerry Garcia – lead guitar, vocals
Donna Godchaux – vocals
Keith Godchaux – piano
Bill Kreutzmann – drums
Phil Lesh – bass, vocals
Pigpen (Ron McKernan) – organ, harmonica, vocals
Bob Weir – rhythm guitar, vocals
Merl Saunders – organ (later studio overdubs)

Produced by the Grateful Dead

WITH THE SUCCESS OF THE previous year's live album *Skull & Roses* still fresh in their minds and an era of studio work temporarily set aside, the Dead set sail for Europe, arriving in April of 1972 with "the mysterious glamor of their psychedelic history flying beside the boisterous, 45-strong crew," according to the tour program that accompanied the band's nearly two-month journey.

Each note of the 22-show run was dutifully recorded on a mobile 16-track machine by engineer Bob Matthews. The resulting triple-album release, originally known as *Over There* before the Dead settled on the Fodor's-worthy *Europe '72*, chronicled one of the more memorable expeditions in the band's ongoing trip. In addition to the certified Pigpen covers that would mark some of the bluesman's last performances with the Dead, the album featured a crop of originals appearing for the first time, including "He's Gone," "Jack Straw," "Brown-Eyed Women," "Ramble On Rose," "Mr. Charlie," and "Tennessee Jed."

Though a decision to sweeten the mix with studio overdubs upon the band's return to the States later offended concert purists, *Europe '72* reached No. 24 in the American charts, becoming the Dead's highest-charting live album and second to be certified gold.

Stanley Mouse and Alton Kelley did the cover art for *Europe '72*. Their initial concept involved a military patch incorporating the stealie logo *(see page 158)*, in keeping with the album's working title, *Over There*, a reference to George M. Cohan's hyper-patriotic World War I song. Another concept involved a *National Geographic* magazine-style jacket, but this was tabled for legal reasons, and the "Rainbow Foot" image was ultimately used.

The back cover featured the now-iconic "Ice Cream Kid," inspired by a (rather politically incorrect) joke the two artists heard at a costume party. The album included a four-color insert with photos by Mary Ann Mayer and quirky notes from Robert Hunter.

Tuesday November 7
President Richard Nixon wins a second term as president, easily beating Democratic challenger George McGovern in the polls.

Sunday November 12
Monday November 13
Soldiers and Sailors Memorial Hall, Kansas City, Kansas

The band's first shows in Kansas, and the first at this venue.

8 – 11   12   13

14   15   16   17

Tuesday November 14
Wednesday November 15
Oklahoma City Music Hall, Oklahoma City, Oklahoma

The band's first shows in Oklahoma.

Friday November 17
Century II Convention Hall, Wichita, Kansas

Right: Sunday December 31; Bob Weir at Winterland Arena, San Francisco, California.

Saturday November 18
Sunday November 19

Hofheinz Pavilion, Houston, Texas

The Allman Brothers Band were to be on the bill for at least one of the Hofheinz Pavilion shows, but they had to cancel due to Berry Oakley's tragic death the preceding week.

Sunday December 10
Monday December 11
Tuesday December 12

Winterland Arena, San Francisco, California

On Sunday with High Country, on Monday with Sons of Champlin, and on Tuesday with the Rowan Brothers plus David Grisman.

Sunday December 31

Winterland Arena, San Francisco, California

The New Year's Eve show is technically the New Year's Day show as the band kicks off after Bill Graham leads the audience in the midnight countdown. David Crosby guests on guitar through much of the second set, which closes with "Morning Dew."

| 18 | 19 | 20 | 21 | 22 | 23 | | 1 ~ 9 | 10 | 11 | 12 | 13 | 14 | 15 | 16 | 17 | 18 | 19 | 20 | 21 ~ 30 | 31 |

Friday November 24
Dallas Memorial Auditorium, Dallas, Texas

Wednesday November 22
Austin Municipal Auditorium, Austin, Texas

| 24 | 25 | 26 | 27 ~ 30 |

Sunday November 26
San Antonio Civic Auditorium, San Antonio, Texas

Friday December 15
Long Beach Arena, Long Beach, California

Tuesday December 19
The Apollo 17 astronauts—the last humans, so far, to walk on the Moon—return safely to Earth.

Wednesday December 20
President Nixon orders a halt to the bombing of North Vietnam.

December 1972

151

Pinked Out

By the start of 1973 Bear was out of jail and Dan Healy was back with the band, so together with Bob Matthews and the Alembic crew, the technical team started to put together a major new sound system, which made its debut at the February 9 show at Stanford University. At the heart of the system was an array of specially modified Electro Voice tweeters which, with $20,000 worth of new amps and other gear, was specifically designed to create pink noise—leveling out highs and lows to create an even, distortion-free signal. At the first notes of the "Promised Land" opener, however, the entire tweeter array blew, erasing about half of that twenty-grand investment in a mere matter of seconds. It was time to go back to the drawing board, with the continued support of the band. Still, the smoked system was an important evolutionary step toward the mother of all sound systems, the Wall of Sound *(see page 166)*.

Friday February 9
Roscoe Maples Pavilion,
Stanford University, Palo Alto, California

The performance year begins with the band's biggest multiple breakout—seven new Garcia and Hunter songs: "Wave That Flag," the lineal ancestor of "U.S. Blues"; the loping, reggae-influenced "They Love Each Other" and "Row Jimmy"; the lilting "Eyes of the World"; "Loose Lucy," an R&B-propelled jailbait story in the manner of the late Pigpen; and "Here Comes Sunshine" and "China Doll." "Sunshine" was informed musically, Garcia later noted, by the Beatles' "sun songs" on Abbey Road ("Here Comes the Sun," "The Sun King"); the lyrics recalled Hunter's childhood experience of fleeing the Vanport, Washington, flood of 1949. The buzzkill in this upbeat set was "China Doll," which Hunter dubbed "The Suicide Song."

Saturday January 27
The US combat role in the Vietnam War is effectively ended today with an official ceasefire agreement signed in Paris.

"U.S. BLUES"
GARCIA/HUNTER

As red, white, and blue as the best of Irving Berlin or George M. Cohan, "U.S. Blues" added a different kind of patriotic slant to the Great American Song Catalog, with a rocking picture of the iconographic Uncle Sam that was a bit different from the patented, finger-pointing version. "Red and white, blue suede shoes," the Garcia/Hunter collaboration begins. "I'm Uncle Sam, how do you do? Give me five, I'm still alive. Ain't no luck, I learned to duck." Originally attached to the song that became "One More Saturday Night" *(see page 438)*, Hunter reclaimed the title when Weir decided to rewrite his first effort. A version of the song called "Wave That Flag" came and went in 1973 before the revised and retitled draft debuted live on February 22, 1974. It also appeared as a studio track on *From The Mars Hotel* (1974). "We have our pantheon, and one of the figures in the pantheon is Uncle Sam," Weir said in 1991. "He's sort of like the godfather of American culture, so we actually have a fair bit of respect for him. And he comes around in different guises." He continued to come around in the form of "U.S. Blues" until July 8, 1995, with a total of 323 performances.

Monday February 19
International Amphitheatre, Chicago, Illinois

Nudie's of Hollywood has outfitted the royalty of Nashville and Hollywood with their rhinestone-studded stagewear since Elvis first hit the scene. The Dead commissioned "Nudie suits" of their own, complete with sinuous skeletons, but only got to wear them for this show.

19   20   21   22

Wednesday February 21
★ **Thursday February 22**
Assembly Hall, University of Illinois, Champaign-Urbana, Illinois

Thursday sees the first performance of "U.S. Blues."

Monday February 26
Pershing Municipal Auditorium, Lincoln, Nebraska

All pictures:
Monday February 19,
International Amphitheatre,
Chicago, Illinois

Thursday February 15 ★
Dane County Coliseum, Madison, Wisconsin

Saturday February 17
St. Paul Auditorium, St. Paul, Minnesota

15   16   17   18

23   24   25   26   27   28

Saturday February 24
Fieldhouse, University of Iowa, Iowa City, Iowa

Wednesday February 28
Salt Palace, Salt Lake City, Utah

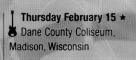

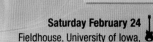

Grateful Dead Records, Round Records, and Big Business

As the '60s turned into the '70s and rock music took on elements of high art as well as becoming big business, groups longed to follow the example of the Beatles in establishing their own record companies. Who wouldn't want to do their own thing, in their own time, without the suits breathing down their necks ranting about studio budgets, promotional appearances, and how long it's been since the last single? The Grateful Dead, greatly valuing autonomy in all things, were no exception, thought it wasn't a band member but wheeler-dealer "Cadillac Ron" Rakow *(see page 82)* who first proposed the idea of Grateful Dead Records on July 4, 1972 in a report he titled "The So What Papers." (No doubt the canny Rakow was making a point about "Independence.") This 93-page proposal was met with apathy by most of the band, but Jerry Garcia got behind the idea and the rest of the boys followed along; Phil Lesh later summed up the collective attitude that it was "worth trying." So Grateful Dead Records was born. Now they had to get financing. Rakow thought that they could get a government small-business loan if "hippies" were classified as a "minority." (He also proposed that GDR distribute its releases through ice-cream trucks.) Eventually Rakow talked the Bank of Boston into a loan. One business associate who raised a problem with GDR was Hal Kant, who pointed out a major conflict of interest when Jerry and Ron created Round Records, a parallel partnership for solo and side projects. Hal was shunted aside as record company attorney (he remained the band's attorney), and they moved on. Steve Brown, a fan and friend since the Haight, joined as GDR jack-of-all-trades. Besides GDR and Round Records, the band set up Fly by Night Travel (run by Bob Weir's girlfriend Frankie and Rosie McGee) to serve as its travel agent, and Out of Town Tours (run by Sam Cutler) to do its booking.

"My interview for the job at Grateful Dead Records was about seeing if there was common ground and cohesion—what we all liked. It was a fitting, not an interview."
STEVE BROWN, 2003

153

Jerry Garcia
ROUND RECORDS
BOX 1166, SAN RAFAEL, CA 9490

Pigpen 1945 - 1973

THREE DECADES AFTER HIS PASSING, Pigpen has become such a legendary character, so enshrined in the mythos of the Grateful Dead, that in assessing his life and legacy there's almost a perverse desire to find some flaw, some crack in that formidable façade. But Pigpen resists debunking. He was what he was, and he was the soul of the Grateful Dead in its formative years. He was the one who convinced his Mother McCree's bandmates to trade in their banjos and washboards for electric axes; he programmed the Warlocks' repertoire around the blues and R&B he loved so much; and onstage, he was the anchor when the early Grateful Dead threatened to founder in seas of psychedelia.

Pigpen differed from his bandmates in that he was essentially a performer in a group of musicians. This is not to denigrate his musicianship, but to Pigpen, the audience was as much of an instrument as his voice or his keyboard—and he played the audience with all the skill and brilliance of Jerry executing a lightning solo or Phil firing a salvo of bombs. But while the rest of the band began exploring exotic time signatures and searching for the sound of thick air, Pigpen's motorcycle boots remained solidly planted in the bedrock of American music. In the tradition of the performers he revered—Big Joe Turner, Wilson Pickett, Otis Redding—he saw his job as helping the audience have a good time—to get them off. And boy, did they get off. Oliver Trager put it perfectly in *The American Book of the Dead*: "Anyone who had the experience of seeing Ron 'Pigpen' McKernan rise from his Hammond B-3 organ, swagger across the stage, and commence belting out a torrid 'Turn on Your Love Light' while the band percolated behind him will likely take that fearsome, jaw-dropping sight to the grave—the tie-dyed memories slowly fading to sepia."

That was Pigpen, but there was also "Blue Ron" McKernan. This isn't to suggest that "Pigpen" was a put-on persona; again, he was what he was. But there was the hard-living Pigpen who caroused all night with bikers in his room behind the kitchen at 710 Ashbury, packed a Beretta, and carried his bottle of Southern Comfort in a black doctor's bag. And then there was the sweet, shy, Ron McKernan who loved chess and science fiction, and about whom no one ever seems to have said a bad word.

Cliché though it is, it has to be said that Pigpen not only performed the blues, he lived them, and ultimately

that life killed him. Pigpen may have started on the bottle (at age 12 or so) in emulation of old-time bluesmen, but alcohol became an end to itself, and even though he heroically separated himself from the bottle, his booze-raddled insides doomed him to an inexorable decline. His last months were filled with pain and loneliness. He had lived a life worthy of any of his musical heroes, but the cost was death at a heartbreakingly young age. But the sadness of his death can't obscure the awesome exuberance and sheer foot-stompin', testifyin' joy he brought to shows as the Grateful Dead's frontman. The love light still shines.

"He was our anchor... he was like gravity... Pigpen was like a warm fire, a cozy fire." JERRY GARCIA TO BLAIR JACKSON, *1993*

"If I could have one wish in the world, it would be that Pigpen was still with us. I think it's safe to say we *all* miss Pigpen."

PHIL LESH TO BLAIR JACKSON, *1981*

This page: Jerry Garcia, Phil Lesh, and Bob Weir play The Spectrum, Philadelphia, Pennsylvania, on Saturday March 24.

In spring '73, unknown Irish folk group the Chieftains came to the US. Jerry already knew and liked the group and fixed them radio interviews and an opening slot at an Old & In the Way show. Jerry and Tom Moloney, the chief Chieftain, became lifelong friends.

Friday March 30
Community War Memorial, Rochester, New York

APRIL '73

30 | 31 | 1 | 2 | 3 | 4 | 5 ~ 30

Monday April 2
Boston Garden, Boston, Massachusetts

Wednesday March 28
Springfield Civic Center Arena, Springfield, Massachusetts

Saturday March 31
War Memorial Auditorium, Buffalo, New York

27 | 28 | 29

Thursday March 27
Jerry Garcia and Robert Hunter decide to drive from Baltimore to Springfield, but are pulled over for speeding on the New Jersey Turnpike. The police find pot in Jerry's briefcase and he's arrested (Hunter isn't charged). New Jersey promoter John Scher bails Jerry out.

155

Saturday March 10
A wake for Pigpen is held at Bob Weir's new house in Mill Valley; it turns into a party the dear departed would have loved. It becomes a *de facto* outdoor event, with 500 people spilling out of Weir's property and onto nearby hills—drinking, dancing, and making love in the rain.

Monday March 12
Pigpen had a traditional Roman Catholic funeral in a church in Corte Madera, attended by his family, the band members, and a miscellany of scenesters, including some Hells Angels. In his open coffin, Pigpen reposed in his leather jacket, his cowboy hat on the pillow. On his gravestone in Alta Mesa cemetery these words are inscribed: "Pigpen was and is now forever one of the Grateful Dead."

MARCH '73

1 ~ 7 | 8 | 9 | 10 | 11 | 12 | 13

Thursday March 8
Dave Parker, Pigpen's friend and bandmate from Mother McCree's, gets a call from Pigpen's landlady, worried that her tenant hadn't left his home lately. On arrival at Pigpen's Corte Madera apartment, Parker found Pigpen's body. Cause of death was massive internal bleeding—even though he'd been sober for a year and a half, his drink-damaged system had finally failed. He was 27. Pigpen's last weeks had been lonely. Chess remained a passion, when he could find a partner. Early in March he'd shown up at a rehearsal, but the interaction with his bandmates was awkward. Increasingly tired and weak, he spent most of his time in his apartment, working on his solo album; one of his last songs included the lines "Seems like there's no tomorrow/Seems like all my yesterdays were filled with pain."

Sunday March 18
An impromptu supergroup—NRPS with Jerry Garcia and Bob Weir, Keith and Donna Godchaux, and folk legend Ramblin' Jack Elliott—plays the Felt Forum, Madison Square Garden, New York, New York.

Wednesday March 21
Thursday March 22
Utica Memorial Auditorium, Utica, New York

14 | 15 | 16 | 17 | 18 | 19 | 20 | 21 | 22 | 23 | 24 | 25 | 26

Thursday March 15
Friday March 16 ★
Monday March 19
Nassau Veterans Memorial Coliseum, Uniondale, New York

Three days after Pigpen's funeral, the band is on tour, giving little time to grieve and adjust, which they could have used. Even though Pigpen hadn't performed with the band since 6/17/72, and all are aware of how sick he became, the loss of someone who'd meant so much at such a young age is a shock. On Thursday, they play a halting "He's Gone" in his memory. This is the first of 42 gigs at this venue—and Phil Lesh's 33rd birthday.

Saturday March 24
The Spectrum, Philadelphia, Pennsylvania

The gig sees the first "Spanish Jam" since 2/11/70.

Monday March 26
Baltimore Civic Center, Baltimore, Maryland

Old & In the Way

In spring '73 Jerry, musically voracious as ever, picked up his banjo and began playing bluegrass with John Kahn, David Grisman, and Peter Rowan, who'd played guitar for bluegrass honcho Bill Monroe. (Peter was the brother of the Rowan Brothers, Chris and Lorin, whom Grisman had managed.) The quartet began gigging around Marin. Richard Greene joined on fiddle, briefly, but when he left for L.A., the group, dubbed Old & In the Way, brought aboard a true bluegrass star—Vassar Clements, a veteran who'd played with Monroe, Flatt & Scruggs, and other greats. The group clicked, with a mainly traditional bluegrass repertoire, and some interesting twists, like the Rolling Stones' "Wild Horses" and the New Riders' "Panama Red," which Rowan had written. The group's life was short—27 gigs, all in '73, most on the West Coast—but sweet; all who heard them agreed they had something special. They recorded an album at Mickey Hart's studio, but didn't release it—Grisman felt it was "rushed"—but three live albums (two released in '97) captured the acoustic magic. In a sad twist of fate, Jerry was considering re-forming the group shortly before his death.

Right and insets: Sunday May 20, Campus Stadium, University of California at Santa Barbara. That's Steve Brown in the tie-dye manning the Dead's information booth.

🎸 **Sunday May 13**
Iowa State Fairgrounds, Des Moines, Iowa

MAY '73

1 – 12 | 13 | 14

Monday May 14
The U.S. launches the 85-ton Skylab 1, its first crewed space station.

May 1973

156

🎸 **Sunday May 20**
Campus Stadium, University of California, Santa Barbara, California

An afternoon show with NRPS.

🎸 **Saturday May 26**
Kezar Stadium, San Francisco, California

Another afternoon concert, with NRPS and Waylon Jennings.

15 | 16 | 17 | 18 | 19 | 20 | 21 – 25 | 26 | 27 – 31

John Kahn

The 25-year relationship between Jerry Garcia and bassist John Kahn began in 1970 when they were both part of a loose jam band led by jazz keyboardist Howard Wales that played at the Matrix Club in San Francisco. Kahn (b.1947) had grown up in Beverly Hills, the son of Hollywood talent agents, and moved to San Francisco in 1966 to attend the Conservatory of Music. Initially a jazz fan, his interests shifted to rock and R&B in the late '60s, and he was in a series of now-forgotten Bay Area bands. Garcia once said that he and Kahn barely spoke to each other the first year they played together, yet they became best friends and musical partners—Kahn played bass in all of Garcia's solo bands, from the group with organist Merl Saunders beginning in 1971 through the last Jerry Garcia Band in the '90s. The taciturn but witty bassist produced and wrote most of the arrangements for Garcia's second solo album (*Compliments*, 1974) and also helped the Dead complete *Shakedown Street* in 1978. Alas, he shared Garcia's appetite for opiates and other drugs, and died in his sleep in 1996, a year after Garcia passed away.

Friday May 18
Watergate hearings begin and are televised; JG and others become addicted to coverage and tune in regularly throughout the summer.

Below: Deadheads having a good time at Campus Stadium, University of California at Santa Barbara, Sunday May 20.

Tuesday June 26
Seattle Center Arena, Seattle, Washington

| 26 | 27 | 28 | 29 | 30 |

Friday June 29
Saturday June 30
Universal Amphitheatre, Universal City, California

Saturday June 9
Sunday June 10 ★
Robert F. Kennedy Stadium, Washington, D.C.

The Allman Brothers play both nights. On Sunday, Merl Saunders and the Allmans join the band for a third set.

| 22 | 23 | 24 | 25 |

Sunday June 24
Portland Memorial Coliseum, Portland, Oregon

| 9 | 10 | 11 | 12 – 21 |

Friday June 22
PNE Coliseum, Vancouver, British Colombia, Canada

FIRE UP
Merl Saunders
Released by Fantasy (9421) in 1973

Side One

1. **After Midnight**
   (Cale)
2. **Expressway (To Your Heart)**
   (Gamble/Huff)
3. **Charisma (She's Got)**
   (Saunders)
4. **Soul Roach**
   (Saunders/Shanklin)

Side Two

1. **Chock-Lite Puddin'**
   (Saunders)
2. **Benedict Rides**
   (Saunders/Carrier)
3. **The System**
   (Saunders/Carrier)
4. **Lonely Avenue**
   (Pomus)

Personnel

Merl Saunders – electric piano, organ, ARP (flute), arp (band), clavinet
Jerry Garcia – guitar, vocals
Tom Fogerty – rhythm guitar
John Kahn – bass
Bill Vitt – drums
Gaylord Birch – congas, drums, tambourine
Chuck Rainey – bass
Walter Hawkins and sisters (Tramaine, Lynette and Feddie) – background vocals
Mike Howell – guitar, rhythm guitar
Ken Nash – percussion
John Kahn – electric piano
Christopher Parker – drums
Bill Somers – percussion
Bill Kreutzmann – drums

Produced by Merl Saunders

JUNE '73

| 1 | 2 | 3 | 4 | 5 | 6 | 7 | 8 |

Tuesday June 5
In between Dead shows, Old & In the Way begins its only real "tour," playing two nights at Boston's Orpheum Theatre, followed by gigs in New Jersey, Connecticut, Pennsylvania, and Virginia.

Below: Jerry Garcia on tour with Old & In the Way.

TAKING THE LIVE CAMARADERIE they'd continued to develop back into the studio, keyboardist Merl Saunders recruited Garcia for six of the eight songs on this Fantasy Records release. Drummer Kreutzmann sat in for a cover of the Doc Pomus song "Lonely Avenue." Besides advancing a musical friendship that would prove to be one of Garcia's most cherished outside of the Dead, Saunders would later remember the guitarist's words of encouragement when he was confronted with creative differences from his label. "Jerry always encouraged me to write material for the group," he told Blair Jackson. "Fantasy was saying stuff like, 'The music is great, but these words about ecology and whatnot, you gotta tone 'em down.' I said, 'I like the words.' And Jerry's attitude was, 'Yeah, fuck 'em! Do what you want, Merl!' He was really my inspiration to do things the way I wanted to do them. I would maybe be leaning toward giving in to the record company and he'd say, 'Merl, you wrote these songs from the heart, so fuck 'em. It's your music, man. Put it out the way you want to.' I needed to hear that." One of the highlights was a smoldering version of "After Midnight," a song Garcia would continue to play in his solo shows through 1983.

★ **Friday July 27**
Saturday July 28
Grand Prix Racecourse,
Watkins Glen, New York

Sunday July 29
JG appears in a New Jersey courtroom and receives a one-year suspended sentence for his 3/27 possession rap (and is ordered to see a psychiatrist). State Trooper Richard Procachino tells the court that Jerry "was such a nice guy, we hated to bust him."

Sunday July 1
Universal Amphitheatre,
Universal City, California

Friday July 13
History of the Grateful Dead, Vol. 1 (Bear's Choice) is released.

Tuesday July 31
Wednesday August 1
Roosevelt Stadium,
Jersey City, New Jersey

The Band opens both nights; first night of the run is Jerry's 31st birthday.

History of the Grateful Dead, vol. I (Bear's Choice)

HISTORY OF THE GRATEFUL DEAD, VOL. 1 (BEAR'S CHOICE)

Grateful Dead

Released by Warner Bros. (BS-2721) on July 13, 1973

Side One
1. **Katie Mae**
   (Hopkins)
2. **Dark Hollow**
   (Browning)
3. **I've Been All Around This World**
   (Traditional, arr. Grateful Dead)
4. **Wake Up Little Susie**
   (Bryant/Bryant)
5. **Black Peter**
   (Garcia/Hunter)

Side Two
6. **Smokestack Lightnin'**
   (Burnett)
7. **Hard To Handle**
   (Redding/Isabell/Jones)

Personnel

Jerry Garcia – acoustic guitar, lead guitar, vocals
Bob Weir – acoustic guitar, electric guitar, vocals
Pigpen (Ron McKernan) – acoustic guitar, organ, percussion, harmonica, vocals
Phil Lesh – bass
Mickey Hart – drums
Bill Kreutzmann – drums

Produced by Owsley Stanley

B ESIDES OFFERING THE BEST supplemental consciousness-shifters in town, one Augustus Owsley Stanley III, a.k.a "Bear," had by 1966 assumed the duties of soundman in the Dead's cast of behind-the-scenes magicians, experimenting with the latest in cutting-edge equipment that the profits from his psychedelic wares had afforded him. True to its title, *Bear's Choice* was just that—a selection of songs hand-picked by the man who'd so meticulously recorded them, with an emphasis on Pigpen, who passed away while the album was being prepared.

The cover, by R.D. Thomas, was a pre-fractal rendering of the nickname "Good Old Grateful Dead" in a circle with a bull's-eye containing the skull-and-bolt logo that would soon be dubbed a Stealie, while the back cover marked the first appearance of the multicolored dancing bears that would later adorn countless bumpers and windshields as a wordless symbol among knowing Dead fans. The music was a pristine collection of country, blues, R&B, and rock covers (only "Black Peter" appears from the band's list of originals) recorded during two legendary Fillmore East shows in New York on February 13 and 14, 1970.

The result was an album that complements the shift in direction found on the two studio records released later the same year (*Workingman's Dead* and *American Beauty*), though by the time of its 1973 appearance the band was splitting from Warner Bros. to create its own label.

"Some people feel that the series of Fillmore East concerts in 1970 are the finest of all," Bear wrote in the liner notes of a recently re-released version of the album. "I'm not going to say I totally agree, but I do think they are definitely among the top few."

Below: Dancing bears appear for the first time on the back cover.

Watkins Glen

It was the biggest rock concert of all the time—a final head count of 600,000—and the end of the era of giant festivals that had begun six years earlier at Monterey. The inspiration for Watkins Glen (or "Summer Jam '73," as it was officially called) came when 22-year-old Jim Koplik saw the Dead and the Allman Brothers at Dillon Stadium on 7/16/72. Koplik and his friend Shelley Finkel were convinced they could sell, say, 100,000, maybe 150,000 tickets to a one-day festival uniting the Allmans and the Dead. And they had a venue, too—the Grand Prix Racecourse outside Watkins Glen in the Finger Lakes region of western New York State. The Dead and the Allmans, offered $110,000 apiece, signed on, with the Band opening. Like Woodstock, Watkins Glen became a *de facto* free festival when the ticketless hordes descended. Luckily, Bill Graham was in charge of the logistics and there was enough water, food, and medical help on hand to avoid disaster. On Friday night, in a pouring rain, the Dead played a couple of brief sets—the famous "sound check." Saturday was the big day, and while those close enough to the stage to actually hear the music felt that the Allmans outdid the Dead, the Dead acquitted themselves well. When the Allmans finished in the wee hours of Sunday morning the Dead joined them for a final jam ("NFA">"Mountain Jam">"Johnny B. Goode").

"I'd never seen that much humanity spread out across a landscape—it was unimaginable." STEVE BROWN, *2003*

Below: Garcia, Lesh, and Weir have picked up some excess baggage as they struggle to get through pre-show traffic.

DRAWN FROM A HANDFUL of live shows recorded at the Keystone Berkeley in 1973, this series (the original double album was later split into two CDs and augmented by two additional volumes, *Keystone Encores*) captures Garcia in a favorite setting doing what he loved—jamming with friends. Featuring mostly covers ranging from Dylan's "Positively 4th Street" to Rodgers and Hart's American songbook staple "My Funny Valentine," the shows allowed him further musical exploration. "When I started playing with Merl I went to a more organ-style trio," he told *Guitar Player* in 1988. "I played big, fat chords and did a lot of that walking-style chord shifting on the blues numbers and things that Merl's so good at. My style is much more conventional, in a way, with him, and it's very satisfying for me to play and hear myself as a conventional player. It's a kind of playing that I don't do in the Grateful Dead." In a 1997 interview, Saunders doted fondly on his unique liaison with Garcia. "We still had it down to the end," he said. "The first time we ever met we had this love for one another. It was charismatic. It was an unbelievable bond. It's hard to describe it, but you can hear it musically. We could do anything musically together and make it sound good."

LIVE AT KEYSTONE
Merl Saunders/Jerry Garcia/John Kahn/Bill Vitt
Released by Fantasy (F-79002) in 1973

Side One
1. Keepers
   (Saunders/Kahn)
2. Positively 4th Street
   (Dylan)
3. The Harder They Come
   (Cliff)

Side Two
1. It Takes A Lot To Laugh, It Takes A Train To Cry
   (Dylan)
2. Space
   (Saunders/Garcia/Kahn/Vitt)
3. It's No Use
   (Clark/McGuinn)

Side Three
1. That's Alright Mama
   (Crudup)
2. My Funny Valentine
   (Rodgers/Hart)

Side Four
1. Someday Baby
   (Hopkins)
2. Like A Road Leading Home
   (Nix/Penn)

Personnel
Jerry Garcia – guitar, vocals
Merl Saunders – keyboards
John Kahn – bass
Bill Vitt – drums
David Grisman – mandolin

Produced by
Merl Saunders
and John Kahn

Recording the Wake

The band spent most of August at the Record Plant studio in Sausalito to record what would become *Wake of the Flood*. Now beholden to no one but themselves, business-wise, they went to it with a will, collectively spending some 300 hours in the studio. Another impetus to getting it together, according to Rock Scully in *Living with the Dead*, was other band members' desire to get in on the publishing, which the Hunter/Garcia partnership had dominated. Keith Godchaux collaborated with Hunter on "Let Me Sing Your Blues Away" (Keith's only songwriting credit not shared with the other instrumentalists), and a good chunk of the finished product would be taken up by Bob Weir's three-part "Weather Report Suite," with lyrics from both John Perry Barlow and folk singer Eric Andersen.

Tuesday September 11 |
Wednesday September 12 🎸
College of William and Mary,
Willamsburg, Virginia
First show with horns (and Mickey
Hart's 30th birthday).

Saturday September 15 🎸
Providence Civic Center,
Providence, Rhode Island

Monday September 17 |
Tuesday September 18 |
Onondaga County War Memorial,
Syracuse, New York

🎤 **Friday September 7** |
🎸 **Saturday September 8**
Nassau Veterans Memorial Coliseum, Uniondale, New York

The band's fall tour has something new—a horn section. In an effort to bring the feel of *Wake of the Flood* onstage, the band brings in sax man Martin Fierro and trumpeter Joe Ellis, both from Doug Sahm's band, the tour's opening act, to play on songs from the new album. Fan reaction is mixed: Some appreciate the broadened lineup, but most feel the horns don't fit in with the band's sound. After 12 shows the horns are dropped. Fierro (who played on Jerry Garcia and Howard Wales' *Hooteroll?*) will remain a frequent partner of Jerry and Merl Saunders and a member of Zero. Friday sees the first "Let It Grow" from "Weather Report Suite." Saturday sees the live breakout of Part I of "Weather Report Suite" and "Let Me Sing Your Blues Away."

Right: It's a new story *the crow told me:* promotional poster for Wake of the Flood *by Rick Griffin, his first Dead cover since* Aoxomoxoa.

🎤 **Thursday September 20** |
🎸 **Friday September 21**
The Spectrum,
Philadelphia,
Pennsylvania

🎸 **Monday September 24**
Pittsburgh Civic Arena, Pittsburgh, Pennsylvania

The first "Nobody's Fault But Mine" since 7/17/66.

🎸 **Wednesday September 26**
War Memorial Auditorium, Buffalo, New York

Last-ever "Sing Me Back Home."

Friday September 21
The Senate confirms Henry Kissinger as America's Secretary of State—it's the first time a naturalized citizen has held this office.

160

Wednesday October 10
U.S. Vice President Spiro T. Agnew resigns, having pleaded no contest to a count of federal income tax evasion. Agnew is later convicted and sentenced to three years probation and fined $10,000. President Nixon names Gerald Ford as the new vice president.

Left: The fall of 1973 (these shots are from October) finds the band playing most of the songs from Wake of the Flood *with some regularity, but also some of the most "out there" versions of both "Dark Star" and "Playing in the Band."*

GRATEFUL DEAD

WAKE OF THE FLOOD

Grateful Dead

Released by Grateful Dead Records (GD-01) on October 15, 1973

Side One

1. **Mississippi Half-Step Uptown Toodeloo**
   (Hunter/Garcia)
2. **Let Me Sing Your Blues Away**
   (Hunter/K. Godchaux)
3. **Row Jimmy**
   (Hunter/Garcia)
4. **Stella Blue**
   (Hunter/Garcia)

Side Two

1. **Here Comes Sunshine**
   (Hunter/Garcia)
2. **Eyes Of The World**
   (Hunter/Garcia)
3. **Weather Report Suite**
   – Prelude
      (Weir)
   – Part 1
      (Weir/Andersen)
   – Part 2 – Let It Grow
      (Weir/Barlow)

Personnel

Jerry Garcia – lead guitar, vocals
Bob Weir – guitar, vocals
Phil Lesh – bass, vocals
Keith Godchaux – keyboards, vocals
Donna Jean Godchaux – vocals
Bill Kreutzmann – drums
Bill Atwood – trumpet
Vassar Clements – violin
Joe Ellis – trumpet
Martin Fierro – alto and tenor saxophones
Sarah Fulcher – vocals
Matthew Kelly – harmonica
Frank Morin – tenor saxophone
Pat O'Hara – trombone
Doug Sahm – 12-string guitar
Benny Velarde – timbales

Produced by the Grateful Dead

DEAD HEADS
P.O. BOX 1065
SAN RAFAEL, CA
94902

Ignore Alien Orders

Wake of the flood~

WITH A BRAND NEW LABEL INTENT ON changing the music industry as they knew it, the Dead's inaugural indie adventure beckoned as they headed into the studio to record *Wake of the Flood*, their first full-length studio release in three years and the first without Pigpen. "We never related to the record company way of thinking and they never related to us," Garcia would tell *Melody Maker* after the album came out. "We figured that even fumbling around we could sell records better than they could."

With its old-timey accompaniment by the likes of violinist Vassar Clements, sax player Martin Fierro, trumpet players Bill Atwood and Joe Ellis, and others, the album was a game attempt to harvest the latest bounty of new material, though still mild compared to the readings that songs like the shuffling "Mississippi Half-Step Uptown Toodeloo" and Beatlesque "Here Comes Sunshine"

would get in concerts that year. Tentatively titled *You Are The Eyes of the World* in reference to one of the more lasting songs from the disc, the band eventually settled on *Wake of The Flood*.

The album, which included an artfully rustic Rick Griffin cover with a reaper-and-wheat motif that bore a marked difference from the artist's lysergic-driven flying eyeballs of yore, would reach #18 in the U.S., helping prove Garcia's point that the band could move units on its own.

Still, critics weren't exactly kind. "The poor bastards can still barely sing," Jim Miller wrote in *Rolling Stone*. "And that's not all! The lyrics on much of *Flood* plumb new depths of dull-witted, inbred, blissed-out hippy-dippyness." In an interesting footnote, a proliferation of bootleg copies of *Wake* led to an unholy alliance between the Dead and the FBI, who briefly worked together to combat the problem.

Sunday October 21
Omaha Civic Auditorium, Omaha, Nebraska
Last-ever "You Ain't Woman Enough (To Take My Man)."

Tuesday October 23
Metropolitan Sports Center, Bloomington, Minnesota

Saturday October 27
State Fair Coliseum, Indianapolis, Indiana

| 11 | 12 | 13 | 14 | **15** | 16 | 17 | 18 | **19** | 20 | 21 | 22 | 23 | 24 | 25 | 26 | 27 | 28 | 29 | 30 | 31 |

Monday October 15
Wake of the Flood is released. "Let Me Sing Your Blues Away"/"Here Comes Sunshine and Eyes of the World"/"Weather Report Suite (Part 1)" are released as singles.

★ Friday October 19
Oklahoma City Fairgrounds Arena, Oklahoma City, Oklahoma
The first "Mind Left Body Jam."

Thursday October 25
Dane County Coliseum, Madison, Wisconsin

Monday October 29
Tuesday October 30
Kiel Auditorium, St. Louis, Missouri

In Business

In the last months of 1973 it seemed like the band's drive for autonomy and solvency was succeeding. Sales of *Wake of the Flood* helped pay off the lingering debt from the '72 European tour, and in September the band's bank balance was well in the black. Ron Rakow took the credit, telling the *Wall Street Journal* that "We were making about 33 cents an album" with Warner Bros., but "Now we make about $1.22 per album." The balance might have been even bigger if some unknown operator (to this day uncaught) hadn't managed to get thousands of bootleg *Wakes* into the stores—relatively easy to do, since GDR distributed the album through independent distributors. This put the band in the unusual position of urging Deadheads, in a mailing, to play narc on the band's behalf: *"Our record is being counterfeited, and the authorities move too slowly not recognizing that our survival is at stake. We need your diligent efforts. The counterfeit has square (not round) corners on the stickers and a white (not orange) 0598 on the spine. Check all stores and immediately report phonies to us. Thanks, GDR."*

It was so much simpler in the days before CD burners and MP3s….

Despite the uptick in their fortunes the Grateful Dead were still a band, not a business; some wondered if (to paraphrase a later headline) modest success would spoil the group. "[This] ain't exactly what we had in mind," said Jerry Garcia in a *Rolling Stone* interview. "12,000-seat halls and big bucks. We're trying to redefine. We've played every conceivable venue, and it hasn't been it. What can we do that's more fun, more interesting?"

Left: *November 9–11, Winterland Arena, San Francisco, California.*

Friday November 23
County Coliseum, El Paso, Texas

Above and right: *November 9–11, Winterland. The band has played only one previous show (on May 26) in San Francisco the entire year.*

Tuesday November 20
Wednesday November 21
Denver Coliseum, Denver, Colorado

20	21	22	23	24	25	26	27	28	29

Sunday November 25
Feyline Field, Tempe, Arizona

Saturday November 17
President Nixon tells an Associated Press managing editors meeting in Orlando, Florida, that "people have got to know whether or not their president is a crook. Well, I'm not a crook. I've earned everything I've got."

Hank Harrison

These days Hank Harrison is best known for his troubled relationship with his daughter, singer/actress Courtney Love. His connection with the Dead goes back to the band's beginnings. A friend of Phil Lesh's during the bassist's pre-Dead days, Harrison was briefly the manager of the Warlocks, and he has exploited that tenuous affiliation ever since. In 1971 he put out the first-ever book about the group—*The Dead Book*, an odd but interesting mishmash of interviews, memories of the early '60s Palo Alto scene, and ramblings about the Dead's evolution from Beat culture. A second volume about the group had much less to offer.

15	16	17	18	19

Friday November 9
Saturday November 10
Sunday November 11 ★
Winterland Arena, San Francisco, California

The band revives "To Lay Me Down," last heard on 9/20/70.

Saturday November 17
Pauley Pavilion, University of California, Los Angeles, California

Having done an analysis of the upcoming gig at the Boston Music Hall, Bob Matthews points out to the band that their current on-stage setup (which by now included some 200 separate amps) wouldn't fit on the hall's stage. The sound system would have to move *behind* the musicians.

...am and Great Western present
THE GRATEFUL DEAD
...vember 23, 1973 — 7:00 p.m.
PASO COUNTY COLISEUM
Advance $5.00
No Refunds or Exchanges
25

DECEMBER
'73

30	1	2	3

Friday November 30
Saturday December 1
Sunday December 2 ★
Boston Music Hall, Bosto... Massachusetts

NOVEMBER
'73

1	2 - 8	9	10	11	12	13	14

Thursday November 1
McGaw Memorial Hall, Northwestern University, Evanston, Illinois

Wednesday November 14
San Diego Sports Arena, San Diego, California

December 1973

163

Tuesday
🎸 **December 4**
Cincinnati Gardens,
Cincinnati, Ohio

Saturday December 8
🎸 Cameron Indoor
Stadium, Duke University,
Durham, North Carolina

Wednesday December 12
🎸 The Omni, Atlanta, Georgia

Monday December 31
Cow Palace, Daly City, California

JG & BK sit in with the Allman Bros.

| 4 | 5 | 6 | 7 | 8 | 9 | 10 | 11 | 12 | 13 | 14 | 15 | 16 | 17 | 18 | 19 | 20 ~ 30 | 31 |

Thursday December 6
🎸 Cleveland Convention
Center, Cleveland, Ohio

Monday December 10
Charlotte Coliseum, 🎸
Charlotte, North Carolina

Tuesday December 18 🎸
Wednesday December 19 🎸
Curtis Hixon Convention Center, Tampa, Florida

Gathering and Spilling

The first full year of independence for the Grateful Dead began with a meeting on where to go, what to do, and—with the band enjoying a positive cash flow—how much to spend, and on what. Dennis McNally records, in *A Long Strange Trip*, some of the funding decisions taken at Fifth and Lincoln in early '74: "The next gigs, in February, would generate funds for a down payment for Keith and Donna's new home, a computer for musical experiments Phil Lesh and Ned Lagin were conducting, and a donation to old KSAN friend Milan Melvin's program for Napa schools." One funding request that did not win approval was for money to buy property for a sort of "homesite" for the band and Family, an idea promoted by Alan Trist.

Another item on the agenda at the January meeting was approval for funding for a new speaker system. In retrospect, it would be one of the most significant in the band's history, as it would lead inexorably to the creation of the Wall of Sound, the sound system that was intended to help the band achieve autonomy but wound up as a millstone around its collective neck.

Despite the balanced books and ambitious plans, all was not sweetness and light as the band began 1974. Part of the price of being on their own, with their own label and several ancillary operations, was that they were…on their own, and thus subject to internal politics and dynamics that quickly led to conflict.

Factionalism came into play. Phil Lesh would later talk about the "Stinson Beach Mafia"—Ron Rakow and Richard Loren—who had their knives out for Sam Cutler, director of Out of Town Tours (OOT), the booking agency. At a January meeting it was decided that OOT would be "taking a vacation" for a few months, but in effect, Cutler was forced out of the organization, with the tacit approval of Jerry Garcia, who continued to hold Rakow in a kind of awe.

Beyond increasing tensions in the office, there were the workaday stresses of operating a record company on top of the strain of touring, recording the next studio album, and the demands of various band members' solo projects. In Rock Scully's words, "[We] have to stop and order vinyl, book time at pressing plants, and figure out how to get the airplay necessary to push the album—all this, combined with the pressure on the band to finish the album fast enough… Jesus, we've become Mo Ostin." (Ostin was Joe Smith's boss, the head of Warner Bros.)

Right: Ron Rakow. The one-time New York Stock trader convinced the band to start their own record company.

"NOT FADE AWAY"

PETTY/HOLLY

When songwriter Charles Hardin, better known to most as Buddy Holly, sat down to write his upbeat ditty "Not Fade Away" with producer Norman Petty, he never could have envisioned the second life the tune and its repeating line "Love is real, not fade away" would enjoy with Grateful Dead fans in the years to come. Holly had already scored a No. 1 song in 1957 with "That'll Be The Day" and a follow-up No. 3 hit with "Peggy Sue" when "Not Fade Away" appeared later that year as the B-side of a third single, "Oh, Boy!" A decade after his tragic death in a 1959 plane crash, the Dead started working the lost classic into their sets. Between 1970 and February '74 it was often played around "Goin' Down That Road Feeling Bad," then linked with "St. Stephen" over a dozen times in 1976 and '77, before settling into its most common spot right after "Drums/Space," where it stayed through most of 1982. It then proved to be the perfect match for Weir and Barlow's "Throwing Stones," which usually preceded the song when it wasn't being saved for an encore. After a five-beat rhythm cycle mirroring its refrain became an audience participation standard, fans often guided the Dead into an "'NFA' encore" by collectively clapping the pattern while they waited for the band to return.

Flying Solo

Setting a pattern that would continue (with exceptions) for the rest of the band's career, the first month or so of 1974 was a time for solo projects. Jerry Garcia was recording his second solo album, which would come to be known as *Compliments of Garcia*, with John Kahn (who selected and arranged the songs) and a roster of top-flight studio musicians, while playing club dates with Merl Saunders. Bill Kreutzmann joined up with Garcia and Saunders for a Keystone gig on 1/17 and settled into the lineup, providing the beat until mid-August. Bob Weir, his appetite for writing whetted by "Weather Report Suite," worked on some new songs with John Perry Barlow. Phil Lesh vacationed in Hawaii while preparing to continue his avant-garde experiments with Ned Lagin. The islands, incidentally, became a favorite rest-and-relaxation spot for several band members, and Kreutzmann would move to Hawaii in later years.

February sees the release of guitarist David Bromberg's *Wanted Dead or Alive;* Bill Kreutzmann, Phil Lesh, Jerry Garcia, and Keith Godchaux play on four tracks.

1 2 3 4 5

Monday February 4
Newspaper heiress Patricia Hearst is kidnapped in Berkeley, California, by the Symbionese Liberation Army.

SKELETONS FROM THE CLOSET

Grateful Dead

Released by Warner Bros. (W-2764) in February 1974

Side One
1. **The Golden Road (To Unlimited Devotion)**
   (Garcia/Lesh/Weir/Kreutzmann/McKernan)
2. **Truckin'**
   (Garcia/Lesh/Weir/Hunter)
3. **Rosemary**
   (Garcia/Hunter)
4. **Sugar Magnolia**
   (Weir/Hunter)
5. **St. Stephen**
   (Garcia/Lesh/Hunter)

Side Two
1. **Uncle John's Band**
   (Garcia/Hunter)
2. **Casey Jones**
   (Garcia/Hunter)
3. **Mexicali Blues**
   (Weir/Barlow)
4. **Turn On Your Love Light**
   (Malone/Scott)
5. **One More Saturday Night**
   (Weir)
6. **Friend Of The Devil**
   (Garcia/Dawson/Hunter)

Personnel

Jerry Garcia – lead guitar, pedal steel guitar, vocals, piano
Bill Kreutzmann – drums, percussion
Phil Lesh – bass, vocals, piano, vocals
Pigpen (Ron McKernan) – keyboards, harmonica, vocals, congas, organ
Bob Weir – guitar, rhythm guitar, vocals
Mickey Hart – drums, percussion
Tom Constanten – keyboard
Donna Godchaux – vocals
Keith Godchaux – piano
Dave Torbert – bass

IF WARNER BROS. WAS REALLY TRYING to present an overview of what the Dead had accomplished during its years with their label, this 11-song best-of package wasn't it. As if favoring studio tracks from four of the band's albums ("Mexicali Blues" from Weir's solo debut *Ace* also appears) over concert fare wasn't bad enough, a further blasphemy occurs in one of the album's two live tracks, a truncated version of *Live/Dead*'s "Lovelight" that had appeared on the 1970 Warner Bros. sampler *The Big Ball.* Though the album appears in the collection of countless rock fans vaguely familiar with the Dead's representation and feeling obligated to acknowledge said rep by buying at least one of the band's releases, newbies who know better are advised to buy virtually any of the dozens of live *Dick's Picks.*

At least the title is fitting; true to the cliché, the Dead may have preferred to leave some of these particular skeletons put away in light of what the band was creating on its own with the just-released *Wake of the Flood* and the upcoming *From The Mars Hotel.*

February 1974

165

Left and below: February 22–24, Winterland, the last shows before the Wall of Sound was introduced.

10 – 21   22   23   24   25   26   27   28

🎸 **Friday February 22**
🎸 **Saturday February 23**
Sunday February 24
Winterland Arena, San Francisco, California

A three-night run at Winterland begins the performance year and, as usual, the band break out the songs worked on over the winter, or whenever. On Friday the band debuts three tunes, or perhaps more correctly, two and a half, since one of them is "U.S. Blues," introduced the preceding year in somewhat different form as "Wave That Flag." (Steve Brown described the song as "The Dead's State of the Union Address for '74.") The others are "It Must Have Been the Roses," a Hunter love/loss meditation written in a style so timeless it could be a Child Ballad (Hunter also wrote the tune) and "Ship of Fools," whose antiauthoritarian lyrics were perhaps influenced by the ever-deepening Watergate scandal. Sunday marks the final time the "Not Fade Away" *(see opposite)* is sandwiched by "Goin' Down That Road Feeling Bad."

Wall of Sound

Undeniably the most famous (or infamous) sound system in the history of music, the Wall of Sound was the collective brainchild of Bear, the other Alembic wizards, Dan Healy, Bob Matthews, and McCune Sound. It was the culmination of the better part of a decade's worth of research and experimentation motivated by the desire to give the Grateful Dead and its audiences the best possible concert experience.

The WOS served two purposes. The first (which may seem paradoxical, given the WOS's size) was to simplify the stage layout. As Bob Matthews had pointed out to the band, the array of amps and monitors (nearly 200 at the average '73 gig—not counting the PA) was starting to exceed the available space onstage. A modular system would move the "amp line" behind the band and eliminate the need for stage monitors—which meant no feedback—or even a mixing board. Whether you were Jerry or a 'Head in the nosebleed section, the music sounded the same.

More important, the WOS would reproduce the band's music with the utmost clarity in the largest of venues. The band still felt a certain guilt that they had outgrown the clubs, ballrooms, and college gyms in which they'd acquired their devoted following; the WOS would permit them to give large audiences much the same experience (in purely musical terms at least) even in drafty, acoustically inert stadiums and coliseums.

In scale and appearance, the WOS was staggering. Dennis McNally described it as "[An] electronic sculpture. To walk into a facility for a Dead concert [in 1974] was to see something like the pylon on the moon in Stanley Kubrick's *2001*, something so grand, so elegant, so preposterous, that words simply fail."

The WOS was actually the aggregate of six separate systems tied in to each of the instruments, plus vocals. Together the WOS comprised 604 speakers, from 5" to 15", and an array of tweeters, crossovers, differentials, and so on that collectively drew almost 27,000 watts of power.

So how did it sound? After it was first tested (3/22, prior to the 3/23 Cow Palace show) notes from an Alembic tech reported that the WOS "[Produced] quite an acceptable sound at a quarter of a mile without the wind and an extremely fine sound up to 500 to 600 feet, where it begins to be injured by wind."

Those who were in the audience at shows where the WOS used will swear that it was the best live sound they've ever heard. Not until the advent of digital technology would any band replicate this kind of pure, distortion-free sound.

But '74 was the analog age, and the system was so heavy and complex that it took three or four 18-wheeler trucks to move it and as many as 26 crewmen 14 hours to set it up. (There were actually two stages for the Wall of Sound; one would be set up at the next show while the one at the previous show was being packed up and trucked to the show after the next show, and so on). And the cost—$350,000 to build it (or them), and another $100,000 a month to keep it all working and moving.

The Wall of Sound was used for only 37 shows, all of them in '74. Technically, it was a brilliant achievement. Musically, it was a dream (Phil Lesh described playing while connected to the WOS as "like piloting a flying saucer"). From a business standpoint, though, it was a disaster.

> **"We ended up actually developing a system so that the band could hear themselves and play better. And if it hadn't been for Owsley, and if it hadn't been for Dan Healy, and Bob Matthews and so on, we would've sounded lousy forever."** ROCK SCULLY TO TONI A. BROWN

Right: March 23, the Wall of Sound at the Sound Test, Cow Palace, San Francisco, California. The speakers above the drums replaced the usual stage monitors.

Saturday March 23
Cow Palace, Daly City, California

First Wall of Sound show. Breakout of two songs destined to be much played, and much loved by 'Heads—"Cassidy" (see right) and "Scarlet Begonias" *(see page 204).*

Recording *Mars Hotel*

After the Wall of Sound's trial run, the band repaired to CBS Studios on Folsom Street in San Francisco to record the next studio album. They'd already worked out arrangements and rehearsed the material, and now they alternated between further rehearsals at Studio Instrument Rentals and recording sessions with engineer "Uncle Roy" Seigel. For the band, the main attraction at CBS was a pair of 16-track tape machines which, as Rock Scully noted in *Living with the Dead*, could be twinned to give the band up to 30 tracks to work with. Once again, the band was about to "take a step back" in the studio, in this case to the *Workingman's Dead/American Beauty* format of discrete, short-form (by Grateful Dead standards) songs and away from the free-flowing and heavily instrumental feel of *Wake of the Flood*.

The album got its eventual title, *Grateful Dead from the Mars Hotel*, from a seedy boardinghouse in the Mission District that figured in the Beat mythos. Kelley and Mouse's art for the back cover showed the band not in the Mars Hotel, but in a similar establishment, the Cadillac Hotel, where Jerry Garcia had once stayed while visiting the city back in the Palo Alto days. The lettering on the back reads "Ugly Rumors"—it was originally "Ugly Roomers," a self-deprecating pun on the band's appearance, but was changed to "rumors" when some sensitive soul observed that "Ugly Roomers" might be construed as disrespecting the Mars Hotel's denizens.

Great American String Band

Jerry Garcia's newest side band included Garcia on banjo, David Grisman on mandolin, Richard Greene on fiddle, David Nichtern on guitar, and Buell Neidlinger on bass (Taj Mahal played bass for one show, 4/20 at Hollywood's Pilgrimage Theater). The group had a wide repertoire of folk, blues, novelty tunes, and Grisman compositions, but the outfit was short-lived, logging just five performances between April and June.

"CASSIDY"

WEIR/BARLOW

April sees the release of the Jerry Garcia-produced *Home, Home on the Road* by the New Riders of the Purple Sage. "Kick in the Head," one of the tracks on the album, is written by Robert Hunter, who also supplies the lyrics.

APRIL '74

1 - 7   8

10

Monday April 8
Hank Aaron of the Atlanta Braves hits his 715th career home run. The Hammer's towering drive against the Los Angeles Dodgers breaks Babe Ruth's 39-year old record.

Owing its namesake to a Beat legend of the past and a member of the Dead family born at the time of its writing, "Cassidy" was one of a handful of songs from Bob Weir's solo debut *Ace* (1972) that the Dead officially adopted, eventually becoming one of the most popular of Weir and Barlow's early efforts. The track serves in part as a biographical nod to hard-living Beat figure Neal Cassady, who'd already made a guest appearance in the earlier Dead expedition "That's It For The Other One," and Cassidy Law, the baby daughter of two members of the band's entourage. "There were the chords which Bobby had strung together the night she was born," Barlow remembered in 1980. "I was still wrestling with the angel of Cassady." Cassady, who had died of exposure two before Law was born, inspired a counterpoint for what Barlow called "necessary dualities... dying and being born, men and women, speaking and being silent, devastation and growth, desolation and hope. It is about a Cassady and a Cassidy." Debuted live at the Cow Palace in Daly City, California, on March 23, 1974, the song remained a Weir standard with the Grateful Dead and beyond, appearing regularly in his solo sets and sporadically with The Other Ones on numerous tours.

Sunday May 12
Mackay Stadium,
University of Nevada,
Reno, Nevada

Tuesday May 14 ★
Adams Field House,
University of Montana,
Missoula, Montana

Sunday May 19
Portland Memorial
Coliseum, Portland, Oregon

Saturday May 25
Campus Stadium, University of
California, Santa Barbara, California

Maria Muldaur supports.

1 | 2 | 3 | 4 | 5 | 6 | 7 | 8 | 9 | 10 | 11 | **12** | 13 | **14** | 15 | 16 | **17** | 18 | **19** | 20 | **21** | 22 | 23 | 24 | **25** | 26 | 27 | 28 | 29 | 30 | 31

Friday May 17
PNE Coliseum,
Vancouver, British
Columbia, Canada

The debut of
Weir/Barlow's
"Money Money,"
originally titled
"Finance Blues."

Tuesday May 21
Edmundson Pavilion,
University of Washington,
Seattle, Washington

Possibly the longest version of
"Playing in the Band" and the
last "Money Money."

Saturday May 25
Jerry Garcia's "Let It
Rock/Midnight Town" single
is released to promote his
forthcoming second solo
LP *(see page 170)*.

Round and Round

Grateful Dead Records and its quasi-subsidiary,
Round Records, used the band's close
relationship with its fan base to promote
upcoming Grateful Dead albums, solo projects,
and the cause of the Dead in general. A mailing
list was compiled from the 'Heads who
responded to the "Dead Freaks Unite" write-in
campaign from the *Skullfuck* album *(see page
137)*, and by some accounts this generated as
many as 25,000 responses.

In May '74, Deadheads on the list got a
delightful surprise: a sampler EP with rough
mixes of tracks from two upcoming solo albums,
Robert Hunter's *Tales of the Great Rum Runners*
and Jerry Garcia's second effort, the so-called
Compliments of Garcia. The Round Records
sampler mailing went out under the name
"Anton Round," which was the alias used by
Ron Rakow. "Anton Round" reportedly also
had a plan to send radio DJs "Mars Bars" to
promote the upcoming Grateful Dead album,
but that scheme apparently foundered.

*Above: John McKuen, comedian Steve Martin,
and Garcia do some pickin' backstage at the
Golden State Bluegrass Festival, April 27, 1974.*
*Opposite page: The Wall of Sound in all its glory at Campus
Stadium, UCSB, Santa Barbara, California, on Saturday May 25.*

*Left and below: Garcia in a studio session for his second solo
album, which was produced by John Kahn over a period of several
months in the Bay Area and Los Angeles, and in general featured
players with no previous association with Garcia or the Grateful Dead.*

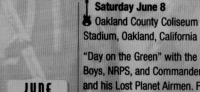

Saturday June 8
Oakland County Coliseum Stadium, Oakland, California

"Day on the Green" with the Beach Boys, NRPS, and Commander Cody and his Lost Planet Airmen. First of 71 shows at this venue.

1 - 7 | 8 | 9 | 10 | 11 | 12 | 13 | 14 | 15

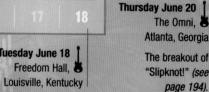

Sunday June 16
Iowa State Fairgrounds, Des Moines, Iowa

16 | 17 | 18

★ **Tuesday June 18**
Freedom Hall, Louisville, Kentucky

19 | 20

Thursday June 20
The Omni, Atlanta, Georgia

The breakout of "Slipknot!" (see page 194).

Saturday June 22
Sunday June 23
Jai–Alai Fronton, Miami, Florida

Sunday marks the only performance of Chuck Berry's "Let It Rock," the lead track on Jerry Garcia's just-released second solo album. Phil Lesh and Ned Lagin (see page 182) had lately been experimenting with synthesizer-based avant-garde music and tonight, during the set break, they let the monster out of the laboratory. (Reportedly, Phil was reluctant to go live with the stuff just yet, but he became chemically convinced that the time had come.) This "Phil & Ned," the predecessor to Seastones (see page 182), was an explosion of white noise, pink noise, high frequency, low frequency, atonal, polytonal, and ultratonal sound. Mickey Hart dubbed it "Warp 10"; Rock Scully called it the "Insect Fear Interlude" and the "Assault of the Grisly Outer Space Noises."

21 | 22 | 23

Below: Saturday June 8, Oakland County Coliseum Stadium, Oakland, California.

June 1974

170

RATHER THAN APPROPRIATE MATERIAL WRITTEN with Hunter that might otherwise appear on future Dead recordings, Garcia concentrated entirely on covers for his second solo album, from Chuck Berry's "Let It Rock" to friends John Kahn and Robert Hunter's "Midnight Town." The guitarist allowed Kahn to pick material to consider for the record, resulting in a broad collection of varied artists. "I would present him with a bunch of ideas, and he'd take the ones he liked and work on those," Kahn later told Blair Jackson and Regan McMahon in *The Golden Road.* "It was mainly stuff that he wouldn't have ordinarily thought of, and I think that was part of the challenge for him, to try something that was really new to him." Though not always successful, the album did have its highlights, including a George Harrisonesque rendering of Smokey Robinson's "When The Hunter Gets Captured By The Game" with Larry Carlton on guitar, and an unlikely take of Irving Berlin's "Russian Lullaby" that Django Reinhart would have appreciated. Wrapped in a vibrant cover by psychedelic artist Victor Moscoso, the album was originally called *Garcia* until promo copies stamped "Compliments of" led to a nickname that finally stuck with its official adoption for the 1989 CD release.

GARCIA (COMPLIMENTS OF GARCIA)

Jerry Garcia

Released by Round (RX 102) on June 6, 1974

Side One

1. **Let It Rock**
(Berry)
2. **When The Hunter Gets Captured By The Game**
(Robinson)
3. **That's What Love Will Make You Do**
(Thigpen/Banks/Marion)
4. **Russian Lullaby**
(Berlin)
5. **Turn On The Bright Lights**
(Washington)

Side Two

1. **He Ain't Give You None**
(Morrison)
2. **What Goes Around**
(Rebbenack)
3. **Let's Spend The Night Together**
(Jagger/Richard)
4. **Mississippi Moon**
(Rowan)
5. **Midnight Town**
(Kahn/Hunter)

Personnel

J. Garcia – vocals, guitar; A. Adams – guitar; T. Adams – cello; B. Benay – guitar; L. Carlton – guitar; M. Clayton – vocals; G. Connors – trombone; M. Dye – viola; A. Egilsson – bass; N. Ellis – viola; A. Garrett – trombone; R. Greene – violin; W. Green – clarinet; B. Hall – percussion; Judiyaba – cello; J. Kahn – bass; J. Kelso – saxophone; C. King – vocals; M. Moore – trumpet; G. Muldaur – clarinet; M. Muldaur – vocals; M. O'Martian – keyboards; S. Page – violin; C. Pedersen – violin; G. Ray – clarinet; J. Rotella – clarinet; N. Rubin – violin; M. Saunders – organ; R. Siegal – bass; J. Speer – bass clarinet; J. Tepp – clarinet; R. Tutt – drums; E. Van Valkenburgh – violin

Produced by John Kahn

GRATEFUL DEAD FROM THE MARS HOTEL

GRATEFUL DEAD FROM THE MARS HOTEL

Grateful Dead

Released by Grateful Dead Records (GD-102) on June 27, 1974

Side One

1. **U.S. Blues**
   (Hunter/Garcia)
2. **China Doll**
   (Hunter/Garcia)
3. **Unbroken Chain**
   (Lesh/Peterson)
4. **Loose Lucy**
   (Hunter/Garcia)

Side Two

1. **Scarlet Begonias**
   (Hunter/Garcia)
2. **Pride Of Cucamonga**
   (Lesh/Peterson)
3. **Money Money**
   (Weir/Barlow)
4. **Ship Of Fools**
   (Hunter/Garcia)

Personnel

Jerry Garcia – lead guitar, vocals
Bob Weir – guitar, vocals
Phil Lesh – bass, vocals
Keith Godchaux – keyboards
Donna Jean Godchaux – vocals
Bill Kreutzmann – drums
John McFee – pedal steel on "Pride Of Cucamonga"

Produced by the Grateful Dead

Below: Artist Alton Kelley transformed the band into God-knows-what on the back cover.

IF AT FIRST YOU DON'T SUCCEED, try again. When the Dead entered CBS Studios in San Francisco to record a second album for their own record label, they were nearing the end of a physically and creatively demanding decade together. Named after a real place located at 4th and Howard near the studio, *From The Mars Hotel* was technically solid but relatively average, despite the inclusion of such patented barn-burners as "U.S. Blues" and "Scarlet Begonias" and fan favorites "China Doll" and "Loose Lucy." "That record, we rehearsed a lot before we went into the studio," Garcia would later tell Blair Jackson. "We rehearsed all the tunes for about a month before we recorded them, so we had them pretty fully arranged." The intricacies of songs like Lesh's "Unbroken Chain" helped ease the pain incurred by Weir and Barlow's awful "Money Money," an ironic title considering the scales of artistic integrity and economic liability the band were trying to keep balanced in the months before they retreated into temporary retirement later that year.

Though *Mars Hotel* was not without its moments (one critic at the time even crowed that it was "the group's best album since *Workingman's Dead*"), Garcia lumped it in with other near-misses in the recording studio, telling *Circus* that such records were "something we do the same way you'd go and make a model airplane. It isn't exactly illustrative." Observant fans would later note that the hotel itself, depicted on the cover illustration floating in some sort of crater-pocked landscape, was the same building that was seen being symbolically torn down in the band's 1977 concert flick *The Grateful Dead Movie*.

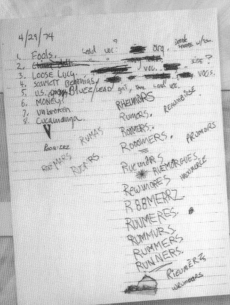

Left: Garcia's notes on a prospective track listing for the Mars Hotel album, dated April 29, 1974.

Wednesday June 26 ★
Providence Civic Center,
Providence, Rhode Island

Thursday June 27
"US Blues/Loose Lucy" single is released
at the same time as the album.

26   27   28   29   30

Thursday June 27
Grateful Dead From The Mars Hotel album is released.

Friday June 28 ★
Boston Garden, Boston, Massachusetts

Sunday June 30
Springfield Civic Center Arena,
Springfield, Massachusetts

Friday July 19
Selland Arena,
Fresno, California

Sunday July 21
Hollywood Bowl,
Hollywood, California

Maria Muldaur with John
Kahn and Commander
Cody and his Lost Planet
Airmen open.

Thursday July 25
International Amphitheatre,
Chicago, Illinois

Monday July 29
Capital Centre, Landover, Maryland

First of 29 shows at this venue (later the USAir Arena).

Saturday July 27
Roanoke Civic Center,
Roanoke, Virginia

Wednesday July 31
Dillon Stadium,
Hartford, Connecticut

1 ~ 18   19   20   21   22 ~ 24   25   26   27   28   29   30   31

July 1974

172

TALES OF THE GREAT RUM RUNNERS

Robert Hunter

Released by Round Records (RX 101) in 1974

Side One

1. **Lady Simplicity**
   (Hunter)
2. **That Train**
   (Hunter)
3. **Dry Dusty Road**
   (Hunter)
4. **I Heard You Singing**
   (Hunter/Freiberg)
5. **Rum Runners**
   (Hunter)
6. **Children's Lament**
   (Hunter)
7. **Maybe She's A Bluebird**
   (Hunter)

Side Two

1. **Boys In The Barroom**
   (Hunter)
2. **It Must Have Been The Roses**
   (Hunter)
3. **Arizona Lightning**
   (Hunter)
4. **Standing At Your Door**
   (Hunter)
5. **Mad**
   (Hunter/Hart)
6. **Keys To The Rain**
   (Hunter)

Personnel

Peter Albin – bass; **Rodney Albin** – vocals, fiddle; **Maureen Aylett** – vocals, spoons; **Mario Cippolina** – saxophone; **T. Will Claire** – vocals; **Hadi El Sadoon** – trumpet; **John Farey** – saxophone; **Milt Farrow** – saxophone; **Snooky Flowers** – saxophone; **David Freiberg** – bass; **Bruce Gapinski** – saxophone; **Jerry Garcia** – guitar; **Donna Godchaux** – vocals; **Keith Godchaux** – keyboards; **Mickey Hart** – drums; **David Kessner** – saxophone; **Barry Melton** – guitar; **Jamie Paris** – harp; **Steve Schuster** – saxophone; **Ray Scott** – saxophone; **Markee Shubb** – mandolin; **Rick Shubb** – banjo; **Jeff Slattery** – saxophone; **Randall Smith** – saxophone; **Bill Steele** – saxophone; **Robbie Stokes** – guitar

Directed by Robert Hunter

THE SECOND RELEASE FROM THE DEAD'S offshoot label Round Records was also the first for long-time lyricist-in-hiding Robert Hunter, though not quite the swashbuckling adventure suggested by the title. Like the rest of the Dead-related solo releases, the album was surrounded by family, with the recordings taking place at Hart's Rolling Thunder studio, soundmen Dan Healy and Bob Matthews manning the boards, and participation from Hart on drums, Garcia on guitar, and the Godchauxs, Keith and Donna, on keyboards and vocals, along with almost two dozen additional guest musicians. (The Dead, meanwhile, had been playing Hunter's wonderful ballad "It Must Have Been The Roses" since February of 1974, four months before *Rum Runners* was released.) Not one to subscribe to the notion that the documented musical past is forever set in vinyl, Hunter enthused about tweaking the album for a compact disc reissue during a 1988 interview with Mary Eisenhart. "I want to like duck some of my vocals back, because some of those brash vocals on it... and bring out some of the instrumental interplay that's going on there, 'cause there's a hell of an album there," he said. "I LOVE the record. I like it better than anything I've done. I hated it for years and years, and I finally just listened to it and I thought HEY! 'Cause I'm far enough away from it now that all my body cells have changed entirely two times over, and I can look at it the way other people look at it now." The result was still a spin only the faithful could love.

"I didn't have any idea what I was doing when I was producing that. It was my first crack at the studio, and the rhythms are all off and it's rough and ready. As one critic said, it sounds like it was recorded in a bathroom."
ROBERT HUNTER TO MARY EISENHART ON *RUM RUNNERS*, FROM *THE GOLDEN ROAD*, 1984

Above: *July 21, Hollywood Bowl. Maria Muldaur (center) led a band that included John Kahn (to her left) to open for the Dead.*

Urobouros

By the end of the summer tour it was clear that something had to give. In a '73 Dead Heads mailing, Robert Hunter (in the guise of St. Dilbert) had likened the state of the band, with its ever-increasing payroll and operating costs, to the Urobouros, the mythical beast that feeds on its own tail. Noting that record royalties accounted for less than a third of the band's income, Hunter pointed out that "gigs offer the only means to earn more money when it is needed to maintain our operation in all its particulars. We cannot sell more records at will, but we can go on the road, within the limits of energy: so that we must play larger halls, with more equipment, and a bigger organization, requiring more gigs…" The creation of Grateful Dead Records and the Wall of Sound were intended to control the Urobouros; instead they stoked the Beast's appetite. The WOS was sucking major money out of the organization, studio time and related costs were spiraling upward, while the "Energy Crisis" that began in '73 sent the price of oil (and thus vinyl) through the roof.

But the problems weren't just economic. Cocaine use had now reached blizzardlike proportions among the band, crew, and staff, with the attendant paranoia and self-aggrandizing among the heavy users. And there were lots of heavy users. In a somewhat related problem, the road crew had become a power unto themselves and were frequently abrasive (to put it mildly) with venue staff and anybody else whom they decided they didn't like. At a band meeting in August, Danny Rifkin (who'd rejoined the organization as a member of the crew) proposed a break in touring. The consensus was that a "hiatus" was a good idea, but the timing and circumstances were left vague.

So Far, a compilation album by Crosby, Stills, Nash and Young, is released. Garcia plays on one track.

Legion of Mary

Jerry Garcia's next solo band included Merl Saunders on keys, the ubiquitous John Kahn on bass, Martin Fierro on sax and flute, and Paul Humphrey on drums (replaced later by Ron Tutt). With an eclectic repertoire oriented toward jazz, reggae, and R&B, the Legion played about a hundred shows from July '74 to July '75. As for the name: "[It was] my idea, but it backfired on us," John Kahn later told Blair Jackson. "We played our first gig under that name at the Keystone Berkeley and these people showed up who were really part of this religious group called the Legion of Mary. I thought I'd made it up!" The Legion of Mary marked the end of Garcia's association with Merl Saunders until John Kahn formed Reconstruction in 1979.

AUGUST '74

1   2   3

Friday August 2
Heavy rain starts before the show, and the band can't take the stage without danger of electrocution. Unfortunately, the tickets say "Rain or Shine." Bob Weir, attempting to explain the situation to the angry audience, gets conked in the head by a bottle. A bad night in Deadworld.

Sunday August 4
Monday August 5
Civic Convention Hall Auditorium, Philadelphia, Pennsylvania

4   5   6   7   8   9 – 31

★ **Tuesday August 6**
Roosevelt Stadium, Jersey City, New Jersey

Makeup show for the rained-out 8/2.

Thursday August 8
President Nixon announces his resignation as a result of damaging revelations in the Watergate scandal. Gerald R. Ford is sworn in as the 38th U.S. president the following day, saying: "Our long national nightmare is over."

RAE - 777

BACKSTAGE
AUG 6 1974

Europe '74

The band's second European tour was a brief (three countries, seven shows) but messy affair that in effect confirmed the tentative decision to stop touring and generally "take a step back." If the '72 tour seemed in retrospect a loopy, loony excursion, '74 had the air of a drugged-out, doomed forced march.

Warner Bros. wasn't picking up the tab this time, so '74 was a stripped-down affair (in personnel terms at least—they did bring the Wall of Sound), with only the band members and essential crew and staff instead of the whole tribe. The absence of wives, girlfriends, and kids fueled a boys-behaving-badly scene in London, where the tour kicked off. The ravages of cocaine were such that Rex Jackson and/or Ram Rod (accounts vary) challenged everyone to burn their stashes after a soundcheck at the Alexandra Palace. (They did, but there were plenty of people on the scene ready to top them up again).

Across the channel things got worse. In Munich, the considerable friction between managers and some band members—Jon McIntire, Richard Loren, and Rock Scully—finally erupted. McIntire quit and Loren and Scully were ousted for a time, leaving Hal Kant and Chesley Milliken, who'd survived the purge of Out of Town Tours, to run the rest of the tour. Tensions among the band were hardly better. Phil Lesh and Bill Kreutzmann had a dust-up, and in Paris Kreutzmann went on a rampage that included tossing a moped through a shop window.

And yet, measured by the music, it was a fine tour. The three "Ally Pally" (Alexandra Palace) shows, especially, saw some outstanding jamming. Phil & Ned's interset electronic experiments, however, continued to get a mixed reaction:

"At the concert in Munich's Olympic Hall, Phil Lesh and Ned Lagin's electronic space set... turned into a super-loud sonic onslaught, reminiscent of the WWII bombardment of Germany all over again. It started to really upset the German audience. They hooted, whistled, shouted and began to throw stuff toward the stage. At the end of the concert that night the crowd trashed the place. It was a mess, but we won the war and got out alive."

STEVE BROWN, *2003*

174

Deadheads of the 70s

By the mid-70s the band had essentially attracted a second generation of fans—Deadheads for whom the Acid Tests, the Haight, and the big festivals were legendary events, and for whom the arrival of "tour" was not just the chance to hear great music and party with old friends and new, but also a sign of continuity with what was already starting to seem like a glorious bygone era. For some, Deadheadism was a family affair, with an older sibling spinning *Workingman's Dead* or *Europe '72* for a younger brother or sister. For others, the hookup came in a smoky dorm room—colleges and universities were now and would remain bastions of Deadheadism. Whether old 'Heads or new, however, all had one question on their mind as the hiatus loomed—would the Dead be back?

Right: October 16–20, Winterland Arena, San Francisco. The final pre-hiatus show was the forty-second show the Dead had played there since 1967.

SEPTEMBER '74

| 1 | 2 | 3 | 4 | 5 | 6 | 7 | 8 | 9 | 10 | 11 |

Monday September 9
Tuesday September 10
★ Wednesday September 11
Alexandra Palace, London, England

The first show of the run includes only one set because of a late start. Material from all three Ally Pally shows appears on 1997's *Dick's Picks Volume Seven*. On Tuesday, the band fall into what is arguably the Grateful Dead sans Garcia jam of all time. Ned Lagin plays on electric piano on Wednesday.

Wednesday September 18
Parc des Expositions, Dijon, France

| 12 | 13 | 14 | 15 | 16 | 17 | 18 | 19 | 20 | 21 |

Saturday September 14
Olympiahalle, Munich, West Germany

Friday September 20
Saturday September 21
Palais des Sports, Paris, France

Ned Lagin plays keys through the entire third set on Saturday.

1 - 15	16	17	18	19	20

Wednesday October 16 🎸
Thursday October 17 🎸
★ **Friday October 18**
Saturday October 19
Sunday October 20
Winterland Arena, San Francisco, California

The "Farewell Shows." Mickey Hart (after much persuasion) reunites with the band for the last show, tickets for which are stamped with the words "The Last One"—not an encouraging omen for Deadheads. All five shows are filmed for what would become *The Grateful Dead Movie (see page 207)*. Fourteen songs, recorded across the five nights, appear on 1976's *Steal Your Face (see page 193)*. The 10/18 show sees the last-ever performances of "Weather Report Suite: Prelude" and "Part 1"; "Tomorrow is Forever" left the rotation after 10/19.

"CUMBERLAND BLUES"
HUNTER/GARCIA/LESH

Among the many standout cuts from the Grateful Dead's pivotal disc *Workingman's Dead* (1970), "Cumberland Blues" showcases Hunter and Garcia at their everyman best, spinning a tale of hard-luck miners who "make good money, five dollars a day" and dream of moving up in life as they consider whether the hardships of a livelihood spent underground are worth returning to. During a 1991 interview, Garcia welcomed comparisons of the song to "Working Man Blues" by Merle Haggard. "Absolutely," he said. "Certainly there was a conscious decision, and then that of course led Hunter and me into the gradual discovery process of crafting a song, putting a song together that… has the thing of being able to communicate at once at several levels." The tune was part of the Dead's playlist during more than 200 shows between 1969 and 1995 (although it was retired for a while from October 18, '74 until August '81), and Hunter later cited it as prompting the best compliment he'd ever gotten when a real former Cumberland mine worker said to him, "I wonder what the guy who wrote this song would've thought if he'd ever known… the Grateful Dead was gonna do it." The Other Ones dusted the soot off of "Cumberland Blues" in 2002 and continued to play it in their new incarnation as The Dead in 2003.

Tuesday October 29
Muhammad Ali regains the world championship by knocking out George Foreman in the epic "Rumble In the Jungle" contest in Kinshasa, Zaire.

29	30	31

The Hiatus Begins

And so, nine years and five months after the Warlocks played Magoo's Pizza Parlor, the Grateful Dead sent the Urobouros into hibernation. How long it would remain in that state remained unsettled. (One reason the band didn't set a timetable was, reportedly, to encourage some of those employees on the band's bloated payroll to seek gainful employment elsewhere rather than just sitting out the break.)

It was also the end of the line for the Wall of Sound, the edifice which, perhaps even more than cocaine, high overhead, and internal politics, had pushed the band over the edge. The WOS was retired after the Winterland "Farewell" shows. Most of the setup was given away to other groups. (In *Skeleton Key*, Dan Healy remarked that "there are probably 25 little bands running around that got outfitted by that system."

For many of the crew and staff, many of whom had been making very good money for a couple of years, it was a hard landing. (To help, the band earmarked part of the gate from the Farewell shows for house down-payments for several crew members, as well as for Bill Kreutzmann.)

There'd be no break for Jerry Garcia. Driven by his relentless need to play, he was at the Keystone with Legion of Mary two days after the 10/21 Winterland show, and if the Dead weren't touring that fall, Jerry sure was, playing 23 Legion shows on the East Coast in November alone.

While all the band members with the exception of Kreutzmann would shortly be at work on solo projects of their own, Jerry's musical hyperactivity was not necessarily admired within the band. In September, during the European tour, Garcia gave an interview to the British music paper *Melody Maker* in which he said, "The most rewarding experience for me these days is to play in bars and not be Jerry Garcia of the Grateful Dead." Not a sentiment likely to endear. Also, if one of the main reasons for the hiatus was to allow everyone to recuperate from nearly a decade of near-constant performance, Jerry Garcia, in his various bands, played 103 shows in 1975 alone. (The Dead averaged 80 shows per year from '71 through '73.)

In the end the hiatus would last a bit under 20 months, from 10/20/74 through 6/3/76. During this period the band released a studio album and played three shows, while Jerry Garcia released two solo albums, Bob Weir and Phil Lesh one solo album apiece, plus one from Robert Hunter. Perhaps the hiatus wasn't that much of a rest, but it was a change, and as the old saying goes, a change is as good as a rest.

The idea of the Grateful Dead "breaking up"—I really don't see how that would come about. After ten years of touring, we've decided to cut that way down. A gig here and there—a solstice or an equinox, perhaps… At least a six-month vacation to just cool out and survey what we've been up to. Building and carting that sound system is, in my head, akin to building a pyramid. It's the world's greatest hi-fi system, and there's no one who would deny that. Recording and practices will go on as usual, leaving space for diversified personal musical projects.
ROBERT HUNTER IN A LETTER PUBLISHED IN *CRAWDADDY, 1/75*

Hiatus Heartaches

As Rock Scully put it in *Living with the Dead*, "The hiatus may have been necessary, but stopping a juggernaut like the Grateful Dead creates many problems. There's far too much time to brood and get fucked up." So it's not coincidental that the hiatus witnessed the collapse of some long-standing personal relationships among the band. Bill and Susila Kreutzmann split up. Around the same time Bob Weir and his longtime companion Frankie separated as well. Jerry and Mountain Girl had a second daughter, Trixie, in 1974, but by fall of that year their relationship, too, was in crisis. Part of the problem was Jerry's constant gigging, which, as we've seen, continued apace even after the Dead went off-road. The bigger problem was Jerry's relationship with Deborah Koons, a young woman whom he'd met in New York in '73 and with whom he began an affair in the summer of '74.

Dead Relix Magazine

One of the consequences of the hiatus was to spur the growth of the nascent network of tape traders—with the band off the road, perhaps permanently (as far as most Deadheads knew), tapes took on a new significance. (In the early '70s, the band's attitude toward taping was ambivalent; Bob Weir, for example, was known to point out the "sweet spot" for mic placement if he spotted Tapers in an audience, while Bear might rip the tape out of someone's deck.) In '74, two Brooklyn Tapers, Les Kippel and Jerry Moore, began publishing the newsletter *Dead Relix* as an adjunct of their Grateful Dead Tape Exchange. At first oriented toward Tapers, *Dead Relix* later became *Relix* and expanded its focus to the whole Dead scene (and related bands), and in the 80s, under the editorship of Toni Brown, *Relix* became a fully-fledged magazine and one of the primal publications in Deadworld. In 2001, Les Kippel sold his interest in the magazine to publisher Steve Bernstein. Today, it is a slick, well-regarded magazine devoted primarily to the jam band scene.

Above: Two early Dead Relix covers. The magazine later shortened its name to Relix to include non-Dead groups.

Sarangi: The Music of India by Ustad Sultan Khan is released, produced and engineered by Mickey Hart.

NOVEMBER '74

| 1 - 25 | 26 | 27 | 28 |

Thursday November 28
John Lennon makes what proves to be his last concert appearance at an Elton John concert at New York's Madison Square Garden.

DECEMBER '74

| 29 | 30 | 1 | 2 | 3 | 4 | 5 |

Kingfish

In '73 NRPS bassist Dave Torbert left the group and hooked up with longtime friend and musical partner Matt Kelly—a singer, guitarist, and harmonica man—who'd also been playing with NRPS. With Robbie Hoddinott on lead guitar, Chris Herold on drums, and Mick Ward on keys, he formed a new group called Kingfish. Sadly, Ward died in a car crash as the band was still getting under way. Bob Weir (who'd known Matt Kelly as a kid) showed up at some of their Bay Area gigs in the summer of '74 and, with the Dead's hiatus coming up, joined Kingfish on vocals and rhythm guitar. They played their first show with Weir in the lineup on 11/17 at the Lion's Share in San Anselmo. The Kingfish repertoire consisted primarily of cover tunes—they drew from R&B, blues, country, early rock 'n' roll, and a few Weir-sung songs from the Dead. They were basically a good-time party band; they jammed minimally, though Hoddinott was an excellent guitarist.

Right and far right: Matthew Kelly and David Torbert joined with Bob Weir to form Kingfish. Weir played with the group between 1974 and 1976; Kelly kept the band going many years after that.

OLD & IN THE WAY
Old & In the Way

Released by Round Records (RX 103) in February 1975

Side One
1. **Pig In A Pen**
   (Traditional)
2. **Midnight Moonlight**
   (Rowan)
3. **Old And In The Way**
   (Grisman)
4. **Knockin' On Your Door**
   (Traditional)
5. **The Hobo Song**
   (Bonus)

Side Two
1. **Panama Red**
   (Rowan)
2. **Wild Horses**
   (Jagger/Richard)
3. **Kissimmee Kid**
   (Clements)
4. **White Dove**
   (Stanley)
5. **Land Of The Navajo**
   (Rowan)

Personnel
Jerry Garcia – banjo, vocals
David Grisman – mandolin, vocals
Peter Rowan – guitar, vocals
Vassar Clements – fiddle
John Kahn – acoustic bass

Produced by David Grisman

YEE-HAW! THERE'S ROOTS AND THEN THERE'S *ROOTS*, and for this live hoedown taken from an October 8, 1973 show at the Boarding House in San Francisco, Garcia and company heavily favored the italicized variety. Though their name showed they had a sense of humor about their down-home alter-egos (Garcia was a grizzled 31-year-old when the album was recorded), Old & In the Way (Garcia on banjo, long-time collaborator David Grisman on mandolin, future Garcia band member John Kahn on bass, Seatrain's Peter Rowan on guitar, and Vassar Clements on violin) were serious about their music, a mix of traditional bluegrass ("Pig in a Pen," "Knockin' On Your Door"), non-Garcia originals (Clements' "Kissimmee Kid," Grisman's title cut theme and three Rowan originals, including the New Riders' soon-to-be classic "Panama Red") and even a Rolling Stones tune ("Wild Horses") thrown in for good measure. The cover, a caricature of the band jamming in a general store by Greg Irons that was strongly reminiscent of Jack Davis's work for *Mad Magazine*, conveyed the feel-good vibe of the music within. "It's been eight years since I've played banjo," Garcia explained in a 1973 interview. "We all used to be heavily into bluegrass, so we got together a little over a month ago, started playing and then decided, 'Shit, why don't we play a few bars and see what happens?'" The third release on Round Records, the album provided a worthy side trip for Dead and country fans alike. "The music on this disc...embodies the spirit of that original Blue Grass quest," Grisman wrote in the album's liner notes, "and a genuine affection for that superlative acoustic blend of banjo, guitar, fiddle, mandolin, string bass and voice(s). We hope you dig." Fans who did were later treated to two more archival releases, *That High Lonesome Sound* (1996) and *Breakdown* (1997).

Unfortunately, the album came out when Round Records was on the verge of implosion and Grisman was never properly paid for his role as producer, which caused a rift between Grisman and Garcia that lasted for 15 years.

> "Like a comet shining briefly for too short a spell, Old & In the Way made an all too short appearance in the bluegrass universe."
>
> OLIVER TRAGER, *THE AMERICAN BOOK OF THE DEAD*

JANUARY '75

| 1 ~ 10 | 11 | 12 | 13 | 14 | 15 | 16 | 17 | 18 | 19 | 20 | 21 ~ 31 |

FEBRUARY '75

Wednesday February 12
Lenny Hart dies. Natural causes claimed Mickey's father, who'd been teaching music in Marin County after serving his sentence for embezzlement. Mickey gives Lenny a rhythmic sendoff, drumming a few patterns on his coffin.

| 1 ~ 10 | 11 | 12 | 13 | 14 | 15 | 16 | 17 | 18 | 19 | 20 | 21 ~ 28 |

| 1 ~ 22 | **23** | 24 | 25 | 26 | 27 | 28 | 29 | 30 |

Sunday March 23 ★
🎸 Kezar Stadium, San Francisco, California

The first of three San Francisco shows during the touring hiatus, this is the all-star SNACK (Students Need Athletics, Culture, and Kicks) benefit *(below)* for San Francisco's public schools, which have had their budgets for nonacademic activities slashed. Also on the bill are Bob Dylan, Neil Young, the Doobie Brothers, Jefferson Starship, Joan Baez, Mimi Farina, and Graham Central Station. The Dead roll out "Blues for Allah" and "Stronger than Dirt (Or Milkin' the Turkey)," with help from Merl Saunders and Ned Lagin.

"BLUES FOR ALLAH"
GARCIA/HUNTER

Though the Dead had never followed the same musical path long enough for anyone to pigeonhole the group, what was to come from the band after a self-imposed hiatus in late 1974 and early 1975 took everyone by surprise. Conceived as a requiem for King Faisal of Saudi Arabia, whose 1975 assassination affected the group personally, "Blues For Allah" served as the title cut for the group's album that same year, though its droning, desert wind cadence was less accessible than even some of their most bizarre early fare. That may help explain why the group only played the tune during the four San Francisco appearances (starting March 23) that constituted all of the Dead's live shows in 1975, despite one critic's speculation that the song might join "Dark Star" as one of the group's "most exciting onstage set pieces." Hints of the song appeared in a "Blues For Allah"-type jam a couple of times in the early '80s, though it never fully returned to the group's setlist. "That song was a bitch to do," Garcia said in 1991. "In terms of the melody and phrasing and all, it was not of this world."

Tuesday April 29
U.S. forces pull out completely from Vietnam. The U.S. embassy in Vietnam is evacuated as North Vietnamese forces fight their way into Saigon.

| 1 ~ 22 | 23 | 24 | 25 | 26 | 27 | 28 | **29** |

KEITH AND DONNA
Keith and Donna Godchaux
Round Records RX 104

In true Dead family fashion, the Godchaux duo recruited band members Jerry Garcia and Bill Kreutzmann into a side project that came to be known as Keith and Donna. Though manager Jon McIntire half-joked with *Rolling Stone* at the time that the band might be renamed the Godchaux-Kreutzmann Band to "make it more interesting," former Wings skinsman Denny Seiwell had taken over on drums by the time the duo began work on their self-titled 1975 LP, with Garcia still in tow. The guitarist also provided a whimsical drawing on the forehead of the Godchauxs' son Zion that would comprise the album's front cover, and the sessions enjoyed a similarly comfortable intimacy, since they were mostly recorded at Keith and Donna's home.

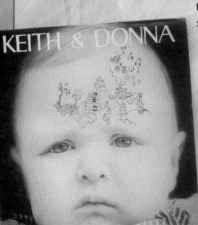

Diga Rhythm Band

A pioneering ensemble of what would latterly be termed World Music, the all-percussion Diga Rhythm Band formed around Zakir Hussain, son of Ustad Allah Rakha, the master musician who had introduced Mickey to Indian instruments and time signatures in '67. Mickey met tabla master Zakir Hussain in '70 and Zakir later invited him to join the Tal Vadyum Rhythm Band, which performed regularly at the Ali Akbar Khan College of Music. (Other members included Jordan Amarantha, Peter Carmichael, Aushim Chaudhuri, Jim Loveless, Vince Delgado, Joy Shulman, Ray Spiegel, and Arshad Syed.) In April '75 the group changed its name to Diga Rhythm Band before their first public gig—opening for the Jefferson Starship.

TIGER ROSE
Robert Hunter

ROUND TWO OF THE Robert Hunter solo show featured another stellar cast of players, with the return of Garcia and Hart, who co-produced, along with Donna Godchaux, Pete Sears (Jefferson Starship), David Freiberg (Quicksilver Messenger Service), Dave Torbert (NRPS), and David Grisman. (Hart was also credited as drummer under the *nom de tambour* of B.D. Shot.) The album's ten originals, none of which would ever appear in the Dead's live rounds, suffered just one little problem—Hunter's hastily recorded vocals.

Released by Round Records (RX 105) in March 1975

Side One
1. **Tiger Rose**
   (Hunter)
2. **One Thing To Try**
   (Hunter)
3. **Rose Of Sharon**
   (Hunter)
4. **Wild Bill**
   (Hunter)
5. **Dance A Hole**
   (Hunter)

Side Two
1. **Cruel White Water**
   (Hunter)
2. **Over The Hills**
   (Hunter)
3. **Last Flash Of Rock 'N' Roll**
   (Hunter)
4. **Yellow Moon**
   (Hunter)
5. **Ariel**
   (Hunter)

Personnel

Robert Hunter – guitar, vocals, mandolin, synthesizer
David Freiberg – bass, piano, celeste, vocals
Jerry Garcia – guitar, piano, synthesizer, pedal steel, vocals
Donna Godchaux – vocals
David Grisman – mandolin
Mickey Hart – percussion
Pete Sears – piano, bass, organ, tack piano, clavinet
B.D. Shot – drums (B.D. Shot is Mickey Hart)
David Torbert – bass

Produced by Jerry Garcia and Mickey Hart

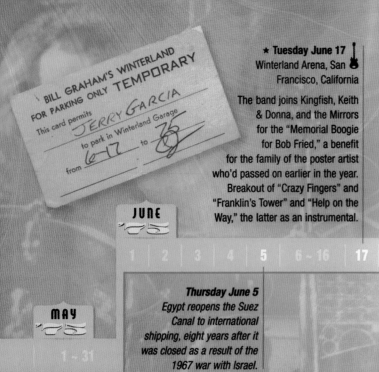

★ **Tuesday June 17**
Winterland Arena, San
Francisco, California

The band joins Kingfish, Keith
& Donna, and the Mirrors
for the "Memorial Boogie
for Bob Fried," a benefit
for the family of the poster artist
who'd passed on earlier in the year.
Breakout of "Crazy Fingers" and
"Franklin's Tower" and "Help on the
Way," the latter as an instrumental.

JUNE '75

| 1 | 2 | 3 | 4 | 5 | 6 - 16 | 17 | 18 |

MAY '75

1 - 31

Thursday June 5
Egypt reopens the Suez
Canal to international
shipping, eight years after it
was closed as a result of the
1967 war with Israel.

Recording Blues For Allah

In 2003, Steve Brown recalled a typical day at Ace's, Bob Weir's home studio, where the band began laying down the new album in early '75:

"[The studio was] a separate trapezoidal structure located above his garage at the end of a very steep driveway. Whoever pulled their car in first was subjected to being the last to be able to leave, unless they could rope me into doing the old 'car shuffle' for them. Recording engineer Dan Healy would start setting up the mixing console and get the recording tapes out. Robbie Taylor would start setting up the mics and baffles. Ram Rod was busy with the drum set and guitar amps.

I'd make fresh Dark French Roast coffee and get the remote cassette recorder in Weir's living room ready to record the day's studio activities. The band members usually arrived before noon and would get out their instruments and plug in, tune up and start noodling awhile to warm up for the day's session. Jerry often had a humorous weirdness to share. Phil was about ready for his first Heineken. Bobby would chase his dog Otis out of the studio again. Otis liked to sing along at times. Keith was hovering quietly over his piano keyboard, smoking. Bill, living far up north in Mendocino County, was grousing about having to deal with his logistics of recording and having to stay overnight in Mill Valley . . .

So eventually, after the latest news, stories, jokes and laughs were shared, gripes were aired, coffee, cigarettes, Heineken and joints were consumed, the "song du jour" was slowly launched into by the band. Sometimes just a 'tricky' musical section from a song from the previous day would be the first thing attempted... "

"Of course being at their own home studio meant the band's local musician friends often came by to visit, like good ol' David Crosby, Van Morrison or John Cipollina. More getting high, more jokes and funny stories and maybe some sharing of each others new songs and jamming on them together. By now everyone was really hungry for lunch."

STEVE BROWN, 2003

Anton Strikes Again

Assuring fans that the band was still making music collectively and individually, mailings and samplers went out to the Dead Heads mailing list twice in '75; the first, a Deadhead update and a Round Records sampler set (once again courtesy of "Anton Round") was sent in February. It included four 45s with work-in-progress tracks from Old & In the Way, Keith & Donna, Tiger Rose, and Seastones. In July, a Grateful Dead Records mailing announced the release of *Blues for Allah* and included a 45 with "Help on the Way" and "The Music Never Stopped." The July mailing also told 'Heads about the distribution deal with United Artists and the "nearly completed" movie.

May/Jun 1975

180

Below: *Calendar of Dead-related activities for May and June 1975, during the group's "working hiatus."*

The Movie Gets Moving

In addition to his musical endeavors, Jerry Garcia, always something of a cineaste, started work on the film to be assembled from the footage of the Winterland Farewell shows. (It might have been *The Grateful Dead Movie*, but it was definitely Jerry's project.) In true auteur form, Jerry clashed with the original director, Leon Gast, over creative control, and Gast (though he would share directorial credit with Garcia on the finished project) ceased active involvement. Working out of Round Reels Studios (a rented house in Mill Valley) Jerry and editor Susan Crutcher began the process of crafting a movie out of several hundred hours of raw footage taken by nine separate cameras. Jerry was especially taken with the footage of the Deadheads themselves. Susan Crutcher would recall, "We had names for the dancers. It was fun, because it personalized it for us, and we got to know them. Jerry loved that part of it."

JULY '75

1 - 23 | 24

Thursday July 24
An Apollo spacecraft
splashes down in the
Pacific, so completing
a mission that
included the first-ever
docking with a Soyuz
capsule from the
Soviet Union.

BLUES FOR ALLAH

Grateful Dead

*Released by Grateful Dead Records
(LA-494) in August 1975*

Side One
1. **Help On The Way**
   (Hunter/Garcia)
2. **Slipknot!**
   (Garcia/K.Godchaux/Kreutzmann/Lesh/Weir)
3. **Franklin's Tower**
   (Hunter/Garcia)
4. **King Solomon's Marbles**
   (Lesh)
5. **Part I: Stronger Than Dirt**
   (Hart/Kreutzmann/Lesh)
6. **Part II: Milkin' The Turkey**
   (Hart/Kreutzmann/Lesh)
7. **The Music Never Stopped**
   (Weir/Barlow)

Side Two
1. **Crazy Fingers**
   (Hunter/Garcia)
2. **Sage and Spirit**
   (Weir)
3. **Blues For Allah**
   (Hunter/Garcia)
4. **Sand Castles and Glass Camels**
   (Garcia/K.Godchaux/D.Godchaux/Kreutzmann/
   Lesh/Weir)
5. **Unusual Occurrences In The Desert**
   (Hunter/Garcia)

Personnel

Jerry Garcia – guitar, vocals
Keith Godchaux – keyboards, vocals
Donna Godchaux – vocals
Mickey Hart – percussion, crickets
Bill Kreutzmann – drums, percussion
Phil Lesh – bass, vocals
Bob Weir – guitar, vocals
Steven Schuster – reeds, flute

Produced by the
Grateful Dead

*Right: Although
Mickey Hart
played on the
album, his
face was not
included on
the back cover.*

The THIRD AND FINAL STUDIO release on the Dead's own label was also probably the most fully realized, an apogee in terms of studio creativity that came on the tail end of the band's touring hiatus. It reflected a new level of dedication that paid enticing dividends, with the legendary troika of "Help On The Way," "Slipknot" and "Franklin's Tower" and another unofficial theme song, Weir and Barlow's "The Music Never Stopped." Excursions like the delicate acoustic instrumental "Sage and Spirit" and a suite of wind-swept, desert-inspired fare were hardly rock radio stuff at the time, but the album marched to a personal high of No.13, thanks to a new distribution deal with United Artists and a network of plugged-in fans and curious outsiders who'd wondered what the band had been up to during its mysterious disappearing act.

The end product was something they felt they could stand behind, too. "It's the first of our albums that's really grown on me," Lesh admitted. "It indicates a new point of departure for our music." Garcia agreed. "The next level of development was when we went to *Blues For Allah*," he told Blair Jackson in 1988. "There we came up with some very interesting, other, alternate ways to invent openness that would be developmental." The album's name was inspired by the recently-deceased Saudi Arabian leader King Faisal (the original gatefold was unique in being the only one ever printed in English, Arabic, and Sanskrit), and its cover had another classic icon with its eerie visage of a red-robed, skeletal violinist by Philip Garris. The album was recorded at Ace's and engineered by comrade-in-sound Dan Healy.

Breakup Blues

A strong-willed, independent woman if ever there was one, Mountain Girl had tolerated—though not exactly accepted—Jerry Garcia's occasional infidelities over the years as an occupational hazard of being a rock star's significant other. By the summer of '75, though, it was clear that Jerry's relationship with Deborah Koons was no fling. As usual, Jerry fled from confrontation, even though for a while he was still living with Mountain Girl while seeing Deborah. Finally, Jerry and Deborah rented a place in Tiburon and Jerry left for good.

AUGUST '75

| 1 | 2 | 3 | 4 | 5 | 6 | 7 | 8 | 9 | 10 | 11 | 12 | **13** |

★ **Wednesday August 13**
Great American Music Hall, San Francisco, California

Essentially the release party for *Blues for Allah*, the GAMH show sees the Dead back in a small hall (400 seats) for the first time in years. "The Music Never Stopped" (which quickly became an iconic song for Deadheads) and "Sage and Spirit" (the instrumental named, incidentally, for Rock Scully's daughters) get their live rollout, and the album's title track (complete with a mic'd tank of crickets) is performed for the second—and last—time.

| 14 ~ 26 | **27** | 28 ~ 31 |

Wednesday August 27
*Haile Selassie, last emperor of
Ethiopia's 3,000-year-old
monarchy, dies at age 83, almost
a year after he was overthrown in
a military coup. Crowned emperor
in 1930, he was by tradition a
descendant of King Solomon
and the Queen of Sheba.*

SEASTONES

SEASTONES
Ned Lagin

Released by Round Records (RX 106) in April 1975

1. Seastones (9 sections)

Personnel

Ned Lagin – piano, clavichord, organ, prepared piano, percussion, synthesizers, computers
David Crosby – guitar, voice
Spencer Dryden – percussion
David Freiberg – voice
Jerry Garcia – guitar, voice
Mickey Hart – percussion
Phil Lesh – bass
Grace Slick – voice

Produced by Ned Lagin

As this one-off project by Lesh and Ned Lagin proves, certain adventures just weren't meant to be accessible. Even the Dead family couldn't describe it, as evidenced by the newsletter that said Lesh and Lagin were "taking their art slowly but surely to the further reaches of its limitations which, of course, are impossible for the human intelligence to define." As abstract as the splotch and squiggle cartoon universe by Ruth Poland on its cover, *Seastones* remains one of the least commercial efforts from the Dead's extended camp, rivaling Garcia's sonic forays from his self-titled debut, and this despite the participation of Garcia, Hart, and even Spencer Dryden, David Crosby, and Grace Slick. It also has the unique distinction of being the only album ever to be recorded at Ace's, Rolling Thunder, and MIT. "'Seastones' is like an Alexander Calder mobile," Lagin valiantly tried to explain during a 2001 David Gans interview. "The score is subject to the physical manipulation of the components, resulting in a number of different valid realizations of the score." A 1990 CD re-release of *Seastones* would include a second version for those who didn't get enough the first time around.

182

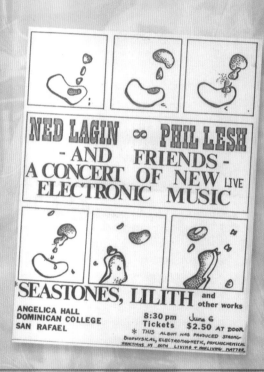

NED LAGIN ∞ PHIL LESH
- AND FRIENDS -
A CONCERT OF NEW LIVE
ELECTRONIC MUSIC

*SEASTONES, LILITH and other works

ANGELICA HALL
DOMINICAN COLLEGE
SAN RAFAEL

8:30 pm   June 6
Tickets $2.50 AT DOOR
* THIS ALBUM HAS PRODUCED STRONG BIOPHYSICAL, ELECTROMAGNETIC, PSYCHOCHEMICAL REACTIONS IN BOTH LIVING & NONLIVING MATTER.

Ned Lagin

A scientist, an aspiring astronaut, and a musician deeply into jazz, classical, electronic, and early music, Ned Lagin met the Dead when they came to MIT, where he was a student, in May 1970. He hit it off with Lesh and Garcia, and when Lagin flew to the Bay Area a month later, Garcia invited him to play piano for a couple of tracks on *American Beauty*. Later he involved members of the Dead in Seastones, a bizarre sound construction involving layers of electronically treated instruments and vocals that came out on the Dead's Round Records label in 1975. Lagin and Lesh also performed bass/electronics duets between sets at a number of Dead shows in 1974.

Below, bottom, and below right: September 28, Lindley Meadows, Golden Gate Park. The band onstage; Keith and Donna relax before the show.

| 1 | 2 | 3 | 4 | 5 | 6 | 7 - 17 |

18

Monday September 1
Today sees the release of two Grateful Dead singles, "Help on the Way/Franklin's Tower" and "The Music Never Stopped/Franklin's Tower."

Thursday September 18
Police and FBI arrest heiress Patty Hearst, William and Emily Harris, and Wendy Yoshimura in San Francisco. Hearst was later convicted of bank robbery and served more than 22 months in federal prison (President Carter commuted her sentence in 1979).

Jerry Garcia Band

In the summer of '75 Merl Saunders and Martin Fierro moved on to other projects, effectively ending the Legion of Mary. Jerry Garcia, John Kahn (bass), and Ron Tutt (drums) continued to gig, bringing in the legendary Nicky Hopkins on keys; the quartet played its first gig under the Jerry Garcia Band name at the Keystone on 8/5/75. Hopkins—an English session man who'd worked with The Who, the Stones, and, most recently, Quicksilver—was a brilliant player but was so deep into cocaine and booze that he was cut loose at the end of the year. The JGB would continue, in various lineups, until Jerry's death. For Jerry, the JGB provided a vehicle to play the small clubs and theaters that his "main band" had outgrown, as well as a means of exploring his diverse musical tastes—the JGB's repertoire would range over R&B, gospel, Dylan, the Stones, and much else, plus some Hunter/Garcia originals like "Deal" and "Reuben and Cherise."

Jerry and John

During the JGB's run at New York's Bottom Line, Jerry Garcia met John Lennon. Accounts of what happened vary; according to one story, Lennon told Jerry how much he liked Jerry and Merl Saunders's cover of "Imagine" on *Heavy Turbulence*, and Jerry invited John to sit in at the next night's show, though he failed to show up. John Kahn would remember it differently, describing a drunk Lennon baiting Jerry in his dressing room before going off to party with the local Hells Angels.

New Riders Of The Purple Sage release *Oh, What A Mighty Time*. Jerry Garcia plays on three of the album tracks; Bob Weir contributes one song.

Above and left: Garcia on tour with the Jerry Garcia Band, Halloween '75. That's Nicky Hopkins in the foreground above.

OCTOBER '75

| 28 | 29 | 30 | 1 | 2 | 3 ~ 31 |

🎸 **Sunday September 28**
Lindley Meadows, Golden Gate Park, San Francisco, California

With Jefferson Starship and as part of the "New Age Bicentennial Unity Fair," the Dead play their first free outdoor show since 10/21/72 at Vanderbilt University. Matt Kelly guests on harmonica on "The Music Never Stopped" and "Beat it On Down The Line," and the crowd—estimated at 25,000 to 40,000—was treated to the first "Eleven" jam since 1/16/70.

NOVEMBER '75

| 1 ~ 19 | 20 | 21 ~ 30 |

Thursday November 20
After almost four decades of absolute rule in Spain, General Francisco Franco dies. Juan Carlos, grandson of King Alfonso, is proclaimed king of Spain two days later.

Release of *Silver* by Silver: the first album from a group that includes future Grateful Dead keyboardist Brent Mydland.

DECEMBER '75

| 1 ~ 26 | 27 | 28 | 29 | 30 | 31 |

Wednesday December 31
Keyboard player Nicky Hopkins leaves the Jerry Garcia Band to be replaced, briefly, by James Booker. A further reshuffle occurs early the following year when Keith and Donna Godchaux join the ranks.

Finance Blues

By the middle of '75 it was clear that the Grateful Dead's experiment in minding its own business had failed. *The Grateful Dead Movie*, still far from completion, was sucking almost as much cash out of the organization as the Wall of Sound had. In addition to "the Movie," Round Reels was at work on another film, *Hell's Angels Forever*, that was also proving a money pit. On the record side, the profits from Grateful Dead Records' *Wake of the Flood* and *Mars Hotel* were more than offset by the poor performance of most of the Round Records solo records. Ron Rakow (who by now had the nickname "Cash Flow Ron Rakow") managed a bailout in the form of a distribution deal with United Artists Records. That solved, for the time being, the money and logistical problems. As the July '75 Dead Head mailing put it: "Anton Round (ex-record czar) formally ate a roast crow at a dinner with other top record executives, to whom he had boasted that the small, independent record company could handle a band's product more efficiently and with greater margin for profit than larger companies with their redundant bureaucratic overflap. The crow, you will remember, was an early emblem of GD records." The UA deal may have cost the band some of its autonomy, but it also liberated the band from the endless workload of monitoring distribution so that they could concentrate on Job No. 1: the music.

Jan/Feb 1976

184

Bam Magazine and Bammies

Founded by a musician named Dennis Erokan in January 1976, BAM magazine started out as a resource guide for Bay Area musicians, but quickly grew to become one of the most successful regional music magazines in America. BAM covered the Dead extensively, even devoting a column to the band—"Dead Ahead"—for a while.

In 1978, Erokan staged the first Bay Area Music Awards, handing out trophies to local musicians. Through the years the Bammie ceremonies attracted many top names, including the Dead, Santana, John Lee Hooker, the Dead Kennedys. BAM folded in 1999, but the Bammies live on as the California Music Awards.

Below: Dennis Erokan, founder of BAM magazine.

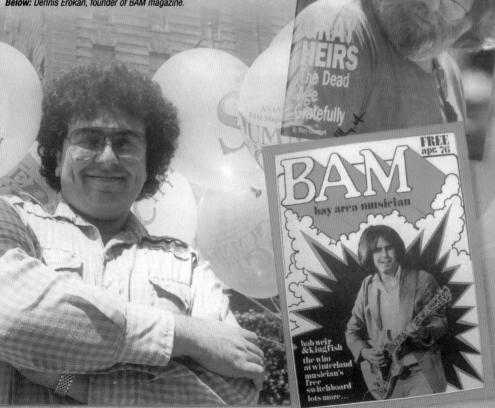

REFLECTIONS
Jerry Garcia

Garcia's third solo album is inadvertently schizophrenic, featuring the Dead as the backup band on part of the album and sidemates John Kahn, Ron Tutt, Larry Knetchel, and Nicky Hopkins included elsewhere. "The album was supposed to be a Jerry Garcia Band album but it sort of fell apart in the middle," Kahn said later, "so it ended up being half that band and half Grateful Dead." Garcia later described the band's involvement as a result of the enjoyment they'd just had working on their most recent LP, *Blues For Allah*, though where "Allah" was meticulous, here the Dead are blowing off steam. Not surprisingly, five of the album's songs would make their way into the Dead's shows, including "Might As Well." Cover artwork was by Mike Steirnagle.

Released by Round Records (RX 107) on February 3, 1976

Side One

1. **Might As Well**
   (Garcia/Hunter)
2. **Mission In The Rain**
   (Garcia/Hunter)
3. **They Love Each Other**
   (Garcia/Hunter)
4. **I'll Take A Melody**
   (Toussaint)

Side Two

1. **It Must Have Been The Roses**
   (Hunter)
2. **Tore Up Over You**
   (Ballard)
3. **Catfish John**
   (McDill/Reynolds)
4. **Comes A Time**
   (Garcia/Hunter)

Personnel

Jerry Garcia — lead guitar, acoustic guitar, rhythm guitar, organ, synthesizer, chimes, percussion, bells, vocals
Donna Jean Godchaux — vocals
Keith Godchaux — piano, fender rhodes, tack piano
Mickey Hart — drums, percussion, fire extinguisher, box
Nicky Hopkins — piano
John Kahn — bass, synthesizer, vibes, organ, clavinet
Larry Knetchel — fender rhodes, piano
Bill Kreutzmann — drums
Phil Lesh — bass; **Ron Tutt** — drums
Bob Weir — guitar, vocals

KINGFISH
Kingfish

In 1976 Weir emerged as a member of Kingfish, a San Francisco-based side group that he hooked up with long enough to record a self-titled debut album that year. Formed by New Riders bassist Dave Torbert and Weir's childhood buddy Matt Kelly, Kingfish's album featured two Weir/Barlow songs ("Lazy Lightning" and "Supplication") that would become part of the Dead's set list three months after the album's March release. Weir's involvement with the band would be brief. "I never really found just exactly what I was going to be doing with Kingfish," Weir told David Gans in 1977. "The problem was that I didn't spend enough time with them... I never really homed in on what my place was in that outfit and what the outfit was really up to."

Released by Round Records (United Artists) (RX-108) on March 3, 1976

Side One

1. **Lazy Lightnin'**
   (Weir/Barlow)
2. **Supplication**
   (Weir/Barlow)
3. **Wild Northland**
   (Torbert/Hovey)
4. **Asia Minor**
   (Carter/Gilbert/Quigley/Hovey)
5. **Home to Dixie**
   (Kelly/Cutler/Barlow/Weir)
6. **Jump For Joy**
   (Carter/Gilbert)

Side Two

1. **Good-Bye Yer Honor**
   (Torbert/Hovey/Kelly)
2. **Big Iron**
   (Robbins)
3. **This Time**
   (Torbert/Kelly)
4. **Hypnotize**
   (Torbert/Kelly)
5. **Bye and Bye**
   (Traditional arr. Weir/Barlow)

Personnel

Bob Weir – guitar, vocals; **Dave Torbert** – bass, vocals
Matthew Kelly – guitar, harp, vocals
Robby Hoddinott – guitar, slide guitar
Chris Herold – drums, percussion

Produced by Dan Healy and Bob Weir

Ⅴarying beat time signatures, anyone? The man behind "The Main Ten" offers up some more of 'em ("Sweet Sixteen," "Magnificent Sevens") on the last Round Records release, an offspring of Hart's work with the rich ensemble of percussionists known as the Diga Rhythm Band. The album's global array of instruments (Dig Delgado's doumbek, dude!) fed the spirit of the burgeoning world music movement most kindly, and like Hart's previous release, *Rolling Thunder* (1972), the album served as a point of inspiration for more Dead material, in this case the transformation of "Happiness Is Drumming" into the band classic "Fire On The Mountain." With Garcia along for the ride on that track and the Arabian-inspired "Razooli," the album, with cover artwork by Jordan De La Sierra, was a sonic safari for adventurous Deadhead ears, seamlessly managing to fuse influences of Indian rhythmic cycles and Balinese gamelan orchestras. In an interview with Doug Heselgrave almost 25 years later, Mickey Hart said: "To create a new kind of gamelan, something that I could relate to that was more culturally specific to what I was involved in...that was always the carrot."

Pistol Packin' Mama by The Good Old Boys, a bluegrass album produced by Garcia, is released this year. It is the only Round Records release that does not include a playing contribution from one of the members of the Grateful Dead.

APRIL '76
1 – 4 | **5** | 6 | 7

Monday April 5
Eccentric, reclusive billionaire Howard Hughes dies in Houston at age 72.

MARCH '76
1 – 25 | 26 | **27** | **28** | **29** | 30 | 31

DIGA
Diga Rhythm Band

Released by Round Records (RX 110/ RX-LA600-G) in March 1976

Side One

1. **Razooli**
   (Spiegel)
2. **Happiness Is Drumming**
   (Hart/Diga Rhythm Band)
3. **Tal Mala**
   (Diga Rhythm Band)

Side Two

4. **Sweet Sixteen**
   (Diga Rhythm Band)
5. **Magnificent Sevens**
   (Diga Rhythm Band)

Personnel

Jordan Amarantha – congas, bongos
Peter Carmichael – tabla
Aushim Chaudhuri – tabla
Vince Delgado – doumbek, table, talking drum
Tor Dietrichson – tabla
Mickey Hart – traps, gongs, timbales, tympani
Zakir Hussain – tabla, folk drums, tar
Jim Loveless – marimbas
Joy Shulman – tabla
Ray Spiegel – vibes
Arshad Syed – duggi tarang, nal
Jerry Garcia – guitar (on "Razooli" and "Happiness Is Drumming")
Jim McPherson – vocals (on "Razooli")
Kathy McDonald – vocals (on "Razooli")
David Freiberg – vocals (on "Razooli")

Produced by Mickey Hart

"It's twentieth century gamelan."

Mickey Hart

Dead Return

An early '76 Deadheads mailing made it official: "[V]acationing is too exhausting too continue, meaning the Grateful Dead has decided to get back into touring . . . The date is not yet agreed upon, or the place, but it will be somewhere around the middle of '76."

The meltdown of the band's various self-run enterprises had something to do with the decision, but the return to touring was equally an artistic decision. As Jerry Garcia put it, "We all miss Grateful Dead Music. We want to be the Grateful Dead some more." (Jerry also noted, however, that the return was something of a "compromise," since the band couldn't come up with an alternative way of performing.) Mickey Hart was back with the band as well, and the group, now a septet, rehearsed intensively in the runup to the "Comeback Tour."

"We're horny to play."

Jerry Garcia

PLAYING IN THE BAND

May 1976 – April 1980

The Dead began their first San Francisco post-hiatus show with Bob Weir's "The Music Never Stopped," and it represented more than just a good inside joke. Playing with another band, Kingfish, during the hiatus had given Weir an increased measure of musical self-confidence, and he accelerated his forward momentum within the Dead. Post-"vacation," their newly returned percussionist and Lesh's decision to discontinue singing due to vocal cord problems led to changes in the repertoire. As things settled out, a significant portion of the most popular new material turned out to be Weir's, including his cover of the Rev. Gary Davis's "Samson and Delilah," and "Lazy Lightning," a tune he'd written with Kingfish. It came about, said Weir, "because I got this thing

The septet, mid-'70s. Weir began to step out more as a songwriter during this era, penning tunes for both the Dead's and his own solo albums.

called a trinome. It was a little plastic box—the dingclicker. You could play in 7/4 with it. And so I got completely wigged out with 7/4... And I'd learned a bunch of new basically jazz chords from Robbie Hoddinott, who was the Kingfish guitar player. I threw a bunch of these new chords into a 7/4 R&B rhythm and had something that was actually kinda fresh sounding." This is probably not the standard ASCAP method of songwriting, but it made an excellent song, one of a number Weir would contribute over the next few years.

Weir occupied an often-underappreciated yet truly fulcrumatic role in the Dead. The man that the women in the audience most noticed— standing between two instrumental geniuses who were rarely thought of as sexy—he was at times dismissed as a rocker who could only rev up a Chuck Berry tune and close a show. Not so. Just as, for instance, Bill Kreutzmann would rarely attract the attention of Deadheads or the media due to his

"We weren't done playing but the tune was over... [so] the first thing we learned was to rattle on in one chord change for a while until we were done punching it around." BOB WEIR TO DENNIS MCNALLY

understated style and disinclination to be interviewed, Weir made any number of essential contributions over the years that tended to be overshadowed by the attention paid to Garcia. But Weir gave the Dead a necessary creative alternative. If Garcia had been the only singer and songwriter, it would not have been the Grateful Dead.

Weir had been adopted into an upper-class family—his first exposure to music came from his black nanny, Luella—who lived in a wealthy suburb of San Francisco. From the first, "Blob Weird" was a wayward youth who went his own way, "the only guy I know," he said of himself, "who was drummed out of the Cub Scouts." As he entered his teens, he turned toward music, but only on his own terms; lessons were out. Yet once he settled on the guitar, it became a part of him, and he formed the youngest part of the gang that followed the action at the Palo Alto folk club called The Tangent where the star was a guy named Jerry Garcia. Weir began to hang out at Morgan's, the music store where Garcia gave lessons, and when Pigpen and Garcia started a Rolling Stones–style blues-oriented rock band, Weir was there to play rhythm guitar and sing—and supply a healthy dose of Beatles orientation to leaven the bluesier influences.

One reason Weir didn't always get his due was his offbeat sense of humor, the essence of dry understatement. He once described the band's swift decision to become an improvisational group as "we weren't done playing, but the tune was over... [so] the first thing we learned was to rattle on in one chord change for a while, until we were done punching it around." In more high-falutin' circles, this is called modal jamming. The main reason the Dead would sound so different was that each member came from a different musical genre, and they each taught themselves (and each other) how to play rock 'n' roll. Typically, when Weir decided to really train for the Dead, he studied not Keith Richards or John Lennon but McCoy Tyner, the legendary pianist of John Coltrane's greatest band.

As "the kid," it took Weir a while to step forward—and in fact, as late as 1968 there was a period in which he (and Pigpen, as it happened) were theoretically not part of the band. In Owsley "Bear" Stanley's view, this was silly because the band was indivisible: "You can't fire your left hand for not writing as well as your right." Weir practiced hard, and the issue swiftly became moot. Still, the criticism he'd endured definitely stunted his songwriting, ironically so because his first major song, "The Other One," was an essential element of the early Dead, and one of the few pre-Hunter lyrics that would endure. He effectively withdrew from composition, so that there is nothing credited to him on *Aoxomoxoa* or *Workingman's Dead*. It was not until 1970's "Sugar Magnolia" that he would take full credit for the music on a song— "Truckin'" was ultimately written by the entire band. But it was arguments with the esteemed lyricist Robert Hunter that would turn him loose.

Early in 1971, having already written the superb "Playing in the Band" without major incident, Hunter and Weir began to argue backstage one night about the song "Greatest Story Ever Told." As Weir's prep-school buddy John Barlow told it, "Hunter went into one of his apoplexies, and says, 'Barlow, you wrote poetry in college, right?' 'Well, yeah.' 'So you could write songs, probably, hunh?' 'Well, maybe. I know they're different.' 'Take him, he's yours.'" Added Weir, "That was pretty much it... I had no more disregard for Hunter's first drafts than Garcia did. It was just simply that Hunter couldn't put up with another one."

Weir finished a song he'd begun with Hunter called "One More Saturday Night," then resumed work on a song he'd begun in the summer of 1970, when he'd been privileged to be present for the birth of a young woman named Cassidy Law. Her mother Eileen, one of Weir's housemates, had taken the name from the film *Butch Cassidy and the Sundance Kid* because it was equally suitable for either gender. At one point Hunter had offered Weir some card-playing lyrics, but Bob didn't dig 'em. Barlow started in, but his first stab was equally off—"Ten pound rat in a trashcan, nuclear war Neanderthal man..." "I thought it was a little heavy-handed for the melody," remarked Weir. When Barlow connected Cassidy with the Dead's inspiration from the Merry Pranksters, Neal Cassady, the song turned into a meditation on generations—as Cassady passed on, Cassidy arrived—and became an instant winner for the new songwriting team.

As the songs collected, Weir got a contract for a solo album, which he would record in January 1972. The Dead's manager convinced him that the smart thing to do was to make it an all-Weir-vocal Dead album. Mind you, in most bands songwriting is a jealously guarded prerogative, the road to riches and the source of half of all conflict (the other half is volume on stage). As in all things, the Dead were different. Weir was encouraged to write, especially by Garcia. Said Weir, "Here was the kid in the band who was starting to develop into a songwriter and a performer. I was starting to hit my stride, and he was proud." Added Barlow, "'Cause he understood something important, which was that if it was just gonna be him and Hunter, it was going to be a monoculture. As juvenile or puerile or whatever that I could be, the whole deal was going to be a lot more interesting if we were part of the mix." The kid not only stayed in the picture, he became a full partner, although never as prolific as Hunter–Garcia.

When the Dead resumed normal touring life they also decided they had to reenter the "normal" life of having a regular record company. The Grateful Dead Record Company was a (mostly fond) memory in late 1976, but it was time to let someone else take care of business. They began to negotiate with Clive Davis, the outstanding former Columbia Records executive who had meantime started Arista Records. Davis would become legendary for his direct contributions to many careers, most especially the pop diva Whitney Houston's; at first glance, he and the Dead was not a promising relationship. Actually, it worked out quite nicely over the next twenty years and more, in considerable part because in those early days Bob Weir acted as something of a liaison between the band and record company, attending record company conventions and generally cooperating with the program.

Arista only insisted on an outside record producer for the next album, and Keith Olsen, who'd recently done a good Fleetwood Mac album, was quickly selected. Early in 1977 they began recording, and Weir quickly contributed a gem, yet another 7/4 beauty about a psychedelicized madman called "Estimated Prophet." Soon after, Hunter and Garcia came in with the masterpiece "Terrapin Station," and they

were off to the races. Eventually, their producer would, as Garcia put it, "put the Dead in a dress," by adding an orchestra (tolerable) and a chorale (not) to the final version, making it yet another of those flawed Dead masterpieces.

As 1977 passed, they'd gotten musically in touch with their "new" configuration, and their spectacular June shows at Winterland showed a band that was hot and going places. Just as Garcia finished his movie and the new album, *Terrapin Station*, was ready for a July release, with a summer of touring planned to regain their financial bearings, fate struck. On June 20th, driving home from a Norton Buffalo show, Mickey Hart drove off the road. Fortunately, there was a tree available to stop him from a 300-foot drop. Unfortunately, by the time his car nestled into the tree, he had a broken collarbone, arm, and ribs, a punctured lung, and an ear half-torn from his scalp. He began to convalesce, and the Dead suddenly found themselves with the summer off. Garcia went into the Dead's own Front Street warehouse and produced an exquisite album called *Cats Under the Stars* that was so poorly promoted and sold he would never again take seriously a solo recording project. Weir approached things differently.

Bob had warmed to Keith Olsen, and with his lyricist partner John Barlow, he decided to make a genuine late-'70s overdone L.A. studio solo extravaganza, which became *Heaven Help the Fool*, complete with a Richard Avedon portrait on the cover. In a time of drink-and-drug excess, they managed to write some really good songs—"Heaven Help the Fool," "Shade of Grey," "Bombs Away"—and record them with some of the best session cats in L.A.—even though, of course, they were horrendously overdone. As Weir told an interviewer, "Really, what concerns me is a chance to do things my way. Not that I object to not being able to do things my way with the Grateful Dead, because it's valuable working with a group of people like that... and it keeps us from being too inbred and stuff like that."

As the year progressed, the band became caught up in the slow process of recovering from their "vacation," the collapse of the record company, and the expense of the movie. Naturally, there was only one solution to such a dreary outlook—find an adventure,

The late '70s saw the introduction of such Weir–Barlow classics as "Estimated Prophet," "I Need a Miracle," "Feel Like a Stranger," and the combo of "Lost Sailor" and "Saint of Circumstance."

something outrageous, something incredible, something Dead. Ever since their visit to Stonehenge in 1972, Garcia and most particularly Lesh had been interested in geomancy, a study of power spots on the earth. Now, in 1978, they pulled off a coup; the Dead were going to go to one of the great power spots on the globe, the Great Pyramid in Gizeh, Egypt, and play three shows. On the last night, their light show at intermission would be a full eclipse of the moon. That's an adventure. In the words of their friend David Freiberg, who went along for the ride, "It was heaven... It was just like a dream... the music seemed to be completely secondary to the whole feeling."

That was just as well, since the music was not remotely their greatest. Kreutzmann had broken his arm that summer playing basketball and was not at the top of his game. The piano was out of tune. In general, the band were simply not playing well, which became all the clearer when they woke up from their dream and went home. First they had to finish their newest

"We play for the moment. None of us is playing by rote, and each of us is considering what we're doing afresh each time." BOB WEIR TO BLAIR JACKSON, *1989*

album, *Shakedown Street*, which, while it had some good material—"Fire on the Mountain" and the title song, among other things—was overall distinctly lacking in inspiration. The live album from Egypt that was going to pay for their adventure did not materialize, quite simply because their playing wasn't good enough to justify its release. Consequently, they had to play too many shows in order to pay off their debts. From within, the band had never seemed more swept by torment and chaos. Drugs had hit them hard. Garcia in particular had started a struggle with opiates that would interfere with his creativity for the rest of his career, although almost everyone else drank or consumed too much of something or other. Keith and Donna had both been eaten alive by the rock and roll lifestyle monster, and in early 1979 concluded that they needed to leave the band in order to save their own lives.

And Weir came to the rescue. Although he would never be as obsessive as Garcia with his side projects, Weir had followed up *Heaven Help the Fool* by working with a band of L.A. studio professionals that included a keyboard player named Brent Mydland. In October 1978, Weir's band opened for the Jerry Garcia Band at three shows in the Pacific Northwest, and Garcia noticed the quality of the keyboard player. In March 1979, Keith and Donna left the band—as with T.C., it was an entirely mutual decision—and Brent Mydland became the fourth Dead keyboard player. A gifted player with a rather too-sweet voice, he was prey to too many of the same sorts of insecurities as Keith. Still, he was game. Weir thought he fit because of his "ding!, who hit me?—world view. He hadn't been there enough, as were the rest of us really, to be intimidated." Brent also didn't have time to be intimidated by his new role, since had had a great deal to learn. He debuted in April on two weeks' rehearsal, and learned on the road—quickly.

Integrating a new band member and new material at the same time had always proven difficult for the band— in 1971, they'd not bothered with a studio album, so that *Europe '72* had been full of songs that never did get that sort of treatment. But in 1979/80, they began almost immediately to work on the album called *Go to Heaven*, and the results were predictable. Though some of the material was quite good, especially Garcia's "Althea" and two of Weir's tunes, the paean to night-crawling, "Feel Like a Stranger," and the rocking "Saint of Circumstance," the Brent material was so lyrically mainstream that no one could quite grasp it. More to the point, the band simply hadn't yet jelled around their new member.

As Weir's lyricist John Barlow said of the recording of *Heaven*, "they came together over a long period of time and they kept seeming like they were together and then they weren't. And the GD were in the studio for, Jesus, two years, and they had the same amount of material two weeks before they finished as they did two years before... doing overdubs like demented people. And I just lost all faith in it." With the exception of *In the Dark*, which was completed so quickly no one had the chance to gripe, Barlow's remarks probably applied to all of the Dead's studio recording projects. But whether the song was the anarchist diatribe "Throwin' Stones," or his dark meditations on urban life like "Picasso Moon," or his collaboration with Willie Dixon, "Eternity," Weir would continue to provide the Dead with an alternative, and personify the code: "You just keep truckin' on."

Above: The group used the reintroduction of Mickey Hart into the band as an excuse to re-learn some long-forgotten songs and introduce a number of new ones.

Rakow Runs Out

The coup de grace to the tottering Grateful Dead Records/Round Records company came in early '76 when the Bank of Boston, which had provided the startup capital, called in its loan. There are conflicting accounts of the various machinations and manipulations that followed—none of them pretty. While Ron Rakow schemed to keep the operation afloat, Bear and Phil Lesh struggled with an impossible deadline and terrible source material to produce the live album the band owed United Artists: the result would be the ludicrous *Steal Your Face*. Mickey Hart, mixing *Diga*, the first album from the Diga Rhythm band *(see page 179)*, faced an even more absurd dilemma. Rakow was leaning on him to deliver the finished product ASAP. Mickey complied by taking over his room at Wally Heider's studio, deploying a phalanx of Hells Angels to bar the door to anyone who might disturb him, including the other artist—Maria Muldaur—who was supposed to be working there. Four sleepless days and nights later, the siege of Wally Heider's ended when Mickey and his unlucky engineer emerged with the album. Ron Rakow's part in the process was less dramatic, and also less successful. His schemes having come to naught, the band furious over *Steal Your Face*, and having lost the support of Jerry Garcia, Rakow was fired in June. He did not wait to negotiate a severance package; having just picked up $275,000 due to the band from United Artists, he wrote a check to himself for $225,000 and said hasta la vista. Rakow claimed the money was owed him, and perhaps all or some of it was, but his action eviscerated the record company, which finally collapsed despite the heroic efforts of Steve Brown and others to keep it going. And like Lenny Hart's earlier betrayal, Rakow's scam-and-scram took a heavy psychic toll on the band, particularly on Jerry, who'd been his chief supporter.

On the Road Again

During the hiatus the band had explored various schemes that would allow them to continue performing live, but on their own terms. One idea was to build their own venue somewhere in the Bay Area, designed, maybe, by Buckminster Fuller, father of the geodesic dome—what could be cooler than that? Another idea, referenced in the July '75 Dead Heads mailing, was to do unannounced "Hit and Run" shows—a concept the band would return to many years later. In the end, however, financial considerations prevailed and the decision was taken to resume touring that June in a more-or-less conventional manner, but to book into smaller venues, with a scaled-down crew (six, as opposed to twenty) and with rented gear (tweaked by Dan Healy). The band also decided to give those fans on the Dead Heads mailing list—now up to 45,000—priority in obtaining tickets from GDTS.

Monday May 24
The first commercial supersonic transport, the Anglo-French Concorde, lands at Dulles International Airport, Washington.

MAY '76

23

| 24 | 25 | 26 | 27 | 28 | 29 | 30 | 31 | 1 | 2 | 3 | 4 | 5 |

JUNE '76

Thursday June 3
Friday June 4
Paramount Theatre, Portland, Oregon

The band come back with the breakout of five new songs, many of them from solo projects; "Might as Well," the opener, from Hunter/Garcia, which had its origins on the Festival Express and which would first hit vinyl on Jerry's *Reflections* album; "Lazy Lightning" and "Supplication," Weir/Barlow songs for Kingfish, which the Dead would usually perform twinned; the Hunter/Garcia/Kreutzmann "The Wheel," from *Garcia*; and "Samson & Delilah." The band also retired "Dancin' in the Street" after 123 known performances.

Same, But Different

The "Comeback Tour" was also called the "Deadheads Only Tour," as tickets were available only through Grateful Dead ticket services. In terms of management and logistics, the tour reflected the changes to the band's organization. With Out of Town tours out of the picture, for example, Bill Graham Productions booked shows west of the Rockies, with John Scher taking care of the rest of the continent. The Dead also benefited from the experience of the Jerry Garcia Band, which had toured regularly during the hiatus; Richard Loren and John Scher had developed (in Dennis McNally's words) "a self-contained touring setup" that worked well for the JGB, and which the Dead copied. There were also some changes to the band's performance style in the first post-hiatus tours. The pace of the music was slower, partly because of the nature of the new material in the rotation, and partly because it took time for the band to regain their rhythmic feet as a dual-drummer outfit. (Kreutzmann noted that "Things maybe didn't flow as easily for awhile.") There was also less pure jamming and the sets tended to be shorter than in the early '70s. No matter; the fans were delighted to have the boys (and Donna Jean) back in town, live and in person.

★ **Wednesday June 9**
Thursday June 10
Friday June 11
Saturday June 12
Boston Music Hall, Boston, Massachusetts

First "High Time" since 7/12/70 and first "St. Stephen" since 10/31/71.

| 6 | 7 | 8 | 9 | 10 | 11 | 12 |

"SAMSON AND DELILAH"
TRADITIONAL/ARR. WEIR

Though a Grateful Dead concert might not be the first place you'd think to go to hear a rousing Negro spiritual, that's exactly what the band delivered with their incendiary take on the song starting on June 3, 1976. The earliest known version of this traditional appears in a turn-of-the-century song sheet titled "Samson Tore The Building Down," followed in the 1920s by Blind Willie Johnson's "If I Had My Way I'd Tear The Building Down." Other versions were recorded by a number of artists between the late 1920s and early 1940s (half of them bore credentials like Reverend and Deacon) before a reworking by Reverend Gary Davis drew the Dead to the song. "Delilah was a woman, she was fine and fair," it begins, bringing the classic biblical story from *Judges* 16 into a hard-grooving musical context. "She had good looks—God knows—and coal black hair." "I've always loved the story," Weir told David Gans just before the song came out on *Terrapin Station* (1977). "It's fun to sing. Once it gets rolling, it's impossible to stop it. I find myself real sorry that it's as short as it is." The Dead usually took care of that, with versions that sometimes exceeded ten minutes.

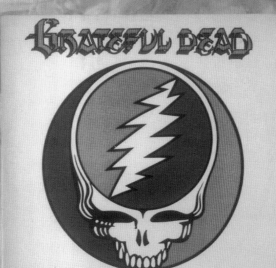

STEAL YOUR FACE
Grateful Dead

Released by Grateful Dead Records (LA-620) in June 1976

Side One
1. **Promised Land** (Berry)
2. **Cold Rain And Snow** (Traditional arr. Grateful Dead)
3. **Around And Around** (Berry)
4. **Stella Blue** (Hunter/Garcia)

Side Two
1. **Mississippi Half-Step Uptown Toodeloo** (Hunter/Garcia)
2. **Ship Of Fools** (Hunter/Garcia)
3. **Beat It On Down The Line** (Fuller)

Side Three
1. **Big River** (Cash)
2. **Black-Throated Wind** (Weir/Barlow)
3. **U.S. Blues** (Hunter/Garcia)
4. **El Paso** (Marty Robbins)

Side Four
1. **Sugaree** (Hunter/Garcia)
2. **It Must Have Been The Roses** (Hunter)
3. **Casey Jones** (Hunter/Garcia)

Personnel

Jerry Garcia – lead guitar, vocals
Bob Weir – guitar, vocals
Phil Lesh – bass, vocals
Keith Godchaux – keyboards, vocals
Donna Jean Godchaux – vocals; **Bill Kreutzmann** – drums

E VEN THE DEAD COULDN'T blow a live album, right? Guess again. Their first concert release on the Grateful Dead label was also one of their weakest, a widely panned collection of 14 songs from the band's "farewell" run in October 1974 at Winterland in San Francisco. Part of the problem was the song selection, a standalone mix of recent originals and old country and rock covers; the real problem was the poor sound quality of the tapes that mixers Lesh and Owsley Stanley had to work with under duress from product-driven GD Records prez Ron Rakow. "Phil and I hated that stuff and didn't want to work on it, but Ron Rakow insisted that he had to have them mixed in nine days, which was inconceivable." Owsley later told Adam Block. "None of us liked it," agreed Garcia to Block. "But there it was. I think part of it was we were not working, and we didn't have anything else to deliver." The album's title, taken from a line in "He's Gone" is which the main character is deemed so unscrupulous that he'll "steal your face right off your head," was rumored to be Lesh's swipe at Rakow, who would part ways with the band soon thereafter.

Monday June 14
Tuesday June 15
Beacon Theatre,
New York, New York

Monday June 21
Tuesday June 22
Wednesday June 23
Thursday June 24
Tower Theatre, Upper Darby, Pennsylvania

| 14 | 15 | 16 | 17 | 18 | 19 | 20 | 21 | 22 | 23 | 24 | 25 | 26 | 27 | 28 | 29 | 30 |

Thursday June 17
Friday June 18
Saturday June 19
Capitol Theatre,
Passaic, New Jersey

Saturday June 26
Sunday June 27
Monday June 28
Tuesday June 29
Auditorium Theatre,
Chicago, Illinois

The band's only performance of "Happiness Is Drumming," a Diga Rhythm band song that formed the foundation of "Fire on the Mountain."

"HELP ON THE WAY/SLIPKNOT/FRANKLIN'S TOWER"

HUNTER/GARCIA/K. GODCHAUX/KREUTZMANN/LESH/WEIR

The Holy Trinity of Dead songs lovingly known to fans as "Help/Slip/Frank" marked one of the most dramatic musical turns in the band's 30 years together. Debuted as a work-in-progress during a rare 1975 performance at the Winterland Arena in San Francisco and released on *Blues For Allah* (1975) that September, the tracks were part of an ambitious new effort resulting from the band's self-imposed retirement, during which they resolved to challenge the boundaries of their musicianship. The result was an opus rivaled only by "That's It For The Other One" and "Terrapin Station," a symbolically rich journey that begins with the beckoning line, "Paradise waits on the crest of a wave" before venturing into an intricate instrumental passage and finally to a mythological tower where the listener is encouraged to "roll away the dew." Along the way, the music drifts from jazz to rock and even calypso. Hints of Garcia's wordless "Slipknot" had popped up as an introduction to other songs in 1974 before it found its place here, and theories persist that some fragmentary Hunter verse that includes a reference to a "slipknot gig" may have been intended for the song at some point. For six years of shows between 1977 and 1983 and four more from 1985 to 1989, "Franklin's Tower" (with lyrics penned by Hunter with the US bicentennial in mind) was the only survivor of this triple play, and the entire trilogy was ultimately performed just over 100 times. It returned with some new twists by The Other Ones in 2002 and The Dead in 2003, who sandwiched time-tested covers like "Turn On Your Lovelight," "Knockin' On Heaven's Door," and "Hard To Handle" amid the classic trio.

Below: The band rehearses at the Orpheum Theatre in San Francisco for their 1976 "Comeback Tour."

Right and above: The band rehearsing at the Orpheum. Note Garcia's Travis Bean guitar.

JULY '76

| 1 | 2 | 3 | 4 | 5 | 6 | 7 | 8 | 9 | 10 | 11 | 12 | 13 | 14 | 15 | 16 | 17 | 18 | 19 | 20 | 21 | 22 | 23 | 24 | 25 | 26 | 27 | 28 | 29 | 30 | 31 |

Sunday July 4
A day of national revelry marks 200 years of U.S. independence. In New York, more than 200 sailing ships from 30 nations parade up the Hudson River in Operation Sail. In Washington, D.C., meanwhile, thousands of visitors grace the new National Air and Space Museum and a spectacular firework display illuminates the night sky over the Lincoln Memorial.

Monday July 12
Tuesday July 13
Wednesday July 14
Friday July 16
Saturday July 17
Sunday July 18 ★

Orpheum Theatre, San Francisco, California

The first night back in town sees the first "New Minglewood Blues" since 4/29/71. Friday's show has the last "Stronger Than Dirt (Or Milkin' the Turkey)" and Happy Birthday is sung to Bill Graham. Donna Jean sits out the second set on Saturday, while Sunday's show sees the Dead at their finest, and by the close, the band members are grinning ear to ear at one another.

Here (S)he comes . . .

The band's five-show run at San Francisco's Orpheum was highly anticipated, since they were the first Grateful Dead performances in the Bay Area (other than the Farewell Shows and the three one-offs during the hiatus) since February '74. At the end of the last show, Bill Graham led six bikini-clad "bathing beauties" onstage, each draped with a banner, beauty-contest style, with the name of a band member—"Miss Phil," "Miss Jerry," and so on. In a spirit of gender inclusiveness, Graham, in a tuxedo, wore a banner proclaiming himself "Mr. Donna Jean." The show was also broadcast live over KSAN.

Below: Wednesday August 4, Roosevelt Stadium, Jersey City, New Jersey. The venue was a decaying one-time minor league baseball park that drew big crowds from the New York metro area.

Wednesday August 4
Roosevelt Stadium, Jersey City, New Jersey

1 2 3 4 5 6 7 8

9 | 10 | 11 | 12 | 13 | 14 | 15 | 16 | 17 | 18 | 19 | 20 | 21 | 22 | 23 | 24 | 25

Monday August 2
Colt Park, Hartford, Connecticut

Rex Jackson

Rex Jackson had been a member of the road crew since '68 and had recently become road manager, the first roadie to "rise through the ranks" to that position, and the loss of such a close friend and brother shook the Grateful Dead family. He left a living legacy in the form of Cole, his son by Betty Cantor, and Cassidy, his daughter by Eileen Law. The band would later establish the Rex Foundation (see page 295) to honor his spirit.

Thursday September 23
Cameron Indoor Stadium, Duke University, Durham, North Carolina

★ **Saturday September 25**
Capital Centre, Landover, Maryland

Thursday September 30
Mershon Auditorium, Ohio State University, Columbus, Ohio

23 24 25 26 27 28 29 30

Friday September 24
College of William and Mary, Williamsburg, Virginia

Monday September 27
Community War Memorial, Rochester, New York

Tuesday September 28
Onondaga County War Memorial, Syracuse, New York

Thursday September 9
Mao Tse-tung, Chinese Communist party chairman since 1949, dies in Beijing at age 82. He was responsible for launching the controversial Cultural Revolution in 1965, an often-brutal campaign to reform Chinese society.

Monday September 6
Crew member Rex Jackson dies in a car crash

SEPTEMBER '76

1 2 3 4 5 6 7 8 9 10 11 12 ~ 22

September 1976

Saturday September 4
George W. Bush, future U.S. president, is arrested and pleads guilty to driving under the influence of alcohol in Kennebunkport, Maine.

198

All pictures: October 9–10, Oakland Coliseum Stadium. Billed as the eighth and ninth "Days on the Green" (Bill Graham Presents' multi-act stadium extravaganzas), the Dead shared the bill with headliners The Who. The Dead played two long, different sets each day, whereas The Who played two nearly identical "hits" sets.

BILL GRAHAM PRESENTS
DAYS ON THE GREEN #8 AND #9

THE WHO
The GRATEFUL DEAD

SAT-SUN OCTOBER 9-10
OAKLAND STADIUM
GATES OPEN 9 AM SHOW TIME 11 AM

Sunday October 3
Cobo Arena,
Detroit, Michigan

1 | 2 | 3 | 4 | 5 | 6 | 7 | 8

Saturday October 2
Riverfront Coliseum, Cincinnati, Ohio

Friday October 1
Market Square Arena, Indianapolis, Indiana

Saturday October 9
Sunday October 10
Oakland COunty Coliseum Stadium, Oakland, California

Day on the Green shows: The Who follow the Dead on both days, with the Dead going on at 11:00 a.m. While there was no interband play, as there would be the next time the two groups appeared on the same bill *(see 3/28/81)*, the Who dedicated their 10/10 encore, "Shakin' All Over," to the Dead.

9 | 10 | 11 | 12 | 13 | 14 | 15 | 16

Thursday October 14
Friday October 15
Shrine Auditorium,
Los Angeles, California

It's no "Nights on the Green" at the Shrine as the LAPD cracks down, proclaiming that the venue is "not a pot-smoking sanctuary."

Disunited Artists

Grateful Dead Records/Round Records officially called it quits in September, leaving the band in need of a label. In fact, none of the major labels had much interest in signing a group whose album sales were modest by industry standards and who had a certain … reputation for doing it their way regardless of corporate etiquette or commercial concerns. But there was one label, a modest startup called Arista, that did court the Dead. (Arista's head, Clive Davis, had tried to lure the Dead to Columbia Records, where he was working at the time, from Warner Bros. in the late 60s, but then-manager Lenny Hart reportedly chose not to tell the band. Hal Kant et al. negotiated a multi-record contract which, when signed in October, terminated the deal with United Artists. The band remained with Arista, in a generally good if occasionally bumpy relationship, for the rest of its career.

17 | 18 | 19 | 20 | 21 | 22 | 23 | 24 | 25 | 26 | 27 | 28 | 29 | 30 | 31

Who's Skylarking?

The Who had had a great spring run at the Winterland, so the ever-canny Bill Graham decided to team them up with the Dead for a pair of shows, "Day on the Green No. 8 and No. 9," at the Oakland Coliseum in October. Graham promoted the gigs with a series of enigmatic ads in Bay Area papers urging readers to "watch the skies"—and on the day tickets went on sale, planes appeared over the bay announcing the double bill. The Dead, of course, remembered The Who from Monterey—at which the autodestructive Brit rockers upstaged the Dead, only to have the Jimi Hendrix Experience upstage both bands—and from Woodstock. Members of the two bands got to hang out together during the "Days on the Green," and by all accounts they had a great time.

NOVEMBER '76

| 1 | 2 | 3 | 4 | 5 | 6 | 7 |

Tuesday November 2
Former Georgia governor Jimmy Carter narrowly defeats Republican incumbent Gerald Ford to become the 39th president of the U.S. and the first to be elected from the Deep South since the Civil War.

All pictures: New Year's Eve at the Cow Palace. Below, Bill Graham, Carlos Santana, Bob Weir, and others share a moment backstage. The show marked the final appearance by the Dead at the widely reviled venue, which was better for rodeos than for concerts.

Eric Andersen's album *Sweet Surprise* is released during this year. Two tracks feature future Dead member Brent Mydland on backing vocals.

DECEMBER '76

| 1 | 2 | 3 | 4 | 5 | 6 | 7 | 8 | 9 | 10 | 11 |

"I wanted to give them one minute of purée rather than soup that was watered down, so we stressed the actual New Year's moment—that last minute where you count down from 60 and then from 30. Through the years it changed and became more elaborate." BILL GRAHAM

26 | 27 | 28 | 29 | 30 | 31

Friday December 31
Cow Palace,
Daly City, California

It's the first NYE show since '72 and a fine performance, including a "One More Saturday Night">"Uncle John's Band">"We Bid You Goodnight" encore. Santana and Soundhole are also on the bill. Bill Graham pops out of a giant hourglass for the midnight countdown. The New Year is welcomed in with a soaring version of "Sugar Magnolia."

"ESTIMATED PROPHET"
WEIR/BARLOW

Like most songs on *Terrapin Station* (1977), the studio version of "Estimated Prophet" was a pale representation compared to the maniacal energy the track took on live. Written by Weir and Barlow in January 1977, the tune deals with a common sight at Dead shows—the messianic tripster who has a message from a higher source. "The basis of it is this guy I see at nearly every backstage door," Weir said in 1977. "Every time we play anywhere there's always some guy that's taken a lot of dope, and he's really bug-eyed, and he's having some kind of vision… He's got some rave that he's got to deliver. So I just decided that I was going to beat him to the punch." With its visions of prophets, fire wheels, and angels, the song was an instant hit with fans, with a May 8, 1977 performance at Cornell University in New York considered the band's all-time best. Garcia cited it as his favorite Weir song in 1989, and the Dead played it nearly 400 times between 1977 and 1995. "If there's a point to 'Estimated Prophet,'" Weir once said, "it is that no matter what you do, you shouldn't take it all that seriously."

All pictures: Sunday February 27, Robertson Gym, University of California, Santa Barbara. This show marked just the second performances of both "Terrapin Station" and "Estimated Prophet."

★ **Saturday February 26**
Swing Auditorium, San Bernardino, California

The year's first show sees the breakout of "Estimated Prophet" and "Terrapin Station."

FEBRUARY '77

| 1 ~ 20 | 21 | 22 | 23 | 24 | 25 | 26 | 27 | 28 |

Sunday February 27
Robertson Gym, University of California, Santa Barbara, California

A show remembered for its "St. Stephen," for which the band reverted to the pre-'70 arrangement sans the bridge.

Monday January 3
The Steven Jobs/Steve Wozniak-founded Apple Computer Company is incorporated. The company produces the first preassembled, mass-produced personal computer.

Monday January 17
Gary Gilmore, convicted for a double murder, is shot by a firing squad at Utah State Prison. It is the first U.S. execution in a decade.

JANUARY '77

| 1 | 2 | 3 | 4 | 5 | 6 | 7 | 8 | 9 | 10 | 11 | 12 | 13 | 14 | 15 | 16 | 17 | 18 ~ 31 |

"TERRAPIN STATION"
GARCIA/HART/HUNTER/KREUTZMANN

The last true opus of the Dead's 30-year career arrived in 1977 with "Terrapin Station." Encompassing over 16 minutes and five time signatures, the title track for the band's first album for Arista Records begins, "Let my inspiration flow/ in token lines suggesting rhythm/ that will not forsake me/ till my tale is told and done." Thus begins a panoply of baroque symbolism in this mythical tale of a soldier and a sailor in pursuit of the same object of desire, a mysterious "lady with a fan." Despite the song's length, Garcia would use only a portion of Hunter's complete lyric for the piece, perhaps explaining why the album version includes "Part 1" at the end of its title. "'Terrapin' came in on a pure beam," Hunter said the year the song debuted. "I started with an invocation to the muse, because if it wasn't going to come from there, it was going to come from nowhere. The invocation carried me all the way through. I must have written a thousand words on it, eight 12-inch pages—song after song after song." Musically, Garcia had a similar experience in creating the masterpiece. "The whole thing came as a completely orchestrated idea," he said in 1981. "I got the idea driving my car. I drove home real fast and sat down with the guitar and worked it all out real quick so I wouldn't forget it, because it was all there." Ultimately, the studio track would incorporate seven subsections and utilize a full orchestra and the English Chorale. Although the song was pared down to a simpler structure for live takes, it still stretched to over 20 minutes on occasion between its February 26, 1977 debut and its appearance in the band's second-last show on July 8, 1995 after just over 300 performances. "There's a good deal more where that came from," Hunter once told David Gans. "That's another one of those projects that could have gone on and become a triple album if I'd had my way. I had a lot to say about Terrapin Station."

Terrapinned

Between January and April the Grateful Dead recorded their first material for Arista. The tracks laid down at these sessions were to become the band's eighth studio album—*Terrapin Station*. Clive Davis suggested the boys use an outside producer, and the band, eager to avoid some of the pitfalls of past studio efforts, agreed. Several producers were considered before the band tapped Keith Olsen, who was riding high off the success of Fleetwood Mac's multiple-platinum eponymous 1975 album. Perhaps the thinking was that if Olsen could reinvent the hard-edged, blues-oriented Mac as radio-friendly popsters, he was the man to get a great studio album out of the Dead. Despite his undeniable gifts as a producer, however, Olsen was unfamiliar with the Dead's musical dynamics. The band recorded at Olsen's own studio in the Van Nuys neighborhood of L.A. while camping out at a nearby motel.

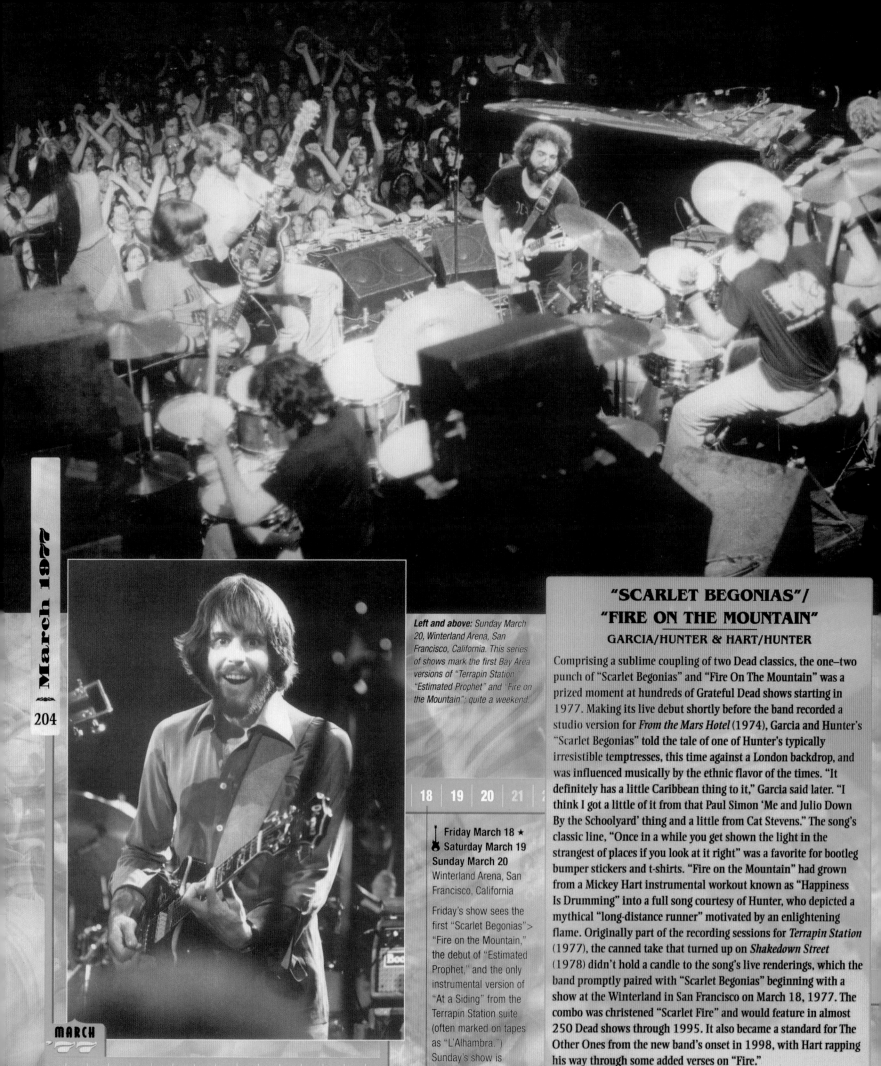

Left and above: Sunday March 20, Winterland Arena, San Francisco, California. This series of shows mark the first Bay Area versions of "Terrapin Station," "Estimated Prophet" and "Fire on the Mountain": quite a weekend.

18	19	20	21	2

🎸 **Friday March 18** ★
🥁 **Saturday March 19**
Sunday March 20
Winterland Arena, San Francisco, California

Friday's show sees the first "Scarlet Begonias">"Fire on the Mountain," the debut of "Estimated Prophet," and the only instrumental version of "At a Siding" from the Terrapin Station suite (often marked on tapes as "L'Alhambra.") Sunday's show is broadcast on the *King Biscuit Flower Hour*.

"SCARLET BEGONIAS"/ "FIRE ON THE MOUNTAIN"
GARCIA/HUNTER & HART/HUNTER

Comprising a sublime coupling of two Dead classics, the one–two punch of "Scarlet Begonias" and "Fire On The Mountain" was a prized moment at hundreds of Grateful Dead shows starting in 1977. Making its live debut shortly before the band recorded a studio version for *From the Mars Hotel* (1974), Garcia and Hunter's "Scarlet Begonias" told the tale of one of Hunter's typically irresistible temptresses, this time against a London backdrop, and was influenced musically by the ethnic flavor of the times. "It definitely has a little Caribbean thing to it," Garcia said later. "I think I got a little of it from that Paul Simon 'Me and Julio Down By the Schoolyard' thing and a little from Cat Stevens." The song's classic line, "Once in a while you get shown the light in the strangest of places if you look at it right" was a favorite for bootleg bumper stickers and t-shirts. "Fire on the Mountain" had grown from a Mickey Hart instrumental workout known as "Happiness Is Drumming" into a full song courtesy of Hunter, who depicted a mythical "long-distance runner" motivated by an enlightening flame. Originally part of the recording sessions for *Terrapin Station* (1977), the canned take that turned up on *Shakedown Street* (1978) didn't hold a candle to the song's live renderings, which the band promptly paired with "Scarlet Begonias" beginning with a show at the Winterland in San Francisco on March 18, 1977. The combo was christened "Scarlet Fire" and would feature in almost 250 Dead shows through 1995. It also became a standard for The Other Ones from the new band's onset in 1998, with Hart rapping his way through some added verses on "Fire."

MARCH
'77

1	2	3	4	5	6	7	8	9	10	11	12	13	14	15	16

Right and above: Saturday April 23, Springfield Civic Center Arena, Springfield, Massachusetts.

Just a Mile (or Reel) to go...

When not working on *Terrapin Station* in Van Nuys, Jerry Garcia spent the spring of '77 across town in Burbank, going through (with Dan Healy) the complicated process of synching up the audio for *The Grateful Dead Movie* and otherwise finishing off the project, which was now at least a year overdue and several hundred thousand dollars over budget. (The other band members had taken to referring to the movie as "Jerry's jerk-off.")

It was also around this time that Jerry—who had progressed from snorting cocaine to freebasing—encountered Persian Base, a potent, highly pure, smokable form of heroin. Jerry may have turned to the new drug as a way of blunting cocaine's effects and/or as a means of getting through an incredibly demanding work schedule. In any case, it was the start of a love affair with opiates that would plague Jerry—with occasional clean periods—until his death.

Jerry's relationship with Deborah Koons also went up in smoke during this period. She would later say that she had "lost [her] identity in Jerry's life" but those around at the time recall an ugly, drawn-out breakup that ended with Jerry fleeing to Richard Loren's place to avoid Koons's wrath.

Friday April 22
The Spectrum, Philadelphia, Pennsylvania

First performance of the classic blues "I Got My Mojo Workin'"—written by Preston Forster, recorded by everybody, but most closely associated with Muddy Waters—sandwiched in a "Dancin'" jam.

22	23	24	25	26	27	28	29	30

Saturday April 23
Springfield Civic Center Arena, Springfield, Massachusetts

Monday April 25
Tuesday April 26
Wednesday April 27
Capitol Theater, Passaic, New Jersey

Friday April 29
Saturday April 30
The Palladium, New York, New York

Norton Buffalo releases the album *Lovin' in the Valley of the Moon* in 1977; Mickey Hart plays on two tracks.

Right: Wednesday April 27. Although the band often played arenas in this era, they almost always played the much smaller Capitol Theater, too.

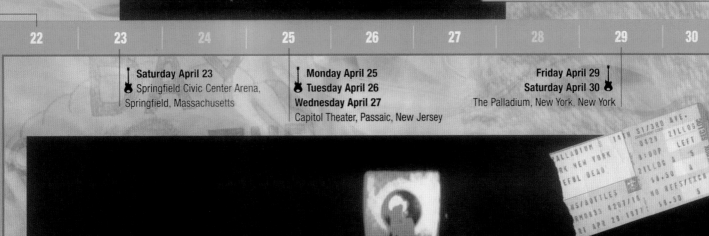

Cornell University Show

The Grateful Dead's 1977 shows are rightly remembered as some of the best in the band's career, and in the considered opinion of some Deadheads, the spring tour may have been the band's finest outing of the post-hiatus period. *The Grateful Dead Movie* was finally in the can; the kinks that had been evident in the '76 "Comeback Tour" had been worked out following extensive band time together under Keith Olsen's strict regime while recording *Terrapin Station*; the boys had returned to extended second-set jamming; and new songs like "Estimated Prophet" and "Terrapin Station," and segues like "Scarlet Begonias">"Fire on the Mountain" received a rapt reception.

The highlight of the tour—indeed, the whole year—was the 5/8 show at Cornell University, prized especially for the closer, "Morning Dew." The night is consistently rated as an all-time favorite show by various Deadworld surveys, although, interestingly, the Feedback Results section of *DeadBase X* lists 5/8/77 as both the "Favorite Tape" and "Most Overrated Show" by Deadhead respondents.

Above: *Saturday May 28, Hartford Civic Center, Hartford, Connecticut.*

May 1977

MAY '77

★ **Thursday May 5**
New Haven Coliseum, New Haven, Connecticut

★ **Sunday May 8**
Barton Hall, Cornell University, Ithaca, New York

Monday May 9 ★
War Memorial Auditorium, Buffalo, New York

Sunday May 1
Tuesday May 3
Wednesday May 4
The Palladium, New York, New York

Sunday's show sees the first "Sunrise," a Donna Godchaux composition that was inspired by the untimely death of road manager Rex Jackson *(see page 198).*

206

Saturday May 7 ★
Boston Garden, Boston, Massachusetts

A show that nearly doesn't happen because crew member Peter "Craze" Sheridan (who, as his nickname implies, was one of the more colorful of the many colorful characters to join the Dead family) "fires" the union stagehands. It takes considerable palm-greasing before the union men resume work—or more accurately, allow the crew to set up. It's also Bill Kreutzmann's 31st birthday.

Wednesday May 11
St. Paul Civic Center Arena, St. Paul, Minnesota

Thursday May 12
Friday May 13
Auditorium Theatre, Chicago, Illinois

Friday sees the breakout of "Jack A Roe," a traditional folk song from the British Isles by way of Appalachia that tells of a well-off young woman who dons masculine garb to follow her lover into battle. The song would also became a Garcia/Kahn acoustic standby.

Sunday May 15
St. Louis Arena, St. Louis, Missouri

The first performance of what would become a warhorse of the rotation—the New Orleans classic "Iko Iko," which, with its African origins, is among the oldest songs performed by the Dead. The show also sees the first "Passenger," from Phil Lesh with lyrics by Peter Monk, which Weir later said was taken from an idea in Fleetwood Mac's "Station Man."

Tuesday May 17
Coliseum, University of Alabama, Tuscaloosa, Alabama

Wednesday May 18 ★
Thursday May 19 ★
Fox Theatre, Atlanta, Georgia

Saturday May 21
Lakeland Civic Center Arena, Lakeland, Florida

★ **Sunday May 22**
Sportatorium, Pembroke Pines, Florida

Much of this concert is on *Dick's Picks Vol 3*

Wednesday May 25
Mosque, Richmond, Virginia

Thursday May 26
Baltimore Civic Center, Baltimore, Maryland

Saturday May 28
Hartford Civic Center, Hartford, Connecticut

Left: *The Dead hang out in Boston around their Boston Garden concert on Saturday May 7.*

Monday May 30
The 800-mile trans-Alaska pipeline is completed at a cost of $8 billion.

Saturday June 4
The Forum,
Inglewood, California

Tuesday June 7
Wednesday June 8
Thursday June 9 ★
Winterland Arena, San
Francisco, California

JUNE
'77

| 1 | 2 | 3 | 4 | 5 | 6 | 7 | 8 | 9 | 10 |

Wednesday June 1
The Grateful Dead Movie is released.

Reggae Music Scene

Nineteen seventy-seven proved to be a high-water year for reggae—Bob Marley's *Exodus* album reached the Top 20 in the U.S. and sold millions around the world. With fellow Jamaican artists Jimmy Cliff, the Mighty Diamonds, Toots & the Maytals, Burning Spear, and others touring the globe independently, reggae had truly become an international sensation. That year, too, the Grateful Dead introduced "Estimated Prophet," Bob Weir's dark, off-kilter reggae-influenced tune in 7/4 time, and Jerry Garcia cut a sunny, mellow Robert Hunter-John Kahn song called "Love in the Afternoon" that sounded like Tin Pan Alley reggae.

Like many Americans, Garcia became infatuated with reggae through the 1972 film and album *The Harder They Come*, which featured songs by Cliff (who also starred in the movie), The Maytals, The Slickers, The Melodians, and Desmond Dekker. Reggae was still fairly new at that point, even in Jamaica—it had bubbled up from the shantytowns, clubs, and recording studios of Kingston in the late '60s, a natural evolution from earlier local styles including mento, ska, and rock steady. Like those styles, reggae was a polyglot of African and Caribbean rhythms, American R&B, and more.

As early as 1973, Garcia was incorporating Cliff's "The Harder They Come" into his solo band repertoire, and reggae had crept into his own writing as well—both "They Love Each Other" and "Row Jimmy" are nods to the genre. Later, the Garcia Band would cover Cliff's "Sitting In Limbo" and "Struggling Man," and The Slickers' "Johnny Too Bad."

O N JUNE 1, 1977, AFTER two-and-a-half years in production and at a cost of $600,000, *The Grateful Dead Movie* premiered at New York's Ziegfeld Theater. For the final print of just over two hour's length, Jerry Garcia & Co. culled the best moments of more than 100 hours of footage shot at the October 1974 Winterland "Farewell Shows" and interspersed them with historical clips of the band, backstage and offstage glimpses, and lots of shots of the Deadheads themselves. The opening sequence—seven minutes of jaw-dropping animation from Gary Gutierrez, set to "U.S. Blues"—was a special treat. (It also cost about $60 per second to create.) At Jerry's insistence, *The Grateful Dead Movie* wasn't distributed in the conventional manner, but instead was booked into rented theaters, concert-style, and only into theaters with good sound systems and a substantial Deadhead population in the local community (John Scher and Richard Loren were charged with this undertaking). Most critics dismissed the film as self-indulgent, or even boring, but some pundits did "Get It," including Robert Christgau, who wrote in the *Village Voice* that the movie "[lays] out enough information for anyone who is genuinely curious to find out what the Dead are really about."

THE GRATEFUL DEAD MOVIE
Grateful Dead
Released June 1, 1977

1. **U.S. Blues**
(Garcia/Hunter)
2. **Going Down the Road**
(Traditional)
3. **Eyes of the World**
(Garcia/Hunter)
4. **St. Stephen**
(Garcia/Lesh/Hunter)
5. **The Golden Road**
(Skjellyfetti)
6. **Stella Blue**
(Garcia/Hunter)
7. **He's Gone**
(Garcia/Hunter)
8. **Morning Dew**
(Dobson/Rose)
9. **Late for Supper**
(Garcia)
10. **The Wheel**
(Garcia/Hunter/Kreutzmann)
11. **One More Saturday Night**
(Weir)
12. **Truckin'**
(Garcia/Weir/Lesh/Hunter)
13. **Sugar Magnolia**
(Weir/Hunter)
14. **Ripple**
(Garcia/Hunter)
15. **Playing in the Band**
(Weir/Hunter)
16. **Casey Jones**
(Garcia/Hunter)
17. **It Must Have Been the Roses**
(Hunter)
18. **Johnny B. Goode**
(Berry)
19. **Eep Hour**
(Garcia/Kreutzmann)

Personnel

Producer – Eddie Washington
Directors – Jerry Garcia, Leon Gast
Executive producer – Ron Rakow
Animation – Gary Gutierrez
Cameras – Jonathan Else, Thomas D. Hurwitz, Kevin Keating, Don Lenzer, Stephen Lighthill, Albert Maysles, David Myers, Richard Paup, Robert Primes
Editors – Susan Crutcher, John Nutt, Lisa Fruchtman

June 1977

207

Below: Bill Kreutzmann and Saturday Night Live's Al Franken in New York City, May 1977.

Sunday June 20
While driving home from a Norton Buffalo show, Mickey Hart loses control of his car, which goes over a guardrail and drops onto a tree some 20 feet below. Mickey is severely injured, with a broken arm and collarbone, cracked ribs, and a punctured lung. His life was probably saved by his passenger, Rhonda Jensen, who managed to get help.

Right: Wednesday June 8, Winterland Arena.

GRATEFUL DEAD

SPARTY 1016

IT'S PROBABLY SAFE TO SAY that the Dead never created anything quite as grandiose in the studio as *Terrapin Station*. It's also safe to say that "Grateful Dead" and "grandiose" were never meant to be in the same sentence in the first place, at least not in the way that producer Keith Olsen envisioned them. Olsen was the first of three outside knob-turners that the band would use as part of their new deal with upstart major Arista Records, which had proudly touted the addition of these love generation vets to their roster with print ads that blared "A New Dead Era Is Upon Us." Olsen also proved to be the most overbearing of the band's producers, imposing preferences on the group that would rankle them long after the album was finished. "Keith Olsen was a good producer and a good engineer," Mickey Hart told David Gans in 1982. "He was the most qualified. But he had a problem; he didn't know the Grateful Dead, and he wanted to mold the Grateful Dead in his own image." That image included an inappropriately slick producing style that should have been

apparent with the first playback of "Dancin' In The Streets," the revived cover classic whose new album incarnation was more suited to Studio 54 than to hometown dance halls of yore. Olsen expanded his views in an interview with the *San Francisco Chronicle* that appeared the day after the album's release. "The Dead are good musicians who have never been exposed as such—especially Weir," Olsen said. "He had never been able to play a rhythm guitar, partly because he had to cover the chord for Phil Lesh, whose bass parts tend to get a little esoteric at times." But while some of the originals appearing on the album would enjoy limited exposure live (in particular, Donna Godchaux's ballad "Sunrise," written in honor of the recently departed Rex Jackson, and Phil Lesh's "Passenger"), the strongest material survived Olsen's meddling to become classic concert fare, including Weir's fiery "Estimated Prophet" and versions of the tasty title cut that did just fine without backup from The English Choral and the Martyn Ford Orchestra. Kelley and Mouse produced the cover artwork.

TERRAPIN STATION
Grateful Dead

Released by Arista (AL-7001) on July 27, 1977

Side One

1. **Estimated Prophet**
   (Weir/Barlow)
2. **Dancin' In The Streets**
   (Stevenson/Gaye/I. Hunter)
3. **Passenger**
   (Lesh/Monk)
4. **Samson and Delilah**
   (Traditional arr. Bob Weir)
5. **Sunrise**
   (D. Godchaux)

Side Two

1. **Terrapin Station**
   – **Lady With A Fan**
   (Garcia/Hunter)
   – **Terrapin Station**
   (Garcia/Hunter)
   – **Terrapin**
   (Garcia/Hunter)
   – **Terrapin Transit**
   (Hart/Kreutzmann)
   – **At A Siding**
   (Hart/Hunter)
   – **Terrapin Flyer**
   (Hart/Kreutzmann)
   – **Refrain**
   (Garcia)

Personnel

Bob Weir – guitar, vocals
Phil Lesh – bass, vocals
Jerry Garcia – guitar, vocals
Donna Godchaux – vocals
Keith Godchaux – keyboards
Bill Kreutzmann – drums
Mickey Hart – drums
Tom Scott – lyricon and saxophones
Martyn Ford Orchestra
The English Choral

Produced by Keith Olsen

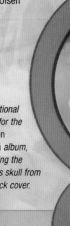

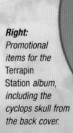

Right:
Promotional items for the Terrapin Station album, *including the cyclops skull from the back cover.*

1 ~ 22	23	24	25	26	27

Wednesday July 27
The band releases two 7-inch singles featuring tracks from *Terrapin Station*—"Dancing in the Streets"/"Terrapin Station" and "Passenger"/"Terrapin Station."

Wednesday July 27
Terrapin Station by the Grateful Dead is released.

28	29	30	31

Right: *Donna Godchaux, August 1.* **Below:** *August 12, Jerry Garcia Band, Greenpeace Benefit, Pier 31, San Francisco.* **Bottom:** *Bob Weir in L.A., August 7.*

The Rowans record their 1977 LP *Jubilation* at Mickey Hart's studios, The Barn.

David Gans

Bay Area journalist/radio host/musician David Gans started writing about the Dead in the summer of 1977, when he took over BAM magazine's "Dead Ahead" column and parlayed his interest in the band into a series of in-depth interviews. His first book about the group, *Playing in the Band*, was published in 1985. Subsequent works included *Conversations With the Dead* and *Not Fade Away: The On-line World Remembers Jerry Garcia*. Since 1985, Gans has hosted the popular syndicated *Grateful Dead Hour* radio program, which has disseminated thousands of hours of unreleased Grateful Dead music from the band's own vaults and kept Deadheads all over the world informed through insightful interviews and relevant news. A musician and songwriter himself, Gans can be credited with coaxing Phil Lesh out of retirement following Garcia's death by having the bassist sit in with some of Gans' musical friends in the Broken Angels. That then became a jumping-off point for Phil Lesh & Friends.

Solo Studio Time

With Mickey Hart recuperating from injuries sustained in his June car crash *(see page 207)*, the band had to cancel the remainder of their summer shows, which opened up some time for solo projects. Bob Weir had decided to make a straight-up commercial album, with Keith Olsen (who better?) chosen to occupy the producer's hot seat. Before heading to L.A. for the recording sessions, Bob decided to woodshed at John Perry Barlow's ranch to work up some songs and also help his friend and lyricist celebrate his wedding to Elaine Parker. After an all-night bachelor party fueled by bourbon and grain alcohol, Barlow, upset that Weir had gone to sleep, decided to wake up his slumbering friend by firing his pistol into the concrete floor of his room. Weir took a bit of ricocheting concrete in the shoulder but survived to record *Heaven Help the Fool*. Meanwhile, Jerry (with John Kahn, the Godchauxs, Merl Saunders, and Ron Tutt) began laying down what would become *Cats Under the Stars* at the Grateful Dead's Club Front rehearsal studios.

Tuesday August 16
Elvis Presley dies at his Graceland Mansion in Memphis, Tennessee. The king of rock 'n' roll succumbs to a drug overdose at age 42.

15 | **16** | 17 | 18 | 19 | **20** | 21

Saturday August 20
The U.S. launches Voyager 2, an uncrewed spacecraft carrying a phonograph record containing greetings in a host of languages, together with samples of music and sounds of nature. The craft is scheduled to pass Jupiter and Saturn.

Above: *September 3, Raceway Park, Englishtown, New Jersey.*

3 | 4 | 5 | 6 | 7 | 8 ~ 11 | 12 | 13 ~ 27 | 28 | 29 | 30

★ **Saturday September 3**
Raceway Park, Englishtown, New Jersey

The Dead's first show following Mickey Hart's car accident *(see page 207)* is a monster gig with 150,000 in attendance. Mickey is on drums, though his arm isn't totally healed, and Donna Jean, recovering from surgery, vocalizes from a chair. Although the band haven't played together in a while, this is a fine show: Phil Lesh plugs the new album (despite the boys' upset with Keith Olsen's post-production excesses), and there is an unusual "Terrapin Station" encore. The Marshall Tucker Band and NRPS also play.

Wednesday September 7
In Washington, D.C., President Carter and General Herrera sign the Panama Canal treaties, which call for the U.S. to eventually turn over control of the waterway to Panama.

Monday September 12
Political dissident Steven Biko dies while in police custody in South Africa.

Wednesday September 28
Thursday September 29
Paramount Northwest Theatre, Seattle, Washington

OCTOBER

1 | 2 | 3 | 4 | 5 | 6

Saturday October 1
★ **Sunday October 2**
Paramount Theatre, Portland, Oregon

Sunday sees the first "Dupree's Diamond Blues" since 7/12/69.

Thursday October 6
Activity Center, Arizona State University, Tempe, Arizona

Friday October 7
University Arena, University of New Mexico, Albuquerque, New Mexico

7 | 8 | 9 | 10 | 11

Sunday October 9
McNichols Sports Arena, Denver, Colorado

Tuesday October 11
Lloyd Noble Center, University of Oklahoma, Norman, Oklahoma

Keeper of the Vault Dick Latvala *(see page 307)* considered this performance to be among the band's absolute best—true Primal Dead. While this has been contested by many, it's still a killer show in anyone's estimation—especially "Not Fade Away"—with a brilliant performance from Bill and, particularly, Mickey, who was still recovering from his recent injuries.

Bob Weir plays on Kingfish's 1977 release, *Live 'N' Kickin'*. The album, containing live songs recorded in 1976, is reissued in 1981 with Weir's guitar parts erased, except on the songs where he sings.

SEPTEMBER
77

Punk Music Scene

"I… want to be… anarchy!" It sounds like a sentiment the Dead could relate to, but roaring out of the mouth of Johnny Rotten, as the Sex Pistols clashed noisily behind him, it seemed more like a threat—with the release of the Pistols' *Never Mind the Bollocks*, the punk revolution had arrived. Punk rock was, in part, a reaction against bands like the Dead, as well as the progressive rock virtuosos of the early and mid-'70s. Punk appealed to a generation of young people who didn't want to hear long guitar solos, didn't care about intricate song arrangements, and couldn't relate to '60s values and ideals. They wanted their own music and their own look. They wanted songs that reflected their cynicism about the world and popular culture.

Musically, punk drew inspiration from the '60s garage-band ethos—play loud and fast; it's all about energy and attitude. Punk progenitors included Iggy Pop, the Velvet Underground, and even the glam-rock New York Dolls. The buzz-saw approach of New York's Ramones had a huge influence on the Sex Pistols; the Pistols, in turn, inspired the formation of The Clash, the movement's greatest socio-political force. By the middle of 1977 there were punk bands—and clubs where they could play—in nearly every major U.S. and European city. The ripples of punk also led directly to the more eclectic New Wave, an umbrella that included the likes of Elvis Costello, Graham Parker, Blondie, Devo, Television, Patti Smith, Talking Heads, and hundreds of others.

Wednesday October 12
Manor Downs, Austin, Texas

12 · 13

Friday October 14
Hofheinz Pavilion,
Houston, Texas

14 · 15

Sunday October 16
Assembly Center,
Louisiana State University,
Baton Rouge, Louisiana

Bob Weir's 30th birthday.

Saturday October 15
Moody Coliseum,
Southern Methodist Univ.,
Dallas, Texas

16 · 17 ~ 27 · 28

Friday October 28
Soldiers and Sailors
Memorial Hall, Kansas
City, Kansas

29

Saturday October 29
Evans Field House,
Northern Illinois University,
DeKalb, Illinois

30 · 31

Sunday October 30
Assembly Hall, Indiana University,
Bloomington, Indiana

"BLACK PETER"
GARCIA/HUNTER

Taking its place among the best folk rock dirges of all time, "Black Peter" found its way into the Grateful Dead's setlist in December of 1969 before appearing on the band's stripped-down 1970 masterpiece *Workingman's Dead*. The tale of a man on his death bed who just wants to spend his final days with family and friends, the song also comments on the transient nature of mankind with great lines like, "See here how everything lead up to this day, and it's just like any other day that's ever been." Robert Hunter later said that the song was never intended to be so slow-paced. "I wrote this as a brisk piece," he commented in his book *A Box of Rain*. "Garcia took it seriously though, dressing it in subtle changes and a mournful tempo." "Black Peter" disappeared in the mid-1970s just before the tour hiatus began, before resurfacing during the October 1, 1977, show. It continued to feature as an electric and acoustic number until its final outing in Boston on September 28, 1994. As an homage to Garcia, veteran proto-punk icon Patti Smith performed the song in the weeks after Garcia's death.

THOUGH BETTER THAN ITS best-of predecessor, 1973's *Skeletons In The Closet*, this after-the-fact Warner Brothers two-fer was more a history lesson than anything else. Issued three months after the band's return to the majors with the release of *Terrapin Station* for Arista, the album basically amounted to a time capsule that was limited to the years the Dead were with the House That Bugs Built (1965 to 1972), thus by necessity ignoring the new era the band had entered into with their music since. Forgiving a studio take of "Dark Star" that, while interesting in its own right, couldn't have been less befitting of the song's legendary live status, *What A Long Strange Trip It's Been* did present a better balance of that period, mixing nine studio cuts with as many concert songs taken from the Dead's four live releases for the label. Unfortunately, its dark, brooding cover, which includes the band's name in blood-red Old English-style lettering, bears more resemblance to something one might expect from Black Sabbath or Bauhaus, and single-handedly did more to misrepresent one of the most colorful groups in rock history than perhaps any artwork since the Beatles' aborted butcher cover for *Yesterday... and Today.*

WHAT A LONG STRANGE TRIP IT'S BEEN—THE BEST OF THE GRATEFUL DEAD
Grateful Dead

Released by Warner Bros. (2W-3091) in October 1977

Side One
1. **New, New Minglewood Blues**
   (McGannahan Skjellyfetti)
2. **Cosmic Charlie**
   (Garcia/Hunter)
3. **Truckin'**
   (Garcia/Lesh/Weir/Hunter)
4. **Black Peter**
   (Garcia/Hunter)
5. **Born Cross-Eyed**
   (Grateful Dead)

Side Two
1. **Ripple**
   (Hunter/Garcia)
2. **Doin' That Rag**
   (Garcia/Hunter)
3. **Dark Star**
   (Garcia/Hunter)
4. **High Time**
   (Garcia/Hunter)
5. **New Speedway Boogie**
   (Garcia/Hunter)

Side Three
1. **St. Stephen**
   (Garcia/Lesh/Hunter)
2. **Jack Straw**
   (Weir/Hunter)
3. **Me and My Uncle**
   (Phillips)
4. **Tennessee Jed**
   (Garcia/Hunter)

Side Four
1. **Cumberland Blues**
   (Garcia/Lesh/Hunter)
2. **Playing In The Band**
   (Weir/Hart/Hunter)
3. **Brown-Eyed Woman**
   (Garcia/Hunter)
4. **Ramble On Rose**
   (Garcia/Hunter)

Personnel

Jerry Garcia – lead guitar, acoustic guitar, pedal steel guitar, vocals, piano
Bill Kreutzmann – drums, percussion
Phil Lesh – bass guitar, piano, vocals
Pigpen (Ron McKernan) – keyboard, harmonica, acoustic guitar, vocals, organ, percussion, congas
Bob Weir – rhythm guitar, acoustic guitar, vocals
Mickey Hart – percussion, drums
Robert Hunter – vocals
Tom Constanten – keyboard
Donna Godchaux – vocals
Keith Godchaux – piano
Merl Saunders – organ
John Dawson (Marmaduke) – supporting musician
David Nelson – supporting musician
Peter Grant – supporting musician; **Wendy** – supporting musician; **Debbie** – supporting musician; **Mouse** – supporting musician; **David Grisman** – guest musician; **Howard Wales** – guest musician

October 1977

211

As part of the band's overseas distribution deal with United Artists, UA repackage *Wake of the Flood* and *Grateful Dead from the Mars Hotel* into a double LP for sale only in Europe.

Above: *Saturday November 5, Community War Memorial, Rochester, New York*

Disco Music Scene

The rhythmic juggernaut known as disco originated in New York's gay nightclub scene in the mid-'70s, but quickly became the dominant musical force in R&B, as artist after artist succumbed to the insistent thumping beat and adopted the style. Disco clubs popped up everywhere, and a new art form was born—the elaborate remixing of songs and artful sequencing of tunes by club DJs, designed to keep happy dancers grooving all night.

What made disco into a mainstream phenomenon, however, was the success of the 1977 film *Saturday Night Fever* and its soundtrack album, which was dominated by catchy disco numbers by the Bee Gees, of all people. From there, the floodgates opened and everyone from the Rolling Stones to Rod Stewart dabbled in it. The Dead, who always embraced different R&B styles, first flirted with disco in 1976, when they re-arranged "Dancing in the Streets" disco-style. In 1978, Hunter and Garcia made their own twisted contribution to the genre, "Shakedown Street." The success of disco caused a tremendous backlash among some rockers ("Disco sucks!" was a popular catchphrase) but the Dead never disavowed it; indeed Hunter joked that he enjoyed "abusing the audience and their expectations."

Though many of the particulars of dance music have changed through the years, it can be convincingly argued that the disco clubs of the '70s were the direct ancestors of today's rave, trance, electronica, trip-hop, and other dance clubs.

NOVEMBER '77

1 | 2 | 3 | 4

Tuesday November 1
Cobo Arena, Detroit, Michigan

Wednesday November 2
Field House, Seneca College, Toronto, Canada

Friday November 4
Cotterell Gym, Colgate University, Hamilton, New York

Saturday November 5
Community War Memorial, Rochester, New York

The phocus is on Phil tonight as the bassmaster lets loose several bomb-dropping solos, as well as leading the "Take a Step Back" ditty—which the Dead traditionally deploy when overenthusiastic crowds start to crowd the stage—before the second set.

5 | 6 | 7 ~ 21

Sunday November 6 ★
Broome County Arena, Binghamton, New York

TRUE ★ TALENT
COLGATE UNIV. SOCIAL COMM.
proudly presents
GRATEFUL DEAD
NOV. 4, 1977 – COTTEREL COURT
GUEST

Tuesday November 22
Regular passenger service between New York and Europe on the supersonic Concorde begins on a trial basis.

22 | 23 ~ 30

DECEMBER '77

1 | 2 | 3

Bob Weir releases two solo singles during 1977, "Bombs Away"/"Easy To Slip" and "I'll Be Doggone"/"Shades of Grey." Promos of each are also distributed.

Bob Weir
BOMBS AWAY
ARISTA

Blair Jackson

A Dead fan since 1970, Blair Jackson first met Garcia in 1977; at the time, Jackson was an editor for *BAM* magazine. His first book, *Grateful Dead: The Music Never Stopped*, was the first comprehensive history of the band when it was published in 1983. A year later, Jackson and his wife, journalist Regan McMahon, started the Dead fanzine *The Golden Road*, widely regarded as the preeminent source for Dead news, in-depth interviews, arcane history, and irreverent humor for the next nine years, encompassing 27 issues. A compilation of articles from the magazine, called *Goin' Down the Road: A Grateful Dead Traveling Companion*, was published in 1993. Jackson's most recent book is *Garcia: An American Life*, published in 1999. His other writings about the Dead have appeared in numerous books and magazines through the years. With fellow Dead scribes David Gans and Steve Silberman, Jackson co-produced the Dead's five-CD box set *So Many Roads: 1965–1995*.

This page: Saturday December 31, Winterland Arena, San Francisco, California. Bill Graham flies in on a motorcycle as Uncle Sam. The New Year's Baby is getting a little long in the tooth.

🎸 **Tuesday December 27**
🎸 **Thursday December 29**
Friday December 30
Saturday December 31
Winterland Arena, San Francisco, California

Music from Thursday and Friday's shows appears on 1998's *Dick's Picks Volume 10*. Saturday's New Year's Eve show also sees NRPS on the bill.

| 27 | 28 | 29 | 30 | 31 |

New Year's Eve

For those Deadheads fortunate enough to get into the New Year's Eve show—only the second since '72—the year 1977 would start a little late. On the way into Winterland, everyone got handed a card with a Stealie logo on one side and the words "Good things come to those who wait. Midnight will come at 12:30." After the set break the Dead jammed in darkness while spots lit up Bill Graham, costumed as Uncle Sam, who was lowered from the rafters aboard a Harley. When he hit the stage—at 12:30—the band launched into "Sugar Magnolia" as thousands of balloons dropped. New Year's Eve 77/78 set the pattern for those to come, establishing "NYE" as the biggest holiday in the Deadhead calendar.

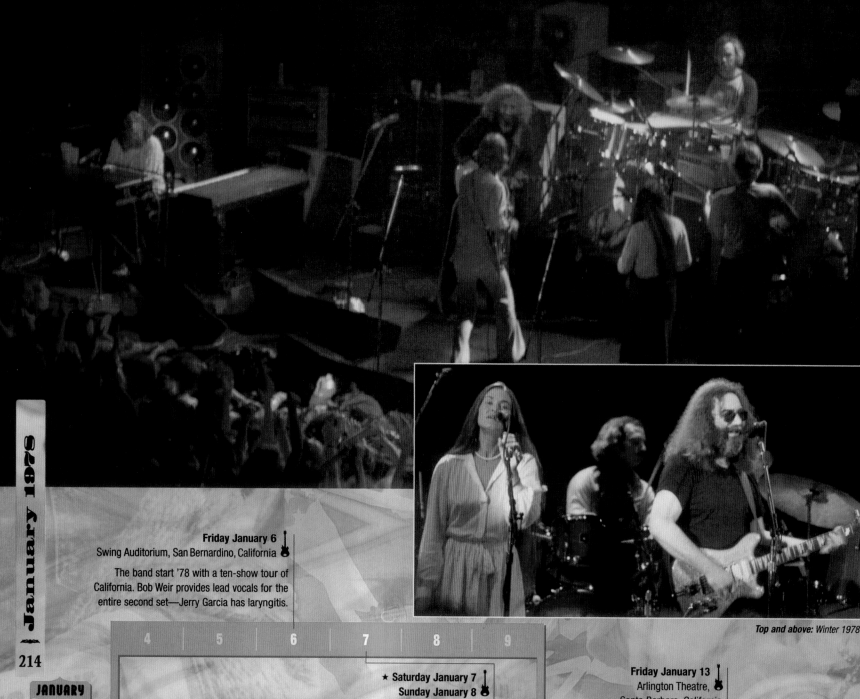

Top and above: Winter 1978.

Friday January 6
Swing Auditorium, San Bernardino, California

The band start '78 with a ten-show tour of California. Bob Weir provides lead vocals for the entire second set—Jerry Garcia has laryngitis.

214

JANUARY '78

4 | 5 | 6 | 7 | 8 | 9

1 | 2 | 3

★ **Saturday January 7**
Sunday January 8
Golden Hall, Community Concourse, San Diego, California

Jerry can't sing at either show but still plays, and Bob continues to carry it off. The 1/8 show is Bill Graham's birthday, and Bob announces a new nickname—"Uncle Bobo."

Friday January 13
Arlington Theatre, Santa Barbara, California

A benefit for the Pacific Alliance's anti-nuclear power campaign.

Sunday January 15
Selland Arena, Fresno, California

"Drums/Space"

Deadheads often had a love/hate relationship with "Drums/Space," the extended instrumental stretch that first appeared on the band's documented setlists in 1969 and became a constant during the second half of the group's concerts beginning in 1978. Alternatively known as "Drumz," the span served as a sonic laboratory which the group used to explore uncharted realms of rhythm and sound, though the effect on the listener could vary greatly depending on the content of the experiment and the extracurricular activities said listener may have indulged in. "I'm trying to be as spontaneous as I can from night to night, and not repeat myself," drummer Mickey Hart offered in 1990. "It's more dangerous that way, and maybe not as fulfilling sometimes... but when you do hit it, you know you've got something original." Despite the free-form nature of "Drums/Space," Garcia acknowledged in 1984 that the band sometimes used abstract themes as a starting point. "Before we started using that idea, that music would tend to get dispersed so far that you couldn't relate to it at all." Though The Other Ones continued to include this improvisational component through their last performance on December 31, 2002, the band's first concert as The Dead on Valentine's Day 2003 was also the first in nearly 25 years to eschew the tradition after over 1,500 shows.

10 | 11 | 12 | 13 | 14 | 15

Tuesday January 10
Wednesday January 11
Shrine Auditorium,
Los Angeles, California

Saturday January 14
Bakersfield Civic Auditorium,
Bakersfield, California

The Dead play rural Bakersfield, California's country capital (it's the hometown of Merle Haggard and Buck Owens) while back in S.F. the Sex Pistols are playing the last show of their infamous eight-date U.S. tour—which turns out to be their last show, ever. The Winterland audience—in which, reportedly, curious hippie types outnumbered actual punks—watch the group self-destruct, with Johnny Rotten leaving the stage with the immortal remark, "Ever get the feeling you've been cheated?"

Timeline

Tuesday January 17
Sacramento Memorial Auditorium, Sacramento, California

Keith stays onstage for "Drums."

Wednesday January 18
Stockton Civic Auditorium, Stockton, California

Monday January 30
Tuesday January 31
Wednesday February 1
Uptown Theatre, Chicago, Illinois

The Uptown Theatre is a band favorite, and they play five more runs there in the next four years (a total of three runs in 1978) until fears about the building's structural integrity force its closure.

Friday February 3
Dane County Coliseum, Madison, Wisconsin

It has been almost four and a half years since the Dead last visited Mad City.

Above: John Kahn and Jerry Garcia perform with the Jerry Garcia Band at the Marin County Veterans Auditorium, San Rafael. Robert Hunter's group Comfort open the show.

Sunday January 22 ★
McArthur Court, University of Oregon, Eugene, Oregon

Remembered as "the UFO Show," thanks to Jerry's playing of the "doo-dee-dee-doo-doo" alien–human communication riff from Steven Spielberg's *Close Encounters of the Third Kind* during "Space" (where else?). Later, Jerry (who is actually skeptical about UFOs) reads an article about Jacques Vallee, the inspiration for Francois Truffaut's character in the film, which references the biblical figure Melchizedek. Not long after Jerry gets in a taxi and the driver's name is—you guessed it—Melchizedek. Synchronicity.

Working Like a Cat

From the middle of 1977 and into early 1978, the Jerry Garcia Band spent literally hundreds of hours at the Club Front studio in San Rafael working up new songs—all of them originals—for the band's first album, *Cats Under the Stars*. The album became a favorite of Garcia's.

"We put so much blood into that album," John Kahn would recall to Blair Jackson. "When we were inside we didn't know if it was day or night except for this one little crack in the ceiling that would allow you to see if it was light or dark. I remember one stretch where it changed three times before I left the studio."

Saturday February 4
Milwaukee Auditorium, Milwaukee, Wisconsin

Sunday February 5 ★
Uni-Dome, University of Northern Iowa, Cedar Falls, Iowa

215

BOB WEIR — Heaven Help The Fool

HEAVEN HELP THE FOOL

Bob Weir

Released by Arista (AB 4155) on January 13, 1978

Side One

1. **Bombs Away** (Barlow/Weir)
2. **Easy To Slip** (George/Kibbee)
3. **Salt Lake City** (Barlow/Weir)
4. **Shade Of Grey** (Barlow/Weir)

Side Two

1. **Heaven Help The Fool** (Barlow/Weir)
2. **This Time Forever** (Barlow/Weir)
3. **I'll Be Doggone** (Moore/Robinson/Tarplin)
4. **Wrong Way Feelin'** (Barlow/Weir)

Personnel

Bob Weir – guitar, vocals
Mike Baird – drums
Bill Champlin – organ, keyboards, background vocals
David Foster – keyboards
Lynette Gloud – background vocals
Tom Kelly – background vocals
Dee Murrey – bass
Nigel Olsson – drums
David Paich – keyboards
Mike Porcaro – bass
Peggy Sandvig – keyboards
Tom Scott – winds
Carmen Twilley – background vocals
Waddy Wachtel – guitar

Produced by Keith Olsen

BOB WEIR HAD WAITED six years between the release of the Dead-backed *Ace* and his second solo album, *Heaven Help The Fool*. He'd enjoyed working with Keith Olsen on the just-finished Dead album *Terrapin Station*, so for *Heaven*, he went for a Los Angeles–session-style approach, and corralled a list of notable guest musicians that included ex-Elton John rhythm section Nigel Olsson and Dee Murray, Toto bassist Mike Porcaro and keyboardist David Paich, more keys from studio whiz David Foster, and session guitarist extraordinaire Waddy Wachtel. "What I'm doing here is going fishing," Weir told David Gans at the time. "With the Grateful Dead, when I do a song, I throw it up to them and it's subject to whatever interpretation it gets... but when I get into the studio with a bunch of musicians, I can say, 'I want this.'" Unfortunately, the slick Richard Avedon portrait of Weir on the cover hinted at the album's overproduced sheen. Weir would continue to play a few of the songs from the album in non-Dead performances (most notably an elegant cover of Lowell George's "Easy to Slip"), but only the title track and "Salt Lake City" would ever find their way to a Dead stage.

Below: Deadheads on the road, cramming as many people as possible into a small motel room.

Egypt Beckons

Believers in the psychedelic truism that the setting is as important as the set, the Grateful Dead had long been interested in playing unusual and mystically charged venues—without much success. Band members had visited Stonehenge on the '72 European tour and Jerry Garcia later wanted to play there, for example, but had been turned down by the British authorities. ("I don't know why they wouldn't let us play there. It'd be fun!" Jerry told *The [London] Times.*)

The genesis for what would become the Dead's greatest single adventure began when Richard Loren and some friends toured Egypt. The easygoing people, the timeless cycle of life along the Nile, and above all the feeling of being in the presence of great antiquity and yet being connected to something infinite and eternal—all convinced Loren that the Dead just had to play the Great Pyramids at Gizeh. There was even a stage in place, built for sound-and-light shows for tourists. Phil Lesh was a devotee of geomancy, which posits that certain places on earth are "power spots" with a heightened connectivity to the cosmic. The Pyramids were maybe the ultimate power spot. Lesh loved Loren's idea. So did Ice Nine publisher Alan Trist. This being the UFO-crazed America of the late '70s, they dubbed themselves the MIBS (Men in Black Suits) and set about making it happen.

Which would not be easy. There were the obvious logistical problems of mounting a major concert in a developing country that was, in 1978, very poor and with a limited infrastructure. Also, the Camp David Accords were still a year in the future; the Arab nations—and Egypt—were still technically at war with Israel, and the last shooting war in the region had taken place just five years earlier. Fortunately, Alan Trist had friends with connections in both Cairo and Washington, and in February and March '78 the MIBS traveled to both capitals to begin laying the groundwork for the shows.

On March 21, the MIBS sent a telegram home:

"Two count them Two open air concerts at the great pyramid sphinx theatre in lower egypt confirmed repeat confirmed for September 14 and 15."

In fact, the Dead would play three shows at the Great Pyramid...

March 1978

216

MARCH '78

4 5 6 7 8 9 10 11 12 13 14 15 16 17-31

1 2 3

JGB Switch

Around the same time *Cats Under the Stars* was released, the Jerry Garcia Band underwent a lineup change. Drummer Ron Tutt left and was replaced by Buzz Buchanan, and Maria Muldaur (who'd sung on two *Cats* tracks) came on board full-time. The combination of Muldaur and Donna Jean Godchaux gave the JGB a powerful vocal punch, but as John Kahn later put it, "It didn't end up being a good idea to have two couples in the band." (Kahn was romantically involved with Muldaur at the time.)

Left: John Kahn and Garcia at a Garcia Band gig at the Warner Theatre in Washington, D.C..
Right: Mickey Hart's grandmother turns up at the Haight Street Fair, April 1978.

APRIL '78

1 2 3 4 5 6 7 8 9 10 11 12

Wednesday April 12
Cameron Indoor Stadium, Duke University, Durham, North Carolina

Saturday April 8
Veterans Memorial Coliseum, Jacksonville, Florida

Thursday April 6
Curtis Hixon Convention Hall, Tampa, Florida

Friday April 7
Sportatorium, Pembroke Pines, Florida

Monday April 10
Tuesday April 11
Fox Theatre, Atlanta, Georgia

Monday's soundcheck is "Salt Lake City."

13 14

Friday April 14
Cassell Coliseum, Virginia Polytechnic Institute, Blacksburg, West Virginia

The band encore with a picture-perfect "Johnny B. Goode."

Emmett Grogan 1944 – 78

Founding member of the Diggers and associate of the band back in the Haight *(see page 59)*, Emmett Grogan was found dead of a heroin overdose in a New York subway car in April. (Grogan and some other Diggers considered heroin use a form of rebellion.) It was a sad end for one of the must unique and talented individuals to emerge in the ferment of the Bay Area in the mid-'60s.

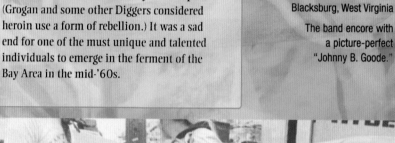

CATS UNDER THE STARS

Jerry Garcia Band

Released by Arista (AB 4160) in April 1978

Side One
1. Rubin And Cherise
   (Garcia/Hunter)
2. Love In The Afternoon
   (Kahn/Hunter)
3. Palm Sunday
   (Garcia/Hunter)
4. Cats Under The Stars
   (Garcia/Hunter)

Side Two
1. Rhapsody In Red
   (Garcia/Hunter/Kahn)
2. Rain
   (Godchaux)
3. Down Home
   (Kahn)
4. Gomorrah
   (Garcia/Hunter)

Personnel

Jerry Garcia – guitar, vocals
Donna Jean Godchaux – vocals
Keith Godchaux – keyboard, vocals
John Kahn – basses, keyboards, guitars, orchestration
Ron Tutt – drums, percussion
Merl Saunders – organ
Maria Muldaur – vocals on "Gomorrah" and "Love In The Afternoon"
Steve Schuster – flute, clarinet, saxophone
Brian Godchaux – violin
Candy Godchaux – violin

FOR HIS FIRST SIDE PROJECT under the Arista banner and first with the newly christened Jerry Garcia Band, the Dead guitarist took to the "studio" (actually the warehouse at Dead headquarters) with a renewed sense of purpose. Kicking off with "Rubin and Cherise," a take on the Orpheus legend that had been in the making for years, the album was arguably the best of Garcia's four solo efforts, featuring a pleasant enough mix of songs worked up by Garcia, Hunter, and bassist John Kahn in various combinations. It also included another welcome cast of friends, with appearances by Ron Tutt, Merl Saunders, and Keith and Donna Godchaux, whose odd pop trifle "Rain" appeared on the album, and a classic new Kelley/Mouse cover of a stately, silhouetted black cat that would become a common decal among Jerry fans.

Though the group's best efforts seem to have had little influence on the album's modest sales, Garcia continued to include many of the songs in his set lists and professed *Cats* to be his favorite of his albums for years to come.

"The record I worked hardest at and liked best was *Cats Under The Stars*," he said later. "That was kind of like my baby. It did worse than any other record I ever did. I think I probably gave away more copies than I sold. It was amazingly, pathetically bad. I've learned not to invest a lot of importance in 'em, although it's nice to care about your work." Like Weir's *Heaven Help The Fool*, the album would provide little in terms of Dead fodder, though both the title track and "Rubin and Cherise" were included in the 1978 promo Grateful Dead Sampler.

"Cats Under the Stars, as far as I'm concerned, is my most successful record—even though it's my least successful record... I've always really loved it and it just never went anywhere."

JERRY GARCIA TO BLAIR JACKSON, *1991*

Above and right: Sunday May 14, Providence Civic Center, Providence, Rhode Island. Mickey and Billy lock in to each other. Phil makes some pre-show preparations.

MAY '78

1 | 2 | 3 | 4

May 1978

218

Friday May 5
Thompson Arena, Dartmouth College, Hanover, New Hampshire

Tuesday May 9
Onondaga County War Memorial, Syracuse, New York

Thursday May 11
Springfield Civic Center Arena, Springfield, Massachusetts

Saturday May 13
The Spectrum, Philadelphia, Pennsylvania

5 | 6 | 7 | 8 | 9 | 10 | 11 | 12 | 13 | 14 | 15

Saturday May 6
Patrick Gymnasium, University of Vermont, Burlington, Vermont

Sunday May 7
Field House, Rensselaer Polytechnic Institute, Troy, New York

Bill Kreutzmann's 32nd birthday.

Wednesday May 10
New Haven Coliseum, New Haven, Connecticut

Sunday May 14
Providence Civic Center, Providence, Rhode Island

16 | 17 | 18 ~ 31

Tuesday May 16
Wednesday May 17
Uptown Theatre, Chicago, Illinois

A show scheduled for 3/18 is canceled after an altercation between Bill Kreutzmann and Keith Godchaux ends with the drummer flying home. Godchaux's drug use and general attitude are increasingly troubling to the band. Jerry Garcia will cut him from the JGB before the end of the year.

Left: Eileen Law at the Dead office in San Rafael, 1978. Eileen was (and still is) the Dead's liaison with their fans.

Left and above: Sunday June 4, Campus Stadium, University of California, Santa Barbara. Mickey listens in at the monitor mixing position. The woman at right is sound engineer Betty Cantor-Jackson.

19 | 20 | 21 | 22 | 23 | 24 | **25** | 26 ~ 30

Sunday June 4

Campus Stadium, University of California, Santa Barbara, California

An afternoon concert with Warren Zevon, Elvin Bishop, and Wah-Koo. The Dead would play "Werewolves of London" twelve times and the tune would also be in heavy JGB rotation, but its auteur—the acerbic, highly literate singer-songwriter Warren Zevon—made few friends at this show when he appeared onstage visibly wasted. (Jerry, who really loved "Werewolves," would later play on Zevon's '89 *Transverse City* album.)

Sunday June 25

Autzen Stadium, Eugene, Oregon

The first rock concert at this football stadium also includes Eddie Money, Santana, and the Outlaws. Prankster Ken Babbs brings the Thunder Machine in from Kesey's place to enliven "Drums." Also the first "Nobody's Jam" since 7/21/74.

JUNE
'78

1 | 2 | 3 | **4** | 5 | 6 | 7 | 8 | 9 | 10 | **11** | **12** | 13 | 14 | 15 | 16 | 17 | 18

Red Rocks

Of all the venues in which the Dead played regularly in the post-hiatus era, probably only UC Berkeley's Greek Theatre rivaled Red Rocks Amphitheatre in the affection of Deadheads. Just outside the mile-high city of Denver, Red Rocks is not only relatively intimate (9,000 seats) and austerely beautiful, but it's one of those "power spots" where the magical moments seem to happen regularly—the site figured largely in the cosmology of the local Native American peoples. The band played 20 shows here, with annual runs ('80–'81 excepted) until they outgrew it after '87. Phil Lesh and Friends played Red Rocks in '99 and '01 and The Dead had a five-show run there in July '03, to the delight of fans old and new.

Friday July 7 ★
Saturday July 8 ★
Red Rocks Amphitheatre, Morrison, Colorado

The first Red Rocks show establishes the venue's reputation for bringing out the "X Factor"; this is considered one of the best shows of the year.

| 6 | 7 | 8 | 9 | 10 | 11 | 12 | 13 | 14 | 15 | 16 | 17 | 18 | 19 | 20 | 21 |

JULY '78

| 1 | 2 | 3 | 4 | 5 |

Saturday July 1
Arrowhead Stadium, Kansas City, Missouri

Waylon Jennings, Jessie Colter and Willie Nelson also perform; it's Willie Nelson's annual July 4 picnic, though off by a couple of days.

Monday July 3
St. Paul Civic Center Arena, St. Paul, Minnesota

Wednesday July 5
Omaha Civic Auditorium, Omaha, Nebraska

Right: The band onstage at Red Rocks Amphitheatre, July 7–8.

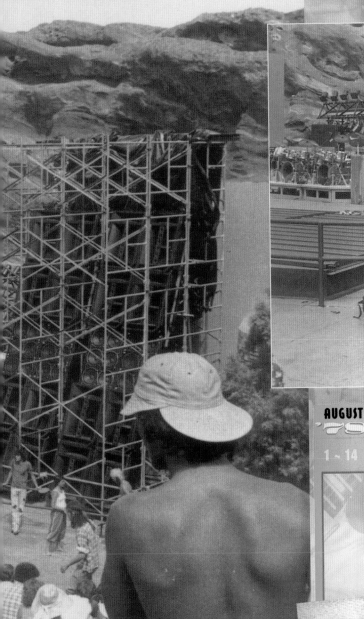

Above: As the equipment is set up onstage at Red Rocks on July 7, these two find time for some juggling.

Wednesday August 30
Thursday August 31

Red Rocks Amphitheatre, Morrison, Colorado

The band debuts three new songs on Wednesday: the Weir/Barlow "I Need a Miracle" *(see page 353)*; "Stagger Lee," Hunter/Garcia's fresh take on one of the most venerable songs in the American folk canon; and the Hunter/Garcia "If I Had the World to Give," an uninspired ballad that would be retired after three shows. Thursday sees two more breakouts: Donna Godchaux's "From the Heart of Me," her second (and not very successful) self-penned effort for the band, and the Hunter/Garcia "Shakedown Street." "Shakedown Street" always sounded better live than on the album version and, "Disco Dead" comments aside, would stay in the rotation for the rest of the band's career.

Above: View of the stage from the crowd at Red Rocks Amphitheatre. The upper seats in the bowl have a spectacular view of Denver in the distance.

Tuesday July 25
Louise Joy Brown, the world's first test-tube baby, is born in Oldham, England, having been conceived through in vitro fertilization.

| 22 | 23 | 24 | **25** | 26 | 27 | 28 | 29 | 30 | 3 |

BACKSTAGE

Red Rocks
MORRISON, COLORADO

AUGUST 31, 1978

Club Front and Lowell George

221

In August the band began recording its second album for Arista, ultimately titled *Shakedown Street*, at Club Front, the combination practice space/recording studio/tape archive/clubhouse in San Rafael. Acquired in '74, the building was located on Front Street (hence the name), in a rundown industrial area frequented by hookers, bikers, dopers, and other members of the Marin County demimonde.

Shakedown would be the first Grateful Dead album recorded at Club Front. Once again the band brought in an outside producer, but in an effort to avoid the problems they'd had with Keith Olsen on *Terrapin Station*, they tapped someone who, seemingly, would be more simpatico personally and musically—Lowell George. A child prodigy, George had played with Zappa before forming Little Feat, a band which, like the Dead, drew on a variety of influences and was known for amazing live performances. Unfortunately George was so drugged out— even by the standards of the Grateful Dead in and around 1978—that it didn't work out. On one occasion George and Mickey Hart got into a fight after George criticized the *Diga* album. In the end George hit the road with Little Feat and left the unfinished album in the Dead's hands. The talented but self-destructive George died of a heart attack in June '79.

"If we were working on a song and Lowell didn't feel it was going right, he'd just grab a guitar and come into the studio and show us how he felt it. That was one of the ways he'd communicate, and it worked great. I had a tremendous amount of respect for him."
BILL KREUTZMANN

Egypt '78

The Egyptian odyssey began on September 4, only two days after it was announced following the Giants Stadium show—the first press conference since the 710 Ashbury bust. No one in the Grateful Dead Family was about to miss this adventure, so the two charter planes that took off that day carried 174 people (some other friends and family traveled separately) making the Europe '72 contingent look like a skeleton crew.

The entourage included Ken Kesey, Ken Babbs, Mountain Girl, Bear, Deadhead hoops star Bill Walton, and Bill Graham (as a private citizen—he'd been offered the chance to run the event, but begged off). Out of the usual suspects, only Robert Hunter decided to give this particular trip a pass, and Rock Scully didn't make it due to "logistical difficulties." Following the band et al. were a cohort of the most Deadicated 'Heads, some of whom reportedly mortgaged their homes to pay for the trip.

The Men in Black were correct: it was love at first sight for the Grateful Dead and Egypt, and the laid-back populace reciprocated. "No cops, no parents!" was how Jerry Garcia described Egypt—a Deadhead's paradise. Even the omnipresent beggars and souvenir hawkers were generally mellow—though Mountain Girl recalled that she and the other women were subjected to "lots of petting and fondling and grabbing" from the local men.

The expedition's HQ was Mena House, originally a lodge for Victorian tourists, about a quarter-mile from the actual pyramids. In the ten-day run-up to the shows, the intrepid travelers explored the crowded streets and markets of Cairo (where hashish was sold in candy-bar-sized slabs) and desert villages, introduced Egyptian kids to Frisbees, rode camels (Mickey Hart, the expert horseman, preferred Arabian stallions), and generally immersed themselves in a timeless and fascinating culture—or, in Bob Weir's words (to Steve Sutherland in *Melody Maker*), "stepped out of the twentieth century for a good few days."

"The concert site was just perfect, immediately to the left of the Sphinx with an incredible backdrop of pyramids illuminated by the almost full moon... the next day we explored the site and caught glimpses of Bobby Weir jogging around the pyramid!"
IAN FRY, DEADHEAD AND INTREPID EXPLORER

Right and middle right: Saturday September 2, Giants Stadium, East Rutherford, New Jersey.

In '78 Robert Hunter toured with a group called Comfort. Hunter recorded an album, *Alligator Moon*, accompanied by Comfort on some tracks; however, it was not released. Three songs from the album appear on Hunter's 1982 compilation *Promontory Rider*.

CRANSTOCK LOVES THE DEAD

SEPTEMBER '78

1 2 3

September 1978

224

Saturday September 2
Giants Stadium, East Rutherford, New Jersey

New Riders of the Purple Sage and Willie Nelson also on bill.

4 5 6 7

Thursday September 7
The Who's flamboyant drummer, Keith Moon, dies of an overdose, aged 31.

8 ~ 13

Left: Jerry Garcia takes time out in Egypt to try his hand at camel-riding.

14 15 16

Thursday September 14
Friday September 15
Saturday September 16
Sound and Light Theatre, the Great Pyramid at Giza, Cairo, Egypt

Hamza El-Din, master of the tar drum, and an ensemble of Nubian music perform all three nights, introducing the ancient tune "Ollin Arrageed" in Dead's repertoire on on the first night. A total eclipse occurs during the show, which also includes the last performance of Donna Jean's "Sunris

The Pyramid Shows

"Take a perfect setting," said Jerry in Blair Jackson's *Garcia: An American Life*. "What could be better? What could be more amazing? A total eclipse, a full moon, the Great Pyramid: everything perfect and we went and played shitty." For neither the first nor the last time in the Grateful Dead's history, and for various acute reasons, the performance failed to match the occasion. Bill Kreutzmann was drumming with one arm (he'd broken the other playing basketball), Keith's piano was out of tune, and Jerry's playing wasn't helped by the fact he was coping with separation from Persian by gulping prescription painkillers. And in this most unique of venues, the band stuck with its standard rotation material, with no surprises or special treats. But, as Jerry also noted, "It didn't really matter. We had a wonderful time… we got a lot out of it. We got off like bandits." So did the audiences—a mix of tourists, Cairene sophisticates, expats, Deadheads, and curious Bedouins from the nearby villages, as only a plastic rope separated the 700 seats of the Sound and Light Theatre from the surrounding desert.
"The whole area was up all night for a whole week—the desert was echoing with the sound. There is an Egyptian proverb that says: 'If you are not convinced about something you want to say, you shout. Those who are sure, talk quietly.' After hearing the Grateful Dead, Egyptians realized that the group is dealing with volume—the Dead mission shows there can be strength in the shouting! In Egypt, they accept anything!" HAMZA EL-DIN

Above: Sunday October 22, Winterland Arena, San Francisco, California. "From Egypt With Love"—Mickey Hart, Hamza El-Din, and members of the Sufi Choir.

| 17 | 18 | 19 | 20 | 21 | 22 | 23 ~ 31 |

🎸 Tuesday October 17
🎸 Wednesday October 18
Friday October 20
Saturday October 21 ★
Sunday October 22
Winterland Arena, San Francisco, California

The Dead's first run back in the U.S. is billed as "From Egypt with Love," and Hamza El-Din performs at the last two shows. Lee Oskar guests on Wednesday, Saturday, and Sunday; John Cipollina also guests on the last night. Wednesday sees the first "Mojo Jam" (incorporating "Mind Left Body Jam") and Sunday the last.

Below: Onstage at the Pyramid shows, September 14–16, Sound and Light Theatre, the Great Pyramid at Giza, Cairo, Egypt.

7 ~ 30

The Music of Upper and Lower Egypt and Hamza El-Din's *Eclipse* were recorded and engineered by Mickey Hart during the band's Egypt trip.

OCTOBER '78

| 1 | 2 | 3 | 4 | 5 | 6 ~16 |

Post-Pyramid Blues

After the last Egypt show Bill Graham threw an after-party, during which a race took place between Graham and Mickey Hart, each of whom was carrying a waiter's tray. Mickey and MERT (the mobile engineering and recording team) then went to the Sudan to record Nubian music, while another contingent took in the sights along the Nile aboard a felucca dubbed "Ship of Fools." The Dead left Egypt with wonderful memories and the thanks of the Egyptian government, but memories and thanks don't pay the bills. The whole trip put the band about $500,000 in the red.

A live album of the shows, which was supposed to amortize the cost of the event, never materialized, largely because of Jerry Garcia's unhappiness at the quality of the performances. The band also canceled the eleven-show European tour planned to follow the Pyramids run. And the Egypt trip was soon followed by *Shakedown Street*'s November release. The Egyptian adventure was something that couldn't be quantified on a balance sheet, of course, but when the band got home they faced the same problem's they'd left—most notably, tight cash-flow and the increasing drug problems of Jerry Garcia, Keith Godchaux, and others in the organization.

Above: October 17–22, Winterland Arena, San Francisco

SHAKEDOWN STREET
Grateful Dead

Released by Arista (AB-4198) on November 15

Side One
1. **Good Lovin'**
   (Resnick/Clark)
2. **France**
   (Hart/Weir/Hunter)
3. **Shakedown Street**
   (Garcia/Hunter)
4. **Serengetti**
   (Hart/Kreutzmann)
5. **Fire On The Mountain**
   (Hart/Hunter)

Side Two
1. **I Need A Miracle**
   (Weir/Barlow)
2. **From The Heart Of Me**
   (D. Godchaux)
3. **Stagger Lee**
   (Garcia/Hunter)
4. **All New Minglewood Blues**
   (Tradition arr. Bob Weir)
5. **If I Had The World To Give**
   (Garcia/Hunter)

Personnel
Jerry Garcia – guitar, vocals
Donna Godchaux – vocals
Keith Godchaux – keyboards
Mickey Hart – drums, percussion
Robert Hunter – lyrics
Billy Kreutzmann – drums, percussion
Phil Lesh – bass, vocals
Bob Weir – guitar, vocals
Jordan Amarantha – percussion
Matthew Kelly – harp
Steve Schuster – horn on "From The Heart Of Me"
John Kahn – horn arrangements, maybe keyboards

Produced by Lowell George

"Lowell... was like a member of the band."
BILL KREUTZMANN TO BLAIR JACKSON

AFTER THE OVERBLOWN antics of *Terrapin Station,* fans had a right to expect something a little more real from their antiheroes for *Shakedown Street,* especially when they learned it was recorded at the band's homey Club Front (a cartoonish street scene depicting life outside of the facility by underground comic legend Gilbert Shelton graced the disc's front cover) with none other than Little Feat's Lowell George wearing the requisite producer's hat. Unfortunately, the combination proved to be detrimental both musically and personally, with cocaine use clouding the proceedings.

"Lowell George was mad," Hart told David Gans in 1983. "He was no producer—certainly not for the Grateful Dead. He did too much coke. There's no way for him to have any kind of rational judgment." The result was an album that bade poorly from the start, kicking off with a limp version of the old Dead favorite "Good Lovin'" and finishing with the sappy love song "If I Had The World To Give." Perhaps the biggest surprise was that the album's title cut would eventually transcend its dance pop vinyl rendering to become a fan favorite, as would Hart and Hunter's "Fire On The Mountain." Called at turns "an artistic dead end," "a rambling, shambling, under-exercised goddam yawn" and "the worst Dead album ever" by various critics, Weir was still gamely trying to defend the disc in the months after its release. "People say every album is more 'commercial' or whatever, than the previous," Weir told *Billboard.* "What we do is try to include as much musical information as we can in each song, and if it sounds more commercial, or sells better, it is because we are playing better." Now that's a shakedown.

Saturday November 11
Saturday Night Live, NBC Studios, New York, New York

It's the band's first appearance on the show, which at the time is still wildly popular (60 million viewers on this night) and certifiably hip. They play three songs—"Casey Jones," "I Need a Miracle," and "Good Lovin'"—whose (relative) brevity and energy come across well on TV. Afterward, the band parties with the cast at the Blues Brothers Bar, Dan Aykroyd and John Belushi's private dive.

Monday November 13
Tuesday November 14
Boston Music Hall, Boston, Massachusetts

JG's drug use is badly affecting his health and the shows; his respiratory problems will force several gigs to be canceled. The strife between Keith and Donna adds to the bad vibe.

Wednesday November 15
A 7-inch single, "Good Lovin'"/"Stagger Lee," is released on the same day as *Shakedown Street.* A second single, "Shakedown Street"/"France" is subsequently released.

Friday November 17
In the afternoon, Bob, Phil Lesh, Mickey Hart, and JG, billed as "Bob Weir & Friends," play a Hunger Week benefit in a tiny university rec room in Chicago, the first acoustic gig in years.

Thursday November 16
Friday November 17
Saturday November 18
Uptown Theatre, Chicago, Illinois

Monday November 20
Cleveland Music Hall, Cleveland, Ohio
Last "If I Had the World to Give."

A promotional LP of tracks taken from Arista Dead albums and solo projects is released under the title *Grateful Dead Sampler* (Arista SP 35), a.k.a. Recently Dead.

DECEMBER '78

Saturday December 16
Nashville Municipal Auditorium, Nashville, Tennessee

Wednesday December 13
Curtis Hixon Convention Hall, Tampa, Florida

Sunday December 17
Fox Theatre, Atlanta, Georgia

Thursday December 21
The Summit, Houston, Texas

Saturday December 30
Pauley Pavilion, University of California, Los Angeles, California

Hamza El-Din and Lee Oskar play on some songs.

| 29 | 30 | 31 |

| 1 ~ 11 | 12 | 13 | 14 | 15 | 16 | 17 | 18 | 19 | 20 | 21 | 22 | 23 ~ 26 | 27 | 28 |

★ **Friday November 24**
Capitol Theater, Passaic, New Jersey

Hamza El-Din joins for "Ollin Arrageed"; the show is broadcast nationwide. The next day Jerry's flu turns to bronchitis and he's in the hospital; five shows are canceled, including that evening's, in New Haven. The audience is already seated as Bob Weir announces the news; they take it beautifully—a single rose is tossed onstage as the 'Heads peacefully file out.

Tuesday November 21
Community War Memorial, Rochester, New York

| 21 | 22 | 23 | 24 | 25 ~ 30 |

Thursday November 23
Capital Centre, Landover, Maryland

Only jam ever on "Ollin Arrageed."

Tuesday December 12
Jai-Alai Fronton, Miami, Florida

Friday December 15
Boutwell Auditorium, Birmingham, Alabama

Tuesday December 19
Memorial Coliseum, Mississippi State Fairgrounds, Jackson, Mississippi

Friday December 22
Convention Center Arena, Dallas, Texas

Wednesday December 27
Thursday December 28
Golden Hall, Community Concourse, San Diego, California

★ **Sunday December 31**
Winterland Arena, San Francisco, California

Winterland

Once upon a time the Winterland, with its 5,000 seats, represented the Big Time to Bay Area bands used to the cozier confines of the Avalon or the Fillmore. With the ballrooms gone, Winterland had become a link back to that golden age, but now Winterland's days, too, were numbered. It was basically falling apart from age, and the owners wanted the property razed for condos. Bill Graham was put on notice. Winterland's last show would be, of course, the Grateful Dead on New Year's Eve—the band's 61st show at the venue.

Below: Sunday December 31, Winterland Arena, San Francisco, California. The last-ever show at this venue.

They're not the best at what they do, they're the only ones that do what they do.
Cheers, Bill + the Winterland Gang
P.S. And so are you!

1535 DAYS SINCE LAST SF DARK STAR

227

Happy New Year—and Goodbye Winterland

Demand for the NYE show was intense; Bill Graham said there were as many as 500,000 ticket requests. As an extra treat, Graham promoted the event as an all-night party, "Breakfast Served at Dawn." The Dead's new pals, the Blues Brothers (Aykroyd and Belushi with a killer backup band) would open, followed by NRPS, with the whole shebang broadcast on KQED TV and KSAN radio. The main attraction almost didn't make it: a bomb scare at the airport in L.A. grounded the Dead for several hours. When they did arrive, they were tired and stressed but gamely brought out "Dark Star" (the first since 10/18/74) and other faves, while an all-star roster of Bay Area greats, including John Cipollina, guested. Confirming the NYE tradition of outlandish pre-countdown appearances, Bill Graham rode down from the ceiling in a huge papier-mâché joint complete with roach clip. Three sets, two encores (the last being the first "We Bid You Goodnight" since NYE '76), and the show finished around 9:00 a.m.

Left: New Year's Eve show, Winterland Arena. Bill Graham descends from the ceiling on a papier-mâché joint.

Above: The New Year's Eve show 1978, Winterland Arena. "We Bid You Goodnight."
Left: Saturday January 20, Shea's Theater, Buffalo, New York.

Wednesday January 17
New Haven Coliseum,
New Haven, Connecticut

Thursday January 18
Providence Civic Center,
Providence, Rhode Island

Monday January 15
Springfield Civic Center
Arena, Springfield,
Massachusetts

17   18   19   20   21   22 ~ 31

Saturday January 20
Shea's Theater,
Buffalo, New York

Sunday January 21
Masonic Temple,
Detroit, Michigan

14   15   16

Sunday January 14
Utica Memorial Auditorium,
Utica, New York

Below: Press conference at the New York Hilton in January. Besides playing shows, the group also spent time in New York recording Go To Heaven.

Wednesday January 10
★ **Thursday January 11**
Nassau Veterans Memorial Coliseum,
Uniondale, New York

Friday January 12
The Spectrum,
Philadelphia,
Pennsylvania

Sunday January 7
Monday January 8
Madison Square Garden,
New York, New York

The first of 52 shows
at this venue.

10   11   12   13

JANUARY
'79

1 2 3 4 5 6 7 8 9

Friday January 5
The Spectrum,
Philadelphia,
Pennsylvania

Reconstruction

The Jerry Garcia Band would have their own hiatus for most of '79, largely because of the departure of Keith and Donna Godchaux from both the JGB and the Grateful Dead. Jerry's chief "side band" this year would be funky Reconstruction, which Merl Saunders put together with Gaylord Birch on bass, John Kahn on drums, Ed Neumeister on trombone, and Ron Stallings on sax.

Saturday February 17 ★
Oakland Coliseum Arena,
Oakland, California

The "Rock for Life" benefit against pollution-caused cancer is the last show for Keith and Donna Godchaux. It also sees the first "Big Railroad Blues" since 10/19/74, the first "Greatest Story Ever Told" since 10/18/74, and the last-ever "From the Heart of Me."

FEBRUARY '79

| 1 | 2 | 3 | 4 | 5 | 6 |

Saturday February 3
Market Square Arena,
Indianapolis, Indiana

Sunday February 4
Dane County
Coliseum, Madison,
Wisconsin

Tuesday February 6
Tulsa Pavilion,
Tulsa, Oklahoma

THE MAIDEN VOYAGE

two incredible evenings with

The Grateful Dead

FRIDAY, FEBRUARY 9 & SATURDAY, FEBRUARY 10
MEMORIAL HALL—KANSAS CITY, KANSAS
SHOWTIME 7:00 P.M. PROMPTLY
RESERVED SEATS $9.00 and $10.00

Wednesday February 7
SIU Arena, Southern Illinois
University, Carbondale, Illinois

The band revives the chestnut "Don't Ease Me In" *(see right)*, dormant since 8/6/74.

Friday February 9
Saturday February 10
Soldiers and Sailors
Memorial Hall,
Kansas City, Kansas

| 7 | 8 | 9 | 10 | 11 | 12 |

Sunday February 11
Kiel Auditorium,
St. Louis, Missouri

Below: Saturday January 20, Shea's Theater, Buffalo, New York. Miserable on the road, Donna Godchaux abruptly left the tour before this show, also missing the next night's concert in Detroit. The handwriting was on the wall...

The Godchauxs Leave

Musically and personally, as individuals and as a couple, Keith and Donna Godchaux were bottoming out by the time '78 turned into '79. Keith's drug use had progressed from cocaine to heroin and anything else he could get his hands on. His once-formidable chops had declined precipitously under the chemical onslaught, to the point where he had difficulty keeping time, and instead of the shimmering fills he used to play, at some shows he was so far gone he just parroted Jerry's solos at the keyboard.

As for Donna Jean, she was drinking heavily, and her role in the band had always been an issue with some. No one could deny the power of her voice on a good night, but she was basically a great studio singer who often got out of her depth on stage and was frequently off key as a result.

Needless to say their marriage was falling apart, and their constant fighting (frequently physical) was another downer in a band already beset by Jerry Garcia's own drug use and myriad other problems. Also, the Godchauxs now had a son, Zion, and factoring parenthood into life with a touring band—even without all their other problems—was proving impossible.

Donna and Keith decided the first step in straightening out and preserving their marriage was to remove themselves from the band and the anything-goes environment that surrounded it. At a February band meeting, they told the others they were leaving, and no one argued. Donna would later say she felt that "about a million pounds had been lifted off me."

| 21 | 22 | 23 | 24 | 25 | 26 | 27 | 28 |

"DON'T EASE ME IN"
GARCIA

Taking a page from the songbook they used in their pre-Dead days as Mother McCree's Uptown Jug Champions, the traditional "Don't Ease Me In" became one of the first songs the band ever released on record when it was used for the B-side of "Stealin'," another traditional that the group had issued as a single on Scorpio Records in 1966. The earliest known version of this rural Texas blues had appeared on a 1928 recording by Henry Thomas (1974–1930), a relatively obscure African-American artist whose recorded body of work consisted of 23 songs that ran the gamut from Negro spirituals and ballads to reels and dance songs. Though his output was minimal compared to some other artists of the time, it was also invaluable to blues musicologists trying to track down the genre's origins, thanks in part to Thomas's background as a child of former slaves. His "Bull Doze Blues" informed another 1960s California band, Canned Heat, who reworked that song's guitar riff for their own 1968 hit "Going Up The Country." Over 300 versions of "Don't Ease Me In" would eventually make their way into Dead concerts between '1966 and 1995.

Above: *The lineup of the band in 1979, with new keyboardist Brent Mydland at the bottom. Brent had played a few Dead tunes in Bob Weir's band but was basically unfamiliar with the repertoire before he joined the band. He was the only player who auditioned.*

230

MARCH '79

8 ~ 22	23	24	25	26	27	28	29	30	31

Monday March 26
The Camp David peace treaty is signed by Israeli Prime Minister Menachem Begin and Egyptian President Anwar Sadat at the White House.

Wednesday March 28
America's worst commercial nuclear accident—almost a meltdown—occurs at the Three Mile Island plant near Middletown, Pennsylvania. Thousands living nearby left the area during the 12-day crisis, which saw some radioactive water and gases released. It cost more than $1 billion and took more than a decade to remove the damaged nuclear fuel.

1	2	3	4	5	6

Thursday March 1
Today marks Keith Godchaux's "official" resignation from the band and the beginning of Brent Mydland's stint in the "Hot Seat." The new keyboard player has about seven weeks to get up to speed on the rotation—which has now grown to the extent that the band can (when it chooses) play a couple of consecutive shows without repeats.

Brent Mydland

Keyboardist Brent Mydland had been a journeyman player in a number of fairly obscure bands (remember Batdorf & Rodney, or the country-rock group Silver?) when he was tapped by Bob Weir to join his solo band in 1978. Then, when Keith and Donna Godchaux departed from the Dead in early 1979, Weir invited Brent to audition for the vacant keyboard chair. There was little debate over the matter, for Mydland was both a fine colorist—especially on the Hammond B-3—and a strong harmony singer. His first tour with the band in the spring of 1979 was quite well received by Deadheads, and over the next decade he developed a large and loyal following.

Garcia, in particular, always encouraged Mydland to write for the group, and his output included such tunes as "Easy to Love You," "Far From Me," "I Will Take You Home," "Tons of Steel," and "Just A Little Light." Brent's downfall was a lack of self-confidence—even after years in the band he still seemed to view himself as "the new guy." Alcohol was his main tool for self-destruction, but by 1990 he'd turned to hard drugs, and he died of a morphine overdose in July of that year.

The Beast

In October '78 Bill Graham invited director Francis Ford Coppola to a Dead show at Winterland. Coppola was sufficiently impressed with the Rhythm Devils, a.k.a. Bill Kreutzmann and Mickey Hart, that he engaged the drum duo to provide some music for the soundtrack of *Apocalypse Now*, with a brief to "make the jungle come alive!" To do so, the drummers assembled a massive circular drum/percussion array, soon dubbed "the Beast," which in '79 was incorporated into the onstage arsenal for "Drums."

Above and left: Sunday April 22, Spartan Stadium, San Jose, California. First time that "the Beast," a giant ring of drums, is used in performance.

Below and below right:
Sunday April 22, Spartan Stadium, San Jose, California. This is Brent's first show, after just a few rehearsals, but he acquits himself well.

APRIL '79

1 ~ 8	9	10	11	12	13	14	15	16	17	18	19	20	21

Sunday April 22
Spartan Stadium, San Jose, California

The Greg Kihn Band and the Charlie Daniels band also perform. This is Brent Mydland's first show with the Grateful Dead. With Brent in the band, the sound of the Hammond organ returns to Dead shows for the first time in the post-Pigpen era; Brent also introduces synths, heretofore unused onstage. This show also marks the debut of "the Beast."

22	23	24	25 ~ 30

APRIL '79
STONED AGAIN
KSAN95FM

Jerry and Rock

After briefly reuniting with Mountain Girl, Jerry moved into Rock Scully's house on Hepburn Heights in San Rafael. Rock, who had served some time on drug charges, is now the band's "press liaison," although most view his real function as keeping Garcia and reality far, far apart. Jerry continues to gig with Reconstruction, but his descent into opiates (in which he's accompanied by John Kahn) leads to a split: Merl Saunders recalled to Blair Jackson, "He [Jerry] seemed pretty clean at first, but then I saw him start to slip, and there was a night he didn't show up for a gig… and shortly after that he and John [Kahn] started a different group and I sort of lost touch with him."

Below: Friday May 4, Hampton Coliseum, Hampton, Virginia.

Tuesday May 8
Recreation Hall, Penn State University, University Park, Pennsylvania

Wednesday May 9
Broome County Arena, Binghamton, New York

7 | 8 | 9 | 10 | 11

Monday May 7
Kirby Field House Lafayette College, Easton, Pennsylvania

John Cipollina joins the Dead for two songs.

Friday May 11
Billerica Forum, Billerica, Massachusetts

Saturday May 12
Alumni Stadium, University of Massachusetts, Amherst, Massachusetts

Roy Ayers' Ubiquity then Patti Smith open.

14 ~ 24 | 25

Friday May 25
275 people die in America's worst domestic air disaster when an American Airlines DC-10 crashes on takeoff at Chicago's O'Hare International Airport.

12 | 13

Sunday May 13
Cumberland County Civic Center, Portland, Maine

MAY '79

1 | 2 | 3 | 4 | 5 | 6

Friday May 4
Hampton Coliseum, Hampton, Virginia

Saturday May 5
Baltimore Civic Center, Baltimore, Maryland

Thursday May 3
Charlotte Coliseum, Charlotte, North Carolina

Friday May 4
Conservative Party leader Margaret Thatcher becomes Great Britain's first female Prime Minister.

Right: May 6. Bob Weir and Brent Mydland in Washington, D.C., for a "No Nukes" rally. Neither perform at the rally.

Above: *Thursday June 28, Sacramento Memorial Auditorium, Sacramento, California.*

Monday June 11
Actor John Wayne, born Marion Morrison in Iowa, dies of cancer aged 72.

Below: *Keith Godchaux (right), by now no longer in the band, of course, and Bill Kreutzmann chilling out in May 1979.*

THE GRATEFUL DEAD

McGuinn, Clark and Hillman
David Bromberg Band

1

PORTLAND INTERNATIONAL RACEWAY
PORTLAND, OREGON

JUNE 30, 1979

233

Saturday June 30
Portland International Raceway, Portland, Oregon

With David Bromberg and McGuinn, Clark & Hillman.

Thursday June 28
Sacramento Memorial Auditorium, Sacramento, California

Left and below: August 4–5, Oakland Auditorium, Oakland, California. Garcia switches from his Doug Irwin "Wolf" guitar to this beauty, nicknamed "Tiger."

Heavenly sessions

In July the band went into Club Front to start recording the next studio album for Arista, *Go to Heaven*. Despite collective dissatisfaction with the way *Terrapin Station* and *Shakedown Street* turned out, the band again brought in an outside producer, Gary Lyons, best known for his work with Foreigner. (Lyons took the job despite the fact that, in his words, the Dead were "a Bermuda Triangle" for producers.) Lyons told Blair Jackson: *"I don't think I was really aware of their music at all at that point. I'd been living in America about a year, but when I told my assistant engineer, Peter Thea, that I was going out to talk to the Dead, he flipped—it turns out he was a Deadhead."*

The biggest problem facing the band was lack of original material. Garcia and Hunter had written four songs for the JGB's *Cats Under the Stars (see page 217)*, but the duo's output flagged as Jerry went dry. As a result, Bob Weir and John Perry Barlow, and Brent Mydland (on his own and with Barlow) took up the songwriting slack.

🎸 **Saturday August 4**
🎸 **Sunday August 5**
Oakland Auditorium, Oakland, California

Two breakouts: Hunter/Garcia's "Althea," a musically mellow meditation on love and communication, and Weir/Barlow's "Lost Sailor," which would usually be paired with "Saint of Circumstance" in performance.

The Sound of Oakland

The Grateful Dead had played twice (6/28/67 and 3/5/71) at the Oakland Auditorium before returning to play the first of 57 shows at the venue, which changed its name to the Henry J. Kaiser Convention Center at the start of 1985. Oakland Auditorium/the Kaiser replaced Winterland as home base for the Dead, and West Coast Deadheads, for the remainder of the band's career, not least because Bob Barsotti of Bill Graham Presents (as Bill Graham Productions was now called) allowed 'Heads to camp in the small park adjacent to the venue (camping at shows was to become an established Deadhead custom). The five-show run during the last week of 1979 further rubber-stamped the venue's popularity.

The August 4–5 mini-run was also significant, however, because it marked the first major advance in performance technology since the Wall of Sound: the introduction of Meyer Sound Lab equipment designed by John Meyer. Dan Healy also had a new partner in sound— mixing-board engineer Don Pearson.

Left: These cheery skeletons greeted concert-goers as they entered the Oakland Auditorium for the Dead's New Year's series in December.

🎸 **Sunday July 1**
🎸 Seattle Center Coliseum, Seattle, Washington

Sunday August 12
Red Rocks Amphitheatre
Morrison, Colorado

Monday August 13
Tuesday August 14
McNichols Sports Arena,
Denver, Colorado

9	10	11	12	13	14	15	16	...	27	28	29	30	31

Above: Sunday August 12, Red Rocks Amphitheatre, Morrison, Colorado. Though it's sunny in the picture, Red Rocks became famous for its downpours during Dead shows.

Friday August 31
Glens Falls Civic Center,
Glens Falls, New York

First "Saint of Circumstance," another Weir/Barlow navel-gazer with spiritual overtones.

Right and below: August 25. Hanging around and up to no good at Club Front, between tours. That's Bob's dog Otis, later immortalized on Reckoning.

Left: August 25. Billy at Front Street enjoying a brewski.

Brothers and Sirens

It's a busy time in New York for the Grateful Dead and no mistake: working on the new album at Media Sound Studios by day in a valiant (but unavailing) effort to get it in stores by Christmas, playing sold-out shows at Madison Square Garden and Nassau Coliseum at night, and then getting down to serious partying with their new friends from *Saturday Night Live* at the Blues Brothers Bar, the anything-goes private club owned by Aykroyd and Belushi. (According to Rock Scully in *Living with the Dead*, it wasn't unusual to see a Hells Angel snorting coke off the bar while the local beat cop quaffed on-the-house scotch at the next stool.)

Around this time, Jerry Garcia brought SNL's Deadhead No. 1, Tom Davis, on board as a screenwriter on his latest cinematic obsession, a movie version of Kurt Vonnegut's novel *The Sirens of Titan*, to which he'd optioned the rights, though the film never got made in the end.

SEPTEMBER '79

Sunday September 2
Augusta Civic Center, Augusta, Maine

| 1 | 2 | 3 |

Saturday September 1
Holleder Stadium, Rochester, New York

Greg Kihn, then the Good Rats open the show.

Tuesday September 4
Wednesday September 5
Thursday September 6
Madison Square Garden, New York, New York

Not for the first time, some crank makes a pre-concert death threat against Jerry Garcia. The 9/4 MSG show goes on, with undercover (i.e., tie-dyed) members of New York's finest embedded in the audience.

Above: Tuesday September 4, Madison Square Garden.

| 15 | 16 | 17 | 18 | 19 |

| 4 | 5 | 6 | 7 | 8 | 9 |

| 20 | 21 |

Below and opposite:
Saturday September 1,
Holleder Stadium,
Rochester, New York.

Above, above right, and right:
September 1,
Holleder
Stadium

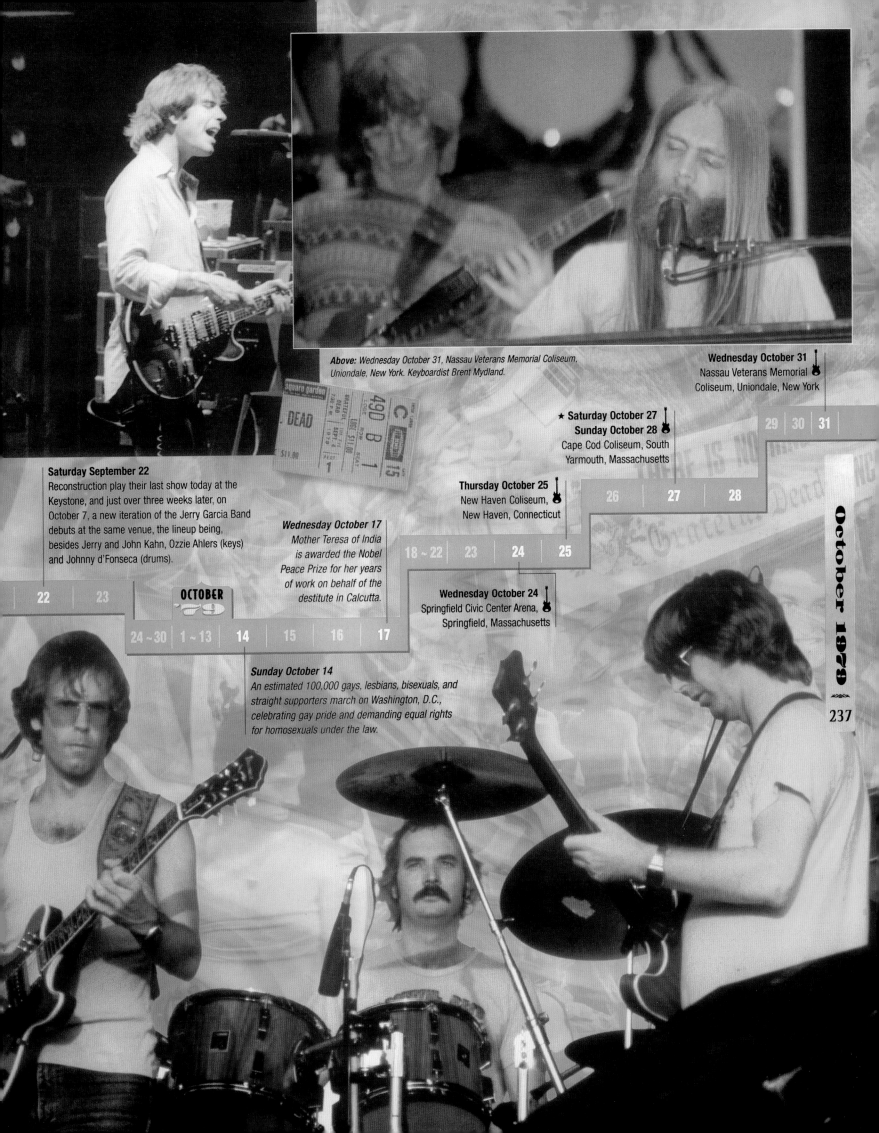

Above: *Wednesday October 31, Nassau Veterans Memorial Coliseum, Uniondale, New York. Keyboardist Brent Mydland.*

Wednesday October 31
Nassau Veterans Memorial
Coliseum, Uniondale, New York

★ **Saturday October 27**
Sunday October 28
Cape Cod Coliseum, South
Yarmouth, Massachusetts

Thursday October 25
New Haven Coliseum,
New Haven, Connecticut

Wednesday October 24
Springfield Civic Center Arena,
Springfield, Massachusetts

Saturday September 22
Reconstruction play their last show today at the
Keystone, and just over three weeks later, on
October 7, a new iteration of the Jerry Garcia Band
debuts at the same venue, the lineup being,
besides Jerry and John Kahn, Ozzie Ahlers (keys)
and Johnny d'Fonseca (drums).

Wednesday October 17
Mother Teresa of India
is awarded the Nobel
Peace Prize for her years
of work on behalf of the
destitute in Calcutta.

OCTOBER '79

| 22 | 23 | | 24 ~ 30 | 1 ~ 13 | **14** | 15 | 16 | **17** | 18 ~ 22 | 23 | **24** | **25** | 26 | **27** | **28** | 29 | 30 | **31** |

Sunday October 14
An estimated 100,000 gays, lesbians, bisexuals, and
straight supporters march on Washington, D.C.,
celebrating gay pride and demanding equal rights
for homosexuals under the law.

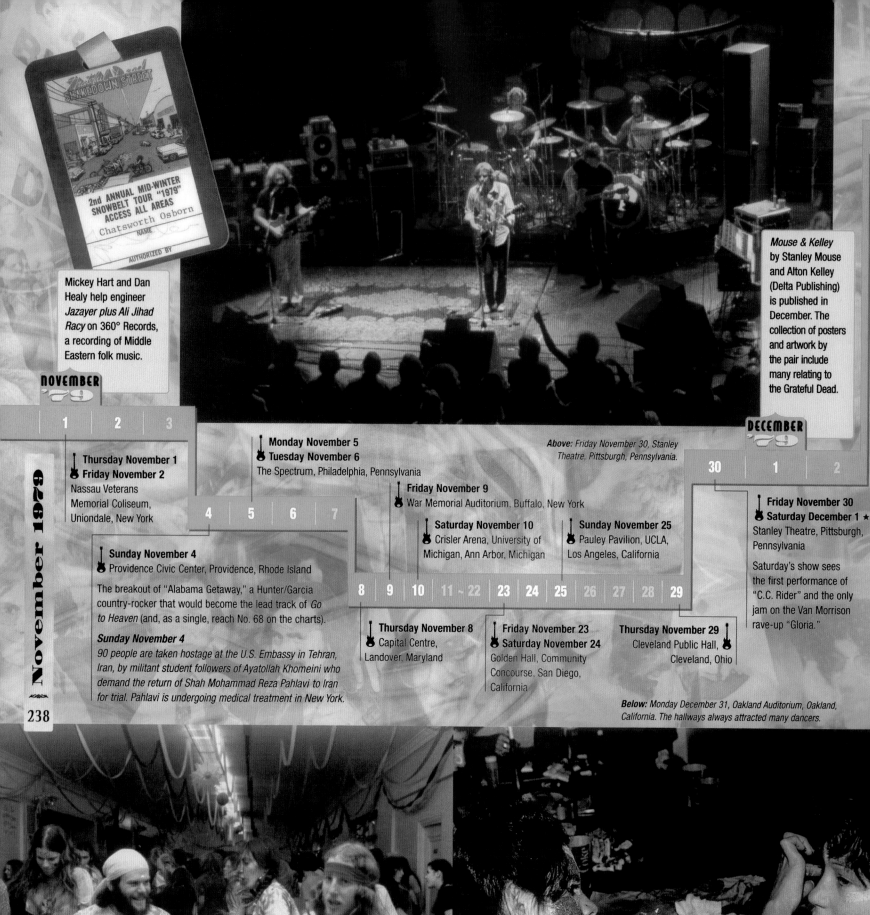

2nd ANNUAL MID-WINTER
SNOWBELT TOUR "1979"
ACCESS ALL AREAS
Chatsworth Osborn
NAME

AUTHORIZED BY

Mickey Hart and Dan Healy help engineer *Jazayer* plus *Ali Jihad Racy* on 360° Records, a recording of Middle Eastern folk music.

Mouse & Kelley by Stanley Mouse and Alton Kelley (Delta Publishing) is published in December. The collection of posters and artwork by the pair include many relating to the Grateful Dead.

NOVEMBER '79

1 2 3

November 1978

Thursday November 1
Friday November 2
Nassau Veterans Memorial Coliseum, Uniondale, New York

4 5 6 7

Sunday November 4
Providence Civic Center, Providence, Rhode Island

The breakout of "Alabama Getaway," a Hunter/Garcia country-rocker that would become the lead track of *Go to Heaven* (and, as a single, reach No. 68 on the charts).

Sunday November 4
90 people are taken hostage at the U.S. Embassy in Tehran, Iran, by militant student followers of Ayatollah Khomeini who demand the return of Shah Mohammad Reza Pahlavi to Iran for trial. Pahlavi is undergoing medical treatment in New York.

238

Monday November 5
Tuesday November 6
The Spectrum, Philadelphia, Pennsylvania

Friday November 9
War Memorial Auditorium, Buffalo, New York

Saturday November 10
Crisler Arena, University of Michigan, Ann Arbor, Michigan

Sunday November 25
Pauley Pavilion, UCLA, Los Angeles, California

8 9 10 11 ~ 22 23 24 25 26 27 28 29

Thursday November 8
Capital Centre, Landover, Maryland

Friday November 23
Saturday November 24
Golden Hall, Community Concourse, San Diego, California

Thursday November 29
Cleveland Public Hall, Cleveland, Ohio

Above: Friday November 30, Stanley Theatre, Pittsburgh, Pennsylvania.

DECEMBER '79

30 1 2

Friday November 30
Saturday December 1 ★
Stanley Theatre, Pittsburgh, Pennsylvania

Saturday's show sees the first performance of "C.C. Rider" and the only jam on the Van Morrison rave-up "Gloria."

Below: Monday December 31, Oakland Auditorium, Oakland, California. The hallways always attracted many dancers.

Monday December 3
🎸 **Tuesday December 4**
Wednesday December 5
Uptown Theatre, Chicago, Illinois

🎸 **Sunday December 9**
Kiel Auditorium,
St. Louis, Missouri

| 12 ~ 25 | 26 | 27 | 28 | 29 | 30 | 31 |

3 | **4** | **5** | **6** | **7** | **8** | **9** | **10** | **11**

Monday December 3
11 people are killed in a
crush of fans at Cincinnati's
Riverfront Coliseum, where
The Who are performing.

Friday December 7 🎸
Indiana Convention
Center, Indianapolis,
Indiana

Monday December 10
Tuesday December 11 🎸
Soldiers and Sailors Memorial Hall,
Kansas City, Kansas

🎸 **Wednesday December 26 ★**
🎸 **Thursday December 27**
Friday December 28
Sunday December 30
Monday December 31
Oakland Auditorium, Oakland, California

Richard Olson and the Flying Karamazov Brothers open the last
NYE show of the '70s. For the midnight countdown, Bill Graham
appears as a butterfly (a van serving as chrysalis.) John Cipollina
guests through most of the third set, and the Grateful Dead
encore with "Good Lovin'" as the band begins its third decade.

Below: Above the entrance of Oakland Auditorium, New Year's Eve.

New Years Eve '79

This year the Grateful Dead introduced what would become a tradition for the rest
of the band's career: multiple year-end shows at a big Bay Area venue—the Oakland
Auditorium/Kaiser, Oakland Coliseum, or San Francisco Civic Auditorium. This way,
'Heads unable to score coveted NYE tickets could at least see a show around the turn
of the year. The first show of the '79 NYE run (December 26) was a benefit for Wavy
Gravy's SEVA Foundation; and it included the first "Brokedown Palace" since
10/14/77 and the first "Uncle John's Band" since 10/06/77. The show
appears in its entirety on 1996's *Dick's Picks Volume 5*. The run was also
significant for the sound system used, a hybrid of the Meyer Sound Lab
gear introduced in August, combined with some other equipment, the
whole tweaked to the peak. Unfortunately, as Dennis McNally noted in
A Long Strange Trip, "Alas, [the
system] could not travel, and
they would spend the next
decade and more trying to
give it wheels."

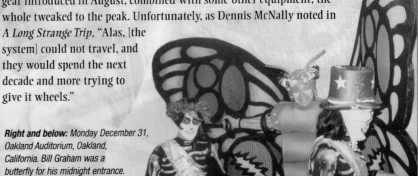

*Right and below: Monday December 31,
Oakland Auditorium, Oakland,
California. Bill Graham was a
butterfly for his midnight entrance.*

December 1979

239

GRATEFUL DEAD
TOUR 1979-1980
ACCESS ALL AREAS
Brent Mydland
NAME
AUTHORIZED BY

Opposite page and inset: New Year's Eve, 1979, Oakland Auditorium. Bill Graham metamorphoses into a butterfly in his now-traditional New Year's flyby.

Sunday January 13
🎸 Oakland County Coliseum Stadium, Oakland, California

Benefit show for Cambodian refugees, also featuring the Beach Boys, Jefferson Starship, and Carlos Santana running solo. John Cipollina and Carlos Santana join the band on "Not Fade Away" and "Sugar Magnolia." The evening's finale sees the Dead, Baez, and the Beach Boys perform "Amazing Grace" together. Broadcast on KSAN radio.

Wednesday February 13
In a stunning upset at the Winter Olympics in Lake Placid, New York, the U.S. hockey team defeats Finland 4–2 (having previously beaten the USSR) to take the Gold Medal.

Left and below: Sunday January 13, Oakland County Coliseum Stadium.

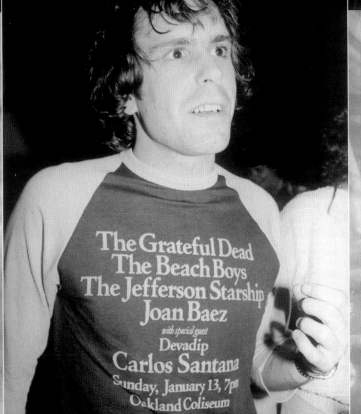

The Grateful Dead
The Beach Boys
The Jefferson Starship
Joan Baez
with special guest
Devadip
Carlos Santana
Sunday, January 13, 7pm
Oakland Coliseum

Dennis McNally

In the fall of 1980, Jerry Garcia ran into a Deadhead named Dennis McNally, who'd written a biography of Jack Kerouac called *Desolate Angel/Jack Kerouac, the Beat Generation, and America.* Kerouac was a critical element in Garcia's life, the hero he'd modeled a large part of his life on, and he'd liked the biography, so—being Garcia—he was extremely interested in talking about the book. A few months later, he sent Rock Scully and Alan Trist to McNally, and they said, "Jerry says, 'Why don't you do us?'" Since McNally had become a Deadhead about the same time he'd begun working on the Kerouac book, it made very good sense to him, and he started researching the Dead. In 1984, with the departure of Rock, the Dead needed a publicist and he needed a job, and was soon busier living with the Dead than researching, so he put the book on the back burner. Finally, in '97 he felt ready to resume work. The final result was published in 2002 by Broadway Books: *A Long Strange Trip/The Inside History of the Grateful Dead.*

Tuesday March 25
Jerry Garcia is voted 1980 Bay Area Musician of the Year in *BAM* magazine's readers' poll.

Above: Jerry, Bammy in hand, with Bill Graham, Tuesday March 25.

| 1 ~ 24 | 25 | 26 | 27 | 28 | 29 |

JACK O'ROSES
Robert Hunter

Dark Star Records 8001

A solo acoustic effort, including alternate and extended versions of "Friend of the Devil" and the entire "Terrapin Station" suite. The album's version of "Terrapin" is even more lyrically rich and allusive than the Grateful Dead version.

242

Above and right: The Dead on stage at the Capitol Theater, Passaic, joined by John Belushi (above left) on Sunday March 30.

CAPITOL THEATRE
126 MONROE STREET, PASSAIC, N.J.
JOHN SCHER
presents
GRATEFUL DEAD
$12.50
NO REFUNDS — NO EXCHANGES
SUNDAY EVENING, MARCH 30, 1980
EIGHT O'CLOCK

Below: March 30–April 1, Capitol Theater, Passaic, New Jersey.

| 30 | 31 | 1 | 2 | 3 | 4 | 5 |

Sunday March 30
Monday March 31
Tuesday April 1
Capitol Theater, Passaic, New Jersey

Sunday's opener sees the first live performance of "Far From Me" and John Belushi joins the band for vocals (and some acrobatics) on encore track "U.S. Blues." Monday's show witnesses the first live "Feel like a Stranger" and Tuesday begins with an April Fool's Day version of "Promised Land": Brent and Jerry are on the drums, Mickey on rhythm guitar and lead vocals, Phil on lead guitar, and Bill on bass.

Saturday April 5
The band perform "Alabama Getaway" and "Saint of Circumstance" on *Saturday Night Live*. It's the second, and last, *SNL* performance for the band.

Friday April 25
Eight American servicemen die in the Iranian desert when a transport plane and helicopter collide during a failed attempt to rescue the Americans being held hostage by student militants in Teheran.

Monday April 28
Boutwell Auditorium, Birmingham, Alabama

The band's Birmingham gig coincides with the release of *Go to Heaven*.

Tuesday April 29
Fox Theatre, Atlanta, Georgia

| 29 | 30 | |

GO TO HEAVEN
Grateful Dead

Released by Arista (AL5-8181) on April 28, 1980

Side One
1. **Alabama Getaway**
   (Garcia/Hunter)
2. **Far From Me**
   (Mydland)
3. **Althea**
   (Garcia/Hunter)
4. **Feel Like a Stranger**
   (Weir/Barlow)

Side Two
1. **Lost Sailor**
   (Weir/Barlow)
2. **Saint Of Circumstance**
   (Weir/Barlow)
3. **Antwerp's Placebo (The Plumber)**
   (Hart/Kreutzmann)
4. **Easy To Love You**
   (Mydland/Barlow)
5. **Don't Ease Me In**
   (Traditional)

Personnel
Jerry Garcia – acoustic guitar, vocals
Bob Weir – acoustic guitar, vocals
Phil Lesh – bass
Brent Mydland – keyboards, vocals
Bill Kreutzmann – percussion
Mickey Hart – percussion

Produced by Gary Lyons

April 1980

243

"Nobody was very happy with *Go to Heaven*. We had kind of a good time making it. It wasn't a total bust, but personally I don't believe I've written any real great songs lately with the exception of 'Althea'" JERRY GARCIA, *MELODY MAKER, APRIL 28, 1981*

ALTHOUGH *GO TO HEAVEN* actually charted (reaching a high of No. 23), neither the band nor the critics found it a particularly divine piece of work. *Rolling Stone* called it "uninspired fluff" and *The Village Voice* called it "an overdelicate, lukewarm dish of leftover boogie." Phil Lesh later called it "dogshit" and faulted Arista head Clive Davis for post-production tinkering to produce a smooth, commercial record.

Go To Heaven was the first album with Brent Mydland in the lineup, and "the new guy" contributed two tracks: his own soulful composition "Far From Me," and the soft-rockish "Easy to Love You," with lyrics by John Perry Barlow. Mydland—still struggling to settle into the band, both onstage and in the studio—caught flack from fans who felt his singing voice and synth

playing pushed *Heaven* into "commercial" territory.

For most fans, the Garcia/Hunter rocker "Alabama Getaway" was the album's standout cut, but the track with the longest pedigree was "Don't Ease Me In." A live staple since the Mother McCree days, "Ease" was a traditional Texas blues number first recorded by Henry Thomas in 1928.

The white disco suits the band wore on the record's cover were a source of much discussion among Deadheads when the album hit the stores. Some interpreted the cover as an ironic comment on the band's less than angelic reputation—or as a sly nod to *Heaven's* smoother and more radio-friendly sound. Others circulated a rumor that the Dead's next album would be titled *Go To Hell* and feature a cover photo of the boys garbed in demonic costumes.

Below: Phil Lesh and "the new guy," Brent Mydland, when he really *was the new guy.*

ROLLING THE THUNDER

May 1980 – June 1987

As show time of the Dead's April 22, 1979, concert at Spartan Stadium approached, Deadheads entered the hall and saw something mysterious onstage. Behind the two already elaborate conventional drum "trap" (short for contraption) sets there was a giant horizontal metal ring roughly six or seven feet in diameter and some six or seven feet in the air. It was festooned with a dozen or more drums mounted at eye level. The "Beast" had been set loose. Although the duo of drummer Bill Kreutzmann and percussionist Mickey Hart had performed drum breaks both individually and as a duo before, from here until the band stopped touring there would be a drum segment in the center of pretty much every second set. For the next decade and a half, Mickey and Billy would

The early '80s saw a flowering of the "Drums" segment of Dead shows, as Mickey Hart and Bill Kreutzmann expanded their rhythmic arsenal.

create what Deadheads called the "Rhythm Devils" segment of the show, starting each night with a double-traps duet, then moving to almost anything. Over the course of that time, this evolved to include tars (African frame drums that looked like tambourines without the jangles), talking drums (an African drum that when squeezed can produce varied pitches), and Inuit hoop drums, all of them instruments which humans have played for centuries. Eventually, they moved from the ancient to the most modern, using sampled electronic sounds—any sound at all, a dog barking, glass breaking—played on drum pads that acted as triggers for material stored in computers. If it had a beat, it was probably worked in at some point. It was an entirely new universe of rhythm every night.

The codification of the Dead's concert structure was pretty well complete by the time the Beast made its debut in 1979—an opening set of individual songs, a second set that generally would jam seamlessly from

"We're not in the entertainment business, we're in the transportation business. We move minds." MICKEY HART TO DENNIS MCNALLY

song to song, with a drum and then atonal "space" section in the middle. The drum duets that would follow wouldn't always be based on the Beast, but from then on there would be some sort of jungle of percussion behind the traps. Jungle was the operative word; the "Beast" had its origin in an extraordinary project that Mickey Hart had been invited to join, the making of an American film masterpiece, *Apocalypse Now*. Director Francis Ford Coppola's incredible fusion of the war in Vietnam and a retelling of Conrad's *Heart of Darkness* was the perfect Mickey Hart project—visionary, challenging, and full of massive risks. Promoter Bill Graham had a part in the film, and then late in 1978 invited Coppola to see the Dead at Winterland. Eleanor Coppola later wrote of sitting behind the drums and encountering the Dead's music as "amazing. It had physical impact." The show reminded her of a night when she'd attended a religious ceremony inside an Ifugao priest's home in the Philippines during filming. "The scale was different, but everyone being joined together by rhythms and images was the same."

Exactly! Coppola had found a drummer/shaman for his project. It was something Mickey had, quite literally, been born to do. His father Lenny had been a champion rudimental (marching band) drummer, but deserted the family when Mickey was quite young. At the age of ten, Mickey found a drum pad and set of sticks in a closet; it was his inheritance, and from that day he drummed, as he put it later, "Obsessively. Passionately. Painfully." After a spell in the Air Force because "that was where the great drummers were," he ended up in San Francisco. One night in 1967 at the Fillmore Auditorium he was introduced to Bill Kreutzmann, and they bonded quickly, roaming the streets raving and drumming on any available surface—cars, garbage cans, light posts— literally playing the city. A month later, Kreutzmann invited him to see a Grateful Dead show at the Straight Theater, in the Haight-Ashbury. Hart was fascinated with the Dead's power, especially the volume, and when he was invited to sit in for the second set, he seized the opportunity. He and Kreutzmann ran off and rounded up a drum set, and in a second set he recalled as hours long, they charged through the songs "Alligator" into

"Caution." Neither Hart nor the Dead were ever the same again. He felt as though he'd been "whipped into a jetstream," and afterwards he felt "so clean, as if I'd taken a long steamy shower."

The addition of a second drummer led the band into the unimaginable complexities of polyrhythm, the perfect example being the contrasting fours (of Kreutzmann) and threes (of Hart) in the classic Dead jam song "The Other One." As Mickey recalled it, "Because I was adding the triple while Billy was playing the shuffle, the backbeat to a sortofakinda shuffle, and I was on the tom tom, which suggested more of a primitive, primal... you had the backbeat, and you also had the rolling 1-2-3-4-5-6." It wasn't merely a new song, although that song was a great vehicle; it was a new way of playing, a new musical language. "Remember," said Hart, "we were doing a lot of acid then, so linear progression was distorted. So we would just drop the one, we would get lost, we would call it the pulse. We would go on the pulse, so all of a sudden the pulse would lead us to a place, and we were completely lost, we didn't know where the original one was, so instead of struggling with the one, we would establish a new one, and that was the telepathy that me and Billy had. And they would catch on to our telepathic one, and they would latch on. When the third person went to it, it became legitimate."

Around this time, Phil Lesh gave Mickey an album called *Drums of North and South India*, featuring Ravi Shankar's tabla partner, Ustad Alla Rakha. Soon Hart approached the master, and brought the unusual (to western ears) time signatures of Indian music to the Dead as well. This excursion into rhythmic complexity catalyzed an enormous evolution, and for the next two or more years the band were one of the great experimental ensembles ever. This was the psychedelic odyssey that Hart summed up perfectly in later years: "We're not in the entertainment business, we're in the transportation business. We move minds." But that experimental mode was incredibly demanding and in a peculiar way, limiting. After all, the band had other strengths. Eventually, the band turned to the songwriting skills of Hunter and Garcia—later others—and grew to encompass more mainstream music forms. Then in 1971 Mickey decided, as he put it, to atone for his father's sins and retire from the road.

After returning to the band in 1974, he tried a first version of a percussion orchestra in 1976 with a band called Diga. His partnership there with his friend and long-time collaborator Zakir Hussain (Ustad Alla Rakha's son) would be at the root of a broad vision of the world's musics that would stimulate and cross-pollinate not only the Dead's work but that of rock in general. It would be one of the primal steps in a road that would lead to American rockers seeking out Cuban or Pakistani or Balinese sounds; world music in the highest sense. Then Coppola's invitation gave him, joined by Lesh, Kreutzmann, and other drummers, a quantum-level shove forward. They began to create new instruments to make war sounds. There was the scritch, a set of vertically mounted metal and glass rods played by rubbing them with a gloved hand. There was a glass harp, wind chimes, devil chasers (shakers) made from bamboo grown at Hart's ranch, and the beam, a solid piece of aluminum 10 feet long strung with piano wire, which made the bomb sounds of napalm. Having constructed a jungle of instruments in front of video screens of the film, Hart led his patrol of intrepid percussionists up the river, playing to the movie; the experience seeped into the music of the Dead for years to come.

As Garcia put it with a chuckle, "Well, Mickey and Bill both have a sort of a weird streak of theatricality which they foist off on us every now and then, and the rest of us have to suffer through it occasionally." That streak brought an ever-evolving stream of ideas, sounds, and musicians into the orbit of the Dead, nurturing a diversity that might not be overtly audible on a day-to-day basis other than in the drum-duet portion of the show, but had a profound influence. Over the course of the '80s and '90s, great percussionists like Airto Moreira and Babatunde Olatunji would sit in with the band, leaving behind traces of a percussive tradition that Mickey would study exhaustively in his books *Drumming at the Edge of Magic* and *Planet Drum.*

Mickey had been going off on field recording adventures at least since he'd gone to his and the band's friend Hamza El-Din's home village in the Sudan after the Dead's Egypt shows in 1978. In 1985, he and Dan Healy made an easier jaunt, going to Amherst, Massachusetts, on a day off during a tour to record the Gyuto Monks of Tibet. The Monks could each sing a chord (three notes, one throat—

can't be done, they can do it), and massed together and amplified by a GD-level sound system, it sounds like the birth of creation. In effect, various members of Grateful Dead Productions adopted the Monks, and Mickey became their U.S. producer and sometime promoter, a relationship that enriched the Dead in ways they'd reflect on for years to come. As Kreutzmann remarked after the monks joined the Dead and "sat in" one night, "The monks are so cool, if they saw a nuclear apocalypse, they might just put on their sunglasses."

For most Americans, the music of the early '80s was best captured by MTV. The Dead, obviously, were heading in a different direction, one Mickey began to articulate as the decade passed in a book he'd publish in 1991, *Planet Drum*. It began, "In the beginning was noise. And noise begat rhythm. And rhythm begat everything else. This is the kind of cosmology a drummer can live with." After tracing some of the uses of drums—for war, for agriculture and fertility, for social rituals like coming-of-age—he arrived at shamanism, at the use of rhythm and dance to alter states of consciousness. In other words, his studies had taken him to exactly what the Dead and Deadheads had been doing for 25 years. Of his own contribution, he said, "People play music for different reasons. I go for the spirit side of things; not necessarily to be perfect. What I'm after is changing consciousness."

In 1986, Mickey and the Dead got an exceptional intellectual validation for what they already knew musically. One of Bob Weir's most interesting neighbors was the head of the Bay Area Jungian Institute, and one night Bob's dinner guest—in addition to Garcia and Hart—was the eminent folklorist, mythologist, and all-around wise elder of the human race, Joseph Campbell. Jerry had been fascinated by Campbell's work since reading *A Skeleton Key to Finnegans Wake* as a young man at Kepler's Bookstore while hanging out with Robert Hunter. Mickey was never all that interested in fiction, so his avenue to Campbell had been through the book *The Way of the Animal Powers*. For all of them, it was one of the encounters of a lifetime, but it got even more interesting when the Dead invited Campbell to a concert. Campbell was a politically conservative scholar who had almost no contact with popular culture—he'd seen his first movie in many years only because George Lucas, the maker of *Star Wars*, had made it as an act of homage. Now Campbell went to a Dead concert and saw that what he'd been saying for years, that the great themes of antiquity such as, for instance, the

The Dead in 1977, one of several different peak years for the group.

"People play music for different reasons. I go for the spirit side of things; not necessarily to be perfect. What I'm after is changing consciousness."

MICKEY HART, FROM *DRUMMING AT THE EDGE OF MAGIC*, 1990

quest for transcendence in the Dionysian rites, endured. Straight and sober, he took a look at the Deadheads in front of the stage and got off like a hippie on 500 mics of the best. "I just didn't know anything like that existed," he told an associate. "This was a real Dionysian Festival." Later, Campbell, Garcia, and Hart would do a show together, mixing music and talk. Campbell would talk about his Dead concert experience, where Deadheads were "25,000 people tied at the heart," and the "antidote for the atom bomb." Over the next year, until Campbell's death in the fall of 1987, he and Hart would share research, as Mickey dug into percussion/shaman mythology—the original shamans of Siberia ride a drum—for *Planet Drum*.

Insatiably curious about the roots of percussion, Hart never stopped digging up ideas and bringing them in to the Dead for consideration. Some of his most interesting work went beyond music into noise. One of his favorite writers, the futurist Luigi Russolo, a prophet of noise, made instruments that reflected a new modern industrial world, which he described in *Planet Drum* as "gurglings of water, air and gas inside metallic pipes, the rumblings and rattlings of engines beating with obvious animal spirits, the rising and falling of pistons." Hart had been doing that sort of thing throughout his career. All the way back to when the Dead played "St. Stephen," there would be a Hartian (pronounced as in Martian) blast of percussion just before the

line "Fortune come a crawling" which was actually produced by a blank shotgun shell in a toy cannon. At times, one of the Dead's roadies would fire up a hotplate and a frying pan full of bacon, then put a microphone close by to get the sound of the sizzle. Once, at Mickey's urging, the sound crew miked up a motorcycle, and one of the roadies joined in a post-drums jam that included roaring throttle—into "Not Fade Away." Some of the "instruments" that Mickey used over the years included children's wind-up toys, whistles, and kazoos. The sound of gargling water might come mysteriously sliding into a drum duet. The limits of what was music were pushed back so that, quite literally, anything could happen.

Mickey was a driven man, and one story captures that drive. The first half of the '80s saw the Dead's audience grow enormously. As Garcia said, following the Dead seemed to be quite possibly the last American adventure. But the Dead even turned up in the very center of the American mainstream culture, television. In 1985 CBS had revived the Rod Serling series *Twilight Zone*, and the Deadhead producer for the show invited the Dead to do the theme music, an updating of the classic "neenerneenerneener" sound signature of the 1950s version. Eventually, they even began to record other elements of the show's soundtrack.

About this time, Mickey had to undergo back surgery, and demanded that the synthesizer equipment he needed to produce soundscape material be put in his hospital room. Aghast, his roadie Ram Rod vetoed the idea, but Mickey pleaded. "When I wake up, I want to go to work." Ram Rod gave in—it's hard to out-argue Mickey Hart—and when he awoke, the medication, he decided, went perfectly with the infinite reverb of his fancy new equipment. "I did the first four episodes in the hospital—it was the best I ever did." A few days later, a CBS executive came to see how things were coming along at the Dead studio, Front Street. Mickey couldn't stay away. He hired an ambulance to bring him to the studio. The driver and his assistant brought him into the control room on a stretcher, still in his hospital bathrobe and slippers. He got up, stood by the control board, and said, "OK, let's roll tape." The stunned look on the executive's face was one of the special satisfactions of Hart's life. When Mickey Hart decides the show must go on, it goes on.

Sunday May 4
🎸 Baltimore Civic Center, Baltimore, Maryland

Tuesday May 6
🎸 Recreation Hall, Penn State University, State College, Pennsylvania

Right: Tuesday May 6, Recreation Hall, Penn State University, University Park, Pennsylvania.

| 1 | 2 | 3 | 4 | 5 | 6 | 7 |

Wednesday May 7
🎸 Barton Hall, Cornell University, Ithaca, New York

Grateful Dead play "Far Above Cayuga's Waters," Cornell's alma mater, while tuning up for "Tennessee Jed." Bill Kreutzmann turns 34.

Friday May 2
🎸 Hampton Coliseum, Hampton, Virginia

Thursday May 1
🎸 Greensboro Coliseum, Greensboro, North Carolina

★ **Thursday May 8**
🎸 Glens Falls Civic Center, Glens Falls, New York

Sunday May 11
🎸 Cumberland County Civic Center, Portland, Maine

| 8 | 9 | 10 | 11 |

Saturday May 10
Hartford Civic Center, 🎸 Hartford, Connecticut

Monday May 12
🎸 Boston Garden, Boston, Massachusetts

| 12 | 13 | 14 | 15 | 16 |

Thursday May 29
Des Moines Civic Center, 🎸 Des Moines, Iowa

Friday May 30
🎸 Milwaukee Auditorium, Milwaukee, Wisconsin

Wednesday May 14
Thursday May 15 🎸
Friday May 16
Nassau Veterans Memorial Coliseum, Uniondale, New York

| 17 | 18 | 19 | 20 ~ 28 | 29 | 30 | 31 |

Monday May 19
A race riot in Miami's Liberty City neighborhood claims 18 lives and results in more than $100 million in damage.

Saturday May 31
Metropolitan Sports Center, 🎸 Bloomington, Minnesota

| 1 | 2 | 3 | 4 | 5 | 6 |

May 1980

250

Left and below: Deadheads outside of Nassau Veterans Memorial Coliseum, Uniondale, New York, Wednesday May 14.

Thursday June 5
🎸 Compton Terrace Amphitheatre, Chandler, Arizona

Warren Zevon *(below)* opens.

NORTHERN STAGE CO. PRESENTS

THE GRATEFUL DEAD
ALASKA 1980
JUNE 19, 20, 21, 7:30
West High Auditorium

TICKETS ON SALE: TEAM ELECTRONICS IN ANCHORAGE
AND FAIRBANKS, AND AT CARR'S MALL IN WASILLA.
FOR MORE INFORMATION CALL 276-4426 EXT. 28

Above: Friday June 20, West High Auditorium, Anchorage, Alaska. When the show ends late at night, it is still light outside.

251

Saturday June 14
Spokane Coliseum, Spokane, Washington

Friday June 20
Bob Dylan's new album Saved *reflects the artist's conversion to "born again" Christianity.*

Friday June 13
Seattle Center Arena, Seattle, Washington

| 13 | 14 | 15 | 16 | 17 | 18 | 19 | 20 | 21 |

Thursday June 12
Portland Memorial Coliseum, Portland, Oregon

| 7 | 8 | 9 | 10 | 11 | 12 |

Blowing the Roof Off

The Mount St. Helens volcano in Washington State erupted at 9:18 p.m., when the band were in the middle of "Fire On The Mountain." Bill Kreutzmann: "It was like I didn't know it was gonna happen... but I knew it was gonna happen." Although this synchronicity is much beloved by Deadheads, the main eruption had in fact taken place on May 18; the June 12 eruption was a sort of "aftershock."

Saturday June 7
Sunday June 8
Folsom Field, University of Colorado, Boulder, Colorado

Although the Boulder shows are billed as a celebration of GD's "official" 15th anniversary, the band apparently forget about the date's significance on the first night. They make it up by kicking off the June 8 show with "Uncle John's Band/ Playing in the Band." Warren Zevon is also on the bill both nights.

Thursday June 19
Friday June 20
Saturday June 21
West High Auditorium, Anchorage, Alaska

The band's only Alaska concerts are performed in a high school auditorium. Afterward, some of the band relaxed in Hawaii, while Mickey Hart took Justin Kreutzmann, Rudson Shurtliff, and his own son Creek on some arctic adventures via bush plane. Mickey also acquired a set of Inuit hoop drums.

Sunday June 30
Featuring an eclectic mix of styles, Bobby and the Midnites play their first proper date, at the Golden Bear in Huntington Beach, California. The genesis of the band came after a one-off performance two years earlier, when Bob Weir put together a pickup group— the "Ibanez All-Star Band"—at the behest of Ibanez Guitar executive Jeff Hasselberger for the National Association of Music Merchants Convention. The impromptu ensemble— including Billy Cobham on drums, Bobby Cochran on guitar, and Tim Bogert on bass— enjoyed performing for the "suits" so much that it was always inevitable that they would begin playing scheduled dates.

| 22 | 23 | 24 | 25 | 26 | 27 | 28 | 29 | 30 |

Saturday June 29
Pauley Pavilion, University of California, Los Angeles, California

Lee Oskar, harmonica virtuoso known for his work with Eric Burdon's War, joins during the second set on "Drums," "The Other One," "Black Peter," and "Sugar Magnolia."

Right: Brent Mydland, Saturday August 16, Mississippi River Festival, Edwardsville, Illinois.

Above and right: *Saturday August 16, Mississippi River Festival, Edwardsville, Illinois. Though billed as a "Festival," the Dead were the only act on the bill.*

Mississippi River Festival, Edwardsville, Illinois

1 2 3 4 5 6 7 8 9 10 11 12 13 14 15 **16**

252

Wednesday July 23
Just four days after his 32nd birthday, Keith Godchaux is killed in a car accident near his home in Marin County, California.

10 ~ 20 | 21 | 22 | **23** | 24 ~ 31

JULY '80

1 2 3 4 5 6 7 8 9

Tuesday July 1
San Diego International Sports Arena, San Diego, California

After the show, Mickey Hart and Bob Weir object to the local law's rough handling of a suspected drug dealer—rather too forcefully, in the opinion of several members of the San Diego Police Department. Mickey and Bob are booked on riot and assault charges; Weir and Danny Rifkin (who tried to stop the fracas) get slapped with additional charges of "lynching," which in this context means "attempting to remove a prisoner from custody." The charges against the three are later dropped.

Keith Godchaux 1948 – 1980

After Keith and Donna Godchaux left the high-pressure world of the Grateful Dead in the winter of 1979, they dropped out of music for six months and vacationed on a lake in Donna's home town of Muscle Shoals, Alabama, in a desperate attempt to regain their health and sanity. When they returned to California, they joined an already existing Marin County group called The Ghosts, which shortly evolved into the Heart of Gold Band, featuring a then-unknown young guitarist named Steve Kimock. The band had been together only a short time when, on July 21, 1980, the car in which Keith was riding with his friend Courtney Pollock (known in Grateful Dead circles for his exceptional tie-dyes) smashed into the back of a flatbed truck parked alongside a Marin County road. Keith, who was just 32, suffered grave head injuries and died two days later; Pollock was also seriously injured, but recovered. The Heart of Gold Band continued to perform for a while after Keith's passing, but eventually broke up. Kimock and drummer Greg Anton went on to form Zero. Donna turned to Christianity for solace and eventually married a Christian musician, David MacKay.

No Mystery Here

Bill Graham Productions takes out a full-page ad in the August 31 San Francisco *Chronicle* announcing a run of shows at the Warfield Theatre in late September and early October. The ad—which is headlined: "They're not the best at what they do, they're the only ones who do what they do"—doesn't mention the name of the group scheduled to perform. However, the accompanying graphic—male and female skeletons, with a garland of roses—leaves little doubt.

Bill Graham Presents in San Francisco
at the

Warfield Theatre

Sept. 25, 26, 27, 29, 30
Oct. 2, 3, 4, 6, 7, 9, 10
all shows at 8 PM

"They're not the best at what they do, they're the only ones that do what they do."

Mail Order Only

Limit six (6) tickets per customer · No refunds or exchanges
Include self-addressed stamped envelope · $1.00 handling charge for each ticket
1st date preference _____ 2nd date preference _____
If above two dates sold out, send best available date. yes ____ no ____

Cashier Checks & Money Orders only
payable to: BASS
Post Office Box 57
Oakland, Ca. 94607

No tape recorders please

Tickets $12.50 & $10.00
All Seats Reserved

Sunday August 17
Kansas City Municipal Auditorium
Arena, Kansas City, Missouri

Tuesday August 19
Wednesday August 20
Thursday August 21
Uptown Theatre,
Chicago, Illinois

Tuesday's show sees the Dead's first performance of "Little Red Rooster" since the Warlocks era.

Saturday August 23
Alpine Valley Music Theatre,
East Troy, Wisconsin

Sunday August 24
Grand Center,
Grand Rapids, Michigan

Tuesday August 26
Cleveland Public Hall,
Cleveland, Ohio

Wednesday August 27
Pine Knob Music Theatre,
Clarkston, Michigan

Friday August 29
Saturday August 30
The Spectrum, Philadelphia, Pennsylvania

Sunday August 31
Capital Centre,
Landover, Maryland

17 18 19 20 21   22 23 24 25 26 27 28 29 30 31

Above: Wednesday August 20, Uptown Theatre, Chicago, Illinois.
Left: "Might as well travel the elegant way." Or not. Deadheads sleep it off after a long night.

Saturday September 6 ★
🎸 Maine State Fairgrounds, Lewiston, Maine

Opening acts include guitarist Roy Buchanan (once billed by his record company as "the best unknown guitarist in the world"), plus Ernie and Earl Cate performing with Levon Helm. In 1983 the Cate Brothers joined Helm, Rick Danko, Garth Hudson, and Richard Manuel to form the second—Robbie Robertson-less—incarnation of The Band.

Above and below: Saturday September 6, Maine State Fairgrounds, Lewiston, Maine.

The Warfield/Radio City Shows

The Dead's real 15th anniversary celebration in 1980 spanned two months, two coasts, and eventually spawned two albums, *Reckoning* and *Dead Set (see pages 261 and 265).* The bicoastal settings for the shows were very different—San Francisco's Warfield Theatre was an intimate house of 2,400 seats, while New York City's Radio City Music Hall was, well, Radio City—but the Dead's performances in both produced some of the most treasured moments of the band's early '80s period.

For both the Warfield and Radio City shows, the band returned to a concert format similar to the "Evening with the Grateful Dead" shows a decade before—minus, this time, the opening set from the New Riders of the Purple Sage. Each performance began with an acoustic set followed by two electric sets. The Dead hadn't done a lot of acoustic work in the 1970s, and they didn't have much time to rehearse before the Warfield run began, so by some accounts the first acoustic sets were somewhat shaky—not that anyone minded.

Demand for both shows was huge. The Warfield run was extended by three nights, and when tickets went on sale for the Radio City shows, the line at the box office practically filled Rockefeller Center—a publicity bonanza for the band. Many media types who'd been counting the Grateful Dead out for years were surprised.

Thursday September 4 🎸
Providence Civic Center, Providence, Rhode Island

First wordless jam around "Supplication," the Weir/Barlow tune introduced in the mid-1970s. In this outing, the jam bridges "Ramble On Rose" and "Estimated Prophet."

Wednesday September 3 🎸
Springfield Civic Center Arena, Springfield, Massachusetts

SEPTEMBER '80

| 1 | 2 | 3 | 4 | 5 |

Tuesday September 2 ★
🎸 Community War Memorial, Rochester, New York

Above: The Dead play 15 dates at the Warfield Theatre in September.

Thursday September 25
🎸 **Friday September 26**
Saturday September 27
Warfield Theatre, San Francisco, California

| 24 | 25 | 26 | 27 | 28 | 29 | 30 |

Monday September 29
🎸 **Tuesday September 30**
Warfield Theatre, San Francisco, California

Monday's show sees the band's first performance of "Heaven Help The Fool," from Bob Weir's 1978 solo album of the same name.

Monday October 6 🎸
Tuesday October 7
Warfield Theatre, San Francisco, California

OCTOBER '80

| 1 | 2 | 3 | 4 | 5 | 6 | 7 | 8 |

Thursday October 2
🎸 **Friday October 3**
Saturday October 4
Warfield Theatre, San Francisco, California

Saturday night and The Dead play "Deep Elem Blues" for the first time in 10 years. Performances of "Deal" and "Feel Like a Stranger" at the same show appear on *Dead Set.*

The final Warfield show saw one of Bill Graham's most inspired acts of showmanship. Returning onstage for the encore, the boys found a table set with glasses and a bottle of champagne—then the house lights came up to reveal the entire audience making a champagne toast to the band.

The otherwise brilliant Radio City run was marred by a bizarre dispute between the band and Radio City's management. The latter objected to promotional posters showing the inevitable skeletons flanking the venerable venue. Evidently not well versed in Grateful Dead iconography, the Radio City execs interpreted the posters as a coded message that the band thought that Radio City's days were numbered, and they slapped the band with a million-dollar lawsuit. The misunderstanding was quickly cleared up.

Bassist bedeviled

The last Radio City night was Halloween, and appropriately enough, technical gremlins kept Phil out of the mix until "It Must Have been the Roses," five songs into the first set.

The show's hosts, Al Franken and Tom Davis, *Saturday Night Live* writers and performers (and Dead fans), conducted a wickedly funny ongoing parody of Jerry Lewis's annual telethon. They targeted his over-the-top appeals on behalf of needy children, known as "Jerry's Kid's." But the donations in this case were a hit of acid and a ticket to the next GD gig. In addition to generating albums the Halloween Radio City was broadcast on closed-circuit TV and simulcast on FM stations. The show was also released on video, *Dead Ahead*, in 1995.

The significance of the Grateful Dead's pioneering return to nonelectric performance wouldn't be fully appreciated until 1989, when MTV's *Unplugged* series began turning on a new generation of rock fans to the delights of acoustic music.

"Radio City, a beautiful and classy venue, brought awe and respect from the 6,000 or so Deadheads who piled in each night. It was also a dreamlike run—every gig had something we dreamed of since we first started lacing up our Grateful Dead sneakers: an acoustic set."
ALAN SHECKTER, MUSIC PHOTOJOURNALIST, 2003

Left: Tour poster for the Dead's October concerts at New York's Radio City Music Hall.

Below: The Dead play eight dates in late October at Radio City Music Hall, New York.

🎸 **Thursday October 9**
🎸 **Friday October 10**
Warfield Theatre, San Francisco, California

Friday's version of "Jack a Roe" appears on *Dead Set*.

| 9 | 10 | 11 | 12 | 13 | 14 | 15 | 16 | 17 |

🎸 **Saturday October 11**
🎸 **Monday October 13**
Tuesday October 14
Warfield Theatre, San Francisco, California

Three extra shows are added to the Warfield run, and John Cipollina joins the band on Saturday night to play "Not Fade Away">"Wharf Rat">"Goin' Down the Road"; the same night's performances of "Deep Elem Blues" and "Loser" turn up on *Reckoning*.

| 18 | 19 | 20 | 21 | 22 | 23 | 24 |

🎸 **Saturday October 18**
🎸 **Sunday October 19**
Saenger Theater, New Orleans, Louisiana

Between the Warfield and Radio City runs, the band take the acoustic/electric/electric format to the Crescent City *(below)* for two nights.

| 25 | 26 | 27 |

🎸 **Saturday October 25**
🎸 **Sunday October 26**
Monday October 27
Radio City Music Hall, New York, New York

Saturday's performance of "Franklin's Tower" appears on *Dead Set*.

🎸 **Wednesday October 22**
🎸 **Thursday October 23**
Radio City Music Hall, New York, New York

| 28 | 29 | 30 | 31 |

🎸 **Wednesday October 29**
🎸 **Thursday October 30**
Radio City Music Hall, New York, New York

Drummer Billy Cobham—a jazz and fusion legend who'd performed with, among others, Horace Silver and Miles Davis—joins Bill and Mickey for the Thursday "Drums."

★ **Friday October 31**
Radio City Music Hall, New York, New York

The night's "Drums"/"Fire on the Mountain" make it onto *Dead Set*.

Wednesday November 26
Sportatorium, Pembroke Pines, Florida

A satisfyingly surprising encore—the Rolling Stones' "Satisfaction," which the boys had performed as the Warlocks but never before under the GD brand.

26 27 28

Friday November 28
Lakeland Civic Center Arena, Lakeland, Florida

1 2 3 4 5 – 25

Tuesday November 4
Republican Ronald Reagan (above) defeats incumbent Democrat Jimmy Carter to become the 40th President of the United States.

Saturday November 29
Alligator Alley Gym, University of Florida, Gainesville, Florida

29 30

★ **Sunday November 30**
Fox Theatre, Atlanta, Georgia

The return of the electric version of the "Bird Song" jam, last performed on September 15, 1973.

November 1980

256

John Lennon 1940 – 1980

If you are of a certain age, you probably remember where you were when you heard the shocking news that John Lennon had been murdered—the first rock 'n' roll assassination. On the night of December 8, 1980, Lennon and Yoko Ono were returning to their apartment overlooking New York's Central Park after a recording session, when an unbalanced and obsessed fan, Mark David Chapman, gunned Lennon down. Not surprisingly, the tragedy touched off a huge wave of memorial events and celebrations of Lennon's life around the world. And at the first Grateful Dead show after the killing, in San Bernardino, California, on December 12, the band played a particularly poignant version of "He's Gone." The Dead attracted more than their own share of crazies through the years and endured a number of death threats, particularly Garcia. In fact, on the Dead's final tour in 1995, a threat against Garcia at one show led promoters to install metal detectors and bring in a large security force to foil a potential gunman.

Right: A man among the crowd at Central Park, New York, gathered to mourn the death of John Lennon.

Monday December 8
A mentally unhinged fan guns down John Lennon in New York City.

1 2 3 4 5 6 7 8

Saturday December 6
Mill Valley Recreation Center, Mill Valley, California

An all-acoustic set including the Delta Blues chestnut "On the Road Again."

9 10 11 12

Friday December 12
Swing Auditorium, San Bernardino, California

John Meyer

The Grateful Dead's ongoing quest for sonic perfection brought them into contact with John Meyer in 1980. A veteran of Harry McCune Sound Service, a well-known Bay Area sound outfit, Meyer spent the mid-'70s studying at the Institute for Advanced Musical Studies in Montreux, Switzerland, before returning to the U.S. to found Meyer Sound Labs in 1979. The following year Meyer introduced the Ultra Monitor, which allowed musicians to hear themselves onstage without the distortion and limited dynamic range of earlier monitors. Meyer's gear was put to good use during the live recordings at the Warfield and Radio City, and MSL equipment became an integral part of the band's setup.

"We were always glad when the Dead arrived at our door to pick up new gear."
JOHN MEYER, *2002*

Saturday December 13 ★
Sunday December 14
Long Beach Arena, Long Beach, California

The Long Beach shows mark the first outing with the Grateful Dead for the great Brazilian percussionist Airto Moreira and his wife, singer Flora Purim—the couple play on "Drumz" both nights. The second show also sees Kingfish kingpin Matt Kelly join in on the Chuck Berry rave-up "Around and Around."

13 14 15 16 17

| 26 | 27 | 28 | 29 |

🎸 **Friday December 26**
🎸 **Saturday December 27**
Sunday December 28
Tuesday December 30
Wednesday December 31
Oakland Auditorium, Oakland, California

| 30 | 31 |

The runup to New Year's Eve features a benefit for the Berkeley-based Seva Foundation on December 26—"an international organization working to alleviate suffering and generate hope through compassionate action."

Bill Graham kicks off the New Year's Eve festivities by riding a giant skull onto the stage. Returning to the acoustic/electric/electric set format for the night, the band are joined by Matt Kelly ("Little Red Rooster") and John Cipollina ("Fire on the Mountain," "Wharf Rat," and "Around and Around") in a second electric set that ends with the first "Sunshine Daydream" since the 1979/80 New Year's Eve show. The band roll out "Satisfaction" again as an encore.

Above, above middle, and top: Wednesday December 31, Oakland Auditorium, Oakland, California. In this park lay the humble beginnings of what would become the Deadhead bazaar.

| 18 | 19 | 20 | 21 | 22 | 23 | 24 | 25 |

Right: Friday December 26, Oakland Auditorium, Oakland, California.

"On New Year's Eve it was important for me to capture Bill Graham's midnight entrance because that was always a lot of what was great about that night. Bill and his crew always put a lot of energy into the midnight entrance. Pretty much every year after '79–'80 I shot New Year's from the balcony on the sides because it was a better angle to capture the whole crazy scene. Over the years the entrances became more elaborate, and visually exciting. This is what really set Bay Area Dead shows apart from what happened elsewhere. The Bill Graham Presents touch." JAY BLAKESBERG, PHOTOGRAPHER, 2003

All pictures: *Wednesday December 31, Oakland Auditorium, Oakland, California. New Year's Eve always found the band playing on a stage full of balloons.*

JANUARY '81

1	2	3	4	5 ~ 15

Thursday January 1
The New Year's Eve party continues through until the early hours of 1981.

Tuesday January 20
Ronald Reagan takes the oath of office as the nation's 40th president.

16	17	18	19	20	21	22	23	24	25	26	27	28	29	30	31

Thursday February 26
Friday February 27
Saturday February 28
Uptown Theatre,
Chicago, Illinois

FEBRUARY '81

1 ~ 25	26	27	28

Reasonable Jerry: The Paul Morley Interview

Sid Vicious may have been dead but punks still stalked the gray streets of London when the Grateful Dead arrived in March for a four-night run at the Rainbow Theatre. Groups like the Sex Pistols and their slicker, synth-powered successors like Joy Division challenged everything the Grateful Dead stood for in terms of musicianship and general attitude toward life—a fact that was very much on the mind of Paul Morley, who interviewed Jerry for the *New Musical Express*.

Famous for his acerbic take-no-prisoners journalism, Morley began baiting Jerry immediately, accusing the Grateful Dead of perpetuating "bland, blanketing myths." Jerry drew Morley's fangs with an amiable, utterly honest rap on the band ("I would be afraid if everybody in the world liked us. I don't want to be responsible for leading the march to wherever. Fuck that.") and on his own insecurities ("I don't think of myself as an adult… I feel like someone who is constantly on the verge of losing it, or blowing it"). As Morley put it, "my heated irrationality [bumped] into Garcia's sheer reasonableness."

Morley later co-founded the proto-techno group The Art of Noise and reportedly masterminded Frankie Goes to Hollywood.

Above: Thursday March 6, Stanley Theatre, Pittsburgh, Pennsylvania.

As winter turns to spring the band head overseas for a European mini-tour—a four-night run at the Rainbow Theatre in London, England, followed by a televised one-night-stand at the Grugehalle, Essen, West Germany. Apart from the Pyramids concerts and a November 2, 1977, show in Toronto, these engagements mark the band's first performances outside the U.S. since 1974.

Saturday March 21
Today show airs; Gene Shalit interviews Jerry Garcia.

Thursday March 5
Friday March 6
Stanley Theatre, Pittsburgh, Pennsylvania

Saturday March 7
Cole Field House, University of Maryland, College Park, Maryland

The band perform a 12-minute jam following "Saint of Circumstance."

| 5 | 6 | 7 | 8 | 9 | 10 | 11 | 12 |

Thursday March 12
Boston Garden, Boston, Massachusetts

Monday March 9
Tuesday March 10 ★
Madison Square Garden, New York, New York

Friday March 13
Utica Memorial Auditorium, Utica, New York

| 13 | 14 | 15 | 16 |

| 19 | 20 | 21 | 22 | 23 | 24 |

Friday March 20
Saturday March 21 ★
Monday March 23
Tuesday March 24
Rainbow Theatre, London, England

On the final night of the Rainbow Theatre run, The Flying Karamazov Brothers—a four-man music/comedy/juggling troupe—perform during "Drums."

Saturday March 14
Hartford Civic Center, Hartford, Connecticut

On the same day as the Hartford show, the band are scheduled to appear on a *Saturday Night Live* episode hosted by friends Al Franken and Tom Davis. The show never airs due to a writer's strike, depriving Deadheads of a couple of live tunes and depriving a national TV audience of what would have been some hilarious (intentionally or not) moments.

Saturday March 28
Grugahalle, Essen, West Germany

The Grateful Dead share the bill with The Who in a concert for the German TV show *Rockpalast* that is broadcast Europe-wide. Pete Townshend jams with the boys through "Not Fade Away">"Wharf Rat">"Around and Around">"Good Lovin'" and The Flying Karamazov Brothers again enliven "Drums" in their unique comic-kinetic style.

| 25 | 26 | 27 | 28 | 29 | 30 | 31 |

Monday March 2
Tuesday March 3
Cleveland Music Hall, Cleveland, Ohio

Right: March 9–10, Madison Square Garden, New York, New York.

Monday March 30
President Reagan is seriously wounded in an assassination attempt outside the Washington, D.C., Hilton Hotel.

GRATEFUL DEAD

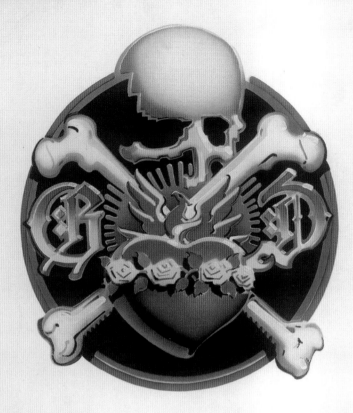

R E C K O N I N G

RECKONING
Grateful Dead
Released by Arista (A2l-8604) on April 1, 1981

Side One
1. Dire Wolf
   (Garcia/Hunter)
2. The Race Is On
   (Rollins)
3. Oh Babe It Ain't No Lie
   (Cotton)
4. It Must Have Been the Roses
   (Garcia/Hunter)

Side Two
1. Dark Hollow
   (Browning)
2. China Doll
   (Garcia/Hunter)
3. Been All Around This World
   (Traditional arr. Grateful Dead)
4. Monkey And The Engineer
   (Fuller)
5. Jack-A-Roe
   (Traditional arr. Grateful Dead)

Side Three
1. Deep Elem Blues
   (Traditional arr. Grateful Dead)
2. Cassidy
   (Weir/Barlow)
3. To Lay Me Down
   (Garcia/Hunter)

Side Four
1. Rosalie McFall
   (Monroe)
2. On The Road Again
   (Traditional arr. Grateful Dead)
3. Bird Song
   (Garcia/Hunter)
4. Ripple
   (Garcia/Hunter)

Personnel
Jerry Garcia – acoustic guitar, vocals
Bob Weir – acoustic guitar, vocals
Phil Lesh – bass
Brent Mydland – keyboards, vocals
Bill Kreutzmann – percussion
Mickey Hart – percussion

Produced by Dan Healy, Betty Cantor-Jackson, and Jerry Garcia

"All of that acoustic stuff that we did... was the result of about three afternoons of rehearsal."

JERRY GARCIA, ON *RECKONING*, APRIL 1981

THE FRUIT OF THE ACOUSTIC SETS from the Grateful Dead's Fall 1980 Warfield Theatre and Radio City Music Hall shows, *Reckoning* (or *Dead Reckoning*, as it's sometimes called) was well received by Deadheads who, in David Shenk's words, felt that it represented "[The band] at its risky best, playing in an environment of complete exposure, total vulnerability." With its mix of blues, folk, and bluegrass covers and new arrangements of GD originals, *Reckoning* was also a record ahead of its time, pointing not only to the "unplugged"

acoustic revival of the 1990s, but also to the renewed interest in "roots music" at the turn of the 21st century. In 1981, however, *Reckoning* was panned by some critics, who saw the release of yet another double live album as proof that the band had run out of gas creatively and/or couldn't get it together in the studio: *Rolling Stone*'s review described *Reckoning* as "[m]ore a document of a once-memorable progressive group grown somewhat sluggish over the years than a compelling aural artifact." Rick Griffin did the cover artwork.

1 | 2 | 3 | 4 | 5 | 6 | 7 | 8 | 9 | 10 | 11 | 12 | 13 | **14**

Wednesday April 1
Reckoning is released.

Tuesday April 14
The Space Shuttle Columbia lands at Edwards Air Force Base in California, completing the first space shuttle mission.

Saturday April 25
Garcia and Weir (along with Kahn, Hart, and Kreutzmann) play an acoustic set for the Sing Out for Sight Benefit at Berkeley Community Theatre in Berkeley. Country Joe McDonald and Kaye Wolf are also on the bill.

15 | 16 | 17 | 18 | 19 | 20 | 21 | 22 | 23 | 24 | **25** | 26 | 27 | 28 | 29 | **30**

Thursday April 30
Greensboro Coliseum, Greensboro, North Carolina

Right and below: Deadheads soaking up the atmosphere.

NOT HERE FOR A LONG TIME
JUST HERE FOR A GOOD TIME
VIVA LAS VEGAS
VIVA LAS VEG...

HONK DEAD
IF YOUR

MAY '81

| 1 | 2 | 3 | 4 | 5 | 6 |

★ **Tuesday May 5**
Glens Falls Civic Center,
Glens Falls, New York

Saturday May 2
Monday May 4
The Spectrum,
Philadelphia, Pennsylvania

Friday May 1
Hampton Coliseum,
Hampton, Virginia

★ **Wednesday May 6**
Nassau Veterans Memorial
Coliseum, Uniondale, New York

Bob Weir dedicates a long
"He's Gone" to Irish "freedom fighter"
Bobby Sands, who died today after a
hunger strike in Belfast's Maze Prison.
Other performance highlights include
the first "Caution (Do Not Stop on
Tracks)"/"Spanish Jam" since July 16,
1976. The entire show can be heard on
Dick's Picks Volume 13.

May 1981

262

| 7 | 8 | 9 | 10 |

Thursday May 7
The band appear on *Tomorrow*, NBC TV's late-
night talk show, for an interview with host Tom
Snyder and to deliver acoustic performances of
"On the Road Again," "Dire Wolf," "Deep Elem
Blues," and "Cassidy."

Friday May 8
Saturday May 9
Nassau Veterans Memorial Coliseum,
Uniondale, New York

On Friday the band's old friend Ken
Kesey joins in on harmonica for
"Drums" and the "U.S. Blues" encore.

SHAKEDOWN ST.

Wednesday May 13
*A gunman shoots and
wounds Pope John Paul II in
Rome's St. Peter's Square.*

| 11 | 12 | 13 | 14 |

Monday May 11
Tuesday May 12
New Haven Coliseum,
New Haven, Connecticut

Tuesday sees another "He's
Gone" deadication, this time
for Bob Marley, who died of
cancer the previous day in
Miami at age 36.

Wednesday May 13
Providence Civic Center,
Providence, Rhode Island

Deadheads in the '80s

Even back in the early 1970s, it was not unusual to find a few hearty souls outside most Grateful Dead shows selling homemade t-shirts, buttons, or bumper stickers to try to earn enough money to follow a Dead tour. But the roots of the truly mammoth bazaars that became a fixture outside the shows from the mid-'80s on can be traced to a small park adjacent to the Oakland [California] Auditorium, where the Dead ushered in New Year's with a series of shows from 1979–1982. Each year during those December runs, the number of merchants hawking everything from tie-dyes to hash pipes to veggie burritos increased exponentially. Then, many sellers found that they could survive and even thrive peddling their wares on tour, so the ever-growing and fabulously entertaining bazaar hit the road and followed the band year-round, much to the chagrin of city officials everywhere.

The early 1980s also saw a huge increase in the number of people taping Dead shows, once the domain of just a handful of surreptitious recordists. Now it was completely out in the open, and even accepted by GD live engineer Dan Healy. By October 1984, however, the sea of microphones had become so large that the Dead set up the first authorized taping section.

All pictures: *The many looks of the Deadheads in the '80s.*

June 1981

263

JUNE '81

1 – 30

15	16	17	18	19	20	21	22	23	24	25

Friday May 15
🎸 Athletic Center, Rutgers University, New Brunswick, New Jersey

Saturday May 16 ★
🎸 Barton Hall, Cornell University, Ithaca, New York

Sunday May 17
🎸 Onondaga County War Memorial, Syracuse, New York

Friday May 22
🎸 Warfield Theatre, San Francisco, California

Billed as Jerry Garcia, Bob Weir, Mickey Hart, and Friends, the boys play a show for nuclear disarmament at the Warfield. John Kahn sits in for Phil on bass during this all-acoustic set.

120 NORTH 17

RACETRACK
DEADHEADS

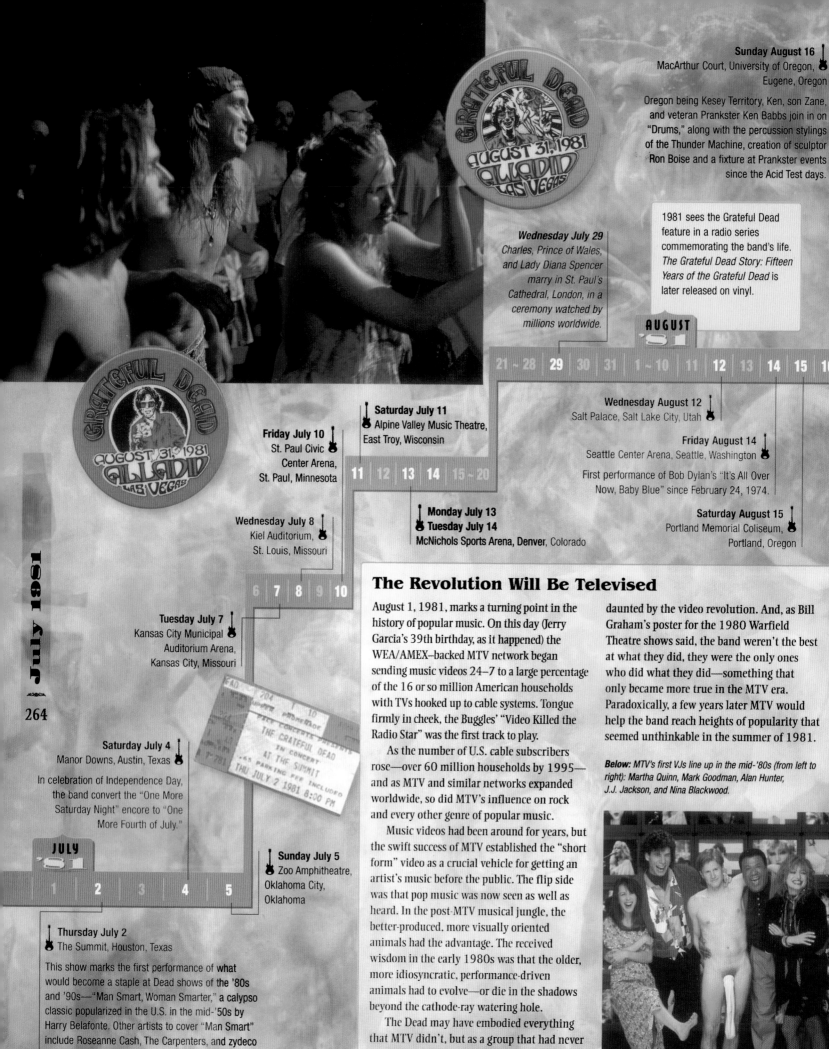

Sunday August 16
MacArthur Court, University of Oregon, Eugene, Oregon

Oregon being Kesey Territory, Ken, son Zane, and veteran Prankster Ken Babbs join in on "Drums," along with the percussion stylings of the Thunder Machine, creation of sculptor Ron Boise and a fixture at Prankster events since the Acid Test days.

1981 sees the Grateful Dead feature in a radio series commemorating the band's life. *The Grateful Dead Story: Fifteen Years of the Grateful Dead* is later released on vinyl.

GRATEFUL DEAD AUGUST 31, 1981 ALLADIN LAS VEGAS

Wednesday July 29
Charles, Prince of Wales, and Lady Diana Spencer marry in St. Paul's Cathedral, London, in a ceremony watched by millions worldwide.

AUGUST '81

| 21 ~ 28 | 29 | 30 | 31 | 1 ~ 10 | 11 | 12 | 13 | 14 | 15 | 16 | 17 |

Wednesday August 12
Salt Palace, Salt Lake City, Utah

Saturday July 11
Alpine Valley Music Theatre, East Troy, Wisconsin

Friday July 10
St. Paul Civic Center Arena, St. Paul, Minnesota

Friday August 14
Seattle Center Arena, Seattle, Washington

First performance of Bob Dylan's "It's All Over Now, Baby Blue" since February 24, 1974.

| 11 | 12 | 13 | 14 | 15 ~ 20 |

Wednesday July 8
Kiel Auditorium, St. Louis, Missouri

Monday July 13
Tuesday July 14
McNichols Sports Arena, Denver, Colorado

Saturday August 15
Portland Memorial Coliseum, Portland, Oregon

| 6 | 7 | 8 | 9 | 10 |

GRATEFUL DEAD AUGUST 31, 1981 ALLADIN LAS VEGAS

Tuesday July 7
Kansas City Municipal Auditorium Arena, Kansas City, Missouri

Saturday July 4
Manor Downs, Austin, Texas

In celebration of Independence Day, the band convert the "One More Saturday Night" encore to "One More Fourth of July."

Sunday July 5
Zoo Amphitheatre, Oklahoma City, Oklahoma

JULY '81

| 1 | 2 | 3 | 4 | 5 |

Thursday July 2
The Summit, Houston, Texas

This show marks the first performance of what would become a staple at Dead shows of the '80s and '90s—"Man Smart, Woman Smarter," a calypso classic popularized in the U.S. in the mid-'50s by Harry Belafonte. Other artists to cover "Man Smart" include Roseanne Cash, The Carpenters, and zydeco great Clifton Chenier.

The Revolution Will Be Televised

August 1, 1981, marks a turning point in the history of popular music. On this day (Jerry Garcia's 39th birthday, as it happened) the WEA/AMEX–backed MTV network began sending music videos 24–7 to a large percentage of the 16 or so million American households with TVs hooked up to cable systems. Tongue firmly in cheek, the Buggles' "Video Killed the Radio Star" was the first track to play.

As the number of U.S. cable subscribers rose—over 60 million households by 1995—and as MTV and similar networks expanded worldwide, so did MTV's influence on rock and every other genre of popular music.

Music videos had been around for years, but the swift success of MTV established the "short form" video as a crucial vehicle for getting an artist's music before the public. The flip side was that pop music was now seen as well as heard. In the post-MTV musical jungle, the better-produced, more visually oriented animals had the advantage. The received wisdom in the early 1980s was that the older, more idiosyncratic, performance-driven animals had to evolve—or die in the shadows beyond the cathode-ray watering hole.

The Dead may have embodied everything that MTV didn't, but as a group that had never scored a Top 10 record and that carried its fans around with it, they weren't particularly daunted by the video revolution. And, as Bill Graham's poster for the 1980 Warfield Theatre shows said, the band weren't the best at what they did, they were the only ones who did what they did—something that only became more true in the MTV era. Paradoxically, a few years later MTV would help the band reach heights of popularity that seemed unthinkable in the summer of 1981.

Below: MTV's first VJs line up in the mid-'80s (from left to right): Martha Quinn, Mark Goodman, Alan Hunter, J.J. Jackson, and Nina Blackwood.

🎸 **Thursday August 27**
🎸 **Friday August 28**
Long Beach Arena,
Long Beach, California

Thursday sees the first live
"Cumberland Blues" since
October 18, 1974. Friday marks
the debut of a cover of Sam
Cooke's "Good Times."

GRATEFUL DEAD

DEAD SET

DEAD SET
Grateful Dead
Released by Arista (A2L-8606) in August 1981

Side One
1. **Samson And Delilah**
(Traditional, arr. Grateful Dead)
2. **Friend of the Devil**
(Garcia/Dawson/Hunter)
3. **New Minglewood Blues**
(Traditional, arr. Grateful Dead)
4. **Deal**
(Garcia/Hunter)

Side Two
1. **Candyman**
(Garcia/Hunter)
2. **Little Red Rooster**
(Dixon)
3. **Loser**
(Garcia/Hunter)

Side Three
1. **Passenger**
(Lesh/Monk)
2. **Feel Like A Stranger**
(Weir/Barlow)
3. **Franklin's Tower**
(Garcia/Kreutzmann/Hunter)
4. **Rhythm Devils**
(Hart/Kreutzmann)

Side Four
1. **Space**
(Lesh/Mydland/Kreutzmann/Hart)
2. **Fire on the Mountain**
(Hart/Hunter)
3. **Greatest Story Ever Told**
(Hart/Weir/Hunter)
4. **Brokedown Palace**
(Garcia/Hunter)

Personnel

Jerry Garcia – acoustic guitar, vocals
Bob Weir – acoustic guitar, vocals
Phil Lesh – bass
Brent Mydland – keyboards, vocals
Bill Kreutzmann – percussion
Mickey Hart – percussion

Produced by Dan Healy, Betty Cantor-Jackson, and Jerry Garcia

THE SECOND DOUBLE LIVE ALBUM from the September and October 1980 Warfield Theatre/Radio City runs, *Dead Set* presented highlights from the shows' electric sets; *Reckoning* (released in March '81) had already covered the acoustic angle. The band had originally planned to release one double LP with both electric and acoustic offerings but, in Jerry Garcia's words, "We really ended up with so much good material that it was a struggle. The idea of just one acoustic and one electric record was sort of pathetic, since our electric tunes are seldom less than eight minutes long. And that meant our fat electric album would have two songs on a side. It was kind of silly."

Although generally considered a less interesting collection than its acoustic counterpart, tracks like "Feel Like a Stranger" and "Franklin's Tower" are still "nicely representative of the band at the time," in Blair Jackson's estimation. A slow-tempo reinterpretation of "Friend of the Devil" was the standout cut for many fans.

As with *Reckoning*, though, *Dead Set* got its share of downed thumbs from the why-do-we-need-another-live-album contingent among the critics. Some Deadheads also felt the release mix had been edited too heavily and thus didn't capture all the nuances present in the actual shows. The album's cover was illustrated by Dennis Larkin.

"A good, if unmemorable, album."

OLIVER TRAGER IN *THE AMERICAN BOOK OF THE DEAD.*

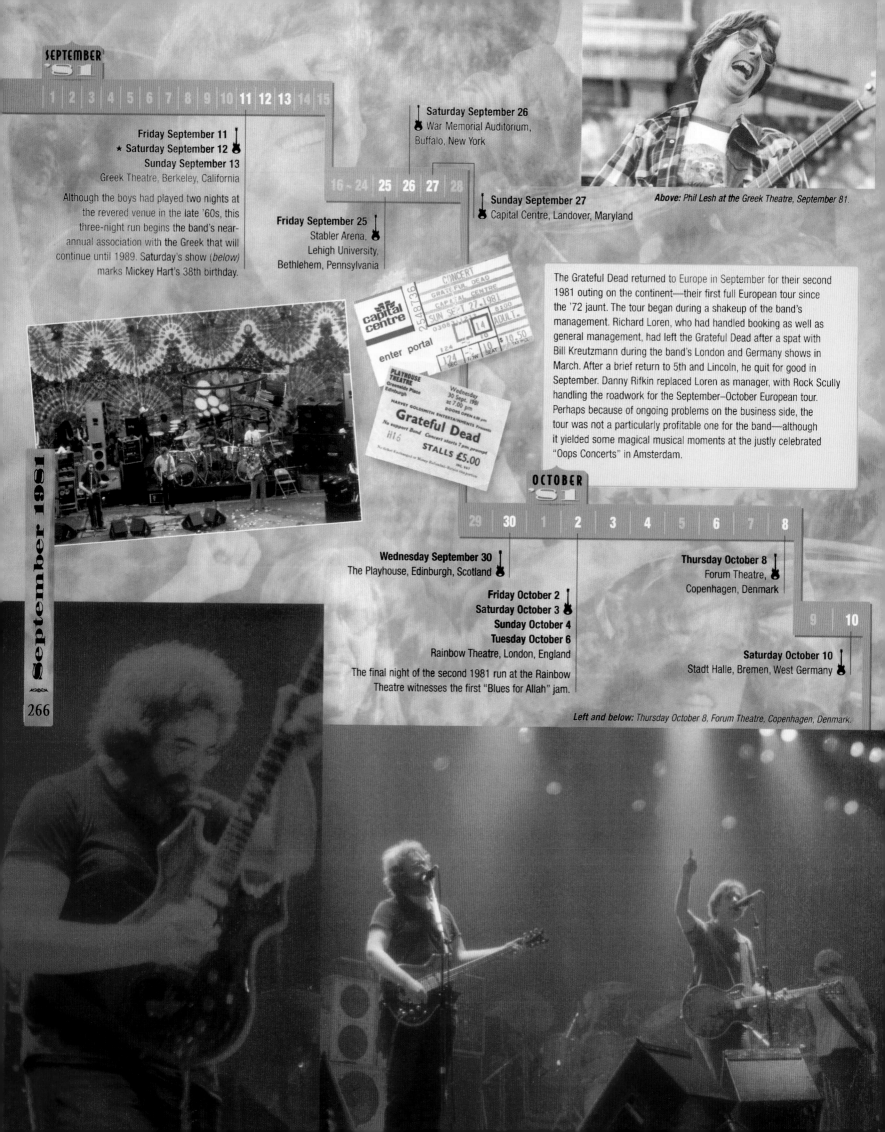

| 1 | 2 | 3 | 4 | 5 | 6 | 7 | 8 | 9 | 10 | **11** | **12** | **13** | 14 | 15 |

Friday September 11
★ **Saturday September 12**
Sunday September 13
Greek Theatre, Berkeley, California

Although the boys had played two nights at the revered venue in the late '60s, this three-night run begins the band's near-annual association with the Greek that will continue until 1989. Saturday's show (*below*) marks Mickey Hart's 38th birthday.

| 16 – 24 | **25** | **26** | **27** | 28 |

Friday September 25
Stabler Arena,
Lehigh University,
Bethlehem, Pennsylvania

Saturday September 26
War Memorial Auditorium,
Buffalo, New York

Sunday September 27
Capital Centre, Landover, Maryland

Above: Phil Lesh at the Greek Theatre, September 81.

The Grateful Dead returned to Europe in September for their second 1981 outing on the continent—their first full European tour since the '72 jaunt. The tour began during a shakeup of the band's management. Richard Loren, who had handled booking as well as general management, had left the Grateful Dead after a spat with Bill Kreutzmann during the band's London and Germany shows in March. After a brief return to 5th and Lincoln, he quit for good in September. Danny Rifkin replaced Loren as manager, with Rock Scully handling the roadwork for the September–October European tour. Perhaps because of ongoing problems on the business side, the tour was not a particularly profitable one for the band—although it yielded some magical musical moments at the justly celebrated "Oops Concerts" in Amsterdam.

| 29 | **30** | 1 | **2** | 3 | 4 | 5 | 6 | 7 | **8** |

| 9 | 10 |

Wednesday September 30
The Playhouse, Edinburgh, Scotland

Friday October 2
Saturday October 3
Sunday October 4
Tuesday October 6
Rainbow Theatre, London, England

The final night of the second 1981 run at the Rainbow Theatre witnesses the first "Blues for Allah" jam.

Thursday October 8
Forum Theatre,
Copenhagen, Denmark

Saturday October 10
Stadt Halle, Bremen, West Germany

Left and below: Thursday October 8, Forum Theatre, Copenhagen, Denmark.

September 1981

266

Oops in Amsterdam

The two nights the band played at the small Melkweg club in Amsterdam rank high on anyone's list of legendary Grateful Dead performances. The gigs got their enduring nickname because they were unscheduled and, in Dennis McNally's words, "financially meaningless" for the band, and also from Phil Lesh's chant of "oops, oops" at the top of the first show—his way of letting the packed house know they were in for something spontaneous and special.

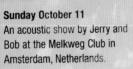

The Oops Concerts happened when a scheduled gig in France had to be canceled. With the night of October 11 free, Jerry and Bob journeyed to Amsterdam to do an acoustic show at the 400-seat Melkweg Club.

A converted dairy, the venue's name literally means "Milky Way," and the club's spacey moniker was well deserved on another level—its menu included hashish. The city's main police station, by the way, was just across the street. Only in Amsterdam…

Garcia and Weir's 35-minute set was well received. Taken with the venue, the crowd, and the Amsterdam ambiance—legal dope, a laid-back citizenry, youth hostels full of EuroHippies and North American backpackers—the guitarists convinced the rest of the band to do two shows at the Melkweg the following week. Cindy Peress, a New York–born singer-songwriter with a wide following in Europe, opened both nights.

After years of playing mostly auditoriums, arenas, and amphitheaters, the band cut loose in the smoky, intimate atmosphere of the club with two sets heavy on blues and rockers, including "Little Red Rooster," "Around and Around," "Johnny B. Goode," and the first-ever performance of Willie Dixon's "Spoonful," encoring with Dylan's "It's All Over Now, Baby Blue." The band's instruments were on their way to Paris for a performance at the Hippodrome, so Bill and Mickey made do with basic drum kits, and Jerry and Bob played on borrowed guitars (a Yamaha 1000 Sunburst and a white Fender Telecaster, respectively). Phil had managed to hang on to his usual ax.

Expanding Milky Way

Word of the Dead's Dutch adventure having spread, the Melkweg was even more packed the second night, with audience members sitting underneath Brent's keyboards. The night marked Bob Weir's 34th birthday, and he received a bouquet of flowers and a chorus of "Happy Birthday" from the audience as the band came onstage. The show began with an acoustic set incorporating most of the songs Jerry and Bob had played as a duo on October 11, with the addition of "Dire Wolf." Totally energized and soon dripping with sweat, the boys turned the second, electric set into a true roof-blower, including their only known performance of the Olympics' "Hully Gully," which segued into the first performance of Van Morrison and Them's garage-band classic "Gloria" since 1968, which segued—to the crowd's joy—into the first post-Pigpen "Turn on Your Lovelight."

When the house lights came up on an utterly spent band and audience at 2:00 a.m., Rock Scully stepped up to the mic and said "This was a very special treat for us and a gift to us from you guys." And so it was.

Now a multi-room "multimedia performance center," the Melkweg frequently hosts contemporary jam bands like Phish.

Above: The band at the Melkweg.
Right: Bill Kreutzmann at the Melkweg.

Sunday October 11
An acoustic show by Jerry and Bob at the Melkweg Club in Amsterdam, Netherlands.

Thursday October 15
Melkweg Club, Amsterdam, Netherlands

16

15

Friday October 16 ★
Melkweg Club, Amsterdam, Netherlands

11

Tuesday October 13
Walter Koebel Halle, Russelsheim, West Germany

Monday October 19
Sports Palace, Barcelona, Spain

By the end of the European tour it was evident that long years on the road, drugs, and hard living in general were pushing members of the band and its extended family toward burnout. The state of Jerry—musical as well as physical—was a particular concern. After the last show, in Barcelona, the band gave Jerry a letter (written by Phil but signed by the whole band) which began: "Dear Sir and Brother: You have been accused of certain high crimes and misdemeanors against the art of music. To wit: playing in your own band; never playing with any dynamics; never listening to what anybody else plays…"

25 ~ 31

12   **13**

17   **18**   **19**   **20**   **21**   **22**   **23**   **24**

Monday October 12
Olympia Halle, Munich, West Germany

Saturday October 17
Hippodrome, Paris, France

Saturday October 24
Hundreds of thousands of demonstrators gather in several European cities to protest U.S. plans to deploy nuclear missiles in Europe.

NOVEMBER '81
1 2 3 4

21 | 22 | 23 | 24 | 25 | 26 | 27 | 28

Saturday November 21
Bobby and the Midnites is released.

Left and above: Garcia and Hart with Joan Baez. Mickey was dating Baez at the time and the Dead backed her on some studio sessions.

Saturday December 5
Market Square Arena,
Indianapolis, Indiana

Thursday December 3
Dane County Coliseum,
Madison, Wisconsin

DECEMBER '81

29 | 30 | 1 | 2 | 3 | 4 | 5

Wednesday December 2
Assembly Hall,
University of Illinois,
Champaign-Urbana, Illinois

Monday November 30
Hara Arena, Dayton, Ohio.

The band lurch shakily into their first and only rendition of the lounge-lizard standby "Mack the Knife," from Kurt Weill and Bertolt Brecht's 1927 *Threepenny Opera.*

Sunday November 29
Pittsburgh Civic Arena,
Pittsburgh, Pennsylvania

BOBBY & THE MIDNITES

Bobby & the Midnites

Released by Arista (AL-9568) on November 21, 1981

Side One
1. **Haze**
   (Cochran/Kelly/Mohawk/Mydland/Shaw/Weir)
2. **Too Many Losers**
   (Cochran/Weir)
3. **Far Away**
   (Cochran/Kelly/Weir)
4. **Book of Rules**
   (Johnson/Llewellyn)
5. **Me, Without You**
   (Barlow/Johnson)

Side Two
1. **Josephine**
   (Weir)
2. **(I Want To) Fly Away**
   (Barlow/Weir)
3. **Carry Me**
   (Weir)
4. **Festival**
   (Weir)

Personnel

B. Weir – guitar, vocals; **B. Cobham** – drums, vocals; **B. Cochran** – guitar, vocals; **A. Johnson** – bass, vocals; **M. Kelly** – harmonica, vocals; **B. Mydland** – keyboards, vocals; J. Barlow – lyrical supervision; Produced by Gary Lyons

In the wake of *Heaven Help the Fool*, Weir organized a touring band that would include, among others, L.A. session guitarist Bobby Cochran (the nephew of rock legend and author of "Summertime Blues" Eddie), old friend and harpist Matthew Kelly, and keyboardist Brent Mydland, who would, soon enough, join the Dead. In 1981, they were joined in the studio by the great drummer Billy Cobham and bassist Alphonso Johnson, and recorded *Bobby and the Midnites*. Though it had a number of catchy tunes, including "Josephine," "Festival," and the reggae "Book of Rules," its sales were only so-so. The album also yielded a single, "Too Many Losers" backed with "Haze," but was ultimately better known for its cover artwork. Weir: "It came to me in a flash… Midnite the Cat was a fixture on a TV show called *Andy's Gang.* I remember it from the very dawn of my memory, when I was a little kid. [The cat] had a little cigar-box podium and he played the fiddle. I guess he was some sort of puppet—had me fooled at the time… that picture [the album cover] more or less came to me. I did a rough sketch and gave it to Vic Moscoso, and he made it just perfect."

Left: Cowboy John Barlow on his ranch.
Right: Thursday December 31, Oakland Auditorium, Oakland, California.

Disarmed Dead

Billed as "Joan Baez and Friends," the Grateful Dead joined Joan Baez (left) for a "Dance for Disarmament" benefit at the San Mateo Fairgrounds on December 12. The band had last played behind Baez during the legendary "Midnight Hour" jam at the Fillmore West on July 16, 1966, although they'd shared the stage with her (and many others) at a number of benefits since.

The show opened with a set by High Noon, a Merl Saunders–Mickey Hart project, with Bill Kreutzmann and Joan Baez guesting. The second set and the Dead's first were acoustic, with the band (minus Brent, and with Jerry sitting out the last couple of songs) backing Joan through a mix of her originals and some covers. These included "Children of the '80s," "Lady Di and I," "Me and Bobby McGee," "The Boxer," and the traditional ballad "Barbara Allen"— a sad, stately song dating back at least 300 years and first mentioned in Samuel Pepys' diary of January 2, 1666.

Matt Kelly joined on several songs during the second electric set and Joan Baez returned for a Jerryless encore of "It's All Over Now Baby Blue."

Left: "Peace man" button made by Lisa Law.

| 20 | 21 | 22 | 23 | 24 | 25 | **26** | **27** | **28** | **29** | **30** | **31** |

Saturday December 26
Sunday December 27
Tuesday December 28
Wednesday December 30
Thursday December 31
Oakland Auditorium, Oakland, California

The band kick off the New Year's run on Boxing Day, dusting off several oldies, including Jimmy Reed's "Big Boss Man" (last performed May 25, 1972) and a jam on "The Eleven" (last performed September 28, 1975). Joan Baez returns for a between-the-sets appearance during Wednesday's show, performing "Me and Bobby McGee," "Lady Di and I," and "Barbara Allen."

Monday December 7
Des Moines Civic Center, Des Moines, Iowa

Saturday December 12
Fiesta Hall, San Mateo County Fairgrounds, San Mateo, California
Dance For Disarmament.

| 6 | 7 | 8 | **9** | 10 | 11 | 12 | 13 | 14 | 15 |

Sunday December 6
Rosemont Horizon Arena, Rosemont, Illinois

Wednesday December 9
Events Center, University of Colorado, Boulder, Colorado

Smokin' New Year's Eve

In an ironic coda to the first year of the just-say-no Reagan era, Bill Graham rode a giant joint onto the stage to kick off the third New Year's Eve show at Oakland. The acoustic first set featured Joan Baez throughout and ended with the band's only performance of "On the Banks of the Ohio," first recorded by Bill and Charlie Monroe in 1936. The boys followed up with three electric sets, with Joan lending her dulcet voice to "Iko Iko" and the closer at 2:00 a.m., "Baby Blue." Usual suspects Matt Kelly (first electric set) and John Cipollina (second electric set) joined in on several tunes. It was a great show, highlighted by the third set opener—the first "Dark Star" since January 20, 1979.

Backstage Wife

The high point of the 1981/82 New Year's Eve Show took place not onstage, but in a backstage dressing room. Between the second and third sets, Jerry and Mountain Girl were married in a Tibetan Buddhist ceremony performed by Jerry's old friend Peter Zimmels. The wedding was probably at least partly a matter of tax benefits as much as a real revival of the couple's relationship—probably the reason for the rush to tie the knot before December 31, 1981, turned into January 1, 1982. Mountain Girl did move into Jerry's Hepburn Heights home, only to move back to Oregon in early January.

"Jerry and I got married but that didn't change a goddam thing... it didn't make a damned bit of difference."
MOUNTAIN GIRL TO ROBERT GREENFIELD IN *DARK STAR*

1 2 3 4 5 6 7 8 9 10

🎸 **Friday January 1**
The New Year's festivities continue into the early hours of today.

GRATEFUL DEAD
BACK STAGE

GRATEFUL DEAD
BACK STAGE

FEBRUARY
'82

1 2 3 4 5 6 7 8 9 10

Opposite page: New Year's Eve, Oakland Auditorium. At the far left is Ken Kesey, descending from the rafters to usher in the New Year.
Top right: Bob Weir at the Warfield Theatre, San Francisco, February 16–17.

WARFIELD THEATRE
982 MARKET STREET - S.F.
BILL GRAHAM PRESENTS
TUE FEB 16 1982 8:00 PM
AN EVENING WITH
THE GRATEFUL DEAD
$25.00
$25.00

🎸 **Tuesday February 16**
🎸 **Wednesday February 17**
Warfield Theatre, San Francisco, California

The band start their 1982 performance year with a pair of benefit performances, with proceeds going to several Bay Area nonprofits.

11 12 13 14 15 **16 17** 18

Left: 1982 would be a good year for Phil Lesh. With his vocal cords finally healed, Phil added his voice to the band's vocals for the first time since 1974, and he adopted what would become his trademark ax from '82 on, a custom six-string bass from Modulus. And in February he invited Jill Johnson, the woman whom he would eventually marry, on their first date—a Dead show, of course.

🎸 **Sunday February 21**
🎸 Pauley Pavilion, University of California, Los Angeles, California

19 20 21 22 23 24 25 26 27 28

🎸 **Friday February 19**
🎸 **Saturday February 20**
Golden Hall, Community Concourse, San Diego, California

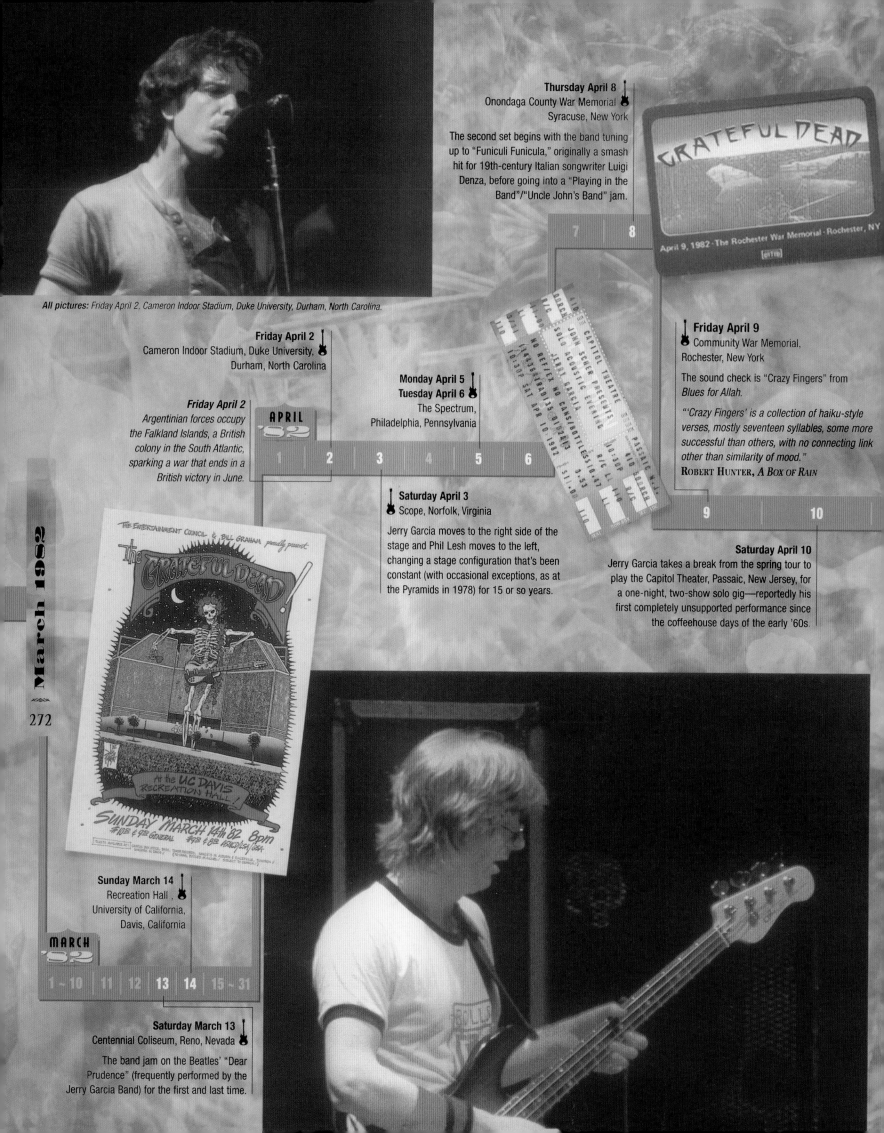

All pictures: *Friday April 2, Cameron Indoor Stadium, Duke University, Durham, North Carolina.*

Thursday April 8
Onondaga County War Memorial
Syracuse, New York

The second set begins with the band tuning up to "Funiculi Funicula," originally a smash hit for 19th-century Italian songwriter Luigi Denza, before going into a "Playing in the Band"/"Uncle John's Band" jam.

GRATEFUL DEAD

April 9, 1982 · The Rochester War Memorial · Rochester, NY

Friday April 2
Cameron Indoor Stadium, Duke University,
Durham, North Carolina

Friday April 2
Argentinian forces occupy the Falkland Islands, a British colony in the South Atlantic, sparking a war that ends in a British victory in June.

APRIL '82

1   2   3   4   5   6

Monday April 5
Tuesday April 6
The Spectrum,
Philadelphia, Pennsylvania

Saturday April 3
Scope, Norfolk, Virginia

Jerry Garcia moves to the right side of the stage and Phil Lesh moves to the left, changing a stage configuration that's been constant (with occasional exceptions, as at the Pyramids in 1978) for 15 or so years.

Friday April 9
Community War Memorial,
Rochester, New York

The sound check is "Crazy Fingers" from *Blues for Allah*.

"'Crazy Fingers' is a collection of haiku-style verses, mostly seventeen syllables, some more successful than others, with no connecting link other than similarity of mood."
ROBERT HUNTER, *A BOX OF RAIN*

7   8

9   10

Saturday April 10
Jerry Garcia takes a break from the spring tour to play the Capitol Theater, Passaic, New Jersey, for a one-night, two-show solo gig—reportedly his first completely unsupported performance since the coffeehouse days of the early '60s.

THE ENTERTAINMENT COUNCIL & BILL GRAHAM *proudly present*

THE GRATEFUL DEAD!

AT THE UC DAVIS RECREATION HALL!

SUNDAY MARCH 14th 82 8pm
#10½ & 9½ GENERAL   #9½ & 8½ PERIODISH/USA

Sunday March 14
Recreation Hall ,
University of California,
Davis, California

MARCH '82

1 – 10 | 11 | 12 | 13 | 14 | 15 – 31

Saturday March 13
Centennial Coliseum, Reno, Nevada

The band jam on the Beatles' "Dear Prudence" (frequently performed by the Jerry Garcia Band) for the first and last time.

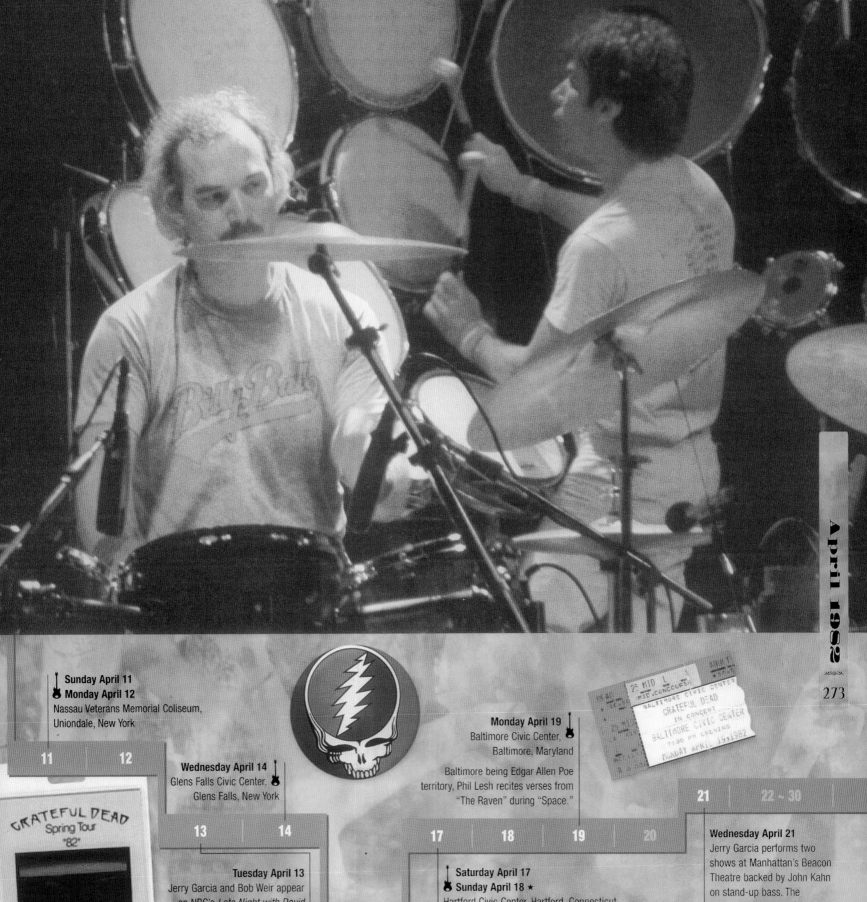

Sunday April 11
Monday April 12
Nassau Veterans Memorial Coliseum,
Uniondale, New York

11   **12**

Wednesday April 14
Glens Falls Civic Center,
Glens Falls, New York

13   **14**

Tuesday April 13
Jerry Garcia and Bob Weir appear
on NBC's *Late Night with David
Letterman*, performing acoustic
versions of "Deep Elem Blues"
and "The Monkey and
the Engineer."

15   **16**

Thursday April 15
Providence Civic Center,
Providence, Rhode Island

Monday April 19
Baltimore Civic Center,
Baltimore, Maryland

Baltimore being Edgar Allen Poe
territory, Phil Lesh recites verses from
"The Raven" during "Space."

17   **18**   **19**   **20**

Saturday April 17
Sunday April 18 ★
Hartford Civic Center, Hartford, Connecticut

Sunday's show sees the famous "Earthquake Space":
noting that the date marks the 76th anniversary of
the 1906 San Francisco earthquake, Phil Lesh (who
else but Phil would make the connection?) attempts
to replicate a seismic incident using the band's PA
system. According to Stephen Peters, the auditory
assault creates "a spontaneous natural disaster
worthy of Kali, shaking the bones of those lucky
enough to have been in attendance."

21   **22 ~ 30**

Wednesday April 21
Jerry Garcia performs two
shows at Manhattan's Beacon
Theatre backed by John Kahn
on stand-up bass. The
acoustic duo gig together
frequently for the remainder
of the year.

GRATEFUL DEAD
Spring Tour
'82'

**ALL AREA
ACCESS**

BEARER'S NAME

AUTHORIZATION

MAY '82

1 - 20	21	22	23	24	25	26	27	28	29	30	31

Friday May 21
Saturday May 22
Sunday May 23
Greek Theatre,
University of California,
Berkeley, California

Friday May 28
Moscone Convention Center, San Francisco, California

The Grateful Dead join Country Joe and Jefferson Starship for a Vietnam Veterans benefit. Although the venue is acoustically awful, the show is memorable, with Boz Scaggs and John Cipollina joining in for the entire second set, including the first performance of Robert Johnson's "Walking Blues" since October 7, 1966, and the only performance of "I Got a Mind to Give Up Livin'" by New Orleans piano legend Alan Toussaint. Airto Moreira plays throughout and Flora Purim joins the Rhythm Devils for "Drums."

All pictures (except below): *Sunday May 23, Greek Theatre, University of California, Berkeley, California.*

Saturday June 12
Three-quarters of a million people demonstrate against nuclear weapons in New York City.

Wednesday June 16
Kicking off proceedings at Music Mountain, Fallsburg, New York, the Jerry Garcia Band, with Bill Kreutzmann in the lineup, play the first of several East Coast dates with Bobby and the Midnites.

GREEK THEATRE
U.C. BERKELEY
BILL GRAHAM & CAL PRES
THE GRATEFUL DEAD
NO CANS·BOTTLES·ALCOHOL
SAT MAY 72 1982 5:00 P
BGZ 10
CA ADULT
GEN 12.00
ADULT
ADM B18APR CA CA-6641 12.00

Bill Graham Presents
GRATEFUL DEAD
May 21·22·23, 1982
Greek Theatre · Berkeley
GREEK HART

12 13 14 15 16 17 18 19 20 21 22 23 24 30

JUNE
'82

1 2 3 4 5 6 7 8 9 10 11

Right: *June 12. Garcia at the Keystone, Palo Alto, for a Jerry Garcia Band gig.*

GEN. ADM.
JULY 25, 1982
THE GRATEFUL
DEAD
COMPTON TERRACE
25
TEMPE, AZ
SUNDAY
7:30 P.M.

BILL GRAHAM/AVALON ATTRACTIONS
BRING YOU
THE GRATEFUL DEAD
VENTURA COUNTY FAIRGROUNDS
VENTURA, CA
0803852
NO REFUNDS/EXCHANGES
SAT JUL 17 1982 4:00P $12.00

Above: July 27–29, Red Rocks
Amphitheatre, Morrison, Colorado.

Saturday July 31
Manor Downs,
Austin, Texas

Saturday July 17
Sunday July 18
Ventura County Fairgrounds,
Ventura, California

"Crazy Fingers" moves from the
sound check to performance proper
(between "Ship of Fools" and
"Drums" in the second set) for the
first time since September 30, 1976.

Sunday July 25
Compton Terrace
Amphitheatre, Chandler, Arizona

| 25 | 26 | 27 | 28 | 29 | 30 | 31 |

Tuesday July 27
Wednesday July 28
Thursday July 29 ★
Red Rocks Amphitheatre,
Morrison, Colorado

On Wednesday the crowd is
treated to a few bars of "C. C.
Rider" between "Big Railroad
Blues" and "Lazy Lightning."

JULY
'82

| 1 ~ 15 | 16 | 17 | 18 | 19 ~ 24 |

The Dinosaurs—Old But Not Extinct

In August, Bay Area rock vets Peter Albin (ex-Big Brother bass), Spencer Dryden (ex-Jefferson Airplane and New Riders drummer), and Barry Melton (ex-Country Joe & the Fish guitarist) performed together at a festival on the Russian River. The trio grew to a quintet with the addition of Robert Hunter and ex-Quicksilver frontman John Cipollina. Dubbed "The Dinosaurs" by Melton—commentary on the fact that the practitioners of the "San Francisco sound" were now entering their third decade as performers—the group soon began gigging locally. At the end of the year The Dinosaurs shared the stage with the Grateful Dead at the traditional Oakland Auditorium concert *(see page 280)*, during which Country Joe McDonald added his voice to "Save the Whales"—making the show a true gathering of San Francisco rock royalty.

"Though the Dead's contribution failed as a whole to match the magnificent vibe created by the Keseys and their production crew and, in turn, the audience, this concert was still the most magical gathering of Deadheads I've ever attended."

JOHN DWORK ON THE FIELD TRIP II IN *THE DEADHEAD'S TAPING COMPENDIUM, VOL II*

Field Trip Flashback

On August 28 the Grateful Dead returned to the Veneta, Oregon, site (or thereabouts) of the legendary August 27, 1972, "Field Trip" benefit for Chuck Kesey's Springfield Creamery *(see page 147)* to play an event billed as "Springfield Creamery Presents the Second Decadenal Field Trip." Other acts to perform on the two stages that day included the Robert Cray Band (who were still relatively unheard-of in the early '80s), The Flying Karamazov Brothers, Peter Rowan, Strangers With Candy, and Tatoo.

Besides bringing out "Dupree's Diamond Blues" for the first time since April 14, 1978, Field Trip II saw the premiere of two new band originals that would eventually make their way onto the *In the Dark* album: "West L.A. Fadeaway" and "Keep Your Day Job." The latter tune was not particularly well received, as the lyrics ("Keep your day job/Until your night job pays") seemed antithetical to the off-the-grid philosophy of most Deadheads.

"This song was dropped from the Grateful Dead's repertoire at the request of fans. Seriously."
ROBERT HUNTER ON "DAY JOB" IN
A BOX OF RAIN

Tuesday August 10 ★
Fieldhouse, University of Iowa, Iowa City, Iowa

In what may have been a salute to their midwestern fans, the band tune up to "Beer Barrel Polka" before going into "On the Road Again."

10 11   13

Left: Brent Mydland shows his true colors.

277

Wednesday August 4
Kiel Auditorium, St. Louis, Missouri

The band perform the first "Stagger Lee'" since December 4, 1979.

★ Tuesday August 3
Starlight Theatre, Kansas City, Missouri

Friday August 6
St. Paul Civic Center Arena, St. Paul, Minnesota

AUGUST '82

1 2 3 4 5 6 7 8 9

Sunday August 1
Zoo Amphitheatre, Oklahoma City, Oklahoma

Jerry's 40th birthday.

GRATEFUL DEAD
SUMMER TOUR 1982

ALL AREA
Mr. Infinity #1 NAME
AUTHORIZED BY

Saturday August 28
Oregon Country Fair Site, Veneta, Oregon

28 29 30 31

Sunday August 29
Seattle Center Coliseum, Seattle, Washington

★ Saturday August 7
Sunday August 8
Alpine Valley Music Theatre, East Troy, Wisconsin

On Sunday, Zakir Hussain, Mickey Hart's longtime friend and Diga musical partner, adds his tabla to "Drums" and "The Other One"—his only performance with the full band. John Cipollina joins in on the second-set "Not Fade Away," "Wharf Rat," and "Good Lovin'," and the encore—"Satisfaction" (with the lyrics to Willie Dixon's "Wang Dang Doodle" instead of the usual verses) seguing into "Brokedown Palace."

JOHN BAUER CONCERT COMPANY (PRESENTS)
THE GRATEFUL DEAD
SEATTLE CENTER COLISEUM
SUNDAY EVE 7:30 P.M.
GENERAL ADMISSION
$10.50
AUGUST 29 1982
NUMBER

Sunday September 5
Glen Helen Regional Park, Devore, California

The US Festival.

The U.S. Festival

Apple Computer co-founder Steve Wozniak managed to hang onto his hippie values while becoming one of the nation's wealthiest techno-entrepreneurs. (Actually, it was Woz's partner Steve Jobs who did most of the entrepreneuring, while Woz, a brilliant engineer, came up with the hardware.) In 1981, Woz conceived a giant rock festival—a "Woodstock West," as he called it. The inspiration behind the mega-event was Woz's desire to see off the selfish '70s (the so-called "Me Decade") and generate a more altruistic vibe for the '80s—hence the "U.S. Festival."

When Woz couldn't find a suitable venue for the event, he took out his checkbook and had one custom-built in a park outside San Bernardino. The festival took place on September 3–5, 1982, featuring a mix of established acts (Fleetwood Mac, The Kinks) and new-wavey newcomers (The Police, Talking Heads) on the bill. In addition to the music, the festival included a "Technology Expo"—an indication of the growing synergy among music, computers, and (counter) culture.

Woz put on a second US Festival the following year, sans the Grateful Dead. By that time, the '80s were on their way to becoming known as the "Decade of Greed" instead of the "Us Decade." At least Woz tried.

Left: Phil Lesh kicks off the band's two sets at the US Festival at 9:30 a.m., telling the bleary crowd to "Settle down and spread, it's breakfast in bed with the Grateful Dead!" The start time, however, is not the band's earliest (see November 26, 1982).

Not Morning People

The Grateful Dead weren't originally scheduled to play the US Festival, but when Bill Graham took over the event's booking, he brought the band on board. (They needed little convincing: Woz was paying top dollar.) However, adding the Grateful Dead to the September 5 bill meant that the boys had to start at the ungodly hour of 9:30 a.m. According to Blair Jackson, the band didn't bother to go to bed the night before, "and so were in an appropriately ragged frame of mind for the 150,000 people who had camped out at the site overnight and were heavy-lidded themselves."

Above: Bill Graham, Steve Wozniak, and Mickey Hart.

Thursday September 9
Saenger Theatre,
New Orleans, Louisiana

Saturday September 11
West Palm Beach Civic Center,
West Palm Beach, Florida

Mickey Hart turns 39.

Sunday September 12
Lakeland Civic Center Arena,
Lakeland, Florida

Tuesday September 14
University Hall,
University of Virginia,
Charlottesville, Virginia

Wednesday September 15
Capital Centre, Landover, Maryland

The band encore with the first live performance of "Touch of Grey."

Friday September 17
Cumberland County Civic
Center, Portland, Maine

First performance of "Throwing Stones."

9   10   11   12   13   14   15   16   17

CADOGAN LIMITED presents at THE DOWNS AT SANTA FE

GRATEFUL DEAD

SUNDAY, OCTOBER 17 AT 1 PM

DESIGN: D.L.RAWLS & D.SNYDER

© 1982 Marthe Fine Arts/C.O.P.

TICKETS AVAILABLE FROM GIANT TICKET OUTLETS

SANTA FE
THE GENERAL STORE
THE AUTHORITY
SF INFO: (415) 457-6388

ALBUQUERQUE
THE GENERAL STORE
WILDWEST RECORDS
THE CLUB AT U.N.M.
ALB. INFO: 243-3266

DEAD HEAD INFO: (415) 457-6388 or (201) 777-8653

Saturday September 18
Boston Garden,
Boston, Massachusetts

*Above and right: Sunday
October 17, Downs of
Santa Fe, Santa Fe,
New Mexico.*

Monday September 20
Tuesday September 21
Madison Square Garden,
New York, New York

| 18 | 19 | 20 | 21 | 22 | 23 | 24 | 25 | 26 | 27 | 28 | 29 | 30 |

Thursday September 23
New Haven Coliseum,
New Haven, Connecticut

Friday September 24
Carrier Dome, Syracuse University,
Syracuse, New York

*Right: "Doctors Smoke It" button
handmade by Lisa Law.*

DOCTORS SMOKE IT

OCTOBER '82

| 1 ~ 8 | 9 | 10 | 11 | 12 | 13 | 14 |

Saturday October 9
Sunday October 10 ★
Frost Amphitheater,
Stanford University,
Palo Alto, California

Sunday October 17
Downs of Santa Fe,
Santa Fe, New Mexico

| 15 | 16 | 17 | 18 | 19 | ... | 22 | 23 | 24 |

279

"THROWING STONES"
WEIR/BARLOW

Although the visions of a peaceful blue planet that open this Weir/Barlow song from *In The Dark* (1987) may sound a tad idealistic, by the time the refrain of "Throwing Stones" arrives we get a grimmer look at a struggling race in a nuclear age. Presenting a tempered reassessment of the optimistic '60s that ultimately acknowledges "the future's here, we are it, we are on our own," the song's coda craftily co-opts a line from an old children's ditty to put annihilation in terms that anyone can understand: "Ashes, ashes, all fall down." "This is more or less just an anarchistic diatribe," Weir said in 1985. "Governments are acting in the most inhumane and ludicrous manner. That got me pissed, and that rattled around in the back of my head for a while and a few lines emerged." Days after its September 17, 1982 debut, Weir would punctuate this dire warning in upbeat clothing by occasionally pairing it with the hopeful strains of "Not Fade Away," the Buddy Holly classic that often followed "Stones" in Dead sets and during shows by The Other Ones. Today, Weir uses "Throwing Stones" as a set closer with his band Ratdog.

CADOGAN LIMITED PRESENTS THE GRATEFUL DEAD
17
NEW MEXICO
SUNDAY
1:00 P.M.
$13.00
TUFF CLUB

*Above: The Dead bus on
Saturday October 9 at the Frost Amphitheater, Stanford.*

RUN FOR THE ROSES

Jerry Garcia Band

Released by Arista (AL9603) in November 1982

Side One

1. **Run For The Roses**
   (Garcia/Hunter)
2. **I Saw Her Standing There**
   (Lennon/McCartney)
3. **Without Love**
   (McPhatter)
4. **Midnight Getaway**
   (Garcia/Kahn/Hunter)

Side Two

1. **Leave The Little Girl Alone**
   (Kahn/Hunter)
2. **Valerie**
   (Garcia/Hunter)
3. **Knockin' On Heaven's Door**
   (Dylan)

Personnel

Jerry Garcia – guitar, vocals
Merl Saunders – organ
John Kahn – bass, synthesizer, piano, clavinet
Roger Neuman – trumpet
Michael O'Martian – clavinet, piano
Melvin Seals – organ
Julie Stafford – vocals
Liza Stires – vocals
Ron Tutt – drums, tambourine, percussion
James Warren – piano, clavinet

Produced by Jerry Garcia and John Kahn

ONLY THE SECOND studio album from the Jerry Garcia Band (and, unfortunately, the last), *Run for the Roses* was something of a pastiche: two of the tracks (Clyde McPhatter's "Without Love" and a reggae-infused version of The Beatles' "I Saw Her Standing There") were actually updated outtakes from the recording sessions for 1974's *Compliments of Garcia*. The album's uneven quality was likely a reflection of the drug problems and general malaise both Jerry Garcia and John Kahn were suffering through during this period. *Run for the Roses* sold poorly and, in Oliver Trager's words, "suggested that Garcia had long settled into the idea that his solo career was a side trip, enjoyable for him and Deadheads, but not in any serious competition with the Dead."

Bad Blues Band

The last show of the year was one of the best shows of the year in the opinion of many fans. After the opening Bill Graham entrance (this time aboard a giant mushroom) and performances by Bay Area faves The Dinosaurs and Brazilian percussion ensemble Batucaje, the band did two sets, with John Cipollina and Matt Kelly guesting. The scorching third set was what made the night unforgettable. The Grateful Dead, again augmented by the Tower of Power horns, transformed themselves into Etta James's backup band—"the baddest blues band in the world," in her words—and ripped through "Turn On Your Lovelight," "Tell Mama," "Baby, What You Want" (the first since September 7, 1969), "Hard to Handle," and "In the Midnight Hour" (the first since April 29, 1971). Somewhere, Pigpen was smiling. The Dead turned back into themselves to close with "Brokedown Palace" in the wee hours of January 1, 1983.

Sunday December 26
Monday December 27
Tuesday December 28
★ **Thursday December 30**
Friday December 31
Oakland Auditorium, Oakland, California

Giving the audience a taste of what was in store for New Year's Eve, the December 30 show sees the band (plus the Tower of Power horns) back up the legendary Etta James for a two-song encore: "Hard to Handle" (the first since August 26, 1971) and the first-ever "Tell Mama," one of Etta's signature songs.

DECEMBER '82

1 – 25	26	27	28	29	30	31

Wednesday November 10
Leonid Brezhnev, longtime ruler of the Soviet Union, dies in Moscow, aged 75.

NOVEMBER '82

1	2	3	4	5	6	7	8	9	10	11 – 23	24	25	26	27	28	29

Below: Bob Weir and Mickey Hart chill out with Sly Dunbar at the Jamaica World Music Festival in Montego Bay, Freeport Zone.

Friday November 26
Montego Bay, Freeport Zone, Jamaica

The Grateful Dead join homegrown stars like Jimmy Cliff and Peter Tosh and acts like the B-52s and Gladys Knight at the Jamaica World Music Festival. The schedule becomes so snarled that the band doesn't go on until sometime between 2:00 and 4:30 a.m. (accounts vary) on the morning of the 26th—despite being booked to play the previous evening. Given the beautiful setting and the ganja-stoked affinity between the Grateful Dead and the reggae community, the band's performance could have been a memorable outing, but the late (or early) start and problems with the sound system mar the two sets. The island was also undergoing a period of political violence, and the presence of machine gun–toting guards is a further buzzkill.

PROMONTORY RIDER

Robert Hunter

Relix Records RRLP-2002

Released in 1982 and subtitled "A Retrospective Collection," *Promontory Rider* gathered songs from Hunter's three previous solo albums, plus a live version of "Touch of Darkness" recorded a year before in New York City. Jerry Garcia, Mickey Hart, Keith and Donna Godchaux, Dave Torbert, and Dave Grisman were among the members of the Grateful Dead and their musical family backing Hunter on the various tracks. The album, with cover art by Gary Kroman, was released on red vinyl and as a picture disc as well as on conventional vinyl and CD.

Opposite page: Friday December 31, Oakland Auditorium, Oakland, California. Bill Graham's makes his midnight entrance as Father Time on a giant, rolling mushroom.

It's in the Mail, Man

The March 1983 Warfield Theatre shows (benefits for Bay Area causes, as in 1982) marked a new development in the Grateful Dead's relationship with its fans—the inauguration of GDTS (Grateful Dead Ticket Service), a mail-order ticket office for Dead concerts. In *A Long Strange Trip*, Dennis McNally notes that manager Danny Rifkin's decision to begin selling tickets by mail was a reflection of changing demographics: many Deadheads now had jobs and families and couldn't drop everything to get in line at a box office. Initially directed by Eddie Washington (producer of *The Grateful Dead Movie*) and later by Frankie Accardi and Steve Marcus, and run by four longtime members of the Dead family (Calico, Mary Knudsen, Carol Latvala, and Janet Wishnoff), the office sold 25,000 tickets in 1983, a number that would rise to more than 500,000 a year by the '90s, by which time the office's hotline number, (415) 457-6388, was engraved on every Deadhead's memory.

No riots at the Hyatts

As with the 1971 "Dead Freaks Unite!" mailing, the establishment of GDTS was a true innovation and an example of the band's close relationship with (and respect for) its fans. However, it put the band at odds with the monolithic Ticketron organization (known to Deadheads as "Ticketmonster" or "Ticketbastard"), which had exclusive contracts with many of the venues that hosted the Grateful Dead. This led to mutual accusations of antitrust violations between Ticketron and the band's management. The band's attorney, Hal Kant, suggested to John Pritzker (whose family owned both Ticketron and the Hyatt Hotel chain) that he wouldn't want "five thousand crazed Deadheads staying at Hyatt hotels unhappy with you," which gave Pritzker and Ticketron head Fred Rosen a lot to think about, and, in the end, an accommodation was reached.

Opposite page: The New Year's Eve Show, 1992, Oakland Auditorium.
This page: Beautifully designed envelopes sent by Deadheads to Grateful Dead Ticket Services.

Tuesday March 8
In a speech in Orlando, Florida, President Reagan states his belief that the Soviet Union is an "evil empire."

Friday March 25
Compton Terrace Amphitheatre, Chandler, Arizona

The first "Help is on the Way">"Slipknot!">"Franklin's Tower" sequence since October 11, 1977. The evening also sees the first performance of "My Brother Esau," a Weir/Barlow meditation on the Vietnam War's impact on American society cast as a retelling of the story from Genesis. "[It's] an allegory about what happened to members of our generation, where one brother went off and fought a war and one brother stayed home and more or less minded the store," Weir told Blair Jackson in 1985.

My Brother Esau

"My Brother Esau" exists in a sort of limbo on commercial Grateful Dead recordings. Despite serving as the B-side of the "Touch of Grey" single, it was left off the vinyl and CD versions of *In the Dark*—but it was included as the final track on the cassette version.

Saturday March 26
Aladdin Hotel Theatre, Las Vegas, Nevada

Sunday March 27
Irvine Meadows Amphitheatre, Irvine, California

Saturday April 9
Hampton Coliseum, Hampton, Virginia

The band jams briefly on Howlin' Wolf's "Smokestack Lightnin'" but there are no vocals this time around.

Tuesday March 29
Wednesday March 30
Thursday March 31
Warfield Theatre, San Francisco, California

Sunday April 10
Coliseum, West Virginia University, Morgantown, West Virginia

All pictures: Thursday March 31, Warfield Theatre, San Francisco, California.

Tuesday April 12
Broome County Arena, Binghamton, New York

Wednesday April 13
Patrick Gymnasium, University of Vermont, Burlington, Vermont

Jerry Garcia, Phil Lesh, and Bob Weir take a break while Brent Mydland introduces his "Maybe You Know." The song (which never makes it onto an album), will be performed only five more times.

March 1983

284

🎸 **Friday April 15**
Community War Memorial,
Rochester, New York

First "Bob Star," Weir's
short-lived addition to the
lyrics of "The Other One."

15   **16**   **17**

🎸 **Saturday April 16**
🎸 **Sunday April 17**
Brendan Byrne Arena,
East Rutherford, New Jersey

Stephen Stills makes a surprise appearance
in the second set of both shows. Saturday
night sees Stills add his voice to "Iko Iko,"
"One More Saturday Night," and the "Johnny
B. Goode" encore, and the band backs Stills
on his "Black Queen"—the Grateful Dead's
first performance of the song since Stills
introduced it at L.A.'s Thelma Theater on
December 10, 1969. Stills returns during
Sunday's show to sing "Love the One You're
With," the Dead's only performance of Stills's
free-love anthem, and "Not Fade Away."

🎸 **Tuesday April 19**
Alfond Arena,
University of Maine,
Orono, Maine

🎸 **Wednesday April 20**
Providence Civic
Center, Providence,
Rhode Island

🎸 **Friday April 22**
🎸 **Saturday April 23**
New Haven Coliseum,
New Haven, Connecticut

🎸 **Monday April 25**
🎸 **Tuesday April 26**
The Spectrum,
Philadelphia, Pennsylvania

18   **19**   **20**   **21**   **22**   **23**   **24**   **25**   **26**   **27 – 30**

Grateful Dead:
The Official Book of the Deadheads

Edited by Paul Grushkin, the book collected contributions—letters, photos, artworks, and other documents—from hundreds of Deadheads to present a lavish, loving portrait of the band and the Dead scene. Jerry Garcia provided a preface, and Deadhead readers especially appreciated the book's listing of the 3,000 or so Dead shows performed through 1982.

Thursday June 9
Margaret Thatcher's Conservative Party is victorious in Great Britain's general election.

JUNE '83

1 2 3 4 5 6 7 8 **9** 10 11

Below: Jerry Garcia playing in June 1983.

Main and above: Sunday May 15, Greek Theatre, University of California Berkeley, Berkeley, California.

🎸 **Friday May 13**
🎸 **Saturday May 14**
Sunday May 15
Greek Theatre, University of California, Berkeley, Berkeley, Callifornia

Bob Weir unveils "Hell In a Bucket" for Friday night's show. A jaunty Weir/Barlow/Mydland rocker replete with somewhat kinky (by Grateful Dead standards) imagery, the song quickly becomes a popular first-set opener. Grateful Dead Radio Hour host and longtime Deadologist David Gans contributes to the song's final lyrics by changing the line "kissing the toe of your boot" to "sipping champagne from your boot." The second set of Sunday's show starts with a chorus of "Happy Birthday" for soundman Dan Healy and Airto Moreira adds his percussion punch to "Help">"Slipknot!">"Franklin's" trio and "Samson and Delilah," augmented by Flora Purim and Billy Cobham on "Drums." John Cipollina joins in on closer "Not Fade Away."

MAY '83

1 2 3 4 5 6 7 8 9 10 11 12 **13 14 15** 16 17 18 19 20 21 22 23 24 25 26

SUMMER TOUR 1983

GOOD OL' GRATEFUL DEAD

June 18 • Saratoga Springs, NY

Monday June 20
Tuesday June 21
Merriweather Post Pavillion, Columbia, Maryland.

Final "Bob Star" on Monday. The show took place in pouring rain, and at one point lightning reportedly hit the stage, but despite the extreme weather the show went on, and brilliantly, including a 16-minute "Sugar Magnolia" closer.

Top: Tom Constanten (center) with Dennis McNally (left) and Lou Tambakos (right), later co-producer of "Birth of the Dead" backstage at the Old Waldorf.
Above: T.C., the Dead's keyboard player between 1968 and 1971, performs a solo show at the San Francisco venue, produced by McNally and Tambakos. "Cold Rain and Snow" and "Dark Star" are among the songs performed.

June 1983

287

Saturday June 18
Saratoga Performing Arts Center,
Saratoga Springs, New York.

| 20 | 21 | 22 | 23 |

Wednesday June 22
City Island, Harrisburg,
Pennsylvania

| 12 | 13 | 14 | 15 | 16 | 17 | 18 | 19 |

Saturday June 18
Dr. Sally Ride becomes the first American woman in space when she blasts off aboard the Space Shuttle Challenger.

UPPER LEVEL
SEC ROW SEAT
225   F   6
ADMIT ONE THIS DATE
JUN 25 1983
S C H O N
PRESENTS
THE GRATEFUL
DEAD
ST. PAUL
CIVIC CENTER
BEHIND STAGE
JUN 25 1983
SAT

Saturday June 25
St. Paul Civic Center Arena,
St. Paul, Minnesota

Monday June 27
Tuesday June 28
Poplar Creek Music Theatre,
Hoffman Estates, Illinois

| 24 | 25 | 26 | 27 | 28 | 29 | 30 |

Friday June 24
Dane County Coliseum,
Madison, Wisconsin

The Music Never Stopped

Blair Jackson—Bay Area music journalist, later co-founder of *The Golden Road* fanzine and biographer of Jerry Garcia—penned the first authoritative account of the band, its members, its influences, and its impact on music and on society. Sadly, *The Music Never Stopped* was out of print as of 2003.

Left: Pro basketball star Bill Walton, a Deadhead since the early '70s, at the Greek Theatre in Berkeley. He was, officially, the tallest Deadhead ever.

Above and right: July 30–31, County Fairgrounds, Ventura, California. An infected foot forced Garcia to cancel Jerry Garcia Band shows after the Ventura gigs.

"No, it's just that when I choose to go from one song to another, I like a segue, I like the doorways. Bob doesn't seem to care about them one way or another."

JERRY GARCIA TO BLAIR JACKSON

288

July tour off
A planned tour by the Jerry Garcia Band is canceled when Jerry falls ill.

JULY '83

| 1 | 2 | 3 | 4 | 5 | 6 | 7 | 8 | 9 | 10 | 11 | 12 | 13 | 14 | 15 | 16 | 17 | 18 | 19 | 20 | 21 | 22 | 23 | 24 | 25 | 26 | 27 | 28 | 29 | 30 | 31 |

Saturday July 30
Sunday July 31
Ventura County Fairgrounds, Ventura, California

Hells Angels Forever

The movie, directed by Richard Chase, Leon Gast, Kevin Keating, and Lee Madden, included footage of the Jerry Garcia Band playing at the Angels' September 5, 1973, "Pirate Party" on San Francisco Bay.

A "semi-documentary" that did surprisingly well at the box office, *Hells Angels Forever* was widely criticized for what many felt was an overly positive portrayal of the biker club. For that reason, perhaps, it is not yet available on commercial video or DVD.

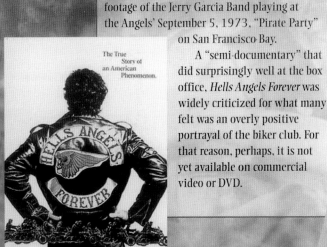

The True Story of an American Phenomenon.

Starring
THE HELLS ANGELS
and Featuring WILLIE NELSON, JERRY GARCIA
JOHNNY PAYCHECK & BO DIDDLEY

hult center house rules:

1. no smoking, drinking, or possession of alcoholic beverages, fireworks or potentially lethal weapons are allowed in the hult center. The presenter of this ticket consents to a reasonable inspection for such items before entry into the hult center.
2. no member of the audience is allowed on stage.
3. aisles must be kept clear.
4. no standing on seats.
5. patron must be in seat designated on ticket.
6. no cameras or recording devices are allowed.
7. no activity which may result in injury to self or others or that may interfere with the performance is allowed.

VIOLATORS ARE SUBJECT TO HAVING THEIR RIGHT to attend this event REVOKED.

Dress to the hilt for the Hult

Friday August 26
Portland Memorial Coliseum, Portland, Oregon

The band's first performance of Willie Dixon's "Wang Dang Doodle." Dixon, who originally wrote this raucous number for Howlin' Wolf, described the origins of "Wang Dang Doodle" in his 1989 memoir *I am the Blues*: "'Wang Dang Doodle' meant a good time, especially if a guy came from the South. A wang dang doodle meant having a ball and a lot of dancing…" The song was also a staple at Kingfish shows.

ENTRY TT
201 F 15
MAIN FLOOR

DOUBLE TEE
AN EVENING WITH
GRATEFUL DEAD
Memorial Coliseum
Portland

AUG 26
PORTLAND, OR
FRIDAY
8:00 P.M.
NO REFUNDS EXCHANGES
NO CAMERAS OR RECORDERS

Monday August 29
Tuesday August 30
Wednesday August 31
Silva Hall, Hult Center for the Performing Arts, Eugene, Oregon

28 | 29 | 30 | 31

Creamery Productions and The Music Bulletin Present
An Elegant Evening with
GRATEFUL DEAD
Hult Center for the Performing Arts
SILVA CONCERT HALL, Eugene, OR
AUG. 29 1983
Admit One
Monday, 8:00 p.m. $15.25
ticket .25
User Fee
TOTAL $15.50
CC 108

Saturday August 27
Seattle Center Coliseum, Seattle, Washington

11 | 12 | 13 | 14 | 15 | 16 | 17 | 18 | 19 | 20 | 21 | 22 | 23 | 24 | 25 | 26 | 27

Phil's Phavorite Bumper Sticker

"My friend Tom Greenleaf made some bumper stickers that featured a cop car chasing some Deadheads in a rental car and said, 'Wherever we go, the people all complain.' After the third Hult show in 1983, we were in the Hilton lobby. Phil was sitting there waiting on his ride and this one Deadhead had a box of bumper stickers he was letting Phil look through. So I told Tom to bring his stickers to the lobby. He hands Phil the aforementioned sticker and Phil says with his big laugh, 'I like this one but I wouldn't put it on my car!' The Deadhead offers Phil his choice of stickers, and Phil says, 'No thanks, man, but I will keep this one.' Two days later in Park City, Utah, we are walking towards the gate when cheers start to be heard as, lo and behold, Phil is cruising up in a dark blue rental and has put Tom's sticker on the rear of the car. Alright Phil! It was Phil's phavorite sticker and we just freaked, yahoo, screaming and waving at Phil's car. Phil gives a nice little wave back. Man, what a laugh… I miss those days."
ERIC SCHWARTZ, DJ, *LONE STAR DEAD RADIO*, DALLAS, TEXAS

Saturday August 20
Sunday August 21
Frost Amphitheatre, Stanford University, Palo Alto, California

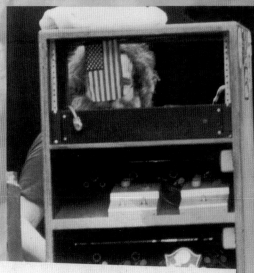

Above: *Garcia and Weir at Frost Amphitheatre, Stanford University, Palo Alto, California, on Saturday August 20.*

August 1983

289

AUGUST '83
1 - 10

WHEREVER WE GO, THE PEOPLE ALL COMPLAIN

STATE POLICE
HURTZ

GEN. ADM. AUG 20, 1983
BGP in Association with STANFORD CONCERT NETWORK Presents
GRATEFUL DEAD
FROST AMPHITHEATRE
AUG 20 1983
STANFORD, CA
SATURDAY
2:00 P.M.
NO CANS, BOTTLES OR ALCOHOL
STANFORD STUDENT I.D. REQUIRED AT GATE

4

Sunday September 4
Park West Ski Resort, Park City, Utah

In honor of the holiday, the "One More Saturday Night" closer becomes "One More Labor Day Night."

Saturday September 10 ★
Sunday September 11
Downs of Santa Fe, Santa Fe, New Mexico

Sunday's show sees Mickey Hart turn 40.

Friday September 2
Boise State University Pavilion, Boise, Idaho

Thursday September 1
A Soviet fighter shoots down Korean Airlines Flight 007 after the 747 strays into Soviet airspace, with the loss of 269 passengers and crew.

Tuesday September 6
Wednesday September 7
Thursday September 8 ★
Red Rocks Amphitheatre, Morrison, Colorado

Tuesday September 13
Manor Downs, Austin, Texas

Sunday September 18
Nevada County Fairgrounds, Grass Valley, California

Saturday September 24
Santa Cruz County Fairgrounds, Watsonville, California

The band's last performance of "Deep Elem Blues."

Saturday October 8
Richmond Coliseum, Richmond, Virginia

The band does a few bars of "Sugar Magnolia" before going into a "Good Lovin'" closer.

Sunday October 9
Greensboro Coliseum, Greensboro, North Carolina

SPEND A ROCKY MOUNTAIN LABOR DAY WEEKEND WITH **GRATEFUL DEAD**

In BOISE, IDAHO, FRIDAY, SEPTEMBER 2, tickets: $10.50, $12.50 reserved, and in PARK WEST SKI RESORT near SALT LAKE CITY, UTAH, SUNDAY, SEPTEMBER 4, tickets: $12.00 advance.

Camping is available between shows at Park West Ski Resort.

Above: Flyer for Park West Ski Resort, Park City, Utah.

September 1983

290

Left and below: Sunday September 11, Downs of Santa Fe, New Mexico. The band played two straight years at this desert race track.

"The Dead show is like an umbilical cord between the people who come. They connect at the gig, then take their plug out and leave...they're like a big family." BILL GRAHAM TO BLAIR JACKSON AND REGAN MCMAHON

10 | 11 | 12 | 13 | 14 | 15

Tuesday October 11 ★
Wednesday October 12
Madison Square Garden,
New York, New York

Tuesday night at the Garden and "St. Stephen" returns to live performance (after "Drums") for the first time since January 10, 1979. Wednesday's show sees a surprise encore: the Beatles' "Revolution." The boys' version (with Garcia on vocals) owes more to the slower "Revolution No. 1" version on *The White Album* than to the Fab Four's single.

Friday October 14 ★
Saturday October 15 ★
Hartford Civic Center, Hartford, Connecticut

Friday's show comprises *Dick's Picks Volume 6*—the first '80s Dead show to make it into the series.

Thursday October 20
Friday October 21
The Centrum, Worcester, Massachusetts

Brent Mydland turns 31. The Rhythm Devils ring changes on *Blues For Allah*'s "Sage and Spirit" instrumental during "Drums."

Dave Harsh

In the second edition of *The Rolling Stone Record Guide*, editor and famously Dead-phobic critic Marsh dissed the band's albums ("virtually worthless") and what he perceived as its "patchouli-oil philosophy," which, he wrote," does nothing more than reinforce solipsism and self-indulgence in its listeners, except when it's nurturing its Hells Angel's fan club—exactly the sort of stuff that gives peace a bad name."

16 | 17 | 18 | 19 | 20 | 21

Tuesday October 18
Cumberland County Civic Center, Portland, Maine

Monday October 17
Olympic Arena, Lake Placid, New York

The band tunes up to Richard Strauss's "Also Sprach Zarathustra" (better known as the opening music for the movie *2001: A Space Odyssey*) before the second set. Deadheads reportedly rename the town by taping over the "P" and "L" on local street signs.

YAMANTAKA

Mickey Hart
Henry Wolff
Nancy Hennings

Celestial Harmonies 13003

Mickey Hart joined with renowned Tibetan bell performers Henry Wolff and Nancy Hennings for this spare, serene album which was released in 1983. It was engineered and mixed by, among others, Dan Healy. Appropriately enough, in Tibetan Buddhism, Yamantaka is the deity of the dead.

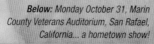

Below: Monday October 31, Marin County Veterans Auditorium, San Rafael, California... a hometown show!

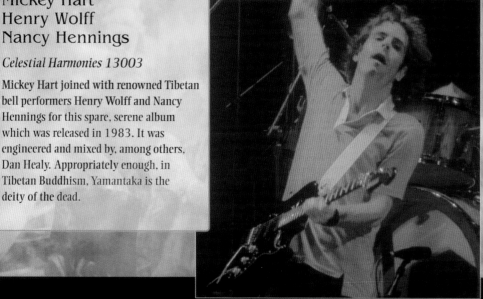

"Isn't it sad that you can't bottle what happens at a Dead show?"

BILL GRAHAM TO BLAIR JACKSON AND REGAN MCMAHON

Saturday October 22
Carrier Dome, Syracuse University, Syracuse, New York

The Band (minus Robbie Robertson, plus the Cate Brothers—*see September 6, 1980*) is the opening act.

Sunday October 23
A suicide bomber destroys the U.S. Marine barracks in Beirut, Lebanon, killing more than 216 American servicemen.

October 1983

291

22 | 23 | 24 | 25 | 26 | 27 | 28 | 29

Tuesday October 25
U.S. forces invade the tiny Caribbean island of Grenada, ostensibly to protect U.S. citizens living there during a pro-Cuban coup d'etat.

30 | 31

Sunday October 30
Monday October 31
Marin County Veterans Auditorium
San Rafael, California

Monday's show marks the band's last performance of "St. Stephen." Airto Moreira also joins on several songs.

GRATEFUL DEAD
SOLD OUT · SOLD OUT
HAPPY NEW YEAR

All pictures: New Year's Eve Show, 1983–84. Some Deadheads are so spaced out, they're still wearing last year's t-shirt!

HAPPY NEW YEARS 82-83

GRATEFUL DEAD

NOVEMBER '83

1 | 2 | 3 | 4 | 5 | 6 | 7 | 8 | 9 | 10 | 11 | 12 | 13 | 14 | 24 | 25 | 26

Wednesday November 2
Congress declares Martin Luther King, Jr.'s birthday a national holiday.

NEW YEARS 1983 GRATEFUL DEAD
ETHAN MIKEL

DECEMBER '83

1 – 24 | 25 | 26 | **27** | **28** | 29 | **30** | **31**

Tuesday December 27
Wednesday December 28
Friday December 30
Saturday December 31
San Francisco Civic Auditorium,
San Francisco, California

Friday's outing sees the first "Mind Left Body Jam" since October 17, 1974, and the year-end show witnesses the band's solitary performance of "Goodnight Irene."

Goodnight 1983

The boys' New Year's Eve extravaganza may have moved to a new venue in downtown San Francisco, but it preserved some old traditions. Bill Graham brought in the New Year by popping out of a giant globe, and after an opening set by The Band, the Dead played three sets, with Rick Danko and Maria Muldaur joining for the entire third set and John Cipollina helping out on the closer—"Goodnight Irene."

Although only performed on this one occasion by the Grateful Dead, "Irene"—originally recorded by Leadbelly *(below)* in 1933— was a song rich with Dead connections. It made frequent appearances at Garcia–Kahn acoustic gigs and also contained the lyric "Sometimes I have a great notion to jump in the river and drown"— the inspiration for the title of Ken Kesey's 1963 novel *Sometimes a Great Notion.*

Further back, as a huge hit for folk quartet The Weavers in 1951, "Goodnight Irene" had been a significant "crossover" record, and its success did much to spark the folk revival of the '50s and early '60s.

Above and right: *The aftermath of the New Year's Eve show, 1983–84, San Francisco Civic Auditorium. It's about 3:30 in the morning.*

Left: *With a studio album now long overdue, the band books some time at Fantasy Records in Berkeley, but "studiophobia" (Bob Weir's neologism) sets in quickly and the session is a bust.*

Zero Plus Many

The proto-jam band Zero formed in 1984 around ex-Ghosts/Heart of Gold Band's Steve Kimock (guitar) and Greg Anton (drums). A Who's Who of Bay Area musical greats rotated in and out of the band's lineup over the succeeding years, including artists such as John Cipollina, Martin Fierro (ex–Legion of Mary), Nicky Hopkins, John Kahn, and Donna MacKay (formerly Godchaux).

"**The inability to come to accord in the studio is a real problem. It's so easy to do onstage because it's demanded of us, but when we're in the studio, we're so pathologically antiauthoritarian, to a man, that when someone makes a suggestion, you generally get an instant six-way factionalization.**" BOB WEIR TO BLAIR JACKSON

JANUARY '84

1 - 31

Monday February 13
Konstantin Chernenko replaces the recently deceased Yuri Andropov as leader of the Soviet Union.

FEBRUARY '84

| 1 | 2 | 3 | 4 | 5 | 6 | 7 | 8 | 9 | 10 | 11 | 12 | **13** | 14 | 15 | 16 | 17 | 18 |

The Rex Foundation

In late 1983 the Grateful Dead and their family began a unique exercise in "Lone Ranger philanthropy"—the Rex Foundation, a homegrown charity devoted to "fostering the power of community, service, and the arts." The foundation's mission statement went as follows: "The Rex Foundation aims to help secure a healthy environment, promote individuality in the arts, provide support to critical and necessary social services, assist others less fortunate than ourselves, protect the rights of indigenous people and ensure their cultural survival, build a stronger community, and educate children and adults everywhere."

In 1994 Mickey Hart discussed the inspiration behind the foundation in the New York *Times*: "We named the foundation after [roadie and road manager] Donald Rex Jackson, who was killed in a car crash in 1976. He embodied this great generous spirit… It's also like that old [TV] show *The Millionaire* where someone you don't know enters your life and gives you the chance to turn it around. I like to think we're doing that through Rex."

Above: David Gans and his wife, Rita Hurault, selling raffle tickets for the Rex Foundation.
Below: The late Rex Jackson, honored in the name of the Dead's charitable enterprise.

The workings of Rex

From the start, the Rex Foundation explicitly eschewed the trappings of conventional charities. It would be a low-overhead, antibureaucratic organization—no paid staff, no celebrity-heavy board of directors, no advertising, no direct mailings. Instead, the receipts from designated Dead shows and other events went into a pool. A "circle of deciders"—mainly the band and their family, plus friends like Bill Walton and Bill Graham—chose beneficiaries. No person or organization could apply for a grant directly: like the millionaire in the TV show, Rex came to the recipient, rather than the other way around.

Gonna Rex you up

From 1984 through 1995 the foundation gave away more than $7 million to several hundred individuals and organizations. In keeping with the foundation's small-scale, grassroots philosophy, most Rex grants were $5,000 or $10,000—sometimes less, rarely more. (The largest single grant, for $91,297, went to Cultural Survival—a group devoted to "protecting the rights, voices, and visions of indigenous people.")

In 1986 the Rex Foundation established the annual Ralph J. Gleason Award, accompanied by a $10,000 grant, for "outstanding contributions to culture." The award honors the man who provided the journalistic voice for the "San Francisco sound," among many other literary achievements. In 1996 the foundation established similar annual awards honoring the memory of Jerry Garcia and Bill Graham.

Rex redux

With the end of touring following Jerry Garcia's death, the Rex Foundation lost its main source of funding, and for several years afterward the foundation's disbursements were limited to the $10,000 grants accompanying the Gleason, Garcia, and Graham awards. After the turn of the millennium, however, the foundation geared up for a new era in giving with The Healing Power of Music concert.

The Diversity of Rex's Generosity
The following list of Rex Foundation grant recipients is completely random, but it gives an idea of the breadth and diversity of the foundation's largesse.

1984: Camp Winnarainbow—Wavy Gravy's "circus and performing arts camp for kids and adults" was a frequent Rex beneficiary.
1985: Chinese Orchestra of San Francisco—the orchestra shared the stage with the Grateful Dead eight times, usually at shows that took place during Chinese New Year.
1986: Berkeley High School's PTA Jazz Fund—Phil Lesh's old school and a mecca for young Bay Area musicians.
1987: Michael Finnissy—this British composer and pianist is one of several contemporary classical composers and musicians helped by Rex.
1988: Friends of the River—an environmental advocacy group devoted to preserving and protecting California's waterways.
1989: Bread & Roses—the organization brings free, live shows to shut-ins, including people in convalescent homes, hospitals, homeless and senior centers, and AIDS facilities.
1990: TreePeople—a Los Angeles–based group promoting "urban forestry."
1991: Project Lighthawk—with the motto "change is in the air," Project Lighthawk champions the role of aviation in environmental causes.
1992: Jan Sawka—an artist working in a variety of media, Sawka designed stage sets for the band in 1989.
1993: Naropa Institute—now Naropa University, "the nation's only accredited Buddhist-inspired university," Naropa is home to the Jack Kerouac School of Disembodied Poetics, co-founded by Allen Ginsberg.
1994: Families Against Mandatory Minimums—founded in 1991, FAMM challenges the "inflexible and excessive penalties required by mandatory sentencing laws" which have put nonviolent, first-time drug offenders—including some Deadheads—in prison.
1995: Forgotten Felines of Sonoma County—a volunteer group "dedicated to the care and control" of the county's feral cat population.

Rock Scully 1941–2014

Rock Scully's nearly 20 years with the Grateful Dead came to an abrupt end in March 1984 when Bill Kreutzmann escorted him to rehab. Drugs had long undercut Rock's effectiveness as road manager, but his ouster was also an attempt to do something about Jerry Garcia's own drug addiction and physical deterioration. (Jerry was by now living as a semi-recluse in the Hepburn Heights house he shared with Scully, and many had come to view Rock as Jerry's co-dependent and enabler.) Although Rock managed to get sober, he was not welcomed back into the Dead's circle. He went on to write a powerful book (with David Dalton) on his time with the band, *Living with the Dead (see page 452).*

"They drove him out of the scene because he was Garcia's supplier. He wasn't allowed to come to the shows for years [afterward]. They couldn't control it all but [Rock] was too close. He was one target they could get a handle on."

OWSLEY IN ROBERT GREENFIELD'S *DARK STAR: AN ORAL BIOGRAPHY OF JERRY GARCIA*

"When I left the Grateful Dead, I left with some resentments. I worked through all of that, and part of that process was the book, but it wasn't a resentful book."

ROCK SCULLY TO TONI A. BROWN IN *RELIX* MAGAZINE, *1996*

GRATEFUL DEAD
Strange Occurances in the Desert
april 6th 84
Aladdin Theater
Las Vegas Nv.

Friday April 6 Aladdin Hotel Theater, Las Vegas, Nevada	**Friday April 13** **Saturday April 14** Hampton Coliseum, Hampton, Virginia

| 6 | 7 | 8 | 9 | 10 | 11 | 12 | 13 | 14 | 15 |

Saturday April 7 Irvine Meadows Amphitheatre, Irvine, California

APRIL '84

| 28 | 29 | 30 | 31 | 1 | 2 |

Wednesday March 28
Thursday March 29
Saturday March 31
Sunday April 1
Marin County Veterans Auditorium, San Rafael, California

The band kicks off the 1984 performance year with a four-night run at the Marin County Veterans Auditorium to benefit the nascent Rex Foundation. During the second set on the first night, Bob Weir and Brent Mydland take a break on "Ain't No Lie." Jerry Garcia and Phil Lesh do the same when Brent premieres "Don't Need Love," a lament on the difficulties of maintaining (or initiating) a relationship. The band will perform the song 16 more times, although it never finds its way onto any "official" release. The second night is marked by the surprise opener—the first performance of Rufus Thomas's "Walkin' the Dog" since November 9, 1970.

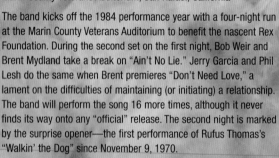

GOOD OL' 1984
APRFOOLS
MARIN VETERANS MEMORIAL AUDITORIUM
GRATEFUL DEAD

Far right: April 23–24, Veterans Memorial Coliseum, New Haven, Connecticut.

GEN. ADM.
APR. 17, 1984
0321

John Scher & Festival East present
Grateful Dead
Niagara Falls
Convention Center
Niagara Falls, NY
Tuesday 7:30 PM
April 17, 1984
Concert #4
Spring East Coast Tour
No Cans, Bottles Or Alcohol.

Tuesday April 17
Niagara Falls Civic
Center, Niagara Falls,
New York

16 17 18 19 20 21

Monday April 16 ★
Community War
Memorial, Rochester,
New York

Thursday April 19
Friday April 20
Saturday April 21
Civic Convention Hall Auditorium,
Philadelphia, Pennsylvania

Left and above: Monday April 30, Nassau Veterans Memorial Coliseum,
Uniondale, New York. Long Island proved to be fertile territory for the
Grateful Dead from 1967 until the end.

Monday April 23 ★
Tuesday April 24
New Haven Coliseum,
New Haven, Connecticut

Again backed by just the
Rhythm Devils, Brent Mydland
presents another self-penned
effort, "Only a Fool," on
Saturday night for its first
and only performance.

LOGE
2
7
2
2

Coast Country Concerts & John Scher present
GRATEFUL DEAD
New Haven Coliseum
New Haven, CT
Monday 7:30 PM
April 23, 1984
Concert #6
Spring East Coast Tour
No Cans, Bottles Or Alcohol.

Sunday April 29
Monday April 30
Nassau Veterans Memorial
Coliseum, Uniondale, New York

23 24 25 26 27 28 29 30

Relix Records

Founded by *Relix* magazine publisher Les Kippel,
Brooklyn-based Relix Records began as an outlet
for albums by musicians associated with the San
Francisco music scene not well-served by the major
record companies. The label's first releases included
works by Robert Hunter, Hot Tuna, Kingfish, and
Jorma Kaukonen, and then grew to encompass
albums by the likes of Tom Constanten, the NRPS,
Merl Saunders, Zero, Big Brother & the Holding
Company, and The Dinosaurs,
as well as non-"Bay Rock"
groups such as Savoy
Brown, Fairport
Convention, and
the Flying Burrito
Brothers—over
100 releases in all.

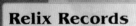

RELIX RECORDS

© 1986
Ice Nine
Pub. Co.

RR45-1A
STEREO
Time: 4:37

from
the album
'Rock
Columbia'

AIM AT THE HEART
ROBERT HUNTER
(Robert Hunter)

Thursday April 26
Friday April 27
Providence Civic Center, Providence, Rhode Island

Thursday sees Brent Mydland again flying (almost) solo on
another of his originals, "Good Times," which many
Tapers' notes list as "Good Time Blues" or "Never Trust a
Woman." (Just to make things more confusing, "Good
Times" is also the title of a Sam Cooke number the band
will cover in the late '80s and '90s. And to add still more
confusion, the Sam Cooke tune is often listed as "Let the
Good Times Roll," even though it bears little resemblance
to the Louis Jordan classic.)

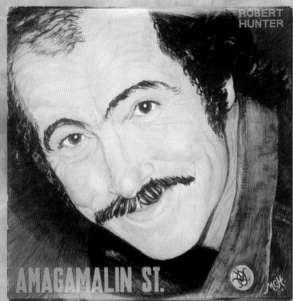

AMAGAMALIN STREET

Robert Hunter

Released by Relix (RRLP-RRCD 2003) in 1984

Side One

1. Roseanne
(Hunter)

Side Two

1. Amagamalin Street
(Hunter)
2. Gypsy Parlor Light
(Hunter)
3. Rambling Ghost
(Hunter)

Side Three

1. Ithaca
(Hunter)
2. Don't Be Deceived
(Hunter)
3. Taking Maggie Home
(Hunter)
4. Out of the City
(Hunter)
5. Better Bad Luck
(Hunter)

Side Four

1. Streetwise
(Hunter)
2. Face Me
(Hunter)
3. Where Did You Go?
(Hunter)
4. 13 Roses
(Hunter)

Personnel

Robert Hunter – acoustic guitar, vocals
Vaclav Berosini – bass
Roy Blumenfeld – drums
John Cipollina – electric guitar
Jorma Kaukonen – electric guitar
Merl Saunders – keyboards
Rodney Albin – violin

I~n~ 1984 MTV, HAIR BANDS, synthesizers, and Springsteen ruled the rock world. "Rock operas" and "concept albums" were laughably passé to the cognoscenti. So give Robert Hunter props for putting out his high-concept *Amagamalin Street* at this juncture. Described by Hunter as a "rock novel," the Dead Poet's fourth solo album (released on CD and double LP) chronicled the intertwined lives of the denizens of said street, most of whom (in true Hunter fashion) are down, if not completely out.

"The idea for Amagamalin Street occurred to me while leaning against a building on Fifth Avenue. I was in one of those ego-flattened mindframes that visit my West Coast psyche when confronted by Manhattan. I began thinking about the values people must assign to themselves, and believe in despite all evidence, in order to cope with the giganticism of Metropolis. I saw a drunk on the other side of the street making a show of himself—and began inventing his story. I had a pencil but no paper—not a problem in New York; I picked up a handbill in the gutter for a show at the Apollo, and began to write on the back of it." ROBERT HUNTER, *A BOX OF RAIN*, 1991

After a 15-minute tutorial on how to handle the press, the Grateful Dead's official historian, Dennis McNally (a.k.a. Scrib), adds "publicist" to his job description.

Saturday June 9
Sunday June 10
Cal Expo Amphitheatre
Sacramento, California

JUNE '84

1 ~ 5 | 6 | 7 | 8 | 9 | 10 | 11

Above and clockwise: *Sunday June 24, Saratoga Performing Arts Center, Saratoga, New York. SPAC, as it was known, was one of the most popular stops on East Coast tours, but eventually problems outside shows there forced the band to abandon the venue.*

MAY '84

1 | 2 | 3 | 4 | 5 | 6 | 7 | 8

9 | 10 | 11 | 12 | 13 | 14 | 15 ~ 31

Sunday May 6
Monday May 7
Tuesday May 8
Silva Hall, Hult Center for the Performing Arts, Eugene, Oregon

During Monday's show a chorus of "Happy Birthday" is sung before "Mama Tried" to commemorate Bill Kreutzmann's 38th birthday. On the last night Ken Kesey and Ken Babbs again haul out the Thunder Machine for "Drums"—just about 20 years after the Great Bus Trip began...

Above: *Ken Kesey with the infamous Thunder Machine percussion contraption, which appeared at Eugene, Oregon, Dead appearances in 1983 and '84.*

12 | 13 | 14 | 15 | 16 | 17 | 18 | 19 | 20

Tuesday June 12
Wednesday June 13
Thursday June 14
Red Rocks Amphitheatre, Morrison, Colorado

The lightning bolts aren't just on the t-shirts: an electrical storm enlivens the second show at this open-air venue. The final night features a second-set surprise after "Playin' in the Band": Traffic's 1967 "Dear Mr. Fantasy." The Dead had some history with Traffic, a Brit outfit comprising Jim Capaldi, Steve Winwood, and Chris Wood. The bands shared the same stage twice in 1970 and also jammed together at a benefit for the New York Hells Angels in the same year. Garcia sings lead for the song's Dead debut, but Brent Mydland takes over during subsequent performances.

Thursday June 21 ★
Kingswood Music Theatre, Maple, Ontario, Canada

The band make their first trip north of the border since 1977 for two shows benefiting the Seva Foundation *(see December 26, 1980)*, with the latest version of The Band (most of whose original members were, of course, Canadian) opening. Although the show takes place on the Summer Solstice rather than Mardi Gras, the band brings out Gary "U.S." Bond's "New Orleans" for the first time since November 12, 1970, as the first song of a three-song encore (the others are "Big Boss Man" and another Crescent City classic, "Iko Iko"). Sylvia Tyson, formerly of the Canadian folk duo Ian & Sylvia, also performs.

Tuesday June 26
Wednesday June 27
Merriwether Post Pavilion, Columbia, Maryland

Going from the sublime to the ridiculous, Phil Lesh debuts his interpretation (sans Jerry) on "Why Don't We Do It in the Road?", Paul McCartney's salacious little ditty from The Beatles' *White Album*—"with hilarious results," according to Blair Jackson.

Saturday June 30
Indianapolis Sports and Music Center, Indianapolis, Indiana

29 | 30

Friday June 29
Blossom Music Center, Cuyahoga Falls, Ohio

21 | 22 | 23 | 24 | 25 | 26 | 27 | 28

Saturday June 23
City Island, Harrisburg, Pennsylvania

Sunday June 24
Saratoga Performing Arts Center, Saratoga Springs, New York

June 1984

299

Tuesday July 3
Starlight Theatre, Kansas City, Missouri

With Rock Scully straightening out and Danny Rifkin about to take some time off to be with his family, the band are once again in need of management help. Jon McIntire, who had been working as a substance-abuse counselor in St. Louis since leaving the Dead *(see page 174)*, is at the Starlight Theatre show. Afterward, Bob Weir persuades the somewhat reluctant McIntire to return and manage the band's upcoming tours.

(see page 174)

Friday July 6
Saturday July 7
Alpine Valley Music Theatre, East Troy, Wisconsin

The first night sees the band's only jam on "Around and Around."

JULY '84

12 13 14 15

6 7 8

Right and below: July 13–15, Greek Theatre, University of California, Berkeley, California. Bob hams it up.

★ **Friday July 13**
Saturday July 14
Sunday July 15
Greek Theatre, University of California, Berkeley, California

Deadhead lore has it that on the first night a shooting star streaked across the sky just as the band launched into the first "Dark Star" since the 1981 New Year's Eve show. On Saturday, Matt Kelly's harp heats up the first-set "Little Red Rooster." The second set of the last night kicks off with Phil's "Why Don't We Do It in the Road?," sung this time, apparently, as "Why Don't We Do It in the Drums?"

1 2 3 4

Sunday July 1
Pine Knob Music Theatre, Clarkston, Michigan

Wednesday July 4
Five Seasons Center, Cedar Rapids, Iowa

0302
GEN. ADM.
JULY 4, 1984

JAM PRODUCTIONS and JOHN SCHER present

Grateful Dead

FIVE SEASONS CIVIC CENTER
370 FIRST AVE. N.E.
CEDAR RAPIDS, IA
JULY 4, 1984
WED. 7:30 P.M.

NO CANS, BOTTLES OR
ALCOHOL PLEASE.

July 1984

300

"AROUND AND AROUND"
BERRY

Also known as "Round and Round," this early Chuck Berry gem certainly made the rounds after its initial release on the rock guitarist's 1959 Chess LP *Chuck Berry Is On Top*. Cover versions by the Animals and the Rolling Stones had already appeared on vinyl by 1964, six years before the Dead added it to their set during the last of six November 1970 shows at the Capitol Theater at Port Chester, New York. It would become the first of five Berry tracks they'd eventually test live, including long-time staples like "Johnny B. Goode" and "The Promised Land," the holiday-themed "Run Rudolph Run," and a one-off take of "Let It Rock" in June of 1974. Berry remembered the song as evolving from a jam session before a show one night: "One of the riffs we struck upon never left my memory, and I waxed in the tune with words about a dance hall that stayed open a little overtime." That up-'til-dawn ethic suited the Dead just fine, and "Around and Around" figured in 412 shows through 1995, making its first formal showing on *Steal Your Face* (1976). The only ever jam on the song was at Alpine Valley in July 1984.

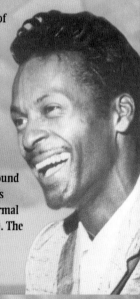

Right: Fan with coffin nail, Sunday July 22, County Fairgrounds, Ventura, California.
Far right: Friday July 13, Greek Theatre, University of California, Berkeley, California.

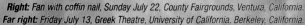

I ♥ BOB WEIR

Bobby & the Midnites
Where the Beat Meets the Street

🎸 Saturday July 21
🎸 Sunday July 22
Ventura County Fairgrounds,
Ventura, California

On Sunday the audience gets a
teaser of Willie Dixon's "I Just Wanna
Make Love to You" (best known in the
1954 Muddy Waters recording), a song last
performed by the band on November 29, 1966,
before "Cassidy" (see October 8, 1984).

WHERE THE BEAT MEETS THE STREET
Bobby & the Midnites

Columbia BFC 39276

Bobby & the Midnites' second—and final—album was a commercially unsuccessful attempt to make a radio-friendly rock record. To that end, co-producer Jeff Baxter augmented the regular band (Weir, Bobby Cochran, Billy Cobham, Alphonso Johnson) with "outsiders" including Steve Cropper, Brian Setzer, and Little Feat's Kenny Gradney. Though Cochran's "Rock in the '80s" and Weir's version of Marvin Gaye's "Ain't That Peculiar" both received some airplay, the album didn't reach many non-Deadheads, and the band broke up a few months later.

Saturday July 28
The Summer Olympics begins in Los Angeles. With the Soviet Union boycotting the games amid renewed Cold War tensions, the U.S. dominates the games.

AUGUST '84

| 16 | 17 | 18 | 19 | 20 | **21** | **22** | 23 | 24 | 25 | 26 | 27 | **28** | 29 | 30 | 31 | 1 ~ 31 |

August 1984

THE GHOSTS PLAYING IN THE HEART OF GOLD BAND
The Ghosts
Whirled Records 01967

Following Keith and Donna Godchaux's departure from the Grateful Dead, the couple hooked up with The Ghosts. While the band's name suggested a life after the Dead, The Ghosts soon started calling themselves The Heart of Gold Band after the acquisition of the Godchauxs—a nod to the Dead's "Scarlet Begonias." This LP presented songs recorded from 1979 through Keith's death in 1980, with the A side credited to The Ghosts and the B-side to The Heart of Gold Band. The tracks were a mix of Ghosts originals, Dylan songs, and—naturally—a cover of "Scarlet Begonias."

Their Words Did Glow

In the winter of 1984 husband-and-wife journalists Blair Jackson and Regan McMahon began publishing *The Golden Road*. Soon established as the Grateful Dead fanzine of record, *The Golden Road* was also, in Dennis McNally's words, "quite possibly the most intelligent and literate rock magazine ever." Jackson and McMahon pulled off the difficult feat of presenting Dead scholarship without losing touch with the playful spirit that animated the band and all its works. Together with the debut of *The Deadhead Hour* radio show (*see November 1984*), *The Golden Road* was a harbinger of the band's amazing mid-'80s revival. It ceased publication in 1993, but many of the best pieces were collected in *Goin' Down the Road: A Grateful Dead Traveling Companion* (Harmony Books, 1992).

The Golden Road was not the only Dead-inspired publication to appear in the 1980s. John M. Dwork (founder of Hampshire College's Grateful Dead Historical Society) and Sally Ansorge Mulvey began publishing *Dupree's Diamond News* in 1986. A successor to earlier 'zines *Dead Beat* and *Terrapin Flyer*, *Dupree's* quarterly issues were supplemented by flyers handed out at concerts. Another new newsletter begun in the same year was *Unbroken Chain*, created by Virginia Deadheads Laura Paul Smith and Wes Wyse.

British and continental Deadheads—a relatively small but highly Deadicated group—also got their own 'zine in 1984 with *Spiral Light: Europe's Grateful Dead Magazine*. Published by a group of British Deadheads, the magazine also sponsored an annual gathering until it ceased publication in 1996.

Sadly, in a period when there was such a flourish in the number of 'zines dedicated to the Dead, the scene lost one of its best-loved publications—*Mikel* (established in 1982). Founder Michael Linah succumbed to cancer in November 1985 and the magazine was forced to fold.

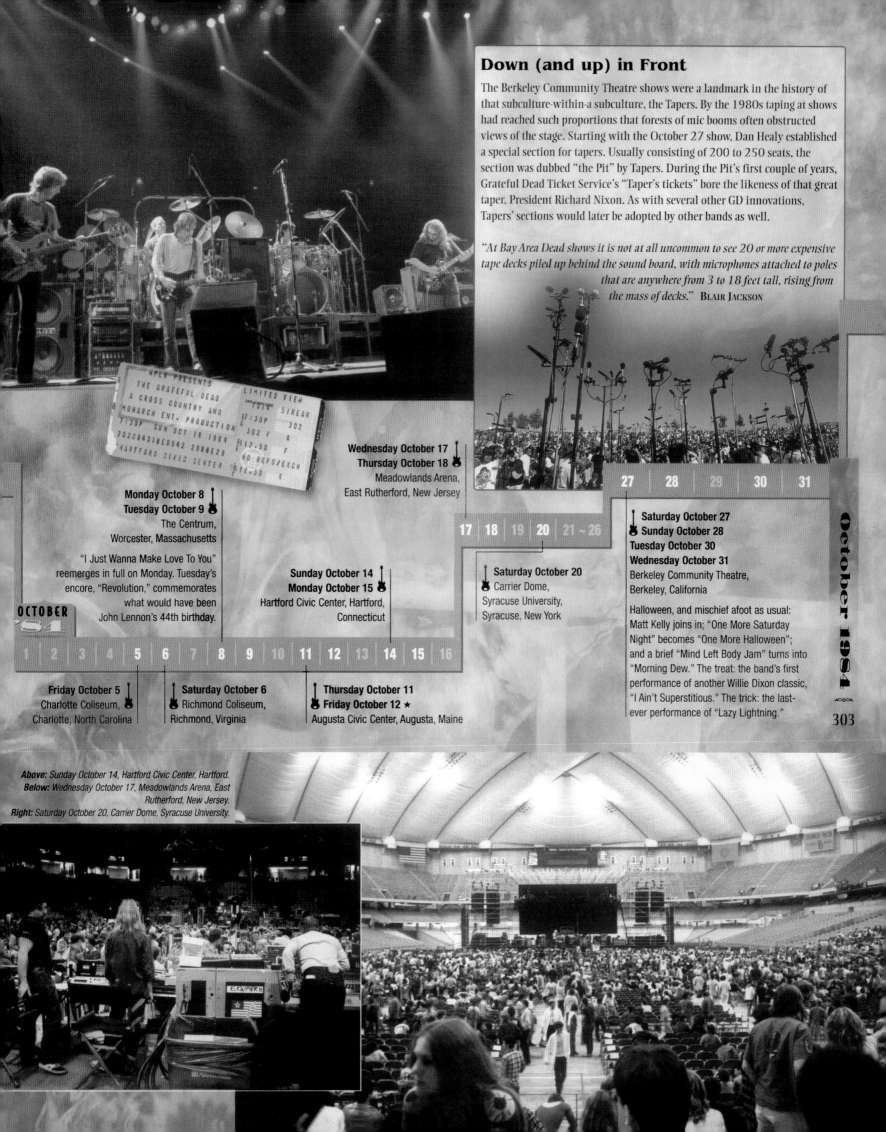

Down (and up) in Front

The Berkeley Community Theatre shows were a landmark in the history of that subculture-within-a subculture, the Tapers. By the 1980s taping at shows had reached such proportions that forests of mic booms often obstructed views of the stage. Starting with the October 27 show, Dan Healy established a special section for tapers. Usually consisting of 200 to 250 seats, the section was dubbed "the Pit" by Tapers. During the Pit's first couple of years, Grateful Dead Ticket Service's "Taper's tickets" bore the likeness of that great taper, President Richard Nixon. As with several other GD innovations, Tapers' sections would later be adopted by other bands as well.

"At Bay Area Dead shows it is not at all uncommon to see 20 or more expensive tape decks piled up behind the sound board, with microphones attached to poles that are anywhere from 3 to 18 feet tall, rising from the mass of decks." BLAIR JACKSON

Wednesday October 17
Thursday October 18
Meadowlands Arena,
East Rutherford, New Jersey

Monday October 8
Tuesday October 9
The Centrum,
Worcester, Massachusetts

"I Just Wanna Make Love To You" reemerges in full on Monday. Tuesday's encore, "Revolution," commemorates what would have been John Lennon's 44th birthday.

Sunday October 14
Monday October 15
Hartford Civic Center, Hartford, Connecticut

Saturday October 20
Carrier Dome,
Syracuse University,
Syracuse, New York

27 28 29 30 31

Saturday October 27
Sunday October 28
Tuesday October 30
Wednesday October 31
Berkeley Community Theatre,
Berkeley, California

Halloween, and mischief afoot as usual: Matt Kelly joins in; "One More Saturday Night" becomes "One More Halloween"; and a brief "Mind Left Body Jam" turns into "Morning Dew." The treat: the band's first performance of another Willie Dixon classic, "I Ain't Superstitious." The trick: the last-ever performance of "Lazy Lightning."

17 18 19 20 21~26

OCTOBER
'84

1 2 3 4 5 6 7 8 9 10 11 12 13 14 15 16

Friday October 5
Charlotte Coliseum,
Charlotte, North Carolina

Saturday October 6
Richmond Coliseum,
Richmond, Virginia

Thursday October 11
Friday October 12 ★
Augusta Civic Center, Augusta, Maine

October 1984

303

Above: Sunday October 14, Hartford Civic Center, Hartford.
Below: Wednesday October 17, Meadowlands Arena, East Rutherford, New Jersey.
Right: Saturday October 20, Carrier Dome, Syracuse University.

In November '84 Bob Weir gigs with the latest incarnation of Kingfish, the New Kingfish Review, featuring Barry Flast (keyboard), Matt Kelly (harmonica), David Margen (bass), Dave Pepper (drummer), and Garth Webber (guitar). Although Brent Mydland and Bill Kreutzmann are pictured here with the band, Weir is not actually featured.

Billy's Band

Bill Kreutzmann's chief solo project this year was Billy Kreutzmann's All-Stars, featuring ex-New Riders guitarist and longtime associate David Nelson, and Larry Murphy, Sr. and Larry Murphy, Jr. on violin and bass, respectively. The quartet performed several highly regarded club shows in early 1984, playing everything from Chuck Berry to Bill Monroe.

1 2 3 4 5

🎸 **Friday November 2** ★
🎸 **Saturday November 3**
Berkeley Community Theatre, Berkeley, California.

The opening night sees the band digging deeper into the Steve Winwood catalog *(see June 14, 1984)*, with Brent Mydland and Phil Lesh sharing vocals on the band's first "Gimme Some Lovin'." On November 3, the band's Willie Dixon binge continues with the first performance of the Mississippi Master's "Down in the Bottom."

GRATEFUL DEAD
MEMORABELIA
SHOW

NOV 2 –
NOV 17

OLD POSTERS
RARE T-SHIRTS
ORIGINAL ART

© 84 1. MOUSE–59

S. MOUSE
STUDIO / GALLERY
652 CANYON RD.
SANTA FE

Sunday November 25
Band Aid—a gaggle of British performers directed by Bob Geldof of The Boomtown Rats—records the single "Do They Know It's Christmas?" to raise funds for Ethiopian famine relief. The song hits No. 1 on the U.S. charts in mid-December and eventually sells 50 million copies worldwide.

19 | 20 | 21 | 22 | 23 | 24 | **25** | 26 | 27 | 28 | 29 | 30

Out of the Fog

The Deadhead Hour, the first regularly scheduled radio show devoted to the Dead, debuts on San Francisco's KFOG FM. In 1985, journalist David Gans appeared as a guest (to discuss the roots of "The Greatest Story Ever Told") and by the end of the year he was hosting the show—or rather serving, in his words, as "scholarly facilitator." Three years later the show won nationwide syndication under the name *The Grateful Dead Hour*. The show reported on all things Dead, but won the hearts of 'Heads by broadcasting songs from the band's archives—though entire sets were *verboten*.

"What I'm doing is highly unusual in the world of intellectual property—for the Dead to give away unpublished stuff on the air every week is pretty cool."
DAVID GANS IN NEWSDAY, 1989.

Below: *Host David Gans with guest Bill Kreutzmann.*

Friday November 16
Jerry Garcia and John Kahn reform their acoustic duo for the first night of a ten-show East Coast tour at Eisenhower Auditorium (Pennsylvania State University), University Park, Pennsylvania, with Robert Hunter as the opening act.

6 | 7 | 8 | 9 | 10 | 11 | 12 | 13 | 14 | 15 | **16** | 1

Tuesday November 6
President Ronald Reagan and his running mate, George H.W. Bush, easily win reelection over Democratic challenger Walter Mondale and his running mate, Geraldine Ferraro—the first woman to be nominated for the vice-presidency by a major party.

Right: *John Kahn, who reformed the acoustic duo with Jerry Garcia in November 1984. Picture taken November 18 in New York.*

Above and right: December 28–31, San Francisco Civic Auditorium.

GRATEFUL DEAD
NEW YEAR'S
SAN FRANCISCO CIVIC
1984
ETHAN MIKEL

1	2	3	4	5	6	7	8	9

Monday December 3
More than 2,000 residents of Bhopal, India, die, and thousands of others are forced to flee after a chemical leak at a Union Carbide insecticide plant.

Support for Deadheads

A classified ad by Don B. in *The Golden Road* eventually led to the formation in 1986 of the Wharf Rats, a 12-step-style support group for Deadheads seeking to live free of drugs and alcohol. The Wharf Rats' information tables *(below)*, yellow balloons (to identify members), and between-the-sets meetings became a familiar part of shows, and a welcome one for Deadheads trying to get—and stay—clean and sober.

Left and above: Dancers twirl in the hallways of the San Francisco Civic Auditorium, which was used for shows while the Oakland Auditorium was being renovated.

Monday December 10
South Africa's anti-apartheid Archbishop Desmond Tutu wins the Nobel Peace Prize.

Friday December 28
Saturday December 29
Monday December 31
San Francisco Civic Auditorium, San Francisco, California

On the first night of the run, another Beatles classic gets rolled out for the encore—"Day Tripper." This New Year's Eve, Bill Graham takes the stage aboard a lightning bolt. The usual three-set year-ender goes out over a nationwide radio hookup. Supporting acts include the acappella group The Bobs, who would later record "The Golden Road (to Unlimited Devotion)" for the *Stolen Roses* tribute album assembled in 2000 by David Gans. This year's New Year's Eve festivities are overshadowed by an awful event—the deaths of stage manager Steve Parish's wife and daughter in a car crash on December 28.

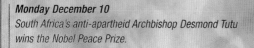

10	11	12	13	14 ~ 20	21	22	23	24	25	26	27	28	29	30	31

Betty on Board

From 1971 through 1978 the Grateful Dead's sound engineer, Betty Cantor-Jackson, recorded more than 200 hours of performance by the band and its various solo/side projects. When she left the band in 1985, the tapes wound up in a rented storage locker. For whatever reason, payments on the locker weren't made, and when the owner auctioned off the locker's contents, most of the tapes went to a cabal of Tapers who had pooled their resources to place the winning bid. And so the now famous and highly sought-after "Betty Boards" found their way into circulation.

Left: New Year's Eve 84–85, San Francisco Civic Auditorium. Bill Graham comes down from the sky on a giant lightning bolt to the stage; fireworks go off and the New Year balloons fall to the floor.

Above: Old House, New Name. The Grateful Dead begin the 1985 performance year with three shows at the former Oakland Auditorium, recently renamed the Henry J. Kaiser Convention Center. The new moniker honors the industrialist who built, among much else, the San Francisco–Oakland Bay Bridge (and who is not to be confused with the avant-garde guitarist with many links to the band).

Friday January 18
Jerry Garcia arrested on drug charges in Golden Gate Park.

JANUARY '85

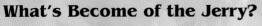
1 | 2 | 3 | 4 | 5 | 6 | 7 | 8 | 9 | 10 | 11 | 12 | 13 | 14 | 15 | 16 | 17 | 18 | 19 ~ 31

What's Become of the Jerry?

As 1985 began Jerry Garcia was in a truly alarming state. Thanks to a diet of cigarettes, ice cream, and candy, his weight was approaching 300 pounds, pushing his respiratory and circulatory systems toward entropy. Captain Trips had become Captain Troglodyte, dozing in front of the TV while freebasing cocaine and "chasing the dragon"—smoking highly pure Persian heroin. Although Jerry was notoriously averse to confrontational situations, band members and family decided that an intervention was needed to convince Jerry to clean up and straighten out.

Mountain Girl described the intervention in Blair Jackson's *Garcia: An American Life*: "It was really organized and everybody participated. We got twelve people to go [to Garcia's Hepburn Heights lair]. A lot of people didn't want to do it, but we talked them into it. I remember how awful it was, and how he ducked it." The intervention was only partly successful: Jerry agreed to get help, but put off entering treatment for several days.

A day before he was scheduled to go into rehab, Jerry Garcia drove his BMW to Golden Gate Park. Noticing that the car was in a no-parking zone, a policeman ran the plates and found that the Beemer's registration had expired. The cop knocked on the window and caught Jerry with small amounts of heroin and cocaine in his briefcase. Jerry was booked on possession charges and released on bail. The charges were later reduced when Jerry agreed to join a support group and play a benefit for the Haight-Ashbury Food Program.

Although Jerry Garcia continued to use drugs after the Golden Gate bust, the attendant publicity and continuing health problems (including swelling in his feet and legs) motivated him to cut back and to take better care of himself, with the help of his live-in housekeeper, Nora Sage. But some in the Dead's family felt that Jerry's long-term recovery would have been better served by a structured rehab program, rather than by leaving the guitarist—a poster boy for passive-aggressive syndrome—to work on his problems mostly in his own way and at his own pace.

The first show of the year takes place exactly a month after Jerry Garcia's bust, and of course every eye in the house is on him. Most observers feel he looks better and shows more energy than he has in a couple of years. He also trades in his customary black T-shirt for a red one. The sartorial choice immediately sends a "trouble ahead, Jerry in red" memo percolating through the Deadhead scene.

The last night is Chinese New Year, and San Francisco's Chinese Symphony Orchestra opens the first two nights, with dragon dances during "Drums" on all three nights. Bob Weir sings the traditional holiday greeting, "Gung Hay Now! Fat Choy Now!" during "Man Smart, Woman Smarter" on the run's second night. (It means "congratulations on prospering in money.")

307

Picking Dick

A one-time postal carrier (as was Phil Lesh—Dead-letter office, anyone?) and full-time Dead Scholar, Dick Latvala got on the bus at the Longshoremen's Hall Trips Festival and stayed for the long haul. While living in Hawaii he got into tape trading, and after moving to the mainland in the late '70s, he befriended the band's roadies. This led to odd jobs at the Front Street office, where his encyclopedic knowledge and excellent (if idiosyncratic) taste in tapes led to his 1985 appointment as official Grateful Dead archivist (*see page 420*).

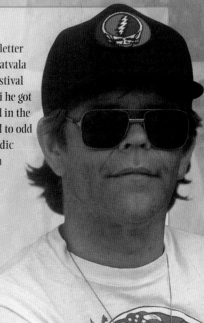

"Who in life can get the only possible job he could do? There's nothing else I know how to do. I can chew Doublemint and sit on a couch longer than anyone, but no one's going to pay money for that."
DICK LATVALA IN THE PHILADELPHIA ENQUIRER, *1995*.

Sunday March 3
Britain's National Union of Mine Workers ends a bitter yearlong strike.

4 ~ 8 | 9 | 10 | 11 | 12 | 13 | 14

Monday March 11
Mikhail Gorbachev becomes leader of the Soviet Union following the death of Konstantin Chernenko.

HAMPTON COLISEUM

MAR 21-22   7 30PM

GRATEFUL DEAD
IN CONCERT

Mickey and the Monks

In-between the Portland and Providence gigs, Mickey Hart meets members of the Gyuto Monks of Tibet at nearby Amherst College, beginning a long association between the monks, the drummer, and the band. Refugees from the Chinese occupation of Tibet, the monks are heirs to a 500-year-old Tantric tradition. Through intense meditation and profound discipline, each monk can sing a complete major chord—something once thought to be beyond the capabilities of the human larynx. In chorus, the monks produce sounds so complex and otherworldly that they go beyond any conventional definition of music.

Later in the year, Mickey Hart produces the first commercial record from the Gyuto Monks, *Tibetan Tantric Choir*, for the new-age Windham Hill label.

Saturday March 9
Sunday March 10
Tuesday March 12
Wednesday March 13
Berkeley Community Theatre, Berkeley, California

These four shows are Rex Foundation benefits, anchoring a spring tradition that would continue over the next decade. On the opening night Merl Saunders accompanies on "Drums" and "The Other One." The Tuesday show features Matt Kelly on "Little Red Rooster" and "Not Fade Away," Kelly returning on the final night for "New New Minglewood Blues," "Deal," "Spoonful," and "Black Peter." The final night also sees Hamza El-Din *(see page 224)* join for "Drums," followed by a haunting performance of the ancient Nubian song "Ollin Arageed"—the first since August 5, 1979.

Thursday March 21
Friday March 22
Hampton Coliseum, Hampton, Virginia

The Dancing Bears officially joined Skull & Roses and Stealie in Dead iconography during the Hampton shows after Jonathan Marks of Grateful Graphics began selling T-shirts featuring the undulating ursines during the 85 Hampton run. The bears first appeared in Bob Thomas's artwork for 1973's *History of the Grateful Dead, Vol. 1 (Bear's Choice)* album, which may in turn have been inspired by designs on blotter acid by Owsley Stanley, a.k.a. Bear.

15 | 16 | 17 | 18 | 19 | 20 | 21 | 22 | 23

Sunday March 24
Monday March 25
Springfield Civic Center Arena, Springfield, Massachusetts

Sunday March 31
Cumberland County Civic Center, Portland, Maine

24 | 25 | 26 | 27 | 28 | 29 | 30 | 31

Wednesday March 27
Thursday March 28 ★
Friday March 29
Nassau Veterans Memorial Coliseum, Uniondale, New York

The shape of tours to come? The re-vocalized Phil Lesh leads the band's first performance of Bob Dylan's "Just Like Tom Thumb's Blues." In subsequent performances Phil often sings "I'm goin' back to San Anselmo" in place of Dylan's original lyric "I'm goin' back to New York City."

Matt Kelly joins the Dead on "Smokestack Lightnin'" on the second night and on the last night returns for the breakout of a Willie Dixon medley—"Down in the Bottom" into "I Ain't Superstitious." This final show of the Uniondale run also sees the return of the first "Supplication Jam" since September 4, 1980, this time as a segue between "Friend of the Devil" and "My Brother Esau."

Siren Song

Together with John Kahn and Richard Loren, Jerry Garcia had optioned the movie rights to Kurt Vonnegut's 1959 novel *The Sirens of Titan* some years before. Jerry cherished the idea of doing a Sirens movie, and by 1985 he and Tom Davis had drafted a screenplay, while Gary Gutierrez, *The Grateful Dead Movie's* animator, worked up storyboards. Although Jerry had some meetings with Hollywood bigwigs, including Mike Ovitz and Bill Murray, the project wound up on the shelf.

Right: Author Kurt Vonnegut, Jr. in New York protesting the imprisonment of Soviet dissidents.

Wednesday April 3
Thursday April 4
Providence Civic Center,
Providence, Rhode Island

Another exercise in Dylanography: Jerry Garcia sings "She Belongs to Me" during Thursday's show, the band's first performance of the song since January 7, 1966.

APRIL '85

1 | 2 | 3 | 4 | 5 | 6 | 7 | 8

Monday April 1
Cumberland
County Civic Center,
Portland, Maine

Saturday April 6
Sunday April 7
Monday April 8
The Spectrum,
Philadelphia, Pennsylvania

WELLcome to Cyberspace

The WELL (Whole Earth 'Lectronic Link), brainchild of SEVA Foundation medico Larry Brilliant and ex-Prankster Stewart Brand, begins operating this month. An early publicly-accessible online service and one of the first Cyber-ventures devoted to fostering a "virtual community," The WELL's Bay Area sensibilities and countercultural connections soon made it a popular online gathering-place for Deadheads (an increasingly wired tribe) to share information about tickets, tour, tapes, setlists, and everything else on the scene.

Saturday April 13
Sunday April 14
Irvine Meadows Amphitheatre,
Irvine, California

9 | 10 | 11 | 12 | **13** | **14** | 15 ~ 25 | 26 | **27** | 28

Saturday April 27
Sunday April 28
Frost Amphitheater, Stanford University,
Palo Alto, California

The first night sees another rare second encore *(see page 325)* as the band, at Bill Graham's behest, follows "U.S. Blues" with "She Belongs To Me."

So Far So Good?

Returning from the East Coast, the band begins work on a long-form video. During three days of shooting, the boys perform more than 50 songs, albeit without an audience, at the Marin County Veterans Auditorium, San Rafael. Len Dell'Amico, videographer for John Scher Productions, was chosen to produce and direct the project, in conjunction with Jerry Garcia, whose interest in the visual arts revived as he struggled to overcome his drug habit.

Tuesday April 30
After years as a private club, the original Fillmore Auditorium reopens with a show by the punk trio Husker Du. Michael Bailey is the resuscitated venue's producer of record.

29 | 30

Left and below: April 28, Frost Amphitheater, Stanford.
Opposite page: Bob Weir at Springfield Civic Center Arena on March 25 (far left); the Grateful Dead at Hampton Coliseum, March 21.

The Grateful Dead almost never cancel shows, but when the dates of a planned Sacramento run conflict with the San Francisco Opera's production of Richard Wagner's *Ring Cycle*, Wagner wins out. The four-opera, 16-hour cycle is such a monumental work that it's rarely performed in full, and Phil Lesh can't pass up the chance to revel in what he called "some of the most transcendental music there is." It is a good call—the SFO's 1985 *Ring*, directed by Nikolaus Lehnoff and conducted by Edo de Waart, now enjoys the same exalted status among opera connoisseurs as, say, the band's February 1970 Fillmore East shows do among Deadheads.

May 1965

310

🎸 Friday June 14
🎤 Saturday June 15
Sunday June 16 ★
Greek Theatre, University of California, Berkeley, California

Left: The pre-show press conference, June 14.
Below: The first night crowd at the Greek Theatre, University of California, Berkeley.

Happy Anniversary

The Grateful Dead marked its "official" 20th anniversary celebration with a three-night run at UC Berkeley's Greek Theatre. The band took the stage the first night to the strains of The Beatles' "Sgt. Pepper's" ("It was 20 years ago today…"), in front of a backdrop by Rick Griffin that reenvisioned Daniel Chester French's sculpture *The Concord Minute-Man of 1776* as a guitar-toting skeleton.

A band press conference (only the third in Grateful Dead history) that preceded the first night's show proved, as recorded by Dennis McNally in *A Long Strange Trip*, that the years had not diminished the boys' disdain for congratulatory platitudes or their irreverence toward the Fifth Estate:

> Q: *"What have the last 20 years taught you?"*
> Phil Lesh: *"It's a good life."*
> Mickey Hart: *"Never take your eyes off the guy to your right or your left."*
> Jerry Garcia: *"Keep your ammunition dry."*
> Bill Kreutzmann: *"Don't swim with piranhas."*

On the first night the band opens with "Dancin' in the Street" and four songs later, in the midst of "Hell in a Bucket," the PA system goes down. After 15 or so minutes the boys return with an anniversary surprise—the first "Keep on Growing," from *Layla and Other Love Songs*, the revered 1970 album by Derek and the Dominoes (a.k.a. Eric Clapton, Duane Allman, Bobby Whitlock, et al.).

For the last night of the anniversary run, the band resurrects the "Cryptical Envelopment" segment from "That's It for the Other One"—the first since September 23, 1972.

"The years are starting to pay off."

JERRY GARCIA TO BLAIR JACKSON

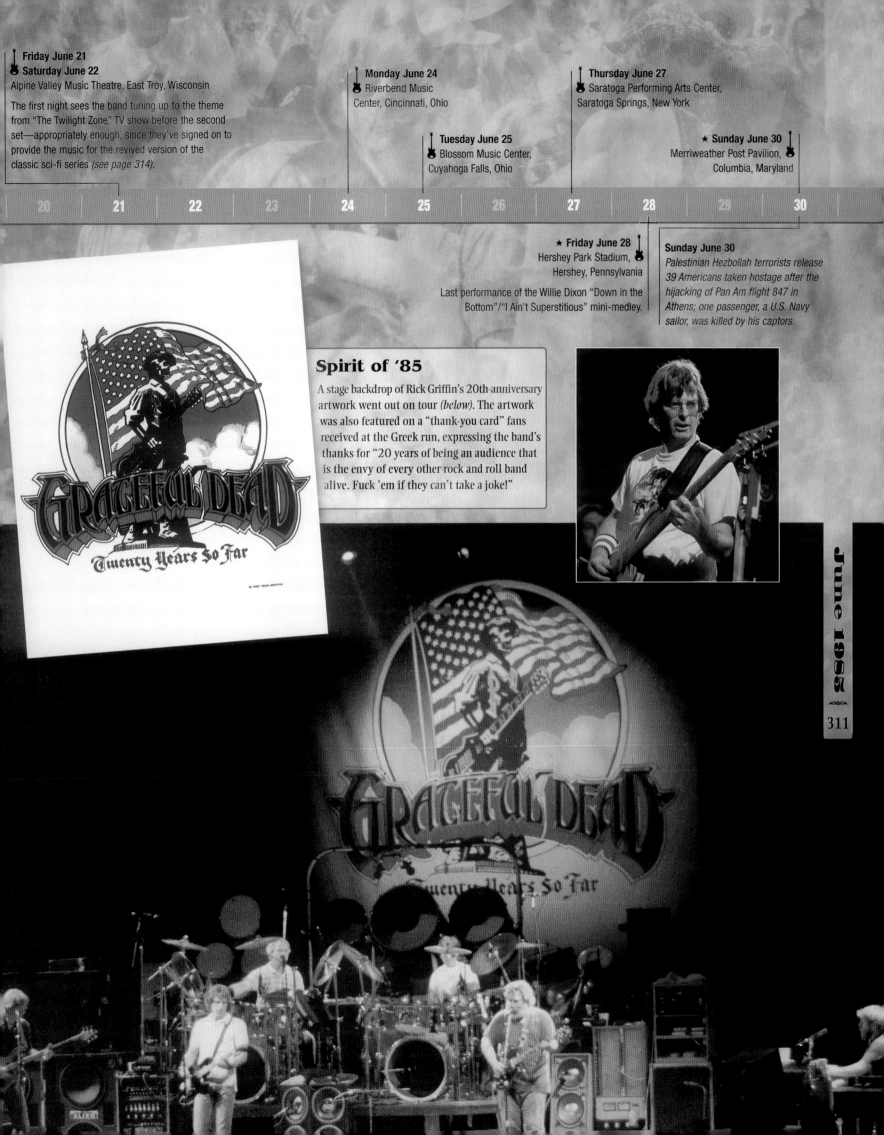

Friday June 21
Saturday June 22
Alpine Valley Music Theatre, East Troy, Wisconsin

The first night sees the band tuning up to the theme from "The Twilight Zone" TV show before the second set—appropriately enough, since they've signed on to provide the music for the revived version of the classic sci-fi series *(see page 314).*

Monday June 24
Riverbend Music Center, Cincinnati, Ohio

Tuesday June 25
Blossom Music Center, Cuyahoga Falls, Ohio

Thursday June 27
Saratoga Performing Arts Center, Saratoga Springs, New York

★ Sunday June 30
Merriweather Post Pavilion, Columbia, Maryland

20	21	22	23	24	25	26	27	28	29	30

★ Friday June 28
Hershey Park Stadium, Hershey, Pennsylvania

Last performance of the Willie Dixon "Down in the Bottom"/"I Ain't Superstitious" mini-medley.

Sunday June 30
Palestinian Hezbollah terrorists release 39 Americans taken hostage after the hijacking of Pan Am flight 847 in Athens; one passenger, a U.S. Navy sailor, was killed by his captors.

Spirit of '85

A stage backdrop of Rick Griffin's 20th-anniversary artwork went out on tour *(below).* The artwork was also featured on a "thank-you card" fans received at the Greek run, expressing the band's thanks for "20 years of being an audience that is the envy of every other rock and roll band alive. Fuck 'em if they can't take a joke!"

GREENPEACE YOU CAN'T SINK A **RAINBOW**

Wednesday July 10
French agents blow up the Greenpeace ship Rainbow Warrior in the harbor at Auckland, New Zealand, to keep it from disrupting nuclear tests in French Polynesia.

Saturday July 13
A galaxy of rock stars perform in Philadelphia and at Wembley Stadium, London, for Bob Geldof's "Live Aid" mega-benefit for Ethiopian famine relief.

| 1 | 2 | 3 | 4 | 5 | 6 | 7 | 8 | 9 | 10 | 11 | 12 | 13 | 14 | 15 | 16 | 17 | 18 | 19 ~ 31 |

Tuesday July 2
Pittsburgh Civic Arena, Pittsburgh, Pennsylvania

Saturday July 13
Sunday July 14
Ventura County Fairgrounds, Ventura, California

Monday July 1
Merriweather Post Pavilion, Columbia, Maryland

Grateful Dead

July 13, 1985
Ventura County Fairgrounds
Ventura, CA

BACKSTAGE

Grateful Dead

August 24, 1985
Boreal Ridge Ski Area
Donner Summit, California

BACKSTAGE

BOREAL RIDGE
HWY. I-80 DONNER SUMMIT
MUSIC FUTURES PRES.
GRATEFUL DEAD
GATES OPEN @ 11:00 AM
SAT AUG 24 1985 2:00PM
ADULT
15.00
GA-4811

Saturday August 24
Boreal Ridge Ski Resort, Donner Summit, California

In the opinion of many Deadheads, Boreal Ridge, a.k.a. the "Summit Conference," was one of the worst shows in the Grateful Dead's history. The combination of a weird venue (a ski resort 7,000 feet above sea level), sound problems, and just plain sloppy musicianship made for a performance so bad that it holds a special place in Deadhead legend and lore.

| 1 ~ 23 | 24 | 25 ~ 29 | 30 | 31 |

Friday August 30
Southern Star Amphitheater, Houston, Texas

Saturday August 31
Manor Downs, Austin, Texas

KLBJ FM &
AUSTIN CHRONICLE
PRESENT
The
Grateful Dead
MANOR DOWNS — MANOR, TX
SAT. — 8:00 PM
AUG 31 1985
GEN. ADM.
$13.00
TAX INCLUDED
CHILDREN AGE 10 YRS. & UNDER ADMITTED FREE
A FURLONG PRODUCTION.
05719

Left and below: July 13–14, County Fairgrounds, Ventura, California.
Opposite page: August 24, Boreal Ridge Ski Resort, Donner's Summit.

SEPTEMBER '85

1 2 3 4

Monday September 2
Zoo Amphitheatre,
Oklahoma City, Oklahoma

Tuesday September 3
Starlight Theatre,
Kansas City, Missouri

The last-ever performance of
"Cryptical Envelopment."

Below: Zoo Amphitheater, Oklahoma City, 9/2/85.
Bottom: Red Rocks Amphitheater, Morrison, 9/5/85

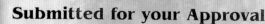

Submitted for your Approval

By 1985 Phil DeGuere, one of the filmmakers behind the
ill-fated *Sunshine Daydream* movie project, was a CBS TV
producer. When CBS decided to do an updated version of
the classic sci-fi series *The Twilight Zone*, DeGuere and
his music director, longtime Dead family member Merl
Saunders, brought the band on board to record a new
version of the original show's main theme (the soundtrack
[left] was released as an album in 1998.) They also did
much of the new show's incidental music.

*"We have done the new main title with music by the Grateful Dead, which is an
extraordinary piece. It's an abstract composition that is entirely in keeping with the
kind of music that was intended for the show in the late '50s. Only now that musical
sophistication has progressed, what we have is a satisfying and exciting interpretation
of those original eight notes of Marius Constant's by one of the most important modern
musical groups around—the Grateful Dead."*
PHIL DeGUERE, IN *THE TWILIGHT ZONE MAGAZINE*, DECEMBER 1985

9 10 11 12 13 14 15 16 17 18 19 20 ~ 25 26 27 28 ~ 30

Tuesday September 10
Wednesday September 11
Thursday September 12
Henry J. Kaiser Convention
Center, Oakland, California

Sunday September 15
Devore Field,
Southwestern College,
Chula Vista, California

Thursday September 19
*A massive earthquake
strikes Mexico City, killing
between 5,000 and
10,000 people.*

Friday September 27
First episode of the
revamped *The Twilight
Zone* airs *(see above).*

5 6 7 8

Thursday September 5
Friday September 6
★ **Saturday September 7**
Red Rocks Amphitheatre,
Morrison, Colorado

The last night sees equipment
glitches holding up the start of the
show, so the band soundchecks with
a revival of the old folk ditty "Frozen
Logger" *(see right)* before the first set.
The show also marks the first time
the "na na, na na na na" finale from
The Beatles' "Hey Jude" is used as a
coda to "Dear Mr. Fantasy."

Thawed Out

The band had played "Frozen Logger"
occasionally in the early 70s, including
an acoustic arrangement; the Red Rocks
soundcheck version was the first since
October 21, 1971. The song, a humorous
lament on the difficulties of loving a
lumberjack, is a traditional Northwest
tune with a variety of verses, although
the best-known version is generally
credited to James Stevens and Ivar
Haglund. (Haglund, by the way, was also
the founder of the Ivar's chain of seafood
restaurants in the Seattle area.)

October 31, 1985
Columbia Coliseum
Columbia, South Carolina

GRATEFUL DEAD
Backstage

1	2	3	4	5	6	7

Monday October 7
The Italian cruise ship Achille Lauro is hijacked by Palestinian terrorists, who kill an American passenger before surrendering to the Egyptian authorities.

"BEAT IT ON DOWN THE LINE"
FULLER

It was a logical move for the Dead, whose roots lay in the burgeoning Bay Area folk and blues scene, to adopt a local favorite like "Beat It On Down The Line" as one of their first electrified numbers. Written by Georgia-born transplant Jesse Fuller, a Bay Area fixture who was already 67 when his seminal album *San Francisco Bay Blues* (1963) put him at the forefront of a blues revival that would share stages with the psychedelic movement in the late 1960s, the track first appeared on Fuller's album *The Lone Cat Sings and Plays Jazz, Folk Songs, Spirituals and Blues* (1961). Its theme of hitting the road to find a better life ("Gonna pack up my bags, gonna beat it on down the line") got bumped up a notch for the Dead's speed-reading on their self-titled 1967 studio debut, as well as in live interpretations dating back to early 1966; on September 11, 1985, Mickey Hart's 42nd birthday was marked by the band playing a 42-beat intro to the song during their show at the Henry J. Kaiser Convention Center in Oakland. After Fuller passed away in Oakland, California on January 29, 1976, the Dead kept his memory alive by playing what fans came to know as "BIODTL" over 100 times through 1994.

Above: October 28, Fox Theatre, Atlanta, Georgia. With its small size and breathtaking architecture, the Fox was a favorite tour spot for years.

Monday October 28
Tuesday October 29
Fox Theatre, Atlanta, Georgia

With the Kansas City Royals having defeated the St. Louis Cardinals the previous day for their first-ever World Series win, the band salutes the victors with their first performance of "Kansas City" on the opening night. This much-covered Jerry Leiber–Mike Stoller number was a chart-topper for Wilbert Harrison in 1959, seven years after it was first released (as "K.C. Loving") by Little Willie Littlefield, "the king of Texas Boogie-Woogie."

24	25	26	27	28	29

30	31

Thursday October 31
Carolina Coliseum Arena, University of South Carolina, Columbia, South Carolina.

The band blasts off with a spooky "Space" as the opener to the first set, into Warren Zevon's "Werewolves of London"—it is, after all, Halloween.

Saturday October 26
Sun Dome, Tampa, Florida

Friday October 25
Sportatorium, Pembroke Pines, Florida

ROBERT HUNTER: LIVE '85
Robert Hunter

Live '85 included eight solo, acoustic-guitar-accompanied performances from Hunter, including versions of "Easy Wind," "Franklin's Tower," "Jack Straw," and "It Must Have Been the Roses." Despite the title the tracks appear to have been recorded at several performances in 1984. The cover artwork is by Maureen Hunter.

Released by Relix (2006) in 1985

Side One

1. **Promontory Rider**
   (Hunter)
2. **Jack Straw**
   (Hunter/Weir)
3. **Red Car**
   (Hunter)
4. **Sweet Little Wheels**
   (Hunter)

Side Two

5. **Amagamalin Street**
   (Hunter)
6. **Rose/Rose (It Must Have Been The Roses)**
   (Hunter)
7. **Easy Wind**
   (Hunter)
8. **Franklin's Tower**
   (Garcia/Hunter)
9. **Boys In The Barroom**
   (Hunter)

NOVEMBER '85

1   2

🎸 Friday November 1 ★
🎸 Saturday November 2
Richmond Coliseum, Richmond, Virginia

The Richmond run is marred by clashes between ticketless gatecrashers and police—a harbinger, unfortunately, of what will become a big problem for the band as the Great Mid-80s Revival hits its stride. (The band will sell out all but a handful of their shows this year, and with a large percentage of the tix bought by hardcore "Tourheads," there's a severe supply/demand imbalance—though that's no excuse for trying to scam in.)

Above and inset: Saturday November 2, Richmond Coliseum, Richmond, Virginia. Despite problems outside, the Richmond shows were among the best of the fall tour.

FLIGHT OF THE MARIE HELENA
Robert Hunter

Relix RRLP-20009

Subtitled "A Musical Narrative," Robert Hunter's metaphor-heavy sixth solo album was released in 1985 and was essentially a long poem set to music.

🎸 Monday November 4
🎸 Tuesday November 5
The Centrum, Worcester, Massachusetts

On Tuesday the band wishes Dead friend Bill Walton (recently traded to the Celtics down the road in Boston) a happy birthday before the second-set opener, "Shakedown Street." "Kansas City" gets its second, and last, airing. Having played several variations on and fragmentations of "Playin' in the Band" since the previous year's fall tour, the band makes it the center of a full-scale jam for the first time.

4   5   6

13 | 14 | 15 | **16** | **17** | 18 | 19

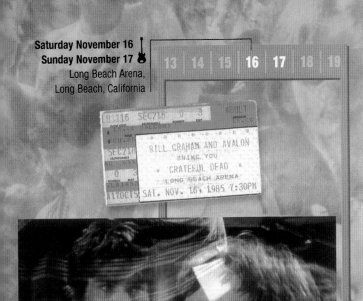

Above: *Following on from work in April, three more days in November were spent shooting the So Far video, directed by Len Dell'Amico, at the Marin County Veterans Auditorium, San Rafael.*

🎸 **Thursday November 7** ★
🎸 **Friday November 8**
Community War Memorial Auditorium, Rochester, New York.

Thursday sees the last performance of Jimmy Reed's "Baby What You Want Me To Do."

Tuesday November 12
As many as 20,000 people die when a volcanic eruption outside of Bogota, Columbia, triggers mudslides.

7 | **8** | 9 | **10** | **11** | **12**

🎸 **Sunday November 10**
🎸 **Monday November 11**
Brendan Byrne Arena, East Rutherford, New Jersey

The first night sees more trouble between police and security and the crowd. Although most of the rowdies are drunken football fans from the nearby Giants Stadium, not Deadheads, the press plays up the incident; the band and its attendant scene are now getting tagged, fairly or not, as a problem act for venues and surrounding communities.

New Year's Run

Kesey inkoherent

The 1985/86 New Year's Eve show was also a celebration of the band's anniversary, so Bill Graham made his pre-midnight entrance inside a 20-foot-tall "birthday cake." As the cake rolled to stage, Ken Kesey—who had apparently been celebrating pretty hard—commandeered the PA system for a rather profane Pranksterish rant.

In the (post) midnight hour

The "midnight set" was beamed out over the USA cable network's *Night Flight* show. The time difference from the West Coast meant that Deadheads elsewhere in the country had to wait till the wee hours of January 1 for their dose.

Fade up

After opening sets by Babatunde Olatunji and the Neville Brothers, the audience showed its birthday love by launching into the "Not Fade Away" chant—usually an end-of-show tradition—as the band took the stage. Suitably touched, the boys responded by opening with "Not Fade Away" into "Touch of Grey."

Short but sweet?

The band came in for some mild grumbling for not playing the usual three New Year's Eve sets, although defensive Deadheads noted that the boys packed 11 songs into the second set. In Bob Weir's words, "If we keep things fairly succinct, we don't drag our stuff out quite so long and we pack a little more music in a little less time. That's kind of neat. I like that myself, rather than dragging it out."

317

🎸 **Wednesday November 20**
🎸 **Thursday November 21**
Friday November 22
Henry J. Kaiser Convention Center, Oakland, California

Thursday's first set kicks off with the first "Big Boy Pete" since September 20, 1970. An occasional outing for Pigpen, the song was originally written and recorded by Don Harris and Dewey Terry in 1960; the Olympics had a hit with it the same year. Big Boy Pete was also the *nom de rock* of British musician Peter Miller, best known for the 1968 single "Cold Turkey," a psychedelic number in the early Pink Floyd vein. The show is "Pete's" swan song—ditto for "She Belongs to Me" and "Walking the Dog."

Monday December 30 🎸
Tuesday December 31 🎸
Oakland Coliseum Arena,
Oakland, California

At the penultimate show of the year the band does "The Mighty Quinn" for the first time—and the sound check includes "Quinn" and "All Along the Watchtower."

DECEMBER '85

20 | **21** | **22** | 23 ~ 30 | 1 ~ 29 | **30** | **31**

| 1 | 2 | 3 | 4 | 5 | 6 | 7 | 8 | 9 | 10 | 11 | 12 | 13 | 14 | 15 | 16 | 17 | 18 |

Mix Up

Starting with shows in 1986, soundman Dan Healy introduced a new live recording technique, known to most tapers as "Healy Ultramix" or "Ultra Matrix." Healy used specially designed equipment from Ultra Sound to mix soundboard and "ambient" audio feeds in perfect synchronization, producing recordings that faithfully captured the experience of hearing the band live while retaining the pristine characteristics of a soundboard recording. Healy returned to more conventional techniques in 1991, making recordings from the Ultra Matrix period especially prized by tapers.

Above and main image:
New Year's Eve show at the Oakland Coliseum Arena.

Tuesday January 28
The Space Shuttle Challenger *explodes shortly after launch from Cape Canaveral, Florida, killing all seven on board.*

| 19 | 20 | 21 | 22 | 23 | 24 | 25 | 26 | 27 | 28 | 29 | 30 | 31 |

1 | 2 | 3 | 4 | 5 | 6 | 7 | 8 | 9 | 10 | 11 | 12 | 13 | 14 | 15 | 16

THE HEART OF GOLD BAND

The Heart of Gold Band

Relix 2020

Keith Godchaux only played one gig with the Heart of Gold Band before his death in 1980; this album documents that show. It contains jammy workouts on a pair of Dylan tracks, Bob Marley's "Stir It Up," and two others. More material was included on the 1989 Relix release *Double Dose*.

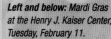

🎸 Saturday February 8
🎸 Sunday February 9
Tuesday February 11 ★
Wednesday February 12
Friday February 14

Henry J. Kaiser Convention Center, Oakland, California

The first two nights celebrate the Chinese New Year. Tuesday is Mardi Gras, and opening act the Neville Brothers bring some Crescent City spice to the show. The Nevilles join the band for a "Drums"-into-"Iko Iko" second-set opener. Friday sees the last performance of Derek and The Dominoes' "Keep on Growing."

February 25
The "People Power" revolution sweeps the Philippines as Corazon Aquino replaces longtime dictator Ferdinand Marcos.

25 | 26 | 27 | 28

February 28
Swedish Prime Minister Olof Palme is assassinated in Stockholm.

Left and below: Mardi Gras at the Henry J. Kaiser Center, Tuesday, February 11.

Books for Yew

In 1986 Mountain Girl, Alan Trist, and members of the Hoedad tree-planting cooperative established Hulogosi Books, later known as Hulogosi Communications, in Eugene, Oregon. ("Hulogosi" is the word for "yew tree" in the language of the Yahi Indians.) Over the next decade, Hulogosi will publish works by Dead wordsmiths Robert Hunter, Bobby Petersen, and Alan Trist, as well as Tom Constanten's "Autobioodyssey," *Between Rock & Hard Places*.

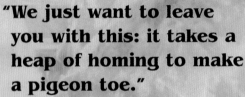

★ Wednesday March 19
★ Thursday March 20
Friday March 21
Hampton Coliseum, Hampton, Virginia

The first night sees the debut performance of Bob Dylan's "Visions of Johanna." The following show has the crowd rejoicing as the band breaks out "Box of Rain" for the first time since July 28, 1973. The resurrection is preceded by Bob Weir's announcement, "Now we're going to prove that practice makes perfect." "Box" will be a frequent and much appreciated encore for the rest of the year. The final night includes the first performance of the Holland-Dozier-Holland chestnut "(I'm a) Road Runner," which Bob Weir and Jerry Garcia have occasionally covered with their side bands.

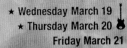

MARCH '86

| 1 | 2 | 3 | 4 | 5 ~ 14 | 15 | 16 | 17 | 18 | 19 | 20 | 21 |

Saturday March 15
The band goes to the Bammies.

Saturday March 1
Bob Weir and Kingfish play shows at New Jersey's Capitol Theater, a longtime Dead-friendly venue, followed by gigs at the Ritz in New York and in Pennsylvania.

March 1986

Below: Wavy Gravy and the band at the Bammies.

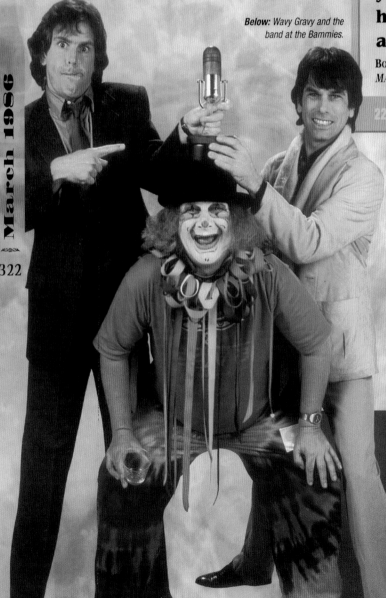

"We just want to leave you with this: it takes a heap of homing to make a pigeon toe."

BOB WEIR'S INTRO TO THE "KEEP YOUR DAY JOB" ENCORE, *MARCH 28*

Maine Force

Some 200 people were arrested during the '86 Portland run for drug selling, gatecrashing, and other offenses. The fact that most of those busted were from out of state was not lost on the local press. *Relix* commented: "Most of the trouble with the Deadhead scene lies with the inadequately prepared transient populace following the band from city to city, not with, by and large, the band's loyal fans that live in each city and see the Dead only in their hometowns or nearby towns."

| 22 | 23 | 24 | 25 |

Sunday March 23
Monday March 24
Tuesday March 25
The Spectrum, Philadelphia, Pennsylvania

The last night in Philadelphia sees continued exercises in Dylanology as the band takes on the magnificent, meandering "Desolation Row," in which Dylan name-checks everyone from Bette Davis to Ezra Pound. The second set starts with "Scarlet Begonias" into "Touch of Grey" rather than the usual "Fire on the Mountain."

Below: Jerry Garcia at The Spectrum, March 24.

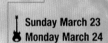

Thursday March 27
Friday March 28
Cumberland County Civic Center, Portland, Maine

The band's first night in Portland witnesses their only performance of "Revolutionary Hamstrung Blues," originally written by Bobby Petersen for Phil Lesh but redirected to Brent Mydland. It is Petersen's final lyrical turn for the band.

"["Revolutionary Hamstrung Blues"] is a period piece about people fighting among themselves, instead of fighting who they should be fighting."
BOBBY PETERSEN IN *THE GOLDEN ROAD*

| 26 | 27 | 28 |

Friday March 28
Adventures in *The Twilight Zone* continued with the airing of an episode written by Robert Hunter. "The Devil's Alphabet" was adapted from "The Everlasting Club," a short story published by one "Ingulphus" in 1919. ("Ingulphus" was the pen name of Sir Arthur Gray, a Cambridge professor and writer of ghost stories.) Fittingly, the plot of "The Devil's Alphabet" involved a sort of dead poets' society.

Left The Grateful Dead at the Cumberland County Civic Center, March 27 and 28

Right: Phil Lesh at Hartford Civic Center, Thursday April 3.

Thursday April 3
Friday April 4
Hartford Civic Center, Hartford, Connecticut

The band retires "Keep Your Day Job" *(see August 28, 1982)* after its outing on the second night.

Saturday April 12
Sunday April 13
Irvine Meadows Amphitheatre, Irvine, California

Tuesday April 15
U.S. warplanes raid Tripoli, Libya, in retaliation for terrorist acts thought to be sponsored by the nation's leader, Colonel Muammar Qaddafi.

Saturday April 26
A nuclear plant at Chernobyl in the Ukraine suffers a major failure, spreading radioactivity throughout the area.

Monday April 28
"Bob Weir and Friends"—including Tom Constanten and David Nelson—play an acoustic show at Wolfgang's, Bill Graham's San Francisco nightclub.

27 28 29 30

24 25 26

3 4 5 6 7

8 9 10 11 12 13 14 15 16 17 18 19 20 21 22 23

Friday April 18
Saturday April 19
Monday April 21
Tuesday April 22
Berkeley Community Theatre, Berkeley, California

Four nights of Rex Foundation benefits. The first night includes an Elvis medley—"My Baby Left Me" (in its only GD performance) into "That's Alright Mama," done by the Dead on June 10, 1973, and not again after tonight. During the Monday show Brent Mydland remains onstage during "Drums," then begins a disturbingly personal and over-the-top rendition of his "Maybe You Know" (the song's last performance.) The band covers Brent's breakdown with—appropriately enough—"Goin' Down The Road Feeling Bad." Jose Lorenzo of Batucaje joins for most of the second set.

APRIL '86

29 30 31 1 2

Sunday March 30
Monday March 31
Tuesday April 1
Providence Civic Center, Providence, Rhode Island

In a rare episode of audience rowdiness—most of the crowd problems starting to plague the band take place in the parking lot—someone throws a bottle at Bill Kreutzmann during Monday's "Truckin'">"Johnny B. Goode" closer. The drummer is unhurt but the show is encore-less.

April 1986

323

Left and below: Berkeley Community Theatre, April 18.

♦ **Saturday May 3**
🎸 **Sunday May 4**
Cal Expo Amphitheatre,
Sacramento, California

Saturday is Kentucky Derby Day, and
the band revives the tradition of playing
"The Race Is On." Technical problems
sabotage the "Sugar Magnolia"
finale and the band leaves
the stage without an
encore. The second show
starts with what would
have been the previous
evening's encore—
"One More Saturday
Night"—even
though it's Sunday.

CAL EXPO AMPHTHR-SACTO
NO OVERNIGHT CAMPING
BILL GRAHAM PRESENTS
GRATEFUL DEAD
NO CANS/BOTTLES/ALCOHOL
SUN MAY 4 1986 2:00PM
ADULT
GEN ADM ** 16.00

5 | 6 | 7 | 8 | 9 | **10** | 11

★ **Saturday May 10** 🎸
Sunday May 11 🎸
Frost Amphitheater, Stanford University,
Palo Alto, California

Psyched by Phil Lesh's return to full vocal
duties, "Let Phil Sing!" chants and
placards are now a fixture on the scene.
As the band takes the stage on Sunday,
Phil jokes with the crowd that "it's not a
matter of letting me sing as much as
making me sing." But the band gives the
bassist's phollowers what they want,
opening with "Gimme Some Lovin'" with
Phil on lead vocal.

324

12 | 13 | 14 | **15** | 16 | 17 | 18 | 19 | 20 | 21 | 22 | 23 | 24 | 25 | 26 | 27 | 28 | 29 | 30 | 31

ROCK COLUMBIA
Robert Hunter

Relix RRCD 2019

A fine return to conventional pop-rock for Robert
Hunter after the challenging, high-concept outings
Amagamlin Street and *The Flight of the Marie
Helena*. Highlights of the eight-song set include
"What'll You Raise"—written in the early '70s
and cut by the Dead (but ultimately rejected) for
Go to Heaven; the moving ballad "Aim at the
Heart," one of Hunter's strongest love
songs; and the introspective "End of
the Road," which is shrouded with
mystery and filled with sharp
imagery. David Nelson plays lead
guitar throughout and keyboardist
Rick Myers anchors the simple but
effective arrangements. Johnny
deFonseca, who played briefly in
the Jerry Garcia Band in the late
'70s, is the drummer.

Thursday May 15
Jerry Garcia, Bob Weir, and Mickey Hart join a host of Bay
Area associates including John Kahn, Jorma Kaukonen, and
Jack Casady at the Berkeley Community Theatre for an event
billed as "Wavy Gravy's Benefit for Just About Anything."

*Below: Tie-dyes for sale on
Shakedown Street, outside Cal Expo
in Sacramento, California.*

Saturday June 28
Sunday June 29
Alpine Valley Music Theatre,
East Troy, Wisconsin

A bit of sublime weirdness as East Troy is also hosting a convention of fans of *Mr. Ed*, the 1960s TV show starring Mr. Ed the talking horse. Both sets of fans mix amicably.

Monday June 30
Riverbend Music Center, Cincinnati, Ohio

Thursday June 26
Hubert H. Humphrey Metrodome, Minneapolis, Minnesota

First gig of summer mini-tour with Bob Dylan and Tom Petty and the Heartbreakers. The next date on the tour is July 2.

26 | 27 | 28 | 29 | 30 | 31

Friday June 20
Saturday June 21
Sunday June 22
Greek Theatre, University of California, Berkeley, California

On Saturday, the band plays a "He's Gone" Deadication to Len Bias, the college basketball star who had died (at age 22) on June 19. As the hall empties out on the last night, the band does a surprise second encore of "Box of Rain."

Above: Various scenes from the Greek Theatre.

Above right: Jerry Garcia at the Frost Amphitheater.

Below and right: The party and the aftermath at the Greek Theatre.

JUNE '96

1 – 15 | 16 | 17 | 18 | 19 | 20 | 21 | 22 | 23 | 24 | 25

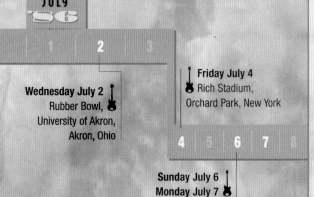

Above and top: The Grateful Dead, Bob Dylan, and Tom Petty.

JULY
'96

| 1 | 2 | 3 |

Wednesday July 2
Rubber Bowl,
University of Akron,
Akron, Ohio

Friday July 4
Rich Stadium,
Orchard Park, New York

| 4 | 5 | 6 | 7 | 8 |

Sunday July 6
Monday July 7
Robert F. Kennedy Stadium,
Washington, D.C.

Bob, Tom, and The Boys

Inspired by Jerry Garcia's growing friendship with Bob Dylan, the Grateful Dead announced a five-night summer mini-tour of big venues of a triple bill with Tom Petty and The Heartbreakers. As with the 1987 "Dylan and The Dead Tour," most Deadheads will consider the five shared shows more significant historically than musically.

The first show, June 26, with Tom Petty and Bob Dylan, takes place in the Metrodome in Minneapolis, a huge stadium infamous for its wretched acoustics. The Grateful Dead open, playing a rare single set. The Dead/Dylan/Petty mini-tour continues on July 2, with Dylan joining the band for "Little Red Rooster," "Don't Think Twice, It's All Right," "It's All Over Now, Baby Blue," and, in the second set, a Jerry-less "Desolation Row."

Part of the triple bill's July 4 show is broadcast (or rather cablecast) on VH-1 as part of a telethon benefiting Farm Aid, including the Dead's "Samson and Delilah," "The Wheel," and "I Need a Miracle." The Dead follow Dylan and Tom Petty, with no inter-performance July 6.

The Dead again close the show on July 7, with Bob joining on the first-set "It's All Over Now, Baby Blue" and "Desolation Row."
"...They played 'Satisfaction' for an encore you could've heard on the moon. Maybe it's because it was the last show before Jerry's illness, but that was one to cherish." PHIL DeGUERE IN DEADBASE

Right: Bob Dylan jams with the Dead.

Thursday July 10
Jerry Garcia falls into a coma.

Jerry Feels the Heat

Brutal heat and humidity followed the band everywhere this summer, taking a particular toll on Garcia. His kidneys had already begun to fail, although apparently no one on the tour noticed that he was alternating bouts of dehydration with frequent urination. Jerry had also begun to use cocaine and heroin again on the tour, in addition to the codeine he had been prescribed for a tooth problem.

After two hot shows (temperature-wise if not musically) at RFK stadium, the band returned to California to play the annual run at the Ventura County Fairgrounds in Ventura. But on July 10, Jerry Garcia's overloaded body systems shut down. Found unconscious in his Hepburn Heights bathroom by Nora Sage, he was rushed to Marin General Hospital. By the time Garcia reached the ER, he was comatose.

Jerry's coma would later be diagnosed as diabetic in origin, but on the morning of July 11, doctors at Marin General weren't sure what was wrong with him—though it was clear he was near death. That afternoon, he got a shot of valium in preparation for a CAT scan. Jerry, however, was allergic to that particular drug and he flatlined. He was revived, but still in danger.

Jerry would be on life support for 48 hours, with his temperature going as high as 105 degrees, and he did not fully emerge from his coma for four days. When he awoke he found Mountain Girl, who had flown down from Oregon on July 11, by his bedside. His first post-coma words were "I'm not Beethoven." Jerry Garcia was indeed neither deaf nor dead, but he now faced a long recovery, mentally as well as physically.

Rocker Jerry Garcia in diabetic coma

GREENBRAE, Calif.—Jerry Garcia, 43, lead guitarist for the Grateful Dead rock band, remained in Marin General Hospital yesterday after he slipped into a diabetic coma caused by an infection which began in an abscessed tooth, a band spokesman said.

"Jerry Garcia is in the hospital receiving treatment for a sudden onset of diabetes and a general systemic infection as a result of an abscessed tooth and exhaustion following a road tour," said band spokesman Dennis McNally. "He's really sick, but he'll be okay," McNally said.
The Associated Press

REFUND NOTICE

We are very sorry, but due to Jerry Garcia's recent illness we have had to cancel the following concerts: Ventura County Fairgrounds July 12 & 13, the Fox Theatre in St. Louis August 6 & 7, and Red Rocks Amphitheatre August 11, 12 & 13.

The enclosed refund is for the face value of each ticket plus our $1.25 per ticket service charge. Postal charges for orders sent back by registered mail are not refundable.

Again, we are very sorry for this inconvenience and we really appreciate the patience and understanding that you all have been showing. We are ALL looking forward to Jerry getting well, and we hope to see you at that time.

Thank you and please...

STAY in TOUCH

HOTLINE INFORMATION: 415 457-6388 WEST COAST
201 777-8653 EAST COAST
415 457-8034 PROBLEMS

AUGUST '86
1 | 2 | 3 | 4 | 5 | 6 | 7

Above: Official GD letter canceling gigs like Red Rocks (right) after Garcia's illness.

3459
GEN. ADMISSION
AUG 13, 1986

GRATEFUL DEAD
RED ROCKS AMPHITHEATRE
MORRISON CO
WED - AUG 13, 1986-7 PM

$16.50
GEN. ADMISSION
3459

Friday August 1
After three weeks in the hospital, Jerry Garcia is finally able to go home, in Mountain Girl's *(right)* care, on his 43rd birthday. In the weeks ahead, as Jerry's body slowly heals, Merl Saunders takes the lead in reintroducing Jerry to his guitar. It is a halting process, as Jerry's near-death experience has affected his nervous system.

"I didn't feel any pain. I didn't feel sick. I just felt tired. Then, when we got back from the tour, I was just really tired. One day, I couldn't move any more, so I sat down. A week later I woke up in the hospital and I didn't know what happened. It was really weird."

JERRY GARCIA TO BLAIR JACKSON

THE WAY IT IS

Bruce Hornsby and The Range

RCA 8058

The debut album from future Grateful Dead member Bruce Hornsby and his band The Range was a huge commercial success that yielded two hit singles, the title track and "Mandolin Rain."

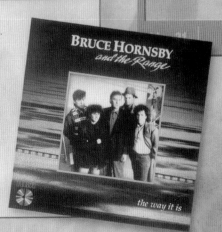

BRUCE HORNSBY and the Range

the way it is

Healing for Jerry

In early September various friends hold a "healing ritual" for Jerry Garcia—Ranch Rock '86—at a Paiute Indian reservation in Nevada. Bob Weir appeared with Kingfish (on vocals only, having recently cracked his shoulder in a bike accident), while Mickey Hart led a pickup band dubbed Mickey and the Daylights. A roster of Bay Area bands, including Zero, came to help beam some get-well vibes to the ailing guitarist.

Another healing event for the Bay Area Deadhead community took place in early September: a "Night of the Living Deadheads" at Wolfgang's, Bill Graham's San Francisco club. David Gans's band Crazy Fingers and some other Deadcentric acts provided music, band memorabilia was auctioned off to benefit the Rex Foundation, and Phil Lesh gave a videotaped update on Jerry's condition—followed by a stern condemnation of hard drugs.

Above: Billy Kreutzmann's All-Stars playing at the Ritz, New York, in September.

328

1	2	3	4	5	6	7

Below: Jerry first show since he left the hospital garners much interest.

Saturday October 4
Sunday October 5
In late September the Jerry Garcia Band announces a show at The Stone in North Beach, San Francisco, on October 4, and when the show sells out in an hour, a second gig is added for the following night. Although some Deadheads are concerned that Jerry is returning to the stage too soon—it is barely two months since he left hospital—his healthy appearance and generally strong playing and singing soothe concerns.

Monday October 13
A summit meeting between President Ronald Reagan and Soviet leader Mikhail Gorbachev ends abruptly when Reagan refuses to discuss halting the planned "Star Wars" antimissile system.

10	11	12	13

Below: Merchants sell their wares outside a Jerry Garcia Band show at Henry J. Kaiser Convention Center in Oakland, October '86.

First Base

During the 1986 Portland run *(see March 1986)*, Dead spokesperson Dennis McNally met a Dartmouth graduate student named John Scott, who sought the band's blessing (enthusiastically bestowed) for a computer-science class project — a complete database of Grateful Dead shows and setlists. The meeting marked the genesis of *DeadBase*.

John W. Scott's setlist-database class project hit print this year as *DeadBase: The Complete Guide to Grateful Dead Song Lists.* Compiled with database master Stu Nixon and pioneer setlist collector Mike Dolgushkin (and help and support from the Dead family, especially Dick Latvala), and with input from a legion of Deadheads, *DeadBase* instantly became "the Bible" for Deadheads and, especially, Tapers. *DeadBase* would subsequently be published yearly and eventually go online.

Joy in Deadville

Wolfgang's hosted a second "Night of the Living Deadheads," this one highlighted by a videotaped interview with Jerry Garcia. Deadheads were overjoyed to see the newly healthy Jerry and delighted when he announced that the Grateful Dead were really, really, really going to start recording a new album in January.

While Jerry Garcia recovered, the rest of the band kept busy with various solo projects throughout the fall—partly out of financial necessity, since the cancellation of the Dead's summer and fall tours drove the band deeply into the red. Go Ahead, Brent Mydland and Bill Kreutzmann's project with members of Santana, played a 15-show tour in October, while Bob Weir gigged with Brian Melvin's Nightfood (including the great jazz bassist Jaco Pastorius) from late September through November.

Although by mid-October Jerry Garcia had performed live three times, everyone knew the real comeback show would be when he took the stage with the Grateful Dead, so there was joy in Deadville when, in mid-October, the band announced three mid-December shows at the Oakland Coliseum Arena to precede the year-end run at the Kaiser.

"I used to be a bluegrass music freak, and I spent a lot of time taping bands. I loved being able to do it, and I loved having the tapes afterwards and being able to trade them around. I think that's healthy stuff."

JERRY GARCIA TO STEVE MARCUS AT THE SECOND "NIGHT OF THE LIVING DEADHEADS," *GOLDEN ROAD, FALL 1986.*

On The Panel

Mickey Hart and Jerry Garcia joined a distinguished panel of scholars and performers at mythologist Joseph Campbell's conference on "Ritual and Rapture" (apt description for a tasty show) at San Francisco's Palace of Fine Arts on November 1 *(below)*. Mickey and multimedia artist Rand Weatherwax followed Campbell's presentation with an improv piece called "The African Queen Meets the Holy Ghost," and Jerry jammed with several musicians behind vocalist Susan Deihim.

Jerry Garcia and Mickey Hart were fans of Joseph Campbell (1904–87), author of seminal works on mythology including *The Power of Myth* and *The Hero's Journey*, long before he became a fan of the band. (They initially hooked up when Bob Weir met one of Campbell's associates while jogging.) Campbell came to a show in '85 and was blown away, proclaiming the Deadheads "the world's newest tribe." Campbell was also a friend of George Lucas, who cinematized much of Campbell's thought in the *Star Wars* saga.

"The Deadheads are doing the dance of life and this, I would say, is the answer to the atom bomb."

JOSEPH CAMPBELL

Above: A fan's car spotted and snapped outside the Henry J. Kaiser Convention Center, Oakland, Saturday December 27.

Saturday November 22
Mickey Hart, Jerry Garcia, and Bob Weir play "Deep Elem Blues," "Throwing Stones," and "Ripple" at a Warfield Theatre benefit for the family of Jane Dornacker. A Bay Area comedian and actress, Dornacker had recently died in a helicopter accident while working as a traffic reporter in New York City. (In 1968 Dornacker had a brief moment of national celebrity when she became the first female mail carrier—another Dead-U.S. Postal Service connection.) Among the other bands performing are The Tubes, including future Grateful Dead member Vince Welnick.

DECEMBER '86
1 2 3 4 5 6 7 8 9

Thursday November 27
The band and family gather for the annual Thanksgiving party at a log cabin in San Anselmo. After dinner there is an impromptu reunion of most of the Black Mountain Boys *(see March 1964)* as Jerry Garcia, Robert Hunter, David Nelson, and Sandy Rothman entertain with a little old-fashioned acoustic pickin', in a moment of healing for all.

22 23 24 25 26 **27** 28 29 30

Thursday November 13
Scandal strikes the Reagan administration when reports surface that the U.S. has secretly sold arms to Iran, using the proceeds to provide illegal funding for anticommunist guerrillas in Nicaragua.

Friday November 21
Jerry Garcia, Mountain Girl, and friends take in Los Lobos (soon to score a major hit with an updated version of Richie Valens's "La Bamba") at New George's in San Rafael. Jerry can't resist the urge to jam and winds up onstage playin' with the band for several tunes.

330

NOVEMBER '86
1 2 3 4 5 ~ 10 11 12 **13** **14** 15 16 17 18 19 20 21

Saturday November 1
"Ritual and Rapture" Conference, Palace of Fine Arts, San Francisco, California *(see above).*

Friday November 14
Jerry Garcia and John Kahn do the acoustic thing at a benefit for the Bread & Roses Foundation at Marin County Veterans Auditorium, San Rafael.

"We just got out the banjos and guitars... There was no pressure and we were remembering the old tunes and it turned out Jerry remembered more words than we did. It was really incredible."

DAVID NELSON, IN ROBERT GREENFIELD'S *DARK STAR: AN ORAL BIOGRAPHY OF JERRY GARCIA*

The Comeback Show

When Garcia sang "I will survive," from the "Touch of Grey" opener, the joyful noise of 14,000 Deadheads rose to the rafters. For many in attendance, the most emotional moment of the night came during "Candyman," when Jerry saluted the crowd while singing "Won't you tell everyone you meet that the Candyman's in town?" The show also saw the debut of "When Push Comes to Shove" and "Black Muddy River." *"A bit thinner, more mobile, and with plenty of breath in his lungs after a few months of clean living, Garcia shined. He smiled more and played with more purpose to his guitar playing than he had in several years."* ALAN SHECKTER, MUSIC PHOTOJOURNALIST, 2003

🎤 **Monday December 15** ★
🎸 **Tuesday December 16**
Wednesday December 17
Oakland Coliseum Arena, Oakland, California

Jerry wavers on Wednesday singing "I was laying in my bed and dying" in "Black Peter"—audience members are tearful.

| 10 | 11 | 12 | 13 | 14 | **15** | **16** | **17** | 18 | 19 | 20 |

"TOUCH OF GREY"
GARCIA/HUNTER

The first track on *In the Dark* (1987) and the Dead's only major hit single, this Garcia/Hunter composition was first performed on September 15, 1982, and heralded an upsurge in the Dead's fortunes in the '80s. Its insouciance, "Oh well a touch of grey, kinda suits you anyway, that's all I've got to say, it's alright," matched a mood of durability, depicting the '60s survivors sliding into a comfortable middle age. An underlying theme of resilience, echoed in the chorus "I will get by, I will survive," made the song a favorite after Garcia recovered from a coma in 1986, especially when he opened his return show with it that December 15, leaving, said Jerry, "not a dry eye in the house." Although Garcia was "appalled" at the Dead's high profile after the song entered the U.S. Top 10 in August of 1987, Hunter seemed to take it in stride. "I think we genuinely got ourselves a hit," he said later, "and a hit does what a hit's supposed to do: propels a band to the top." "Touch of Grey" remained a keynote song for the Dead, airing over 200 times and featuring as the opener for the Dead's last show with Garcia on July 9, 1995.

🎤 **Saturday December 27**
🎸 **Sunday December 28**
Tuesday December 30
Wednesday December 31
Henry J. Kaiser Convention Center, Oakland, California

The New Year's Eve eve show on Tuesday is opened by the Neville Brothers, who join on the second-set "Iko Iko," "Woman Smart, Man Smarter," and the "Johnny B. Goode" encore. Hamza El-Din and Jose Lorenzo join for "Drums." New Year's Eve itself is a joyful yet poignant night as band and fans reflect on how close Jerry Garcia came to not seeing another new year, and the "Brokedown Palace" encore is the highlight for many. Bill Graham makes his entrance swooping to the stage as a giant eagle, and David Crosby and the Neville Brothers open. No one jams with the Dead during their set—it's their night, as in many ways the year ahead will be their year.

| 26 | 27 | 28 | 29 | 30 | 31 |

This page: December 27–31, Henry J. Kaiser Convention Center, Oakland, California. Below are the balloons for the New Year's Eve show, before and after.

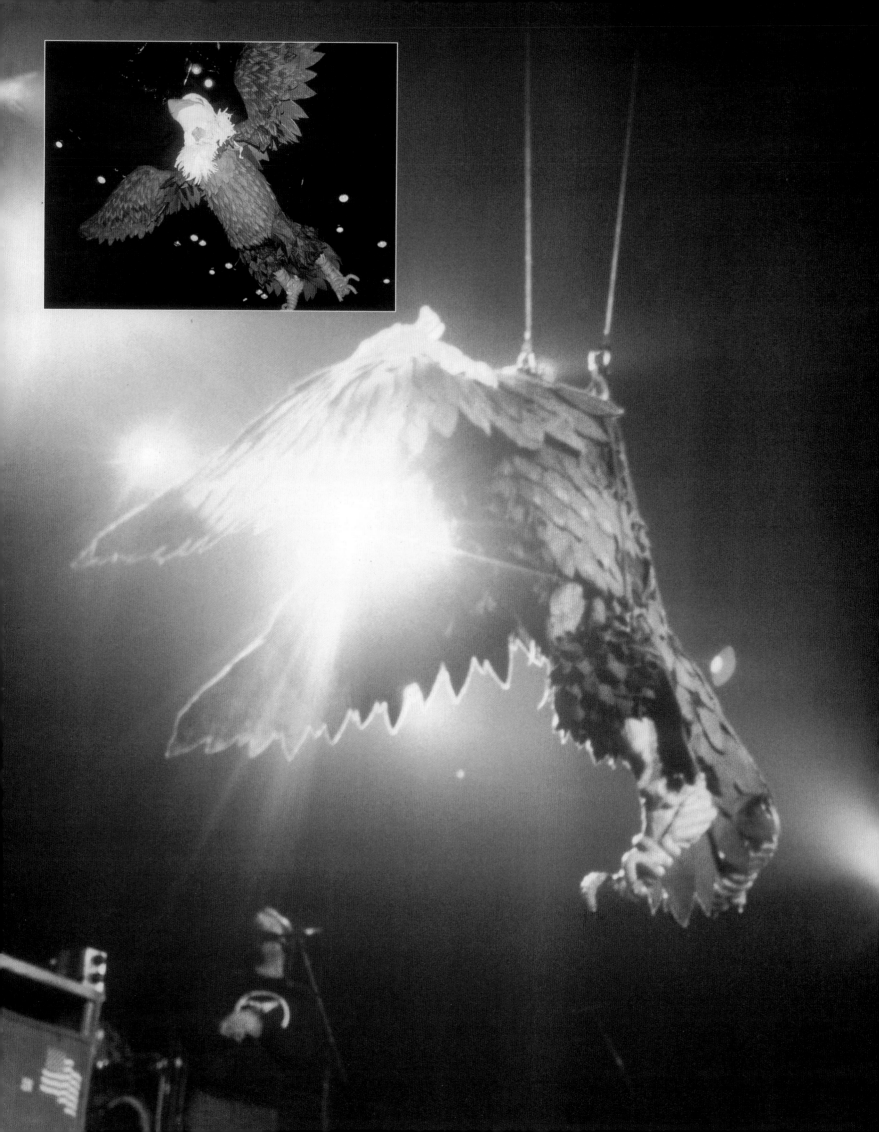

"The Grateful Dead wrote a fuckin' hit!"

INCREDULOUS, OVERJOYED ARISTA RECORDS EXEC UPON HEARING A TAPE OF "TOUCH OF GREY" FROM THE *IN THE DARK* SESSIONS, AS RELATED BY DENNIS MCNALLY IN *A LONG STRANGE TRIP*.

Dark Stars

The band returned to the Marin County Veterans Auditorium to lay down tracks for the new album. Recording in an actual venue in concert setup alleviated the "studiophobia" that hampered the February 1984 recording attempts, and the sessions went well: the inspired idea of doing the basic recording on a stage instead of in a studio solved (insofar as it could be solved) the Great Grateful Dead Record Dilemma—how to capture the band's live dynamics within the confines of a "traditional" rock 'n' roll album.

The band decided on *In the Dark* as the title after they jammed with the house lights down—an episode instigated by the eternally experimenting Mickey Hart. It was the band's 19th album, the first studio album in seven years, and the first "official" GD release of any kind since 1981's *Reckoning*.

> How do you like them Apples...? According to a feature article on Apple Computers in *Business Week*, "Apple engineers recently entertained members of the Grateful Dead, who now compose some of their songs with the help of Macintosh."

The Real Ice Cream Kid

Further proof that the '60s generation had successfully infiltrated American commerce came when Ben Cohen and Jerry Greenfield, socially conscious purveyors of all-natural ice cream, introduced a new flavor: *Cherry Garcia*. The ice cream (cherry with cherries and chocolate flakes) was an instant hit. However, Ben & Jerry failed to secure any kind of permission to use Jerry Garcia's name. The guitarist was apparently not much concerned over the misappropriation (however well-intentioned) of his moniker, but the band's legal eagles worked out an arrangement that got him some royalties, half of which he redirected to the Rex Foundation. According to David Shenk and Steven Silberman's *Skeleton Key*, the idea for Cherry Garcia came from Maine Deadhead Jane Williamson MacDonald.

"At least they didn't name a motor oil after me." ATTRIBUTED TO JERRY GARCIA

Monday January 12
Bobby Petersen, poet and "road pirate" (as described by his long-time friend Phil Lesh), passes away in San Francisco. Petersen's lyrical contributions to the band include "New Potato Caboose," "Pride of Cucamonga," "Revolutionary Hamstrung Blues," and "Unbroken Chain."

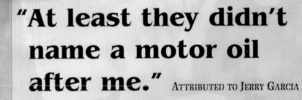

Wednesday January 28
Thursday January 29
Friday January 30
San Francisco Civic Auditorium, San Francisco, California

On the first night, Bob Weir handles the lead vocal (in a somewhat ragged manner) on the band's only performance of The Beatles' "Get Back." San Francisco's Chinese Symphony Orchestra opens the Chinese New Year show on the 29th. Bill Graham tells the press that the Grateful Dead intend to play in China in 1988, but the plans fall through, and the Great Wall remains a fantasy venue.

Above: On February 15, Carlos Santana and Garcia sang "Fire on the Mountain" at a Petaluma benefit concert.

Above and right: *January 28–30, San Francisco Civic Auditorium, San Francisco, California. The Chinese New Year show is on the 29th.*

Left: *Bill Graham descends as an eagle at the New Year's Eve show 1986, at the Henry J. Kaiser Convention Center, Oakland, California.*

Sunday February 15
Jerry Garcia, Bob Weir, and Mickey Hart join Carlos Santana, Hamza El-Din, and Bobby Vega to back up Babatunde Olatunji and his Drums of Passion at a benefit for World Music in Schools at the Veterans Memorial Auditorium, Petaluma, California.

334

Tuesday March 3
Bob Dylan is a frequent visitor to the band's Front Street office in January 1987, and he does a photo shoot with the Dead at the Mardi Gras show at the Kaiser, fueling speculation among Deadheads that a Dylan/Dead tour is in the works. For once the rumors are true; confirmation comes when the town government of Foxboro, Massachusetts, announces approval for a July 4 show at Schaefer Stadium.

MARCH '87

1   2   3

Sunday March 1
Monday March 2
Tuesday March 3
Henry J. Kaiser Convention Center, Oakland, California

Right: Sunday March 1, Henry J. Kaiser Convention Center.

5   6   7   8   9   10   11   12   13   14   15

Friday March 6
The Jerry Garcia Band (gigging regularly in the Bay Area and occasionally as far afield as L.A. and Reno) play a type of venue that probably would have been unthinkable in the Summer of Love—the aircraft carrier USS *Carl Vinson*, anchored in San Francisco Bay.

The '87 East Coast Tour

More indications that the band's resurgence had its troubling side emerged when the Dead headed east in March. The parking-lot scene, in particular, was getting out of control. Professional t-shirt sellers and other "merch" vendors out for a fast buck started to outnumber the Tourheads who sold homemade crafts or whole foods for tickets and traveling money. And the ever-growing crowds at shows (including many decidedly unmellow characters with no real interest in the band's music) were beginning to make Grateful Dead *group non grata* at some venues.

Below: Vendors at the East Coast Tour

Main picture, left and above: Tuesday March 3, Mardi Gras madness at Kaiser Convention Center, Oakland, California.

Wednesday March 18
Jerry Garcia and John Kahn join David Nelson and Sandy Rothman for an acoustic show at the reopened Fillmore—a benefit for Artist's Rights Today.

18   19   20   21   22   23   24

Sunday March 22
Monday March 23
Tuesday March 24
Hampton Coliseum, Hampton, Virginia

The second set on the first night opens with "Sugar Magnolia" and closes with the "Sunshine Daydream" coda for the first time since the 1982 New Year's Eve show.

Thursday April 9
🎸 **Friday April 10**
Saturday April 11
UIC Pavilion, Chicago, Illinois

"Ultimately, what has won the Dead their place in rock history is their sound, a stylistic amalgamation that's both highly distinctive and nearly always danceable."
CHICAGO TRIBUNE REVIEW OF THE FIRST UIC PAVILION SHOW

| 9 | 10 | 11 | 12 | 13 | 14 | 15 | 16 | 17 | 18 | 19 | 20 ~ 30 |

Friday April 17 🎸
Saturday April 18 🎸
★ **Sunday April 19**
Irvine Meadows Amphitheatre, Irvine, California

Several hundred people rush a fence the first show of the Irvine run, many of them getting through to the amphitheatre. Just as bad as the gatecrashing, in the opinion of many Deadheads, is that many in the outdoor venue's audience cheer the gatecrashers on. Scott Allen commented in *Relix*: "What? Did this actually happen on the West Coast? I guess the East Coast doesn't have an exclusive on over-enthusiastic Deadheads."

🎸 **Monday April 6**
🎸 **Tuesday April 7**
Brendan Byrne Arena,
East Rutherford, New Jersey

Friday sees the band retire Martha & the Vandellas' "Dancin' in the Streets." Perhaps a subtle comment on the crowd-control problems outside shows? The second night at the Brendan Byrne Arena in the Meadowlands complex is broadcast live on New York's WNEW and WXRK—sponsored by Ben & Jerry's.

April 1987

335

APRIL '87

| 1 | 2 | 3 | 4 | 5 | 6 | 7 | 8 |

🎸 **Thursday March 26**
🎸 **Friday March 27**
Hartford Civic Center, Hartford, Connecticut

During the '87 Hartford run, Jerry Garcia's friendship with Manasha Matheson (they met at a 1978 show when she gave Jerry a pumpkin) turns into romance.

🎸 **Thursday April 2**
🎸 **Friday April 3**
Saturday April 4 ★
The Centrum, Worcester, Massachusetts

| 25 | 26 | 27 | 28 | 29 | 30 | 31 |

Sunday March 29 🎸
Monday March 30 🎸
Tuesday March 31
The Spectrum, Philadelphia, Pennsylvania

Bill Walton worked praise for the band into a *Sunday New York Times* interview on 29th: "As you get older, you get better. Their creativity, their spontaneity, their ability to create the speed, the space, to create the environment around them is unbelievable. They took their first break from touring in twelve years—from last summer to the beginning of this year—and they're starting to play again and, boy, it's better than ever."

Above and right: *Saturday April 7, Meadowlands Arena, East Rutherford, New Jersey.*

The band spend the latter part of May woodshedding with Bob Dylan at Front Street to prepare for the upcoming six-show tour. (According to Blair Jackson, Dylan got tagged with the nickname "Spike" because the band already had one Bob.) Although they rehearse scores of songs—his, theirs, everyone's—the eternally unpredictable Dylan would, while on tour, pull out the one song he and the Dead had never played together *(see July 26).*

(see July 26)

MAY '87

| | 1 | 2 | 3 | 4 | 5 | 6 | 7 |

Saturday May 2
Sunday May 3

Frost Amphitheater, Stanford University, Palo Alto, California

On the second night, Bob Weir tunes up to "Little Bunny Foo-Foo" before the first-set "Peggy-O," with Brent singing along—no doubt triggering summer-camp singalong flashbacks in many audience members.

Saturday May 9 ★
Sunday May 10

Laguna Seca Raceway, Monterey, California

A two-show run to celebrate the 20th anniversary of the Monterey Pop Festival (which actually took place on June 16–18, 1967). Bruce Hornsby and The Range and slide-guitar master Ry Cooder open both shows. After the band leaves the stage on the first night, the audience forms a huge circle of now-legendary proportions. During the shows, the band prepares to enter the MTV Age by shooting a short-form video for "Touch of Grey." Garry Gutierrez's concept for the video envisioned the band as—what else?—life-size performing skeletons. After a run-through of the song, a group of puppeteers re-create the band's movements for the camera, much to the delight of a group of Deadheads camping nearby, who are invited to serve as the audience.

| 8 | 9 | 10 | 11 | 12 |

Above: Saturday May 9, Laguna Seca Raceway, Monterey, California

Sunday May 24

It's the 50th anniversary of the opening of the Golden Gate Bridge. Bill Graham had organized an anniversary concert, which included the Grateful Dead, but the event is canceled when San Francisco authorities reportedly back out of a promise to halt traffic on the bridge during the performances.

| 13 | 14 | 15 | 16 | 17 | 18 | 19 | 20 | 21 | 22 | 23 | **24** | 25 |

| 26 | 27 | 28 | 29 | 30 | 31 |

Below and right: The 20th anniversary of Monterey Pop Festival, held on May 9–10, Laguna Seca Raceway, Monterey, California.

May 1987

336

Radio Station KPFA, Berkeley, begins broadcasting "Eyes of Chaos"/"Veil of Order." Hosted by Phil Lesh and Gary Lambert (editor of the *Grateful Dead Almanac*), the monthly program showcases the work of "avant garde" 20th century composers and performers.

Friday June 12
Saturday June 13
Sunday June 14
Ventura County Fairgrounds, Ventura, California

The band adds another dense, dark Dylan number to its repertoire with the first performance of "When I Paint My Masterpiece" on the second night.

Cameron Sears

For a band that built its business operation mostly hiring close friends and relatives, the addition of Cameron Sears to the organization in 1987 was rather unusual: he had been a white-water river rafting guide and environmental lobbyist before he was hired as an assistant to Grateful Dead road manager Jon McIntire. Before long, McIntire quit and Sears took his place, so becoming responsible for the day-to-day functioning of the group on the road. During the challenging early and mid-'90s he became a more all-encompassing manager for the band. Since Garcia's death he has continued to work with the band members, serving as Ratdog's manager and, at the tail end of 2001, being elevated to President/CEO of Grateful Dead Productions.

| 1 | 2 | 3 | 4 | 5 | 6 | 7 | 8 | 9 | 10 | 11 | 12 | 13 | 14 |

Friday June 12
Prime Minister Margaret Thatcher's Conservative Party wins Great Britain's general election.

Tuesday June 30
Kingswood Music Theatre, Maple, Ontario, Canada

| 26 | 27 | 28 | 29 | 30 |

Friday June 19
Saturday June 20
Sunday June 21
Greek Theatre, University of California, Berkeley, California

The countdown to the Dylan & the Dead tour continues with the first performance of "All Along the Watchtower" from 1968's John Wesley Harding (and magnificently covered by Jimi Hendrix on *Electric Ladyland* from that same year), marking the second night. The crowd goes wild. Sunday offers a rare afternoon show— especially delightful in a venue renowned for its ambiance.

Friday June 26
Saturday June 27
Sunday June 28
Alpine Valley Music Theatre, East Troy, Wisconsin

Below: The big ticket for the Dead's show on June 21 at the Greek Theatre.

| 15 | 16 | 17 | 18 | 19 | 20 | 21 | 22 | 23 | 24 | 25 |

Tuesday June 16
"Touch of Grey"/"My Brother Esau" is released.

Friday June 19
MTV's usual acts grab their hairspray and run for the exits as the video network declare a "Day of the Dead" for the premiere of the "Touch of Grey" video, which is soon programmed into heavy rotation. Later in the summer MTV presents a "Dawn of the Dead Weekend" featuring various clips from previous band film and video ventures, including *The Grateful Dead Movie*.

"MTV recently devoted an entire day to the band, which once would have seemed as remote a possibility as an MTV special on Sun Ra."
STEVE SILBERMAN IN THE *SAN FRANCISCO SENTINEL*.

Suddenly, it's Hip to be a Hippie

The Arista single "Touch of Grey" backed with "My Brother Esau" hit the stores four years and nine months after the A-side's live debut *(see December 1986)*. With the release of the single, the song assumed the status of an anthem, linked in the public's mind both with the band's perseverance into its third decade and with Jerry Garcia's remarkable recovery from his nearly fatal coma. Heavy rotation of the video on MTV *(see June 19)* and major airplay hammered the point home further. "Touch of Grey" eventually reached No. 9 on the charts, giving the band its first-ever top 40 appearance. The success of the single (and the video, and *In the Dark*) brought the band a horde of new fans—soon known to old-guard Deadheads as "Touchheads."

"It was the Dead's peculiar luck to produce "Touch of Grey" at precisely the time MTV's hierarchy decreed that some old guys would be nice."
DENNIS McNALLY

"The nice thing about the second set (drum solo) is that it's a nice place to experiment. I can do anything that I want that I feel like playing. My rule to myself is be as musical as I can. I'm not up there just trying to play a million hot licks to show I'm the fastest." BILL KREUTZMANN TO BLAIR JACKSON, 1989

KEEPER OF THE BEAT

July 1987 — December 1995

The late 1980s was a very special era for the Grateful Dead and Deadheads. In a sense it felt like borrowed time—or, more accurately, added time—for in the summer of 1986 the circus tent almost came crashing down for good when Garcia slipped into a diabetic coma and came close to dying. As Garcia noted a couple of months after the episode, "The doctors said they'd never seen anybody as sick who wasn't dead." With the Grim Reaper kept at bay (this time), Garcia spent the fall of 1986 recuperating, recharging his tired batteries, and reevaluating his reckless lifestyle, and everyone—band and fans alike—counted their blessings that the Grateful Dead would go on; indeed, the late '80s would usher in a true renaissance for the band, both musically and in terms of their popularity.

From the late '80s and through the '90s Kreutzmann and Hart used MIDI effects to create new soundscapes that added an extra dimension to the band.

The particulars of the group's spectacular comeback have been oft-recounted: the triumphant spring '87 East Coast tour; the mega-success of *In the Dark* and "Touch of Grey" (the band's only true hit single); a hit conceptual video, *So Far*; landing on the cover of *Rolling Stone* for the first time since the mid-'70s; and the sold-out stadium tour with Bob Dylan. This is the period when the Dead went from being an arena band to (gasp!) a stadium band, so large was their following in the East and Midwest. Garcia could only laugh at the sheer improbability of it all: "We're sort of like the town whore who has finally become an institution; we're finally becoming respectable."

"I can't tell you what it means to have been to the point where it looked like there wasn't going to be any more Grateful Dead, and then to come back like this and to have it be as good as it is now," Bill Kreutzmann said in 1988. "I don't think before that we ever really took it for granted— I mean, we all know how special it is—but now it has a different feeling. We're playing better. We're healthier—all of us, not just Jerry—and we have

"We'll be back there saying 'Earthquake!' or 'World War III!' and we'll do big bomb shots on the big toms... That's some of the influence from (working on) *Apocalypse Now*. It's kind of fun to have a theme going through your mind." BILL KREUTZMANN TO BLAIR JACKSON, *1989*

Bill Kreutzmann has always been passionate about music, from the Warlocks in the mid-'60s through to The Dead in 2003, and no doubt way into the future.

more energy: I know I do. I feel great! I feel young!"

By 1988, Kreutzmann's onstage world had evolved into a gargantuan maze of large and small mounted drums, hand percussion instruments, and state-of-the-art electronic gear. Thanks to Bob Bralove, who signed on as one of the band's sound wizards in 1986, Billy (and his partner in rhythm, Mickey Hart) now had a huge range of natural and electronic sound samples at his fingertips—or, more accurately, sticktips—that he could trigger at his whim and mix in any combinations he chose, making the "Rhythm Devils" segment in the second set a sonic landscape with truly limitless possibilities. The antiquated notion of a "drum solo" didn't begin to capture what Kreutzmann and Hart served up every night deep in the heart of the show. Each night brought a completely different percussion journey—it might move from the primordial ooze to the farthest nebulae, with a dozen side trips in between. There might be electronically altered versions of church bells or a natural soundscape with birds and insects, or the hypnotic clanging of an Indonesian gamelan. It was always a completely new and free creation, improvisation at its highest, and still, it seemed, rooted firmly to the psychedelic abstraction of the ol' Acid Test mentality, which had been chemically etched into their DNA so many years ago.

Like Bob Weir, Bill Kreutzmann was just a teenager when he hooked up with the Warlocks back in 1965. His earliest memory of playing music was pounding the quarter-time on an Indian tom-tom while his mother— a choreographer who taught dance at Stanford University in Palo Alto— worked on new dance moves. He started taking drum lessons at 12, and by his mid-teens was playing in rock and roll and R&B cover bands at local dances—one group, The Legends, even wore matching red coats and black pants: very slick! By 1964, when he turned 18, he was married and had a baby girl, and was struggling to make ends meet working at a wig shop and teaching drums at Dana Morgan's Music Shop, where Garcia (another new dad) also taught guitar and banjo. Billy counted himself as a fan of Mother McCree's Uptown Jug Champions—"I really got off on those guys; my heart just said, 'This music is really cool'"—so it wasn't too much of a surprise that when Garcia, Weir, and Pigpen plugged in and became the Warlocks, they'd call on Bill Kreutzmann to be their skinsman. It was, needless to say, quite a change from playing tight, four-minute R&B songs.

"We played extended pieces from the very beginning," he said of the Warlocks. "We just never thought of stopping; it never crossed any of our minds to play three-minute songs. We played this bar called the In Room that was a terribly weird gig on some levels, but a great learning gig for us— six nights a week, five sets a night. The weekends were all these straight juicer types, and they'd be looking up at us as we played all these long, long songs and they didn't know what to make of us. They wanted us to quit, but the men didn't want to admit they were tired and look shitty to their girls. We played every new Rolling Stones song that's come out, and Pigpen would sing some blues. We just kept playin'." It helped that under the tutelage of Phil Lesh, Kreutzmann had started listening to lots of adventurous jazz—he especially liked the subtle but intricate stick work of Elvin Jones, drummer on some of John Coltrane's greatest works. "He was a major influence on me, no question about it," he said.

Not surprisingly, playing drums under the influence of LSD at the Acid Tests (and after) presented a great challenge for Kreutzmann. Acid, he noted with a laugh, "changed the tempo a lot. Actually, a lot of time there was no tempo. It also created more extendedness and amplified what was going on—it made things go on longer, or just seem like a blink, depending... When you're high on acid you can't really be expected to be too analytical about things; you're going more with the free-flow, and sometimes that would be synchronous with what the other guys were playing, and sometimes you'd just be in your own world playing. I remember once when I was high on acid it took me what seemed like fourteen years to take my drums apart. It seemed like lifetimes had gone by—I'd gone gray, grown old, died, been reborn all in the time it took to put one cymbal in the case!"

There's no question that the Dead would not have developed the way they did had Kreutzmann not been such a supple and reflexive drummer. He could keep time with the best of them on the Dead's shorter songs, but it was his elasticity on the more extended and open-ended pieces that allowed the group to move so easily from one rhythmic mode to the next. The guitarists never had to worry about whether the beat was going to be there—even if Billy wasn't playing on the two or the four (or the whatever, if it was stranger), he was always at least cruising in the vicinity of the time, a handy reference for the others. As he once explained it, "I can almost be like two people sometimes. I can sit up there and be the time-keeper and let that happen. Though actually I'm not really keeping the time—I'm playing with it. The time is already there—you're just picking out parts to show people. And then I can also be real excited inside and that makes me play in another way."

When Mickey Hart joined the group in the fall of '67, the whole rhythmic apparatus of the Grateful Dead moved into a new dimension. Kreutzmann is the first to admit that he learned much from Hart: together they brought a palpable intensity to the new material the band were working on at that time, and an increased rhythmic sophistication to the many cover tunes the group still played. "What happened was during that period we really rehearsed a lot at the old Potrero Theater," Kreutzmann recalled, "and a lot of what we'd do was rehearse different times—we'd do sevens, or nines, and I think 'The Eleven' came out of that stint. We'd play for hours until it was

"We played extended pieces from the very beginning. We just never thought of stopping; it never crossed any of our minds to play three-minute songs." BILL KREUTZMANN TO BLAIR JACKSON, *1989*

practically flawless." This period also produced "The Other One," which is credited to Kreutzmann and Weir. Surprisingly, though, the drummer said he was not that enamored with *Anthem of the Sun*, the album where that song/jam first appeared: "It wasn't my cup of tea, particularly."

More to his liking was the shift to the more concise musical statements of the *Workingman's Dead* era, 1969 and '70. "It was a neat period," he says. "We were adding so many new songs and the whole feeling of the music was very different from what we'd been doing. For me, it was a lot more satisfying."

When Mickey Hart left the group beginning in 1971, Billy went back to being the sole drummer, and the music immediately felt lighter and freer—the band as a whole became more nimble, able to turn musical corners with greater fluidity. Their jams opened up tremendously during the early '70s, incorporating more dissonance, irregular rhythms, and jazzier textures. "I had a sense that the music became a little more clear," Kreutzmann said. "The rhythms and the grooves had a clarity you can hear on tapes from that period... It was definitely the most open music we've played. It's never quite been that way again—which is fine; you want things to be different, to change."

By 1973, too, the band's original songs were starting to move away from the simple structures of their "Americana" period, in favor of more exotic world rhythms—from reggae to Latin and Brazilian-influenced tunes. Kreutzmann handled the multiplicity of rhythm shifts with typical aplomb. His drumming never really called much attention to itself, yet it always seemed perfect. If you listened closely, though, it was hard not to agree with Phil Lesh's assessment of the Europe '72 Bill Kreutzmann, who "played like a young god... He was everywhere on the drums, and just kickin' our butts every which way, which is what drummers live to do."

Still, Kreutzmann always maintained that he was delighted when Mickey Hart returned from his self-imposed exile in 1974 at Winterland, and then during the Dead's year-and-a-half "retirement" from performing. When the band went back onto the road in mid-'76 with both drummers and a fistful of new arrangements that capitalized on the double-drum

attack, "things maybe didn't flow as easily for a while," Billy said. "It was a little more cumbersome, which I think you'd expect, but it smoothed out over time." Indeed, 1977 was another peak year for the band, and by the time the '80s rolled around, the drumming tandem was at full strength again and moving in new, creative directions with each passing month, as they built up their arsenal of percussion instruments, and took their second set jams farther and farther away from the simple drum duels of years past. "It's so good up there," Billy enthused in the summer of '79, "that if you fell down, with any luck at all you'd make tons of music!"

"Billy and I really listen well to each other," Mickey commented in 1990. "We don't even have to look at each other. We're hearing it all. Sometimes we'll crack each other up. We have our own little musical conversation going most of the time. Sometimes it lasts the whole evening and we'll never talk about it, but we've talked about it in the drums. We have complete conversations—it's how we move the rhythms, what we do to what, who treats what which way... there are a million things that go on every night between us. It can be very satisfying because you're doing it with somebody else."

Just as Garcia and Weir would sometimes predetermine a vague "theme" for the "Space" jam that always followed the "Rhythm Devils" segment, Billy and Mickey would sometimes discuss a certain approach to their solo before the show, or grab inspiration from a headline in the papers, or from the possibilities presented by a new piece of gear. "We'll be back there saying 'Earthquake!' or 'World War III!' and we'll do big bomb shots on the big toms," Kreutzmann said in the late '80s. "That's some of the influence from [working on] *Apocalypse Now*. It's kind of fun to have a theme going through your mind. The other thing we do is program rhythms, sometimes before the show, or during the break. We'll be back there doing these rhythms that are stored [by computer] and then we use them during the drum solo."

For the bulk of the show, though, Kreutzmann would be at his trap set, laying down simple but slippery beats that neatly propelled the songs but also left plenty of room for melodic and rhythmic ornamentation by the other players. In the grand Dead tradition, he always saw himself as playing with each band member individually at the same time he contributed to a grand gestalt. "Through the years, I've learned how to play with all the other musicians at the same time," he explained in 1988. "The bass drum goes with the bass—with Phil—and I'll do the right hand lead stuff with Jerry, complemented on cymbals or crashes with Bobby, and then I'll use the left hand hi-hat stuff for the rhythm pocket with Brent and the bass and the rhythm guitar. I'll do all of that at the same time. I found myself doing that once [many years ago] and I thought it was a cool thing to do instead of dedicating the drum set to one player and then moving it around the band that way. It's not something I could ever teach another drummer, because it's really a matter of listening and being able to separate the functions…

"To me, the neatest thing is playing with everyone in the band—true ensemble playing. When we're really playing well is when we take the most chances, and that's the most fun for me. I love to go out and take a gigantic risk someplace in a song. Sometimes they make it and sometimes they don't. When they make it, it's amazing. Jerry once described it: 'Kreutzmann, it's wonderful—you sound like you're falling down a flight of stairs but landing on your feet!'" Which isn't a bad metaphor for the Grateful Dead's entire career.

It was that elegant, nuanced playing that was the heart of the Dead's rhythm section for 30 years, and made Kreutzmann so central to the band, despite his modest profile. It was no surprise that in the bleak months after Garcia's body gave up the struggle and he died, a smile on his face, in August 1995, that it was Kreutzmann who ultimately led

the band to its first post-Garcia decision, by declaring himself retired—a decision, happily, he rescinded a few years later.

"I just love music," he said in the same interview. "I love listening to it and I love playing it. I feel incredibly lucky that I've been able to spend my life in music. And it's still getting better for me; that's the best part.

"We've been having such a good time lately; that's a big reason [we've been playing well]. And also we've been playing a lot, which is important. You gotta keep playin'. I don't like sitting around in hotels on an off-day watching TV. It's like, 'What the fuck am I doing here?'" he chuckled. "I can get in a weird headspace. But on show days I usually wake up and all day I look forward to playing. Playing is what makes it all worthwhile."

Dylan and the Dead

Officially called the Alone and Together Tour but universally referred to as Dylan and the Dead, the six July 1987 shows united two of music's most venerated acts. As with other episodes in the Grateful Dead's career—like the Pyramid shows—the quality of the actual performances didn't match the historical significance of the event.

The problem wasn't the Grateful Dead, who played well throughout, but with Dylan, who, according to Dennis McNally, "forgot his own lyrics, and the keys the songs were played in."

The choice of songs was also, perhaps, not what it could have been. During rehearsals *(see page 336)* Dylan and the band had run through upwards of a hundred songs, but without much thought as to which they would actually perform: "When we went on the road we didn't have the slightest idea of what we were going to do," said Bob Weir.

Some fans and critics also imputed an ulterior motive to Dylan's collaboration with the Dead; Dylan's own shows weren't selling out and his most recent album, *Knocked Out Loaded*, had had a poor commercial and critical

reception. Could it be that Dylan was trying to ride the Mega-Dead's coattails to boost his own career? If so, it was a reversal of fortune that would have seemed unthinkable 20 or even 10 years earlier.

The shows themselves were mixed in quality, but the Meadowlands and Anaheim outings were generally regarded as the strongest performances. Some Deadheads were disappointed over the first two dates when the band played only one set before backing Dylan; this was remedied at the July 12 show, in front of 70,000, when the Dead added a second set prior to the Dylan/Dead slot—retaining the format for the rest of the run.

The encores at all the shows—"Touch of Grey," "Knockin' on Heaven's Door," and "All Along the Watchtower," singly or in combination—were always enthusiastically received, as was Jerry's use of the pedal steel guitar. At Foxboro on July 4, Garcia played the instrument behind Dylan on "I'll be Your Baby Tonight" for the first time in nearly twenty years. The pedal steel had another outing on July 10 before Garcia's final public appearance with it and the band at the Meadowlands show on July 12.

"[The Grateful Dead] taught me to look inside these songs I was singing that, actually at the time of that tour, I couldn't even sing... I realized that they understood these songs better than I did at the time."

BOB DYLAN TO DENNIS MCNALLY

*Top left: July 19, Autzen Stadium, Eugene, Oregon. **Above, top:** July 24, Oakland County Coliseum Stadium, Oakland, California. **Above, bottom:** July 12, Giants Stadium, East Rutherford, New Jersey.*

344

Grateful Dead with Bob Dylan

Backstage

*July 12, 1987
Giants Stadium
East Rutherford, NJ*

| 14 | 15 | 16 | 17 | 18 | **19** | 20 | 21 | 22 | 23 | **24** | 25 | **26** | 27 | 28 | 29 | 30 | 31 |

Sunday July 12
Giants Stadium,
East Rutherford, New Jersey

The show features the only-ever performances of "Wicked Messenger" and "Tomorrow is a Long Time," and the band tunes up to the *Addams Family* TV show theme after the second set opener, "Morning Dew."

Friday July 10
JFK Stadium, Philadelphia, Pennsylvania

Saturday July 4
Schaefer Stadium,
Foxboro, Massachusetts

Sunday July 19
Autzen Stadium,
Eugene, Oregon

Another *Addams Family* tuning, this time before the first-set (and Dylan-less) "When I Paint My Masterpiece." The show sees the only Grateful Dead performance of "Heart of Mine."

Friday July 24
Oakland County
Coliseum Stadium,
Oakland, California

Only Dead performance of "Shelter from the Storm."

Sunday July 26
Anaheim Stadium,
Anaheim, California

Bob Dylan has a little surprise for the boys on the last show of the tour—he launches into "Mr. Tambourine Man," which they've never rehearsed. It's the only GD performance of the song.

| 4 | 5 | | | 9 | 10 | 11 | 12 | 13 |

JULY '87

| 1 | 2 | 3 |

| 6 | 7 | 8 |

**Tuesday July 7
Wednesday July 8**
Roanoke Civic Center, Roanoke, Virginia

Monday July 6 ★
Pittsburgh Civic Arena, Pittsburgh, Pennsylvania

It's the official release day for *In the Dark*, and the band keeps its contrarian cred by not playing any tracks from the new album. Members of the Neville Brothers guest for most of the second set, which sees the breakout of Harry Belafonte's '50s calypso classic, "Day-O."

Thursday July 2
Silver Stadium,
Rochester, New York

COL724
1X 718
ADULT
98

GA   GEN ADM   20.00
GEN.   ADM.   ADULT
BILL GRAHAM PRESENTS
BOB DYLAN/GRATEFUL DEAD
NO BOTTLES CANS ALCOHOL
OAKLAND COLISEUM
STADIUM
FRI JUL 24 1987 7:00PM

Tuesday August 11
Wednesday August 12
Thursday August 13
Red Rocks Amphitheatre, Morrison, Colorado

The '87 run is the last at this beautiful outdoor venue.

Thursday August 20
Park West Ski Resort,
Park City, Utah

Saturday August 22
Sunday August 23 ★
Calaveras County Fairgrounds,
Angel's Camp, California

Carlos Santana plays two songs both nights.

Sunday August 30
The Jerry Garcia Band plays the
Greek Theatre, University of
California, Berkeley, California,
with Bonnie Raitt guesting.

Saturday August 15
Sunday August 16
Town Park, Telluride, Colorado

Tuesday August 18
Compton Terrace Amphitheatre,
Chandler, Arizona

Saturday August 29
The first performance of the Jerry Garcia Acoustic Band
(see March 18, 1987) with the Jerry Garcia Band, at
French's Camp, Eel River, Piercy, California.

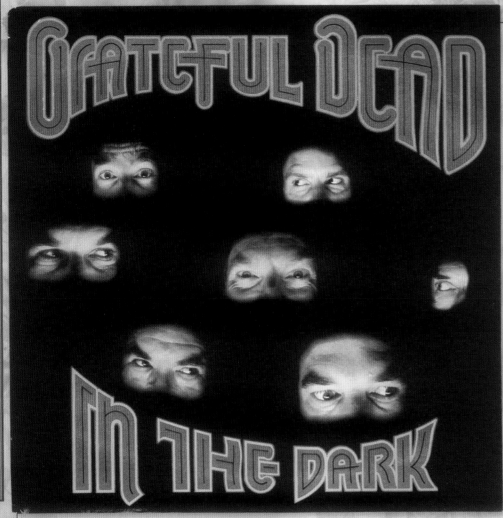

IN THE DARK
Grateful Dead

*Released by Arista (AL-8452)
on July 6, 1987*

Side One

1. **Touch of Grey**
   (Garcia/Hunter)
2. **Hell in a Bucket**
   (Weir/Barlow/Mydland)
3. **When Push Comes to Shove**
   (Garcia/Hunter)
4. **West L.A. Fadeaway**
   (Garcia/Hunter)

Side Two

1. **Tons of Steel**
   (Mydland)
2. **Throwing Stones**
   (Weir/Barlow)
3. **Black Muddy River**
   (Garcia/Hunter)

Personnel

Jerry Garcia – acoustic guitar, vocals
Bob Weir – acoustic guitar, vocals
Phil Lesh – bass
Brent Mydland – keyboards, vocals
Bill Kreutzmann – percussion
Mickey Hart – percussion

Produced by Jerry Garcia and John Cutler

HOW MANY BANDS RELEASE their "breakthrough" albums 22 years after getting together? In commercial terms, *In the Dark* was a late-bloomer's triumph, reaching No. 6 on the charts and going platinum shortly after it was released. Big sales were never a huge concern for the Dead, of course, so what made the album's success sweeter was the warm reception it got from critics who had long ago dismissed the band as noodling nostalgiasts. Rolling Stone's review was typical: "[In the Dark] bespeaks an effortlessness long absent from their oeuvre… Despite nods to technology, this sounds more like a Dead record than anything they've done in years."

But the band was never much concerned with the critics, either; it was the Deadheads' reaction that counted. And among the band's longtime fans, response to *In the Dark* was enthusiastic—mostly. There were the usual comments along the lines of

"It's no *American Beauty*," but most Deadheads understood that the boys were trying to capture something different—in Jerry's words, "the way the band sounds today—a lean rock 'n' roll sound [but with] real range, too." On that level the majority acknowledged that *In the Dark* was a success.

Still, as Blair Jackson would later note in *The Golden Road*, there were Deadheads who hoped *In the Dark* would flop, out of fear that a hit album would accelerate the band into the mainstream and further damage the "always-fragile GD ecosystem."

In theme with the album's title, Herb Greene's cover depicted the band's eyes seemingly glowing in the dark. The 13th eye belongs to Bill Graham—he came to the photo shoot to talk business and wound up on the cover. *In the Dark* was dedicated to the memory of roadie Paul Roehlk. The Otis mentioned in the "Farewell to Otis" on the sleeve was Bob Weir's dog, who passed away early in 1987.

Below: A version of the cover with upside down eyes.

1987 sees Robert Hunter add "translator" to his resume with the Hulogosi-published translation of Austrian poet Rainer Maria Rilke's (1875–1926) *Duino Elegies*. In September Kitaro's *The Light of the Spirit*, an album produced by Mickey Hart, is released.

1 | 2 | 3

Friday September 11
Saturday September 12
Sunday September 13
Capital Centre, Landover, Maryland

On the first night Jerry Garcia and Phil Lesh play "Happy Birthday" for Mickey's 44th birthday. Sunday marks the only full-band performance of Little Willie John's "You Give Me Fever," sung by Bob Weir, who often performs the song with his side bands.

Thursday September 17
Jerry Garcia and Bob Weir yak it up with late-night TV talk-show host David Letterman in an appearance on NBC's *Late Night With Letterman* highlighted by a bit of special effects trickery in which Bob "levitates" Jerry.

10 | 11 | 12 | 13 | 14 | 15 | 16 | 17 | 18 | 19 | 20 | 21

Sound and Vision

The Dead released "Hell in a Bucket" as a 12-inch promo single in September, with "West LA Fadeaway" on the flip side. Alongside the liner notes on the back was a small black and white *In the Dark* album cover with the "eyeballs" printed upside-down. The single was also filmed as a short-form video that was broadcast in September, featuring various members of the band's office staff and extended family *(below and right)*.

Tuesday September 15
Wednesday September 16
Friday September 18 ★
Saturday September 19
Sunday September 20
Madison Square Garden, New York, New York

The opening show halts temporarily when Bob Weir blows out his speakers after the first-set "When Push Comes to Shove." The New York City Percussion Ensemble opens the following night, and on Friday, referring to the previous night's *Letterman* appearance *(see above)*, Bob announces to Phil, "Hey, Rocky! Watch me levitate Garcia!" Part of the second set of the Sunday show is broadcast live as part of the Farm Aid III benefit, including, appropriately enough, Dylan's "Maggie's Farm."

> ## "You know those occasional pistachio nuts that are really tough to open? Now I just throw them out." BOB WEIR ON THE PERKS OF COMMERCIAL SUCCESS

346

4 | 5 | 6 | 7 | 8 | 9

Monday September 7
Tuesday September 8
Wednesday September 9
Providence Civic Center, Providence, Rhode Island

The first night of the Fall East Coast Tour sees the Dead break out their own cover of Richie Valens's "La Bamba," a recent mega-hit for the East LA band (and Dead friends) Los Lobos. It's also a "Playin' in the Band" jam, as a first-set sandwich between "Uncle John's Band" and "Drums." At the next show the Dylan Slot is filled by the first "Queen Jane Approximately" played without Dylan himself. The last night sees Brent Mydland premiere what will become something of a signature tune for him: the peppy "Hey Pocky Way," a traditional New Orleans Mardi Gras chant first recorded by the Meters (with Art Neville in the lineup) in 1974. The first set ends with another surprise, or rather two of them: Brent leading the band through "Good Golly Miss Molly" and "Devil with a Blue Dress On" in the rave-up medley arrangement popularized by Mitch Ryder and the Detroit Wheels.

Bob Bralove

After a stint as Stevie Wonder's synthesizer technician, Bob Bralove was hired by Merl Saunders in 1986 to help with production of the Dead's *Twilight Zone* music. Impressed by Bralove's musicianship (he's an accomplished keyboardist) and technical brilliance, the band hired him to work with Brent Mydland's keyboards and on *In the Dark*, and he would stay with the band until 1995. His primary contribution to the band's latter-day sound was the introduction (1987–89) of MIDI (Musical Instrument Digital Interface), which gives instruments an infinite palette of sound through sampling and processing. So Garcia, say, could transform his guitar sounds into those of trumpet, sax, or flute, or, for that matter, a flute capturing the sounds of a flock of birds during "Bird Song." In 1991, Bralove collaged live versions of "Space" and "Drums" to produce *Infrared Roses (see page 396)*, perhaps the most complex Dead Album since *Anthem of the Sun*. In 1996 Bralove and Tom Constanten formed Dose Hermanos, "the world's premiere psychedelic keyboard duo," and released several albums. Bralove has also performed and recorded with Second Sight, an ensemble including Henry Kaiser, and with the electronica outfit Mobius Cubed.

> "[The Grateful Dead] understood the idea of infinite sounds intuitively... they were already masters of the conceptual realm. So for me, the task was to say, 'All right. How do you see your music, and how can I make the technology apply to the picture of that?'"
>
> BOB BRALOVE, INTERVIEWED IN *THE DEADHEAD'S TAPING COMPENDIUM, VOLUME III*

Video of The Video

During filming for the "Touch of Grey" promo, Bill Kreutzmann's filmmaker son Justin had been on hand to document the videomaking process. The resulting film, *The Making of the "Touch of Grey" Video*, was released as a video in September and was itself a notable critical and commercial success.

Tuesday September 22
Wednesday September 23
Thursday September 24
The Spectrum, Philadelphia, Pennsylvania

The first night sees Spencer Davis add guest vocals on the second-set opener—"Gimme Some Lovin'," his own huge 1967 hit with the Spencer Davis Group. The show also sees the band's first jam on the traditional tune variously known as "Two Soldiers" or "The Handsome Cabin Boy." Wednesday's show marks the retirement of "La Bamba" and Brent Mydland's "Tons of Steel."

OCTOBER '87

1 2 3 4 5 6 7 8

Friday October 2
Saturday October 3
Sunday October 4
Shoreline Amphitheatre, Mountain View, California

Saturday sees the last "My Brother Esau," while Sunday marks the final "Good Golly Miss Molly"/"Devil With a Blue Dress On" medley.

Live on Video

So Far, a 55-minute video featuring live concert footage mixed with animation sequences is released this year. Among the tracks included are "Uncle John's Band," "Playing in the Band," "Throwing Stones," and "Not Fade Away."

Nuts To Success

"Touch of Grey" cracked the Top 10 during the sold-out Fall '87 MSG run, precipitating one of the band's least favorite activities—a photo-op with Arista Records executives. Despite the band's wariness about committing to a multi-album deal, their management inked a deal with Arista for three more albums, at a royalty rate of $3.50 per CD—the highest yet commanded by any performer. (A far cry from the Lenny Hart era…). The new contract included a clause, also unprecedented in pop-music history, permitting the band to release archival recordings—an arrangement that launched the *From the Vault* and *Dick's Picks* series.

Left and below: October 31, Jerry Garcia Acoustic Band/Jerry Garcia Band at Lunt-Fontanne Theater

Jerry on Broadway

Jerry Garcia Acoustic Band/Jerry Garcia Band perform at the Lunt-Fontanne Theater, New York, New York (including two shows a day on October 17, 21, 25, 28 and 31).

According to David Nelson, it started as a bit of a joke: when Bill Graham praised the performance of the Garcia/Kahn/Nelson/Rothman acoustic ensemble at the Artists Rights Today benefit at the Fillmore (*see March 18, 1987*), saying he had to "take this somewhere," Jerry Garcia facetiously suggested Broadway, and the proverbial light bulb went on over Bill's head. (In fact, Bill may have already been mulling over the idea of a Broadway theater run for Jerry—he was looking for a New York venue that didn't have ties to his competitor John Scher.)

Bill didn't just get Jerry on Broadway—he booked him into one of the jewels of the Great White Way, the elegant and historic Lunt-Fontanne Theater, for an epic stint of eighteen shows over 16 days, including five "matinee" performances. What's more, each show would comprise a set from Jerry's acoustic band (Jerry and David Nelson on guitar, John Kahn on upright bass, Sandy Rothman on banjo, mandolin, and dobro, Kenny Kosek on fiddle, supplemented on some numbers by the electric JGB's drummer, David Kemper, on snare), followed by an electric set from the JGB, whose lineup at the time included Jerry, John Kahn, David Kemper, Melvin Seals on keyboards, and backup singers the "Jerryettes"—Gloria Jones and Jaclyn LaBranch.

A rock star performing in a venerable "legitimate" theater was a novel idea, but it all worked. Despite a relatively high ticket cost—$30.00—when tickets went on sale, they were snapped up so fast it set a Broadway box-office record. Photographer Herb Greene produced a brilliant Broadway-style playbill for the shows, its cover depicting Jerry as a magician conjuring an electric guitar from his hat. Matrons from Greenwich and Great Neck on their way to see "Cats" may have been a bit discomfited by the sight of throngs of Deadheads sparking up along 46th Street, but no untoward incidents marred the run.

For the audiences, rarely have so many been entertained by so broad a spectrum of music in a single show. The acoustic band's sets included bluegrass, country blues, and folk, from Flatt & Scruggs ("Gone Home") to Elizabeth Cotten ("Oh Babe it Ain't No Lie") to Leadbelly ("Goodnight Irene"); the JGB electric band's material ranged from reggae (Jimmy Cliff's "The Harder They Come") to Dylan ("Tangled Up in Blue") to Los Lobos ("Evangeline"), to soul ("Respect"), with a few Hunter/Garcia numbers ("Deal," and, at three shows, "Ripple").

For Jerry, it was an invigorating, if somewhat grueling, experience. He only had four days off during the entire run, and on days that included both matinee and evening performances, he had to catch as many Z's as he could between shows in a dressing room that once sheltered Mary Martin and Vivien Leigh.

A triumph on all levels, the Broadway shows were ample proof that Jerry was well and truly back on track, both with the Grateful Dead and on his own—with a little help from his friends.

9 | 10 | 11 | 12 | 13 | 14 | 15 | 16 | 17 | 18 | 19 | 20 | 21 | 22 | 23 | 24 | 25 | 26 | 27 | 28 | 29 | 30 | 31

"I thought it would be tiring and maybe it would be rough switching back and forth between electric and acoustic, but everyone was so relaxed, and the crowds were so great. It was the most fun I ever had playing in New York, that's for sure, and I think Jerry had a lot of fun too." JOHN KAHN TO BLAIR JACKSON

PROD. **THROWING STONES**

HRS   MIN   SEC   FRS

20   2   6

SCENE   TAKE   ROLL   SYNC   MOS

DELL'AMICO   LIGHTHILL   11–5

DIRECTOR   CAMERA   DATE

Dcode   TS-1   DENECKE INC.   Adolph Gasser   CA

🎸 **Friday November 6**
🪘 **Saturday November 7 ★**
Sunday November 8
Henry J. Kaiser Convention Center, Oakland, California

Three Rex Foundation benefit gigs.

6	7	8	9	10	11	12	13	14	15

Friday November 13 🎸
Saturday November 14 🎸
Sunday November 15
Long Beach Arena, Long Beach, California

16 – 26

Above: *Sunday November 8, Henry J. Kaiser Convention Center, Oakland, California.*

November 1987

348

Above: *On the set of the video shoot for "Throwing Stones."*

1	2	3	4	5

Thursday November 5
The band shoots a short-form video for "Throwing Stones" in Oakland, costumed in voluminous coats and a motley assortment of headgear. The chief backdrop to the shoot is "an apocalyptic mural they'd painted on a wall" of an abandoned school, in the words of photographer Jay Blakesberg. Bill Kreutzmann couldn't make it to the shoot, so roadie Robbie Taylor understudied the drummer in a mask.

Below: *Garcia's acoustic/electric shows at the Warfield.*

DECEMBER '87

27	28	29	30	1	2	3	4	5	6	7

Friday November 27
Saturday November 28
Sunday November 29
Thursday December 3
Friday December 4
Saturday December 5
Sunday December 6
Jerry Garcia reprises the Broadway run's acoustic/electric shows on the West Coast with a three-show stint at the Warfield followed by four nights at LA's Wiltern Theatre.

Top: The New Year's Eve show, Oakland Coliseum Arena, Oakland, California.
Above: At "Joan Baez and Friends, a Christmas Concert," an AIDS benefit.

STAFF
GRATEFUL D·E·A·D
NEVILLE BROTHERS
LOOTERS
OAKLAND COLISEUM
NAME *Pilar Law*
DEPT. *BGP*

8	9	10	11	12	13	14	15	16	**17**	18	19

Sunday December 27 ★
Monday December 28
Wednesday December 30
Thursday December 31 ★
Oakland Coliseum Arena, Oakland, California

The '87 New Year's Eve show—broadcast nationwide on FM radio and pay-per-view television—is one of the best in recent years, interspersing solid performances with comedy courtesy of *Saturday Night Live* alums Tom Davis and Al Franken, including a cooking-show spoof wherein Jerry Garcia shares his pigs-in-a-blanket recipe with the audience. Bill Graham makes his entrance riding a huge float celebrating the 50th anniversary of the Golden Gate Bridge. Unfortunately, Ken Kesey's running kommentary is once again somewhat inkoherent (this time he misplaced his notes), and when a hundred or so white doves are released from the float, at least one of them gets shredded by an overhead ventilation fan. The Neville Brothers (who also open, along with the Looters) add some early-morning New Orleans spice to the post-midnight third set, including the only GD performance of Bobby Freeman's "Do You Wanna Dance." (Freeman was a Bay Area R&B performer before "Do You Wanna Dance," and a Deadhead rumor that a young Garcia had actually played on the 1958 hit could not be confirmed by Garcia, though he could remember backing Freeman on a demo.) The show contains the last "Day-O." Composer Mason Williams also performs.

Thursday December 17
"Joan Baez and Friends, a Christmas Concert" is held at the Warfield Theatre, San Francisco, California. This benefit concert for the AIDS Emergency Fund of Humanitas International, founded by Joan Baez in 1979, includes an acoustic ensemble of Jerry Garcia, Bob Weir, and John Kahn playing "When I Paint My Masterpiece," "Deep Elem Blues," "Victim or the Crime," "Bird Song," and backing up Joan on "Dark Hollow," "Turtle Dove," and "Knockin' on Heaven's Door."

20	21	22	23	24	25	26	**27**	28	29	**30**	**31**

Sunday December 20
Jerry Garcia becomes a father for the fourth time—daughters all— when Manasha Matheson gives birth to Keelin Noel Garcia.

Above: NYE 1987, Oakland Coliseum Arena.
Below: Boz Scaggs and Garcia, January 21.

Jerry Garcia, Mountain Girl, and their daughters Annabelle and Trixie spend a post-New Year's vacation in Hawaii, where Jerry indulges in what is becoming a consuming passion—scuba diving.

"[Diving] takes up some of this space that drugs left, insofar as it's like going to a different world. You're in a different place. It's very sensual. There's lots of new information there... And physically it's good for you." JERRY GARCIA TO BLAIR JACKSON, 1992

| 1 | 2 | 3 | 4 | 5 | 6 | 7 | 8 | 9 | 10 | 11 |

"IKO IKO"

TRADITIONAL

Of the nearly three dozen documented traditional covers the Dead would deliver in their three decades together, few had the ethnic flavor of "Iko Iko." The band had often mined material from the plentiful source of uncredited artifacts that dated back to the early 20th century and further, but "Iko Iko" predated even those with origins whose roots may lie with slavery-era call-and-response chants, giving the song one of the longest pedigrees of any GD cover. Variants eventually ended up in New Orleans, where Mardi Gras "tribes" engaged in verbal sparring based on the indigenous rituals of their forbears. The song had appeared in many forms before the Dead started playing it in St. Louis on May 15, 1977. The first recorded version was titled "Jock-O-Mo" after the Cajun patois that appears in its chorus and was released in 1954 by James Crawford, a New Orleans singer who worked under the name of Sugar Boy and the Cane Cutters. Another take by the New Orleans female vocal trio the Dixie Cups hit #20 in 1965. The band would eventually play 185 rousing versions of this crowd favorite—often at Mardi Gras shows—through 1995, while The Dead kept the history alive by including "Iko Iko" in their first show on February 14, 2003.

| 25 | 26 | 27 | 28 | 29 | 30 | 31 |

Saturday January 23

Jerry Garcia and Bob Weir guest alongside Santana, Bonnie Raitt, Randy Jackson, Tower of Power, Boz Scaggs, and others at the Henry J. Kaiser Convention Center in Oakland. Garcia, Weir, Carlos Santana, Chester Thompson, and the Tower of Power horn section form a one-shot supergroup for Blues for Salvador, a benefit for war-ravaged El Salvador. Wayne Shorter, Randy Jackson, NRBQ, and Bonnie Raitt join for a first-set jam that morphs into "Turn on Your Lovelight," and NRBQ and Bonnie Raitt remain for the second set.

| 15 | 16 | 17 | 18 | 19 | 20 | 21 | 22 | **23** | 24 |

Saturday February 13
Sunday February 14
Tuesday February 16
Wednesday February 17
Henry J. Kaiser Convention Center,
Oakland, California

The Tuesday show is marked by a Mardi Gras parade during "Drums" (with Batucaje)>"Iko Iko." The Chinese Symphony Orchestra open the final show (it's Chinese New Year), and a Dragon dance takes place during "Drums."

BILL GRAHAM PRESENTS
GRATEFUL DEAD
FEBRUARY 13, 14, 16, 17 1988
HENRY J. KAISER CONVENTION CENTER

Below: The Mardi Gras Parade, February 16, Henry J. Kaiser Convention Center.

Fame, the Ticketless, and the Touchheads

1988 saw the start of the "Mega-Dead" period. Mega-success brought continuing mega-problems at shows for the band whose biggest commitment was still making live music. The amazing upsurge in the band's popularity had transformed its fan base. Steve Marcus of Grateful Dead Ticket Sales once estimated that the average age of people at concerts had been about 27 before 1987 but that it now dropped to 18. The new fans—called "In the Darkers" or "Touchheads" by the old skool—not only neglected finer points of "Deadiquette," but were rowdy. Many, in Blair Jackson's words, dissed the "fragile ecosystem" that had evolved around the band. At every venue, a torrent of bad publicity was generated—by blatant drug use and dealing, overnight parking, rip-off artists in the parking lot, and general disrespect for neighborhoods.

Bigger meant worse, too. With more fans, the band was now playing stadiums and other high-capacity venues where crowd control and security were problematic. Dealing with the ticketless was the biggest problem, especially at auto-centric venues, such as Wisconsin's Alpine Valley Music Theatre, where checking for tickets would cause unholy gridlock. Ticketless fans who weren't content to wander outside waiting for a miracle (wandering around the parking lots with a finger in the air, a universal gesture), would try to "scam in" or, occasionally, create ugly gatecrashing episodes.

The band were in a classic double bind. They were simply doing what they'd done for decades, playing music for people. Their job ended at the edge of the stage. And—whatever critics might think—they weren't the leaders of a mobile, mangy hippie cult, since the Deadhead scene had created itself. No way could they turn authoritarian and accept responsibility for their fans' behavior. On the other hand, something had to be done or they'd be banished from various communities, including some long-standing no-hassle Dead venues.

The band's response was, in its characteristic grass-roots, direct-action fashion, to mail out SOS Deadhead communiqués and hand out show flyers telling people to cool out. Similar unequivocal messages hit rock stations in tour towns and the band also created a sort of tribal council, including Deadheads and Hog Farmers Calico and Goose, to deal with people directly in the parking lots. This so-called Minglewood Town Council passed out garbage bags, picked up trash, remonstrated with rowdies, and generally tried to keep things mellow. The 1988 concerts were mostly peaceful—but the problems were to grow worse over time.

Sunday February 21
Tearful "televangelist" Jimmy Swaggart admits to consorting with prostitutes—just one of several sex and financial scandals plaguing American TV preachers.

Sunday February 28
Portions of the '87 New Year's Eve show are broadcast on the nationwide King Biscuit Flower Hour radio show. A CD of the broadcast is released later in the year.

| 21 | 22 | 23 | 24 | 25 | 26 | 27 | **28** | 29 |

February 1988

351

Above: Chinese New Year at the Henry J. Kaiser Convention Center, Oakland, on February 17.

The Bammies

The 12th annual Bay Area Music Awards (Bammies) were a triumph for the band in general and Jerry Garcia in particular. Phil Lesh won Best Bassist, Bill Kreutzmann and Mickey Hart shared Best Drummer accolades, "Touch of Grey" and *In the Dark* took Best Song and Best Album, and Jerry Garcia was named both Guitarist of the Year and Musician of the Year. The band's well-known antipathy toward awards was evident in their acceptance remarks: Phil told the crowd that he intended to give his statue to "my little son Graham for him to play with in the bathtub." Upon receiving his Best Guitarist award, Jerry said, "I don't think of music as being a competition. I didn't enter a contest to win this. This is for Deadheads everywhere and my partners, The Grateful Dead." Among the evening's musical highlights was a rendition of "Touch of Grey" in an orchestral arrangement, performed by Dick Bright (musical director of the Fairmont Hotel) and his Sounds of Delight. They also played "Good Morning Little Schoolgirl" and "Turn On Your Lovelight" with Huey Lewis, then finished with "Long Tall Sally" with Huey Lewis and John Fogerty. The evening ended with the Dead, Huey Lewis and the News, Merl Saunders, John Fogerty, and others onstage for a jam which, in the words of *Relix* magazine, "will go down in history as one of the great ones."

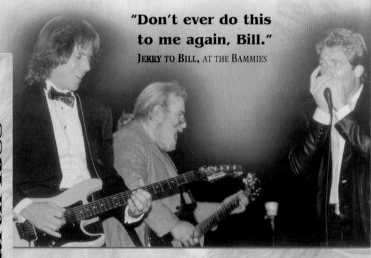

"Don't ever do this to me again, Bill."
JERRY TO BILL, AT THE BAMMIES

LIBERTY
Robert Hunter
Relix 2029

Considered by most fans to be one of Robert Hunter's best solo outings, *Liberty* included several lyrics from the batch the Grateful Dead cherry-picked for *In the Dark* (and from which Bob Dylan appropriated "Silvio" and "Ugliest Girl in the World" for *Down In the Groove*). Jerry Garcia played guitar on the album, and the title track would become a Grateful Dead staple, especially as an encore, in the band's last years. All the songs are Hunter originals: *Liberty*'s "When a Man Loves a Woman" is not the Calvin Lewis-Andrew Wright composition made famous by Percy Sledge.

Saturday March 26
★ Sunday March 27
Monday March 28
Hampton Coliseum, Hampton, Virginia

Saturday sees the first and last GD performance of Bob Marley and the Wailers' "Stir it Up" as a first-set sandwich between "Sugaree" and "New Minglewood Blues." Sunday is another highly regarded '88 show, and it is highlighted by the first Dylan-less performance of "Ballad of a Thin Man," with Bob Weir on lead vocal.

| 21 | 22 | 23 | **24** | 25 | **26** | **27** | **28** | 29 |

Thursday March 24
The Omni, Atlanta, Georgia

"Many doors have been closed to us in the last several months due to the trash and boogie behavior of new fans who have no regard for the way the Dead do things... We intend to step on it—hard!" ROBERT HUNTER

Below: Sunday March 27, Hampton Coliseum, Hampton, Virginia.

March 1988

352

MARCH '88

Friday March 4
Organist Howard Wales, Jerry Garcia's collaborator on the 1971 *Hooteroll?* album, joins the Jerry Garcia Band at the Warfield Theatre, San Francisco, California, for a jam.

Saturday March 12
San Francisco Civic Auditorium, San Francisco, California

The Bammies.

| 1 | 2 | 3 | **4** | 5 | 6 | 7 | 8 | 9 | 10 | 11 | **12** | 13 | 14 | 15 | **16** | **17** | **18** | 19 | 20 |

★ Wednesday March 16
Thursday March 17
Friday March 18
Henry J. Kaiser Convention Center, Oakland, California

With the Spring Tour about to begin, Robert Hunter includes a message from the band in the March Deadheads' mailing. It says that negative elements have entered the scene and that action would be taken to control them: "Understand that we are doing what must be done to ensure our rights and yours." The first night is a classic show but unfortunately, local complaints about the parking-lot scene and inconsiderate Deadhead behavior (i.e., pissing in public) abound. The second falls on St. Patrick's Day, and the band plays in front of a leprechaun banner. Irish band Train to Sligo opens, Hamza El-Din joins for drums, and the band introduces a Dylan-less take on "Stuck Inside of Mobile with the Memphis Blues Again."

Wednesday March 30
Thursday March 31
Friday April 1
Brendan Byrne Arena,
East Rutherford, New Jersey

The last night of the run is the final
outing for "Ballad of a Thin Man."

Thursday April 7
Friday April 8
Saturday April 9
The Centrum, Worcester,
Massachusetts

| 7 | 8 | 9 | 10 | 11 |

APRIL '88

| 30 | 31 | 1 | 2 | 3 | 4 | 5 | 6 |

Monday April 11
Joe Louis Arena,
Detroit, Michigan

Sunday April 3
Monday April 4
Tuesday April 5
Hartford Civic Center, Hartford, Connecticut

On the last night, the band brings out the frat-rock classic "Louie Louie," with Brent Mydland on lead vocals. First recorded by Richard Berry in 1956 and popularized by the Kingsmen in 1963, it is played for the first time in a long time. Just how long is a matter of interpretation: the first known GD performance of the tune was at Awalt High School *(see May 18, 1967)*. They joined with members of the Jefferson Airplane for a rendition at a Family Dog show *(see September 7, 1969)*; and jammed on it at the June 7, 1970, Fillmore West show.

Below: Tuesday April 5, Hartford Civic Center, Hartford, Connecticut.

"I NEED A MIRACLE"
BARLOW/WEIR

Weir and Barlow's straight-up rocker about needing a woman (actually many of them, in all shapes and sizes) fared better as a live crowd-rouser that in its passable take on the Dead's 1978 album *Shakedown Street*, which one critic likened to "an Engelbert Humperdinck reject" despite some great harp work by Matthew Kelly, a friend of Weir's and future guitarist for his side band Ratdog. Though the song's eager demands could be misconstrued as sexually aggressive, Weir insisted it was meant in good spirit. "I don't take it all seriously," he said in 1981. "If there are sexual overtones, it's just something to sing about. Hopefully I can make it fun. Those are the songs I try to have fun with." Besides popping up in 271 Dead shows between 1978 and 1995, the track also provided the perfect rallying cry for Deadheads in search of a free ticket, of which there were many in the late '80s. They could be frequently found circling any given venue with a single finger in the air and a hastily-scrawled sign reading "I need a miracle!"

LIVE AT THE KEYSTONE
Merl Saunders, Jerry Garcia, John Kahn, Bill Vitt

Volume 1 (Fantasy FCD 7701-2), Live At The Keystone Volume 2 (Fantasy FCD 7702-2), Keystone Encores (Fantasy FCD 7703-2)

Originally recorded during the Saunders–Garcia band's 1973 shows at Berkeley's Keystone Club, these three CDs essentially comprise an expanded and augmented version of the 1978 double LP *Live at Keystone*. Highlights include David Grisman joining on mandolin for Dylan's "Positively Fourth Street" and a jammy version of "My Funny Valentine."

Wednesday April 13
Thursday April 14
Friday April 15 ★
Rosemont Horizon Arena, Rosemont, Illinois

The '88 Spring Tour sees the band varying the set list, and the last night of the Rosemont run is no exception, with a first-ever "Scarlet Begonias">"Fire on the Mountain" opener.

| 12 | 13 | 14 | 15 | 16 | 17 | 18 | 19 | 20 | 21 |

Dead Head TV

The first regular Grateful Dead–themed television program, *Dead Head TV*, makes its first appearance on a San Francisco public-access station. Produced by Scott Wiseman and Kathleen Watkins, the monthly show featured interviews with the likes of Dan Healy and Robert Hunter, profiles of Deadheads, tour updates, and anything and everything Dead-related. Wiseman and Watkins made tapes available, gratis, to cable-TV systems across the country; at the show's peak (no pun intended) it airs regularly in more than 15 cities.

Friday April 22
Saturday April 23
Irvine Meadows Amphitheatre,
Irvine, California

Tuesday April 26
The Black Mountain Boys—Jerry Garcia, David Nelson, and Sandy Rothman, with John Kahn—perform at Marin County Veterans Auditorium, San Rafael, California. They perform an acoustic set at a benefit for Creating Our Future, a new organization devoted to creating "a shared vision of world peace" among students. (Creating Our Future is the creation of Sat Santokh Singh Khalsa, who, as Burt Kanegson, worked for the band's management from 1967 to 1969.) Also on the bill are Hot Tuna and Brent Mydland and Bob Weir flying solo. Brent and Bob join the Black Mountain Boys for the encores—the Beatles' "Blackbird" and Sam Cooke's "Good Times."

| 22 | 23 | 24 | 25 | 26 | 27 | 28 | 29 | 30 |

Saturday April 30 ★
Frost Amphitheater,
Stanford University,
Palo Alto, California

A strong show highlighted by the full-band premiere of Sam Cooke's "Good Times" (with Jerry Garcia, Bob Weir, and Brent Mydland trading verses) and capped by an exceedingly rare triple encore of "China Cat Sunflower"> "I Know You Rider">"One More Saturday Night."

Bruce Hornsby

When Brent Mydland died in 1990 the Dead needed a keyboardist—and Bruce Hornsby, a long-time fan and collaborator, stepped in to help them through a tough period of a year and a half. His high-end musicianship, on grand piano and squeezebox, contributed to some fine musical moments.

Born in 1954 in Williamsburg, Virginia, Bruce was already an accomplished keyboardist when in 1973 he was so inspired by a Dead gig that he and his brother formed a cover band, Bobby Hi-Test and the Octane Kids.

After moving to Hollywood, Bruce Hornsby's new incarnation with his band The Range achieved (unlike the Dead!) instant success with the April 1986 Huey Lewis–produced album *The Way It Is*, which went multiplatinum and yielded three hit singles. In 1987 and 1988 Bruce opened gigs for the Dead, and a rap with fellow aficionado Phil Lesh about Scott Joplin led to an invitation to sit in. Bruce's fearless improvisation and multi-genre fluency brought him instant rapport with the band, and between '88 and '90 he sat in several more times, before his brief but crisis-busting stint as band member.

Right: Bruce Hornsby at the Shoreline Amphitheater, Mountain View, California, in May 1991.

Friday June 17
Metropolitan Sports Center, Bloomington, Minnesota

The kickoff of the Summer Tour sees the premiere of one of the more controversial Grateful Dead songs of the '80s, "Victim or the Crime." Jerry wasn't too keen on it.

"It's a hideous song It's very angular and unattractive-sounding. It's not an accessible song… And it is strange. It has strange steps in it, but that's part of what makes it interesting to play. Bob's songs sometimes don't make sense in a direct, traditional way."
JERRY GARCIA TO BLAIR JACKSON, *1988*

Tuesday May 31
US President Ronald Reagan arrives in Moscow for his first visit to the Soviet Union.

JUNE '88

| 26 | 27 | 28 | 29 | 30 | 31 | 1 | 2 | 3 | 4 | 5 | 6 | 7 | 8 | 9 | 10 | 11 | 12 | 13 | 14 | 15 | 16 | 17 |

Monday May 16
Soviet troops start to withdraw from Afghanistan, the beginning of the end of more than eight years of war and occupation.

Origins of a Controversial Song

Written by Bob Weir with lyrical contributions from actor Gerrit Graham, "Victim or the Crime" had dark lyrics and an abrasive sound (the latter, according to Weir, influenced by Stravinsky and Bartok) that contrasted starkly with the generally more melodic and upbeat tunes produced by the band during the *In the Dark/Built to Last* period. Many Deadheads especially hated the opening lines, "Patience runs out on the junkie/The dark side hires another soul," interpreting the passage as commentary on Jerry Garcia's dope problems, which Weir denied. John Perry Barlow so hated the song, it reportedly led to a rift between Weir and his long-time collaborator. Despite, or because of, the controversy, "Victim or the Crime" became the single most performed song from *Built to Last*, with 96 outings.

May 1988

354

| 7 | 8 | 9 | 10~15 | 16 | 17 | 18 | 19 | 20~25 |

Friday May 6
Howard Wales joins the Jerry Garcia Band at the Fillmore, San Francisco, California, for "Don't Let Go."

MAY '88

| 1 | 2 | 3 | 4 | 5 | 6 |

Monday May 2
A "Week of Dead" interviews and music is aired on the radio. Highlights are released as a double LP—*Rock Stars No. 15*—in June.

Sunday May 1
Frost Amphitheater, Stanford University, Palo Alto, California

Right and above: Sunday May 1, Frost Amphitheater, Stanford University, Palo Alto, California.

Sunday June 19

Monday June 20

Wednesday June 22

Thursday June 23

Alpine Valley Music Theatre, East Troy, Wisconsin

The '88 four-show Alpine run is remembered both for what happened onstage (a new song broken out every night) and off (clogged parking lots, massive traffic jams, the weather a miasma of rain alternating with triple-digit heat). By some estimates there were half again as many people camped outside the venue (20,000) as inside for each show (40,000) from a Bob Dylan show that preceded the Dead run. On Sunday "Foolish Heart" debuts; the Garcia/Hunter number is destined to be the lead track on *Built to Last* (but not, despite its radio-ready sound, destined for major chart success on the order of "Touch of Grey"). Fortunately, the song works equally well as a launch platform for jamming.

24 25

Saturday June 25

Buckeye Lake Music Center, Hebron, Ohio

Bruce Hornsby and the Range open the concert, and Bruce lends his accordion to a first-set "Sugaree">"Stuck inside of Mobile (with the Memphis Blues Again)"—his performance debut with the band. The band issues another communiqué to fans at the show, which reads, in part: "The Grateful Dead has an awkward, dangerous problem at its door, a situation bad enough to put our future as a touring band in doubt. Part of our audience—a small part, but that's all it takes—is making us unwelcome at show site after show site with insensitive behavior including flagrant consumption of illegal substances (including alcohol), littering, and general disturbances of the environment... More security or more rules isn't the answer—you guys know what righteous behavior is about. Because you created your scene, it is up to you to preserve it."

Top and above: Saturday June 25. The Dead rock America's rural heartland at Buckeye Lake Music Center, Hebron, Ohio.

Studio Time—'88 Releases

Bob Dylan's latest album, *Down in the Groove* (Columbia OC 40957), included two songs with lyrics by Robert Hunter: "The Ugliest Girl in the World" and "Silvio." Jerry Garcia, Bob Weir, and Brent Mydland provided background vocals on the latter track. Hunter wrote the songs in the fall of 1986, shortly before Dylan and the Grateful Dead began woodshedding at Front Street in preparation for the 1987 tour. Dylan recorded the two songs without bothering to tell Hunter in advance—not that it mattered: as Hunter told David Gans in an interview on *The Grateful Dead Hour*, "Bob Dylan doesn't have to ask a lyricist if he can do his tunes! Come on, man!"

Jerry Garcia guests on Ornette Coleman and Prime Time's album *Virgin Beauty* (CBS/Portrait OR 44301), playing on "Three Wishes," "Singing in the Shower," and "Desert Players." "This is dense, complex music but still accessible," in Blair Jackson's estimation. Band members' time in the studio also involved: Pete Sears and Friends—*Watchfire* (Redwood Records RR 8806). Garcia plays on two tracks, Garcia/Hart play on one track. Mickey Hart's 360 Degree Records releases *The Music of Upper and Lower Egypt*, which he'd recorded during the Dead's 1978 visit. He also produced an album for Babtunde Olatunji—*Drums of Passion: The Invocation*—for Rykodisc, among much other work.

Thursday June 30

Silver Stadium, Rochester, New York

A fine show highlighted by the second-set opener, a brief take on the classic R&B instrumental "Green Onions," first recorded by Booker T. and the MG's in 1962.

Tuesday June 28

Saratoga Performing Arts Center, Saratoga Springs, New York

The show is marred by a run-in between gatecrashers and police.

26 27 28 29 30

Sunday June 26

Pittsburgh Civic Arena, Pittsburgh, Pennsylvania

The band breaks out "Gentlemen, Start Your Engines," the evil twin of "I Will Take You Home" (Brent Mydland and John Perry Barlow wrote both songs on the same day). An ode to drinking and hell-raising ("One of these days I'm gonna pull myself together/After I finish tearing myself apart"), activities with which both Brent and John Perry were well acquainted, the song wound up in album-less limbo and was only performed once more *(see July 31, 1988)*.

"The difference between an alcoholic and a normal drinker is that whereas a normal drinker gets to a certain point and thinks, 'Well, that's enough, I just said something weird,' the same little voice in an alcoholic's head says, 'GENTLEMEN, start your engines!'"

JOHN PERRY BARLOW, TO BLAIR JACKSON, 1988

JUNE 1988

Above: *Sunday July 3, Oxford Plains Speedway, Oxford, Maine.*

🎸 **Saturday July 2**
🎸 **Sunday July 3**
Oxford Plains Speedway, Oxford, Maine

A massive crowd camps out at this relatively remote, rural outdoor venue, but the two-show run is peaceful, if boisterous. On Sunday a high-energy show is highlighted by another of those cherished synchronicities: an ultralight plane circles the stage and dips its wings during the first-set closer—"Bird Song."

Monday July 4
A missile accidentally launched from a U.S. warship destroys an Iranian civilian airliner, killing 290.

Below: *Summer wildfires ravage almost 100,000 acres in Wyoming's Yellowstone National Park.*

World Music

Deadheads had been getting lessons in "World Music" since the fall of 1978, when the band went to Egypt and then started to incorporate Arab instruments and rhythms into Mickey Hart's and Bill Kreutzmann's drum solos. In the following years, Hart brought in percussion from Brazil, Africa, Indonesia, India, Tibet, and many other places, and he generously shared the Dead's stage with everyone from Hamza El-Din to Flora & Airto to Babatunde Olatunji. Hart's own *Planet Drum* ensembles mixed percussionists and singers from all over the world; meanwhile, he shepherded a custom record label called The World devoted to world music.

At the same time, World Music was catching on globally. In the early and mid-eighties, African musicians such as King Sunny Ade and Thomas Mapfumo, France's nouveau flamenco sensations the Gipsy Kings, and even the Bulgarian Women's Choir caught on internationally and opened the floodgates for scores of other artists—from Malian singer Salif Keita, to South Africa's Ladysmith Black Mambazo, to the late Qawwali master Nusrat Fateh Ali Khan. World Music has been especially successful and influential in Europe, where large populations from Africa, Asia, and the Middle East have settled and become integrated into existing cultures. Paris, in particular, has been a hub for African musicians and for various Arab-influenced styles, including Rai. In England, Peter Gabriel's Real World label has put out a number of fine World Music releases, and Gabriel's own music has been enriched by the addition of various African performers, such as Senegalese singer Youssou N'Dour.

In the United States, World Music moved from being the exclusive domain of university music programs, to rock clubs and concert halls. A number of American artists have successfully integrated World Music influences into their own sound, with Paul Simon (*Graceland, Rhythm of the Saints*) perhaps the most notable example. Various World Music specialty labels, such as Putumayo and Rough Guide, have also enjoyed considerable success in the U.S., and National Public Radio has been a consistent supporter of World artists.

🎸 **Friday July 15**
🎸 **Saturday July 16**
Sunday July 17
Greek Theatre, University of California, Berkeley, California

Three Rex Foundation *(see page 295)* benefits at the Greek. Saturday sees Babatunde Olatunji join on "Drums." The '88 Rex Run ends the next night with the retirement of "Blackbird"—by most accounts not the most successful of the band's Beatles covers.

Saturday July 16
Jerry Garcia joins Zero (with Merl Saunders and Pete Sears in the lineup) at Golden Gate Park, San Francisco, California, *(below),* to try to cool out the Cold War a little by entertaining a rally in support of the US/USSR Peace Walk—a delegation of antiwar activists who have just set out for San Francisco from Washington, D.C. Mickey Hart is also at the afternoon event with Grace Slick and Paul Kantner.

THOSE WHO KNOW HISTORY ARE DOOMED TO REPEAT IT

Henry Kaiser

SST Records 198

Improvisational guitar whiz Henry Kaiser's "breakthrough" album, *Those Who Know History Are Doomed to Repeat It*, was released in 1988 and included interpretations of the Grateful Dead's "Mason's Children" and "Dark Star." (The later CD version has a longer version of "Dark Star" > "The Other One" with Robert Hunter vocalizing.) Non-Dead-derived tracks include takes on Bobbie Gentry's "Ode to Billie Joe" and "The Fishin' Hole," the theme song to *The Andy Griffith Show*. *Grateful Dead Hour* host, Dead Scholar, and general scenester David Gans backs Kaiser on guitar.

Below: Sunday August 28, Autzen Stadium, Eugene, Oregon.

STAFF

GRATEFUL DEAD
ROBERT CRAY
JIMM D

SUNDAY · AUGUST 28 · 12 NOON
AUTZEN STADIUM
UNIVERSITY OF OREGON IN EUGENE

Above and Left: Saturday July 16, Greek Theatre, University of California, Berkeley, California.

Above: Friday July 29, Laguna Seca Raceway, Monterey, California.

★ Friday July 29
Saturday July 30
Sunday July 31
Laguna Seca Raceway, Monterey, California

The band's second run at Laguna Seca *(see May 1987)* will be its last, thanks to some Deadheads who camp on a nearby military firing range. David Lindley and El Rayo-X are on the bill for all three shows; Los Lobos for the last two. Jerry Garcia joins opening act Los Lobos on Sunday, and Los Lobos' David Hildalgo adds his guitar to the first set "Little Red Rooster" and "West L.A. Fadeaway." The show also sees the second and last performance of "Gentlemen, Start Your Engines."

BILL GRAHAM PRESENTS
GRATEFUL DEAD
LOS LOBOS
DAVID LINDLEY & EL RAYO EX
AT LAGUNA SECA

August 1988

357

Sunday August 28
Autzen Stadium, Eugene, Oregon

A triple bill with Robert Cray and Jimmy Cliff.

1 ~ 25	26	27	28	29	30	31

Friday August 26
Tacoma Dome, Tacoma, Washington

This is the last-ever show at the "Taco Dome," one of those huge but acoustically inert stadiums that were the band's main stomping grounds in the post-*In the Dark* era. The opening act, Santana, goes into overtime, so the Dead don't take the stage until nearly 10:00 p.m. The show is also distinguished as the only occasion on which the band went from "Space" into "Touch of Grey."

20	21	22	23	24	25	26	27

Wednesday July 20
The Iran–Iraq War ends in a cease-fire after eight years of combat that killed about a million people in total.

29	30	31

GEN. ADM. AUG 26, 1988
0204

BILL GRAHAM/M.E.G. Presents
GRATEFUL DEAD
WITH **SANTANA**
TACOMA DOME
TACOMA, WA
AUG. 26, 1988
FRIDAY—6:00 PM

Madison Square Garden

The Dead play nine shows over eleven days at Madison Square Garden—the longest single run since the eight shows at Radio City Music Hall (*see October 1980*) and probably exceeded in length only by their stint at the In Room as the Warlocks (*see page 38*). A huge inflatable King Kong (togged out in tie-dye) greets showgoers as they enter the Garden.

The Rainforest Benefit

The last night of the Madison Square Garden run is a benefit concert devoted to raising consciousness about rainforest preservation and raising money for three organizations—Greenpeace, Cultural Survival, and the Rainforest Action Network. Despite the Grateful Dead's famed resistance to getting sucked into politics, by 1988 the band decided that the accelerating destruction of the planet's rain forests justified bending the rules—especially as they now had the profile to really make an impact.

On September 14, Jerry Garcia, Mickey Hart, and Bob Weir went uptown to the United Nations for a press conference, at which Jerry explained the motivation behind the band's decision: "We've never really called our fans… to align themselves one way or another as far as any political cause is concerned because of a basic paranoia about leading someone… But this, we feel, is an issue strong enough and life-threatening enough that inside the world of human games [there is] the larger question of global survival. We want to see the world survive to play those games, even if they're atrocious."

Bruce Hornsby and the Range open the benefit gig and a galaxy of guest stars join the band. Ex–Rolling Stone Mick Taylor plays guitar on the first set's "West L.A. Fadeaway" and "Little Red Rooster"; the second set opens with the band backing neo-folkie Suzanne Vega on Robyn Hitchcock's "Chinese Bones" and her own "Neighborhood Girls"; Daryl Hall and John Oates vocalize on "Every Time You Go Away" and "What's Going On"; Baba Olatunji and percussionist Michael Hinton join on "Drums," and Baba stays for "Space">"The Wheel">"Throwing Stones">"Not Fade Away," with Bruce Hornsby coming aboard for NFA. The double encore, "Good Lovin'" and "Knockin' on Heaven's Door" includes most of the performers, plus Jack Casady taking over bass duties from Phil Lesh.

The show nets over $600,000, but the band is tired from the epic MSG run—Garcia's voice, in particular, is shot—and the music doesn't rise to the importance of the occasion.

Top: *September 14–24, Madison Square Garden, inflatable King Kong.*
Left: *September 24, Madison Square Garden, Garcia with Suzanne Vega.*

PENN STATION   Amtrak

358

Wednesday September 14
Thursday September 15
Friday September 16
Madison Square Garden, New York, New York

| 13 | 14 | 15 | 16 | 17 |

"RIPPLE"

GARCIA

Perhaps the finest sonic accomplishment in the Grateful Dead's body of recordings. "Ripple" was a shimmering songwriting triumph both live and in the studio. In addition to some fine mandolin flourishes by long-time band friend David Grisman, the studio version also featured members of the Dead's extended clan piping up for a true chorus to go with Hunter's masterful, Zen-like haiku: "Ripple in still water, where there is no pebble tossed, nor wind to blow." "'Ripple' is one of those things of having two halves of a thing and having them come together perfectly," Garcia said in 1971. "Bob Weir had a guitar custom-made for himself and I picked it up and that song came out… next time I saw Hunter he says, 'Here, I have a couple of songs I'd like you to take a look at,' and he had 'Ripple'… it was just perfect." The track had the unique distinction of being one of the band's best-known and least-played; although the version appearing on *American Beauty* (1970) and the B-side of that album's only single, "Truckin'," reaped airplay of its own as a de facto radio song, live takes were to be savored like a fine wine, with less than a dozen logged in 1970 and '71 before a nine-year absence. The tune made a welcome return during a rare acoustic run in 1980, leading to a standout take in New York on Halloween, October 31. A one-off performance during an encore in Maryland on September 3, 1988, marked the last Grateful Dead version of the song, though in an uncommon role reversal Garcia ended up playing it solo 70 times between 1982 and 1992. It was later welcomed like a lost friend in sets by The Other Ones beginning in 1998.

Monday September 5
The Grateful Dead Hour radio show, hosted by David Gans, goes into nationwide syndication (*see page 209*).

| 1 | 2 | 3 | 4 | 5 | 6 | 7 | 8 | 9 | 10 | 11 | 12 |

Friday September 2
Saturday September 3
Monday September 5
Tuesday September 6
Capital Centre, Landover, Maryland

The Fall East Coast Tour kicks off with a four-night run at the familiar Capital Centre. The band varies its usual tour itinerary by playing more nights at fewer venues. After the customary "One More Saturday Night" encore at the Saturday show, the band brings out "Ripple" for the first time since the Melkweg shows in Amsterdam (*see October 16, 1981*) and in its first electric version since the last Fillmore East show (*see April 29, 1971*). There is a sad story behind the revival: it was made at the request of a terminally ill Deadhead. The performance is somewhat ragged (Bob Weir bet that Jerry Garcia would flub the lyrics, and won). The revival is a one-off and the last-ever performance of the much-beloved tune by the band.

Thursday September 8
Friday September 9
Sunday September 11
Monday September 12
The Spectrum, Philadelphia, Pennsylvania

On Sunday it's Mickey Hart's 45th birthday, and Bill Kreutzmann presents him with a cream pie in the face at the end of "Drums."

"Fuck 'em if they can't take a joke. I can sell anything, even my ass, if I want."

THERE IS CONSTERNATION AMONG DEADHEADS WHEN IT'S DISCOVERED THAT JERRY GARCIA HAS LICENSED A SNIPPET OF "EEP HOUR," THE MULTILAYERED INSTRUMENTAL FROM HIS FIRST SOLO ALBUM, FOR USE IN A COMMERCIAL FOR CHER'S "UNINHIBITED" PERFUME. THIS IS JERRY'S RESPONSE TO DENNIS McNALLY.

Above: Sept 24, Madison Square Garden, Baba Olatunji. *Right:* Sept 24, ex–Rolling Stone Mick Taylor with Jerry Garcia.

"For anyone out there who has kids, my son just said 'rock 'n' roll' for the first time."

PHIL LESH, TO THE AUDIENCE AT THE START OF THE SECOND SET, *SEPTEMBER 15*

18	19	20	21	22	23	24	25	26

Sunday September 18
Monday September 19
Tuesday September 20
Madison Square Garden,
New York, New York

Thursday September 22
Friday September 23
Saturday September 24
Madison Square Garden,
New York, New York

Trying To Use The Force

With the Fall Tour behind them and having (more or less) enough new material for an album, thanks largely to the new songwriting partnership of Brent Mydland and John Perry Barlow, the band set to recording. Unfortunately, the technique of recording the basic tracks live that worked so well on *In the Dark* failed them this time out. The band tried out the recording facilities at filmmaker George Lucas's Skywalker Ranch, which had most recently been used by Mick Jagger for some solo work. Even in these high-tech surroundings, however, the old problems of "studiophobia" and intraband squabbling returned to plague the sessions, and little was accomplished before the end of the year. At least one tape of a rehearsal from this period, including versions of about half the tracks that would eventually make it onto the final album, is in circulation.

"The first six months [of recording what would be Built To Last], it seemed like we hung out arguing over how many peanuts should be in the mixed nuts."
BOB WEIR, *THE GAVIN REPORT, 1989*

Thursday September 29
The Space Shuttle Discovery lifts off from Cape Canaveral, Florida, in the first shuttle mission since the loss of the Challenger in January 1986.

Nightfood, Brian Melvin's tribute to the great jazz and fusion bassist Jaco Pastorius, includes Bob Weir contributing vocals on Marvin Gaye's "Sexual Healing" and guitar on Little Willie John's "Fever" and "Mercy Mercy Mercy," the latter written by Joe Zawinul, Pastorius' sometime bandmate in the seminal fusion ensemble Weather Report. (Brian Melvin's ensemble also included Merl Saunders.) Pastorius—whose immense talent was matched by his capacity for self-destructive behavior—played on five tracks, but died in tragic circumstances before the album was released.

OCTOBER '88

27	28	29	30	1	2	3

Friday September 30
Saturday October 1
Sunday October 2
Shoreline Amphitheatre,
Mountain View, California

The tuning before the second set on the last night leads into "Space">"Crazy Fingers," with the band taking off into "Space" again in its usual slot.

Friday October 14
Miami Arena, Miami, Florida

4 – 13	14	15	16

Below: Sunday October 2, Shoreline Amphitheatre, Mountain View, CA.

Saturday October 15
Sunday October 16
Bayfront Center,
St. Petersburg, Florida

It's Bob Weir's 41st birthday on Sunday, commemorated with a chorus of "Happy Birthday" before the encore—Dylan's "The Mighty Quinn." Bob himself marks the occasion by singing the first verse of "Victim or the Crime" as "Patience runs out on the bunny…"

Tuesday October 18
Lakefront Arena,
New Orleans, Louisiana

Members of the Neville Brothers join on "Drums," and surprise guests the Bangles add some girl-group gestalt to the double encore—"Iko Iko" (a natural choice, given the venue) and "Knockin' on Heaven's Door."

17	18	19	20	21	22 – 31

Above: Sunday October 2, Shoreline Amphitheater, Mountain View, California.

Thursday October 20
The Summit, Houston, Texas

The show marks the first performance of what will become the title track for the band's next studio album, the Hunter/Garcia "Built to Last." One of Hunter's "big idea" songs (Jerry's phrase), "Built to Last" is, lyrically, classic Grateful Dead ambiguity—on one level an affirmation of the band's endurance, and on another level (right out of the opening verses of the Bible's *Book of Ecclesiastes*) a reminder that nothing is permanent except change: "One blue star/Sets on the hill/Call it back/You never will/Show me something built to last."

Friday October 21
Reunion Arena, Dallas, Texas

Another October birthday—Brent Mydland's 36th—and another chorus of "Happy Birthday," on this occasion before the second-set opener, "Wang Dang Doodle."

October 1988

359

ALMOST
ACOUSTIC

Jerry Garcia Acoustic Band

Recorded Live

ALMOST ACOUSTIC
Jerry Garcia Acoustic Band

The short-lived Jerry Garcia Acoustic Band is in fine form on this selection of old-time, bluegrass, and even a Grateful Dead tune or two. Sandy Rothman, in particular, shines on dobro, and the group's harmonies are strong throughout.

Released by Consensus Reality/GD Merchandising (GDCD4005) in December 1988

1. **Swing Low Sweet Chariot**
   (Traditional)
2. **Deep Elem Blues**
   (Traditional)
3. **Blue Yodel #9 (Standing On The Corner)**
   (Rodgers)
4. **Spike Driver Blues**
   (Hurt)
5. **I've been All Around This World**
   (Traditional)
6. **I'm Here To Get My Baby Out Of Jail**
   (Davis/Taylor)
7. **I'm Troubled**
   (Traditional)
8. **Oh, The Wind And Rain**
   (Traditional)
9. **The Girl at the Crossroads Bar**
   (Bryson)
10. **Oh, Babe It Ain't No Lie**
    (Cotton)
11. **Casey Jones**
    (Hurt)
12. **Diamond Joe**
    (Logan)
13. **Gone Home**
    (Carlisle)
14. **Ripple**
    (Garcia/Hunter)

Personnel

Jerry Garcia – guitar, vocals
David Nelson – guitar, vocals
Sandy Rothman – mandolin, dobro, vocals
John Kahn – acoustic bass
Kenny Kosek – fiddle
David Kemper – snare drum

Produced by Sandy Rothman

NOVEMBER '88

| 1 – 7 | 8 | 9 – 24 |

Tuesday November 8
Republican George H.W. Bush easily defeats Democrat Michael Dukakis to win election as the 41st president of the United States.

**Friday November 25
Saturday November 26
Sunday November 27**
Jerry Garcia Band performs four nights at the Wiltern Theatre, Los Angeles, California. The shows are opened by a Bob Weir acoustic set.

DECEMBER '88

| 1 | 2 | 3 | 4 |

| 25 | 26 | 27 | 28 | 29 | 30 |

Right: Randall Delpiano, a grifter, is arrested in Oakland for scamming locals out of money and meals by impersonating Bob Weir. He winds up sentenced to fifteen months in the slammer.

Robert Hunter writes forewords to two books published in 1988: *Dead Tour* by Alan Neal Izumi (Relix Books, New York), which is a fictional account of a murder on an East Coast Dead tour, and *Alleys of the Heart: The Collected Poems of Robert M. Petersen* (Hulogosi, Eugene, Oregon).

Sunday December 4
Jerry Garcia, Bob Weir, and bassist Rob Wasserman appear at Oakland Coliseum Arena, Oakland, California. They play an acoustic set ("Wang Dang Doodle," "Friend of the Devil," "Throwing Stones," and "Ripple") at the second annual benefit concert for the Bridge School, Hillsborough, California, an institution devoted to "ensuring that children with severe speech and physical impairments achieve full participation in their communities." (The concert is organized by Neil Young, who joins Jerry, Bob, and Rob on harp and vocals on "Wang Dang Doodle.") Other performers include Billy Idol, Bob Dylan, Tom Petty and the Heartbreakers, Tracy Chapman, and David Crosby, Stephen Stills, and Graham Nash, who join Young for one song.

Left: December 9–11, Long Beach Arena, Long Beach, California.

Below: December 9–11, Long Beach Arena, Long Beach, California.

GRATEFUL DEAD

NOT GOOD FOR ADMISSION
Backstage

December 9, 1988
Long Beach Arena
Long Beach, California

| 5 | 6 | 7 | 8 | 9 | 10 | 11 |

**Friday December 9
Saturday December 10
Sunday December 11**
Long Beach Arena, Long Beach, California

Right: Saturday December 31, Oakland Coliseum Arena, Oakland, California.

Above: Saturday December 31, Oakland Coliseum Arena, Oakland, California.

GRATEFUL DEAD

1988

TOM TOM CLUB

PETER APFELBAUM AND THE HIEROGLYPHICS ENSEMBLE

OAKLAND COLISEUM SATURDAY DECEMBER 31 7PM

| 22 | | | | | 27 | **28** | **29** | 30 | **31** |

Wednesday December 21
A terrorist bomb blows up Pan American Airlines Flight 101 above Lockerbie, Scotland, killing 259 passengers and crew and 11 people on the ground.

| 12 | 13 | 14 | 15 | 16 | 17 | 18 | 19 | 20 | **21** |

Wednesday December 28
🎸 **Thursday December 29**
Saturday December 31 ★
Oakland Coliseum Arena, Oakland, California

On New Year's Eve Clarence Clemons's sax pumps up the energy level during the show, while Baba Olatunji, Sikiru Adepoju, and Kitaro join in on drums (complete with Olatunji leading the crowd in polyrhythmic African chants). The three-song encore is especially well-received—"Wharf Rat," "Goin' Down The Road Feeling Bad," and this New Year's Eve falling on Saturday night, "One More Saturday Night." Bill Graham makes his pre-countdown entrance aboard a giant mirrored "disco ball."

FLOOR GEN ADM
GEN. ADMISSION ADULT
GREAT WESTERN FORUM
BILL GRAHAM & AVALON
PRESENT
GRATEFUL DEAD
CAMPING NOT PERMITTED
SAT FEB 11 1989 8:00 PM

Left: New Year's Eve show, 1988, held at Oakland Coliseum Arena, Oakland, California.

In February, Relix Records continues its release of Dead solo material with two reissues: *Keith and Donna Godchaux – Double Dose* is a CD-only package of the *Ghosts Playing in the Heart of Gold Band* and *The Heart of Gold Band Live* albums; *Kingfish – Double Dose* is also CD-only and contains the *Alive in '85* and *Kingfish* albums on one CD.

Drums of Passion: The Beat by Babatunde Olatunji, a digitally remixed version of *Dance To The Beat Of My Drum* (1986), is released this year. It is produced by Mickey Hart.

FEBRUARY '89

| 1 | 2 | 3 | 4 | 5 | 6 | 7 | 8 | 9 |

JANUARY '89

| 1 - 30 | 31 |

Tuesday January 31
Dylan & the Dead is released.

Sunday February 5
Monday February 6
Tuesday February 7
Henry J. Kaiser Convention Center, Oakland, California

Monday's show marks Chinese New Year and sees the now-traditional opening from San Francisco's Chinese Symphony Orchestra and a dragon dance during "Drums." No report of Bob Weir proclaiming "Gung Hey Fat Choy!", however *(see page 307)*.

Friday February 10
Saturday February 11
Sunday February 12
Great Western Forum, Inglewood, California

Saturday's show sees Airto Moreira, his wife Flora Purim, and their daughter Diana Moreira join for "Drums." Sunday night is full of surprises, with Spencer Davis joining the band for the first performance in nearly 20 years of Leroy Carr and Scrapper Blackwell's classic "How Long, How Long Blues," and also on the Spencer Davis Group's "Gimme Some Lovin'." Bob Dylan guests during the second set, which includes "Monkey and the Engineer" and "Stuck Inside of Mobile (with the Memphis Blues Again)." Japan's Kodo Drummers pound their taikos during "Drums," and Dylan returns for a superb double encore, "Not Fade Away" and "Knockin' On Heaven's Door."

| 10 | 11 | 12 | 13 | 14 | 15 ~ 28 |

Running and Standing

The February 5 show included the first performances of two songs that would make it onto *Built to Last*.

"We Can Run" was an environmentalist anthem from Brent Mydland and John Perry Barlow that combined a pop-country tune with heavy-handed lyrics ("We don't own this place/But we act as if we did/It's a loan from the children/Of our children's kids"). Unsurprisingly, it became the soundtrack to a pro-environment TV spot under the auspices of the Audubon Society. The band performed the song 22 times before its retirement in 1990. (The decidedly un-pacific origin of the song's title originated with boxer Joe Louis's 1946 comment about his opponent for the heavyweight championship, Billy Conn—"He can run, but he can't hide").

The Garcia/Hunter "Standing on the Moon" became one of the best-loved and most-performed songs of the band's last decade. The music is austere ("as minimal as I could make it," in Jerry's words). Hunter's lyrics speak in the voice of a narrator looking at earth from space, reflecting on how peaceful our planet looks from afar but acknowledging the violence and despair below the stratosphere: "I see all of Southeast Asia/I can see El Salvador/I hear the sounds of children/And the other songs of war," but ending on a note that put the personal over the political: "But I would rather be with you/Somewhere in San Francisco/In a back porch in July/Just looking up to heaven/At this crescent in the sky." If "Built to Last" seems to reflect the Old Testament's *Book of Ecclesiastes*, "Standing on the Moon" seems to owe something to *Lamentations*.

"'Standing On the Moon' was one of those neat, sweet, quick things, like 'It Must Have Been the Roses,' where the whole picture just came to me, and I grabbed a piece of paper and got it down. No changes, no nothin'. Out of the head of Zeus, full-born, and clad in armor."
ROBERT HUNTER TO STEVE SILBERMAN, IN *POETRY FLASH*, 1992

The Grateful Dead deferred to Bob Dylan's selections of which performances from the 1987 tour would go onto this live album, with typically uneven, inscrutable results. Most fans felt the album failed to capture even the better moments from the tour; in Oliver Trager's words, "only 'All Along the Watchtower' sprouts wings and soars amidst the ill-chosen track list." For some, the best part of the album was Rick Griffin's cover.

A better documentation of Dylan–Dead dynamics are the several tapes in circulation from the tour rehearsals at the Grateful Dead's Club Front studio. As DeadBase editor Mike Dolgushkin put it in Shenk and Silberman's *Skeleton Key*, "Both the Dead and the Garcia Band have covered Dylan songs since the beginning, and the rehearsals at Front Street gave the band a chance to try their favorites with a playfulness and sense of adventure that was lacking on the tour."

"The Dylan Dead tour was a historic collaboration certainly worth recording for posterity. Dylan & the Dead though makes you wonder what the fuss was about. You really had to be there."
DAVID FRICKE, IN *ROLLING STONE*

DYLAN & THE DEAD

Bob Dylan and the Dead

Columbia OC-45056/Grateful Dead GDCD-41012 (CD)
Recorded at the Dead/Dylan concerts in July 1987

1. **Slow Train**
   (Bob Dylan)
2. **I Want You**
   (Bob Dylan)
3. **Gotta Serve Somebody**
   (Bob Dylan)
4. **Queen Jane Approximately**
   (Bob Dylan)
5. **Joey**
   (Bob Dylan/J. Levy)
6. **All Along the Watchtower**
   (Bob Dylan)
7. **Knockin' on Heaven's Door**
   (Bob Dylan)

Personnel

Bob Dylan - guitar, harmonica, vocals
Jerry Garcia - guitar, vocals
Mickey Hart - drums
Bill Kreutzmann - drums
Phil Lesh - bass
Brent Mydland - keyboards, vocals
Bob Weir - guitar, vocals

Produced by John Cutler and Jerry Garcia

363

Clockwise from right: Garcia and Country Joe McDonald, who both took part in an acoustic set at a benefit for Artists Rights Today on Wednesday March 22. Ron Turner (publisher of Last Gasp Comix) and Victor Moscoso were also in attendance. To the left, the band holds a press conference with Huey Lewis at the Fillmore to promote a benefit for AIDS on May 27.

The Rhythm Devils' *Apocalypse Now Sessions* is released this year. Mickey Hart, Bill Kreutzmann, and Phil Lesh (and others) add bits and pieces to the original recordings for the *Apocalypse Now* soundtrack. Produced by Mickey Hart, it is an expanded CD version of the original 1980 LP.

MARCH '89

| 1 | 2 | 3 | 4 | 5 | 6 | 7 | 8 | 9 | 10 ~ 21 | 22 |

Wednesday March 22

Jerry Garcia, Bob Weir, and John Kahn perform an acoustic set at another benefit for Artists Rights Today *(see page 334)* at Gift Center, San Francisco, California, the campaign to win the great poster artists of the Bay Area their legal and financial due. Country Joe McDonald, the Dinosaurs, and Nick Gravenites also perform; Jerry backs up Country Joe on "Starship Ride" and "Lady with the Lamp."

Below: Thursday March 30, Greensboro Coliseum, Greensboro, North Carolina.

| 23 | 24 | 25 | 26 |

CELLAR DOOR PRODUCTIONS Presents
Grateful Dead
GREENSBORO COLISEUM
GREENSBORO, NC
MARCH 31, 1989
FRIDAY 7:30 PM
Please, No Cans, Bottles, Alcohol, Flash or Movie Cameras and No Video Equipment of ANY Kind.
$18.50
SEC ROW SEAT
GEN. ADM. 0775

Thursday March 30
★ **Friday March 31**
Greensboro Coliseum,
Greensboro, North Carolina

Monday March 27
Tuesday March 28
The Omni, Atlanta, Georgia

| 27 | 28 | 29 | 30 | 31 |

Monday March 27
The oil tanker Exxon Valdez goes aground in Alaska's Prince William Sound, spilling a million gallons of oil and devastating the area's environment and wildlife.

Tuesday April 11
Wednesday April 12
Thursday April 13
Rosemont Horizon Arena, Rosemont, Illinois

9 | 10 | 11 | 12 | 13

Sunday April 9
Freedom Hall, Louisville, Kentucky

The last-ever "Louie Louie" *(see page 353)*.

Saturday April 8
Riverfront Coliseum, Cincinnati, Ohio

5 | 6 | 7 | 8

Wednesday April 5
Thursday April 6
Crisler Arena, University of Michigan, Ann Arbor, Michigan

14 | 15 | 16

Saturday April 15
Sunday April 16
MECCA, Milwaukee, Wisconsin

The two-night run at MECCA (the only shows at this venue) mark the band's return to Milwaukee after almost nine years *(see page 250)*. Maybe it's the fresh surroundings, maybe it's the relatively small (by late-'80s standards) hall, but the band puts on two of the best shows of the year.

17 | 18 | 19 | 20 | 21 | 22 | 23

Monday April 17
Metropolitan Sports Center, Bloomington, Minnesota

Jerry Garcia debuts his first MIDI-equipped guitar *(see page 346)* during "Space."

Above: Monday April 24, Jerry Garcia, James Burton, Pete Sears and Elvis Costello jam together at a party at the Sweetwater club in Mill Valley, California.

Monday April 24

Jerry Garcia and Bob Weir sit in with Brit rocker Elvis Costello at Sweetwater, a Marin County club in Mill Valley, California. The famously eclectic ex–New Waver—who has collaborated with everyone from George Jones to Burt Bacharach—first saw the Grateful Dead at the Bickershaw Festival *(see page 144)* and later contributed a cover of "Ship of Fools" to the 1991 tribute album Deadicated.

I really love his playing—it's very lyrical, humorous, and unpredictable. I like his use of harmonics, and the endless modulations he goes through. But my favorite thing is that sense of fearlessness.—ELVIS COSTELLO ON JERRY GARCIA'S GUITAR STYLE, QUOTED IN DAVID SHENK & STEVE SILBERMAN'S *SKELETON KEY*

April 1989

365

24 | 25 | 26 | 27 | 28 | 29 | 30

Tom Constanten's *Fresh Tracks In Real Time* is released during 1989, a solo piano album that includes, among other things, a version of "Dark Star."

APRIL '89

1 | 2 | 3 | 4

Sunday April 2
Monday April 3
Pittsburgh Civic Arena, Pittsburgh, Pennsylvania

The Pittsburgh run is plagued by "riots" between 3,000 ticketless troublemakers and police, resulting in more than 20 arrests. In fact, the venue management had ignored the band's recommendations for extra security, and the local media roundly criticized the mayor and Pittsburgh law enforcement for using excessive force. Nevertheless, the national news picked up the story and, as Dennis McNally put it, "the image of a violent audience was established."

MUSIC TO BE BORN BY
Mickey Hart
Rykodisc RCD 20112

In 1983 Mickey Hart recorded his unborn son Taro's in utero heartbeat and added his own accompaniment on wooden flute and Brazilian surdo drum, with Bobby Vega on bass. Mickey originally made the recording to help his wife relax and concentrate during delivery. It worked so well that friends began to request copies, and an album was released commercially on Rykodisc six years later. Hart also produced the album.

music to be born by

Friday April 28
Saturday April 29
Sunday April 30
Irvine Meadows Amphitheatre, Irvine, California

Friday's show sees the first airing of "Picasso Moon," credited to Weir, Barlow, and Bob Bralove. It's a rocker in the vein of "Hell in a Bucket" but with even more twisted and obscure lyrics ("tattooed tots and chrome-spike bunnies"). Fans either loved it or hated it but the band would play it live 77 times and it would appear on *Built To Last*, giving that album the distinction of having two moon tunes on it (see February 5, 1989).

John Cipollina 1943 – 1989

On May 29 the Bay Area music scene lost one of its stalwarts when a respiratory ailment claimed the life of guitarist John Cipollina at age 46. Born on August 24, 1943, he was a founding member of Quicksilver Messenger Service *(see page 34)* and one of the originators of the "San Francisco Sound." He went on to play in at least a dozen Bay Area groups, including the Dinosaurs *(see page 277)*, the Heart of Gold Band *(see page 302)*, and Zero, and he sat in with the Grateful Dead 14 times between 1970 and 1983, including every New Year's Eve show from '78 through '83. Cipollina also played on Mickey Hart's 1972 *Rolling Thunder* album and on Robert Hunter's *Amagamalin Street* in 1984.

Left: Mickey Hart shows his support for Deadhead basketball star Bill Walton's team at Oakland Stadium, May 27.

June 18, 1989
Shoreline Amphitheatre
Mountain View California
Backstage
NOT GOOD FOR ADMISSION

Saturday May 27
Oakland Coliseum Stadium, Oakland, California

The band joins Tracy Chapman, John Fogerty, Los Lobos, Joe Satriani, and Tower of Power for the "In Concert Against AIDS" benefit. Clarence Clemons joins the Grateful Dead on half of their songs, and Jerry Garcia and Bob Weir help back up Fogerty.

Friday May 19
Jerry Garcia Band plays at Irvine Meadows Amphitheatre, Irvine, California. Bob Weir and Rob Wasserman open.

| 19 | 20 | 21 | 22 | 23 | 24 | 25 | 26 | 27 | 28 | 29 |

Saturday May 20
Jerry Garcia Band plays at Open Air Theater, San Diego, California. Bob Weir and Rob Wasserman open.

Monday May 29
John Cipollina dies at Marin General Hospital.

Alan Trist's *The Water of Life: A Tale of the Grateful Dead* (Hulogosi Books) is published in 1989.

MAY '89

| 1 | 2 | 3 | 4 | 5 | 6 | 7 | 9 ~ 17 |

| 30 | 31 |

Saturday May 6
Sunday May 7
Frost Amphitheater, Stanford University, Palo Alto, California

At the second of these two Rex Foundation benefit gigs "The Other One" opens with a resurrection of "the Roll," Phil Lesh's rafter-shaking bass run.

Right: Saturday May 6, Frost Amphitheater, Stanford University, Palo Alto, California. This weekend marked the last shows the Dead would play at this beloved venue. Alas, they simply outgrew it.

One of the buses following the band around in the summer of '89 carried Rebecca G. Adams, a sociology professor at the University of North Carolina at Greensboro, and 21 of her students. The roadwork was coursework for what's believed to be the first college-level class devoted to the Grateful Dead and the Deadheads. Adams and Robert Sardiello would ultimately edit a collection of academic studies of Deadheaddom, *Deadhead Social Science: You Ain't Gonna Learn What You Don't Want to Know*, which was published in 2000, with an introduction by Dennis McNally.

1	2	3	4	5	6 ~ 17

The summer tour is preceded by another cautionary Deadhead mailing laying out the band's policy on vending (only where allowed, respect trademarks), taping (in "the Pit" only, no selling for any more than the cost of the blank), and tickets (only buy from authorized sources or you may end up with a counterfeit and won't get in). The missive ends:

"We gratefully invite you to experience this unexpected era of Mega Dead-dom. Take it with the grain of salt it deserves and enjoy watching the ripples as our personal tributary begins mingling with larger currents. It's just as weird for us as it is for you, but, after all, this wasn't meant to be a private party!"

DEADHEAD MAILING, *SUMMER 1989*

Monday June 5
Poland's communist government falls as Solidarity candidate Lech Walesa wins the nation's first free elections in a half-century.

Monday June 5
Hundreds, perhaps thousands, of pro-democracy demonstrators are killed when the Chinese government sends tanks and troops to clear Beijing's Tiananmen Square.

GRATEFUL DEAD

June 19, 1989
Shoreline Amphitheatre
Mountain View California
NOT GOOD FOR ADMISSION
BACKSTAGE

June 1989

367

Above: June 18–21 (stage pic from Sunday June 18), Shoreline Amphitheatre, Mountain View, California.

Sunday June 18
Monday June 19
Wednesday June 21
Shoreline Amphitheatre, Mountain View, California

The opening night sees the band's last-ever performance of "Alabama Getaway." The Summer Solstice show two nights later is the Grateful Dead's first non–New Year's Eve broadcast nationwide on pay-per-view cable TV, and something of a test case: the band is considering doing more pay-per-view performances to cut down on touring and its attendant problems. The numbers, however, aren't great: there is nothing like a Grateful Dead concert, indeed, but only if you're actually there… The broadcast also suffers from technical problems, and so does Bob Weir, who at one point kicks his amp in frustration. Other show highlights include Clarence Clemons's sax for most of the second set and the first (and last ever) performance of Freddie King's "Hide Away" since November 7, 1971.

18	19	20	21	22	23	24	25	26	27	28	29	30

Tuesday July 4
ABC TV's *Nightline* July 4 special includes a videotaped performance of Woody Guthrie's "This Land Is Your Land" by Jerry Garcia, Bob Weir, and Los Lobos—recorded backstage at Sullivan Stadium before the July 2 show.

Friday July 7
JFK Stadium, Philadelphia, Pennsylvania

Bruce Hornsby and the Range opens what would be the Dead's last show at this venue.

Wednesday July 12
Thursday July 13
RFK Stadium, Washington, D.C.

Bruce Hornsby and the Range open both shows, and on the first night Bruce sits in for the second-set starters, "Sugaree" and "Man Smart, Woman Smarter." During the second show Bruce adds his squeezebox to the first set's "Tennessee Jed" and "Stuck Inside of Mobile (with the Memphis Blues Again)."

Monday July 17 ★
Tuesday July 18
Wednesday July 19 ★
Alpine Valley Music Theatre, East Troy, Wisconsin

The first show of what will be the full band's last run at Alpine Valley sees the last-ever performance of "Push Comes to Shove." The evening's rendition of "The Music Never Stopped" appears on 1997's *Fallout from the Phil Zone*. At the end of the second set the band delivers an emotional, ethereal performance of "And We Bid You Goodnight"—the first since the '78 New Year's Eve Show. The crowd's beatific silence—louder, in its way, than any applause—leads Garcia to thank the audience before the band launches into the "Johnny B. Goode" encore. It is an eerily prescient moment: The last night's "Box of Rain" is also included on the *Fallout from the Phil Zone* release.

The Gyuto Monks' *Freedom Chants from the Roof of the World* is released. Produced by Mickey Hart, it is recorded at the Skywalker Ranch owned by George Lucas.

| 4 | 5 | 6 | 7 | 8 | 9 | 10 | 11 | 12 | 13 | 14 | 15 | 16 |

| 17 | 18 | 19 | 20 ~ 31 | 1 | 2 | 3 |

Tuesday July 4
Rich Stadium, Orchard Park, New York

10,000 Maniacs opens. A sunshower accompanies the first-set "Looks Like Rain," cooling out the crowd on a couple of levels.

Sunday July 9
Monday July 10 ★
Giants Stadium, East Rutherford, New Jersey

Los Lobos opens the first show, with the Dead resurrecting the Addams Family theme tune-up before the opener, "Shakedown Street." The Neville Brothers open the second show, and join the Dead for most of the second set.

Below: Sunday July 2, Sullivan Stadium, Foxboro, Massachusetts. It was scorchingly hot, as usual.

Saturday July 15
Deer Creek Music Center, Noblesville, Indiana

The first Dead show at this venue is also Jerry's first with his MIDI guitar, blasting the *Close Encounters of the Third Kind* theme during "Space."

Wednesday August 2
Jerry Garcia joins Carlos Santana and Ruben Blades at a Benefit for the National Hispanic Arts, Education & Media Institute at the Biltmore Hotel, Los Angeles, California.

| 1 | 2 | 3 |

Sunday July 2 ★
Sullivan Stadium, Foxboro, Massachusetts

Los Lobos opens the first show of the tour at a venue recently renamed from Schaefer Stadium.

I peaked at the Greek.

BUMPER STICKER SPOTTED IN THE BAY AREA, *1980s*

Left: The crowd at the Cal Expo Amphitheatre, Sacramento, California, August 4–6.

| 20 ~ 25 | 26 | 27 ~ 31 |

Saturday August 26
Jerry Garcia Band plays at the Greek Theatre, University of California, Berkeley, California. Jimmy Cliff opens and provides lead vocals on his reggae classic "The Harder they Come," a JGB staple.

| 13 | 14 | 15 | 16 | 17 | 18 | 19 |

Thursday August 17
Friday August 18 ★
Saturday August 19
Greek Theatre, University of California, Berkeley, California

| 4 | 5 | 6 | 7 | 8 | 9 | 10 | 11 | 12 |

Friday August 4
Saturday August 5
Sunday August 6
Cal Expo Amphitheatre, Sacramento, California

Three Rex Foundation benefits. Of all the places the Grateful Dead played regularly in the 1980s, the Greek Theatre on the campus of UC Berkeley was probably the most beloved by West Coast Deadheads, and by anybody else lucky enough to see any of the 29 shows the band played there between 1980 and 1989. Built around the turn of the 20th century and really more of an amphitheater than a theater, the Greek is an intimate (about 9,000 seats), bowl-shaped space, with the stage backed by graceful classical columns—hence the venue's name. (The concrete seats, however, could be tough on the backsides of Heads who forgot their blankets and pillows in the car.) Deadheads with kids loved the adjacent picnic area, and luckless miracle-seekers appreciated the band's practice (at some late '80s shows) of setting up a PA system on a nearby soccer field. Unfortunately, the increasing numbers of ticketless made it impossible for the band to continue their traditional three-day summer runs at the Greek after 1989.

Building Built to Last

Following the Summer Tour the band resumed work on the next studio album, which Arista had pegged for a Halloween release. The recording process the band finally settled on was 180° from the live-performance tack they'd taken with *In the Dark*. Now, the band members worked from pre-recorded rhythm tracks (exactly what they'd sought to avoid on the previous album), each musician adding his own parts at Front Street or in their home studios. ("Really, nobody heard this record till we mixed it," said Jerry Garcia—who co-produced with John Cutler—in a *Rolling Stone* interview.) Another contrast with *In the Dark* was that the band's new originals hadn't been in "the rotation" very long—some of the previous album's songs had seven years of live seasoning behind them, while none of the nine tracks that made it onto *Built to Last (see page 371)* predated '88. And then there was the pressure to meet Arista's release date...

"When the real world's gonna-end deadline comes, we keep ignoring it until panic sufficiently motivates us to get to work. Then we make most of our records in about a month and a half. The last two weeks are particularly hellish." BOB WEIR

"I do think *Built to Last* was one of the best *sounding* records we've ever made. You can hear everything real clearly. But it didn't hang together all that well."

PHIL LESH TO BLAIR JACKSON, *1990*

Instruments and Equipment

The second half of the Grateful Dead's career maintained the tradition of experimentation and exploration set in the days of Alembic *(see page 102)* and the Wall of Sound *(see pages 166–167)*. The big news in the late '80s was Bob Bralove's introduction of MIDI *(see page 346)*, which allowed the band to take its on-stage interplay to amazing new heights. Phil Lesh and Jerry Garcia debuted their first MIDI-equipped axes on April 17, 1989, and MIDI was built into "Rosebud," the third in a series of guitars custom-made for Jerry by luthier Doug Irwin, in 1990.

On the drum riser, the Rhythm Devils continued to pound on anything—analog, digital, or hybrid—capable of producing an interesting sound, from the Nubian tar to the South American berimbau to "the Beast," Mickey Hart's *taiko*-style bass drums, leftovers from the *Apocalypse Now* sessions *(see page 231)*. Another addition to the percussion arsenal was "the beam," an electrified aluminum girder rigged with piano strings tuned to various unusual pitches.

At the soundboard, Dan Healy doggedly pursued sonic perfection until his departure from the band in '94. Among his later innovations were the Ultra Matrix system *(see page 320)* and the mid-1980s "in-house FM" system, which transmitted an FM signal from the soundboard to speakers to augment the band's sound. (The system was dropped due to FCC regulations.)

For Tapers, the early '90s brought the advent of portable DAT (Digital Audio Tape) like the Sony D-3, which could record a couple of hours (avoiding the dreaded "flip" inherent in cassette taping) and which, being digital, produced pristine copies with no degradation in copying.

One oft-expressd downside of the Dead's post–*In the Dark* popularity was that the band was forced to play in big, drafty, characterless arenas and amphitheaters. To counteract the decreased intimacy between band and audience as much as possible, the band paid more attention to the visual aspects of the show experience: Candace Brightman's light show was expanded, and the band began to use custom-built stage sets, most notably Polish-born artist Jan Sawka's beautiful "Sunrise to Moonrise" set, which, synchronized with Candace's lights, accompanied the '89 tour.

"[By 1984] their concert sound had gone to levels most bands didn't know existed. That summer a veteran CBS-TV soundman stood in front of the speakers, listening first to the mix in his headphones as beamed from the soundboard, and then to the sound system." DENNIS MCNALLY

Now *group non grata* at two longtime venues, the band decided to take the hard line before the Fall Tour and issued another communiqué:

"There will be no vending and no camping on the Fall Tour. There will be security people representing the Dead who will tell you not to sell anything outside (or inside); listen to them. The parking lots will be cleared every night… The music and dance is important. Being able to buy a t-shirt or camp out is not."

The Fall '89 Tour also saw the first "Guerrilla shows"—with late ticket sales and/or limited mail order—so local fans could get tickets before hardcore "Tourheads" snapped them up.

SEPTEMBER '89

1 ~ 28	29	30

Friday September 29
Saturday September 30
Sunday October 1
Shoreline Amphitheatre, Mountain View, California

Nineteen eighty-nine was a year of revivals, especially in the Fall: Friday sets the tone for shows to come when the band breaks out the Rev. Gary Davis's "Death Don't Have No Mercy in this Land" for the first time since April 26, 1970.

★ **Sunday October 8**
★ **Monday October 9**
Hampton Coliseum, Hampton, Virginia

The highest of the high points: The second set of the first night opens with the first "Help On the Way">"Slipknot!">"Franklin's Tower" medley in four years since September 12, 1985. "Dark Star" shines again on Monday (for the first time since July 13, 1984, at the Greek), and it burns bright. As if this isn't magic enough for a night, the encore is another amazing revival— "Attics of My Life," not performed since September 27, 1972.

OCTOBER '89

1	2 ~ 7	8	9	10	11	12

Wednesday October 11
Thursday October 12
Brendan Byrne Arena,
East Rutherford, New Jersey

Saturday October 14
Sunday October 15
★ **Monday October 16**
Brendan Byrne Arena, East Rutherford, New Jersey

There is great anticipation for the last night of the Meadowlands run, because (1) it's Bob Weir's 42nd birthday, (2) the number 42 is the secret of life, according to Douglas Adams's *The Hitchhiker's Guide to the Galaxy*, a seminal text for many Deadheads, (3) it's the 8th anniversary of the second Melkweg Show *(see October 15–16, 1981)*, (4) Jerry Garcia has hinted, in an interview on New York's WNEW radio station on the afternoon of the show, that the band might break out "Dark Star" again "sooner than you think," and (5) a horse named "Dark Star" ran the day of the show at Meadowlands Racetrack (it showed). And indeed, the show lives up to the prognostications, including "Dark Star," to the huge joy of the always irrepressible New York–area audience.

370

Thursday October 12
"Foolish Heart"/"We Can Run" are released as CD/vinyl/cassette singles. The cassette single includes five playing cards.

Friday October 13
Jerry Garcia and Bob Weir pay another visit to David Letterman on *Late Night with Letterman* at NBC Studios, New York, performing Smokey Robinson's "I Second That Emotion." They also jam with Paul Shaffer and the show band on various numbers, including Pink Floyd's "Another Brick in the Wall." No levitation *(see September 17, 1987)* but Dave does offer them some duck prepared earlier by fellow guest Julia Child.

13	14	15	16	17

18	19	20	21

Wizardry from the Warlocks

The Grateful Dead were billed as "formerly the Warlocks" for two shows at the Hampton Coliseum, reportedly because the venue management said the band had to cut back on the crowds. It seemed like the most transparent ploy in the world, but it worked, helped by the fact that tickets were only sold at three locations; the two shows took three days to sell out, so the audiences were mainly local Deadheads.

And what a pair of nights those 15,000 people were in for. The '89 Hampton shows have passed into Deadhead lore as among the band's best performances of the 1980s.

"ATTICS OF MY LIFE"
HUNTER/GARCIA

With its abstract images of "cloudy dreams unreal," "tastes no tongue can know," and "lights no eyes can see," "Attics of My Life" represents a poetic high point for lyricist Robert Hunter, who penned the song with Jerry Garcia for the Dead's seminal studio disc *American Beauty* (1970). A recurring theme of unconditional companionship appears at the end of each of the track's four verses, with lines like "When I had no wings to fly, you flew to me" suggesting that the subject of the song's appreciation might be some sort of spiritual guide. Hunter appeared to acknowledge as much when he wrote to a fan from a Dead newsgroup in 1996 that "this is not a song about being stoned. It's a song about the soul." Though "Attics of My Life" was only played live a handful of times in 1970 and once in 1972 before being shelved for nearly two decades, the Dead surprised fans by dusting it off in the late 1980s for an additional 26 performances between October 9, 1989 and December 18, 1994.

Tuesday October 17
While the band were between shows on the East Coast, a massive earthquake hit San Francisco at 5:04 p.m. local time. While not as devastating as the 1906 quake and fires, the '89 quake—which measured 7.1 on the Richter scale—left 270 people dead, more than 3,000 injured, and caused up to $3 billion in damage.

Tragedy at the Meadowlands

While the band performs on Saturday, the body of nineteen-year-old Adam Katz is found on a road leading into the Meadowlands complex. The cause of death is a beating, but who administered it, and in what circumstances, is never clearly established, although suspicion falls on the venue's security guards, who have a reputation for roughness. Meadowlands' management eventually reached an out-of-court settlement with Katz's family.

Wednesday October 18
Thursday October 19
Friday October 20
The Spectrum, Philadelphia, Pennsylvania

In a gesture of solidarity with their earthquake-beset hometown, the boys end Friday's first set with Rodney Crowell's "California Earthquake."

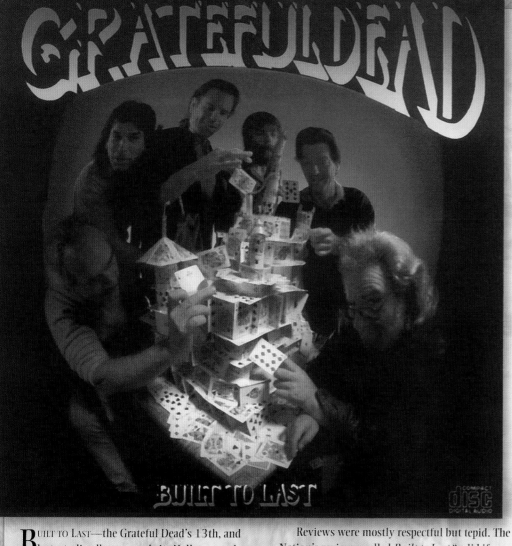

BUILT TO LAST
Grateful Dead

Released by Arista (ARCD-8575) on October 31, 1989

1. **Foolish Heart**
   (Garcia/Hunter)
2. **Just A Little Light**
   (Mydland/Barlow)
3. **Victim Or the Crime**
   (Weir/Graham)
4. **Standing On The Moon**
   (Garcia/Hunter)
5. **Blow Away**
   (Mydland/Barlow)
6. **Picasso Moon**
   (Weir/Barlow/Bralove)
7. **Built To Last**
   (Garcia/Hunter)
8. **I Will Take You Home**
   (Mydland/Barlow)
9. **We Can Run**
   (Mydland/Barlow)

Personnel

Jerry Garcia – guitar, vocals
Mickey Hart – drums
Bill Kreutzmann – drums
Phil Lesh – bass
Brent Mydland – keyboards, vocals
Bob Weir – guitar, vocals

Produced by Jerry Garcia and John Cutler

BUILT TO LAST—the Grateful Dead's 13th, and last, studio album—made its Halloween release date, and most fans regarded it as neither trick nor treat. The record sounded polished and professional, but it lacked *In The Dark*'s underlying sense of spontaneity and collective interplay.

Also, whether for good or ill, *Built to Last* is very much Brent Mydland's album: he co-wrote four of the nine tracks, and his trademark heart-on-sleeve emotionalism gives the album most of whatever soul it had. According to Jerry Garcia, "You always go with whatever your strong suit is, and in this case it was Brent that had the good songs." There were only three Garcia/Hunter songs on the album, and only one, "Standing on the Moon" (*see page 363*), approached the level of their best previous work, in the opinion of most, although "Foolish Heart" had its aficionados. The album might have been stronger if it had included a couple of other songs the band was kicking around at the time, including the Garcia/Hunter "Believe it or Not" and the Weir/Hunter "Shit Happens," heard only on a bootlegged rehearsal tape.

Reviews were mostly respectful but tepid. The Nation's reviewer called *Built to Last* "solid if unspectacular." Rolling Stone summed up the album as "Built to Last, but not for speed."

Some Deadheads wondered if there wasn't some passive-aggressive wish-fulfillment afoot in *Built to Last*—did the band, already having problems coping with success, deliberately or subconsciously make an underwhelming record in order to avoid turning Mega-Dead into Super-Mega-Dead? As Dennis McNally said of *Built to Last*'s reception, "The band was fortunate, really. Another hit and they'd have never been able to tour again."

The house of cards featured on the cover was built by Jerry Garcia's daughter Annabelle and a couple of her friends. Always eager to read hidden symbolic significance into anything Dead-related, Deadheads were quick to note that Jerry Garcia held the Ten of Diamonds, the same card he's pictured holding on the cover of 1972's Garcia solo album. Others had a field day matching the cards up with their equivalents in the Tarot deck.

A "deluxe" version of Built to Last *was sold in an oversized box that also included playing cards.*

Sunday October 22
Monday October 23
Charlotte Coliseum,
Charlotte, North Carolina

The band rumble through "California Earthquake" for its final outing.

22   23   24

25   26   27

Wednesday October 25
Thursday October 26 ★
Miami Arena, Miami, Florida

Donna Godchaux once observed that "In general, the Grateful Dead is not benign." On the second night the band's dark side was definitely in control. Whether it was the set list, the venue (located in a scary neighborhood), the approach of Halloween, or general Karmic disturbance, the adjective most used to describe the last show of the tour is "terrifying."

Tuesday October 31
Built To Last released.

Garcia and Weir are interviewed by Rona Elliot on NBC's *Today Show* at NBC Studios, New York.

GRATEFUL DEAD FAMILY ALBUM

JERILYN LEE BRANDELIUS

A Visual Record

In November Warner Books publishes *Grateful Dead Family Album* by Jerilyn Lee Brandelius. It is a scrapbook of the band's history from the Acid Trips through the late '80s. Oliver Trager calls it "a veritable silver mine of Dead ephemera."

DECEMBER '89

1	2	3	4	5	6

Friday December 1
Saturday December 2
Jerry Garcia Band performs at the Warfield Theatre, San Francisco, California. Clarence Clemons guests on sax both nights.

Saturday December 2
An Evening With the Grateful Dead (KQED and GD Productions) is broadcast by KQED TV in San Francisco. The 90-minute film features the Dead in film and video performances.

Wednesday December 6
Oakland Coliseum Arena, Oakland, California

With Clarence Clemons on sax for most of the second set, the band play to benefit San Francisco's Earthquake Relief Fund. The boys unleash an amazing "earthquake space" but, oddly enough, don't play "California Earthquake."

Tales of the Band

Grateful Dead Folktales, a compilation of 13 Dead tales from different countries, edited by Bob Franzosa, is published in 1989 by Zosafarm Publications.

Radio and TV Exposure

No performances or releases this month, but the Dead appeared in a number of broadcasts:
• Two one-hour Grateful Dead radio shows (music/interviews) were broadcast in the weeks beginning November 20 and 27; these were later available as a release, *Up Close With the Grateful Dead*.
• *Timothy White's Rock Stars* (right) was also broadcast on radio in the week beginning November 20; the 90-minute show covered Garcia/Weir interviews and a studio acoustic version of "The Victim or the Crime."
• *A Latino Session – The Cinemax Specials* (HBO) aired on November 19 on the Cinemax cable network. It featured music by Santana, Linda Ronstadt, and Jerry Garcia (who plays on a number of songs).

372

NOVEMBER '89

1 ~ 8	9	10	11 ~ 30

Thursday November 9
Jubilant crowds surround the Berlin Wall after the East German government opens its border with West Germany.

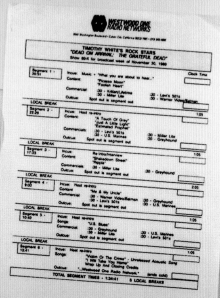

Grunge

As the '80s turned to the '90s the Big New Thing in the somewhat moribund world of rock music was grunge. There were a lot of superficial parallels between grunge and the "San Francisco Sound" of the mid- to late '60s. Like its predecessor, the grunge "scene" was focused largely on a single city (Seattle), it came with its own "look" (ripped jeans, boots, lumberjack shirt, wool watch cap pulled down over long, unkempt hair), had druggy associations (heroin and crystal meth), and supposedly appealed to "a new generation of young people"—in this case, "Generation X," a.k.a. the "Slackers," post–Baby Boomers who, it was said, rejected both the peace-love-and-granola philosophy of the '60s and '70s and the greed-is-good philosophy of the Reagan–Bush I years. And as with the hippie phenomenon, there was a lot of hype and commercialism around grunge. It was another textbook case of record-company suits descending on a small, local, innovative music scene and inflating it into a nationwide marketing extravaganza.

Musically, grunge was mostly an amalgam of '70s hard rock (Black Sabbath, Led Zeppelin) with early '80s hardcore punk, played on the classic guitars/bass/drums lineup, with songs heavy on tormented, nihilistic lyrics. The scene proper began with groups like Green River and Screaming Trees recording on small "indie" labels, then broke nationwide with Nirvana *(below)*, fronted by the troubled and brilliant Kurt Cobain. Nirvana's 1991 album *Nevermind* was grunge's *Surrealistic Pillow*. In 1994, Cobain shot himself. It's amazing to think that Cobain was born the year the Grateful Dead released their first album, and yet he predeceased Jerry Garcia by five months. Following his demise the hype faded and the grunge bands that persevered (most notably Pearl Jam) today are usually just filed under "Alternative."

7	8	9	10

Friday December 8
Saturday December 9
Sunday December 10
Great Western Forum, Inglewood, California

On the first night the band tease "The Other One" going into and out of "Drums." The second show's "Bird Song" appears on 1990's *Without a Net*. The final night, Bruce Hornsby adds his piano and squeezebox to several songs, and Spencer Davis joins on "C. C. Rider" (which he sings, for whatever reason, as "Easy Rider"). The show also sees the band's only performance of "I'm a Man," a transatlantic hit for the Spencer Davis Group in 1965.

On the last night of the Forum run, Patrick Shanahan dies following an altercation with several LAPD officers. Shanahan had left the audience, apparently to seek help for a bad acid trip, when he encountered the police. The authorities ruled the death "a justifiable killing," despite considerable circumstantial evidence that the cops used excessive force. (This was two years before the Rodney King beating focused the world's attention on the LAPD's restraint techniques.) In response, the band severed its ties to the Forum.

BILL GRAHAM AND AVALON ATTRACTIONS PRESENT

GRATEFUL DEAD

GREAT WESTERN FORUM

DECEMBER 8, 9 & 10, 1989

Monday December 11
Garcia and Weir appear on *Rockline*, a live radio call-in interview show in San Francisco.

| 11 | 12 | **13** | 14 | 15 | 16 | 17 | 18 |

Wednesday December 13
Brent Mydland suffers an overdose—maybe morphine, maybe heroin, maybe some combination thereof. He survives and recovers in time for the New Year's Eve run, though his physical and emotional state (he is both drinking heavily and hard-drugging, and separated from his family) adds to the band's worries as an already difficult year comes to an end.

Above: Garcia with saxophonist Clarence Clemons on December 27 at Oakland Coliseum Arena.

Tuesday December 19
Romanians begin an uprising that leads to the downfall and execution of the nation's hated communist dictator, Nicolae Ceausescu.

| 19 | **20** | 21 | 22 | 23 | 24 | 25 | 26 |

Wednesday December 20
U.S. forces invade Panama to oust dictator Manuel Noriega.

Below: Sunday December 31, Oakland Coliseum Arena, Oakland, California.

Wednesday December 27
Thursday December 28
Saturday December 30 ★
Sunday December 31
Oakland Coliseum Arena, Oakland, California

The first show sees Clarence Clemons play sax for most of the second set, with Willie Green of the Neville Brothers guesting on "Drumz" the following night. On Saturday Airto Moreira plays for most of the evening. The New Year's Eve show opens with sets from New Grass Revival and Bonnie Raitt, who also joins the band for the first-set "Big Boss Man." "Drums" includes Airto Moreira and six-year-old Taro Hart (already a recording artist thanks to *Music to Be Born By*—see page 365). Bill Graham enters on a huge egg, which cracks open to disgorge a couple of young folks, one of them being Graham's son Alex. The band caps off a year of amazing revivals by breaking out "Dark Star" again, although the usual third set is ditched in favor of an extended encore ("Brokedown Palace" with the "Sunshine Daydream" coda, "In the Midnight Hour"). "MY BUDDY OVER HERE TELLS ME IT'S THE BEGINNING OF A NEW DICKHEAD—I MEAN DECADE." BOB WEIR TO THE AUDIENCE AS THE GRATEFUL DEAD ENTERS THE 1990s

| 27 | 28 | 29 | 30 | 31 |

GRATEFUL DEAD 1989-1990
LET'S PARTY!
ME TOO!

New Year's Eve 1988-1989

Bob Weir and Rob Wasserman perform "Victim and the Crime" on a January broadcast of the *Night Music* TV show.

Friday January 19
Marion Barry, mayor of Washington, D.C., is caught in a hotel room smoking crack with a prostitute.

Left: New Year's Eve show, 1989, Oakland Coliseum Arena Oakland, California

Monday January 15
First TV broadcast of the video for "Just a Little Light."

Wednesday January 31
The first McDonald's opens in Moscow. The Cold War is truly over.

The American Institution & Famous Deadheads

By 1990, a quarter-century after that first gig at Magoo's, the Dead had become a bona-fide American Institution—as much a part of the cultural landscape as Mount Rushmore or Disneyland. The enduring appeal of the Dead's music to over four decades of fans had seen this come to pass.

Those who got on the bus in the 1960s had a particular role to play in the Dead's national canonization. By the '80s many first-generation fans, Baby Boomers, had assumed positions of power and influence: the rebels had become the establishment. Nevertheless, countless of their number retained a soft spot in their hearts for the Good Ol' Grateful Dead—even if their days now started with a latte and *The Wall Street Journal* instead of a joint and *Workingman's Dead*. Bill Clinton's eventual election as president was a particularly symbolic reflection of this phenomenon.

If one key to the Grateful Dead's endurance had been their ability to attract new fans while retaining the loyalty of the old guard, another was the band's appeal to a very broad spectrum of fans. Yes, there is a popular stereotype of Deadheads, but from the beginning the band's music and gestalt won them a wide fan base. As Carol Brightman writes in *Sweet Chaos: The Grateful Dead's American Adventure*, the diversity is staggering:

"There's so-and-so in the mail room, your seatmate on the plane, the governor of a New England state, the clerk in the bookstore, the inmate of a medium-security prison in Oregon, an astrophysicist in Colorado Springs, a dulcimer player in Denver, students everywhere, a famous chef in Chicago, a Stealth bomber pilot with Dead stickers on his wing (who died in 1996), a cohort of lawyers in San Francisco, a minyan of brokers on Wall Street, a handful of young actors in Hoboken, middle-aged bikers in Vermont, a string of carpenters and fishermen along the Maine coast…"

And by the 1990s the ranks of Dead fans included some very well-known individuals. The shortlist would have to begin with former vice-president Al Gore and (especially) his wife Tipper. Bill Clinton is known to be a fan, while longtime Democratic Senator Patrick Leahy is another Deadhead at the highest level of politics. British PM Tony Blair attended the 11/1/90 London Dead show and played guitar in a *Mars Hotel*–inspired student band called Ugly Rumours.

Bill Walton, the NBA hall-of-famer who played center for the Portland Trailblazers, the San Diego and L.A. Clippers, and the Boston Celtics, is another huge fan, who has become a member of the band's extended family. To the delight of Deadhead basketball fans, Walton would frequently slip Dead references into interviews.

From the arts and sciences, UC Berkeley physicist Owen Chamberlain, co-winner of the 1959 Nobel Prize, was observed at Bay Area shows sitting between Billy and Mickey. Chamberlain said the Rhythm Devils gave him "interesting ideas," thereby triangulating music, mysticism, and mathematics. The late, great graphic artist Keith Haring was a Deadhead—the first entry in his published journal, from 1977, describes his joy at getting tickets to a show. And Joseph Campbell *(see page 330)*, certainly the 20th century's greatest scholar of mythology, famously placed the band and its music in a mythico-religious framework.

And so the list of aficionados goes on, including luminaries from many other walks of life; it just goes to show, you never quite know when or where you're going to meet a Deadhead.

BILL GRAHAM PRESENTS
GRATEFUL DEAD
BALAFON MARIMBA ENSEMBLE MICHAEL DOUCET AND BEAUSOLEIL
MARDI GRAS '90

Sunday February 11
African National Congress leader Nelson Mandela is freed after 27 years in South African prisons.

February 1990

🎤 **Sunday February 25**
🎸 **Monday February 26**
Tuesday February 27
Oakland Coliseum Arena, Oakland, California

On the first night the band play the Rolling Stones' "The Last Time" for the first time since sometime in 1965, while Jerry debuts "Rosebud," his new custom-made, MIDI-equipped guitar *(see page 369)*. On Monday the Balafon Marimba Ensemble opens. Often played by Mickey Hart, the balafon is a West African instrument made of fire-hardened hardwood blocks with resonating gourds below. Cajun combo Michael Doucet and Beausoleil open the Mardi Gras show on Tuesday and sit in on (*naturellement, cher!*) "Iko Iko" and "Man Smart, Woman Smarter."

375

Left and above: Tuesday February 27, Oakland Coliseum Arena, Oakland, California. The Mardi Gras show. Each year, the Fat Tuesday parades became more and more elaborate, incorporating huge papier mâché figures and trippy Dead-related floats.

Wednesday March 14
Thursday March 15
Friday March 16
Capital Centre, Landover, Maryland

The kickoff show is highlighted by the revival of the raunchy "Loose Lucy," last heard on October 19, 1974, in a punched-up arrangement that becomes a singalong favorite. The second night it's Phil's phiftieth birthday (he's the first band member to hit the half-century mark) and the show sees a couple of surprises—the first performance of Brent's "Easy to Love You" since September 30, 1980, and the first Beatles' "Revolution" since November 8, 1985. This entire show will be released on a special three-CD set in 1997, *Terrapin Limited*, to raise money for an interactive museum/performance center to be called Terrapin Station—which remains unbuilt as of this writing. The show's "Althea" is released on *Without a Net* later in the year. The last night sees another tune shelved since October 19, 1974 getting an airing—the Weir/Barlow road odyssey "Black-Throated Wind."

| 14 | 15 | 16 | 17 |

Branford Marsalis

A member of the "first family of jazz" (brother of trumpeter Wynton, drummer Jason, trombonist Delfeayo, and son of pianist and composer Ellis), Branford Marsalis established himself early on as a master of all music playing with Art Blakey's Jazz Messengers, Dizzy Gillespie, and in Wynton's band, but also serving a stint as leader of NBC TV's *Tonight Show* band, performing on records by Sting and other rock and pop stars, and (like Wynton) periodically venturing into classical territory. With his versatility and their shared influences (Ornette Coleman, John Coltrane—*see page 32*), Branford was a natural partner for the Grateful Dead, and he would share the stage with them five times.

"Of all the great musicians who shared the Dead's Stage through the years . . . none embodied both the Dead's adventurous, questing spirit and their obsession with beautiful melodies and accessible structures quite like Branford did."
BLAIR JACKSON

Above: Some of lighting designer Candace Brightman's trippy handiwork.

Wednesday March 21
Thursday March 22 ★
Copps Coliseum, Hamilton, Ontario, Canada

This is the band's first performance at this venue and a relatively rare excursion north of the border. (Not that there aren't plenty of Deadheads beneath the Maple Leaf Flag—but the road crew hates the hassles of getting all that equipment through the border checkpoint.) The second night is considered by many to be one of the best shows of a very good tour, and it also sees the band's final performances of "Believe it or Not." Brent decides to stretch the "Hey Jude" coda following "Dear Mr. Fantasy" into the whole song—the first performance of the song in its entirety since March 1, 1969.

Saturday March 24 ★
Sunday March 25
Monday March 26
Knickerbocker Arena, Albany, New York

Saturday marks the first of the band's 13 shows at the Knick. The entire second set (plus "Walkin' Blues" from the first set), eight songs from the next night, and six from the last show were released as *Dozin' at the Knick* in 1996; "One More Saturday Night" from the Saturday show is also found on 1990's *Without a Net*. The last gig at the Knick sees the band's final rendition of "Built to Last."

Wednesday March 28
Thursday March 29 ★
Friday March 30
Nassau Veterans Memorial Coliseum, Uniondale, New York

Located in Long Island, serious Deadhead Country, and adjacent to the whole New York metro area, Nassau Coliseum in the late '80s seemed fated to to be lost to the band, too, due to the local law enforcement community's pronounced dislike for the annual run. Thankfully, a cooperative venue management saved the relationship. The band played 42 shows at Nassau Coliseum between 1973 and 1994.

The second night is a truly special show, thanks to a truly special guest, Branford Marsalis, who brings his brilliant tenor sax to the first-set "Bird Song" and the entire second set.

"The entire band seemed galvanized by Marsalis's presence, and the crowd—even those who had, like, no idea who the dude with the horn was— settled down for an evening of exploration."
ERIC POOLEY'S REVIEW OF THE MARCH 29 SHOW IN *NEW YORK* MAGAZINE.

The "Eyes of the World *(see page 383)*" from this show and the "Help on the Way">"Slipknot!"> "Franklin's Tower" opener from the final show appear on *Without a Net*.

MARCH '90
| 1 – 13 |

Songs of Amber by The Latvian Women's Choir comes out this month. The LP, which comprises traditional and modern Latvian songs, is produced by Jerry Garcia and Mickey Hart. It is recorded at the Skywalker Ranch studio.

March also sees the video release of *The Acid Test*. A Ken Kesey production originally released in 1966, the video includes film footage of the Grateful Dead at the infamous Acid Tests.

| 18 | 19 | 20 | 21 | 22 |

Sunday March 18
Monday March 19
Hartford Civic Center, Hartford, Connecticut

| 23 | 24 | 25 | 26 | 27 | 28 | 29 | 30 | 31 |

Sunday March 25
A fire in the Happy Land Social Club in New York City claims 87 lives.

T-shirts and Bumper Stickers

Of all the items sold in the mobile *souk* that accompanied latter-day Dead shows, from veggie burritos to balloons of nitrous oxide, the most ubiquitous had to be the t-shirt. Whether it was an individual creation silk-screened in a friend's basement, or one of a thousand mass-produced models sold off a rolling rack; be it festooned with the iconic bears or skull-and-lightning-bolt; or imprinted with the date and venue of the show as a wearable souvenir; or a platform for announcing the wearer's aesthetic tastes or philosophical convictions, the t-shirt was practically *de rigueur* Deadwear. (The now-mighty Grateful Dead Merchandising empire, it should be remembered, began with the Pigpen t-shirts produced by the band's first fan club, the Golden Road to Unlimited Devotion, in 1966. *"Yeah, I hear there's something called the 'Pigpen t-shirt'...does that mean you've arrived or something?"* exclaimed a long-since-forgotten DJ in '66.)

Tie-dye is the popular stereotype, but tie-dye really wasn't seen much at shows until the '80s, and the band itself never went in for the look much, at least on the basis of available visual evidence. But tie-dye took off in a big way in the Mega-Dead period, and Deadheads gathering for a "Tie Party" was a sure sign a tour was about to start, or that the band was headed to town.

And then there were bumper stickers—t-shirts for your vehicle. Some Deadheads covered the bumpers *and* the quarter-panels *and* the hood with them. With the War on Drugs raging, though, driving a vehicle with Dead stickers was like asking to be pulled over by John Law in many places, so it was hardly surprising that many Deadheads eschewed them in favor of "driving stealth." Another option for the devoted 'Head was to outfit his or her Deadmobile with vanity license plates.

| 1 | 2 | 3 | 4 ~ 21 |

🎸 **Sunday April 1**
🎸 **Monday April 2**
Tuesday April 3
The Omni, Atlanta, Georgia

Monday marks the last-ever performance of "Death Don't Have No Mercy." The last night is the final show of the tour and the band ends with a "We Bid You Goodnight" encore.

| 22 | 23 | 24 |

Sunday April 22
Earth Day sees the broadcast of the Audubon Society's public-service video, including images of oil and pollution-ravaged wildlife and other environmental disasters, set to "We Can Run" *(see page 363).*

BLUES FOR THE RAINFOREST
Merl Saunders

Released by Sumertone Records (S2CD-01) in April 1990

Jerry Garcia plays guitar (electric MIDI and acoustic) on all but one of the tracks on the album, which is subtitled "A Musical Suite." This marked the first time Garcia and Saunders had worked together since their band Reconstruction in 1979. Garcia was delighted to be improvising again with his old friend and was moved by the ecological theme of the album.

"I wanted to re-create the falling of trees and the crying of the forest. It's as if the forest is talking and telling the people who are exploiting it to get lost."
MERL SAUNDERS IN AN INTERVIEW WITH JIM ROSENTHAL, *RELIX*, 1990.

Above: Thursday March 22, Copps Coliseum, Hamilton, Ontario, Canada.
Right: Thursday March 29, Nassau Veterans Memorial Coliseum, Uniondale, New York.

Heirs Apparent & The Ph Phactor

In the '80s and '90s various rootsy bands with a reputation for hot live shows got tagged in the rock press as being potential "successors" to the Grateful Dead (whatever that was supposed to mean), including Los Lobos, the Dave Matthews Band, and Blues Traveler.

Phish, which formed in 1983–84 at the University of Vermont, was the band generally considered "first in the line of succession" from the Grateful Dead following Jerry Garcia's death. Even before then, Phish had to contend with a "Grateful Dead, Jr." perception on the part of some rock fans. Indeed, there was a fair amount of overlap in the fan bases of the two bands, and a number of similarities between them: both made their musical bones through their live shows and jamming; both attracted highly devoted fans, the most hardcore of whom followed the band on tour; and a thriving Taper subculture sprang up around both. And of course, Phish shared with Jerry Garcia the distinction of inspiring a Ben & Jerry's ice-cream flavor. (Dave Matthews eventually got his own flavor, too.)

Although Phish's members loved the Dead, they went out of their way to deflect comparisons with the Dead—not covering any Dead songs, for example. The similarities were in fact superficial, rooted more in image than in music. As Phil Lesh put it in a May 1999 interview with *Rolling Stone Online's* Jaan Uhelszki, "They're different. They have their own characteristic. They're more together than we were. I don't think they're so much the ragged hippies as we were. But, I mean, their musical sensibilities are refined in a certain direction that ours never were. Our stuff was more rootsy because most of the guys, with the exception of myself, came from roots music. I was a jazz and classical musician."

But the Grateful Dead were certainly one of the main inspirations, indeed THE inspiration, for the jam band movement that emerged in the '90s, including Rusted Root, String Cheese Incident, moe, Widespread Panic, God Stret Wine, Gov't Mule, and Medeski, Martin and Wood—many of whom would share the stage with Phil Lesh & Friends, The Other Ones, the Dead, and other post-'95 Grateful Dead iterations.

Saturday May 5
Sunday May 6
California State University,
Dominguez Hills,
Carson, California

It's Kentucky Derby Day on the first night, so "The Race Is On" is played in the first set.

| 1 | 2 | 3 | 4 | 5 | 6 | 7 ~ 28 | 29 | 30 | 31 |

Tuesday May 29
Boris Yeltsin is elected president of the Russian Republic.

Busy Tom

Tom Constanten released *Outsides* in 1990, a recording of one of his live solo piano recitals. He also received a credit on The Henry Kaiser Band's *Heart's Desire*, released the same year. Constanten played on a version of "Dark Star."

| 1 ~ 7 | 8 | 9 | 10 | 11 | 12 | 13 | 14 |

Friday June 8 ★
Saturday June 9
Sunday June 10
Cal Expo Amphitheatre,
Sacramento, California

The band starts the summer with the now-traditional three-show run to benefit the Rex Foundation, this time at the Cal Expo Amphitheatre, having outgrown the Greek. The Cal will gain a reputation as one of the best venues for shows.
One of the items going through the endlessly grinding Deadhead Rumor Mill has it that Phil Lesh is going to quit the band. Phil takes the final show as the opportunity to squash such scurrilous talk and announces "It's a bullshit lie!" before "Dire Wolf." Without missing a beat, Jerry shoots back, "Yeah, it's the rest of us that are quitting." Deadheads sporting "Phil's Last Show" T-shirts are spotted throughout the summer.

BILL GRAHAM AND THE REX FOUNDATION PRESENT
GRATEFUL DEAD
JUNE 8
JUNE 9
JUNE 10
1990
CAL EXPO AMPHITHEATRE

A NIGHT ON THE TOWN
Bruce Hornsby and The Range
RCA/BMG 2041-2-R

When Garcia went into the studio to lay down a fiery guitar solo for Bruce Hornsby's radio hit "Across the River," he had no idea the pianist would become a member of the Grateful Dead that fall. Garcia also contributed guitar to "Barren Ground." Other luminaries helping Hornsby and his group on this album were Wayne Shorter, Bela Fleck, Shawn Colvin, and Charlie Haden.

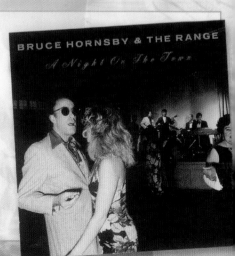

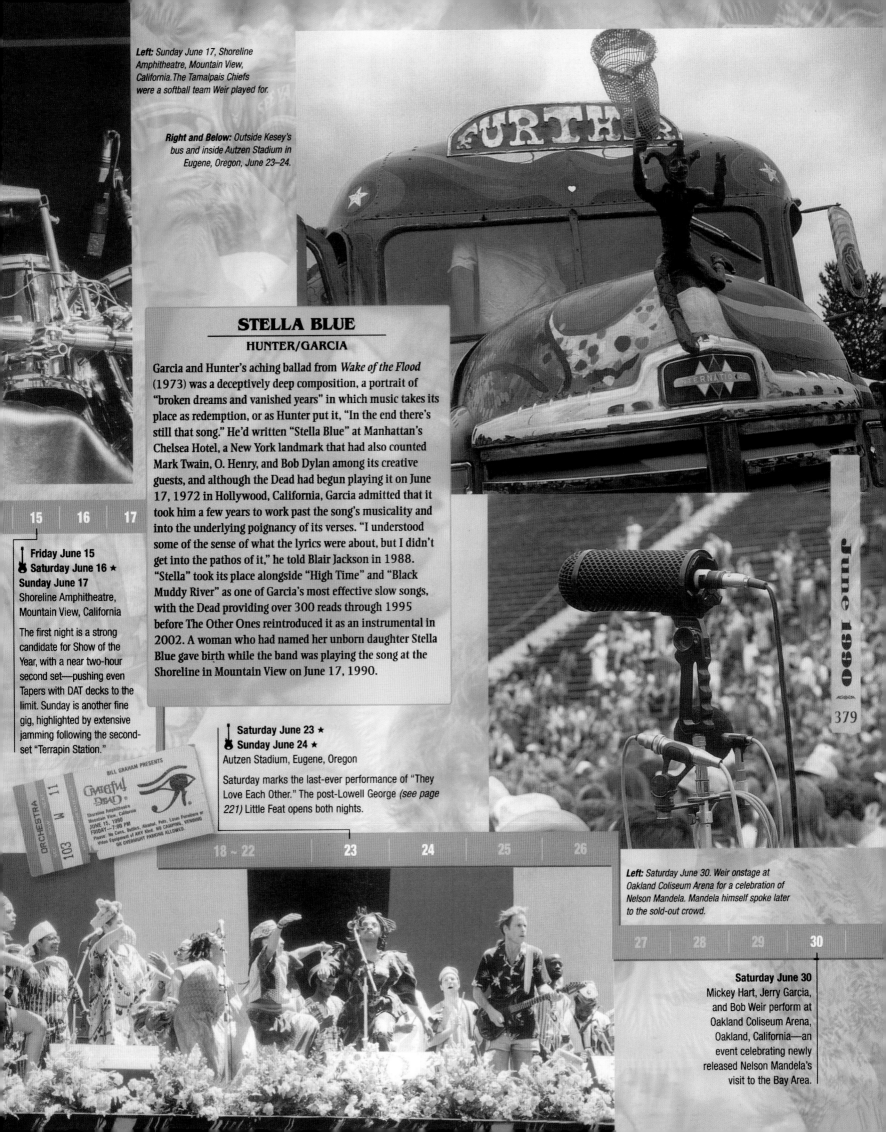

Left: Sunday June 17, Shoreline Amphitheatre, Mountain View, California. The Tamalpais Chiefs were a softball team Weir played for.

Right and Below: Outside Kesey's bus and inside Autzen Stadium in Eugene, Oregon, June 23–24.

STELLA BLUE
HUNTER/GARCIA

Garcia and Hunter's aching ballad from *Wake of the Flood* (1973) was a deceptively deep composition, a portrait of "broken dreams and vanished years" in which music takes its place as redemption, or as Hunter put it, "In the end there's still that song." He'd written "Stella Blue" at Manhattan's Chelsea Hotel, a New York landmark that had also counted Mark Twain, O. Henry, and Bob Dylan among its creative guests, and although the Dead had begun playing it on June 17, 1972 in Hollywood, California, Garcia admitted that it took him a few years to work past the song's musicality and into the underlying poignancy of its verses. "I understood some of the sense of what the lyrics were about, but I didn't get into the pathos of it," he told Blair Jackson in 1988. "Stella" took its place alongside "High Time" and "Black Muddy River" as one of Garcia's most effective slow songs, with the Dead providing over 300 reads through 1995 before The Other Ones reintroduced it as an instrumental in 2002. A woman who had named her unborn daughter Stella Blue gave birth while the band was playing the song at the Shoreline in Mountain View on June 17, 1990.

15 | 16 | 17

Friday June 15
Saturday June 16 ★
Sunday June 17
Shoreline Amphitheatre, Mountain View, California

The first night is a strong candidate for Show of the Year, with a near two-hour second set—pushing even Tapers with DAT decks to the limit. Sunday is another fine gig, highlighted by extensive jamming following the second-set "Terrapin Station."

Saturday June 23 ★
Sunday June 24 ★
Autzen Stadium, Eugene, Oregon

Saturday marks the last-ever performance of "They Love Each Other." The post-Lowell George *(see page 221)* Little Feat opens both nights.

18 ~ 22 | 23 | 24 | 25 | 26

BILL GRAHAM PRESENTS

GRATEFUL DEAD
Shoreline Amphitheatre
Mountain View, California
JUNE 15, 1990
FRIDAY—7:00 PM
Please: No Cans, Bottles, Alcohol, Pets, Lawn Furniture or
Video Equipment of ANY Kind. NO CAMPING, VENDING
OR OVERNIGHT PARKING ALLOWED.

ORCHESTRA
11 M
103

379

Left: Saturday June 30. Weir onstage at Oakland Coliseum Arena for a celebration of Nelson Mandela. Mandela himself spoke later to the sold-out crowd.

27 | 28 | 29 | 30

Saturday June 30
Mickey Hart, Jerry Garcia, and Bob Weir perform at Oakland Coliseum Arena, Oakland, California—an event celebrating newly released Nelson Mandela's visit to the Bay Area.

Brent Mydland 1952 – 1990

Shortly after the end of the Summer Tour, Brent Mydland was found dead of an overdose from a speedball—a mix of morphine and cocaine. He was 37 years old. He left behind his wife, Lisa, from whom he was separated, and two daughters. When Brent died, some who knew of his history of emotional problems suspected suicide, but those closest to him believed he overdosed through inexperience—Brent had only started on hard drugs recently. He'd preferred alcohol, and it may have been the prospect of a short jail term for DUI that pushed him, fatally, into "chasing one last binge," in Dennis McNally's words. As the news spread, the band issued a brief statement: "We have lost a brother in music and we grieve for him and his family"—and groups of Deadheads gathered to light candles and mourn.

Brent's relationships with the band and with the fans were often difficult. He had never fully gotten over being "the new guy," although Jerry Garcia noted that the band members had never treated him that way. Fans had mixed reactions. Some liked his soulful vocals and B-3 organ playing. But detractors felt his aggressive and even hostile vibe, as shown in some of his songs, was out of place at Dead shows.

But Brent's relationship with himself was more difficult still. He had low self-esteem and was highly sensitive—and did not cope easily with the strains of life—especially life with the band. Brent wasn't the only member with a penchant for self-destructive behavior. But the others had a range of outside interests and projects to help provide some balance. Brent did pursue some solo projects, but nothing seemed to provide solace beyond the drinking and, finally, the drugs that killed him.

With three premature deaths to date, Deadheads dubbed the seemingly-jinxed keyboardist's bench "The Hot Seat."

"[Brent] was a bigger contributor than anyone was willing to state. He had a genius for providing exactly the right kind of color. He was brilliant. . . but there was something that was fundamentally unsatisfiable about him."
JOHN PERRY BARLOW IN DAVID SHENK & STEVE SILBERMAN'S SKELETON KEY.

"It was heartbreaking when Brent died, because it seemed like such a waste. Here's this incredibly talented guy—he had a great natural melodic sense, and he was a great singer. And he could've gotten better, but he just didn't see it."
JERRY GARCIA TO JAMES HENKE IN ROLLING STONE, 1991.

Wednesday July 4
Sandstone Amphitheatre, Bonner Springs, Kansas

The summer tour starts off with a hot show… literally. It's over 100°F in the shade and an early-evening start time, with the sun still high in the sky, doesn't help. The opener is "Cold Rain and Snow," but on this occasion music doesn't trump meteorology. The band takes a long break between sets to let the sun go down. Even so, it's a fine show, capped by a "U.S. Blues" encore in slightly ironic celebration of Independence Day.

Sunday July 8
Three Rivers Stadium, Pittsburgh, Pennsylvania

Crosby, Stills and Nash open the show.

1 2 3 4 5 6 7 8 9 10 11

John Perry Barlow and software tycoon Mitch Kapor, founder of Lotus, establish The Electronic Frontier Foundation—"a nonprofit civil liberties organization working in the public interest to protect privacy, free expression, and access to public resources and information online, as well as to promote responsibility in new media."

Friday July 6
Cardinal Stadium, Louisville, Kentucky

Bruce Hornsby and The Range open. Outside, camping Deadheads (Jerry's Witnesses?) share facilities with a Jehovah's Witnesses conclave.

Tuesday July 10
Carter-Finley Stadium, Raleigh, North Carolina

Bruce Hornsby and the Range open, and Bruce sits in on accordion for most of the show, including a "Promised Land" interrupted by a power outage. The show also sees the final performance of "We Can Run." It's another blazing hot day, though storm clouds are on the horizon, so Jerry and Bob tailor the lyrics of Jack Straw to fit the day: "Leavin' Texas/*Tenth* day of July/Sun so hot, clouds so low…"

Saturday July 21
Sunday July 22
Monday July 23
World Music Theatre, Tinley Park, Illinois

Final outings for "Just a Little Light" and "Dear Mr. Fantasy" on the first night, "Far From Me" and "Hey Pocky Way" the second night, and "Good Times" on the last night, which is the end of the tour—and Brent Mydland's last show. Deadheads will later find significance in the fact that it's the tenth anniversary of Keith Godchaux's death, and that in the encore, "The Weight," Brent sang the "I gotta go, but my friend can stick around" verse.

17 18 19 20 21 22 23

Thursday July 12 ★
RFK Stadium, Washington, D.C.

Edie Brickell and New Bohemians open. The Dead attaches the "Hey Jude" coda to "Dear Mr. Fantasy" for the last time.

12 13 14 15 16

Wednesday July 18 ★
Thursday July 19
Deer Creek Music Center, Noblesville, Indiana

The last-ever performance of "Easy to Love You."

Monday July 16
Rich Stadium, Orchard Park, New York

Crosby, Stills & Nash open, and it's the final performance of "Blow Away."

Saturday July 14
Foxboro Stadium, Foxboro, Massachusetts

Edie Brickell and New Bohemians open at the newly renamed Foxboro Stadium (previously the Schaefer and originally the Sullivan). The show sees the final performance of Brent Mydland's tender "I Will Take You Home"—poignant, in retrospect at least, given that he would soon be going home for good.

Above: Tuesday July 10, Carter-Finley Stadium, Raleigh, North Carolina. Tapers often complained about having to set up behind the soundboard.

Thursday July 26
Brent Mydland dies of
a drug overdose at his
home in Lafayette,
California.

AUGUST
'90

| 26 | 27 | 28 ~ 31 | 1 | 2 |

Thursday August 2
Iraqi forces invade and occupy Kuwait;
a week later, President George H. W.
Bush begins a buildup of U.S. and
Allied forces in the Persian Gulf.

Vince Welnick

Born on February 21, 1951, and raised in Phoenix, Arizona, Vince Welnick learned piano from his mother and absorbed a variety of influences (John Coltrane, McCoy Tyner) and genres (blues, jazz, rock 'n' roll), which would stand him in good stead when he inherited the Hot Seat. He progressed to a local group that moved to San Francisco and changed its name from the Beans to the Tubes. They were as eccentric as their music was eclectic, combining funk with jazz fusion and hard rock. Their gonzo stage presence made them look like mutant offspring cloned from the combined DNA of George Clinton, Frank Zappa, Monty Python, and assorted characters from John Waters films. Their costumes and stage antics frequently got them into trouble, as did their songs, including numbers like "Mondo Bondage," "Don't Touch Me There," and their breakout song, 1975's "White Punks on Dope." By 1985, the Tubes had fallen on hard times, and Vince drifted away. He played on a couple of albums by Todd Rundgren, who had produced the Tubes' last album, but in the summer of 1990 he was broke and practically homeless. And then, like something out a movie, came the call from the Grateful Dead .

Some fans were surprised at his selection in 1990—imagine going from a band that wore costumes to the Dead! Yet from the start he clicked with the Deadheads, who liked his hard-working team ethic, his adept handling of high harmonies and some excellent chops on MIDI keyboards. He was too resilient to suffer from New Guy Syndrome and continued to play with side bands, such as Zero, which on Garcia's death provided a nucleus, along with ex-Tubes Prairie Prince, for Vince's new band, Missing Man Formation.

AT THE EDGE
Mickey Hart

Released by Rykodisc (RCD 10124) in August 1990

1. **#4 For Gaia**
   (Hart)
2. **Sky Water**
   (Hart/Hussain)
3. **Slow Sailing**
   (Hart/Hussain)
4. **Lonesome Hero**
   (Hart)
5. **Fast Sailing**
   (Hart/Hussain)
6. **Cougar Run**
   (Hart)
7. **The Eliminators**
   (Hart/Creek Hart/Taro S. Hart/Garcia)
8. **Brainstorm**
   (Hart/Olatunji)
9. **Pigs in Space**
   (Moreira)

Personnel

Mickey Hart – whistles, rainstick, processed bell, rattles, forest zone (processed crickets), matrix-12, roland d-50, remo toms, raindrops, slit gongs (hollow log), engelhart cornet bells (metal percussion), kalimba (thumb piano), cowbells, dundun (talking drum), panpipes, trap set, agogo (double bell), balafon (pentatonic marimba), shekere (beaded gourd rattle), devil chasers (bamboo concussion sticks), bass drum, wood blocks, tar, spatial processing
Sikiru Adepoju – dundun
Jerry Garcia – guitar, forest zone, guitar synthesizer
Creek Hart – linn 9000 drum samples
Taro S Hart – kawasaki electronic drums
Zakir Hussain – tar (frame drum), tabla, processed tabla, duggi tarang, shakers, dholak (double-headed cylinder drum)
Jose Lorenzo – berimbau (musical bow)
Airto Moreira – extended voice and beast
Babatunde Olatunji – djembe (wooden hour glass drum), cowbell, shekere (beaded gourd rattle), engelhart hex bells

Produced by Mickey Hart

MICKEY HART'S FIRST ALBUM of percussion music was designed to be a "companion" to his book *Drumming at the Edge of Magic*, his memoirs/history of percussion released around the same time. "I didn't specifically try to re-create things I was writing about the book," he said. "It was more the spirit of what I was writing about… It was like me waking up in the forest as the first man, before there was sound, and the world slowly coming alive for me."

Over the course of nine very different percussion soundscapes, Hart and some of his musical friends explore the very roots of rhythm—the sounds of nature—and then move through a number of rhythmic worlds with varying degrees of complexity and sophistication. Helping out are future Planet Drum members Zakir Hussain and Sikuru Adepoju, Jose Lorenzo, Airto, Babatunde Olatunji, Hart's sons Creek and Taro, and, on three tracks, Jerry Garcia. Besides the requisite shakers, rattles, berimbau, hand drums, bells, and gongs, *At the Edge* also features various pieces of electronic technology—samplers, sound processors, a guitar synthesizer, and electronic drums to create a subtle but spellbinding blend of the primitive and the modern. "I wanted people to drift," Hart said of the album. "That's what this is all about to me—the flow of consciousness."

The New New Guys

To the delight of Deadheads the band announced the day after Brent Mydland's death that the Fall tour would go on. (The band did cancel a couple of scheduled shows at the Shoreline Amphitheatre rather than play without a keyboardist.) The band had to find Brent Mydland's successor in a hurry. As it happened, they found two.

The band had been extremely impressed by Bruce Hornsby *(see page 354)*, and Jerry Garcia and Phil Lesh importuned Bruce into joining up shortly after Brent's death. Bruce, however, had a lot on his plate and couldn't commit to doing every tour and show, so the band decided to recruit another full-timer.

As it happened, they auditioned only a few prospects before settling—unanimously—on Vince Welnick *(see above)*, best known as a member of the Tubes, in late August.

The Fall East Coast Tour is one of the best since the '70s. The entire performance year, in fact, is marked by excellent shows, with consistently high energy levels onstage and lots of good old-fashioned jamming, punched up by new-fashioned MIDI. The addition of Vince Welnick and Bruce Hornsby following Brent Mydland's death in July had an invigorating effect; Jerry Garcia formed a tight musical bond with Bruce, and Bruce's fearless, fluent playing seemed to inspire Jerry's solos. The two-keyboard Dead went on to celebrate some stormin' shows, not least a titanic run at Madison Square Garden. The shows on the European leg of the tour aren't quite as spectacular, but the band's three December shows at Denver's McNichols Sports Arena vie with the MSG shows as the best run of a great performance year.

Friday September 7
Saturday September 8
Richfield Coliseum, Richfield, Ohio

The tour kickoff is Vince Welnick's first show, and he gets a warm welcome from the crowd ("Yo, Vinnie!") as Jerry Garcia introduces him "officially" after "Bird Song." A fine show that boded well for the future.

September 1990

382

THE BAND'S 22ND ALBUM (discounting *Skeletons From the Closet*), ninth live album, and, in a sense, the last "real-time" Grateful Dead album— apart from *Infrared Roses*, Bob Bralove's 1991 post-processed exploration of "Space," it would all be from the archives after this. Phil Lesh picked the songs, and while some Deadheads (who of course will quibble over anything) had issues with the selection, *Without a Net* was generally hailed as a fine collection of songs from one of the latter-day Dead's best periods of performance. The standout track (and on this there is little quibbling) is the exquisite "Eyes of the World" featuring Branford Marsalis (see page 376).

Without a Net was dedicated to "Clifton Hanger,"

the alias Brent Mydland used in signing hotel registers on the road.

The excellent old-timey cover was the work of the great Rick Griffin, also responsible for the *Aoxomoxoa* cover, who died not long after the album's release.

WITHOUT A NET
Grateful Dead

Released by Arista (ACD2-8634) in September 1990

Disc One
1. **Feel Like A Stranger**
   (Barlow/Weir)
2. **Mississippi Half-Step Uptown Toodeloo**
   (Garcia/Hunter)
3. **Walkin' Blues**
   (Johnson arr. Weir)
4. **Althea**
   (Garcia/Hunter)
5. **Cassidy**
   (Barlow/Weir)
6. **Bird Song**
   (Garcia/Hunter)
7. **Let It Grow**
   (Barlow/Weir)

Disc Two
1. **China Cat Sunflower**
   (Garcia/Hunter)
2. **I Know You Rider**
   (Traditional arr. Grateful Dead)
3. **Looks Like Rain**
   (Barlow/Weir)
4. **Eyes Of The World**
   (Garcia/Hunter)
5. **Victim Or The Crime**
   (Graham/Weir)
6. **Help On The Way**
   (Garcia/Hunter)
7. **Slipknot!**
   (Garcia/Lesh/Weir/Kreutzmann/Godchaux)
8. **Franklin's Tower**
   (Garcia/Hunter/Kreutzmann)
9. **One More Saturday Night**
   (Weir)
10. **Dear Mr. Fantasy**
    (Capaldi/Wood/Winwood)

Personnel

Jerry Garcia – guitar, vocals
Mickey Hart – drums
Bill Kreutzmann – drums
Phil Lesh – bass, vocals
Brent Mydland – keyboards, vocals
Bob Weir – guitar, vocals
Branford Marsalis – tenor and soprano saxophone on "Eyes Of The World"

Produced by John Cutler and Phil Lesh.

"Despite a hint of jazz and funk, [*Without a Net*] is the Dead that Deadheads cherish..."
NEW YORK TIMES REVIEW, NOVEMBER 1990.

EYES OF THE WORLD
HUNTER/GARCIA

Riding on a bright, jazzy chord progression and a heartening message of self-reliance, "Eyes of the World" was another of a handful of Hunter/Garcia gems from *Wake of the Flood* (1973) that would remain an integral part of the Dead's repertoire for the remainder of their days together. "There comes a redeemer, but he slowly too fades away," the track offers at one point, adding later, "Sometimes the songs that we hear are just songs of our own." Originally considered for the title of *Wake*, the song's Buddhist bent resonated with Deadheads who saw their association with "the family" in terms of a more global purpose. "'Eyes of the World' was quite mystical," Hunter said in 1986. "It's a song about compassion as I understand it, being able to see things from someone else's point of view. It's always a right message, but I think it can be overdone. It can be made corny. Of course, there are eternal verities. You can't avoid those too much if you want to say something." The Dead ended up saying it almost 400 times between 1973 and 1975, it appeared on *Without A Net* (1990), and The Other Ones brought the song back into the fold in the fall of 2002.

OCTOBER '90

1	2	3

In October the band jets off to Europe for their first tour of the continent in nine years, and the first since the end of the Cold War.

Friday September 14
Saturday September 15
Sunday September 16
Tuesday September 18
Wednesday September 19 ★
Thursday September 20 ★
Madison Square Garden, New York, New York

At the Saturday show, the already soaring energy level gets kicked up when Bruce Hornsby debuts as an "official" band member. The two keyboardists settle the division of labor they'll keep to in most shows when they're both onstage—Vince tackles the synthesizer, Bruce tickles the ivories of a grand piano. The show also sees the only post-Mydland "Gimme Some Lovin'." The entire Sunday show is available on *Dick's Picks, Volume Nine*. The last (and maybe the best) night of a legendary run is highlighted by a post-"Drums" jam that weaves in and out of "Dark Star" and capped by "Turn on Your Lovelight" in a rare encore slot.

10	11	12	13	14	15	16	17	18	19	20	21 ~ 30

Monday September 10
Tuesday September 11
Wednesday September 12 ★
The Spectrum, Philadelphia, Pennsylvania

The final night at the Spectrum sees an extreme rarity in the second set—a jam on "Two Soldiers" (a.k.a. "Handsome Cabin Boy"), a "mainstay of the Garcia-Grisman band, but never part of the Dead's repertoire," morphing into "Morning Dew."

Wednesday October 17
Grugahalle, Essen, West Germany

Rested and back on track, the band returns to the site of the famous double-bill with The Who (see page 260), including the first "Maggie's Farm" since November 14, 1987.

4 ~ 12	13	14	15	16	17

Saturday October 13
Ice Stadium, Stockholm, Sweden

Even a great year has its bad nights. Travel-tired and sans Bruce Hornsby, the band starts the tour with a show often described as "somnolent." According to Blair Jackson, Bob Weir joked that the Grateful Dead had been replaced by a Swedish band called "Jetlag."

Wednesday October 3
A midnight ceremony in Berlin marks the reunification of East and West Germany.

Left: Garcia with his daughter Keelin in London (October 30 and 31 at Wembley Arena).

Above: The Dead with a poster for their Europe 1990 tour.

Friday October 19
Saturday October 20
Internationales Congress Centrum, Berlin, Germany

Monday October 22
Festhalle, Frankfurt, Germany

First performance of Bruce Hornsby and The Range's "Valley Road."

Wednesday October 24
Sporthalle, Hamburg, Germany

18	19	20	21	22	23	24	25	26	27	28	29	30	31

Saturday October 27
Sunday October 28
Zenith, Paris, France

The last night elicits another breakout of a Bruce Hornsby original, "Stander on the Mountain."

Tuesday October 30
★ Wednesday October 31
Wembley Arena, London, England

At the opening show the PA somehow picks up a cell phone conversation between two clubbing girls during "Drums," much to the crowd's amusement. Wednesday… Halloween… London… The encore… "Werewolves of London." So obvious you almost wish they hadn't done it.

October 1990

383

Above: October 27–28, Zenith, Paris, France.
Right: Wednesday September 12, The Spectrum, Philadelphia.

GRATEFUL DEAD NO CAMPING

"So much the literal song of any place I ever wanted to be."

ROBERT CREELEY, BOLLINGEN PRIZE-WINNING AMERICAN POET
ABOUT *A BOX OF RAIN*

A Box of Rain

From a literary standpoint, the publication of Robert Hunter's *A Box of Rain* (Viking Penguin, New York) in 1990 was in its way as significant as the start of the release of archival Grateful Dead performances in 1991 was from a musical standpoint. The book gathered all of Hunter's lyrics in one elegant volume for the first time, and reading those words on their own, instead of hearing them sung or seeing them with notation in a songbook, just reinforces the Deadhead reader's innate understanding that Hunter is a true poet. Many of the lyrics are accompanied by Hunter's own notes and comments, showing how Hunter's writing evolved over the course of his life, and how the events and passages of his life emerged in his writing. Deadhead deconstructionists have had a field day noting how Hunter's original texts differ from the versions performed by the band, as well as poring over the lyrics to unperformed or unreleased songs. A revised edition, with lyrics up to 1993, was published in that year.

"A unique talent, a sculptor whose finely sanded lines resemble nothing else on the rock 'n' roll landscape." FROM THE *BOSTON GLOBE*'S REVIEW

A BOX OF RA[IN]
Collected Lyrics of
ROBERT HUNTER

Monday December 3
Tuesday December 4
Oakland Coliseum Arena, Oakland, California

On the first night Sikiru Adepoju plays on "Drums" and "Stander on the Mountain" is performed for the last time. The second night sees Huey Lewis playing harmonica on "Turn on Your Lovelight."

NOVEMBER '90

| 1 | 2 | 3 | 4 | 5 | 6 | 7 | 8 | 9 | 10 ~ 30 |

Thursday November 1
Wembley Arena, London, England

At this gig the band again bring out "Maggie's Farm," interpreted by some as a sly dig at British PM Margaret Thatcher.

DECEMBER '90

| 1 | 2 | 3 | 4 | 5 | 6 | 7 | 8 | 9 | 10 | 11 | 12 | 13 | 14 | 15 | 16 |

November 1990

Mickey's Input

During 1990, several albums to which Mickey Hart had contributed to in various ways were released. On *Various Artists—Folkways: The Original Vision* (Folkways/Smithsonian), he transferred original masters to CD. The sleevenotes to the album incuded the line, "Special thanks to Mickey Hart of the Grateful Dead."

Hariprasad Chaurasia and Zakir Hussain's *Venu* was also re-released in 1990. It had been co-produced and recorded by Mickey Hart in 1974 and was now released on CD.

384

Saturday December 8
Sunday December 9
Compton Terrace Amphitheatre, Chandler, Arizona *(below)*

Wednesday December 12 ★
Thursday December 13
Friday December 14
McNichols Sports Arena, Denver, Colorado

"WHARF RAT"
HUNTER/GARCIA

Possibly the greatest tragic figure in the Dead's vast kingdom of the persecuted, the lead character of "Wharf Rat" is also one of the most hopeful, an alcoholic dock-dweller named August West whose low lot in life hasn't extinguished the inner spirit that prompts him to declare amid his personal chaos, "I'll get up and fly away." Introduced on February 18, 1971, during the same Capitol Theater show in Port Chester, New York, that yielded a number of debuts, the song appeared later that year on the band's second live release, *Grateful Dead*. It was another happy product of the incredible symbiosis that was going on between Garcia and Hunter at the time. "'Wharf Rat' was almost completely instantaneous," Garcia later told David Gans. "Just about the time I had those musical ideas worked out and showed them to Hunter, he happened to have lyrics that, with a little alteration, a little fooling around, fit perfectly." As with the milder "goddamn" in "Uncle John's Band," the word "fucker" in the "Wharf Rat" lyrics led some radio stations to ban the song. The Dead had played "Wharf Rat" almost 400 times by 1995, with The Other Ones adding another dozen between 1998 and 2002. Fittingly, sober Deadheads recovering from alcohol and drug dependencies assumed the song's name for an AA-like group called The Wharf Rats that was established in 1986. A Garcia drawing inspired by the song titled "August West (Wharf Rat)" was listed on auction website eBay for $55,000 in late 2001.

Anniversary Books

A number of books are published during 1990 to mark the 25th anniversary of the band. These include *Book of the Dead: Celebrating 25 Years With The Grateful Dead* (Delacorte Press & Delta Books) containing more than 150 black and white photographs by Herb Greene chornicling the changes and constants of the band, and with a foreword by Robert Hunter; *The History of The Grateful Dead* by William Ruhlmann (Gallery Books), a short history of the band produced to coincide with the Dead's 25th anniversary; and *Built To Last: Grateful Dead 25th Anniversary Album 1965–1990* by Jamie Jensen (Plume), a history of the Dead with photographs.

Thursday December 27
Friday December 28
Sunday December 30
Monday December 31 ★
Oakland Coliseum Arena, Oakland, California

Hamza El-Din joins the band on "Drums" on the opening night, which also marks the first "Comes a Time" since July 8, 1987. The Rebirth Brass Band opens the New Year's Eve show, followed by Branford Marsalis, who wields his tenor to the usual great effect for the first-set closing sequence, "Bird Song" and "Promised Land," and the entire second set, which also includes Hamza El-Din on "Drums." Fire dancers and jungle-themed props appear onstage as the midnight countdown approaches, and Bill Graham descends from the rafters in a huge black cauldron, garbed as a witch doctor. A couple of similarly clad bungee jumpers bounce over the audience just after 1990 turns into 1991.

All in all, the second-to-last New Year's Eve show is considered one of the best and it goes out nationwide on radio, hosted by Ken Nordine, pioneer of " Word Jazz." In the late '50s, using his amazing voice and matching talent for free-association the way the bop instrumentalists used their trumpets and saxes, Ken recorded four hit records and played packed clubs. Although he was a fixture on Chicago-area radio and TV, Ken had largely fallen off the national radar screen before Dan Healy—with Garcia's enthusiastic blessing— recruited him to host the New Year's broadcast. Ken would ultimately release two new Word Jazz albums on Grateful Dead Records and perform his unique and inimitable verbalism onstage with the band *(see March 11, 1993)*.

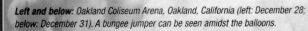
Left and below: *Oakland Coliseum Arena, Oakland, California (left: December 28; below: December 31). A bungee jumper can be seen amidst the balloons.*

December 1990

385

The Gulf War Shows

The band's first run of the year, at the Oakland Coliseum, will become known to Deadheads as the "Gulf War Shows." The air war against Iraq had begun about two weeks before the first show; major ground combat had yet to begin, but no one doubted that it was coming. The shows took place in an atmosphere of tension, and of anticipation—would the band break their default apolitical stance to comment overtly on the conflict? Or would they express their views through their music? All three shows were played without Bruce Hornsby.

Masters of Rock

Masters Of Rock: Grateful Dead by Elin Wilder is published; this series of articles collected from magazine interviews includes a discography and an illustrated bibliography.

Left and above: December 31, 1990, Oakland Coliseum. Garcia and sax great Branford Marsalis.

Tuesday February 19
Wednesday February 20
Thursday February 21
Oakland Coliseum Arena, Oakland, California

Deadheads expecting a musical statement on Tuesday are not disappointed. The first set ends with the first "New Speedway Boogie" since September 20, 1970, and the first electric version since July 11, 1970. The "One way or another/This darkness got to give" takes on special significance with war clouds in the air. The second-set "All Along the Watchtower" and the "U.S. Blues" encore hammer home the point. The following night, Baba Olatunji and Sikuru Adepoju play on "Drums" and "Space." It may be life during wartime, but Thursday is also Chinese New Year, with the traditional opener and "Drums" dragon dance from San Francisco's Chinese Symphony Orchestra. Airto Moreira joins for most of the second set, and the encore is "Knockin' on Heaven's Door," which most see as a parting comment on the tragedy and futility of war—"Mama take these guns off of me/I won't shoot them any more…"

FEBRUARY '91

| 1 | 2 | 3 | 4 | 5 | 6 | 7 | 8 | 9 | 10 | 11 | 12 | 13 | 14 | 15 | 16 | 17 | 18 | **19** | **20** | **21** | 22 ~ 28 |

Ned Lagin's *Seastones* is released on CD this year, an extended version of the 1975 album with contributions from Garcia, Hart, and Lesh.

JANUARY '91

| 1 ~ 21 | 22 | 23 ~ 31 |

Tuesday January 22
Instant Recall TV program is aired. Nationally syndicated, it includes interviews with Garcia, Ken Kesey, David Gans, and others.

Saturday February 2
Sunday February 3
Having played publicly just once before (in a Mill Valley music store), Jerry Garcia and David Grisman bring their new acoustic group (including Jim Kerwin on bass and Joe Craven on fiddle) to the Warfield for two nights. In a nod to the darkening war clouds in the Middle East, the shows include the traditional "Two Soldiers." This will be a heavy performance year for Jerry: in addition to 77 shows with the Grateful Dead, he'll play 29 Jerry Garcia Band shows (including a tour of the Northeast and Midwest in November) and four more Garcia/Grisman gigs.

Below: The Garcia-Grisman acoustic group played their first shows in February 1991. Here, they're joined by Bela Fleck at Squaw Valley in August '91.

"NEW SPEEDWAY BOOGIE"
HUNTER/GARCIA

By far the most pointed commentary ever to emerge from the Dead camp, "New Speedway Boogie" was a spontaneous Hunter/Garcia collaboration prompted by the tragedy that took place at California's Altamont Speedway on December 6, 1969, during which a free concert headlined by the Rolling Stones and featuring the Dead and the Jefferson Airplane turned into a melee in which a man was killed by Hells Angels acting as security guards. "It was completely unexpected," Garcia later recalled. "That was the hard lesson there: that you can have good people and good energy... and still have it all weird." Hunter later cited an article by music writer Ralph J. Gleason that was critical of the incident as the true impetus of the song, which begins, "Please don't dominate the rap, Jack, if you got nothing new to say." "'New Speedway Boogie' is one of those miracle songs," Garcia said. "It's one of those 'once-through' ones. The words were just so right." Debuted live exactly two weeks after the tragedy and later appearing in studio form on *Workingman's Dead* (1970), the band played the song just over two dozen times before retiring it from 1970 to 1991. It returned for another two dozen performances between 1991 (February 19) and 1994 (and later with The Other Ones in 2002).

Amid problems with unruly fans and gate-crashers during the Dead's final months together, the group sent out a foreboding flyer in 1995 invoking one of the song's classic lines: "One way or another, this darkness got to give."

Four nights at the Cap Centre kick off the annual springtime East Coast expedition. Bruce Hornsby is out until the March /April shows at the Greensboro Coliseum. All in all, the band will take in $35 million in ticket sales in 1991, making the Grateful Dead the top-grossing touring band in the country while other "monsters of rock" are actually losing money on their tours—which many will try to remedy through inflated ticket prices and a growing reliance on corporate sponsorship. The Good Ol' Grateful Dead, however, barely stay in the black: the band's huge payroll and expensive logistics continue to drain the coffers almost as soon as they're filled.

Above: Limited edition packaging.

DEADICATED
Various Artists
Released by Arista (ARCD 8669) in April 1991

1. **Bertha** *(Los Lobos)*
(Garcia/Hunter)
2. **Jack Straw** *(Bruce Hornsby & The Range)*
(Weir/Hunter)
3. **U.S. Blues** *(Harshed Mellows)*
(Garcia/Hunter)
4. **Ship Of Fools** *(Elvis Costello)*
(Garcia/Hunter)
5. **China Doll** *(Suzanne Vega)*
(Garcia/Hunter)
6. **Cassidy** *(Suzanne Vega)*
(Weir/Barlow)
7. **Truckin'** *(Dwight Yoakam)*
(Garcia/Weir/Lesh/Hunter)
8. **Casey Jones** *(Warren Zevon/David Lindley)*
(Garcia/Hunter)
9. **Uncle John's Band** *(Indigo Girls)*
(Garcia/Hunter)
10. **Friend Of The Devil** *(Lyle Lovett)*
(Garcia/Hunter)
11. **To Lay Me Down** *(Cowboy Junkies)*
(Garcia/Hunter)
12. **Wharf Rat** *(Midnight Oil)*
(Garcia/Hunter)
13. **Estimated Prophet** *(Burning Spear)*
(Weir/Barlow)
14. **Deal** *(Dr. John)*
(Garcia/Hunter)
15. **Ripple** *(Jane's Addiction)*
(Garcia/Hunter)

Right: Standard CD cover.

MARCH '91

1~16	17	18	19	20	21	22 ~ 26

March 1991

388

Sunday March 17
Monday March 18
Wednesday March 20
Thursday March 21
Capital Centre, Landover, Maryland

The opening show brings a pleasant surprise for JGB fans— the first Grateful Dead rendition of "Reuben and Cherise," the Hunter/Garcia retelling of the myth of Orpheus and Eurydice in New Orleans at Mardi Gras. Following Thursday's "Scarlet Begonias">"Fire on the Mountain" the band keep the Caribbean vibe alive with the first-ever jam on Bob Marley's "Stir it Up."

P RODUCED BY RALPH SALL (who was also credited with the "concept"), the first Grateful Dead tribute album sold 400,000 copies, got generally excellent reviews, and gave the band some positive media spin at a time when the media focused mainly on crowd-control and other problems on tour. The best covers, in the opinions of most, came from Elvis Costello, Dwight Yoakam, and Jane's Addiction. The artists all donated their shares of the proceeds to Cultural Survival and the Rainforest Action Network.

"I think this album's a great thing because it will draw attention to the fact that these guys are great songwriters and that there are a lot of people who feel that way—a lot of musicians, a lot of their peers who obviously feel the same way I do." FROM BRUCE HORNSBY'S LINER NOTES.

27	28	29	30

Wednesday March 27
Thursday March 28
Friday March 29
Nassau Veterans Memorial Coliseum, Uniondale, New York

Evidently there is a Terrapin Station on the Long Island Rail Road: on Thursday the band encore with "Terrapin" for the first time since July 8, 1978, at Red Rocks.

April sees the broadcast, on PBS, of *Deadheads—An American Subculture*, a feature produced by the Institute of American Popular Culture. Also released on video, this one-hour documentary is not just an intriguing treatise in Deadhead sociology, but also a compelling portrait of the Deadhead scene during the Mega-Dead era.

The Mickey Hart-produced *Voices of the Rainforest* comes out on Rykodisc this year, featuring recordings of the Kaluli tribe in Papua New Guinea.

Sunday April 7
Monday April 8
Tuesday April 9
Orlando Arena, Orlando, Florida

The band's first performances at this 15,000-seat venue. Tuesday marks the last-ever "Stir it Up" jam.

APRIL '91

31	1	2	3	4	5	6	7	8	9	10 ~ 25	26	27	28	29	30

★ **Sunday March 31**
★ **Monday April 1**
Greensboro Coliseum, Greensboro, North Carolina

If the tour so far had seen a few tepid shows, the band make up for them in Greensboro, thanks to the rejuvenating presence of Bruce Hornsby. April Fool's notwithstanding, the second night is one for the ages. The first set is capped by a soaring 16-minute "Bird Song," and the second set is a treat for connoisseurs of the Old School Dead: all the songs are pre-1973, "Dark Star" crashes into "Drums" and "Space" and reenters the atmosphere before a "Playing in the Band" reprise, and the set ends with "Turn on Your Lovelight."

Wednesday April 3
Thursday April 4
Friday April 5
The Omni, Atlanta, Georgia

Saturday April 27
Sunday April 28
Sam Boyd Silver Bowl, Las Vegas, Nevada

Carlos Santana opens both shows, and on the second night he joins in on "Bird Song," the first-set closer. Appropriately enough for the band's first Vegas run in seven years (see April 6, 1984) the second set includes "Deal" and a "Space" featuring the MIDI-fied sounds of slot machines.

FROM THE VAULTS

The arrival of *One From The Vault*—the first "official" release of a complete show from the band's tape archives—marked the start of a new era for Deadheads. The album opened the floodgates: together with the *Dick's Picks* series *(see pages 420–421)*, Grateful Dead Records (GDR) would go on to issue 45 albums of previously unreleased live performance (as of Spring 2003) not counting additional material on the *So Many Roads* and *Golden Road* compilations and David Gans' *Best Of The Grateful Dead Hour* CD (2000), which is available only to public radio and TV stations.

The choice of show for the kickoff *Vault* release surprised some Deadheads. August 13, 1975, at the Great American Music Hall in San Francisco (one of only four shows during the '74–'76 hiatus) circulated among Tapers, and much of the show appeared on the bootleg *Make Believe Ballroom*.

While Deadheads are happy with *any* archival release, the appearance of the *Vault* and *Dick's Picks* series did spark some debate in the Deadhead community, between two camps that David Shenk and Steve Silberman, in *Skeleton Key*, dubbed the Completists and the Perfectionists. The former felt that past performances should be released "as is," without any alteration of song sequence or correction of flaws in either the performance or the source recording. The latter were more inclined to favor aesthetic considerations over historical purism. And of course there's also the fierce (if good-natured) debate among Deadheads about just which shows merit inclusion in either series, a debate that's usually thrashed out online these days.

One From The Vault GDCD-4013-2
Released April 15, 1991, by GDR (2 CDs). Produced by Dan Healy. Recorded on August 13, 1975, at the Great American Music Hall, San Francisco, California.

Two From The Vault GDCD-4016-2
Released May 1992 by GDR (2 CDs). Produced by Dan Healy. Recorded live on August 24, 1968, at the Shrine Auditorium, Los Angeles, California.

Hundred Year Hall GDCD-4020-2
Released September 1995 by GDR (2 CDs). Recorded live on April 26, 1972, at Jahrhundert Halle, Frankfurt, West Germany.

Dozin' At The Knick GDCD-4025
Released October 1996 by GDR (3 CDs). Produced by John Cutler and Phil Lesh. Recorded live March 24–26, 1990, at Knickerbocker Arena, Albany, New York.

Below: Dick Latvala in the Grateful Dead Vault.

Fillmore East 2-11-69 GDCD-4054
Released October 1997 by GDR/Arista (2 CDs). Produced by John Cutler and Phil Lesh. Recorded live on February 11, 1969, at the Fillmore East, New York, New York.

View From The Vault GDCD-4077
Released June 2000 by GDR (3 CDs). Produced by Dan Healy. Recorded live at Three Rivers Stadium, Pittsburgh, Pennsylvania, on July 8, 1990, and Cardinal Stadium, Louisville, Kentucky, on July 6, 1990.

Ladies And Gentlemen...The Grateful Dead Arista-4075
Released October 2000 by GDR/Arista (4 CDs). Produced by David Lemieux. Recorded live at Fillmore East, New York City, April 25–29, 1971.

View From The Vault II GDCD-4080
Released June 2001 by GDR (3 CDs). Produced by Dan Healy. Recorded live at RFK Stadium, Washington, D.C., on June 14, 1991, except last three tracks, which were recorded live at RFK Stadium, Washington, D.C., on July 12, 1990.

View From The Vault III GDCD-4087
Released August 2002 by GDR (3 CDs). Produced by Dan Healy. Recorded live at Shoreline Amphitheatre, Mountain View, California, on June 16, 1990; the last six tracks are from the same venue's October 3, 1987, show.

Terrapin Station GDCD-4055
A limited edition GDR release (3 CDs), comprising the entire 3/15/90 Grateful Dead show at the Capitol Centre, Landover, Maryland, to raise money for the proposed Terrapin Station museum/performance center. Released September 1997.

Fallout From The Phil Zone GD/Arista-1405-2
A 2-CD release of live material from 1967 to 1995 as personally selected by Phil Lesh. Released on June 17, 1997.

Nightfall Of Diamonds 2001 GDCD-4081
A 2-CD release of the October 16, 1989, show in East Rutherford, New Jersey. Released on September 25, 2001.

Stepping Out With The Grateful Dead 2002 GDCD-1408-4
A 4-CD set of music from seven UK shows during the 1972 tour of Europe. Released July 9, 2002.

Go To Nassau GDCD-1408-5
A two-CD set of music from the May 14, 15, and 16, 1980, shows at Nassau Veterans Memorial Coliseum, Uniondale, New York. Released October 22, 2002.

View From The Vault IV GDCD-4089
Released on April 8, 2003. A 4-CD issue of the Dead's Oakland County Coliseum Stadium July 24, 1987, show and the Anaheim Stadium July 26, 1987, performance. Bob Dylan does not feature.

1	2

3	4	5	6	7	8

Friday May 3
Saturday May 4
Sunday May 5
Cal Expo Amphitheatre,
Sacramento, California

The band return to California for
the traditional three-night run of
Rex Foundation benefits, minus
Bruce Hornsby. Sunday's
Kentucky Derby Day show
is celebrated with the usual
"The Race is On."

One More Saturday Night

The Sandy Troy-penned *One More Saturday Night:
Reflections With The Grateful Dead,
Dead Family and Deadheads* is
published by St. Martin's Press this
year. It features interviews with
members of the Dead and others in the
"family" plus extensive photographs.

Friday May 10
Saturday May 11
Sunday May 12
Shoreline Amphitheatre, Mountain View, California

On the final night the Dylan Slot is filled by the revival of
"It Takes a Lot to Laugh, It Takes a Train to Cry," for the
first time (without Bob on vocals) since June 10, 1973.

9	**10**	**11**	**12**	13	14	15	16	17	18	19	20 ~ 31

Below: Spring tour 1991: "The kids they dance,
they shake their bones..."

1	2	3	4	5	6	7	8	9

Thursday June 6
Friday June 7
Deer Creek Music Center,
Noblesville, Indiana

Saturday June 1
L.A. Memorial Coliseum,
Los Angeles, California

The band's only LA-area
performance in 1991 sees
the last-ever "Rubin and
Cherise." South African
singer Johnny Clegg and his
band Savuka opens.

Sunday June 9
Buckeye Lake Music
Center, Hebron, Ohio

The Violent Femmes open.

Thursday June 13
New York's finest raid a mobbed-up Queens print shop and seize thousands of counterfeit tickets to the upcoming Giants Stadium shows—another backhanded compliment to the band's popularity.

Right: Friday June 14, RFK Stadium, Washington, D.C.

| 10 | 11 | 12 | 13 |

Tuesday June 11
Wednesday June 12
Charlotte Coliseum, Charlotte, North Carolina

Friday June 14 ★
RFK Stadium, Washington, D.C.

Dwight Yoakam opens, and promoter John Scher takes the mic to threaten the band won't come back for a second set unless people clear the aisles. They don't, but the band plays on.

| 14 | 15 | 16 | 17 | 18 | 19 | 20 |

Sunday June 16
Monday June 17 ★
Giants Stadium, East Rutherford, New Jersey

Little Feat opens the first night but the second night is a truly great show, all the more remarkable for taking place in this cavernous, soulless football stadium. Among the delights are the first first-set "Eyes of the World" since August 13, 1975, and the first "Dark Star Jam" (adumbrated by a tease before the first-set "When I Paint My Masterpiece") since June 23, 1974.

Below: Wednesday June 19, Pine Knob Music Theatre, Clarkston, Michigan. Sure doesn't look like the Detroit area.

Wednesday June 19
Thursday June 20
Pine Knob Music Theatre, Clarkston, Michigan

Aesthetics of the Grateful Dead

Aesthetics of the Grateful Dead: A Critical Analysis was written by David Womack and published by Flying Public Press in '91. This heavy-sounding tome was split into two sections, the first examining attitudes to the Dead and the band's ethos, the second (lighter) section reviewing Grateful Dead and bandmember solo albums up to January 1989.

Saturday June 22
Soldier Field, Chicago, Illinois

Ex-Byrdman Roger McGuinn opens.

| 21 | 22 | 23 |

Monday June 24
Tuesday June 25
Sandstone Amphitheatre, Bonner Springs, Kansas

| 24 | 25 | 26 | 27 | 28 | 29 | 30 |

Friday June 28
Mile High Stadium, Denver, Colorado

Santana open.

Below: The Tapers entrance at Pine Knob Music Theatre, Clarkston, Michigan.

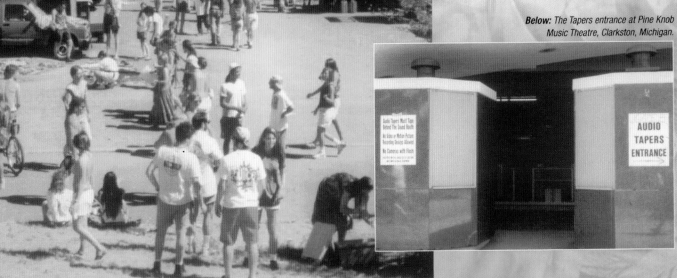

AUDIO TAPERS ENTRANCE

Hip-Hop Music Scene

What is it about hip-hop? In the annual Deadbase polls, normally eclectic Deadheads consistently identify hip-hop as their least favorite genre. Maybe it's the reliance on heavy, processed beat. Maybe it's the (usual) foregrounding of words rather than music. Or maybe it's the aggressive style and content of the rap music that emerges from hip-hop culture. It is, after all, a rare Deadhead who prefers the nine-millimeter to the six-string.

To define terms: hip-hop means the whole package (dress, art, dance, etc.) of which rap is the musical component—but over the years hip-hop has become shorthand for rap. Hip-hop began in the '70s in the Boogie Down Bronx in New York City, when MCs at street parties took to improvising rhymes over the rhythmic accompaniment of DJs, who used their turntables to "scratch" a beat on vinyl records. (Rapping itself has origins in Jamaican "toasting," the boating contests known as "the dozens," and other Afro-American-Caribbean sources.) In the '80s the music broke out of the 'hood following the chart success of the Sugar Hill Gang's "Rapper's Delight" (Grandmaster Flash and Melle Mel, Kurtis Blow, Afrika Bambaata, and others also made their mark.)

And as with jazz and other genres that began in the African-American community, hip-hop got watered down somewhat as it hit the mainstream—remember M.C. Hammer?—but at the same time groups like NWA and, especially, Public Enemy emerged with a hard-edged sound and an aggressive political agenda to match. And then came "gangsta" rap-aggression, but without the politics... along with other sub-genres, including Old Skool, essentially a return to hip-hop's roots.

In the '90s hip-hop, once an urban curiosity to most Americans, was firmly established as one of the country's (and the world's) most dynamic and influential musical movements, and one that had a major and ongoing influence on popular culture. And in one of those ironies with which American music is rife, by the turn of the 21st century, the nation's top rapper was a white guy—Marshall Mathers, a.k.a. Eminem.

But what of its links to the Grateful Dead? It may be poison to your average Deadhead, but common ground is not hard to find. Pigpen's mastery of improvised blues lyrics drew, of course, on the same traditions as the extempore inventiveness of rap. Hip-hop's use of pre-programmed rhythm and sampling is akin to some of the Dead's own experimentation, such as the MIDI-heavy "Spaces" of the '90s. And, of course, the fans in both camps share a love of the Chronic, be it blunt or bong.

Left: Cypress Hill are one of many hip-hop bands who are open about their fondness for good weed.

Above and right: Monday August 12, Cal Expo Amphitheatre, Sacramento, California. This small, grassy venue was a favorite of many Heads.

AUGUST '91

| 1 | 2 | 3 | 4 | 5 | 6 | 7 | 8 | 9 | 10 | 11 | 12 | 13 | 14 | 15 |

Thursday August 1
Mickey Hart speaks to the U.S. Senate Special Committee on Aging to promote drum circles as a therapeutic activity for the elderly. Mickey's testimony is a catalyst in the founding of Rhythm for Life, a coalition including the National Association for Music Therapy, the National Association of Music Merchants, and Remo, Inc.

Monday August 12
Tuesday August 13
Wednesday August 14
Cal Expo Amphitheatre, Sacramento, California

"We are embedded within a rhythmical universe... It is there in the cycles of the seasons, in the migration of the birds and animals, in the fruiting and withering of plants, and in the birth, maturation and death of ourselves. Rhythm is at the very center of our lives."

MICKEY HART'S SENATE SPEECH

The first collection of Robert Hunter's poems, *Night Cadre*, is published by Viking/ Penguin USA this year.

JULY '91

| 1 | 2 | 3 | 4 | 5 | 6 – 24 |

Friday July 5
ABC TV's late night *In Concert* program includes video of the band performing "Eyes of the World" and "Saint of Circumstance" at the June 17 Giants Stadium show.

JERRY GARCIA AND DAVID GRISMAN
Jerry Garcia and David Grisman
Acoustic Disc ACD 2

Jerry Garcia and David Grisman was the tasty fruit of reconciliation between the two pickers, reportedly over accounting issues dating back to the *Old and In the Way* days. Backed by Joe Craven on fiddle and percussion and James Kerwin on bass, Jerry and Dave played a mix of old-timey tunes, originals, and a version of "Friend of the Devil." The album, and the quartet's live shows, revived a musical partnership that would continue until Jerry's death. To promote the album, Justin Kreutzmann directed a video of "The Thrill is Gone." *Jerry Garcia and David Grisman* was a surprise hit, selling about 100,000 copies. Grisman plowed most of his return back into his Acoustic Disc label.

jerry GARCIA
david GRISMAN

★ **Friday August 16** ★
Saturday August 17
Sunday August 18

Shoreline Amphitheatre, Mountain View, California

On the opening night "Dark Star" rises in the first set for the first time since November 15, 1971, though the performance is somewhat brief and lackluster.

16	17	18	19	20	21	22	23

JERRY GARCIA BAND
Jerry Garcia Band

Recorded during a run at San Francisco's Warfield Theatre in the spring of 1990, *Jerry Garcia Band* was the first solo album to showcase Jerry's electrified side since the JGB's 1982 studio release, *Run for the Roses*. It's a notable album both for the performances and for the sheer breadth of the material, always a characteristic of Jerry's solo work—everything from standards ("That Lucky Old Sun") to a Los Lobos tune ("Evangeline"), with a version of "Deal" thrown in.

Released by Arista (18690-2) in August 1991

1. **The Way You Do The Things You Do**
   (Robinson Jr/Rogers)
2. **Waiting For A Miracle**
   (Cockburn)
3. **Simple Twist Of Fate**
   (Dylan)
4. **Get Out Of My Life**
   (Toussaint)
5. **My Sisters And Brothers**
   (Johnson)
6. **I Shall Be Released**
   (Dylan)
7. **Dear Prudence**
   (Lennon/McCartney)
8. **Deal**
   (Garcia/Hunter)
9. **Stop That Train**
   (Tosh)
10. **Senor (Tales Of Yankee Power)**
    (Dylan)
11. **Evangeline**
    (Hidalgo/Perez)
12. **The Night They Drove Old Dixie Down**
    (Robertson)
13. **Don't Let Go**
    (Stone)
14. **That Lucky Old Sun**
    (Gillespie/Smith)
15. **Tangled Up In Blue**
    (Dylan)

Produced by Jerry Garcia, John Kahn, and John Cutler

A BOX OF RAIN
Robert Hunter

Released by Rykodisc (10214) in August 1991

1. **Box Of Rain**
   (Hunter/Lesh)
2. **Scarlet Begonias**
   (Garcia/Hunter)
3. **Franklin's Tower**
   (Garcia/Hunter/Kreutzmann)
4. **Jack Straw**
   (Hunter/Weir)
5. **Brown Eyed Women**
   (Garcia/Hunter)
6. **Reuben And Cerise**
   (Garcia/Hunter)
7. **Space**
   (Hunter)
8. **Deal**
   (Garcia/Hunter)
9. **Promontory Rider**
   (Hunter)
10. **Ripple**
    (Garcia/Hunter)
11. **Boys In The Barroom**
    (Hunter)
12. **Stella Blue**
    (Garcia/Hunter)

Robert Hunter's third album for Rykodisc, *A Box of Rain* was released to accompany the book of the same title *(see page 384)* and featured the wordsmith doing solo acoustic turns on an even dozen of his best-known songs, most of them among the Dead repertoire. Nine of the songs were recorded live in December 1990 at the Warfield and at a show in Boston, while the remaining three were studio recordings.

"SUGAR MAGNOLIA"
HUNTER/WEIR

Taking up where the unnamed dancing girl from the earlier "Golden Road (To Unlimited Devotion)" left off, this first Weir–Hunter collaboration captures a timeless portrait of a seemingly magical Dead girlfriend. "She can dance a Cajun rhythm, jump like a Willys in four wheel drive," Weir enthuses. "She's a summer love in the spring, fall and winter, she can make happy any man alive." Unlike other songs that had a chance to gestate live before being recorded, "Sugar Magnolia" developed a different way. "We took it into the studio and recorded it, and I wasn't altogether pleased with what it came out like," Weir told David Gans almost seven years after its debut on *American Beauty* (1970). "I didn't know how to tell anybody that, but as soon as we took it out on the road, it immediately evolved into a whole lot more than what we'd just put down on vinyl." That evolution included a coda dubbed "Sunshine Daydream" which, after a point, was occasionally played independently of the main song, often on New Year's Eve. "Sugar Magnolia" would ultimately take the stage more than any other Dead original, with 576 plays between June 7, 1970, and the band's last show on July 9, 1995. It was Bill Graham's favorite Dead song and was played at his funeral on October 27, 1991.

Panther Dream

Bob and Wendy Weir's book, subtitled *A Story Of The African Rainforest*, was published this year. A children's book with accompanying audio cassette (read by Bob Weir), it was inspired by the Dead's Rainforest Benefit concert in 1988.

Right: *Monday October 28, Oakland Coliseum Arena, Oakland, California.*

September 1991

394

| 1 | 2 | 3 | 4 | 5 | 6 | 7 |

🎸 **Wednesday September 4**
🎸 **Thursday September 5**
Friday September 6
Richfield Coliseum, Richfield, Ohio

SEPTEMBER '91

With the two-guitar, two-keyboard lineup now well established, the band heads East for a tour centered around the usual Homeric run at Madison Square Garden—this year, nine nights. The tour includes some good shows, though Garcia shows signs of fatigue. The tiredness is real but also exacerbated by drugs. Accounts vary about when he began using again, and just what he was using (prescription painkillers, his old favorite Persian base, or both), but at the end of the tour he starts a methadone maintenance program and enters counseling.

| 8 | 9 | 10 | 11 | 12 | 13 | 14 | 15 | 16 | 17 | 18 | 19 |

🎸 **Sunday September 8**
🎸 **Monday September 9**
Tuesday September 10 ★
Thursday September 12
Friday September 13
Saturday September 14
Monday September 16
Tuesday September 17
Wednesday September 18
Madison Square Garden, New York, New York

The first night of the Garden run sees the year's first "Attics of My Life," as the encore. On Tuesday Branford Marsalis plays the whole show, and proves once again *(see page 376)* that he's among the finest—if not *the* finest—guests to ever sit in with the band, in terms of musical empathy.

Below: *Noted neurologist and author Oliver Sacks at Madison Square Garden, September 1991.*

| 20 | 21 | 22 | 23 | 24 | 25 | 26 | 27 - 30 |

🎸 **Friday September 20**
🎸 **Saturday September 21**
Sunday September 22
Tuesday September 24
Wednesday September 25
Thursday September 26 ★
Boston Garden, Boston, Massachusetts

During a period when the band and its fans live in fear of losing access to venues, the Grateful Dead are *invited* to play by the Boston Garden's management, with the support of most of the area's businesses, which are hemorrhaging money in the early-90s recession. Reportedly, the only call to a special "complaint hotline" comes from a Deadhead looking for ducats. It is the band's first time at the venue in nine years. The last time they'd played *(see September 18, 1982)* it was a fairly big hall by the band's standards; in the Mega-Dead era, it's practically an intimate space. Perhaps for this reason, the opening show is one of the tour's best, and some consider the band's six nights at the Garden as the last of the great runs. On Sunday the band breaks out "Nobody's Fault But Mine" for the first time since September 3, 1985. Wednesday's second-set surprise is the first performance of "That Would Be Something," from Paul McCartney's eponymous 1970 solo album. The final show of the tour is the best, in the opinion of many, capped with a double encore: "Brokedown Palace" and "We Bid You Goodnight"—the last performance of the latter.

The Garden

Bill Graham 1931 – 1991

Bill Graham and his girlfriend Melissa Gold were returning from a Huey Lewis concert at the Concord Pavilion in a helicopter piloted by Steve "Killer" Kahn on October 25, 1991, when high winds forced the craft into power lines. All three died instantly. Graham was 60.

Graham had bestridden the world of rock like a colossus for a quarter century, in the process joining an elite group of non-performers who did as much for the music as any band or artist. The list of his achievements goes on and on: promoting the Bay Area music scene into national prominence; managing perhaps the most celebrated venues in rock history, the Fillmores; and, ultimately, helping to bring rock (for better or worse) into the era of multi-thousand-seat stadiums and multi-million-dollar tours. Graham's ceaseless innovation, relentless attention to detail, and gift for the graceful gesture made him beloved of audiences and performers alike. Who else would have put Miles Davis on a double bill with the Grateful Dead? Or pulled off a Thanksgiving Dinner for 5,000 at the Band's famous 1978 "Last Waltz" concert? Or masterminded the audience toast to the Grateful Dead at the conclusion of the Warfield acoustic/electric shows in 1980?

Graham could be abrasive—what impresario isn't?—and he made no bones about being a businessman, but it was his love of music, and respect for the people who made music, that was behind everything he did.

If Graham's death was a loss for rock music in general, it was a particularly sorrowful event for the Dead. Bill Graham had always had a special relationship (if not always an easy one) with the band, something he acknowledged in a 1985 interview in *The Golden Road*: "I always thought they were different. They make my body move and feel good. They did that from day one." And while the public perception was that Graham had "given the Grateful Dead their start," the mutual ties were deeper and longer than that. As Dennis McNally notes in *A Long Strange Trip*, Graham's support (including financial help) was not only ongoing, but critical in helping the band weather the rough patches in its career.

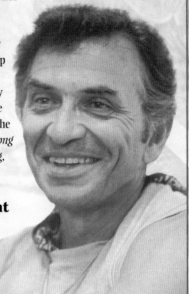

"I think he's checking laminates in heaven right now. They got a lot of rock stars up there. They need somebody to get it organized, that's all." WAVY GRAVY TO BLAIR JACKSON, *1992*

PLANET DRUM
Mickey Hart

The CD released to accompany Mickey Hart's landmark book brought together perhaps the most stellar group of percussionists ever assembled, including many who'd played with the Grateful Dead over the years, like Airto Moreira, Flora Purim, Zakir Hussain, Babatunde Olatunji, and Sikiru Adepoju. Planet Drum went on to win a Grammy for Best World Music Album in 1991, the year that the category was introduced.

Released on Rykodisc (10206) in late 1991

1. **Udu Chant**
   (Adepoju/Hart/Hussain/Moreira)
2. **Island Groove**
   (Adepoju/Hart/Hussain/Moreira/Olatunji)
3. **Light Over Shadow**
   (Moreira/Olatunji/Purim)
4. **Dance Of The Hunter's Fire**
   (Adepoju/Moreira/Olatunji/Purim/Vinayakram)
5. **Jewe "You Are the One"**
   (Olatunji)
6. **The Hunt**
   (Adepoju/Hart/Hussain/Moreira/Olatunji/Vinayakram)
7. **Temple Caves**
   (Adepoju/Hart/Hussain/Moreira/Olatunji)
8. **The Dancing Sorcerer**
   (Hussain/Moreira)
9. **Bones**
   (Hart/Hussain/Olatunji/Purim)
10. **Lost River**
    (Adepoju/Hart/Hussain/Moreira/Olatunji/Purim)
11. **Evening Samba**
    (Adepoju/Hart/Hussain/Olatunji/Vinayakram)
12. **Iyanu "Surprises"**
    (Olatunji)
13. **Mysterious Island**
    (Hart/Moreira/Purim/Sterling)

Produced by Mickey Hart

OCTOBER '91

| 1 | 2 | 3 | 4 | 5 | 6 ~ 24 | 25 |

Friday October 25
Bill Graham dies.

Ouija Boards Not Needed?

Conversations With the Dead: The Grateful Dead Interview Book by *Grateful Dead Hour* radio-show host and all-around scenester David Gans, is published by Citadel Underground/Carol Publishing Group. (An updated paperback edition was published in 1999 by Da Capo Press.) The book is a fascinating collection of interviews, not just with band members but also with the likes of Bear, Ned Lagin, Robert Hunter, and John Perry Barlow. Hunter's Pranksterish hijacking of a 2/25/88 GDH interview is a special treat.

Sunshine Daydreams

Subtitled *A Grateful Dead Journal*, Herb Greene's '91 publication on Chronicle Books included many of Greene's own photos as well as ticket stubs and album covers.

★ **Sunday October 27**
Monday October 28
Wednesday October 30
★ **Thursday October 31**
Oakland Coliseum Arena, Oakland, California

The opening show is the first following Bill Graham's death, and it finds the band grieving but in good form. The opener is "Sugar Magnolia"—Bill's favorite Grateful Dead song. Carlos Santana and ex-Quicksilver Messenger Service guitar slinger Gary Duncan join for the second-set "Iko Iko," into "Mona," the Bo Diddley tune last played by the band (backing Bo) at the celebrated American Indian benefit concert at Winterland on March 5, 1972. "Mona" was also a QMS standby. At the final show, Gary Duncan joins for part of the second set, and during "Dark Star" Ken Kesey takes the mic to declaim a tribute to Bill Graham, which ends with him quoting the last line of e.e. cummings' poem *Buffalo Bill's/defunct*: "How do you like your blueyed boy/Mr. Death." But it's Halloween, and the band encores with "Werewolves of London" (the last-ever performance.)

| 26 | 27 | 28 | 29 | 30 | 31 |

 October 1991

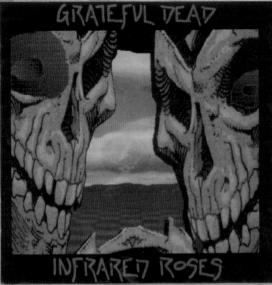

Fired by the same experimental spirit that inspired *Aoxomoxoa* and *Blues for Allah* but armed with state-of-the-art electronic gadgetry, MIDI-master Bob Bralove (see page 346) assembled this sonic collage from pieces of "Drums" and "Space" taken from various shows in 1989 and 1990. In a particularly adept touch, Bralove also brought in the sounds of Deadheads themselves—parking lot vendors hawking, drum circlers pounding—for the "Crowd Sculpture" segment that begins the album. The result is definitely not for all tastes but it presents the band's most adventurous music in an entirely new and compelling way. Robert Hunter provided the poetic track titles.

"The secret to the success of Infrared Roses is MIDI guru Bob Bralove, who waded through five years of drums/space to assemble it. And assemble is the right word here, because Bralove did more than simply choose a dozen interesting jams. Instead, he isolated selected passages from dozens of jams, and used them as compositional elements to create a series of four symphonic pieces of three movements each."
GUITAR PLAYER EDITOR JON SIEVERT, IN SHENK & SILBERMAN'S SKELETON KEY

INFRARED ROSES
Grateful Dead

Released by Grateful Dead Records (GDCD-40142) on November 1, 1991

1. **Crowd Sculpture**
   (Bralove)
2. **Parallelogram**
   (Hart/Kreutzmann)
3. **Little Nemo In Nightland**
   (Garcia/Lesh/Weir/Bralove)
4. **Riverside Rhapsody**
   (Garcia/Hart/Kreutzmann/Lesh/Mydland/Weir)
5. **Post-Modern Highrise Table Top Stomp**
   (Garcia/Green III/Hart/Kreutzmann/Lesh/Mydland/Weir)
6. **Infrared Roses**
   (Garcia/Lesh/Mydland/Weir/Bralove)
7. **Silver Apples Of The Moon**
   (Hornsby/Welnick)
8. **Speaking In Swords**
   (Hart/Kreutzmann/Bralove)
9. **Magnesium Night Light**
   (Garcia/Lesh/Mydland/Weir)
10. **Sparrow Hawk Row**
    (Garcia/Hart/Healy/Kreutzmann/Lesh/Mydland/Weir/Bralove)
11. **River Of Nine Sorrows**
    (Hart/Kreutzmann/Bralove)
12. **Apollo At The Ritz**
    (Garcia/Hart/Kreutzmann/Lesh/Marsalis/Mydland/Weir)

Personnel

Jerry Garcia – guitar, electronic percussion, synthesizer
Bruce Hornsby – piano, synthesizer
Mickey Hart – trap drums, beast, beam, electronic percussion, talking drum
Bill Kreutzmann – trap drums, timbales, electronic percussion, toms, synthesizer
Phil Lesh – bass, synthesizer
Brent Mydland – keyboards, midi keyboard, synthesizer
Bob Weir – guitar, midi guitar, synthesizer
Vince Welnick – synthesizer
Bob Bralove – drum machine sequencing
Willie Green III – kick snare hat
Dan Healy – processing
Branford Marsalis – tenor saxophone, soprano saxophone

Produced by Bob Bralove

Bill Graham Memorial Show

On November 3, more than 300,000 people packed Golden Gate Park's Polo Field (*below*) for "A Benefit for Laughter, Love, and Music"—a farewell tribute for Bill Graham, Melissa Gold, and Steve Kahn, featuring the Grateful Dead and a galaxy of musical stars. (It was, in fact, the third-largest crowd the Grateful Dead ever played for, exceeded only by Woodstock and Watkins Glen, and the lineup of other acts wasn't announced until just before the event.)

The Dirty Dozen Brass Band led off, playing from a flatbed truck in an updated version of the traditional New Orleans jazz funeral procession. Jackson Brown, Santana (with members of Los Lobos), and Tracy Chapman followed. The first part of the concert ended with Crosby, Stills, Nash, and Young—particularly touching because Bill's death brought them back together as a quartet after several years.

The Grateful Dead took the stage for 90 minutes. John Popper of Blues Traveler joined on harp for "Wang Dang Doodle," after which the band backed up John Fogerty for a four-song Creedence medley. The set ended, fittingly, with the "Sunshine Daydream" coda from Bill's favorite, "Sugar Magnolia," followed by an emotional encore of "Forever Young" and "Touch of Grey," with Neil Young helping out on vocals.

Other performers included Journey, Aaron Neville, Robin Williams, and ballerina Evelyn Cisneros.

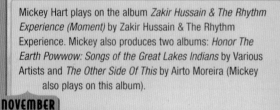

Mickey Hart plays on the album *Zakir Hussain & The Rhythm Experience (Moment)* by Zakir Hussain & The Rhythm Experience. Mickey also produces two albums: *Honor The Earth Powwow: Songs of the Great Lakes Indians* by Various Artists and *The Other Side Of This* by Airto Moreira (Mickey also plays on this album).

NOVEMBER '91

1 2 3 4 5 6 7 8 9

Sunday November 3
The Bill Graham Memorial Show is held at Polo Field, Golden Gate Park, San Francisco, a farewell tribute to Bill Graham, Melissa Gold, and Steve Kahn.

Wednesday November 27
Mickey Hart and the Planet Drum Band (Babatunde Olatunji, Airto Moreira, Zakir Hussain, Vikku Vinayakram, Sikiru Adepoju, Giovanni Hidalgo, and Flora Purim) cap their tour with a triumphant performance at New York's Carnegie Hall.

| 25 | 26 | **27** | 28 | 29 | 30 |

Jerry Garcia stars in a TV commercial for Levi's 501 jeans. As with his licensing of "Eep hour" for a Cher perfume commercial *(see page 359)*, purist Deadheads treat the spot as a sign of the Apocalypse. JG had advertised Levi's before, however: in 1987 he featured in a 30-second radio commercial, along with Sandy Rothman, David Nelson, and John Kahn.

Sonatas by Tom Constanten, is released this month; it is, unsurprisingly, a solo recital of Sonatas.

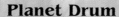

Planet Drum

Nothing less than a portrait of the planet in percussion, *Planet Drum*, by Mickey Hart, Frederick Lieberman, and D.A. Sonneborn was the brilliant realization of Mickey Hart's lifelong exploration of the role that drumming has played in human society from prehistory to present. Longtime Dead fan Elvis Costello once said that writing about music is like dancing about architecture, but *Planet Drum* is that rare example of a book that conveys a musician's passion and knowledge to a wide audience. Following a performance to promote the book at the American Booksellers Association Convention in New York City, Mickey and his partners in percussion led the normally buttoned-down publishing-industry crowd in an exuberant snake dance through the atrium of the Marriott Marquis Hotel. *"Original and provocative thinking permeates this magnificently illustrated and fascinating volume."* WALTER CRONKITE

Friday December 27
Saturday December 28
Monday December 30
Tuesday December 31 ★
Oakland Coliseum Arena, Oakland, California

The band are without Bruce Hornsby for the year-end run. A surprise revival on Saturday: the first "The Same Thing" (a raunchy traditional blues popularized by Muddy Waters) since New Year's Eve '71, with Bob Weir inheriting Pigpen's lead vocal. Airto Moreira joins the penultimate show of '91 for "Drums" and stays to provide percussion and vocals on "Stalla Blue." Babatunde Olatunji opens on Tuesday, followed by banjo maestro Bela Fleck and his Flecktones. The band play two sets and close out a year clouded by the loss of Bill Graham with "Knockin' on Heaven's Door."

DECEMBER '91

| 1 – 11 | 12 | 13 | 14 | 15 | 16 | 17 | 18 | 19 | 20 | 21 | 22 | 23 | 24 | 25 | 26 | **27** | **28** | 29 | **30** | **31** |

Clockwise from left:
Mountain Girl, Carlos Santana, the crowd, and the Dead onstage at the Bill Graham Memorial Show.

The Last New Year's Eve

This would be the Grateful Dead's last New Year's Eve show; it was a tradition too closely associated with Bill Graham to continue. (They'd been doing NYE shows since '66, with '67 and '73, '74, and '75 excepted.) In fact, it was a tradition that the Dead were probably glad to retire. The last show of the year (1) was often a logistical nightmare; (2) disrupted the holiday season (and all the band and most of the crew had families by now); (3) fell at a time when the boys were usually still recovering from fall touring and solo work; and (4) despite (or maybe because of) the massive popularity of the NYE show and attendant hype, they were rarely at their musical best—despite some fine moments over the years. (Dennis McNally compared the NYE shows to the Super Bowl— "so often a mediocre game because of the excessive preceding tension.") But the band had soldiered on, December 31 after December 31, out of loyalty to Bill Graham, who loved making his costumed, prop-supported pre-countdown entrances; it was the one moment of the year that Bill could step out and take center stage.

Left and below: The last New Year's Eve show, at Oakland Coliseum Arena, Tuesday December 31.

December 1991

397

Jerry Garcia plays on three tracks on *Bluegrass Reunion,* a compilation that is released in February.

FEBRUARY '92

| 1 ~ 15 | 16 | 17 |

Monday February 17
Cannibal serial killer Jeffrey Dahmer receives 15 life sentences—one for each of his victims—in a Milwaukee courtroom.

Aces Back To Back

Scott Allen's *Aces Back To Back: A Guide To The Grateful Dead* was published by Pierce Axiom this year, an offbeat look at the Dead through a series of essays about the band.

JANUARY '92

| 1 ~ 31 |

Noodling with Ken

Jerry Garcia and David Grisman backed up the extraordinary spoken stylings of Ken Nordine (*see December 31, 1990*), originator of "word jazz" and a hero of the young Jerry, on Nordine's *Devout Catalyst* album, released in January. Joe Craven and Jim Kerwin, Jerry and Dave's acoustic sidemen, contributed percussion and bass, respectively, with Howard Levy on keyboards. Tom Waits added his own brand of inimitable vocals to two tracks.

Left: *February 24, Oakland Coliseum Arena. The Dead celebrate Mardi Gras with another colorful parade.*

Saturday February 22
Sunday February 23
Monday February 24
Oakland Coliseum Arena, Oakland, California

Bruce Hornsby sits out the three-night run at the Oakland Coliseum that kicks off the performing year. The first show introduces two new originals. "So Many Roads" is a well-received Garcia/Hunter song full of allusions to old-time blues, folk, and jug band music. In *A Box of Rain*, Robert Hunter recalled the song's long gestation period:

"One afternoon, Jerry was playing some structured changes on the piano. Figuring they might be forgotten otherwise, I clicked on my tape recorder. Ten years later I found the tape and listened to it, liked it, and set these words to it."

The second new song, Hunter and Lesh's "Wave to the Wind," is one of the less successful originals of the band's last years. Neither the tune (which some Deadheads liken to the theme from *The Love Boat*) nor the lyrics (which read like the poetry of an oversensitive high-school freshman) find favor with '90s audiences who were, in Stephen Peters's words, "looking to boogie its collective ass off." The band retires "Wave to the Wind" after twenty more outings.

On the second night Babatunde Olatunji joins on "Drums" for a show in which two more originals, "Corinna" and "Way to Go Home," are unveiled. The first (and final) song from the creative troika of Messrs. Hunter, Hart, and Weir since "Playin' in the Band" and "The Greatest Story Ever Told," the laid-back, funky "Corinna" may or may not, according to the listener's perspective, have its roots in the much-covered folk-blues tune of the same name. "Way to Go Home" marks Vince Welnick's first songwriting credit for the band. A literal and figurative road song, Welnick and Bralove worked up the tune in a hotel room and mailed the resulting tape to Robert Hunter for versification.

Below: *A Deadhead takes a break at the Mardi Gras show 1992.*

February 1992

399

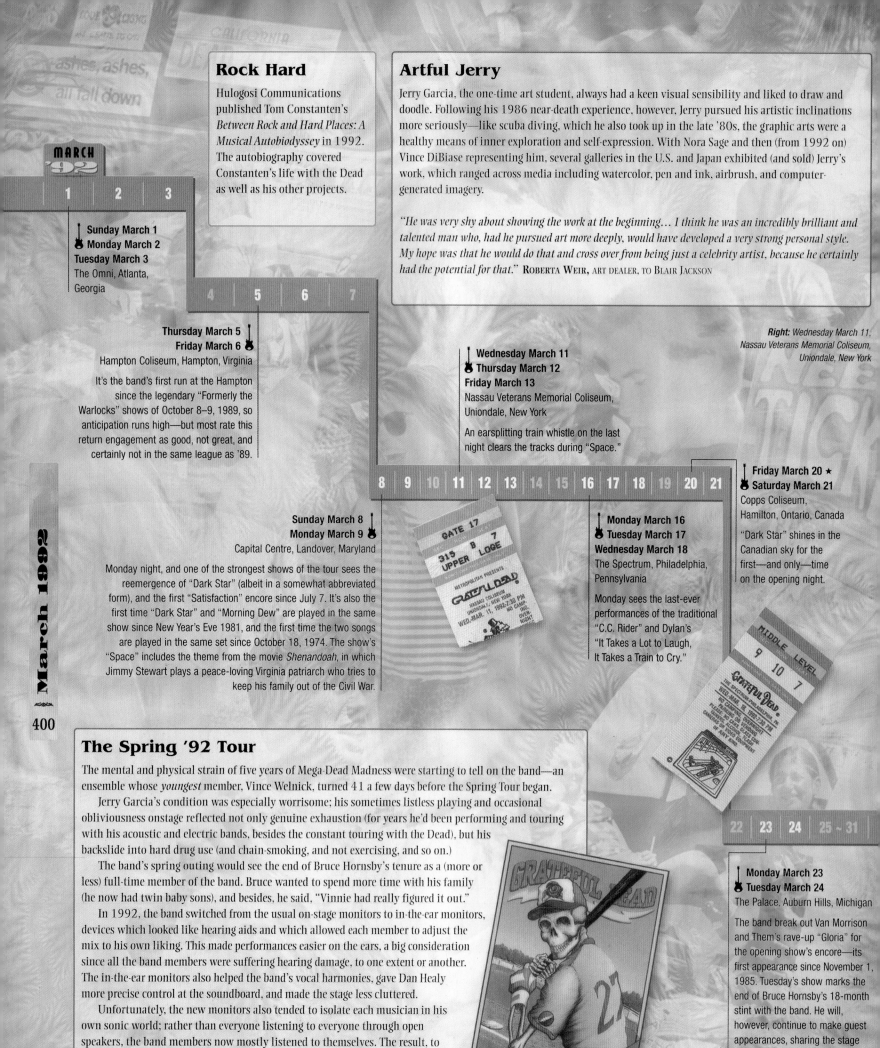

| 1 | 2 | 3 |

Rock Hard

Hulogosi Communications published Tom Constanten's *Between Rock and Hard Places: A Musical Autobiodyssey* in 1992. The autobiography covered Constanten's life with the Dead as well as his other projects.

Artful Jerry

Jerry Garcia, the one-time art student, always had a keen visual sensibility and liked to draw and doodle. Following his 1986 near-death experience, however, Jerry pursued his artistic inclinations more seriously—like scuba diving, which he also took up in the late '80s, the graphic arts were a healthy means of inner exploration and self-expression. With Nora Sage and then (from 1992 on) Vince DiBiase representing him, several galleries in the U.S. and Japan exhibited (and sold) Jerry's work, which ranged across media including watercolor, pen and ink, airbrush, and computer-generated imagery.

"He was very shy about showing the work at the beginning… I think he was an incredibly brilliant and talented man who, had he pursued art more deeply, would have developed a very strong personal style. My hope was that he would do that and cross over from being just a celebrity artist, because he certainly had the potential for that." ROBERTA WEIR, ART DEALER, TO BLAIR JACKSON

Sunday March 1
Monday March 2
Tuesday March 3
The Omni, Atlanta, Georgia

| 4 | 5 | 6 | 7 |

Thursday March 5
Friday March 6
Hampton Coliseum, Hampton, Virginia

It's the band's first run at the Hampton since the legendary "Formerly the Warlocks" shows of October 8–9, 1989, so anticipation runs high—but most rate this return engagement as good, not great, and certainly not in the same league as '89.

Wednesday March 11
Thursday March 12
Friday March 13
Nassau Veterans Memorial Coliseum, Uniondale, New York

An earsplitting train whistle on the last night clears the tracks during "Space."

Right: Wednesday March 11, Nassau Veterans Memorial Coliseum, Uniondale, New York

| 8 | 9 | 10 | 11 | 12 | 13 | 14 | 15 | 16 | 17 | 18 | 19 | 20 | 21 |

Friday March 20 ★
Saturday March 21
Copps Coliseum, Hamilton, Ontario, Canada

"Dark Star" shines in the Canadian sky for the first—and only—time on the opening night.

Sunday March 8
Monday March 9
Capital Centre, Landover, Maryland

Monday night, and one of the strongest shows of the tour sees the reemergence of "Dark Star" (albeit in a somewhat abbreviated form), and the first "Satisfaction" encore since July 7. It's also the first time "Dark Star" and "Morning Dew" are played in the same show since New Year's Eve 1981, and the first time the two songs are played in the same set since October 18, 1974. The show's "Space" includes the theme from the movie *Shenandoah*, in which Jimmy Stewart plays a peace-loving Virginia patriarch who tries to keep his family out of the Civil War.

Monday March 16
Tuesday March 17
Wednesday March 18
The Spectrum, Philadelphia, Pennsylvania

Monday sees the last-ever performances of the traditional "C.C. Rider" and Dylan's "It Takes a Lot to Laugh, It Takes a Train to Cry."

March 1992

The Spring '92 Tour

The mental and physical strain of five years of Mega-Dead Madness were starting to tell on the band—an ensemble whose *youngest* member, Vince Welnick, turned 41 a few days before the Spring Tour began.

Jerry Garcia's condition was especially worrisome; his sometimes listless playing and occasional obliviousness onstage reflected not only genuine exhaustion (for years he'd been performing and touring with his acoustic and electric bands, besides the constant touring with the Dead), but his backslide into hard drug use (and chain-smoking, and not exercising, and so on.)

The band's spring outing would see the end of Bruce Hornsby's tenure as a (more or less) full-time member of the band. Bruce wanted to spend more time with his family (he now had twin baby sons), and besides, he said, "Vinnie had really figured it out."

In 1992, the band switched from the usual on-stage monitors to in-the-ear monitors, devices which looked like hearing aids and which allowed each member to adjust the mix to his own liking. This made performances easier on the ears, a big consideration since all the band members were suffering hearing damage, to one extent or another. The in-the-ear monitors also helped the band's vocal harmonies, gave Dan Healy more precise control at the soundboard, and made the stage less cluttered.

Unfortunately, the new monitors also tended to isolate each musician in his own sonic world; rather than everyone listening to everyone through open speakers, the band members now mostly listened to themselves. The result, to many Deadheads, was a decline in the kind of spontaneous, collective playing that made the band's live shows so magical.

| 22 | 23 | 24 | 25 ~ 31 |

Monday March 23
Tuesday March 24
The Palace, Auburn Hills, Michigan

The band break out Van Morrison and Them's rave-up "Gloria" for the opening show's encore—its first appearance since November 1, 1985. Tuesday's show marks the end of Bruce Hornsby's 18-month stint with the band. He will, however, continue to make guest appearances, sharing the stage with the band nine more times, including one complete show *(see June 20, 1992).*

Fit to be Tied

First ice cream, now this: in the summer of 1992, Stonehenge Ltd. introduced a line of neckties with designs based on Jerry Garcia's artworks. Jerry had dismissed the idea when Stonehenge originally approached him with a proposal (reportedly, he compared ties to a hangman's noose), but somehow, it happened. The ties were a huge hit, selling in the hundreds of thousands at upscale department stores. The media had a field day, with headlines rarely failing to make some sort of lame tie/tie-dye reference. As Blair Jackson noted in his biography of Jerry, however, few accused him of "selling out." Instead, the Jerry Garcia tie became a sort of icon of stealth counterculture— wearers "[E]njoyed the ties for their subversive nature: if you had to wear a tie in your job, you could at least wear one designed by someone far removed from the Fortune 500 culture."

"The tie thing was something that more or less got away from him… [Stonehenge] took little pieces of a piece of art and duplicated the design and then added their own colors. Jerry said he wouldn't even recognize his own art on those ties."
SUE STEPHENS IN ROBERT GREENFIELD'S DARK STAR: AN ORAL BIOGRAPHY OF JERRY GARCIA.

Sunday April 12
More than 100 million people worldwide tune in to watch the opening ceremonies at Euro Disneyland, the U.S. company's $4-billion theme park outside Paris.

Thursday April 30
Today sees the first full day of rioting in the city's South-Central neighborhood following the acquittal of four Los Angeles police officers accused of beating an African-American motorist, Rodney King. Three days of violence, vandalism, and looting leave 37 people dead, more than 1,500 injured, and as much as $1 billion in property damage.

J. GARCIA
COLLECTOR'S EDITION

NIGHTFALL OF DIAMONDS
Tom Constanten

Released by Relix (RRCD 2046)
on May 15, 1992

1. **Cold Rain And Snow**
   (Traditional/Ramsey)
2. **Play The Game**
   (Mcshee/Portman-Smith)
3. **Wild Flowers**
   (Kallick)
4. **Ashokan Farewell**
   (Ungar)
5. **Dejavalse**
   (Constanten)
6. **Graceful Ghost**
   (Bolcom)
7. **Winter Shade Of Pale**
   (Brooker/Reid)
8. **Friend Of The Devil**
   (Dawson/Garcia/Hunter)
9. **Boris The Spider**
   (Entwistle)
10. **Dejavalentino**
    (Constanten)
11. **Oriental (Spanish Dance #2)**
    (Granados)
12. **Butterfly Rag**
    (Chopin)
13. **Chopped Liver**
    (Ryan)
14. **Fake Fur Elise**
    (Constanten)
15. **Speaking**
    (Forrester)
16. **Prelude In E Flat, Opus 23 #5**
    (Rachmaninoff)
17. **I Know You Rider**
    (Traditional)
18. **Goin' Home**
    (Jagger/Richards)
19. **Dark Star**
    (Grateful Dead/Robert Hunter)
20. **And We Bid You Goodnight**
    (Traditional)

Produced by Tom Constanten

PLAYING SOLO PIANO (with Henry Kaiser on guitar on an interstellar version of "Dark Star" and the Rolling Stones' bluesy "Goin' Home"), T.C. pitches a big musical tent under which Chopin and Rachmaninoff mingle with The Who ("Boris the Spider"), Procol Harum ("Whiter Shade of Pale") and, of course, T.C.'s old bandmates. The album is a luminous showcase for T.C.'s dexterity, imagination and sly sense of humor. He dips into a folk bag on versions of "Friend of the Devil," "Cold Rain and Snow," "I Know You Rider," and the lilting "Ashokan Farewell" (popularized on the Ken Burns documentary series *The Civil War*). Many of the other pieces show his affection for both classical and modern composers; in the latter category are works by Terry Ryan, William Bolcom, and T.C. himself. The disc's tracks move easily from simple melodic flights to abstract and dissonant space music, with plenty of twists and turns and unusual tangents in between; capped by a lovely arrangement of the song the Dead used to close many of their concerts during T.C.'s tenure with the band: the old Bahamian spiritual "And We Bid You Goodnight."

Idiot's Delight

The second collection of Robert Hunter's poems to be published, *Idiot's Delight*, comes out through Hanuman Books.

Saturday May 23
Sunday May 24
Monday May 25
Shoreline Amphitheatre, Mountain View, California

| 23 | 24 | 25 | 26 | 27 |

Above: *Sunday May 31, Sam Boyd Silver Bowl, Las Vegas, Nevada.*
Right: *Pictures from the Summer '92 Tour.*

| 28 | 29 | 30 | 31 |

Friday May 29
Saturday May 30
Sunday May 31 ★
Sam Boyd Silver Bowl, Las Vegas, Nevada

Play it again, Sam: the band's second run at this 42,000-seat outdoor Vegas venue yields what many consider the best shows of the year. Steve Miller opened all three nights. On Sunday Steve Miller joins in the second set and contributes some particularly tasty guitar to the "Baba O Riley"/ "Tomorrow Never Knows" encore.

| 18 | 19 | 20 | 21 | 22 |

MAY '92

| 1 ~ 14 | 15 | 16 | 17 |

Friday May 15
Release of *Nightfall of Diamonds* by Tom Constanten (Relix 2046).

Tuesday May 19
Wednesday May 20
Thursday May 21
Cal Expo Amphitheatre, Sacramento, California

Spring forward to summer: most Deadheads feel that the Summer '92 Tour sees the band in far better form than on the Spring Tour—although a number of 'Heads continue to profess disappointment at the changes in sound wrought by the introduction of in-the-ear monitors.

That other perpetual Deadhead concern, the state of Jerry Garcia's health, seems to hold cause for cautious optimism as well; he looks and plays better than he had in the Spring shows, though by July he is essentially running on fumes.

After the Spring Tour the band returns to Cal Expo for the annual run of Rex Foundation benefits. This year, each night's opening act is the winner of a Rex Foundation award or beneficiary of a Rex Foundation grant: Peter Apfelbaum, founder of Hieroglyphics Ensemble (Ralph. J. Gleason Award, 1989), David Grisman (Ralph J. Gleason Award, 1990), and Pharoah Sanders (grant beneficiary, 1992).

The first night opens with the David Grisman Quintet and closes with a terrific surprise: Vince Welnick leading the band in an encore medley of The Who's anthemic "Baba O Riley" and the Beatles' psychedelic "Tomorrow Never Knows." Vince later tells *The Grateful Dead Almanac* that the pairing is spontaneity followed by serendipity: "With 'Baba O Riley' I just started playing the intro and Billy just jumped right in. Pretty soon the whole band was all over it like a cat on a mouse. The way it got put together with 'Tomorrow Never Knows' was just a coincidence; Bobby Weir happened to bring that song into rehearsal on that same day." The crowd-pleasing combo will fall into the encore slot 11 more times.

Pete Townshend pays tribute to both his spiritual guru (Meher Baba) and his musical guru (minimalist composer Terry Riley) in the title of "Baba O Riley," the leadoff track on The Who's 1971 masterpiece *Who's Next*. Riley's electronic composition *A Rainbow in Curved Air* (1968) inspires Townshend to explore the possibilities the synthesizer had for rock music.

The Hieroglyphics Ensemble, the acclaimed free-jazz orchestra founded by Peter Apfelbaum (like Phil Lesh, a Berkeley High music program alum) in 1977, opens on Wednesday, while Bay Area jazz great Pharoah Sanders, master of the tenor sax and a protégé of John Coltrane, opens on Thursday.

"You know, a day not spent with the Grateful Dead is really missing out on life to some extent." VINCE WELNICK TO BLAIR JACKSON

Saturday June 20 ★
RFK Stadium, Washington, D.C.

The train whistle during "Drums" announces the arrival of the first "Casey Jones" since November 2, 1984. Steve Miller opens, and Miller and Bruce Hornsby (on accordion) for the "One More Saturday Night" closer and the "Baba O Riley"/"Tomorrow Never Knows" encore.

Al's well: among those in attendance at RFK are Al Gore, who will shortly be tapped as Bill Clinton's running-mate in the upcoming presidential race, and his wife Tipper.

| 22 | 23 | 24 | 25 | 26 | 27 | 28 | 29 | 30 |

Monday June 22
Tuesday June 23
Star Lake Amphitheater, Burgettstown, Pennsylvania

"Dark Star" appears for the third time in two weeks on Monday but, as with many of its outings this year, it's a short version.

Thursday June 25
Friday June 26
Soldier Field, Chicago, Illinois

Steve Miller opens and sits in for several second-set songs. So does the great blues harmonica player James Cotton (a.k.a. "Mr. Superharp"), who adds some of that deep-dish Chicago blues flavor to "Good Mornin' Little Schoolgirl" (the first since August 22, 1987), "Turn on Your Love Light," and the encore, "Gloria."

Sunday June 28 ★
Monday June 29
Deer Creek Music Center, Noblesville, Indiana

Sunday is the last-ever "To Lay Me Down"— and an exceedingly fine performance.

Wednesday June 17
Thursday June 18
Charlotte Coliseum, Charlotte, North Carolina

Thursday sees the last-ever "Dark Star Jam."

Thursday June 11
Friday June 12
Knickerbocker Arena, Albany, New York

JUNE '92

| 1 ~ 5 | 6 | 7 | 8 | 9 | 10 | 11 | 12 | 13 | 14 | 15 | 16 | 17 | 18 |

Saturday June 6
Rich Stadium, Orchard Park, New York

Steve Miller opens.

Monday June 8
Tuesday June 9
Richfield Coliseum, Richfield, Ohio

Sunday June 14
Monday June 15
Giants Stadium, East Rutherford, New Jersey

Steve Miller opens both shows.

| 19 | 20 | 21 |

Dance Music Scene

At first sight, there is little in common between the Grateful Dead and the dance music boom that swept the U.S. and Europe in the late '80s and early '90s . The Dead, founded on principles of musicianship, songcraft, and the ability to play one's instrument, seem an antithesis to the latter, with the thud of its repetitive beat and plethora of hard-edged bleeps and bass. But if one delves a little deeper there is plenty of common ground in the culture and ethos behind both.

Dance music was born out of the disco scene, and a fearless sense of exploration by certain individuals (sound familiar?). Among their number was a DJ with a mid-'80s residency at Chicago's Warehouse club—Frankie Knuckles. His pioneering techniques included extending the rhythm sections of disco tracks and creating different effects and beats using drum machines and samplers; the new sound he created would take the name of the nightclub where it was spawned—"house" music had been born. A couple of Chicago house record companies soon sprang up and the new music began to reach a wider audience, especially in New York and Detroit, where it quickly evolved into "garage" and "techno," respectively.

It was inevitable that house and its offspring would go mainstream, but in 1986 the U.S. wasn't ready. Many Americans still associated the music with the black and gay communities,

so in time-honored tradition the music had to cross the water to Great Britain and Europe before it could take off in the States.

The American and European scenes that grew up around dance music in the late '80s and early '90s were very much products of their era and the new music, but they also represented the latest iteration of an older tradition of experimentation and freedom—a wave the Pranksters and the Dead had ridden 20 years earlier during the Acid Tests. In the UK, "Acid House" raves saw thousands dancing in fields and at illegal warehouse parties under the influence of acid and ecstasy; the smiley face became a symbol of turned-on, loved up individuals everywhere. In the U.S. and mainland Europe, similar things were happening, too, although the parties took place more in clubs than the outdoors.

"Anything goes" was the mantra and every Saturday night would see the same setup: decks, DJ, music, light show, drugs, dancing; self-expression, freedom, and togetherness; tabloid terror, establishment paranoia, and parental angst. The spirit of improvisation, spontaneity, and collectivity was still very much alive 20 years on; its older brother may have had the social conscience, but this was Generation X's very own post-punk interpretation—slick and every bit as relevant to its era as the peace and love of the 1960s.

"I'm basically a lazy fuck. Things have to get to the point where they're screaming before I'll do anything... In a way I was lucky insofar as I had an iron constitution. But time naturally gets you, and finally your body just doesn't spring back the way it did..."

JERRY GARCIA TO ANTHONY DECURTIS IN *ROLLING STONE*, OCTOBER 1993.

AUGUST '92

| 1 | 2 | 3 | 4 | 5 | 6 |

Sunday August 2
Jerry collapses at his new home in Marin County.

July 1992

404

JULY '92

| 1 | 2 | 3 | 4 | 5 | 6 | 7 | 8 |

Above: DJs rule the roost in the dance music scene.

Wednesday July 1
🎸 Buckeye Lake Music Center
Hebron, Ohio

Tom Petty opens and guests, along with his longtime harmonica player, Norton Buffalo, one of the great harp virtuosos who's played with (among many others) Merl Saunders and Mickey Hart.

Thursday July 9
Release of *Fire Up Plus* by Merl Saunders and Friends—a compilation of Merl Saunders songs. Jerry Garcia plays on every song.

Right: Wednesday July 1, Buckeye Lake Music Center.

| 9 | 10 | 11 | 12 | 13 | 14 | 15 | 16 | 17 | 18 | 19 | 20 | 21 |

Infrared Sightings

1992 saw the release of *Infrared Sightings*, an 18-minute video of three tracks—"Riverside Rhapsody," "Post-Modern Highrise Table Top Stomp," and "Infrared Roses"—recorded live in 1990 and mixed in with computer animation. It was produced by Len Dell'Amico and Larry Lachman.

> # "I mean, it's a powerful incentive, the possibility that, hey, if you're going the way you are, in two years you're going to be dead."
>
> JERRY GARCIA TO ANTHONY DECURTIS IN *ROLLING STONE, OCTOBER 1993.*

Jerry's Collapse

Jerry Garcia had expressed a desire for a nice long break in an October 1991 *Rolling Stone* interview, but after the Grateful Dead came off the road, he took the Jerry Garcia Band out on a tour of California venues. On August 3 (two days after his 50th birthday) Jerry returned to the palatial new Marin County home he shared with Manasha Matheson.

The next day he could barely move, or breathe. While he didn't go into full-blown coma as he had in 1986, his overtaxed body had once again simply shut down. Jerry would later be diagnosed with an enlarged heart, respiratory problems, and a variety of related ailments.

There was no question of the Grateful Dead performing again until Jerry was up to it, so the band canceled the next 23 announced shows, including what was to have been the third "decennial" trip to Veneta, Oregon (see page 147).

Getting Better, Again

Jerry refused to go the hospital, so Manasha brought in a parade of specialists to attend the ailing guitarist, including a Chinese herbalist, an acupuncturist, and various New Age healers. This didn't go down well with many in the band's organization, who would have preferred a more conventional and rigorous approach to getting Jerry back on his feet. Whatever the merits of the treatments, Jerry did improve. It seemed that he had realized at last that the road of excess might lead not to wisdom, as William Blake had it, but to premature death instead, and that realization gave him a new level of self-discipline. Jerry swore off ice cream and M&Ms in favor of organic vegetables, dropping more than the 60 pounds in five months. He again cut down on his cigarette habit (he once observed that it was harder for him to give up his Pall Malls than his heroin). He relaxed with Keelin, his youngest daughter *(above)*. It was the vacation he had wanted for so long.

21 | 22 | 23 | 24 | 25 | 26 | 27 | 28 | 29 | 30 | 31

7

J. Garcia: Paintings, Drawings and Sketches

Published by Celestial Arts in September '92, and edited by David Hinds, this book presented dozens of Jerry Garcia's artworks, all created between 1985 and 1991. The great poster artist Victor Moscoso—creator of the cover art for Jerry's first solo album and the Jerry Garcia Band's *Run for the Roses*—contributed the afterword. Talking about Jerry, the book's jacket noted: "His work with visual arts has always been a personal amusement, and the notion of selling his paintings has come about in a purely accidental way."

"I hope that nobody takes them too seriously." JERRY GARCIA FROM THE JACKET TO *PAINTINGS, DRAWINGS AND SKETCHES*

Left, above and opposite: Saturday October 31, Oakland Coliseum Arena, Oakland, California.

Backstage Pass

Released in October on Grateful Dead Records, this 35-minute video was directed by Bill Kreutzmann's son, Justin, and contained rare film of the band from 1964 through 1992, as well as animation by Xaos.

Goin' Down the Road: A Grateful Dead Traveling Companion is published. Much of Blair Jackson's book is based on material originally published in *The Golden Road*, the fanzine that he had edited since 1984. The Companion features articles by Steve Brown and Steve Silberman, interviews with members of the band, a guide to the pick of the years' shows for tape collectors, and a section on the cover songs performed by the Dead.

Also published is *Bill Graham Presents: My Life Inside Rock and Out*. This Doubleday-published book by Graham and Robert Greenfield is essentially an autobiography that Graham himself was contributing to until his death in 1991. It consists of quotes and anecdotes from friends and family.

SEPTEMBER '92

1 - 30

OCTOBER '92

1 2 3 4 5 6 7 8 9 10 11 12 13 14 **15** 16 | 17 18 19 20 21 22 23 24 25 26 27 28 29 30 **31**

Thursday October 15
Video release of the Dead's *Backstage Pass* on Grateful Dead Records.

Saturday October 31
The (not so) Big Man is Back: slimmed down and displaying more onstage energy than he's had for years, Jerry Garcia leads the JGB through a Halloween show at the Oakland Coliseum Arena, Oakland, California, that's a welcome treat for all *(right)*. Vince Welnick's new side band, The Affordables, opens.

"The whole month in Hawaii was so unbelievable. It really did feel we'd created a time warp and were right back where we left off." BARBARA MEIER ON HOOKING UP AGAIN WITH JERRY GARCIA IN DECEMBER 1992

The 1992 release of *He's All I Need* by the San Quentin Mass Choir is recorded by Mickey Hart and funded by the Rex Foundation. Music for the album is performed by inmates and staff of San Quentin Prison.

NOVEMBER '92

1	2	3	4	5	6	7 ~ 30

DECEMBER '92

1	2	3	4

Tuesday November 3
Democrat Bill Clinton (and his Dead fan running-mate, Al Gore) defeat Republican incumbent George W. Bush in the presidential election.

Wednesday December 2
Thursday December 3
McNichols Sports Arena, Denver, Colorado

Five months and one day after the Grateful Dead's last performance, the band takes the stage for a show inevitably dubbed "Comeback II" by Deadheads. Besides the elation at Jerry's recovery and the band's resumption of touring, local 'Heads are psyched because it's only the band's second appearance at this venue since '81, and only the second Colorado run since 1987. It's an emotional evening, of course, but the musical highlight is the encore—another Vince-led venture into Beatles territory, in this case "Rain," one of Lennon & McCartney's early (1966) forays into psychedelia. The band's version even replicates—live—the backwards singing on the last verse, which John Lennon achieved with a tape loop on the original: "daeh rieht edih dna nur yeht semoc niar eht fl..." Weir sings this verse, probably inspired by Dave Nelson, whose "party trick" is to speak backwards—or maybe the dyslexia that dogged Weir's school days is now coming in handy.

5	6

Saturday December 5
Sunday December 6 ★
Compton Terrace Amphitheatre, Chandler, Arizona

Sunday's standout show starts with the first "Here Comes Sunshine" since February 23, 1974, in an arrangement courtesy of Vince Welnick; Deadheads are thrilled at the song's revival but divided about the new version.

Below: December 5–6, Compton Terrance Amphitheatre, Chandler, Arizona. Arizona was one of the few places the Dead could play outdoors in December; a treat for tourheads.

November 1992

408

The Comeback Tour

With Jerry Garcia rested and recovered, the band announces its tour schedule for the remainder of the year—four shows in Colorado and Arizona, followed by a five-show mid-December run at the Oakland Coliseum.

Above, right, and below: Photo shoot of Jerry Garcia looking well, taken December 10, 1992, at an opening of Jerry's art work.

Wednesday December 9
U.S. troops land in Somalia in an effort to protect relief supplies in the starving, anarchic East African nation.

Friday December 11
Saturday December 12
Sunday December 13
Wednesday December 16
Thursday December 17
Oakland Coliseum Arena, Oakland, California

At Saturday's show Yothu Yindi, an Australian band that blends rock 'n' roll with Aboriginal music, opens.

Another Kind of Comeback

With no New Year's Eve show to worry about, Jerry Garcia planned to depart for Hawaii at the end of December. Manasha Matheson, however, would not be going with him. Over the last few months, Jerry had resumed his relationship—after three decades—with Barbara Meier, his girlfriend from the Palo Alto days. While Jerry seemed to have acquired the discipline to work on his health problems following his August collapse, his passive-aggressive loathing for emotional confrontation remained unchanged: instead of telling Manasha the news himself, he delegated the ugly task to Vince DiBiase, manager of his art business. This led Jerry to become estranged from Manasha and their daughter Keelin.

Left: Saturday December 5, Compton Terrace Amphitheatre, Chandler, Arizona. Many descendants of the Merry Pranksters' original bus followed the Dead on the road.

December 1992

409

1 ~ 19   20

Wednesday January 20
William Jefferson Clinton is sworn in as the nation's 42nd president. Reportedly, the incoming administration contacted the Grateful Dead about the possibility of playing one of the inaugural events, but the band begged off. Bob Weir and Ron Wasserman do play in D.C. that evening.

Opposite page: Mardi Gras Show, Tuesday February 23, Oakland Coliseum Arena, Oakland, California.

21   22   23   24   25   26

3458
GEN. ADM.
JAN 24, 1993

BILL GRAHAM PRESENTS
Grateful Dead.

OAKLAND COLISEUM ARENA
OAKLAND, CA

JANUARY 24, 1993
SUNDAY • 7:00 PM

NO SMOKING ALLOWED
IN THE ARENA!!

NO CAMPING, OVERNIGHT PARKING OR VENDING.

Sunday January 24
Monday January 25
Tuesday January 26
Oakland Coliseum Arena, Oakland, California

Acrobats open the Chinese New Year's show on Tuesday, which includes the traditional Dragon Dance during "Drums." Another guest is Carlos Santana, who sits in for the second set, post-"Drums."

1 ~ 20   21   22   23

Sunday February 21
Monday February 22
Tuesday February 23 ★
Oakland Coliseum Arena,
Oakland, California

The Oakland run sees the band roll out a bunch of new songs. Sunday marks the debut of "Lazy River Road," "Liberty," and the Willie Dixon collaboration "Eternity," while the second night sees the breakout of another Hunter/Garcia original, "Days Between"—the last of the 61 songs the two wrote together for the Dead. Tuesday is a great show. It's Mardi Gras, and Ornette Coleman, one of the greatest living jazz musicians, is the opening act. Garcia joins Coleman and his band, Prime Time, for the final part of their set, and Coleman joins the Dead for "Drums" and "Space" and the rest of the second set. (Graham Wiggins, multi-instrumental whiz with a PhD in physics, also sits in on drums with his didgeridoo.) And if this isn't enough there's a new song—sung by Phil Lesh, no less—a well-received cover of Robbie Robertson's "Broken Arrow," from the ex-Band-man's self-titled 1987 album. (Yes, the same "Broken Arrow" with which Rod Stewart had a hit.)

Friday February 26
A terrorist bomb explodes in a parking garage underneath the World Trade Center in New York City, killing five and injuring hundreds more.

Above: Tuesday January 26, Chinese New Year Show, Oakland Coliseum Arena, Oakland, California.

24   25   26   27   28

The Willie Dixon Connection

The Grateful Dead shared the stage with scores of great musicians, but Willie Dixon is certainly the most distinguished artist to share a writing credit on one of the band's originals. Even before the collaboration, Dixon had been very much part of the Grateful Dead live experience. The band had eight Dixon numbers in the rotation over the years—more than any other songwriter, Dylan and Lennon/McCartney excepted. The opportunity to work with the blues legend was therefore not to be passed up.

While recording a track for Rob Wasserman's *Trios* album *(see page 423)*, Dixon wrote up some lyrics to a tune Bob Weir was working on. Bob initially thought the lyrics were "awfully simplistic," but matched to the tune they worked perfectly and the song cooked. "Now you see it," Dixon laughed after the first run-through. "That's the wisdom of the blues." "Eternity" was Willie Dixon's last composition; he died on January 19, 1992, just over a year before the song's first performance in Oakland.

> "To know him was to realize he was a true, simple genius in capital letters. Maybe the only one I've ever met."
>
> BOB WEIR

Above: Tuesday January 26, Chinese New Year Show, Oakland Coliseum Arena, Oakland, California.

Left: Ornette Coleman plays the Mardi Gras Show, Tuesday February 23.

The band, and especially the reenergized Jerry Garcia, play well on their 1993 Spring Tour, and if audiences aren't entirely thrilled about some of the band's choices of material (e.g., "I Fought the Law"), several of the new originals and the Garcia-led cover of The Beatles' "Lucy in the Sky With Diamonds" quickly become audience favorites.

The tour begins with Jerry's personal life in turmoil again. His reunion with Barbara Meier turns out to be just a brief idyll and in March the two break up. Jerry has begun seeing another old girlfriend, in this case Deborah Koons, with whom he'd been involved in the '70s, and who is now an independent filmmaker. And, despite his health crisis the previous summer, Jerry is once again backsliding into hard drug use in the spring of '93.

Saving the Music

Mickey Hart, the staff of the Library of Folk Culture, and Rykodisc representatives hold a major event at the Library of Congress' Madison Building to launch the Endangered Music Project, which will release the music of indigenous people from around the world, with Mickey and Dr. Allen Jabbour as curators and producers. The rest of the band and major figures from Congress, including Senator Patrick Leahy, show up to support Mickey. *"The... Project is being launched to highlight Traditional music as an endangered cultural resource throughout the world. Proceeds from the project will be used to support the performers and their cultures, as well as the release of additional recordings in the series."* FROM THE LIBRARY OF CONGRESS' PRESS RELEASE

March saw the release of *Various Artists – The Spirit Cries: Music from the Rainforests of South America & the Caribbean.* Produced and edited by Mickey Hart, this was the first CD to emerge from the Project. *The Spirit Cries* included field recordings (some dating back to the 1940s) of the music of indigenous peoples of Latin America and the Caribbean.

1 | 2 | 3 | 4 | 5 | 6 | 7 | 8 | 9 | 10 | 11 | 1

FLOOR
SEC | ROW | SEAT
3 | 21 | 4

JAM PRODUCTIONS Presents
GRATEFUL DEAD
ROSEMONT HORIZON
ROSEMONT, IL
WED. • MAR. 10, 1993 • 7:30 PM
NO CAMPING, OVERNIGHT PARKING
Please: No cans, glass containers,
alcohol, flash cameras or
video equipment of ANY kind.

Tuesday March 9
Wednesday March 10
Thursday March 11
Rosemont Horizon Arena, Rosemont, Illinois

Wednesday night marks the last ever "Mind Left Body Jam." At the next show, on his home turf—Chicagoland—word-jazz master Ken Nordine takes the mic during "Space" to recite two of his most famous pieces, "Flibberty Jib" and "The Island." (In another bit of Dead synchronicity, "Flibberty Jib" is enjoying new popularity thanks to its use in a Levi's commercial.)

Saturday March 20
Sunday March 21
Monday March 22
The Omni, Atlanta, Georgia

Monday March 15
Library of Congress Endangered Music Project (see above).

13 | 14 | 15 | 16 | 17 | 18 | 19 | 20 | 21 | 22 | 23

"CASEY JONES"
GARCIA/HUNTER

"Drivin' that train, high on cocaine." Combining the tragic story of a real-life turn-of-the-century train wreck with the riding-off-the-rail drug ethos that governed much of the counterculture 1970s, "Casey Jones" became a controversial FM radio staple and one of the Dead's signature songs soon after its appearance on the band's *Workingman's Dead* album in 1970. Unlike the tweaked conductor of Garcia and Hunter's version, the real engineer behind the legend was John Luther Jones (nicknamed "Casey" after his hometown of Cayce, Kentucky), whose tardiness and decision to ignore a signal to stop resulted in a fatal train wreck on the Illinois Central Railroad's Chicago–New Orleans Line in April of 1900. Jones' friend Wallace Saunders wrote the first of many folk songs about the incident days after the actual accident, and the Dead themselves had worked a traditional version of "Ballad of Casey Jones" into their set lists not long after they began presenting their own take on the tale in 1969.

In a 1972 interview with *Rolling Stone*, Garcia attributed the song's popularity to its bouncy tempo and "that sing-songy thing—a little melody that gets into your head... [Hunter] had the words, and the words were just so exquisite. They were just so perfect that I just sat down with the words, picked up a guitar, and played the song. It just came out. It just triggered." Though "Casey Jones" rode through nearly 300 Grateful Dead shows, the group played the song less than three dozen times between 1977 and 1984, with three more passes in 1992 and a final read at the Knickerbocker Arena in Albany, New York, on March 27, 1993. Fans rejoiced when Lesh began working this Dead classic into his Phil and Friends shows in 1999, a treat that was followed by five performances of the cut by The Other Ones in 2002. The newly redubbed Dead also played the song with guest vocalist Joan Osborne during their debut show on February 14, 2003, suggesting that "this old engine" might still have some life in it yet.

Right: Spread from Grateful Dead Comix No.1.

Tuesday March 16
Wednesday March 17 ★
Thursday March 18
Capital Centre, Landover, Maryland

The second (and best) show of a strong run at the Cap Centre features a short-form "Dark Star" and the first "Two Soldiers Jam" since September 12, 1990. The encore is another exercise in psychedelenostalgia courtesy of Mr. Garcia—The Beatles' "Lucy in the Sky with Diamonds," which is a real crowd-pleaser, for obvious reasons. On Thursday, Bruce Hornsby swings by to lay down accordion for the entire second set.

Sunday March 14
Richfield Coliseum, Richfield, Ohio

Bad weather (in Ohio? In March? Who knew...?) forced the cancellation of the previous night's show, but when the Dead do finally appear in Richfield, they break out probably the most disliked encore ever—The Bobby Fuller Four's 1966 outlaw ode "I Fought the Law," (a Garcia favorite) latterly covered by the Clash, the Dead Kennedys, and every bar and frat-party band in the known universe. As a one-off or occasional novelty "IFTL" might be OK... but a three-minute, three-chord rocker with no jamming potential and no particular relevance to the Grateful Dead (or to anything else of significance to most Deadheads) as an *encore*? It was whispered in some quarters that the band (or, more precisely, Jerry) used IFTL as a way of getting offstage ASAP, especially after less than inspiring shows. Despite its bad rep, IFTL turned up 35 more times, always in the encore slot. (For a hilarious account of IFTL's introduction to the rotation, check out Brian Dykke's review of the show in *The Deadhead's Tapiping Compendium, Volume III.*)

HARBOR LIGHTS
Bruce Hornsby

RCA 66114

Without the Range but with an all-star cast of guest musicians, Bruce Hornsby's latest offering included Jerry Garcia on guitar on two tracks, "Passing Through" and "Pastures Of Plenty." Pat Metheny, Phil Collins, and Debbie Harry were among the other musicians who contributed to the album.

BRUCE HORNSBY

HARBOR LIGHTS

Wednesday March 24 ★
Thursday March 25 ★
Dean Smith Center, University of North Carolina, Chapel Hill, North Carolina

24 **25** **26**

Below and right: Monday April 12, singing "The Star-Spangled Banner" at Candlestick Park, San Francisco.

27 **28** **29** **30**

Saturday March 27
Sunday March 28
Monday March 29
Knickerbocker Arena, Albany, New York

Saturday sees the final "Casey Jones" *(see left).*

Wednesday March 31
Thursday April 1
Friday April 2
Sunday April 4
Monday April 5
Nassau Veterans Memorial Coliseum, Uniondale, New York

Touch of... purple? As the second set opens with "Iko Iko" on the April Fool's Day show, Barney the Dinosaur appears onstage wearing Phil Lesh's bass. (However, Phil was *not* the person in the Barney suit.) Given the nature of things, however, this is probably not the first time someone saw a purple dinosaur at a show. On Sunday Babatunde Olatunji guests on "Drums" for what's considered the best show of a strong run at this Deadhead stronghold.

APRIL '93

31 | **1** | **2** | **3** | **4** | **5** | **6** | **7** | **8** | **9** | **10** | **11**

Monday April 12
Candlestick Park, San Francisco, California

Jerry Garcia, Bob Weir, and Vince Welnick take the pitcher's mound at Candlestick Park *(left)* to sing "The Star-Spangled Banner" at the San Francisco Giants' home opener against the Florida Marlins (the Giants won). In an interview with Paul Liberatore of the *Marin Independent Journal*, Vince described an unforeseen consequence of the event: "I can't even go to the grocery store now without a bunch of sports fans jumping on me."

12 | **13 ~ 18** | **19** | **20 ~ 30**

Monday April 19
The FBI assaults the fortified compound of the Branch Davidians religious cult in Waco, Texas, in an effort to end a siege begun on February 28. More than 100 people die in the fire that results.

413

The Grateful Dead's story

Another GD book hit the stores with the publication of *The Story of the Grateful Dead* by Adrian Hall. Published by Magna Books/Longmeadow Press, it was a look back at the history of the band plus photos.

JUNE '93

| 1 | 2 | 3 | 4 | 5 | 6 | 7 |

| 24 | 25 | 26 | 27 | 28 ~ 31 |

Saturday June 5
Sunday June 6

Giants Stadium, East Rutherford, New Jersey

Sting opens both nights. The first night sees the debut of another new original. "Easy Answers," a team effort by Robert Hunter, Bob Bralove, Bob Weir, Vince Welnick, and Rob Wasserman, had already been earmarked to appear on Wasserman's *Trios* album *(see page 423)*, making the song, as Oliver Trager points out in *The American Book of the Dead*, the first Grateful Dead song to be released on another artist's album prior to making it onto a GD disc. "Easy Answers" later found its way into The Other Ones repertoire and a version appears on 2000's *Furthur Most.*

Neil Young had a bit to do with the genesis of "Easy Answers," as Rob Wasserman described in the liner notes to *Trios:*

"The night before this session Bob Weir and I were rehearsing a song idea for our trio with Neil Young. The next day Neil, Bobby and I were sitting in Neil's ancient Cadillac listening to both songs, and we decided to record the newer one from the previous evening which, needless to say, became "Easy Answers." Bobby recorded his lead vocal around midnight. Neil and I wouldn't let him do it over again as we both felt he had captured the true spirit of a preacher in his late night delivery."

Friday May 14
Saturday May 15
★ Sunday May 16
Sam Boyd Silver Bowl,
Las Vegas, Nevada

Sting opens all three shows.

MAY '93

| 1 ~ 12 | 13 | 14 | 15 | 16 | 17 | 18 | 19 | 20 |

| 21 | 22 | 23 |

Friday May 21
Saturday May 22
Sunday May 23
Shoreline Amphitheatre,
Mountain View, California

"Supplication Jam" is played for the first time on Saturday since October 31, 1984—and for the last time.

Tuesday May 25
Wednesday May 26
Thursday May 27 ★
Cal Expo Amphitheatre,
Sacramento California

The X Factor is in evidence on the second night of the annual Rex Foundation benefit run—a show considered by many Tapers to be one of best of the band's last couple of years, especially the second set, and "Playin' in the Band." Thursday is another great show, capped by a rip-roaring "Gloria" encore.

May 1993

414

'90s Deadheads

To paraphrase the classic bumper sticker, who were the Deadheads of the '90s, and why did they keep following the band around?

As always, what constitutes a "Deadhead" and how many of them existed, at whatever level of Deadication, are subjects of irresolvable debate. By the early 1990s the Dead had become both the countercultural establishment and the established counterculture. The 'Heads of the '60s and '70s were now bringing their kids to shows, and a guy who went to shows was the proverbial heartbeat away from the presidency. We were, truly, everywhere. But for the purposes of this discussion, the question is, who were the rank-and-file of the Deadhead subculture in the band's last years, especially the (relatively small) percentage of them who followed the band for as many shows as possible?

It's impossible to construct a profile of the "typical" Deadhead of the 1990s. (As with Newton's Third Law of Motion, for every statement you can make about the band and its fans, an equal and opposite statement can apply.) But certain generalizations can be made. The Deadheads of the '90s tended to be young (teens through early 30s), white, male, (though not outnumbering females by a huge margin), and from middle-class backgrounds—in short, they were drawn from much the same demographic base as most rock fans. Deadheads did tend to be somewhat better educated than other rock fans, and the band attracted a perhaps disproportionate percentage of fans from high-income families. ("Trustafarians" shuttling between shows in dad's Beemer was a '90s Deadhead archetype.)

Prep schools, colleges, and universities were all Dead bastions. (It's no coincidence that the Dead's typical tour itineraries generally overlapped with the parts of the country with the biggest concentrations of institutions of higher learning.) Some areas—Long Island, Western New York State, the Washington, D.C. metro area—also seemed to produce more Deadheads than others.

As to why '90s Deadheads followed the Dead around, there are lots of sociological studies that break it down, but probably the two biggest attractions were (1) the sense of community around the Dead scene, community being an increasingly rare item in

an increasingly stratified and deracinated American society; and (2) adventure. As Jerry Garcia put it: "It is this time frame's version of the archetypal American adventure. It used to be that you could run away and join the circus, say, or ride the freight trains." In the '90s, following the Dead was as close as American middle-class youth could get to Kerouac's joy-and-kicks highway or Whitman's open road.

Devoted spinners

One interesting development in the Deadhead world in these years was the emergence of various subcultures within the subculture. The one that got the most attention was the "Spinners"—or more properly, members of the Family of Unlimited Devotion. The nickname derived from their ecstatic dancing at shows, inevitably compared to that of the Sufi "dervishes," the Islamic mystics who seek experience of Allah through intense motion.

A syncretistic, communal group that eschewed sex and drugs, the Family did not (contrary to popular belief) worship Jerry Garcia as God. They used the band's music in worship services and were a constant presence at shows (and not always a welcome one, thanks to their habit of "scamming in" without tickets).

Jerry had mixed feelings about the Family. He said it was "really neat" that the Dead gave Family members "a place where they can be comfortable enough to do something with such abandon," but when an interviewer asked how he felt about being an object of religious devotion (at least obliquely), he replied, "I'll put up with it until they come for me with the cross and the nails."

8 **9** **10**

🎸 **Tuesday June 8**
🎸 **Wednesday June 9**
The Palace, Auburn Hills,
Michigan

🎸 **Friday June 11**
🥁 Buckeye Lake
Music Center,
Hebron, Ohio

Sting opens.

Sunday June 13
Rich Stadium, Orchard Park, New York

Sting opens, and Jerry Garcia sits in for two songs during the ex-Policeman's set. This is also the last of the band's six shows at this Western New York venue.

🎸 **Tuesday June 15**
🥁 **Wednesday June 16**
Freedom Hall, Louisville, Kentucky

Sting opens both shows at Soldier Field.

11 **12** **13**

15 **16** **17** **18** **19** **20**

🎸 **Friday June 18**
🥁 **Saturday June 19**
Soldier Field, Chicago, Illinois

Friday's show is one of the worst of the year, in the opinion of many Tapers.

21 **22** **23** **24**

Below: Sunday June 13, Rich Stadium, Orchard Park, New York.

🎸 **Monday June 21**
🎸 **Tuesday June 22**
🥁 **Wednesday June 23**
Deer Creek Music Center,
Noblesville, Indiana

🎸 **Friday June 25**
🥁 **Saturday June 26**
RFK Stadium, Washington, DC

Sting opens both shows. Saturday is the last night of the East Coast Summer Tour Masterpiece '93. Bruce Hornsby is onstage with his squeezebox on both days.

June 1993

415

25 **26** **27** **28** **29** **30**

Left: Friday June 25, RFK Stadium, Washington, D.C.. Market stall. At any given Dead show, one could always find many people adept at juggling, a fine pursuit under the influence of pot or psychedelics.

LAWN
0361

BILL GRAHAM
PRESENTS
WITH
FIELD TRIP
PRODUCTIONS
AND DOUBLE TEE

GRATEFUL
DEAD.

WITH SPECIAL GUEST
INDIGO GIRLS
AUTZEN STADIUM • UNIVERSITY OF OREGON
EUGENE, OREGON
SUN. • AUG. 22, 1993 • 2:00 PM
Please: No cans, glass containers, alcohol,
flash cameras or video equipment of ANY kind.
NO VENDING, CAMPING OR OVERNIGHT PARKING.
(PRICE INCLUDES FACILITY FEE)
$26.00

★ Saturday August 21
★ Sunday August 22
Autzen Stadium,
Eugene, Oregon

The Indigo Girls open both shows. On the first
night Huey Lewis plays harp on "Good Mornin'
Little Schoolgirl," "Smokestack Lightning," and
"The Last Time." After the second show *(above
left)*, Kesey, Ken Babbs, & Co. perform Kesey's
new play "Twister" in a Eugene theater, with
some help from Jerry Garcia and Huey Lewis.

Hunter's Publications

1993 saw the release of a number of publications
written or contributed to by Robert Hunter.
Infinity Minus Eleven: Poems was a limited edition
of thirteen of Hunter's poems (each illustrated
by Bob DeVine) published by Cityful Press. The
Hulogosi-published *Duino Elegies/The Sonnets of
Orpheus* saw the original 1989 release of Hunter's
translation of *Duino Elegies* repackaged along with
a new translation of the Sonnets. This collection
was substantially illustrated with block prints by
Maureen Hunter. It was also available as a spoken-
word cassette with Robert Hunter narrating.
*A Box of Rain: Lyrics 1965–1993 (expanded
edition)*, published by Penguin Poets, was an
updated version of the 1990 Viking-published
collected lyrics and notes for Hunter's Grateful
Dead songs as well as his other projects.

416

In August Jerry brings out a new MIDI guitar.
Made by the late luthier Stephen Cripe, it is
decorated with a lightning bolt in a circle, and
is notable for its ultra-clean tone.

AUGUST '93

| 1 | 2 | 3 | 4 | 5 | 6 | 7 | 8 | 9 | 10 | 11 | 12 | 13 | 14 | 15 | 16 | 17 | 18 | 19 | 20 | 21 | 22 |

The Dead Family

The term "Grateful Dead Family" crops up a lot in
this book, and it's used in a very real sense—though
biological ties are only one of the many kinds of
connection between the band and the close-knit
community that came to surround it. The communal
spirit forged at 710 Ashbury and Olompali didn't die
after the "Summer of Love"; instead, it transmuted
into something different but no less significant as the
band members and their closest associates got older,
fell in and out of love, had children, and otherwise
made their way through life onstage and off.
"Everything that happens to a family has happened to
the Grateful Dead," Dennis McNally writes in *A Long
Strange Trip*, "Marriages and divorces, car accidents,
deaths, arrests, graduations, pregnancies, lawsuits,
mortgage payments, wayward children, braces, new
cars, high-school athletics."

As with any family, love and emotional support
are the most important things, but the Grateful Dead
is also a family business in many ways. The band's
studio, office, and various business spinoffs have been
well-stocked with friends, relatives, friends of relatives,
and so on, both during the band's lifespan and
following Jerry Garcia's passing. This is hardly a
matter of conventional music-biz nepotism; who
better to understand the workings of the complex,
contradictory organism that is the Grateful Dead than
someone who has lived the life, either by association
or by upbringing?

Some members of the band's "extended" family, in
fact, got on the bus before there even was a Grateful

Dead: Jerry's older brother Tiff, for example, worked
for the band's organization, while Willy Legate, later
superintendent of the band's Club Front recording
studio, and Alan Trist, later head of Ice Nine, the
band's publishing company, both hooked up with Jerry
Garcia on the Palo Alto scene circa 1961 *(see page 22)*.

Others have remained a part of the family even
after their initial relationship with a particular band
member ended; for example, Rosie McGee (a.k.a.
Florence Nathan), Phil Lesh's girlfriend in the late
'60s, stayed on to work for the band's travel agency
long after they ceased to be romantically involved. And
by the 1980s, the children of the "original" family
members were finding places within the organization,
including Cassidy Law, daughter of Deadhead Den
Mother Eileen Law and roadie Rex Jackson (she's the
"newborn of 1970" Bill Graham refers to below).

*"The family tree of the Grateful Dead would resemble a
cypress, twisted by the winds of time and hanging on by
its roots. The young guy loading the truck in '65 is today
an integral part of the operation. The newborn of 1970
now works in the office. Friends and relatives make their
creative statements through the group and earn their
keep through the scene. Throughout a quarter of a
century, we've experienced the joyful evolution of family
life—the unions, the births, the adventures of the
traveling circus; and also the tragic loss of family
members, who stay on in spirit."* FROM BILL GRAHAM'S
INTRODUCTION TO JERILYN LEE BRANDELIUS'S *THE GRATEFUL
DEAD FAMILY ALBUM, 1989*

July 1993

JULY '93

| 1 | 2 | 3 | 4 | 5 | 6 ~ 31 |

At the end of the Summer Tour Jerry
Garcia, Deborah Koons, and friends
enjoy a refreshing vacation in Ireland.
In a place where practically nobody
knows who he is, Jerry is able to relax
and move around freely—literally miles
away from the pressures of celebrity.

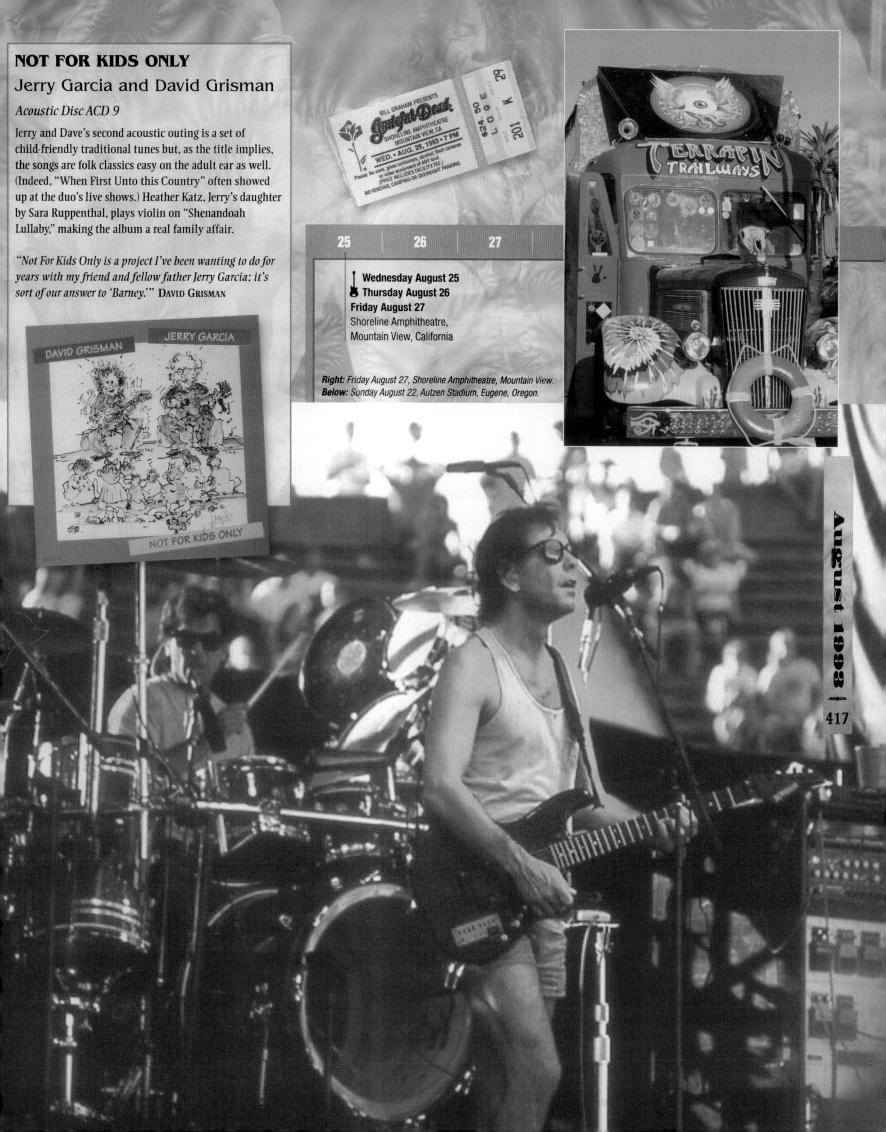

NOT FOR KIDS ONLY

Jerry Garcia and David Grisman

Acoustic Disc ACD 9

Jerry and Dave's second acoustic outing is a set of
child-friendly traditional tunes but, as the title implies,
the songs are folk classics easy on the adult ear as well.
(Indeed, "When First Unto this Country" often showed
up at the duo's live shows.) Heather Katz, Jerry's daughter
by Sara Ruppenthal, plays violin on "Shenandoah
Lullaby," making the album a real family affair.

*"Not For Kids Only is a project I've been wanting to do for
years with my friend and fellow father Jerry Garcia; it's
sort of our answer to 'Barney.'"* DAVID GRISMAN

25   26   27

🎸 **Wednesday August 25**
🎸 **Thursday August 26**
Friday August 27
Shoreline Amphitheatre,
Mountain View, California

Right: Friday August 27, Shoreline Amphitheatre, Mountain View.
Below: Sunday August 22, Autzen Stadium, Eugene, Oregon.

August 1993

417

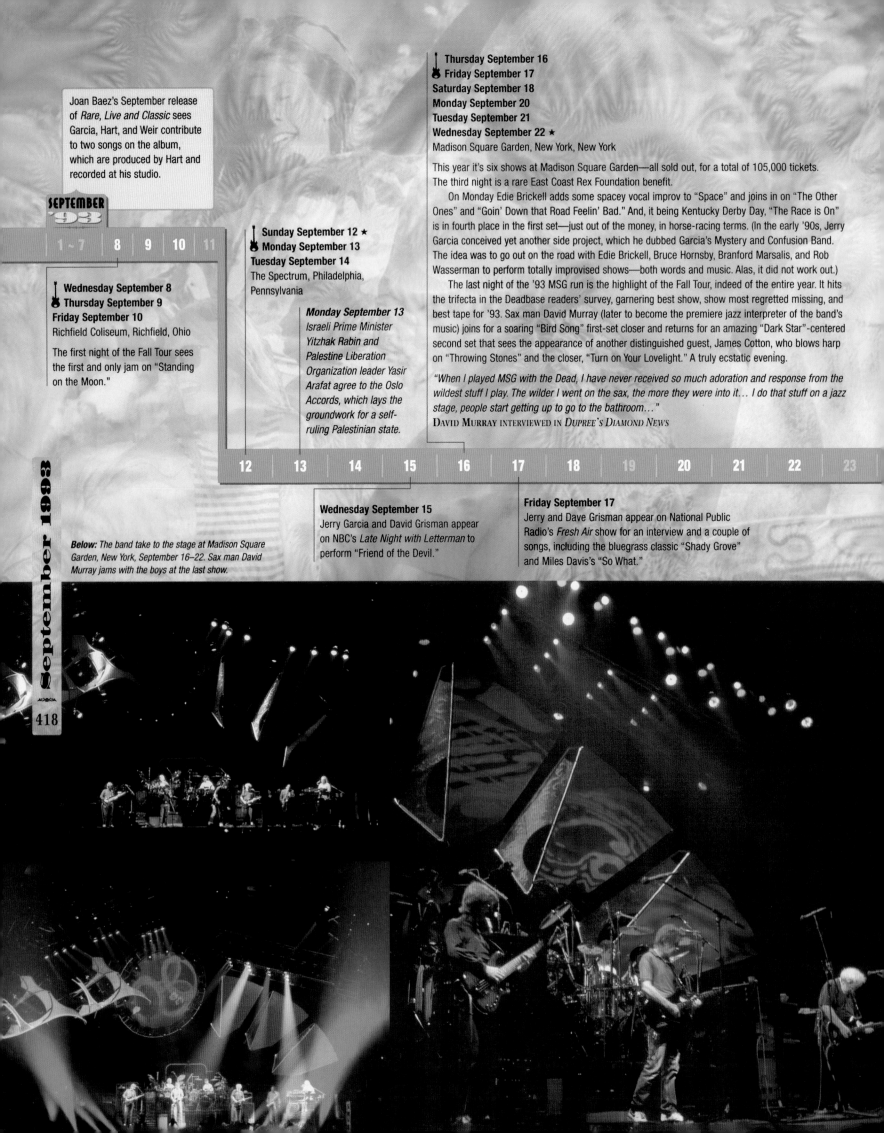

Joan Baez's September release of *Rare, Live and Classic* sees Garcia, Hart, and Weir contribute to two songs on the album, which are produced by Hart and recorded at his studio.

SEPTEMBER '93

| 1 ~ 7 | 8 | 9 | 10 | 11 |

Wednesday September 8
Thursday September 9
Friday September 10
Richfield Coliseum, Richfield, Ohio

The first night of the Fall Tour sees the first and only jam on "Standing on the Moon."

Sunday September 12 ★
Monday September 13
Tuesday September 14
The Spectrum, Philadelphia, Pennsylvania

Monday September 13
Israeli Prime Minister Yitzhak Rabin and Palestine Liberation Organization leader Yasir Arafat agree to the Oslo Accords, which lays the groundwork for a self-ruling Palestinian state.

Thursday September 16
Friday September 17
Saturday September 18
Monday September 20
Tuesday September 21
Wednesday September 22 ★
Madison Square Garden, New York, New York

This year it's six shows at Madison Square Garden—all sold out, for a total of 105,000 tickets. The third night is a rare East Coast Rex Foundation benefit.

On Monday Edie Brickell adds some spacey vocal improv to "Space" and joins in on "The Other Ones" and "Goin' Down that Road Feelin' Bad." And, it being Kentucky Derby Day, "The Race is On" is in fourth place in the first set—just out of the money, in horse-racing terms. (In the early '90s, Jerry Garcia conceived yet another side project, which he dubbed Garcia's Mystery and Confusion Band. The idea was to go out on the road with Edie Brickell, Bruce Hornsby, Branford Marsalis, and Rob Wasserman to perform totally improvised shows—both words and music. Alas, it did not work out.)

The last night of the '93 MSG run is the highlight of the Fall Tour, indeed of the entire year. It hits the trifecta in the Deadbase readers' survey, garnering best show, show most regretted missing, and best tape for '93. Sax man David Murray (later to become the premiere jazz interpreter of the band's music) joins for a soaring "Bird Song" first-set closer and returns for an amazing "Dark Star"-centered second set that sees the appearance of another distinguished guest, James Cotton, who blows harp on "Throwing Stones" and the closer, "Turn on Your Lovelight." A truly ecstatic evening.

"When I played MSG with the Dead, I have never received so much adoration and response from the wildest stuff I play. The wilder I went on the sax, the more they were into it… I do that stuff on a jazz stage, people start getting up to go to the bathroom…"
DAVID MURRAY INTERVIEWED IN DUPREE'S DIAMOND NEWS

| 12 | 13 | 14 | 15 | 16 | 17 | 18 | 19 | 20 | 21 | 22 | 23 |

September 1993

Below: *The band take to the stage at Madison Square Garden, New York, September 16–22. Sax man David Murray jams with the boys at the last show.*

Wednesday September 15
Jerry Garcia and David Grisman appear on NBC's *Late Night with Letterman* to perform "Friend of the Devil."

Friday September 17
Jerry and Dave Grisman appear on National Public Radio's *Fresh Air* show for an interview and a couple of songs, including the bluegrass classic "Shady Grove" and Miles Davis's "So What."

418

Friday September 24
Saturday September 25
Sunday September 26
Tuesday September 28
Wednesday September 29
Thursday September 30
Boston Garden, Boston, Massachusetts

Saturday's show is another East Coast Rex Foundation benefit. On Sunday Bob Weir surprises all by strapping on an acoustic guitar for the first set "Me and My Uncle" and "Maggie's Farm." Wednesday night marks the last "Playin' in the Band" reprise.

With the tour over, Bob Weir now goes off to be operated on (successfully) for that bane of singers, nodes on the vocal cords.

| 24 | 25 | 26 | 27 | 28 | 29 | 30 |

Tom Constanten's *Morning Dew* album comes out on Relix this month. It includes a version of "Mountains of the Moon."

OCTOBER '93

| 2 | 3 | 4 | 5 | 6 | 7 | 8 | 9 | 10 | 11 | 12 | 13 | 14 | 15 | 16 | 17 | 18 | 19 | 20 | 21 | 22 | 23 | 24 | 25 | 26 | 27 | 28 | 29 | 30 | 31 |

Sunday October 3
Eighteen American servicemen are killed in Mogadishu, Somalia, in a failed operation aimed at capturing the country's top warlord.

The Grateful Dead Almanac

The year saw Gary Lambert publish Issue One, Volume One of *The Grateful Dead Almanac*. Available for free to anyone who wrote to the band's office (and eventually available online), the *Almanac* included news about the band and related artists, merchandise for sale, and occasional comics, poems, and essays. Within a couple of years the office was mailing out more than 200,000 copies of each issue.

DEAD EXPRESS
3712   5006
JACK STRAW   MEMBER SINCE ...

Membership has its privileges.

Above: Jerry at Boston Garden, Wednesday September 29.
Right: A fan begs for a ticket outside Boston Garden.
Far right: A fan's t-Shirt.
Below: The band onstage at Madison Square Garden.

WILL SHOW MY TITS 4 A TICKET

SENTINEL
Robert Hunter
Rykodisc 20265

The second in a series of Rykodisc's *Voices* series of spoken-word recordings, *Sentinel* was released in October to accompany the book of the same name. *Sentinel* presented Robert Hunter reading his poetry unaccompanied. The material included selections from three previously published volumes of Hunter's verse (*Idiot's Delight*, *Infinity Minus Eleven*, and *Night Cadre*), in addition to new pieces. The handsome block print on both the book and CD cover was the work of Maureen Hunter.

SENTINEL
ROBERT HUNTER

DICK'S PICKS

The doors to the tape vault opened further with the release of the first of a series of live recordings, chosen by archivist extraordinaire Dick Latvala (*see page 307*). Unlike the *Vault* series (*see page 389*), the recordings released under the *Dick's Picks* imprimatur were recorded mostly on two-track equipment, and did not comprise complete shows, leading to yet more debate between "completist" and "perfectionist" Deadheads. The series was originally sold only via mail order.

Wittily packaged in a CD jewel box designed to look like an old reel-to-reel tape box, Dick's first pick was the December 19, 1973, show at the Curtis Hixon Convention Center in Tampa, Florida. As always, there were those who questioned why this show got the nod to be the premiere release, especially since 1973 was one of the band's best years, but everyone loved "Here Comes Sunshine" and "Weather Report Suite" on the first of the album's two CDs.

"The recording herein has been lovingly remastered directly from the original two-track master tape and is therefore not immune to the various glitches, splices, reel changes, and other aural gremlins contained on said original. Dick's Picks differs from our From The Vault series in that we simply did not have access to complete shows (nor the modern mixing capabilities afforded by multitrack tapes). But we think the historical value and musical quality of these tapes more than compensates for any technical anomalies... In other words what you hear is what you get. And what you get ain't bad!"
FROM THE CD COVER OF *DICK'S PICKS VOLUME ONE*

Dick's Picks Volume 1 GDCD-4018
Released December 1993 by Grateful Dead Records. Produced and Recorded by Kidd Candelario. Recorded at the December 19, 1973, show in Tampa, Florida. The first of the vault releases selected by and named in honor of tape archivist Dick Latvala.

Dick's Picks Volume 2 GDCD-4019
Released March 1995 by Grateful Dead Records. Recorded at the October 31, 1971, show in Columbus, Ohio.

Dick's Picks Volume 3 GDCD-4021
Released November 1995 by Grateful Dead Records. Recorded at the May 22, 1977, show in Pembroke Pines, Florida.

Dick's Picks Volume 4 GDCD-4023
Released February 1996 by Grateful Dead Records. Recorded at the February 13 and 14, 1970, shows at the Fillmore East, New York, New York.

Dick's Picks Volume 5 GDCD-4024
Released May 1996 by Grateful Dead Records. Recorded at the December 26, 1979, show from Oakland, California.

Dick's Picks Volume 6 GDCD-4026
Released October 1996 by Grateful Dead Records. Recorded at the October 14, 1983, show in Hartford, Connecticut.

Dick's Picks Volume 7 GDCD-4027
Released March 1997 by Grateful Dead Records. Recorded at the three London shows on September 9, 10, and 11, 1974.

Dick's Picks Volume 8 GDCD-4028
Released June 1997 by Grateful Dead Records. Recorded at the May 2, 1970, show at Harpur College, Binghamton, New York.

Dick's Picks Volume 9 GDCD-4029
Released October 1997 by Grateful Dead Records. Recorded at the September 16, 1990, show at Madison Square Garden, New York, New York.

Dick's Picks Volume 10 GDCD-4030
Released February 1998 by Grateful Dead Records. Recorded at the December 29 and 30, 1977, shows at Winterland Arena, San Francisco, California.

Dick's Picks Volume 11 GDCD-4031
Released June 1998 by Grateful Dead Records. Recorded at the September 27, 1972, show at the Stanley Theatre, Jersey City, New Jersey.

Dick's Picks Volume 12 GDCD-4032
Released October 1998 by Grateful Dead Records. Recorded at the June 26, 1974, Providence Civic Center, Providence, Rhode Island, and June 28, 1974, Boston Garden, Boston, Massachusetts shows.

Dick's Picks Volume 13 GDCD-4033
Released March 1999 by Grateful Dead Records. Recorded at the May 6, 1981, show at Nassau Coliseum, Uniondale, New York.

Dick's Picks Volume 14 GDCD-4034
Released June 1999 by Grateful Dead Records. Recorded at the November 30 and December 2, 1973, shows at Boston Music Hall, Boston, Massachusetts.

Dick's Picks Volume 15 GDCD-4035
Released October 1999 by Grateful Dead Records. Recorded at the September 3, 1977, show in Englishtown, New Jersey.

Dick's Picks Volume 16 GDCD-4036
Released February 2000 by Grateful Dead Records. Recorded at the November 8, 1969, show at the Fillmore Auditorium, San Francisco, California.

Dick's Picks Volume 17 GDCD-4037
Released April 2000 by Grateful Dead Records. Recorded at the September 25, 1991, show at the Boston Gardens, Boston, Massachusetts. Two additional tracks are from the March 3, 1991, show.

Dick's Picks Volume 18 GDCD-4038
Released June 2000 by Grateful Dead Records. Recorded at the February 3 and 5, 1978, shows in Madison, Wisconsin and Cedar Falls, Iowa. There are also two songs from the February 4, 1978, show.

Dick's Picks Volume 19 GDCD-4039
Released October 2000 by Grateful Dead Records. Recorded at the October 19, 1973, show in Oklahoma City, Oklahoma.

Dick's Picks Volume 20 GDCD-4040
Released January 2001 by Grateful Dead Records. Recorded at the September 25, 1976, show at the Capital Centre, Landover, and the September 28, 1976, show at the Onondaga County War Memorial, Syracuse, New York.

Dick's Picks Volume 21 GDCD-4041
Released March 2001 by Grateful Dead Records. Recorded at the November 1, 1985, show at the Richmond Coliseum, Richmond, Virginia. An extra 35 minutes is included on disc 3 from the September 2, 1980, show at the Community War Memorial, Rochester, New York.

Dick's Picks Volume 22 GDCD-4042
Released June 2001 by Grateful Dead Records. Recorded at the February 22 to 24, 1968, shows at King's Beach Bowl, Lake Tahoe, California.

Dick's Picks Volume 23 GDCD-4043
Released October 2001 by Grateful Dead Records. Recorded at the September 17, 1972, show at the Baltimore Civic Center, Baltimore, Maryland.

Dick's Picks Volume 24 GDCD-4044
Released February 2002 by Grateful Dead Records. Recorded at the March 23, 1974, show at the Cow Palace, Daly City, San Francisco, California.

Dick's Picks Volume 25 GDCD-4045
Released July 2002 by Grateful Dead Records. Recorded at the May 10, 1978, at New Haven, Connecticut, and May 11, 1978, at Springfield, Massachusetts, shows.

Dick's Picks Volume 26 GDCD-4046
Released October 2002 by Grateful Dead Records. Recorded at the Electric Theater, Chicago, Illinois, on April 26, 1969, and Labor Temple, Minneapolis, Minnesota, shows on April 27, 1969.

Dick's Picks Volume 27 GDCD-4047
Released January 2003 by Grateful Dead Records. Recorded at the December 16, 1992, show at the Oakland Coliseum Arena, Oakland, California. Four additional tracks were recorded live at the same venue on December 17, 1992.

Dick's Picks Volume 28 GDCD-4048
Released April 2003 by Grateful Dead Records. Recorded at the Lincoln, Nebraska, show on February 26, 1973, and Salt Lake City, Utah, show on February 28, 1973.

Dick's Picks Volume 29 GDCD-4049
Released June 2003 by Grateful Dead Records. Recorded at the May 19, 1977, Fox Theatre, Atlanta, Georgia, show and the May 21, 1977, Lakeland Civic Center, Nebraska, show.

"Dick knew more about the music than anybody I know. He knew more about the music itself than the people who were playing the music. There's volumes of books that he kept notes on each night—what songs were played, how they were played, the quality of the recordings, or the quality of music." BILL "KIDD" CANDELARIO, *RELIX* MAGAZINE, *AUGUST 2001*

Above: *The Dead didn't play New Year's Eve in '93, so BGP made up this fake in-house poster.*

Mouse's freehand art

Mickey Hart provided the foreword to *Freehand: The Art of Stanley Mouse*, a 1993 book on the artist (*see page 60*), who produced artwork for various Grateful Dead albums and music posters.

Saturday December 11
Bob Weir guests on the *Elwood Blues' House of Blues* radio show.

11 | 12 | 13 | 14 | 15 | 16

Sunday December 12
Monday December 13
San Diego International Sports
Arena, San Diego, California

8 | 9 | 10

Wednesday December 8
Thursday December 9
Friday December 10
Los Angeles Sports Arena, Los Angeles, California

On Wednesday the band revive "I'm a King Bee" (first recorded by Slim Harpo, but closely associated with Muddy Waters) for the first time since December 15, 1971, with Bob Weir on vocals and both Bob and Jerry Garcia giving their slides a workout. On Thursday Ornette Coleman returns to share the stage for a second-set sequence of "The Other One">"Wharf Rat">"Turn on Your Lovelight," and Airto Moreira and Flora Purim guest on "Drums." For the final night Branford Marsalis sits in for the entire show—capping a year that has seen the band performing with some of the greatest names in jazz.

Saturday December 4
Frank Zappa dies of cancer at age 52.

Wednesday January 19
Grateful Dead inducted
into Rock and Roll Hall
of Fame.

Monday January 17
*An earthquake measuring 6.7 on the Richter scale rocks
Northridge, California, leaving more than 50 people dead and
resulting in property damage costing many billions of dollars.*

January 1994

422

Hall of Fame

Performers are eligible for induction into the Rock and Roll Hall of Fame
25 years after their first record is released, so the Grateful Dead could have
been a part of the "Class of '93" rather than '94; the fact that the band had
to wait a year to get enough votes for induction was seen by many 'Heads
as a reflection of the anti-Dead bias exhibited by some critics and other
members of the rock "establishment." Not that Deadheads cared much for
the concept of awards and halls of fames, anyway… and neither did Jerry
Garcia, who declined to attend the ceremony at New York's Waldorf-Astoria
Hotel. (Bob, Bill, Phil, Mickey, and Vince brought along a life-size cardboard
cutout of their absent bandmate.)

Deadly mixture

The band accepted the honor (presented, fittingly, by Bruce Hornsby) with a
mix of pranksterish humor and serious sentiment. After tearing up a fake
speech, Bill saluted the fallen (Keith, Brent, and especially Pigpen), and Phil
offered some words of hope to Deadheads imprisoned due to mandatory
sentencing under ludicrous drug laws.

The Grateful Dead's fellow inductees in the "Class of '94" included the
Animals, Duane Eddy, Elton John, John Lennon (as a solo performer), Bob
Marley, and Rod Stewart.

*"The Grateful Dead wrought a psychedelic revolution upon the cultural landscape
of the Sixties. They also kept the spirit of the Sixties alive in the decades that
followed, building a massive, supportive network of fans known as "Deadheads."
The Dead and their peers on the San Francisco scene helped steer the adventurous
rock audience of the mid-Sixties toward a brave new world of sound in which
albums supplanted singles and concerts became improvisational marathons."*
FROM THE ROCK AND ROLL HALL OF FAME WEBSITE

TRIOS
Rob Wasserman

MCA/GRP 4021

The natural successor to Rob Wasserman's *Solo* (1983) and *Duets* (1988) albums, *Trios* finds the protean bassist cavorting musically in a series of stimulating threesomes, including outings with Jerry Garcia and singer Edie Brickell (two songs improvised on the spot); Bob Weir and Neil Young ("Easy Answers," which the Dead later tackled), Bruce Hornsby and Branford Marsalis, Elvis Costello and Marc Ribot, Brian and Carnie Wilson, and several other groupings (and three triple-tracked "solo" bass excursions). The album, recorded over a period of more than three years, was engineered and co-produced by Grateful Dead engineer John Cutler.

Friday February 25
Saturday February 26
Sunday February 27
Oakland Coliseum Arena,
Oakland, California

No special guests at the Mardi Gras show on Sunday, but the usual parade of outlandish floats enlivens the Coliseum.

FEBRUARY '94

1	1 ~ 13	**14**	15 ~ 2	

Monday February 14
On Valentine's Day, Jerry Garcia ties the knot with Deborah Koons at Christ Episcopal Church in Sausalito. (It's his third, for those keeping count.) The bride wears white; Jerry wears a black suit with no tie. Afterward, the 70 guests repair to a nearby yacht club for the reception.

Left: Sunday February 27, Chinese New Year Show, Oakland Coliseum Arena, Oakland, California.

Dan Departs

Shortly after the '94 Phoenix shows the band gave longtime soundman Dan Healy his walking papers. It was a sudden parting and not an amicable one, which was sad given Healy's amazingly long tenure (from July 1966 on, with a single break of about 18 months in 1969–71) and the fact that he did more than anyone to make the band's live sound the benchmark for all other rock acts. Healy's departure was an especial bummer to Deadheads, among whom he was admired for his brilliance in general ("Healy's a Genius" banners sometimes appeared at shows) and particularly for his friendliness toward Tapers, which extended even to patching decks into the soundboard on occasion.

John Cutler took over at the soundboard, however Cutler was more at home in the studio than on tour, and many Deadheads felt he kept the volume too low, especially in larger venues, where 'Heads in the nosebleed sections often complained they could barely hear the band. Cutler was also perceived (rightly or wrongly) as being less well disposed toward Tapers than Healy.

Many Deadheads would later look upon the '94 Spring Tour as the beginning of the end. While the rest of the band is playing well, Jerry Garcia is clearly a mess. His playing is frequently sloppy, lazy, or both. Many attribute this to drugs, but Jerry is in fact suffering from a couple of medical conditions, including carpal-tunnel syndrome and diabetes, both of which reduce the sensitivity in his fingers.

These conditions can not, however, explain the many occasions when Jerry loses his place in a song, or seems unaware of what song is being performed. Jerry's playing is not uniformly bad; often the old speed and fire do return, and his fingers go racing up and down the neck of his guitar as they always used to.

March 1994

424

MARCH '94

| 1 | 2 | 3 | 4 | 5 | 6 | 7 | 8 | 9 | 10 |

Friday March 4
Saturday March 5
Sunday March 6
Blockbuster Desert Sky Pavilion, Phoenix, Arizona

The three-night run at the Blockbuster Desert Sky Pavilion is the band's only appearance at this venue.

Right: Bill Kreutzmann at the Blockbuster Desert Sky Pavilion, Phoenix, Arizona, March 4–6.

Right: April 6–8, Miami Arena, Miami, Florida.

| 11 | 12 | 13 | 14 | 15 | 16 | 17 | 18 | 19 | 20 | 21 | 22 |

Wednesday March 16
Thursday March 17
Friday March 18
Rosemont Horizon Arena, Rosemont, Illinois

Sunday March 20
Monday March 21
Richfield Coliseum, Richfield, Ohio

Monday's show is an exception—and a big one—to the average and below-average shows of this period.

Wednesday March 23
Thursday March 24
Friday March 25
★ **Sunday March 27**
Monday March 28
Nassau Veterans Memorial Coliseum, Uniondale, New York

"Might as Well" appears for the first time since June 17, 1991, on Wednesday and for the last time ever. On Friday Bruce Hornsby guests on accordion for the entire show. Sunday's second set opens with "Samson and Delilah" (quite appropriate—it's Passover), after which equipment problems force a break before the band returns with "Iko Iko."

Wednesday March 30
Thursday March 31
Friday April 1
The Omni, Atlanta, Georgia

Recedes in the nights of goodbye… The band breaks out "Dark Star" on Wednesday for the 37th time since its resurrection at the October 9, 1989 Hampton show. This will be the last performance of the song that, for most, defines what the Grateful Dead was all about. Thursday's show sees the last-ever "I'm a King Bee."

APRIL '94

| 23 | 24 | 25 | 26 | 27 | 28 | 29 | 30 | 31 | 1 | 2 |

Sunday April 3
Monday April 4
Orlando Arena, Orlando, Florida

Sunday's show is canceled: Bill Kreutzmann has to fly to California to be with his seriously ill father. The last few tours have been mostly free of the crowd-control problems of the early '90s: Monday is the exception. When gatecrashers rush the doors, the Orlando police respond with tear gas and riot sticks. It's the last show at this venue.

Wednesday April 6
Thursday April 7
Friday April 8
Miami Arena, Miami, Florida

Left: Monday April 4, Orlando Arena, Orlando, Florida.

Wednesday April 27
Former U.S. president Richard Nixon dies at age 81.

3 | 4 | 5 | 6 | 7 | 8 | 9 | 10 | 11 | 12 | 13 | 14 | 15 | 16 | 17 | 18 | 19 | 20 | 21 | 22 | 23 | 24 | 25 | 26 | **27**

JUNE '94

| 12 ~ 31 | 1 | 2 | 3 | 4 | 5 | 6 | 7 | 8 | 9 | 10 |

Many of the band's usual arena and stadium venues were hosting World Cup soccer matches in the summer of '94, delaying the start of the Summer '94 Tour. As a result, the band and its audiences had to endure some seriously high temperatures—especially in Las Vegas, where the mercury went as high as 120°F at the first two shows. Thankfully, no one died.

MAY '94

| 1 ~ 10 | 11 |

Wednesday May 11

Phil Lesh is a guest conductor for the Berkeley Symphony Orchestra at a benefit concert for music programs in Berkeley's public schools. Maestro Phil's modernist material includes the concluding section of Igor Stravinsky's 1910 ballet *The Firebird* and contemporary American composer Elliott Carter's "A Celebration of some 100 x 150 Notes." (Born in 1908, Carter was a protégé of another Phil phave, Charles Ives.)

Monday June 6

Release of *Chance in a Million* (Whirled 1960) by Zero. Vince Welnick sits in on some tracks. The album includes five songs with lyrics by Robert Hunter.

Wednesday June 8
Thursday June 9
Friday June 10

Cal Expo Amphitheatre, Sacramento, California

The first show of the annual Rex Foundation benefit run sees the breakout of the year's first original song, "Samba in the Rain." A Latin-flavored groover (though not actually a samba) from Robert Hunter and Vince Welnick, "Samba" leaves Deadheads divided; halldancing types take to it, others are put off by the song's unusual structure and lightweight lyrics ("Samba in the rain/Let's get down and dirty/Don't bother to explain.") The next night and another breakout: "If the Shoe Fits," from Phil Lesh and his friend Andrew Charles. An acerbic breakup song that sounds like it was written by the ghost of Brent Mydland, "If the Shoe Fits" has only 17 outings before retirement. At the final Cal Expo show, the last-ever "Sunshine Daydream" coda closes the second set.

Opposite page: Many stadium venues were hosting World Cup soccer matches during the Summer '94 Tour. Here, Carlos Santana and Bob Weir play at a pre-game celebration at Stanford Stadium, Palo Alto.

Friday June 17
Saturday June 18
Sunday June 19
Autzen Stadium, Eugene, Oregon

Cracker—who covered "Loser" on their 1993 album *Kerosene Hat*—opens all three shows at Autzen.

Monday June 13
Tuesday June 14
Seattle Center Memorial Stadium, Seattle, Washington

Friday June 17

As millions watch on TV, football and movie star O.J. Simpson leads L.A. police on a slow car chase through the city before being arrested in connection with the murder of his ex-wife, Nicole Simpson, and her friend Ron Goldman.

Thursday June 30

A congressional committee declines to charge members of the Clinton administration with wrongdoing in connection with the "Whitewater" real-estate investigation.

Friday June 24
Saturday June 25
★ **Sunday June 26**
Sam Boyd Silver Bowl, Las Vegas, Nevada

Despite some technical problems in the first set, the last night at the Silver Bowl is considered one of the better shows of the year.

Below and inset: June 24–26, Sam Boyd Silver Bowl, Las Vegas, Nevada.

1 | 2 | 3 | 4 | 5 | 6 | 7 | 8 | 9

Friday July 1
Saturday July 2
Sunday July 3

Shoreline Amphitheatre, Mountain View, California

All three Shoreline shows are encore-less, the first two-set shows without encores since May 3, 1986, at Cal Expo. Chief culprit, reportedly, is Bob Weir, who refuses to return to the stage because he is enraged with the drummers, annoyed with the volume on stage, and other stuff.

The opening night sees the final Beatles cover breakout: "I Want to Tell You," from *Revolver*. The instigator this time is Jerry, not Vince, and the songwriter is George Harrison, not Lennon & McCartney. (The Jerry Garcia Band performed the song about a dozen times in the mid-'70s and the mid-'80s.)

Wednesday July 13
Franklin County Airport, Highgate, Vermont

This is something of a stealth show, with little advance publicity, at a field outside an airport on the U.S.–Canadian border. Most of those in attendance feel the leafy ambiance exceeds the performance. The great Senegalese musician Youssou N'Dour opens.

10 | 11 | 12 | **13** | 14

Saturday July 16
Sunday July 17
RFK Stadium, Washington, D.C.

Traffic opens on both nights.

15 | **16** | 17 | 18

Sunday July 17
Brazil wins the first soccer World Cup final to be held in the U.S.

Tuesday July 19
Wednesday July 20 ★
Thursday July 21
Deer Creek Music Center, Noblesville, Indiana

The opening night at Deer Creek (usually voted "Favorite Venue" in *DeadBase's* reader surveys) sees Bob Weir play acoustic on the first-set "Big River" and "Maggie's Farm." Bob again wields an acoustic ax the next night, this time on the second-set "Looks Like Rain." There are two breakouts tonight. The band always had a soft spot for calypso, and tonight they add "Matilda" to "Day-O" and "Man Smart, Woman Smarter" on the list of Harry Belafonte covers (although all these songs were popularized rather than written by Belafonte). "Childhood's End" was Phil Lesh's last songwriting credit for the band and the only song (other than "No Turn Left Unstoned") for which he wrote the lyrics. The song has nothing to do with the Arthur C. Clarke novel of the same title, though the lyrics—with their references to motherships, Mars, and multi-colored moons—are certainly spacey. "Childhood's End" was performed 11 times and has yet to find its way on any official GD release.

Friday July 29
Buckeye Lake Music Center, Hebron, Ohio

Traffic opens (after a brief delay because of rain). Tonight's encore, "The Mighty Quinn," is also the last-ever performance of the song.

Wednesday August 3
Thursday August 4
Giants Stadium, East Rutherford, New Jersey

Traffic opens on Wednesday, joined by Jerry Garcia for "Dear Mr. Fantasy." Traffic opens again on Thursday and this time Jerry guests on "Gimme Some Lovin'" as well as "Dear Mr. Fantasy." Bruce Hornsby sits in (on accordion) for the entire second set.

19	20	21	22	23	24	25	26	27

28	29	30

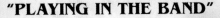

AUGUST '94

31	1	2	3	4	5 - 31

Saturday July 23
Sunday July 24
Soldier Field, Chicago, Illinois

Traffic opens both nights. The first night's encore is the band's last take on "Knockin' On Heaven's Door."

Tuesday July 26
Wednesday July 27
Riverport Amphitheater, Maryland Heights, Missouri

Sunday July 31
Monday August 1
The Palace, Auburn Hills, Michigan

Monday's "(I Can't Get No) Satisfaction" is the band's last outing for the song. For the first time in 12 years, Jerry's birthday (his 52nd) falls on a show day. After the show, Deborah Koons organizes a party for Jerry, but he leaves after five minutes.

Right: Deadheads on tour, July 1994.

Left and above: Wednesday July 13, Franklin County Airport, Highgate, Vermont.

"PLAYING IN THE BAND"
WEIR/HUNTER

One of the best tracks from Bob Weir's solo bow *Ace* (1972) and one of just two co-written with Robert Hunter for the disc, "Playing In The Band" was destined to become a Dead anthem from the day of its debut on February 18, 1971, during a much-acclaimed run in Port Chester, New York. The song's lyrics seem to encapsulate at least part of the Dead experience from the band's eyes. "I can tell your future, just look what's in your hand," Weir jokes at one point, perhaps to those who would look to a rock group for divinatory guidance. "I can't stop for nothing, I'm just playing in the band." Originally inspired by a rhythm pattern that drummer Hart (who also shares a credit here) dubbed "The Main Ten," Hunter later told Jeff Tamarkin, "I wasn't certain it was going to be a Grateful Dead song." But "Playing" would turn up on the band's live album *Grateful Dead* (1971) even before the release of *Ace*, and quickly became an ideal vehicle for another extended, spaced-out ride. The song ended up in the band's rotation almost 600 times, often dissolving into selected detours before returning as a reprise in a long-standing custom that continued with The Other Ones.

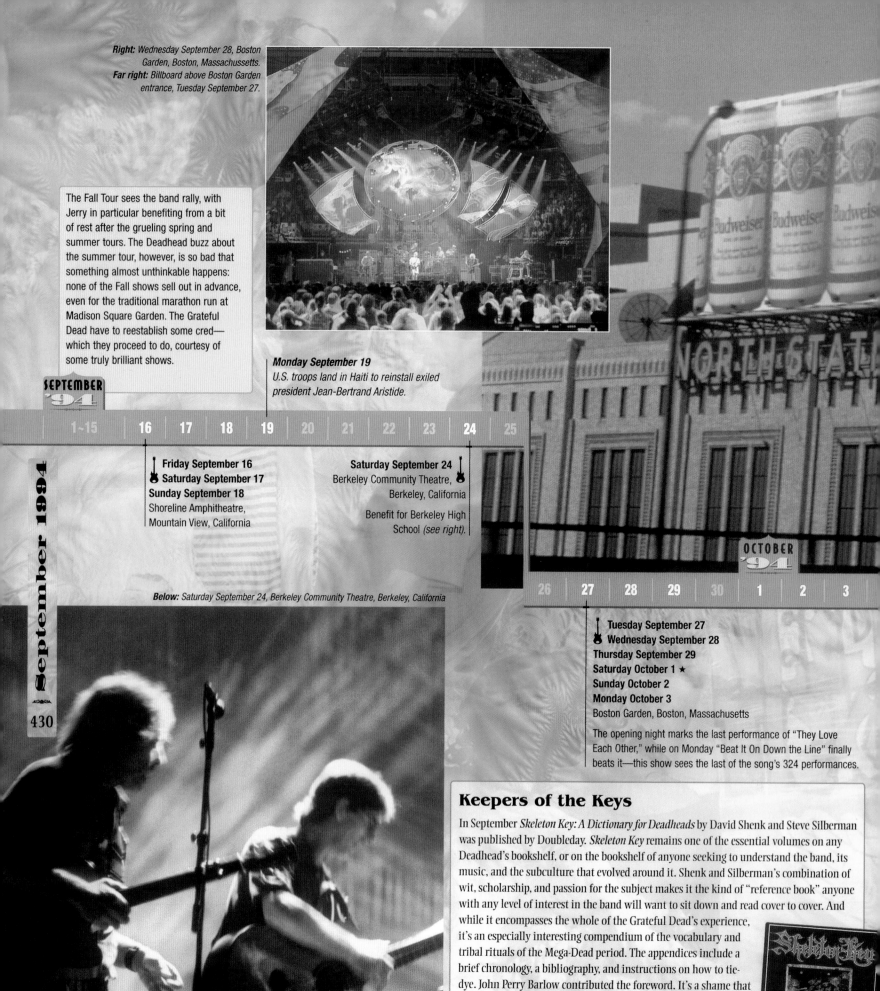

Right: Wednesday September 28, Boston Garden, Boston, Massachussetts.
Far right: Billboard above Boston Garden entrance, Tuesday September 27.

The Fall Tour sees the band rally, with Jerry in particular benefiting from a bit of rest after the grueling spring and summer tours. The Deadhead buzz about the summer tour, however, is so bad that something almost unthinkable happens: none of the Fall shows sell out in advance, even for the traditional marathon run at Madison Square Garden. The Grateful Dead have to reestablish some cred—which they proceed to do, courtesy of some truly brilliant shows.

Monday September 19
U.S. troops land in Haiti to reinstall exiled president Jean-Bertrand Aristide.

SEPTEMBER '94

| 1~15 | 16 | 17 | 18 | 19 | 20 | 21 | 22 | 23 | 24 | 25 |

September 1994

430

Friday September 16
Saturday September 17
Sunday September 18
Shoreline Amphitheatre, Mountain View, California

Saturday September 24
Berkeley Community Theatre, Berkeley, California

Benefit for Berkeley High School *(see right).*

Below: Saturday September 24, Berkeley Community Theatre, Berkeley, California

OCTOBER '94

| 26 | 27 | 28 | 29 | 30 | 1 | 2 | 3 |

Tuesday September 27
Wednesday September 28
Thursday September 29
Saturday October 1 ★
Sunday October 2
Monday October 3
Boston Garden, Boston, Massachusetts

The opening night marks the last performance of "They Love Each Other," while on Monday "Beat It On Down the Line" finally beats it—this show sees the last of the song's 324 performances.

Keepers of the Keys

In September *Skeleton Key: A Dictionary for Deadheads* by David Shenk and Steve Silberman was published by Doubleday. *Skeleton Key* remains one of the essential volumes on any Deadhead's bookshelf, or on the bookshelf of anyone seeking to understand the band, its music, and the subculture that evolved around it. Shenk and Silberman's combination of wit, scholarship, and passion for the subject makes it the kind of "reference book" anyone with any level of interest in the band will want to sit down and read cover to cover. And while it encompasses the whole of the Grateful Dead's experience, it's an especially interesting compendium of the vocabulary and tribal rituals of the Mega-Dead period. The appendices include a brief chronology, a bibliography, and instructions on how to tie-dye. John Perry Barlow contributed the foreword. It's a shame that *Skeleton Key* is (as of spring 2003) out of print; it richly deserves a revised and updated edition to bring it up to the present.

"Skeleton Key is an elegantly written, one-size-fits-all passport to Deadhead culture's rich, weird pageantry."
RICHARD GEHR'S REVIEW IN THE *VILLAGE VOICE*.

SKELETON KEY
DICTIONARY
DEADHEADS

In Boston, Nothing Beats The DEAd.

BOSTON GARDEN

Thursday October 13
Friday October 14 ★
Saturday October 15
Monday October 17
Tuesday October 18
Wednesday October 19
Madison Square Garden, New York, New York

The opening night sees the first "Dupree's Diamond Blues" since March 26, 1990, and the last ever. The X Factor is a capricious entity, and at Friday's show, toward the end of a year full of average or below-average shows, it descends in full force, animating a performance that many Deadheads feel holds up to any in the band's history: not the show as whole, however, but a monumental "Scarlet Begonias">"Fire on the Mountain" in which—reversing the usual—the rest of the band struggles (successfully) to keep up with Jerry.

On Monday Bob Dylan ambles onstage to lead the shambolic encore, "Rainy Day Women #12 and #35," and the always well-stoked MSG audience raises the roof on the "Everybody Must Get Stoned" chorus. It's the first "Rainy Day Women" since July 26, 1987, and the last ever. The show also marks the last "In the Midnight Hour." Tuesday's "Smokestack Lightning" is the last ever, and Wednesday marks the final Grateful Dead show at Madison Square Garden—a venue that hosted the band 52 times.

Phil Lesh and Friends

Berkeley High School's music program has long been acclaimed as among the best, perhaps *the* best, in the nation. Berkeley's classrooms have incubated an amazing roster of top jazz and classical performers, and even a rock star or two, including Country Joe McDonald—and, of course, Phil Lesh, whose parents, unable to afford private instruction for their talented offspring, had moved to Berkeley for the express purpose of getting young Phil into the school.

So when Phil learned that budget cuts had caused the total elimination of the school's music program, he was having none of it. Phil made sure the program got a substantial Rex Foundation grant and volunteered to organize a benefit concert—on September 24, 1994.

Bay Area Deadheads were in raptures when the concert—billed as Phil Lesh and Friends—was announced via *The Grateful Dead Hour*. The band, *sans* Rhythm Devils, would play an acoustic set—it would the band's first acoustic show in the Bay Area since April 25, 1981, and the first time they'd played the lovely, 3,600-seat Berkeley Community Theater since April 22, 1986. Country Joe, the Michael Wolff Trio, the high school's own jazz band, and an all-star alumni band filled out the bill.

Deadheads, jazz fans, and classical aficionados mixed amicably as the doors opened on the night of show. It was very much Phil's night, and he began the proceedings with some typically Leshian remarks—noting, for example, that the music program's very success was evinced by the fact that most of its alumni couldn't come to the concert because they already had gigs that night.

The drummerless Dead closed the show, with Phil toting an acoustic bass (quite a rarity) and Vince at the grand piano. They kicked off with "Walkin' Blues," followed by "K.C. Moan," and then a historic revival that elicited gasps of joyous surprise from the Deadheads in the audience—the first acoustic "Dupree's Diamond Blues" since June 7, 1969, at the Fillmore West. "Childhood's End," Phil's new song, came next, followed by "When I Paint My Masterpiece," "Attics of My Life" (also reverentially received), "Cassidy," "Bird Song," and "Throwing Stones" to close. A great evening for a good cause.

Friends for life

The Phil Lesh and Friends concept has had a life far beyond the initial concert. In 1998, Phil Lesh and Friends became a permanent ensemble with a continually changing lineup which, as of 2003, has included the best of the old breed (Bob Dylan, David Crosby, Jorma Kaukonen) and the new (Trey Anastasio, Jimmy Herring, Susan Tedeschi), as well as Bob, Bill, Vince, and even Donna Jean Godchaux MacKay. The group began touring regularly in 2001 and has so far released two albums, 1999's live *Love Will See You Through* and 2002's *There and Back Again*, Phil's first solo studio album *(see page 465)*.

Sunday October 9
Monday October 10
Tuesday October 11
USAir Arena, Landover, Maryland

The old Cap Centre is now the USAir Arena, another example of the rampant corporate logo-ing of the rock world and the world in general. The opening night is a Rex Foundation benefit, the show also marking the last coming of "Comes a Time." Tuesday sees the last "China Doll"—and is the band's last show at this venue.

Wednesday October 5
Thursday October 6
Friday October 7
The Spectrum, Philadelphia, Pennsylvania

Below: Vince Welnick (left) and Bob Weir, playing in October 1994.

Herb's History

Herb Greene's *Dead Days: A Grateful Dead Illustrated History* came out on Global Interprint this year. Essentially a journal for Deadheads, it contained interviews with Garcia and photographs by Greene.

Tuesday November 29
Wednesday November 30
Thursday December 1
McNichols Sports Arena, Denver, Colorado

Technical problems on the opening night force Jerry to give up during "Tennessee Jed," so the band plays the first-set closer, "Easy Answers," without him. The show sees the last "Baba O Riley"/"Tomorrow Never Knows."

Captain Jerry

Captain Trips: A Biography of Jerry Garcia by Sandy Troy (Thunder's Mouth Press) was another '94 release. It was the first complete biography of Garcia.

Wednesday November 9
In a stunning victory, the Republicans win a majority in both houses of Congress in the midterm elections.

November 1994

432

Once More, Without Much Feeling

Following the tour, the band conclaved at The Site, a Marin County studio, to take another stab at putting a new album in the can. (Many Deadheads expected a new studio release to coincide with the band's 30th anniversary in 1995.)

Despite having a number of new songs worked up (such as "So Many Roads" and "Days Between"), the sessions were no more productive than those of previous years. Jerry Garcia, in particular, acted like the studio was the last place he wanted to be (which was probably the case) and contributed little to the process.

And so it would be that 1989's *Built to Last* was the Grateful Dead's final studio album. Several songs that would have been on the "unfinished album" are now performed by The Other Ones/The Dead.

Thursday December 8
Friday December 9
Sunday December 11
Monday December 12
Oakland Coliseum Arena, Oakland, California

Despite the generally positive buzz about the Fall Tour, the band doesn't return to their home turf in triumph. Three of the four Oakland Coliseum shows fail to sell out, and for the first time in Bay Area memory, there are rows of empty seats at a Dead show. The opening show sees the last "Spoonful." Friday night sees Sikiru Adepoju guesting on a few songs and is also the first time the band uses a Teleprompter. Sikiru Adepoju returns on the last night for "Scarlet Begonias">"Fire on the Mountain" and "Drums."

Thursday December 15
Friday December 16
Sunday December 18
Monday December 19
Los Angeles Sports Arena, Los Angeles, California

The band ends the year with a rare long (four-show) run in Los Angeles. It's also the first time in more than 20 years that the band ends the year outside the Bay Area. At the first show Bob Weir takes his acoustic into "Space." Friday's special guest is Branford Marsalis, who sits in for the second set but bows out before the "Lucy in the Sky with Diamonds" encore. Monday marks the last "Nobody's Fault but Mine."

Main picture: GD on stage at the Los Angeles Sports Arena.
Below: Jerry with Branford Marsalis, December 16.

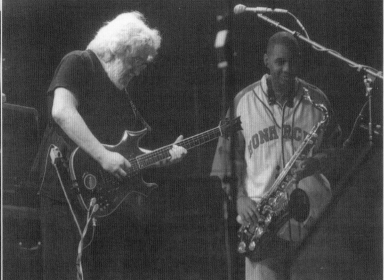

Oakland Snippets

At the first Oakland show the band soundchecked "St. Stephen," which hadn't been performed since Halloween '83, and which, if played, would have been an event on the order of the Hampton revivals of "Box of Rain" (March 20, 1986) and "Dark Star" (October 9, 1989). Rumors raced through the Deadhead network, which now ran at the instantaneous speed of the Internet. However, the band did not break out the Saint, leading the more cynical Deadheads to speculate that the soundcheck might have been a deliberate bit of hype. And although the *DeadBase* surveys consistently vote "St. Stephen" as the song Deadheads would most like to see revived, the song would never be performed again, although it enjoyed a post-Grateful Dead revival thanks to The Other Ones and The Dead, who usually played it into "The Eleven" in the canonical pairing.

If my words did glow, with the cathode-ray tube...
Starting with the December 12 Oakland show, the band began using Teleprompters—video monitors that scroll lyrics—onstage. Forgetting lyrics was a hallowed Grateful Dead tradition, but Jerry Garcia's vocal lapses had reached a point where the device was a necessity. Unfortunately, Teleprompters helped, but didn't solve the problem. They only worked if they were programmed correctly, and they were continually plagued by gremlins. Also, the band only used them for newer songs, and Jerry frequently forgot the words even to the old standbys. The use of Teleprompters (as at the Los Angeles Sports Arena, *left*) was taken by many Deadheads as another worrisome sign that the band was heading deeper into entropy.

Thursday January 19
Driving an unfamiliar car, Jerry Garcia loses control on Highway 101, spins out, and ricochets off the divider, ending up uninjured but badly shaken.

Saturday January 21
The Jerry Garcia Band records two songs for the soundtrack of director (and ex-JGB roadie) Wayne Wang's film *Smoke*: "Cigarettes and Coffee," written by Jerry Butler and best known from Otis Redding's rendition, and Jerome Kern's "Smoke Gets in Your Eyes" (in *Garcia, an American Life*, Blair Jackson observes that this was, most likely, the only occasion on which Jerry performed a song by the man he was named after). The session marks the JGB's last-ever recordings.

Above: Mickey Hart on drums at the Mardi Gras show, Sunday February 26, Oakland Coliseum Arena.

Jerry Garcia and Deborah Koons take a much-postponed honeymoon on the Caribbean island of Bonaire, where Jerry indulges in his passion for scuba-diving. Unfortunately, he is stung on the hand by a jellyfish, the effects of which, combined with his ongoing carpal tunnel syndrome, leave him unable to play. This leads to the cancellation of three Jerry Garcia Band shows at the Warfield; the first cancellation is not announced until after the audience has taken their seats.

Left: Floats at the Mardi Gras show, Sunday February 26, Oakland Coliseum Arena.

Sunday February 19
Monday February 20
Tuesday February 21
Delta Center, Salt Lake City, Utah

For the first time since 1983 the band begins its performance year outside the Bay Area. It's also the first show in Utah since 1983, and the three-night run at the Delta Center will be the band's only visit to this venue. On the first night, the band revives "Alabama Getaway," last heard on June 18, 1989.

There's a surprise opener on Tuesday—the first and only full-band performance of "Salt Lake City" from Bob Weir's *Heaven Help the Fool* solo album. The Barlow-penned lyrics are a hilarious send-up of the Mormon Mecca, and the song is naturally followed by the Hunter-penned "Friend of the Devil" ("Spent the night in Utah…"). It's a rollicking start to an unusually tight, high-energy show. The surprises continue in the second set, with the first (and last-ever) "I Just Want to Make Love to You" since October 8, 1984.

But the real shocker comes out of "Space" when Jerry leads off into Dylan's "Visions of Johanna," played previously only at a couple of '86 shows, the last time being at the Berkeley Community Theater on April 22. The fact that Jerry tackles this complex ten-minute-plus ballad—and nails it—testifies to the fact that the spirit could still burn bright even as the body faded. (Of course, the Teleprompter helped.) It's also Vince Welnick's 44th birthday, and the second set kicks off with a chorus of "Happy Birthday."

The Spring '95 Tour

Given the problems the Grateful Dead experienced in 1994—first and foremost, Jerry Garcia's failing health—the year 1995 would have been an ideal time for the band to call a time-out for a while, as they had in 1974. But it wasn't that easy. Two decades earlier, Robert Hunter had likened the Grateful Dead to the Ouroboros, the mythical snake feeding on its own tail; a more apt metaphor for the band as 1995 began would be the Juggernaut of Hindu mythology—a "terrible, irresistible force" rolling inexorably onward.

Economics powered this juggernaut. The Grateful Dead had grossed more than $52 million from the 1994 tours, with merchandise and record sales bringing in tens of millions more. But it was never enough. The band had a huge payroll to meet. Jerry, the band member who most desperately needed a break, was burdened by various financial obligations. And one of the problems inherent in playing the big venues was that they were booked far in advance. So the juggernaut rolled on into another year of touring.

Nineteen-ninety-five was the band's "30th anniversary," but, as with the 25th anniversary in 1990, they chose not to make a big deal out of it.

435

Thursday February 23
The Dow Jones Industrial Average tops 4,000 for the first time.

Friday February 24
Saturday February 25
Sunday February 26
Oakland Coliseum Arena, Oakland, California

The David Murray Octet opens Sunday's Mardi Gras show and sax man Murray guests through most of the second set. Sikuru Adepoju, Mickey, and Bill provide accompaniment to the parade of floats, which includes a giant Bill Walton.

Left: David Murray at the Mardi Gras show, Sunday February 26, Oakland Coliseum Arena.

"UNBROKEN CHAIN"
LESH/PETERSEN

Long the great missing link of Phil Lesh songs, "Unbroken Chain" was a live no-show for over two decades after appearing on *From the Mars Hotel* (1974). The complex track was the bassist's first collaboration with pal Robert Petersen since 1968's "New Potato Caboose" and was imbued with a wary religious cynicism in lines like "They say love your brother but you will catch it when you try." Although it also marked Lesh's first original since "Box of Rain," he avoided it in concert for 22 years. "'Unbroken Chain' could have really been something," he said during the track's live dry spell. "Some people think it really is, but I wanted it to be what I wanted it to be." By the time the bassist finally presented it to a disbelieving Dead audience at The Spectrum in Philadelphia, Pennsylvania on March 19, 1995 (keyboardist Vince Welnick remembered that Lesh "just got a flash that he'd like to do it"), some fans had subscribed to a superstition that its performance would mark the Dead's last days, a notion borne out by the death of Garcia that August. Lesh continued to play the song with both Phil & Friends and The Other Ones, and established a charity called the Unbroken Chain Foundation in 1997.

Friday March 17
Saturday March 18
★ Sunday March 19
The Spectrum, Philadelphia, Pennsylvania

The band explores the Beatles' psychedelic period with, on Friday, "Lucy in the Sky" as an encore and, on Saturday, the breakout of "It's All Too Much," George Harrison's contribution to the *Yellow Submarine* soundtrack. Sunday's gig is perhaps the show of the year, as it witnesses the totally unexpected, first-ever live performance of "Unbroken Chain" *(see above)*—greeted with euphoria.

6 – 15 | 16 | **17** | **18** | **19**

20 | 21 | **22** | **23** | **24** | 25 | **26** | **27** | 28 | **29** | 30 | 31

Wednesday March 22
Thursday March 23 ★
Friday March 24
Charlotte Coliseum,
Charlotte, North Carolina

Bruce Hornsby sits in for the entire second show, this time on piano rather than accordion.

Sunday March 26
Monday March 27
Wednesday March 29
Thursday March 30
The Omni, Atlanta, Georgia

Left: Jerry and Bob at The Spectrum, Philadelphia, Pennsylvania, March 17–19.

"HIGH TIME"
GARCIA/HUNTER

Despite the misleading title, which seems to suggest a party song on the order of a "Sugar Magnolia" or "The Music Never Stopped," the bittersweet sentiment of love lost that infuses "High Time" instead makes for one of the most plaintive ballads the Dead ever recorded, while its plodding pace left many with the opinion that it was a song only a Deadhead could love. Though a shimmering take appeared on *Workingman's Dead* (1970), where Garcia once again put his new pedal steel skills to good use, the guitarist said that it was his least favorite track on the album. "It's a beautiful song, but I was just not able to sing it worth a shit," he admitted frankly in 1971. "I really can't do justice to that kind of song now. I'm not that good a singer." For whatever reason, the Dead did bring the tune back into its setlist during a June 9, 1976, Boston gig after a six-year absence, and ended up playing it a total of over 100 times between 1969 and 1995 (last played on March 24), even though, as Garcia inadvertently points out in one line from "High Time," "it could always go wrong."

GRAYFOLDED:
TRANSITIVE AXIS/ MIRROR ASHES
Grateful Dead/John Oswald

Released by Swell Artifacts (SW/ART 1969-94) in 1995

Transitive Axis

1. Novature (Formless Nightfall)
2. Pouring Velvet
3. In Revolving Ash Light
4. Clouds Cast
5. Through
6. Fault Forces
7. Phil Zone
8. Estrella Oscura
9. Recedes (While We Can)

Mirror Ashes

1. Transilience
2. 73rd Star Bridge Sonata
3. Cease Tone Beam
4. Speed of Space
5. Dark Matter Problem/Every Leaf Is Turning
6. Foldback Time

Personnel

Tom Constanten, Jerry Garcia, Keith Godchaux, Mickey Hart, Bruce Hornsby, Bill Kreutzmann, Phil Lesh, Ron McKernan (Pigpen), Brent Mydland, Bob Weir, Vince Welnick

Produced by John Oswald

THE BRAINCHILD OF "plunderphonic" maestro John Oswald, *Grayfolded* drew on Vault tapes of more than 100 separate performances of "Dark Star," from 1968 to 1993, to produce a sound that captured the magic of the Grateful Dead at their live best. All tracks were produced with the band's blessing (David Gans brought the project to the band's attention) and credited to Oswald/Skjellyfetti, except "Phil Zone" which saw the ever *avant* Phil Lesh get more involved. *Grayfolded*, in fact, was a two-part project: the first CD, subtitled *Transitive Axis*, was shipped in a double-CD case with an order form for the second disc, *Mirror Ashes*.

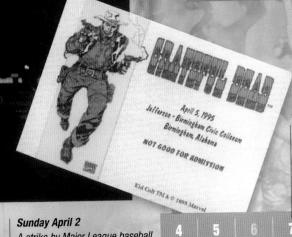

Above and inset: *Saturday March 18, The Spectrum, Philadelphia, Pennsylvania.*

10 ~ 18 | **19** | **20 ~ 30**

Wednesday April 19
A bomb destroys the Alfred P. Murrah federal building, Oklahoma City, Oklahoma, killing 169 people in what was then the worst-ever terrorist attack on U.S. soil.

Deadnet Launched

Deadheads have been active on-line through BBS's, Usenet, and the WELL for years, but now the Grateful Dead staked an "official" claim in cyberspace with the launch of dead.net on the burgeoning World Wide Web. Robert Hunter took on the role of webmaster, and his on-line journals and commentary quickly became one of the most popular parts of the site.

♪ Friday April 7
Tampa Stadium, Tampa, Florida

The Black Crowes open.

Sunday April 2
A strike by Major League baseball players, which forced the cancellation of the 1994 World Series, ends after 234 days.

4 | **5** | **6** | **7** | **8** | **9**

♪ Tuesday April 4
♪ Wednesday April 5 ★
Birmingham-Jefferson Civic Center Coliseum, Birmingham, Alabama

Another return to a Southern city last visited many years ago, in this case April 28, 1980. Neville Brothers' drummer "Mean" Willie Green funks up "Matilda" and "Drums" during Wednesday's gig.

APRIL '95

1 | **2** | **3**

♪ Saturday April 1
♪ Sunday April 2
The Pyramid, Memphis, Tennessee

The band celebrates its first show in Memphis in 25 years with a first-set, locally themed mini-medley *à la* the February 21 show in Salt Lake City: Hunter/Garcia's "Candyman" ("I came in from Memphis…") followed by Al Green's great mix of the sacred and the profane, "Take Me to the River," which the Talking Heads appropriated on 1978's *More Songs About Buildings and Food*.

"ONE MORE SATURDAY NIGHT"

WEIR

An early Bob Weir rave-up and one of the few Dead songs on which the guitarist has sole credit, this offering from Weir's album *Ace* (1972) owes a debt to Chuck Berry, Robert Hunter (who withdrew his involvement with the tune after Weir reportedly mangled his lyrics), and the politically turbulent times in which it was written. "Everybody's dancin' down the local armory, with a basement full of dynamite and live artillery," Weir sings with mock glee in one of the many couplets that are delivered rapid-fire throughout the song. "The temperature keeps risin' everybody gettin' high, come the rockin' stroke of midnight the whole place is gonna fly." Hunter would sharpen a finer political barb with "U.S. Blues" *(see page 153)*, a title that Weir had originally hoped to use for this. Not surprisingly, "One More Saturday Night" often served as the topper during the Dead's Saturday shows, despite its original debut on Tuesday, October 19, 1971. In addition to over 300 go-rounds with the group ending with their last-ever Saturday performance in Chicago on July 8, 1995, "One More Saturday Night" continued to appear in sets by Ratdog and The Other Ones.

The Tour from Hell

It lasted less than a month but it would go down in Deadhead legend as the Tour from Hell: a harrowing passage in which bad fortune stalked the Grateful Dead from Vermont to Chicago, with the media there to report (and hype) every accident and nasty episode.

Onstage, Jerry seemed to be turning into a specter in front of the eyes and ears of the audience: always pale, obviously exhausted, often confused, he sometimes turned his guitar volume down so low in the mix that it was barely audible, as if he wanted to spare Deadheads from the musical evidence of his physical decline. The fact that the band (and Jerry) could still sometimes summon up the X Factor—for a solo, a song, or even a whole show—just made the overall situation seem worse, somehow.

No one, of course, knew then that this would be the band's last tour, but even without the benefit of hindsight, it was clear in June and July of '95 that one way or another, the darkness had to give.

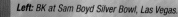

MAY '95

| 1 ~ 16 | 17 | 18 | **19** | 20 | 21 | 22 | 23 |

🎸 **Friday May 19**
🎸 **Saturday May 20**
Sunday May 21
Sam Boyd Silver Bowl, Las Vegas, Nevada

The Dave Matthews Band opens all three shows at the Silver Bowl. The Kentucky Derby didn't fall on a show day this year, but today, Saturday, is the Preakness, and that's good enough reason to bring out "The Race is On." The encore is, naturally, "One More Saturday Night" *(see right)*. On the third night Dave Matthews Band drummer Carter Beauford sits in on "Drums."

🎸 **Sunday May 28**
🎸 **Monday May 29**
Portland Meadows, Portland, Oregon

Chuck Berry, still reelin' and rockin' at 68, opens both Portland shows—despite the hopes of the audience, Chuck doesn't sit in with the band, or vice versa. The last "Good Times" is performed at Monday's show.

May 1995

438

Above: Sound man John Cutler in May 1995.

JUNE '95

| 24 | 25 | 26 | 27 | 28 | 29 | 30 | 31 | 1 | 2 | 3 | 4 | 5 ~ 12 | 13 | 14 | **15** | 16 | 17 | **18** | **19** |

🎸 **Wednesday May 24**
🎸 **Thursday May 25**
Friday May 26 ★
Seattle Center Coliseum, Seattle, Washington

🎸 **Friday June 2**
🎸 **Saturday June 3**
🎸 **Sunday June 4**
Shoreline Amphitheatre, Mountain View, California

The Gyuto Monks take the stage on Friday during "Drums" for ten minutes of otherworldly chanting.

🎸 **Thursday June 15**
Franklin County Airport, Highgate, Vermont

The band's return to northern Vermont set the tone for the tour. Minimal publicity had kept the '94 Highgate audience at a manageable 60,000, but around 80,000 people—including, it seemed, every rowdy between New Jersey and Maine—showed up in '95. The gates had to be opened to prevent a disaster. Musically, it was a lackadaisical exercise—in a reverse of summer '86, many in the audience found Bob Dylan's opening set more enjoyable than the Grateful Dead's two sets. The show also saw the breakout of the band's last cover—the old Delta blues "Rollin' and Tumblin'," recorded by both Muddy Waters and Elmore James.

🎸 **Sunday June 18**
🎸 **Monday June 19**
Giants Stadium, East Rutherford, New Jersey

Bob Dylan opens both nights at Giants stadium. It's 30 years to the day since Phil Lesh, clutching a bass "with a neck like a telephone pole," played his first show with the Warlocks at Frenchy's. Most of the 6/16 version of "The Other One" is performed without Jerry.

The Weirs at Bay

Baru Bay, Australia by Bob Weir/Wendy Weir (Hyperion Books For Children)—a children's book plus audio cassette produced by Bob and Wendy Weir—was published on May 8. The Weirs hoped that the project, a combination of realism and fantasy, would inspire and educate young readers about the need to preserve the fragile balance of the coral reef. Proceeds from *Baru Bay* went to benefit Coral Forest and the Yothu Yindi Foundation.

Below: The Gyuto Monks take to the stage on Friday June 2, Shoreline Amphitheatre, Mountain View, California.

Left and above: *Sunday June 18, Giants Stadium, East Rutherford, New Jersey.*

Friday June 30
Three Rivers Stadium,
Pittsburgh, Pennsylvania

In the final instance of meteorological synchronicity at a show, the heavens open just as the second set opens with "Rain"; the band follows with "Box of Rain," "Samba in the Rain," and "Looks Like Rain."

Tuesday June 27
Wednesday June 28
The Palace, Auburn Hills, Michigan

20   21   22   23   24   25   26   27   28   29   30

Wednesday June 21 ★
Thursday June 22
Knickerbocker Arena, Albany, New York

Outside on the opening night, ticketless fans attempt to rush the gates; several are injured (along with some police) and arrested. Inside, the band plays one of its better shows of the tour.

Saturday June 24
★ Sunday June 25
RFK Stadium, Washington, D.C.

Bob Dylan opens both nights at RFK Stadium. Bruce Hornsby plays the entire first show on grand piano, and the band revives "Black Muddy River," last heard on August 13, 1991. A day later a freak lightning strike hits three people in one of the RFK parking lots before the show. All survive, but the spooky symbolism is lost on no one. Bruce Hornsby again guests on piano. Jerry Garcia, seemingly reenergized for the night, backs up Dylan on "It Takes a Lot to Laugh, It Takes a Train to Cry" and "Rainy Day Women #12 and 35."

"UNCLE JOHN'S BAND"

GARCIA/HUNTER

"Well the first days are the hardest days, don't you worry anymore..." So begins one of the most beloved songs in all of Deaddom. The first track and the melodic linchpin of *Workingman's Dead* (1970), it marked a major transition for the band, with lush harmonies and glimmering acoustics that were a complete turnaround from the acid-soaked days of the past. *Rolling Stone* blithely predicted, "Staunch Dead freaks probably will hate this song." In fact, it became the theme for a sort of Grateful Dead alter ego. "Come hear Uncle John's Band, by the riverside," the refrain invites, manifesting an idyllic setting in any venue. "Got some things to talk about, here beside the rising tide." The song's real origins had more to do with the Greek-Macedonian motifs Garcia was fiddling with on the fingerboard at the time and a drifter Hunter had known of who had a circus of fleas dressed in band uniforms and happened to be named Uncle John. But it made its own history from its first full performance at the Fillmore West in December of 1969. "'Uncle John's Band' was a major effort as a musical piece," Garcia said in 1971. "It's one we worked on for a really long time to get it working right." The time-shifting coda that ends in a wash of voices after a few bars on the album version was opened up in the live arena for some brilliant minor-key jamming that often stretched the song to over 10 minutes long by 1977, and over 12 during an unforgettable performance at the Fox Theatre in Atlanta, Georgia on May 19, 1977. Last played by the Dead at Auburn Hills on June 28, 1995, the song was brought back to an acoustic setting by The Other Ones for Neil Young's Bridge School on October 27, 2002.

"BLACK MUDDY RIVER"

GARCIA/HUNTER

"When the last rose of summer pricks my finger and the hot sun chills me to the bone..." Any misconceptions that the Dead's hit 1987 album *In The Dark* would end on a high note were dashed with "Black Muddy River," a Garcia/Hunter swan song that seemed especially prophetic during the band's last performance with Garcia nine years after it debuted on December 15, 1986. Inspired by a recurring nightmare that Hunter has described as "one of the most chilling experiences that I've had," the wordsmith acknowledged in a 1992 interview that the song was ultimately about the darkness of death. Hunter gave Garcia the song's lyrics while he was recovering from a diabetic coma in 1986; two hours later Garcia had completed the tune. The song routinely appeared during the band's encores and was part of a rare two-song encore on July 9, 1995, Garcia's last concert with the group. Discerning listeners can clearly hear him sing "last muddy river" during one of the verses of this final rendition.

The Last Show

It's an unusually cool July night in Chicago as the Dead take the stage for their 2,318th show (by *DeadBase*'s calculations). The band's misfortunes this tour have been national news, so cameras from 11 news services and TV channels are poised like vultures to capture anything untoward. There's nothing to record. The crowd is well-behaved. The foremost emotion among the band and crew is relief that this is the last show of a wretched tour.

As Jim Egan notes in his *DeadBase* review, this show can't be separated from its historical context. Reading retroactive significance into the band's song choices and other aspects of performance is a favorite Deadhead head game, and of course, more so for this show than any other: did Jerry give some sign that he knew what lay ahead? Probably not—Blair Jackson later observed that if Jerry had some inkling of his approaching demise, he would hardly have chosen the life-affirming "Touch of Grey" as the opener.

But what (some would argue) about Jerry's particularly impassioned performance of "So Many Roads"? Was it just end-of-tour relief at soon being homeward bound, or did he sense something? And then there's the matter of the encore. Most Deadheads were expecting the customary tour closer, "Brokedown Palace," but instead, Jerry sang the unmistakably elegiac "Black Muddy River" *(see left)*, which had been revived, after more than four years, just a few shows earlier. "Black Muddy River" was Jerry's swan song, but it was a double encore, and so the last song ever performed by the Grateful Dead in concert was "Box of Rain," another eloquent mediation on love and loss, written by Phil Lesh and Robert Hunter for Phil's dying father: "Such a long, long time to be gone/And a short time to be here"… As the last notes fade, fireworks—including a giant heart—light up the sky over Lake Michigan, to the accompaniment of the Jimi Hendrix "Star-Spangled Banner" that closed Woodstock.

Bob gives an end-of-tour hug to Jerry, the band leaves the stage, the roadies begin the load-out, and 58,000 fans start to make their way to the parking lots, basking in that post-show glow. As Jerry gets into the van after the show, however, he remarks he's had a great time that night and wished the tour didn't have to end.

Set list: *Set 1:* Touch of Grey, Little Red Rooster, Lazy River, Masterpiece (Weir on acoustic), Childhood's End, Cumberland Blues, Promised Land. *Set 2:* Shakedown Street, Samson & Delilah, So Many Roads, Samba in the Rain, Corrina -> Drums -> Space -> Unbroken Chain, Sugar Magnolia. Encore: Black Muddy River, Box of Rain.

Wednesday July 5
Thursday July 6
Riverport Amphitheater, Maryland Heights, Missouri

In response to the Deer Creek crowd problems, another Deadhead mailing is sent out on July 5: "Want to end the touring life of the Grateful Dead? Allow bottle-throwing gatecrashers to keep thinking they're cool anarchists instead of the creeps they are…" At that night's show, still concerned over the death threats against Jerry, the band play with the house lights on. The show ends without incident, but later that night, at a campground outside, Deadheads crowd onto a cabin porch seeking shelter from the rain. The roof collapses, injuring more than 100, and leaving one person paralyzed.

JULY '95

| 1 | 2 | 3 | 4 | 5 | 6 | 7 |

Sunday July 2
Deer Creek Music Center, Noblesville, Indiana

Local police inform the band that someone has phoned in a death threat against Jerry. The band goes on with the show, trusting to security and metal detectors. (Unaware of the threat, the audience can't grasp the ironic overtones of the first-set "Dire Wolf," with its "Please, don't murder me" refrain.) Unfortunately, about 20,000 ticketless partiers have descended on central Indiana, and halfway through the first set there's a run on the gates by between 1,000 and 5,000 of them. What's worse, many inside the venue help the ticketless get in. Citing danger to themselves, the police refuse to provide security inside the venue for the July 3 show, which is then canceled.

HOT HOUSE

Bruce Hornsby

Released July 18, 1995; (RCA 66584)

Bruce Hornsby's fifth album is released—the second to be credited to just Hornsby, and the third Hornsby album to include a Garcia contribution (on "Cruise Control").

A Stab At Rehab

Back in the Bay Area, Jerry stopped by Dave Grisman's studio on July 16 to record Jimmie Rodgers' "Blue Yodel #9" for a tribute album to the "Singing Brakeman" being put together by Bob Dylan. It was his last recording. The next day Jerry checked into the Betty Ford Clinic in Rancho Mirage, California, in his latest effort to kick his heroin habit. The Grateful Dead Family welcomed the news, since this was Jerry's first inpatient, 12-step-based rehab.

Two weeks into the 30-day initial program, however, Jerry checked himself out, reportedly because he didn't want to spend his 53rd birthday in rehab—which would suggest he didn't fully grasp the recovery paradigm in the first place. Jerry also didn't like the food and the atmosphere. In his last conversation with Robert Hunter, he said that the best thing about the experience was meeting a security guard who had played with Django Reinhardt, one of Jerry's guitar heroes.

| 8 | 9 | 10 | 11 | 12 | 13 | 14 | 15 | 16 | 17 | 18 |

Saturday July 8
Sunday July 9 ★
Soldier Field, Chicago, Illinois
The Band opens both shows.

Monday July 17
Jerry checks into the Betty Ford Clinic.

Right: A day of mourning: grief-stricken Deadheads pay their respects (pictures taken August 9)

Serenity At Last

On August 8, Jerry Garcia checked himself into another rehab facility, Serenity Knolls in Marin County. He picked Serenity Knolls because of its proximity to Lagunitas, where the Grateful Dead had enjoyed good times in '66. Apparently convinced he needed to separate himself from the scene in order to really straighten out, he told almost no one, not even Deborah. Unfortunately, while he was determined to put heroin behind him, drugs were just one of Jerry's chronic health problems, and he was not receiving proper treatment for any of them.

At 4:23 a.m. on August 9, a member of the Serenity Knolls staff did a bed-check and found that Jerry wasn't breathing. Attempts to revive him failed. A week into his 54th year, Jerome John Garcia had died of a heart attack in his sleep.

Later, at the funeral home to which Jerry's body was taken, Deborah Garcia was surprised by Jerry's beatific facial expression. She asked the funeral-home staff if they'd done that to him; no, they replied, he looked that way when he was brought in. So Jerry Garcia passed into eternity with a smile on his face.

In the nights of goodbye…

No Deadhead would ever forget where they were and what they were doing when they heard the news of Jerry Garcia's death.

By mid-morning a tie-dyed flag flew at half-mast over San Francisco's city hall. Flowers were strewn and candles lit in front of 710 Ashbury, in Golden Gate Park, in Strawberry Fields in New York's Central Park. In college dorms, in suburban subdivisions, in city offices, those who had been touched by Jerry's music gathered to share their grief and their memories. Others gathered in cyberspace in mourning no less intense for being "virtual." The tributes began flooding in:

"There is no way to measure his greatness as a person or a player… he really had no equal. To me he wasn't only a musician and friend, he was more like a big brother who taught and showed me more than he'll ever know… His playing was moody, awesome, hypnotic, and subtle. There's now way to convey the loss. It just digs down really deep." BOB DYLAN

"He was a great talent; he was a genius… He also had a terrible problem that was a legacy of the life he lived and the demons he dealt with. And I would hope that all of us who loved his music would also reflect on the consequences of self-destructive behavior."
PRESIDENT BILL CLINTON

The Funeral

A private funeral for Jerry Garcia was held at St. Stephen's Episcopal Church in Belvedere, just north of San Francisco. (The church was chosen not for its name, but for its location and the fact it could accommodate the 250 or so invited mourners.) The Rev. Matthew Fox, who had married Jerry and Deborah Koons just 20 months earlier, led the service.

Among those present, besides the band, crew and office staff, were Ken Kesey, Bob Dylan, Bill Walton, Barbara Meier, Sarah Ruppenthal Katz, Heather Garcia Katz, and Annabelle and Trixie Garcia. Deborah Garcia refused to invite Mountain Girl, though M.G. was able to view Jerry's body at the preceding evening's wake. Deborah also excluded Manasha Matheson and John Kahn; she (and others) considered Kahn one of Jerry's enablers. Kahn attended anyway, staying in the back.

David Grisman (who slipped a guitar pick into Jerry's casket) played "Amazing Grace" and "Shalom Aleichem"; Gloria Jones and Jackie LaBranch, the "Jerryettes" of the Jerry Garcia Band, sang the spiritual "My Living Shall Not Be in Vain" accompanied by Melvin Seals. The eulogies were both touching and irreverent, something Jerry no doubt would have appreciated. For many in the pews of St. Stephen's that summer afternoon, the most emotional moment came when Robert Hunter rose to deliver a eulogy-in-verse to his longtime friend and creative partner:

Now that the singer has gone,
Where shall I go for the song?…
…May she bear thee to thy rest,
beyond the solitude of days,
the tyranny of hours—
the wreath of shining laurel lie
upon your shaggy head,
bestowing power to play the lyre
to legions of the dead.

And with a final standing ovation, the service ended. Jerry's body was cremated; his ashes would be scattered the following spring (see page 452).

Deadheads 'mourning with music,' 1,2D

'FARE THEE WELL'
Generations grieve for Jerry Garcia

'The loss … just digs down really deep.'
— Bob Dylan

DIES AT 53: Jerry Garcia often sang 'fare thee well,' from the Dead song 'Brokedown Palace.'

Right: Cover Story on USA Today

COVER STORY

Grateful Dead founder's death 'end of an era'

Band's future unclear after guitarist dies in clinic; "body gave …"

Wednesday August 9
Bob Weir and Ratdog take the stage of a club in New Hampshire, packed inside and outside with grieving Deadheads. "If our dear, departed friend proved anything to us," Bob tells the tearful crowd, "he proved that great music will remain."

Tuesday August 8
Jerry Garcia goes into rehab again, this time in Serenity Knolls.

Tuesday August 1
Jerry Garcia's 53rd birthday.

Wednesday August 9
Jerry Garcia passes away peacefully in his sleep.

Friday August 11
Jerry Garcia's funeral.

Sunday August 13
Memorial Celebration held in Golden Gate Park.

The Celebration

On the morning of August 13, 25,000 people gathered at the Polo Fields in Golden Gate Park—site of the Human Be-In 28 years earlier—to publicly celebrate Jerry Garcia's life and legacy. Above a small stage loomed a 30-foot-tall painting of a beaming Jerry, holding his guitar as if he was about to launch into a solo. By the end of the day the space in front of the stage had become an impromptu shrine, heaped with flowers, mementos, and messages.

The celebration kicked off with a New Orleans funeral parade around the Golden Gate grounds, followed by rhythmic and vocal invocation by Babatunde Olatunji. One by one, Jerry's fellow bandmates and family members took the stage to address the crowd. Annabelle Garcia thanked the Deadheads, on behalf of herself and her sisters, for putting them through college—"and we didn't have to work at the Dairy Queen." Bob Weir expressed his gratitude to Jerry for "showing me how to live with joy and mischief." Vince Welnick noted that "the first time I ever laid eyes on Jerry, I believed in Santa Claus. He could be ornery at times, but that was his body talking,

not his soul. Because I never met a kinder man in the world."

"If the Grateful Dead did anything," said Mickey Hart, "we gave you the power… You have the groove, you have the feeling. We've been working on it for 30 years now. So what are you going to do with it? That's the question."

"As the ceremony ended, with a drum recessional to the familiar "Not Fade Away" beat, the celebration began, with the assembled throng embracing, crying, smiling and, of course, dancing, to several hours' worth of primo recorded Grateful Dead music, blasting in all its glory through the Dead's powerful P.A. system. The music was lovingly selected by vault archivist Dick Latvala (ably abetted by Grateful Dead Hour *host David Gans). Dick's first pick for the afternoon was, appropriately, the Dead's cover of a Beatles classic: 'It's All Too Much.'*

And indeed, it was. And indeed, it still is."
FROM THE *GRATEFUL DEAD ALMANAC*, VOL. III, NO. 1

"There is not a sentence in the world that could do justice to the life and music of Jerry Garcia." BRANFORD MARSALIS

Jerry Garcia 1942 – 1995

JERRY GARCIA'S DEATH MEANT MORE THAN THE LOSS of a brilliant musician; it marked the passing of an American cultural icon. The Grateful Dead's persistence into the '90s was widely held up as proof that the spirit of the '60s had not entirely died with that decade, but with Jerry gone, a major link in the chain had broken irreparably.

Whether or not the Grateful Dead would go on without Jerry wasn't clear in the immediate aftermath of his death; the band announced the cancellation of the Fall Tour but made no comment about their long-term plans. Whether the band went on or not, however, it would not be the same entity. The Golden Road ended at Golden Gate Park, August 13, 1995.

In the weeks that followed Jerry's passing, it seemed that every pundit and talking head in the country felt obliged to make some comment, to analyze What It All Meant in editorials heavy with pop sociology. A few right-wingers, most notably columnist George Will, sermonized along the lines of the-wages-of-hippiedom-is-death. In their view, Jerry had been a pied piper who for three decades had seduced innocent American youth into a morass of drugs and hedonism, and away from God, the flag, Mom, and apple pie. In fairness, several commentators on the left side of the divide said much the same thing, and it should also be noted that criticism of Jerry's drug use was usually mitigated by the fact that he died in his sleep while trying to straighten out, instead of being found floating in a swimming pool or asphyxiated on his own vomit in customary rock-star fashion.

The harsher voices were largely drowned out by those who looked on Jerry with respect for his artistic achievement and affection for his personality. In a way, though, the sometimes uncritical posthumous praise heaped on Jerry was sometimes as wrongheaded as the judgments passed by George Will and his fellow travelers.

In his last years, Jerry's shaggy visage was familiar to Americans who had never been near a Dead show and who couldn't identify any of the band's songs. In the collective mind Jerry had become, like Vince Welnick said, Santa Claus with a guitar; chubby, white-bearded, avuncular, kindly. The man had an ice cream flavor named after him. You could even buy a cuddly, stuffed Jerry Garcia doll. Nobody was about to market a cuddly, stuffed Bob Dylan doll.

Jerry, of course, was neither wicked pied piper nor rock 'n' roll Santa Claus. He was capable of acts of great grace and generosity, certainly; a man of humor and courtesy, yes. But Jerry's emotional insecurity, his hatred of confrontation, his unwillingness to do it any way but the way he wanted to, all took a toll on the people closest to him, and ultimately on himself. When, at the funeral, Annabelle Garcia described Jerry as "a great man and a shitty father," everyone there knew exactly what she meant—Jerry himself once told an interviewer that "anyone who thinks I'm God should talk to my kids."

And then there was Jerry's famed ambivalence about his leadership role in the Dead and, by extension, in the subculture that evolved around the band. Jerry was technically correct in insisting he was not the leader of the band; but it was a role that fell on him by default, rightly or wrongly. Perhaps if he had accepted this fact—if he had understood just how much he meant to so many people—he might have had the motivation to take better care of himself.

In *Sweet Chaos: The Grateful Dead's American Adventure*, Carol Brightman offers perhaps the most clear-eyed assessment of the forces at work within and without Jerry at the end of his life: "Garcia was an old dog who'd been doing his tricks for too long, with too many bones heaped beside his plate, to summon the energy to walk away. Besides, he was a performer in the archaic sense, who felt he was an instrument of forces outside himself. An ego-driven star would have burned out much sooner. The constant playing was how he justified himself before his gods; he made himself a fit instrument, a worthy vessel."

Jerry had the roles of pop-culture icon and subculture leader foisted on him; all he ever wanted to be was a musician, and his music, ultimately, is the only valid context in which to approach his life. And what music it was. Master of a half-dozen musical idioms, Jerry nevertheless became a true original. He is one of maybe a dozen guitarists whose sound is instantly recognizable. His voice, while not that of the conventional rock singer, is at its best just as expressive as his guitar. It has even been said that the example of Jerry's lead singing has encouraged may thin-voiced aspiring vocalists to persevere.

The breadth of Jerry's musical accomplishment is equally impressive: more than 2,300 Grateful Dead shows from 1965 through 1995; at least 1,300 other performances during this same period, with the Jerry Garcia Band, Old & In the Way, Legion of Mary, Reconstruction, Howard Wales, Merl Saunders, John Kahn, David Grisman, and others; 13 studio albums with the Grateful Dead, and a dozen or so studio solo or collaborative efforts; performances or other contributions to more than 60 other albums; plus the "contemporary" live albums, archival releases, and all those thousands and thousands of hours of tapes… What these numbers can't measure, however, is the sheer joy that Jerry Garcia's music has given, and continues to give; in that respect, the music has not stopped, and never will.

"Jerry was the best musician I ever played with. He was 100 percent music. Every pore, every bit of his body, every molecule, was music, whether he liked it or not." BILL KREUTZMANN

"As far as I'm concerned, he's still here really, inside me and all around. His leadership and his influence isn't something that disappeared with his body. I hear it whenever I'm playing." BOB WEIR

"Where do you begin? There's so much to say about him. He was a genuine, lovable guy and he was also a magic man, a shaman. There was a feeling of going out in the world with kindness that Jerry represented." MICKEY HART

"We never really talked about this, because it was so obvious to all of us, but he knew he wasn't making that music; it was like he was just up there quoting or transcribing what it was that was being given to him or coming through him,

Grateful Dead: A Photofilm

One of the more unusual tributes to appear after Jerry's death (though work had started on it before) was a "photofilm" directed by Paul McCartney, and based on photos taken by Linda Eastman McCartney. In 1967 and 1968 the late Linda McCartney (then Linda Eastman, and a well-known photographer) snapped about 150 shots of the band in New York and San Francisco, both in performance and "candid." With the aid of a computer, Sir Paul "animated" these stills and added various effects to create a nine-minute documentary that was eventually distributed by Miramax.

OCTOBER '95

| 1 | 2 | 3 | 4 | 5 ~ 31 |

Sunday October 1
A Los Angeles jury acquits O.J. Simpson in the murder of his ex-wife, Nicole Brown Simpson, and Ronald Goldman.

Friday September 8
Sanjay Mishra's *Blue Incantation* CD is released today, with Jerry Garcia as special guest. Garcia played on three tracks of this album by guitarist Mishra and his ensemble.

SEPTEMBER '95

| 1 | 2 | 3 | 4 | 5 | 6 | 7 | 8 | 9 | 10 ~ 30 |

Friday September 1
Billed as the "Ratdog Revue," Ratdog (Bob Weir, Matt Kelly on guitar and harmonica, Rob Wasserman on bass, Jay Lane on drums) play two nights at San Francisco's Warfield Theatre (9/1–2) and at the annual Hog Farm Picnic in Laytonville, California. Vince Welnick joins on keys, Prairie Prince guests on percussion, and Henry Kaiser sits in on several numbers on guitar.

Saturday September 9
Kurt Loder of *MTV News* briefly interviews Bob Weir before the MTV Awards show:

"I'm sure he's still singing. I can hear it. I'm sure anyone who was ever exposed to that, you know, joy and that creativity and that wickedness and all that kind of stuff he used to project, that mischief. And the love, it's still there. You know it's in you. You can't lose that—once you catch that it stays in you. And so it's not like he's gone." BOB WEIR

A Pigpen Solo Album?

Pigpen started work on a solo album in 1969, recording "I'm a Loving Man" in a San Francisco studio with a backup band that included Jerry Garcia and Bob Weir. He apparently recorded two more songs in 1970 and three more (recorded in his Corte Madera apartment) shortly before his death in March 1973. These songs circulated on tapes, as did earlier solo and pre-Dead Pigpen material, including at least one song ("McKernan's Blues") from his band the Second Story Men, c.1963. But none of this material was ever collated into a commercially released album. Or was it? An Internet music site includes a listing for a CD titled *Bring Me My Shotgun*, supposedly released by Capricorn Records in 1995. From the track list, it would appear that this album includes the 1969–70 songs as well as some earlier material. Unfortunately, it's impossible to determine the derivation of the music on the CD, or any other details—it isn't available from any retail outlet.

Left: *Memorial Celebration for Jerry Garcia held in Golden Gate Park, Sunday August 13. The day begins with fond speeches from band, family, and crew, and later features hours of taped Grateful Dead music from all eras.*

GD Disband

On Friday December 8, the day after the band meeting when the decision was made to "retire" the Grateful Dead, the Dead office issued the following statement:

"'The wheel is turning and you can't slow down
You can't let go and you can't hold on
You can't go back and you can't stand still...'
'THE WHEEL,' ROBERT HUNTER

"After four months of heartfelt consideration, the remaining members of the band met yesterday and came to the conclusion that the 'long, strange trip' of the uniquely wonderful beast known as the "Grateful Dead" is over. Although individually and in various combinations they will undoubtedly continue to make music, whatever the future holds will be something different in name and structure."

In making this announcement, band members were especially mindful of their partners in this adventure, the Deadheads, urging them to remember that the music, the values, and the spirit of this marvelous shared journey endure.

Tuesday November 7
In 1985, Tom Gehrels, an astronomer at the University of Arizona's Kitt Peak Observatory, discovered a small asteroid orbiting between Mars and Jupiter. For ten years the heavenly body was known only as Asteroid 1985RB1. Shortly after Jerry Garcia's death, two Deadhead astronomers, Ed Olszewski and Simon Radford, came up with the idea of naming some heavenly body for the late great one. There are rules, however; major celestial features can't be named for individuals (though asteroids can) and only discoverers can do the naming. But Gehrels was happy to cede 1985RB1 to Olszewski and Radford, and so the International Astronomical Association re-registered the asteroid as 4442 Garcia. (The Beatles, Eric Clapton, and Frank Zappa have also had asteroids named after them.)

NOVEMBER '95

| 1 ~ 6 | 7 | 8 ~ 28 | 29 | 30 |

Wednesday November 29 – Saturday December 16
Ratdog tour the Southwest and California, with Vince Welnick playing his last show 12/12, in Santa Barbara, California. Edwin McCain, Cindy Wasserman, and Merl Saunders guest at various shows.

Manager Cameron Sears announces that Mickey Hart's new group, Mystery Box, and Bob Weir's group, Ratdog, will tour, with other performers, in the summer of '96 in a traveling festival similar to H.O.R.D.E. or Lollapalooza. Deadheads immediately dub the upcoming tour "Deadapalooza" but the tour is officially called the "Furthur Festival."

DECEMBER '95

| 1 ~ 6 | 7 | 8 ~ 31 |

Thursday December 7
The surviving band members meet to determine the Grateful Dead's future. Bill Kreutzmann tells his bandmates he can't go out on the road again, so the collective decision is made to retire the name "Grateful Dead."

KEEP ON, TRUCKIN'

January 1996 – Future Unknown

On Pearl Harbor Day—December 7, 1995—Bill Kreutzmann dropped a bomb of his own. He told the other remaining members of the Grateful Dead that he wouldn't be flying in from Hawaii to attend the big meeting that had been called to discuss the future of the group in the post-Garcia world; for him, it was over. The next day it was formally announced that the Grateful Dead would no longer tour—and if they did in the future, it would not be under that name. But this did not mean that the Dead organization was about to fade away, nor did it mean the players were retiring from music—far from it. Bob Weir was touring with his group Ratdog at the time of Garcia's death, and he

The Core Four—Kreutzmann, Lesh, Hart, and Weir—are all smiles during a rehearsal break at their Novato, California, studio before their triumphant Summer 2003 tour.

continued on with that band. Mickey Hart had been recording an album with a group he called Mystery Box. Vince Welnick plunged into a dark depression after Garcia's death but eventually regained his footing and went on to form a truly great band—Missing Man Formation.

In the summer of 1996, Weir, Hart, and Bruce Hornsby spearheaded the first Furthur Festival (named after the Merry Pranksters' bus), designed to bring Deadheads together for an eclectic afternoon and evening of music by their respective solo bands and sympathetic friends, but the tour was not a financial success. The following summer's Furthur Festival also failed to draw big crowds.

By the following summer, Phil Lesh had emerged from semiretirement and could be found haunting Bay Area clubs occasionally with an ever-changing aggregation known as Phil Lesh & Friends. Then, for the third Furthur Festival, Lesh joined Weir, Hart, and Hornsby, Ratdog sax player Dave Ellis, Phil's drummer John Molo, and guitarists Steve Kimock and Mark Karan in a group cleverly dubbed The Other Ones. The band's blend of classic and rearranged Dead songs, Hornsby tunes, and originals by Hart and Weir drew rave reviews from most Deadheads, and the tour was a box office hit as well. "The heat coming from the audience was tremendous," Hart said that fall. "They were hungry and we were hungry and we all sat together for a big feast. We were all desperate for that Grateful Dead feeling." Near the tour's end, a visit from Bill Kreutzmann to jam had fans salivating about the prospect of a true reunion of the four surviving core members the next year.

It was not to be. That fall, Lesh became seriously ill with hepatitis C, which he'd first been diagnosed with in 1992, but which had been dormant. Now he was so sick that to save his life he underwent a liver transplant in Florida in late 1998. Phil was becoming increasingly disenchanted with the way the Grateful Dead organization was being run,

though, and he was consistently outvoted by Weir, Hart and Kreutzmann on business matters. Finally, the relationship between Lesh and the others deteriorated into acrimony, and during his recuperation that winter and spring of 1999, Phil decided to completely disengage from the day-to-day affairs of the organization, both business-wise and musically.

Itching to play music again, Lesh revived Phil & Friends with a series of shows in April 1999 that included Trey Anastasio and Page McConnell of Phish jamming out spectacularly on Grateful Dead and other tunes. After a year of shifting lineups, Lesh settled on a group that included Allman Brothers and Gov't Mule guitarist Warren Haynes, former Aquarium Rescue Unit guitarist Jimmy Herring, keyboardist Rob Barraco of the Zen Tricksters, and the one fixture of all the bands—drummer John Molo. After playing on and off for more than two years, this last group had gained a large and devoted following because of their unwavering commitment to bold improvisation.

"There's a whole new world of kids coming up that want to feel it, that want to experience what we have to offer. " MICKEY HART TO BLAIR JACKSON

At the same time as Phil & Friends were crisscrossing the country, Ratdog and two different bands led by Mickey Hart—first, the rockin' Mickey Hart Band, then a wondrous multi-ethnic group known as Bembe Orisha—were touring independently. Ratdog put out a fine album of original material called *Evening Moods* and their playing seemed to grow more adventurous with each passing tour.

In the summer of 2000, The Other Ones hit the road again, this time with Bill Kreutzmann joining the lineup, but without Phil. The tour drew mixed reviews from Deadheads, many of whom seemed hurt and confused by the intensity (and duration) of the internecine squabbling, especially on New Year's Eve—when Phil & Friends played at Kaiser Convention Center in Oakland, while The Other Ones hosted a rival concert across town at the Oakland Arena.

By the middle of 2001, there had been a thaw in the relationship between Weir and Lesh. Ratdog and Phil & Friends toured together that summer. That New Year's Eve, to the delight of the assembled Deadhead throng, both groups were on the same bill, and when midnight rolled around, Phil, Bobby, Mickey, and Billy (and assorted members of Ratdog and Phil & Friends) were all up there onstage together, rocking through "Sugar Magnolia" one more time, smiles all around. "Unity is possible!" Lesh declared from the stage.

Then, in the summer of 2002, came a two-day event at Alpine Valley Music Theatre in Wisconsin—a former GD stronghold—billed as a "Grateful Dead Family Reunion." Ratdog, Phil & Friends, Bembe Orisha, Kreutzmann's solo band The Trichromes, and Robert Hunter were all part of the action. But all eyes (and ears) were on a new version of The Other Ones, this one featuring the Core Four plus a mixture of players from Ratdog and Phil & Friends—guitarist Jimmy Herring and keyboardists Jeff Chimenti and Rob Barraco. The show was a triumph all around, and it was followed that fall by a very successful East Coast tour.

"I thought the tour was a gas," Phil Lesh said in mid-2003. "It was really interesting to see what everyone had learned and how they had grown during the years we hadn't played together. So for me it had the feeling of

New name, new faces: The Dead in 2003. Left to right: Phil Lesh, Bill Kreutzmann, Jeff Chimenti, Bob Weir, Rob Barraco, Mickey Hart, Jimmy Herring, Joan Osborne.

According to Rolling Stone, *each of the four major members of the Dead stood to make upwards of two million dollars from the summer 2003 tour.*

being old and new at the same time. I thought everyone in the band was playing more interestingly than they had been at the end of the Grateful Dead."

In the spring of 2003 came the next step: at Phil's suggestion, the group dropped the name "The Other Ones" and became known simply as The Dead. "It says, 'This is who we are,'" Phil explained, and it still gives a proper amount of respect to Jerry's memory. That group will always be the Grateful Dead. This is something a little different, but still in that line."

For their big 2003 summer tour, The Dead's lineup was strengthened by the addition of Joan Osborne, a soulful belter who broadened the group's palette considerably.

Hovering over everything the surviving Grateful Dead have done since August 9, 1995, is the towering shadow of Jerry Garcia. Every guitarist is, alas, measured against Garcia, every lineup of every group compared to the Grateful Dead. It's an impossible standard, and everybody knows it. Yet they bravely forge on, digging out bits of musical magic from the strangest of places, reaching deep inside to discover the gold of a new alchemy, drawing on a combination of inspiration, synaptic memory, and the invisible bonds of love and friendship to keep on truckin' down that Golden Road.

"I keep hearing Jerry in my ear and he's saying, 'Yeah! Go! Go! Go! Yeah! Yeah! Yeah!'" Hart said with a laugh before the 2003 Dead tour. "Jerry's really loud and he's riding shotgun with me."

Symphony Space

At the invitation of the San Francisco Symphony's musical director, Michael Tilson Thomas, Phil Lesh, Mickey Hart, Bob Weir, and Vince Welnick join the orchestra *(right)* in June for performances of John Cage's "Renga/Apartment House 1776." Another program, "An Afternoon with America's Musical Visionaries," saw the four plus Tilson Thomas debut SPACE for Henry Cowell, in an original "group improvisation." (Menlo Park-born Cowell was an influential modernist composer and teacher, as well as an early exponent of what would later be called "World Music.")

Starting out in an ethereal place, not unlike some "Space" segments of Dead shows, the piece gathered momentum; the 13-minute jam built to a furious crescendo and came to an explosive end—followed by a rapturous ovation that lasted nearly as long as the piece itself.

Ratdog

Bob Weir's duo with Rob Wasserman on bass evolved in the spring of '95 into Ratdog, with Jay Lane on drums and Matt Kelly on guitar, harmonica, and vocals. This lineup soon added Johnnie ("B. Goode") Johnson, once Chuck Berry's pianist, for a year, until he pretty much retired from the road and was supplanted in 1997 by Jeff Chimenti. Dave Ellis joined on sax around this time, and was in turn succeeded by Kenny Brooks. Lead guitarist Mark Karan came over after first appearing with The Other Ones, and in 2003 Robin Sylvester replaced Rob Wasserman. Ratdog built up a strong following through constant performance (nearly 500 shows between mid-'95 and mid-'03); the band's first album, *Evening Moods (see page 461)* appeared in 2000, followed by a live album, *Live at Roseland*, a year later.

The Living Dead

Rock Scully had been fired by the band, so many Deadheads expected his book, *Living With the Dead* (co-written with David Dalton), to be a hatchet job. In fact, it's a witty, vastly entertaining chronicle of the band's life and high (often very high) times from the Acid Tests to the '80s. There's some ax-grinding here and there, but it's a good antidote to the often overserious writings about the band.

Final Farewells

The surviving band members (minus Mickey Hart), Tiff Garcia, Laird Grant, Ram Rod, Francis Shurtliff, Steve Parish, Annabelle Garcia, Theresa Garcia, Sunshine Kesey, Heather Katz, Sue Stephens, Cameron Sears, Cassidy Law, Dennis McNally, Bob Weir, and others gathered at a dock in Marin to take Jerry Garcia's ashes out to sea aboard the *Argosy Venture*. Some of them are scattered over the water at the entrance to the Golden Gate, between Land's End and Point Bonita. Mountain Girl was at the dock, but in a sign of the incipient conflict between the two widows, Deborah Koons Garcia refused to let her board the vessel.

Also in April, a group including Deborah Koons Garcia and Bob Weir went to Benares, India, and scattered part of Jerry Garcia's ashes into the Ganges River, where, in the Hindu tradition, the soul of the departed will swiftly find an auspicious reincarnation.

MARCH '96

APRIL '96

Thursday April 4
"Unabomber" Theodore Kaczynski spends his first full day in custody after his arrest in Montana.

4

Thursday May 30
Death of John Kahn.

Friday May 31
Timothy Leary dies in Los Angeles.

MAY '96

25 30 31

Saturday May 25
Ratdog and Mystery Box (Mickey Hart, Zakir Hussain, Sikiru Adepoju, Giovanni Hidalgo, Dave Garibaldi all on percussion, Bakithi Kumalo on bass, and the vocal group Mint Juleps) perform at the Laguna Seca Raceway, Monterey, California.

JUNE '96

Dark Star: An Oral Biography of Jerry Garcia

Robert Greenfield compiled this chronicle of Jerry's life from interviews with more than 60 friends, family, and associates.

FEBRUARY '96

JANUARY '96

Garcia Still Rolling

Garcia, by editors of *Rolling Stone*, is a handsome, well-designed compilation of the magazine's interviews with and articles on Jerry, from 1970 to shortly before his death.

MYSTERY BOX
Mickey Hart

Rykodisc 10338

Described by Dead scholar Oliver Trager as "Mickey Hart's percussion-vocal fantasy," this ensemble included Giovanni Hidalgo, Zakir Hussain, and the female vocal group the Mint Juleps, plus Bob Weir, Bruce Hornsby, and the usual cast of World Music all-stars in supporting roles. Robert Hunter provided the lyrics for the album's ten tracks.

John Kahn 1948 – 1996

On May 30, 1996, John Kahn died at his Mill Valley home from heart failure. The bassist had outlived his friend and collaborator Jerry Garcia by less than a year and passed on in very similar circumstances.

Kahn had the longest tenure of any of Jerry's many musical partners, beginning with the Matrix jam sessions in '70 through more than 1,000 performances with Old and In the Way, Legion of Mary, and Reconstruction, and he'd been the one constant member of the Jerry Garcia Band through all its lineups. Kahn was also one of Jerry's closest friends, and Jerry spent much time with John and his wife Linda, especially during the last, difficult years of the guitarist's life, when both men were troubled by problems with drug abuse.

Salute to the Fallen

One of the most highly regarded of the post-'95 bands, Vince Welnick's Missing Man Formation—the name comes from the formation flown by military pilots to salute a fallen comrade—originally also included Steve Kimock and Bobby Vega of Zero on guitar and bass, respectively, ex-Tubes drummer Prairie Prince, and Todd Rundgren alum Bobby Strickland on keys and vocals. The band's repertoire featured covers of '60s BritRock classics and old/esoteric Dead songs like "Cream Puff War."

Jerry Garcia Award Winners

In 1996 the Rex Foundation established the Jerry Garcia Award to commemorate the Grateful Dead guitarist and founding Rex board member. This award was designed to honor and support those individuals and groups working to encourage creativity in young people.
The recipients to date are:
Precita Eyes Mural Arts Center, San Francisco (1996)
BRAVA! For Women in the Arts, San Francisco (1997)
La Pena Cultural Center, Berkeley (1998)
Mission Cultural Center for Latino Arts, San Francisco (1999)
Babatunde Olatunji (2000)
Loco Bloco Drum & Dance Ensemble of San Francisco (2001)
MACLA (supporting Latino artists), San Jose (2002)

THE ARISTA YEARS
Grateful Dead

Arista 18934-2

A double CD with 25 songs (plus the entire "Terrapin Station suite") drawn from the albums released by Arista between 1977 and 1981, this compilation is a passable introduction to the latter-day Dead, but it was dissed by Deadheads for its lack of bonus material or unreleased tracks and its selective focus.

Friday July 19
The music for the opening ceremonies of the Olympic Games in Atlanta includes "Call to the Nations," a 12-minute composition contributed by Mickey Hart & Friends.

JULY '96

27

Saturday July 27
A bomb kills two people and leaves more than 100 hurt at the Atlanta Olympics. The explosion occurs near a sound-and-lights setup worked by Candace Brightman and Ultra Sound employees Mike Brady and Don Pearson (they are uninjured).

AUGUST '96

SEPTEMBER '96

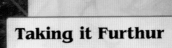

OCTOBER '96

15 29

Tuesday October 15
Second Sight is released on CD. The only album from this electrono-psychedelic outfit comprising Vince Welnick, Bob Bralove, Bobby Strickland, Henry Kaiser, and Marc and Paul van Wageningen, *Second Sight* includes guitar work from Jerry Garcia on two tracks and Bob Weir on one track.

Tuesday October 29
Shady Grove by Jerry Garcia and David Grisman is released. The third album from the duo features 13 traditional songs (and the "hidden track," "Hesitation Blues"), recorded at Grisman's Dawg Studios between 1990 and 1995.

NOVEMBER '96

4

Tuesday November 4
Ticket to New Years video is released by Grateful Dead records. The footage is taken from the 1987 NYE show at Oakland Coliseum Arena.

DECEMBER '96

Playing in the Band

Subtitled *An Oral and Visual Portrait of the Grateful Dead*, Dead scholar and broadcaster David Gans and photographer Peter Simon's book was originally published in 1985. Phil Lesh contributed the foreword.

Taking it Furthur

Inevitably dubbed "Deadapalooza," the mobile Furthur Festival '96 *(left)* rolled through 31 shows from 6/20 to 8/4. Ratdog headlined, with Mickey Hart's Mystery Box, Bruce Hornsby, Los Lobos, Hot Tuna, Alvin "Youngblood" Hart, John Wesley Harding, and The Flying Karamazov Brothers performing. Robert Hunter also played some shows, and Phil Lesh sat in with his old bandmates for a jam at the Shoreline show on 7/30. Each show included seven or eight hours of music, and the interartist jams that ended each event were the highlights for most of those in attendance. Furthur even had its own version of Shakedown Street, with officially licensed vendors, and Deadheads could even call the familiar Grateful Dead Ticket Service hotline for ducats. Still, Furthur '96 was given a mixed reception. Phil Lesh, of course, was conspicuous by his absence, and even though there was some great music to be had, it was only a year after Jerry Garcia's death and many 'Heads weren't ready to go Furthur just yet.

Furthur '97

The lineup for the second Furthur Festival (28 dates in all) included the Black Crowes, Ratdog (in their new lineup with Dave Ellis and Jeff Chimenti), Mickey Hart and Planet Drum, Jorma Kaukonen and Michael Falzarano, vocalist-fiddler Sherri Jackson, and improv quartet moe.. Arlo Guthrie both performed and MC'd, and Robert Hunter played the last leg of the tour—his first public performances in seven years. As he had in '96, Phil Lesh joined for the Shoreline Amphitheatre show, jamming with Bob Weir, Mickey Hart, and Bruce Hornsby, along with Bonnie Raitt. Another high point was the Saratoga New York Performing Arts Center show, in which Bob Weir joined moe. for a workout of the entire "That's It for the Other One" suite. Despite fine performances (especially from a revitalized Ratdog), however, Furthur '97 lost money and got mixed reviews. The decision to have the Black Crowes as the "headline" act was faulted by some, since the Crowes' southern-fried hard rock didn't sync entirely with the jam-band vibe.

Above: Robert Hunter and Bob Weir (center) jamming at Further '97.

Above: Mickey Hart at Further '97.

JANUARY '97

Zabriskie Point: Original Soundtrack is released on two CDs. The first contains an excerpt from "Dark Star" from *Live/Dead* and "Love Scene," a Garcia solo recorded on January 20, 1970. The second CD contains four alternate versions of "Love Scene Improvisations." These were also recorded in January, 1970, but not used in the movie.

454

FEBRUARY '97

Dose Hermanos, the band formed by Tom Constanten and Bob Bralove, release *Sonic Roar Shock*, an album culled from a series of gigs in New York City in January 1996.

18

Tuesday February 18
Release of *Relix Bay Record Shop, Vol. 9: Tribute To Jerry Garcia* by Various Artists. This consists of a mix of music and interviews with the friends and collaborators of Jerry's, including Tom Constanten, Jorma Kaukonen, and Marmaduke Dawson. The CD was intended mainly for radio use but found its way into retail channels.

MARCH '97

6

Thursday March 6
Phil Lesh and Bob Weir guest with the David Murray Octet at the Fillmore, San Francisco, California.

APRIL '97

5

Tuesday April 15
Release of *How Sweet It Is* by the Jerry Garcia Band. This live CD is drawn from 1990 JGB shows at San Francisco's Warfield Theatre.

15

19

Above, top: Bob Weir with Bonnie Raitt at Shoreline during Furthur '97.
Above: Weir with Ratdog saxophonist Dave Ellis and bassist Rob Wasserman.

Jeff Chimenti

Born in South San Francisco, keyboardist Jeff Chimenti is one of the brightest stars of the new generation of Bay Area musicians. At home in every music genre from jazz to blues and funk, Jeff has worked with everyone from R&B divas En Vogue to jazz-fusion pioneers Larry Coryell and Steve Marcus, as well as being a core member of the Bay Area "underground supergroup" Alphabet Soup. Jeff joined Ratdog in late '96 and shortly thereafter became one of The Other Ones and, now, The Dead.

Monday May 5
Allen Ginsberg dies in New York City.

Saturday April 19
Anthem to Beauty, directed by Jeremy Marre, airs on VH-1. A segment in the music channel's Classic Albums series, *Anthem to Beauty* is a fascinating look at how the band and their music evolved from the avant-garde experimentalism of *Anthem of the Sun* to the rootsy, almost-acoustic *American Beauty*. The documentary includes some terrific interviews with band members and others, including Joe Smith of Warner Bros. *Anthem to Beauty* is now available on DVD.

MAY '97

1

Thursday May 1
Tony Blair is elected prime minister of Great Britain.

13

Tuesday May 13
Release of *Furthur* on Hybrid. Not—as one might think from the title—a live CD of performances from the '96 Furthur shows, but instead a compilation of previously released material (both live and studio) from bands and artists that took part in Furthur, including Ratdog, Mickey Hart's Mystery Box, Hot Tuna, Bruce Hornsby, John Wesley Harding, and Alvin Youngblood Hart.

Unbroken Chain Foundation

Taking its name from the song (see page 436), Phil Lesh established the Unbroken Chain Foundation in 1997 as a "nonprofit organization which seeks to perpetuate the long-standing tradition of community service that has been the hallmark of the remarkable three-decade relationship between the Grateful Dead and its audience. The foundation's mission is to generate support for, and public awareness of, groups and individuals that bring hope and inspiration to communities where great need exists, and to create partnerships of people working together for a common good, especially in such areas as the arts, education and the environment." Like the Rex Foundation (see page 295), UBC supports a wide variety of good causes at the grass-roots level, from the Bay Area Women's and Children's Center to UC Berkeley's Young Musicians Program.

The UBC also coordinates Odyssey of the Spirit, which encourages local volunteerism. The UBC is funded primarily through benefit concerts by Phil Lesh & Friends; the first event, "PhilHarmonia" (right), was held at San Francisco's Maritime Hall on December 7, 1997, and included Edie Brickell, David Grisman, Bruce Hornsby, Jackie LaBranch from the Jerry Garcia Band, Donna Jean (Godchaux) MacKay, Graham Nash, and San Francisco Symphony musical director Michael Tilson Thomas. *"My wife Jill said, 'Why don't we have a singalong benefit where the audience is the band, essentially' and so we put that together…"*
PHIL LESH ON THE ORIGINS OF THE FOUNDATION AND THE PHILHARMONIA EVENT, IN AN INTERVIEW WITH *JAMBANDS.COM*

BREAKDOWN
Old & In the Way

Acoustic Disc ACD-28

Garcia plays banjo on this Acoustic Archive Series recording of live performances from 1973. Old & In the Way's eclectic and extensive repertoire is once again well represented: *Breakdown* has 18 previously unreleased tracks and includes a hidden track—"Blue Mule" ends at 4:26, then there is silence before "Catfish John" starts at 5:35.

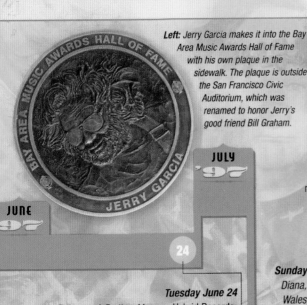

Left: Jerry Garcia makes it into the Bay Area Music Awards Hall of Fame with his own plaque in the sidewalk. The plaque is outside the San Francisco Civic Auditorium, which was renamed to honor Jerry's good friend Bill Graham.

JUNE '97

JULY '97

24

Tuesday June 24
Release of *Furthur More* on Hybrid Records. Like *Furthur*, this is a mix of live and studio from tracks from the artists and performers of Furthur '97, although unlike the first compilation, this disc includes three tracks recorded at Furthur '96 shows: Bruce Hornsby's "Rainbow's Cadillac" and two jams, "All Along the Watchtower" and "Proud Mary" > "Not Fade Away."

AUGUST '97

31

Sunday August 31
Diana, Princess of Wales, dies in car crash in Paris.

SEPTEMBER '97

21

Sunday September 21
Phil Lesh makes the first of several appearances with Broken Angels, a multi-member band led by Dead scholar David Gans and Dead associates Bob Bralove and Gary Lambert, at the Deadhead Community Center Benefit, Ashkenaz, Berkeley, California.

OCTOBER '97

7

Tuesday October 7
Release of *Downhill from Here* video, which includes footage from two July 1989 Grateful Dead shows at the Alpine Valley Music Theatre, Wisconsin.

NOVEMBER '97

DECEMBER '97

7

Sunday December 7
PhilHarmonia Concert at Maritime Hall, San Francisco, California.

The American Book of the Dead

Both wide-ranging and wonderfully written, Oliver Trager's *The American Book of the Dead: The Definitive Grateful Dead Encyclopedia* stands with *DeadBase* and Dave Shenk and Steve Silberman's *Skeleton Key* as essential references for the Deadhead bookshelf. More than 750 alphabetically organized entries in the tome cover albums, songs, people, bands, books, and anything else related to the band, its members, their solo/side projects, and musical influences.

THAT HIGH LONESOME SOUND
Old & In the Way

Acoustic Disc ACD-19

A long overdue release of additional material from the October 1 and 8, 1973, OAITW shows at the Boarding House in San Francisco. The songs include plenty of bluegrass standards, an interesting reworking of the Platters' "The Great Pretender," and a couple of Peter Rowan originals, including the title track, an ode to the joy of bluegrass festivals.

War of the Wives

One of the most unpleasant aspects of Jerry Garcia's passing was the legal/financial wrangles over his estate. The guitarist's final will (drawn up in 1994) divided his estate among his widow Deborah Koons Garcia, his four daughters, Sunshine Kesey, and his brother Tiff. In the months after Jerry's death, however, the estate's executors were inundated with other claims against the estate that ultimately totaled almost $40 million.

The bitterest conflict of all was between Deborah Koons Garcia and Carolyn "Mountain Girl" Garcia over the provisions in Jerry and M.G.'s 1993 divorce agreement—a battle that *People* magazine called "the War of the Wives." The conflict became a media circus thanks to the Court TV cable network's near-continuous coverage of the December '96 hearings, including O.J. Trial–style commentary from legal talking heads. The judge ruled in favor of Mountain Girl, whereupon Deborah Garcia appealed, and it seemed that War of the Wives II was about to start in mid-1998 when M.G. settled the suit.

456

Release data for several 1998 offerings is unavailable, but during the year, various Dead alumni were active in the studio. Bill Kreutzmann's group, Backbone, released an eponymous album on GDR. The band's lineup included Rick Barnett on guitar and lead vocal and Ed Cook on bass and sax.

Donna Jean by the Donna Jean Band: this release from Donna Jean Godchaux MacKay's band, recorded at Muscle Shoals Sound, Alabama, includes a track titled "American Beauty."

Live From California by Dose Hermanos: live tracks recorded at the Fillmore in 1997 from Bob Bralove and Tom Constanten, aided by Joe Gallant (bass), Henry Kaiser (guitar), Steve Kimock (guitar), and Prairie Prince (electronic drums).

Side Trips Volume One: a live album recorded during jams by Howard Wales and Jerry Garcia at the Matrix, San Francisco, in 1971.

JANUARY
'98

13

Tuesday January 13
Release of *Weir/Wasserman Live* by Bob Weir and Rob Wasserman. Most of the tracks on this live CD (which includes several of Weir's Grateful Dead songs, including "Throwing Stones" and "Victim or the Crime," were recorded at the duo's 1988 shows.

Tuesday January 27
Classic Albums: Anthem to Beauty (see page 454) is released on video.

Furthur With The Other Ones

The '98 Furthur Festival—or, more precisely, "The Other Ones on the Further Festival with Hot Tuna and Rusted Root"—comprised 24 shows, starting at Atlanta's Lakewood Amphitheatre and ending with two shows at Shoreline. Most fans found this outing more enjoyable than '96 and '97 festivals. For one thing, there was the joy in seeing Bob Weir, Mickey Hart, Phil Lesh, and Bruce Hornsby in the same band—and a band that played brilliantly. Also, the fact that there were only three main acts meant longer sets, which meant more jamming and exploration.

For Furthur '98, The Other Ones lineup was, in addition to those listed above, John Molo (drums), Dave Ellis (sax), and Steve Kimock and Mark Karan (guitars). Hot Tuna's lineup saw Michael Falzarano (guitar), Pete Sears (piano), and Harvey Sorgen (drums) join Jorma Kaukonen and Jack Casady.

The addition of Rusted Root—a sextet that built their reputation, like the Dead's, on the basis of their incomparable live shows—was an excellent choice, linking the original "jam band" with one of their most acclaimed successors.

FEBRUARY
'98

27

MARCH
'98

Friday February 27
Phil Lesh & Friends (Phil Lesh, Bob Weir, Jeff Chimenti, Dave Ellis, Stan Franks, Jay Lane) perform at the Benefit for Unbroken Chain Foundation, Fillmore Auditorium, San Francisco, California.

APRIL
'98

20   30

Monday April 20
Phil Lesh & Friends (band includes Bruce Hornsby, John Molo, Branford Marsalis, and Bob Weir) perform at the Warfield Theatre, San Francisco, California.

Thursday April 30
A "surprise show" (with Phil Lesh, Bob Weir, Sammy Hagar, Jay Lane, Henry Kaiser, and others) at the Bohemian Club Theater, San Francisco, with a stellar lineup.

MISSING MAN FORMATION
Missing Man Formation
Arista 14058

The only album (so far) by Vince Welnick's solo band—featuring Vince, Steve Kimock, Prairie Prince, and Bobby Vega, with Robin Sylvester, Scott Matthews, Trey Sabatelli, Bobby Strickland, Barbara Mauritz, and Juan Cutler—includes a version of the "Samba In the Rain" (written for the Dead by Welnick and Robert Hunter) and another Welnick/Hunter song, "Golden Stairs," and "Devil I Know" by Welnick with John Perry Barlow and Bob Bralove.

"The word is out. The Grateful Dead are gone, but The Other Ones are worthy successors."

STEVE MORSE IN THE BOSTON *GLOBE*

Friday May 15
Ratdog and Phil Lesh (with David Crosby) perform at this "Sing Out for SEVA" benefit—for Wavy Gravy's SEVA foundation—at the Berkeley Community Theatre, Berkeley, California.

MAY
'98

14   15

Thursday May 14
Frank Sinatra dies in Los Angeles.

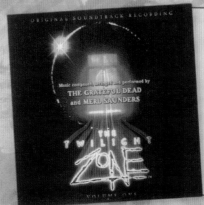

TWILIGHT ZONE SOUNDTRACK
The Grateful Dead and Merl Saunders
Silva Screen Records FILMCD-203

Theme and "incidental" music from the 1985 TV show by the Grateful Dead in various combinations. Merl Saunders was the show's musical director. The soundtrack album was dedicated to the memory of "Rod Serling and Jerry Garcia, two men who have gone beyond *The Twilight Zone* far too soon."

Phil's Ills

In late '98 Phil Lesh began to experience internal bleeding, signaling that his hepatitis C, dormant for most of the decade, had become active. He was hospitalized for a time in September, and rumors raced around the Deadhead Internet community that the bassist was seriously ill—rumors fueled by the fact that his name didn't appear on the bill for a New Year's Eve show at Oakland's Kaiser Auditorium.

On December 7, Phil broke the silence with a post on Dead.net announcing that he was indeed scheduled for liver transplant surgery. He asked fans to direct "healing light" toward him and to give blood. For ten days, Deadheads waited anxiously for news, and on December 17, they learned that Lesh had successfully undergone the surgery that day at the Mayo Clinic in Jacksonville, Florida, and his prognosis was good. Phil's recovery was, indeed, amazingly rapid; he was performing again barely four months after the operation.

MOTHER McCREE'S UPTOWN JUG CHAMPIONS

Released by Grateful Dead Merchandising (GDCD 4064) in 1998

1. **Overseas Stomp**
   (Jones/Shade)
2. **Ain't It Crazy (a.k.a. The Rub)**
   (Hopkins)
3. **Boo Break**
4. **Yes She Do, No She Don't**
   (DeRose/Trent)
5. **Memphis**
   (Berry)
6. **Boodle Am Shake**
   (Palmer/Williams)
7. **Big Fat Woman**
   (Traditional)
8. **Borneo**
   (Donaldson)
9. **My Gal**
10. **Shake That Thing**
    (Jackson/Traditional)
11. **Beat It On Down The Line**
    (Fuller)
12. **Cocaine Habit Blues**
    (Hart/Shade)
13. **Beedle Um Bum**
    (Dorsey)
14. **On The Road Again**
    (Traditional)
15. **The Monkey And The Engineer**
    (Fuller)
16. **In The Jailhouse Now**
    (Rodgers)
17. **Crazy Words, Crazy Tune**
    (Milton Ager/Jack Yellen)
18. **Band Interview**

Personnel

Jerry Garcia – guitar, kazoo, banjo, vocals
Pigpen (Ron McKernan) – harmonica, vocals
Bob Weir – guitar, washtub bass, footcrasher, jug, kazoo, vocals
Dave Parker – washboard, kazoo, tin cup, vocals
Tom Stone – banjo, mandolin, guitar, vocals
Mike Garbett – washtub bass, guitar, kazoo

Produced by Michael Wanger

In 1964 two Stanford students, Michael Wanger and Wayne Ott, had a radio show, *Live from the Top of the Tangent*, on KZSU, the university radio station. The show was not broadcast live, but taped at the Tangent coffeehouse. That July, the duo recorded 16 songs, and an interview with the band—Jerry Garcia, Bob Weir, Pigpen, Dave Parker, Tom Stone, and Mike Garbett. Five years on, Wanger and Vance Frost produced *The Grateful Dead: A Documentary*, broadcast on San Francisco's KSAN. It included a couple of songs from one of the Tangent tapes (which then made their way into circulation among early Tapers) but it seemed that all but one reel of the tapes were lost. Then, in '97, Michael and his brother Pete discovered the lost tapes in the attic of their mother's house. From these tapes Jeffrey Norman and John Cutler produced this CD, which presented the songs as if recorded in continuous performance—although the material was taped over several shows. The typical jug-band songs ("Overseas Stomp," "In the Jailhouse Now") include a couple that made it into the Dead's repertoire (Jesse Fuller's "Beat It on Down the Line" and "The Monkey and the Engineer"). And so a priceless historical document— the first known recording of Jerry, Bob, and Pigpen playing together—made its way into release.

COMPENDIUMS

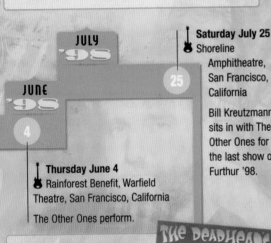

Poet and songwriter Michael M. Getz and *Dupree's Diamond News* publisher John M. Dwork—plus a host of Tapers and associates— produced this truly monumental three-volume work of Dead scholarship: reviews and detailed information on every recorded performance by the band and their predecessors, from a '59 concert by the College of San Mateo Jazz Band (Phil Lesh on trumpet) to July 9, 1995. It also includes interviews with taping luminaries like Dick Latvala and others.

JULY '98

25

Saturday July 25
Shoreline Amphitheatre, San Francisco, California

Bill Kreutzmann sits in with The Other Ones for the last show of Furthur '98.

JUNE '98

4

Thursday June 4
Rainforest Benefit, Warfield Theatre, San Francisco, California

The Other Ones perform.

Friday August 7
Saturday August 8
The Other Ones take on the Phil Lesh & Friends moniker for two shows to benefit the Unbroken Chain Foundation.

AUGUST '98

7   8   18

Friday August 7
First reviews of Mickey Hart and Planet Drum's *Supralingua* (released August 4). It explores the primordial relationship between rhythm and the human voice (the title means "beyond words"). Besides the Planet Drum ensemble, *Supralingua* has contributions from the top ranks of world music, including Zakir Hussain and Baba Olatunji.

Tuesday August 18
Release of *So What*, by Jerry Garcia and David Grisman. The fourth album from the Dawg Duo showcases their jazz side, including no fewer than three versions of the eponymous Miles Davis classic.

SEPTEMBER '98

6

Sunday September 6 – Sunday September 27
Ratdog—with Rob McNabb as the group's first full-fledged lead guitarist—tour the Midwest and West.

OCTOBER '98

13

Tuesday October 13
Release of Bruce Hornsby's *Spirit Trail*. Hornsby returns to his piano roots for his sixth album.

NOVEMBER '98

DECEMBER '98

10   31

Thursday December 31
Ratdog and Mickey Hart and Planet Drum join Hot Tuna, KVHW (Steve Kimock, Bobby Vega, Alan Hertz, and Ray White), Santana, and String Cheese Incident at the Henry J. Kaiser Convention Center, Oakland, California, to usher in the last year of the millennium.

Thursday December 10
Bob Weir, Mark Karan, Steve Kimock, and Mickey Hart and Planet Drum perform at "Forest Aid," Mateel Community Center, Redway, California—a fundraiser for rainforest preservation.

457

THE STRANGE REMAIN
The Other Ones

Grateful Dead Records (Arista) 4062

A live double CD recorded during the July '98 Furthur shows, *The Strange Remain* includes both heavy-rotation Dead material ("China">"Rider") and revived classics ("St. Stephen">"The Eleven"), two Bruce Hornsby songs ("White-Wheeled Limousine" and "Rainbow's Cadillac"), and several Robert Hunter originals: "Only the Strange Remain," written with Mickey Hart, which first appeared on Mickey's '95 *Mystery Box* album; "Banyan Tree," written with Mickey and Bob Weir; and another Hunter/Hart number, "Baba Jingo."

Above: Friday September 17, Shoreline Amphitheatre, Mountain View, California. Phil Lesh bounces with Phish on their trademark trampolines.

What A Long, Strange Trip

Subtitled "The Stories Behind Every Grateful Dead Song," Stephen Peters' *What A Long Strange Trip* is just that—an album-by-album analysis of all the band's original songs, in terms of how they were written, the musical influences informing them, the nuances of the lyrics, performance history, and any other relevant context. *What A Long Strange Trip* includes not only songs from the band's pre-1995 "official" releases but "outtakes," "lost" songs, unrecorded songs, and "performance pieces" like Phil Lesh and Ned Lagin's 1974 electronic explorations. It's the key to the canon.

Tuesday April 27
Phil Lesh, Bob Weir, Mickey Hart, John Molo, Steve Kimock, Jeff Chimenti, Sammy Hagar, Rebecca Mauleon, and Keta Bill perform at an Open Nature Benefit for Bohemia Waterfall Park held at Luther Burbank Center for the Arts, Santa Rosa, California.

Friday June 4
Ken Kesey, Ken Babbs, and a Prankster Party pack Furthur off to England on an expedition in search of Merlin the Wizard (to be filmed for British TV).

APRIL '99

6

20 27

JUNE '99

1 4

Tuesday June 1
Cuba launches a $181.1 billion compensation claim against the US government for deaths and injuries sustained in the 50-year anti-Castro "dirty war."

MARCH '99

Tuesday April 6
Bob Weir and Mickey Hart sit in with the Flying Other Brothers—a conglomeration of Bay Area music scene stalwarts—at a benefit for Al Gore's presidential campaign held in Woodside, California. Tipper Gore, who once played drums for a group called the Wildcats, gives Mickey some help on percussion.

Tuesday April 20
In the worst of a spate of school shootings, two high school boys kill 13 and wound 23 more at Columbine High School, Littleton, Colorado.

MAY '99

29

Saturday May 29
The latest iteration of Phil Lesh & Friends (Lesh, Kimock, Molo, Merl Saunders, Gov't Mule guitarist Warren Haynes, and Donna Godchaux MacKay) perform at the Mountain Aire Festival, Calaveras County Fairgrounds, Angel's Camp, California. Mickey Hart and Planet Drum also perform.

FEBRUARY '99

16

JANUARY '99

Tuesday February 16
Ratdog and Mickey Hart and Planet Drum celebrate Mardi Gras at the Warfield Theatre, San Francisco, California.

Sweet Chaos

From the author of the award-winning *Writing Dangerously: Mary McCarthy and Her World*—and the sister of Candace Brightman, the band's lighting director—Carol Brightman's *Sweet Chaos* is a clear-eyed chronicle of the Dead's odyssey that shows how the band was both a product of its times and a shaper of them. Subtitled "The Grateful Dead's American Adventure," Brightman's examination of the Dead in a political and cultural context strips away some of the warm-and-fuzzy mythology about the band.

Rob Barraco

Keyboardist (and occasional bassist) Rob Barraco has lived the ultimate Deadhead fantasy—to play with the band (or at least a couple of its post-Jerry iterations). Rob attended about 100 shows between '72 and '78. After graduating from the State University of New York at New Paltz, Rob put his chops to work in a diverse series of gigs before taking on keyboard duties with the Zen Tricksters, which used Dead tunes as the basis for jazzy improvisation. In late '99, Phil Lesh tapped Rob for Phil Lesh & Friends, and he stayed on through the 2002 creation of The Other Ones, along with Jeff Chimenti of Ratdog. Barraco and Chimenti remained when The Other Ones became The Dead in the spring of 2003, and they gave both bands a powerful double-keyboard punch. Rob also played bass at several Ratdog shows in February '03.

Garcia: An American Life

Still the only full biography of Garcia to come out since his death, Blair Jackson's *Garcia: An American Life* is not just an authoritative chronicle of Jerry's life and music, but functions equally well as a history of the band as a whole. Jackson's affection for and closeness to his subject is evident throughout, but never clouds his objectivity.

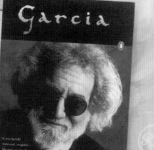

Thursday July 15
Bob Weir marries Natascha Muenter, with Mickey Hart, Phil Lesh, and John Perry Barlow in attendance.

Friday July 23
Saturday July 24
Sunday July 25
Bruce Hornsby and Mickey Hart and Planet Drum perform at the Woodstock '99 festival in Rome, New York, which ends, unfortunately, with rioting, looting, and assorted mayhem.

JULY '99

2   15   23

Friday July 2
Saturday July 3
Phil Lesh & Friends (Lesh, Kimock, Bill Kreutzmann, David Nelson, Mookie Siegel, Barry Sless) perform at the Warfield Theatre, San Francisco. Songs include Phil and Bobby Petersen's "New Potato Caboose," which the Grateful Dead retired in 1969.

Thursday August 12
Bob Weir, Mickey Hart, Henry Kaiser, Greg Anton, Bobby Vega, Bob Bralove, Sandy Rothman, David Nelson, and Pat Campbell perform at the Dick Latvala Memorial, held at the Phoenix Theater, Petaluma, California.

AUGUST '99

6   12

Friday August 6
Vault archivist Dick Latvala dies following a heart attack at age 56, and the Deadhead world loses one of its most colorful—and beloved—characters. The series of archival releases he began in 1993 will continue under the *Dick's Picks* imprint.

SEPTEMBER '99

17   18   30

Friday September 17
Having borrowed Trey Anastasio and Page McConnell back in April, Phil Lesh returns the favor by guesting with Phish at the Shoreline Amphitheatre, Mountain View, California—even taking a bounce or two on Phish's trademark trampoline. Warren Haynes joins Phil and Phish for the "Viola Lee Blues" encore.

Saturday September 18
Bob Weir sits in with "The Sensitive Ones" (Bruce Hornsby, Bonnie Raitt, Shawn Colvin, Jackson Brown, David Lindley, and Wally Ingram) and Phil Lesh sits in with Phish at the Shoreline Amphitheatre, Mountain View, California.

Thursday September 30
With the San Francisco Giants about to move to PacBell Stadium, Phil Lesh, Bob Weir, and Donna Godchaux MacKay sing "The Star-Spangled Banner" to open the final baseball game at Candlestick Park.

SO MANY ROADS (1965–1995)
Grateful Dead
Arista 4066

Produced by three top Dead scholars—David Gans, Blair Jackson, and Steve Silberman—with the help of the late Dick Latvala's archives, this five-CD set was the first major "retrospective" of the band's entire career. The 47 tracks were mostly drawn from live performances and rehearsals (e.g. "Eternity"), but also included the early Warlocks demos (e.g. "Can't Come Down") and studio outtakes (e.g. "Mason's Children," "Believe It Or Not"), many of which hadn't appeared in any "official" GD release. A promo sampler CD was released simultaneously, with one track not on the box set.

Phil Lesh & Friends release *Love Will See You Through* on Grateful Dead Records, a live double CD of mostly Grateful Dead songs, recorded at the Warfield Theatre, San Francisco, shows on June 4–5, 1999. The CD was produced by Lesh and his wife Jill.

OCTOBER '99

Dose Hermanos' *Shadow of the Invisible Man*, essentially a slice of digital psychedelia on DVD, is released. According to Grateful Dead Merchandising, it is "a psychedelic adventure where both sound and pictures are played from the keyboards of the Dose Brothers. Bralove and Constanten give you a view of the future where sound and image dance together so you can see every note they play, in their first studio recording."

NOVEMBER '99

30

Tuesday November 30
Sing Out For SEVA, a compilation of live performances recorded at several benefit concerts for SEVA, is released. Bob Weir, Mickey Hart, and Phil Lesh perform on various songs. David Crosby and Graham Nash perform with Phil Lesh on "Box Of Rain."

DECEMBER '99

5

Sunday December 5
An Unbroken Chain Foundation Benefit is held at Marin County Veterans Auditorium, San Rafael, California. Phil Lesh, Donna Godchaux MacKay, David Crosby, David Grisman, Michael Tilson-Thomas, Rob Barraco, Derek Trucks, Susan Tedeschi, Lisa Vroman, Roslyn Barak, and the Unbroken Chain Children's Choir all perform.

Phil and Phriends

On April 15, Phil Lesh performed in public for the first time since his life-saving liver transplant in December '98 for the first of a three-show run to benefit the Unbroken Chain Foundation. Phil & Friends (or "Phriends," as it appeared on the Warfield's marquee) included Steve Kimock, John Molo, and, to the great delight of all, guitarist Trey Anastasio and keyboardist Page McConnell of Phish. The first show of the run was stellar, starting with a 39-minute "Viola Lee Blues" and ending nearly four hours later. In a pleasant surprise, Donna Godchaux MacKay was a guest vocalist the next two nights, which included duets with Trey Anastasio on "Scarlet Begonias" > "Fire on the Mountain."

Above: On September 30, Phil Lesh, Bob Weir, and Donna Godchaux MacKay sing "The Star-Spangled Banner" at the last Giants game to be held at Candlestick Park.

Monday June 26
Two competing groups of scientists announce they have mapped the human genome.

JUNE 2000

16   **26**

MAY 2000

Friday June 16 – Sunday July 30
Phil Lesh & Friends (Lesh, Molo, Robben Ford, Paul Barrere, Bill Payne; two shows with Jimmy Herring) join with the Bob Dylan Band to tour the nation.

9

Tuesday May 9
Mickey Hart kicks off a national tour with his new rock-oriented ensemble, the Mickey Hart Band, featuring Vince Welnick on keys and vocals. The opening show is at Club 9:30, Washington, D.C.

What Will You Wear, Jenny Jenkins? audio-book by Garcia and illustrated by Bruce Whatley is released.

Tuesday April 18
Tom Constanten's *Grateful Dreams* is released on CD, featuring live tracks from his Fall '99 tour.

APRIL 2000

2   **18**   **24**

The Grateful Dead Reader

David G. Dodd, a college professor (and creator/maintainer of *The Annotated Grateful Dead Lyrics* on the Internet) and his wife, Diana Spaulding, a librarian, compiled and edited this terrific anthology of writings on the band. Part of the *Readers on American Musicians* series, it includes gems from Richard Brautigan's poem about the 710 Ashbury bust and "An Aged Deadhead," an essay by philosopher (and father of Rock Scully) Milton Mayer.

Sunday April 2
Ratdog and the Flying Other Brothers, with Mickey Hart and Bob Weir, perform at a $5,000-per-person Democratic Congressional Campaign Committee fundraiser at Stanford, California. President Bill Clinton is a guest; it's not known if he brought his sax and sat in.

Monday April 24
Bob Weir and Mickey Hart join a cast of performers ranging from Tito Puente to Ralph Stanley at celebrations marking the 200th birthday of the Library of Congress, held at the library's Thomas Jefferson Building in Washington, D.C. Mickey is also honored by the LOC for his ongoing work with the library's musical archives.

MARCH 2000

10

Above: Friday March 10, Benefit for Unbroken Chain Foundation, Henry J. Kaiser Convention Center, Oakland, California. Little Feat guitarist Paul Barrere played at a number of Phil & Friends shows. Phil turns 60 today!

Mickey Hart receives an honorary Doctorate in Humane Letters from the Saybrook Graduate School and Research Center in San Francisco.

Tuesday January 25
The release of *Spirit Into Sound*, the companion CD to Mickey Hart's book *(see page 467)*. It includes 12 tracks performed by Mickey, Rebecca Mauleon, and guests including Bob Weir, Ustad Sultan Khan, and Zakir Hussein. Mickey dedicated the album to the memory of Dick Latvala.

Friday March 10
Phil Lesh becomes the first bandmember to reach 60, and he celebrates this landmark birthday with a hepatitis C research benefit show for the Unbroken Chain Foundation at the Henry J. Kaiser Convention Center, Oakland. Tonight's PL&F lineup includes Bill Payne, Paul Barrere, blues guitarist Robben Ford, and Phish bassist Mike Gordon.

THE PIZZA TAPES

Jerry Garcia
David Grisman
Tony Rice

Acoustic Disc 41

A disc of terrific, relaxed jamming on mostly traditional tunes—interspersed with snippets of conversation—at Grisman's studio in February 1993. The music was already well-known in Taper circles, since a pizza-delivery dude swiped a dupe of the master tape that had been rolling during the session, and it was soon in circulation as the "Pizza Boy Tape." Grisman later decided to "bury the hatchet with the Pizza Boy" and release the material officially from the master tape.

JANUARY 2000

20   **25**

Thursday January 20
Mickey Hart, Bob Weir, Vince Welnick, Steve Kimock, Bobby Vega, Pete Sears, and Big Bang Beat perform at a tribute to Peter and Bob Barsotti at the Warfield Theatre, San Francisco. The Barsottis were longtime Bill Graham Presents associates.

FEBRUARY 2000

26

Saturday February 26
Phil Lesh & Friends (in the new more-or-less permanent lineup of Lesh, John Molo, Warren Haynes, and Jimmy Herring) guest with funky Bay Area faves The Vinyls at a benefit for the Novato Charter School at the Phoenix Theater, Petaluma, California.

Thursday August 17
Mickey Hart leads the delegates in a "drum-in" at the Democratic National Convention in Los Angeles, California.

17 **21**

**Monday August 21 –
Sunday September 24**
Furthur 2000.

Furthur 2000

After skipping 1999, Furthur returns in August 2000, with 21 shows. Furthur 2000 is more like a regular tour than a festival, with a single opening act—Ziggy Marley and the Melody Makers—although Steve Winwood, the Flying Other Brothers Band, Sy Klopps, ekoostik hookah, and Jorma Kaukonen open and/or guest at various shows. In terms of lineup, it was a "win one, lose one" situation for Deadheads. Phil Lesh begged off, although the disappointment over the loss of Lesh was offset by delight at having Bill Kreutzmann (who had developed, in his words, "a slight case of island fever" in Hawaii) joining his rhythm brother Mickey Hart once more. (John Molo was unable to tour because of "scheduling conflicts.") Lesh's replacement on bass was the great Alphonso Johnson, veteran of the pioneer fusion band Weather Report as well as Jazz is Dead and of course, Bobby & the Midnites. Bob Weir, Bruce Hornsby, and the guitar team of Mark Karan and Steve Kimock fill out the Furthur 2000 roster.

EVENING MOODS

Bob Weir and Ratdog

Grateful Dead Records 4072

The first solo studio album from Bob Weir since 1984's Bobby & the Midnites' *Where the Beat Meets the Street*, *Evening Moods* included nine tracks written by various combinations of the band, plus a version of the Hart/Weir/Hunter "Corrina," performed live by both the Grateful Dead and The Other Ones. Mickey Hart and Matt Kelly guested on several songs. *Evening Moods* got a generally good reception.

Friday October 13
Bill Kreutzmann marries Linda Wiley in Hawaii.

Saturday October 14
Grateful Dawg documentary, is released. Directed by Gillian Grisman, it captures Jerry Garcia and David Grisman at work and play, with commentary from various associates.

4 **13** **14** **24**

Wednesday October 4
Bob Weir, mezzo-soprano Frederica von Stade, and Jerry Lawson of the Persuasions sing the "Star-Spangled Banner" to open the first day of the playoffs at Pacific Bell Park, San Francisco, California. (The Giants go on to win the National League West.)

Tuesday October 24
Here Come the Noisemakers, by Bruce Hornsby and The Range, is released.

Left: Even though the Grateful Dead no longer exist, there are still many ghosts from the past surrounding members of the band.

Bob Bralove & Tom Constanten's Dose Hermanos release *Search For Intelligent Life*, which offers more psychedelic keyboard noodling.

VIEW FROM THE VAULT

These concert DVDs and VHS videos were released simultaneously with the CDs.

View from the Vault I
Released 10/10/2000; recorded 7/8/90 at Three Rivers Stadium, Pittsburgh, Pennsylvania.

View from the Vault II
Released 10/9/2001; recorded 6/14/91 at RFK Stadium, Washington, D.C.

View from the Vault III
Released 10/08/2002; recorded 6/16/90, at Shoreline Amphitheatre, Mountain View, California.

View From The Vault IV
Released 04/08/2003; recorded 7/24/87 at Oakland Coliseum Arena, Oakland, California, and 7/26/87, Anaheim Stadium, Anaheim, California.

Dead on the Web

Deadheads had long been early adopters of online technology, from the setlists that circulated on BBSs and Internet ancestors like ARPANET to the establishment of Grateful Dead conferences on the 'WELL and Dead-related newsgroups like rec.music.gdead. In the aftermath of Jerry Garcia's death, the "virtual community" of Deadheads proved that it was no less a true community for being virtual, as people gathered online to mourn, console one another, and share memories, many of which are gathered in David Gans's "Not Fade Away, The OnLine World Remembers Jerry Garcia." The Internet also revolutionized tape trading as Tapers posted their lists online.

From the mid-'90s, on the exponential growth of the World Wide Web led to the creation of some terrific online resources for Deadheads. The invaluable DeadBase (www.deadbase.com) went online with a searchable database of setlists, while the ongoing Deadlists Project (www.deadlists.com), begun in '94, seeks to maintain the most comprehensive collection of detailed information about every Grateful Dead performance. Anyone who wants to know who the doo dah man was, or is, or has any other question regarding the words, can turn to David G. Dodd's *The Annotated Grateful Dead Lyrics* (arts.ucsc.edu/gdead/agdl/) for answers. (With Diana Spaulding, Dodd also edited *The Grateful Dead Reader*, a brilliant compilation of writings about the band). The Grateful Dead Family Discography (www.deaddisc.com) is an invaluable archive not only to the band's music, but, as the name applies, to solo/side bands, bandmembers' contributions to other artists' recordings, and indeed any recordings relating to the Grateful Dead. Ihor Slabicky's justly renowned Compleat Grateful Dead Discography (tcgdd.freeyellow.com/tcgdd.html) is another treasure trove.

Sunday December 31
New Year's Eve presents an upsetting dilemma for West Coast Deadheads. The Other Ones, featuring Hart, Kreutzmann, and Weir, are playing at the Oakland Coliseum, while Phil Lesh & Friends, including Lesh, Molo, Haynes, Herring, and Barraco, are performing up the road at Henry J. Kaiser Convention Center in Oakland. Symbolically the evening marks a nadir in relations between band members, and, importantly, a *glasnost* that would follow shortly after.

30 **31**

Saturday December 30
Universal Amphitheatre, Universal City, California
The Other Ones (Hart, Kreutzmann, Weir, Hornsby, Johnson, and Karan) perform. The Steve Kimock Band opens.

Ken Kesey 1935 – 2001

On November 10, Ken Kesey died of complications from surgery for liver cancer at the age of 66, depriving U.S. culture of one of its great originals, and Deadheads of a revered elder. Kesey first won fame as a novelist in the early '60s with *One Flew Over the Cuckoo's Nest* and *Sometimes a Great Notion*, but he completed only one other novel (*Sailor Song*, published in 1992 to mixed reviews). His other great work, of course, was not written down— it was the social experiment he led when the bus Furthur rolled across the republic in the summer of '64 with Cowboy Neal at the wheel.

Kesey never ceased to be a Prankster and never ceased to create. And not the least of his contributions was to invite those young rock 'n' rollers, the Warlocks, to play the Acid Tests— which, as Jerry Garcia famously said much later, established the Basic Pattern. Pigpen, Jerry, Phil, Bob, and Bill might have continued as a band if they hadn't hooked up with Kesey, but they surely wouldn't have been the Grateful Dead.

"Ken Kesey was kind of a Buffalo Bill character. He liked to put on a great show. He was truly larger than life."
MUSICIAN MASON WILLIAMS

Above and left: New Year's Eve 2001–02. The lineup included Pnf with guest vocalist Susan Tedeschi (left) and the Crusader Rabbit Stealth Band (above).

Timeline

Sunday January 21
Weir & Wasserman perform at the San Francisco Food Show (at the Marriott Hotel) to promote Bob's new culinary side project, Weir's Sauces.

Tuesday January 23
Release of *Don't Let Go* by the Jerry Garcia Band, a double live CD of the JGB's 5/21/76 show at San Francisco's Orpheum Theatre, plus one track recorded at the Keystone on 9/11/76.

Tuesday March 20
Release of *Shining Star* by the Jerry Garcia Band. Another double live CD from the JGB, this one recorded at various shows from 1989 to 1994.

Tuesday March 27 – Friday May 4
Ratdog (Lesh, Rob Wasserman, Mark Karan, Jay Lane, Jeff Chimenti, and Dave Ellis) tour nationwide.

Friday April 27
Phil Lesh, playing himself, makes a cameo appearance in tonight's episode of the TV show *Nash Bridges*. The plot revolves around a robbery at the Fillmore after a Pnf concert, although the taping (which shows the band playing "Bertha") was done at the Great American Music Hall.

Tuesday May 1
Mickey Hart remasters *American Beauty* and *Workingman's Dead* into Dolby 5.1 Surround Sound DVD Audio format.

Tuesday May 15
Mickey Hart and Bob Weir join Hot Tuna, Dr. John, Indigenous, Box Set, Paul Kantner, Diana Mangano, Maria Muldaur, and Zero for Wavy Gravy's 65th Birthday Bash at the Berkeley Community Theatre, with proceeds to benefit the SEVA foundation.

Sunday June 10
In a confirmation of the Core Four rapprochement, a Phil Lesh & Friends show at the Sweetwater Saloon, Mill Valley, California, is taken over by an entity called "The Crusader Rabbit Stealth Band"—Phil Lesh, Bob Weir, John Molo, Rob Barraco, and Jimmy Herring. The quintet tore through two sets glittering with gems like "Mason's Children" and "Maggie's Farm." Warren Haynes joined for the encore, "Promised Land">"I Know You Rider."

Saturday June 2
Ratdog and Bill Kreutzmann play at the Black and White Ball fundraiser for the San Francisco Symphony Orchestra (at the Bill Graham Civic Auditorium San Francisco).

Monday July 9 – Sunday July 22
Ratdog opens seven shows for Phil & Friends, starting in Oklahoma City.

Thursday July 26
Bob Weir and Steve Miller perform at the Bohemia Club, Monte Rio, California.

Bill Kreutzmann's new trio, House of the Spirits, plays local gigs in Hawaii, where Bill spends most of his time scuba-diving and tending to his organic farm, Grateful Greens.

Saturday January 20
George W. Bush is sworn in as the 43rd president of the United States.

Jimmy Herring

Born in 1962, Jimmy Herring began playing guitar at 13. His first influences were hard rockers like Jimmy Hendrix and the Allman Brothers Band, though he then discovered more improvisational jazz and fusion guitarists. After a short stint at Berklee College of Music in Boston and a longer period at the Guitar Institute of Technology in L.A., Jimmy moved to Atlanta. There he hooked up with the legendary Col. Bruce Hampton and became part of the Aquarium Rescue Unit, gigging with, among many others, the Allman Brothers Band and Bruce Hornsby. Herring then started listening to Grateful Dead show tapes but forced himself to stop, fearing that it would compromise his own style. Nevertheless, when T. Lavitz invited him to join Jazz Is Dead, Herring jumped at the chance, absorbing the canon but preserving his own fluid-yet-fiery style. In early 2000 Phil Lesh tapped him for Phil Lesh & Friends and, ultimately, The Other Ones and The Dead.

January 2001

GRATEFUL DEAD

THE GOLDEN ROAD (1965-1973)

Jon Hendricks on "Fire in the City." Each remastered album was accompanied by chronologically linked live versions, outtakes (including some particularly crispy studio jams from the recording of *Aoxomoxoa*), and other rarities, like the single version of "Dark Star," plus ephemera such as radio ads and Bob Weir's infamous "Yeller Dog" story.

Each CD box had well-scaled reproductions of the original jacket artwork plus its own extensive, illustrated notes, and the set included an 80-page, full-color booklet with essays by James Austin, David Lemieux, Dennis McNally, Connie Bonner Mosley, Lou Tambakos, Blair Jackson, Gary Lambert, Lenny Kaye, Steve Silberman, David Gans, Paul Nichols and Hale Milgrim, and Bear, and a discography by Ihor Slabicky.

The Golden Road won kudos from the recording industry for its excellent packaging, programming, and scholarship, while the brilliantly remastered sound and intelligently chosen bonus material led many 'Heads to finally make the leap from vinyl to CD. The individual albums, plus *Birth of the Dead*, soon became available separately from the box set.

"This exquisitely packaged 12-CD set also reveals quite how good [the Grateful Dead] could be away from the stage." CLARK COLLIS IN Q. MARCH 2002

THE GOLDEN ROAD (1965–1973)

Grateful Dead

Released by Rhino Records (Rhino R2 74401) on October 16, 2001

Albums:

Birth of The Dead
Grateful Dead
Anthem of the Sun
Aoxomoxoa
Live/Dead
Working Man's Dead
American Beauty
Grateful Dead (Skull & Roses)
Europe '72
History of the Grateful Dead,
    Vol. 1 (Bear's Choice)

A COLLABORATION BETWEEN Grateful Dead Merchandising and Rhino Records, this 12-CD box set presented digitally remastered versions of the band's nine Warner Bros. albums, from *The Grateful Dead* through *History of the Grateful Dead, Volume 1 (Bear's Choice)*, plus a plethora of previously unreleased material—in fact, of the set's fifteen or so hours of music, about seven hours' worth had not previously left the Vault in sanctioned release.

Besides the nine WB albums, *The Golden Road* included *Birth of the Dead*, a double CD (studio and live) presenting some of the band's earliest and/or rarest recorded music, including the Emergency Crew and Warlocks demos and the Dead backing

December 2001

463

AUGUST '01

SEPTEMBER '01

OCTOBER '01

NOVEMBER '01

DECEMBER '01

Thursday August 23
Release of *Ratdog – Live at Roseland*, a double CD of live performances from April this year.

Tuesday September 11
Release of the *Grateful Dawg* soundtrack, which includes one track from Old & In the Way and one from Bill Monroe.

Friday August 10 – Monday September 3
Ratdog hit the road again on the "So Many Roads/Traveling Furthur Tour"—18 shows from Pennsylvania to Idaho—with Rusted Root, Keller Williams, Karl Denson's Tiny Universe, and DJ Logic, who converted many Deadheads previously dismissive of hip-hop *(see page 392)* with his master turntablist skills.

Tuesday September 11
Al Qaeda terrorists fly two hijacked passenger jets into the World Trade Center in New York and a third into the Pentagon; a fourth crashes in a field in Pennsylvania.

Sunday October 7
U.S. and British forces begin a military campaign against the Taliban, the Islamic fundamentalist group in power in Afghanistan, who are sheltering Al Qaeda and its leader, Osama Bin Laden.

Sunday October 28 – Sunday November 18
Having taken his fill of rock 'n' roll with the Mickey Hart Band, Mickey returns to World Music by touring the South and Northeast with a new ensemble called Bembé Orisha; the name means "Party of the Saints" in Yoruba, a West African language. The band consists of Hart, Azam Ali, and Gladys "Bobi" Cespedes on vocals, Barney Doyle on guitar, Greg Ellis and Humberto "Nengue" Hernandez on percussion, and Rahsaan Fredericks on bass.

Friday October 26
Bill Kreutzmann's latest band, the Trichromes (ex-Journey man Neal Schon on guitar, Mike Di Pirro on bass, and Sy Klopps, also ex-Journey, on vocals), makes its debut at the Fillmore.

Monday December 3
For the last night of the Phil & Friends tour, Bob Weir joins for a benefit at New York's Beacon Theatre for the Unbroken Chain Foundation's 9/11 Relief Fund.

Thursday November 8 – Monday December 3
Phil Lesh & Friends tour the Midwest, South, and East. Susan Tedeschi, Dickey Betts, and Page McConnell guest at gigs; on 11/17, at Stabler Arena in Bethlehem, Pennsylvania, Phil & Friends break out a new song written with Robert Hunter, "No More Do I."

Sunday December 30
Phil Lesh & Friends gig (opened by Ratdog) at Oakland's Henry J. Kaiser Convention Center.

Monday December 31
In contrast to New Years Eve 2000, with its dueling post-Dead bands playing across town from one another, NYE 2001 is a night of joyous togetherness. The Derek Trucks Band opened, followed by Ratdog, and then Pnf, with Susan Tedeschi guesting on the "In the Midnight Hour">"Hard to Handle" set opener. After the Midnight Parade, the Crusader Rabbit Stealth Band (Phil & Friends plus Bob Weir, Mickey Hart, and Bill Kreutzmann) reassembled to prove that, as Phil told the audience, "Unity is possible!"

POSTCARDS OF THE HANGING: GRATEFUL DEAD PERFORM SONGS OF BOB DYLAN

Released by Arista (14069)/Grateful Dead Records (4069) in March 2002

1. **When I Paint My Masterpiece**
   (Dylan)
2. **She Belongs To Me**
   (Dylan)
3. **Just Like Tom Thumb's Blues**
   (Dylan)
4. **Maggie's Farm**
   (Dylan)
5. **Stuck Inside Of Mobile With The Memphis Blues Again**
   (Dylan)
6. **It Takes A Lot To Laugh, It Takes A Train To Cry**
   (Dylan)
7. **Ballad Of A Thin Man**
   (Dylan)
8. **Desolation Row**
   (Dylan)
9. **All Along The Watchtower**
   (Dylan)
10. **It's All Over Now, Baby Blue**
    (Dylan)
11. **Man Of Peace**
    (Dylan)
12. **Queen Jane Approximately**
    (Dylan)
13. **The Mighty Quinn (Quinn The Eskimo)**
    (Dylan)

Personnel

Bob Dylan – acoustic guitar, vocals
Jerry Garcia – guitar, vocals
Mickey Hart – drums
Bill Kreutzmann – drums
Phil Lesh – bass, vocals
Brent Mydland – keyboards, vocals
Bob Weir – guitar, vocals
Keith Godchaux – piano
Dickey Betts – guitar
Butch Trucks – drums

Above and right: The "Core Four" onstage together again at Terrapin Station, held at the Alpine Valley Music Theatre in East Troy, Wisconsin.

The only archival release (so far) to be thematic rather than derived from a particular show, *Postcards of the Hanging* presents the Dead's covers of eleven songs from the Master's pen, all but one of them from the '80s, the decade when (in the latter years at least) Dylan tunes were so heavy in the rotation that Deadheads took to referring to "the Dylan Slot" in the first set. (The exception is "It Takes a lot to Laugh, It Takes a Train to Cry" from 6/10/73, with help from Butch Trucks and Dickie Betts from the Allman Brothers Band.) Compiled by David Gans, *Postcards* also includes one track, "Man of Peace," recorded during the Club Front rehearsals before the summer '87 "Dylan & the Dead" shows. The initial release of *Postcards* was bundled with a bonus CD including "Queen Jane Approximately" and "The Mighty Quinn (Quinn The Eskimo)."

[If] the Dead were not the boldest of Dylan-cover bands—no great liberties are taken in these live tracks, mostly from the 1980s—they were the purest: swinging through the songbook like real fans, finding workingman's poetry in Dylan's most elusive parables. FROM DAVID FRICKE'S REVIEW IN *ROLLING STONE*, MARCH 2002.

Friday June 28 – Thursday July 18
Europe '02: overseas tours have been even rarer for the post-Jerry bands than they were for the Grateful Dead, but summer 2002 sees Bob Weir and Ratdog in Europe for fifteen shows, in England, Scotland, Wales, France, Germany, Italy, and the Netherlands (including, on 7/10, a return to Amsterdam's Melkweg—*see page 267*).

Tuesday June 25
Release of *Big Swing Face*, Bruce Hornsby's eighth album.

JUNE '02

23 **25** **28**

Sunday June 23
Bonnaroo 2002: Phil Lesh & Friends, joined by Bob Weir and Jeff Chimenti, perform at this three-day festival in Manchester, Tennessee, which draws as many as 75,000 people and includes performers from the worlds of hip-hop, gospel, bluegrass, and electronica as well as rock 'n' roll of the jam-band brand (Widespread Panic, Jack Johnson, Gov't Mule, Trey Anastasio, et al.). In contrast to the last rock festival on such an ambitious scale—Woodstock '99—Bonnaroo 2002 passes peacefully, with few arrests and injuries.

JANUARY '02

26

Saturday January 26
The Trichromes, Bill Kreutzmann's latest band, release a three-song CD, *Dice with the Universe*, which includes a version of "New Speedway Boogie."

Mickey Hart visits Cuba (and has dinner with Fidel Castro—"a great hang" according to MH) as part of a cultural delegation led by Senator Barbara Boxer.

Wednesday May 22
Phil Lesh & Friends perform "Night of 1,000 Stars" from *There and Back Again* on *The Late Late Show*—at the CBS Studios, Los Angeles, with Craig Kilborn.

A Long Strange Trip

As a Ph.D. in history, Dennis McNally brought a trained historian's skills to this chronicle of the band's life and times. As the author of *Desolate Angel: Jack Kerouac, the Beat Generation, and America*, McNally was able, in *A Long Strange Trip*, to articulate brilliantly the connections between the band and its (counter-) cultural antecedents and influences.

Just as significantly, McNally ("Scrib," in Deadspeak) was the band's official historian from 1980 (Garcia's admiration for the Kerouac bio helped get him the gig) and their spokesperson from 1984.

FEBRUARY '02

Tuesday April 23
Release of *Over the Edge and Back: The Best of Mickey Hart*. This nine-track compilation ranges across 20 years of the percussion paragon's career, from 1976's Diga Rhythm Band to "Call to the Nations" from the 1996 Olympics.

MAY '02

5 **22** **23**

Sunday May 5
Bob Weir jams with Phil & Friends at the New Orleans Jazz Festival.

Thursday May 23 – Sunday August 4
Phil Lesh & Friends tour the country on the "There and Back Again" tour. Mickey Hart and Bembe Orisha, Robert Hunter, the Trichromes, and Ratdog open various shows.

APRIL '02

MARCH '02

23

THERE AND BACK AGAIN

Phil Lesh & Friends
Lapis Music/Columbia Records

Unless you want to count Seastones (see page 182), Phil Lesh did not pursue much of a solo/side career until the emergence of Phil Lesh & Friends; There and Back Again was in fact his first solo studio album—at age 62. Phil's phreshman solo effort got positive but somewhat muted reviews: phans were delighted to hear their hero on good form, but many of those who had heard the album songs in live performance felt that the studio tracks failed to capture the power of the live versions. Sound familiar?

Phil Lesh & Friends

There and Back Again
LIMITED EDITION

JULY '02

2

AUGUST '02

3 **11**

SEPTEMBER '02

OCTOBER '02

2

Sunday August 11
Mt. Fuji Jazz Festival
Mt. Fuji Speedway, Shizuoka, Japan

Bob Weir brings RatDog to the Land of the Rising Sun for a one-off performance at the Mt. Fuji Jazz Festival, Mt. Fuji Speedway, Shizuoka, Japan.

Saturday August 3
Sunday August 4
The Other Ones play at Terrapin Station 2002

Tuesday July 2
The Trichromes by The Trichromes, the first album from Bill Kreutzmann's latest band, is released. It includes eight songs with lyrics by Robert Hunter.

Left: Bill, Phil and Mickey enjoy themselves at Terrapin Station.
Below: Mountain Girl an John Perry Barlow

Tuesday October 22
Tom Constanten's compilation of previously unreleased live and studio recordings, *88 Keys to Tomorrow* hits the stores. Track 20 is a live version of "Dark Star", recorded at the Somerville Theater in Somerville, Massachusetts, when he was on tour, opening for Robert Hunter.

Thursday October 24
John Lee Malvo and John Allen Muhammad are arrested in connection with ten sniper killings committed earlier in the month in and around Washington, D.C.

22 **24** **27**

Wednesday October 2
In the middle of their nationwide tour Ratdog stop at New York's Roseland Ballroom for an all-star jam at the "Jammys" award show. Bob Weir also accepts the Jammy for Lifetime Achievement on behalf of the Grateful Dead.

Sunday October 27
Shoreline Amphitheatre
Mountain View, California

The Other Ones contribute an acoustic set to this benefit for the Bridge School. Neil Young, James Taylor, Jack Johnson, Ryan Adams, Radiohead's Thom Yorke, Vanessa Carlton, and Tenacious D (a.k.a. Jack Black and Kyle Gass, a.k.a The Greatest Band on Earth!) also perform.

Thursday November 14 – Friday December 6
The Other Ones (Lesh, Weir, Hart Kreutzmann, Herring, Barraco, and Chimenti) go nationwide—fifteen shows, from Virginia to Oakland—on the "Get Back Truckin' On" tour, with Robert Hunter peforming solo acoustic between sets.

NOVEMBER '02

12 **14**

Tuesday November 12
The Other Ones perform "The Wheel" on *Late Night with Conan O'Brien* at NBC Studios, New York.

DECEMBER '02

31

Tuesday December 31
Oakland Coliseum Arena, Oakland, California

A very good show ends a very good year for band and fans. Acoustic Hot Tuna opened (Jorma Kaukonen and Jack Casady) opens, followed by Medeski, Martin and Wood, and then three sets from The Other Ones, capped by an instrumental "Stella Blue" encore.

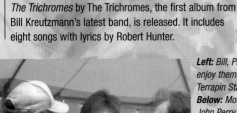

Terrapin Station

Billed as "Terrapin Station: A Grateful Dead Family Reunion," this was the event that brought happiness to all Deadheads and utter joy to the 30,000 'Heads able to be there in person. The venue, the Alpine Valley Music Theatre in East Troy, Wisconsin, had been a Dead Head favorite, but massive traffic jams and hordes of ticketless heads in 1989 had ended shows there, and in 2002 authorities still remembered the mess and initially refused to permit shows.

After intense negotiations that decision was reversed, and local worries proved groundless; the two–day event was totally mellow. The current crop of post–Jerry side/solo bands performed (Mickey Hart and Bembe Orisha, RatDog, Phil Lesh & Friends, the Trichromes, and Robert Hunter in solo acoustic mode), along with jamsters old and new: Jorma Kaukonen, the Disco Biscuits, Warren Haynes, Donna the Buffalo, Karl Denson's Tiny Universe, and Robert Randolph and the Family Band. The highlight, of course, was the return of The Other Ones, playing almost four glorious hours each night.

Given the auspicious occasion, everyone expected a surprise, and they got it; Saturday's TOO performance saw–sandwiched in "Dark Star"—the revival of "Born Cross–Eyed," last heard live on 4/3/68, before many of those boogying in front of the shed were born, probably. "It was more their [the Deadheads] event than anybody's. I was really surprised with the way the audience sort of took the reins. We just kinda helped things along, but they were really doing the driving," said Bob Weir.

A Momentous Announcement From The Other Ones, February 2003

"Seven years ago, when Jerry passed, we made a conscious decision to retire the name Grateful Dead. We did so after some deep soul searching and out of our love and respect for what we had created together. After we played our first shows together at Alpine Valley last year, we were all profoundly affected by a sense of awe and connection that none of us had felt since we played with Jerry.

It was a magical occurrence that no one could have anticipated, yet one we all want to embrace. To us, this was the Grateful Dead—without Jerry. We had stopped being the 'Other Ones' and were on our way to becoming something new but at the same time very familiar.

Grateful Dead conjures up many different emotions and feelings for all of us; it was a BAND; it continues to be a community, an approach to life, an electrical current, a dream—the list goes on. Whenever and wherever we played this past year, we all knew that we were experiencing Grateful Dead in its multiplicity of forms. We also know that this would not have been possible without all of you joining to support us. Therefore, with the greatest possible respect to our collective history, we have decided to keep the name "Grateful Dead" retired in honor of Jerry's memory, and call ourselves: The Dead."

Joan Osborne

Born in Kentucky, Joan Osborne began her professional career while at NYU Film School when her friends goaded her into helping close a bar with a rendition of Billie Holliday's "God Bless the Child." The house pianist invited her to perform regularly, and after some time on the club circuit, she developed a following that led first to some well-reviewed releases on her own Womanly Hips label and then to Mercury, where in 1995 she released *Relish*, which included the soon-to-be-ubiquitous "One of Us," written by her studio guitarist, Eric Bazilian. "One of Us" was a Top 5 single, while *Relish* went double platinum, garnered seven Grammys, and established Osborne as both a popular success and a critical favorite. With her devotion to roots music and warm yet powerful voice, Osborne gave The Dead a vocal range and strength unmatched since the Donna Godchaux era.

JANUARY '03

Right: First show for "The Dead" under their new moniker, Friday February 14, Warfield Theatre, San Francisco.

FEBRUARY '03

1

MARCH '03

13

Thursday March 13 – Sunday April 6
Robert Hunter (solo acoustic) tours the Northeast and Midwest.

20

Thursday March 20
War with Iraq begins as U.S. missiles hit Baghdad.

Saturday February 1
The Space Shuttle Columbia disintegrates in the skies over the southwestern U.S., killing all seven crew.

Right: The First Leg of the Dead Summer Getaway 2003; Phil Lesh and Joan Osborne (above) and Deadheads (below). **Below:** Members of the Grateful Dead organization in March 2003. The entire merchandising wing of the company and a number of other long-time employees were laid off in the spring as a part of a restructuring.

466

14

Friday February 14
Warfield Theatre, San Francisco, California

The Dead's first show under the new handle is a triple-threat benefit for the Rex Foundation, the Unbroken Chain Foundation, and the Furthur Foundation. Robert Hunter opens, Michael Kang guests, and The Dead introduce a new member to the lineup—Joan Osborne.

Changes at Headquarters

In a less joyful development, the Grateful Dead organization began scaling back some of its operations, which unfortunately led to pink slips for a number of longtime employees. Despite the revival of The Other Ones>The Dead and the ongoing stream of archival releases and other merchandise, the decision was made that the organization's infrastructure was just too unwieldy, and so, to avoid having the revived Beast turn into the Orobouros, the dreaded "D-word"—downscaling—came into play, as it has for so many other entities.

MAY '03

APRIL '03

9

JUNE '03

15 19

JULY '03

15 29

Sunday June 15 – Friday July 11
The First Leg of the Dead Summer Getaway 2003 with Joan Osborne includes 18 shows (not counting Bonnaroo), starting in Virginia Beach and ending with a five-show run at one of the (Grateful) Dead's most revered venues, Red Rocks in Colorado. Steve Winwood opens (and frequently jammed with) the Dead through 6/25, handing off to Willie Nelson.

Thursday June 19
The Dead perform "Casey Jones" on *The David Letterman Show.*

Tuesday July 29 – Friday August 8
The Second Leg of the tour includes ten shows, from Florida to Long Island, with Bob Dylan and Robert Hunter (plus more, at the 8/8 show at Darien Lakes Performing Arts Center outside Buffalo).

Wednesday April 9
U.S. Forces occupy Baghdad.

Sunday June 15
Bonnaroo 2002, Manchester, Tennessee

The Dead kick off the first leg of their "Summer Getaway 2003" tour with a triumphant return to the Bonnaroo Festival. A second '03 festival, Bonnaroo Northeast, was planned for early August in Riverhead, New York, with The Dead scheduled to play. Unfortunately, promoters of a festival that was to take place earlier on the same site (Field Day, featuring Radiohead) ran into so many problems with Long Island authorities that they had to move the event; Bonnaroo NE's promoters canceled rather than face the same headaches. To the joy of area 'Heads, however, The Dead announced two three-set shows (including one acoustic set) at Long Island's Jones Beach Theater for 8/9–10.

"This is mostly a festival of backpackers: the world of peaceful collegiate rebellion. Much of it descends from Grateful Dead audience culture; The Dead in fact headlined the final night of Bonnaroo this year. You could theorize that the band provides the logic of the programming: break down the Grateful Dead into its components, follow those aesthetic side roads, and you get Bonnaroo." BEN RATLIF IN THE NEW YORK TIMES, 6/15/03

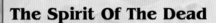

Tuesday July 15
The Dead announce a three-show, West Coast "Third Leg" for Summer Getaway 2003: Verizon Wireless Amphitheatre, Irvine, California (9/18); Shoreline Amphitheatre, Mountain View, California (9/19); and The Gorge, George, Washington (9/21).

Things certainly have come a long way from the days when pioneer Tapers would smuggle in decks in hollowed-out cakes—for most Summer Getaway 2003 shows, concertgoers can pre-order soundboard-derived CDs at whatever show(s) they're attending; at some venues, people will be able to pick up their CDs as they leave the show! Despite the introduction of the OCRS (Original Concert Recording Series), the Good Ol' Grateful Dead were careful to announce that "Our long standing tradition of allowing concert goers to record their concerts for personal use with their own portable audio equipment will continue."

The Spirit Of The Dead

So what lies ahead for the Dead? Two decades on from Jerry's death and other sad losses, the remaining Dead family members keep the flame alive. Despite the closure of GD HQ, Deadnet remains a vital resource for the community. In 2007, the Dead received a Grammy Lifetime Achievement award, and in 2011 their gig at Barton Hall, Cornell University (May 8 1977) entered the Library of Congress's National Recording Registry. The Rex Foundation resolutely pursues its charitable activities; newly mastered live material still flows through; the Grateful Dead Hour (*gdhour.com*) continues to broadcast a "weekly audio postcard"; and the enormous Grateful Dead archive now resides at the University of California, Santa Cruz.

New ventures involving original band members and a host of new musicians, including Jimmy Herring, Warren Haynes, Rob Wasserman, John Madeski, Joe Russo, Joan Osborne, and Jeff Chimenti, means that the Deadhead audience still has a lot of material to play with. Phil Lesh, Bob Weir, Mickey Hart, and Bill Kreutzmann continue to promote imaginative ventures across and beyond the original Dead spectrum.

At the heart of it, the Dead's trip began a long time ago, when the music of slaves and settlers began evolving into folk, country, jazz, blues—in other words American music—the different strands the Grateful Dead wove into a musical fabric that was, and remains, uniquely their own.

The Music (And Words) Never Stopped

Since '95 there's been a steady stream of publications and music exploring and celebrating the life and legacy of the Dead. Below is just a tiny sampling.

Tribute CDs
Several albums include covers of Dead songs by artists in a variety of genres, including *Fire on the Mountain* (reggae) and *Wake the Dead* (Celtic). *The Music Never Stopped* explores the roots music the band drew on, while albums by Henry Kaiser, Jazz is Dead, David Murray, and Joe Gallant and Illuminati brings the Dead's music into the world of cutting-edge jazz.

Books
Elizabeth Zipern's *Cooking with the Dead* is a fascinating look at Deadhead cuisine and culture. From academia came *Perspectives on the Grateful Dead* (Robert Weiner, ed.) and *Deadhead Social Science* (Rebecca Adams and Robert Sardiello, eds.). From the band came *Harrington Street*, Jerry Garcia's posthumous "anecdotal autobiography," ecologically themed kids' books from Bob Weir and his sister Wendy, while Mickey Hart explored the world of music and the music of the world in *Spirit Into Sound* and *Songcatchers*.

December 2003

467

Mystery Box And Beyond

Mickey Hart's inexhaustible, almost archeological, enthusiasm
for "world music," simultaneously exploring rhythms and the
environmental issues that he is married to, remains unabated.
He has written several books about the global cultural significance
of percussion, and helmed the Global Drum Project in 2007.
After creating the Mickey Hart Band as a successor to the
Mystery Box ensemble in 2012, he went on to make two
memorable albums: "Mysterium Tremendum" (2012)
and "Superorganism" (2013).

The Weir Commitment

Quite aside from Bob Weir's
admiration for the kind of democratic
outreach that always characterized
the Dead, both Weir and Phil Lesh
were effectively behind the
"Deadheads for Obama"
concert in 2008, and the
band were invited to
perform at Obama's
inauguration. "Ratdog"
continues as a Weir touring
outfit, and Weir remains an
outspoken political voice in
the Dead arena.

Phil Lesh

The very eclectic and adventurous Phil Lesh Quintet, and the versatile
bass player's Terrapin Crossroads Club, have seen many performances
of Dead covers, the "Planet Jams" material, and other Dead-related music
including jazz-nuanced sets with Rob Wasserman,
and an extended international tour with Peter
Shapiro in 2014. Notable albums have included
"Live at the Warfield" (2006). Lesh, a musical
scholar, has vigorously pushed hard for the
musical recognition of the Dead and
the band's heritage.

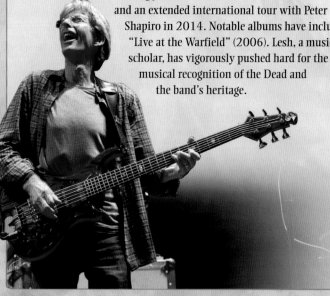

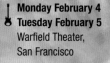

'08

**Monday February 4
Tuesday February 5**
Warfield Theater,
San Francisco

"Deadheads for Obama"
concerts.

Tuesday November 4
Barack Obama (b.1961) elected
44th president of the U.S., the
first African American to achieve
the office of president.

'09

'14

Tuesday January 20
Washington, D.C.

Weir plays at the Obama Inaugural
Ball with other band members.

A Big Deal

The startlingly original drummer for the Dead, but a notably reticent figure, Bill
Kreutzmann announced the publication of his autobiography, *Deal*, in 2015. Its
subtitle promised much—"My Three Decades of Drumming, Dreams, and Drugs
with the Grateful Dead." The fact that Kreutzmann has, like other surviving
members of the band, kept "on rolling" and performing remained both promising
and compromising in equal measure.

A Stanley Mouse "concept" artwork before the final poster for the 2015 50th Anniversary concerts was revealed.

Friday July 3 –
Sunday July 5
Soldier Field, Chicago

Final concert by the surviving members of the Dead announced, twenty years on from Garcia's last performance.

©2015 STANLEY MOUSE

2015: The End Of A Long And Winding Road

After more than two decades of uncertainty over how to handle the legacy of the Dead, especially in the post-Garcia years, and despite outings as "The Dead" and as "Further," the four remaining members of the original band announced a final series of concerts to celebrate the 50th anniversary of the Dead's foundation in Palo Alto in 1965. The concerts would be held on July 3–5, Soldier Field, Chicago (where the Dead played their last concert with Garcia in July 1995, a mere month before he died). Band members were no longer spring chickens, so the choice of venue was understandable and admirable after half a century at the center of American and alternative culture. Once again, Stanley Mouse produced a memorable poster.

Lesh, Weir, Kreutzmann, and Hart would be accompanied by some outstanding sometime fellow travelers: Trey Anastasio (of the notable jam band Phish, among many other ventures), Jeff Chimenti (long-time keyboardist with Weir's Ratdog), and Bruce Hornsby (of The Range and former member of the Dead).

As Phil Lesh said, they were reconvening the band "one last time to celebrate—not merely the band's legacy, but also the community that we've been playing to, and with, for 50 years."

Index

The following abbreviations have been used:
GD – Grateful Dead; JG – Jerry Garcia
Venues are listed under the names of towns/cities.

Picture Credits

Every effort has been made to trace copyright holders. Dorling Kindersley apologises for any unintentional omissions, and would be pleased, if any such case should arise, to add an appropriate acknowledgment in future editions.

All LP covers, books, cds, and memorabilia credited to Dorling Kindersley are from the private collections of Ken Hunt and Chris Jones.

Picture credits source key

All photographs are copyrighted to the individual photographers who took them.

The publishers would like to thank the following or their estates for their kind permission to reproduce their photographs:

AG = Allen Ginsberg; AP = Associated Press; AS = Alan Sheckter; AT = Alan Trist; BCJ = courtesy of Betty Cantor Jackson; BE = Bettmann; BGA = Bill Graham Archive (BG = the Bill Graham numbered series, Bill Graham Archive); BK = William Kreutzmann; BM = Bob Minkin, Robert Minkin Photography; BMe = Brigid Meier; BO = Bill Owens; BPl = Barry Plummer; BPo = Bruce Polonsky, bpphotography.com; BT = Brad Temkin; BW = Baron Wolman, www.photobaron.com; C = Corbis; CBS = Christie Bourne Segal; CI = © Christie's Images Ltd; CL = City Lights Bookstore; DG = David Gans, www.dgans.com; DH = Derek Hatfield; DK = Dorling Kindersley; DKPL = DK Picture Library; DK/SB = Dorling Kindersley/Private collection of Steve Brown; DL = Dennis Larkins; EP = Ed Perlstein/ MusicImages.com; ES = Eric Schwartz/Lone Star Dead Radio KNON 89.3FM Dallas Texas; EV = Erik Van Ophuijsen; FD = Family Dog (Family Dog Productions is the d.b.a. of Chester L. Helms, 771 Bush Street, San Francisco, California 94108); GA = Gene Anthony; GB = Gary Braasch; GDA = Grateful Dead Archive; GJ = Grant Jacobs; GN = Gregg Nixon/Gregg Nixon Photography; HA = Hulton Archive/Getty Images; HD = Henry Diltz; HDC = Hulton-Deutsch Collection; HG = Herb Greene; HU = Hulogosi; IF = Ian Fry; IWS = Ihor W. Slabicky; JAl = Jeff Albertson; JAn = © Jim Anderson photog.com; JB = Jay Blakesberg, Jay Blakesberg Photography/ www.blakesberg.com; JR = John Rottet; JSi = Jon Sievert; JSu = Julian Sutton; KF = Ken Friedman; KH = Ken Hunt; KP = Kevin R. Papa; LFI = London Features International Ltd; LG = Lynn Goldsmith; LL = Lisa Law (tickets & posters Courtesy Lisa Law); LM = Lee Marshall; MAM = Mary Ann Mayer; MB = Morton Beebe; MC = Mark Currie, www.markcurriestudios.com; MF = courtesy of Michael Frisch www.usfestivals.com; MIJ = Marin Independent Journal; MM = Matthew Mendelsohn; MOA = Michael Ochs Archives.com; MV = Michelle Vignes; MZ = Michael Zagaris; NPo = Norman Parkinson; NPr = Neal Preston; OF = Owen Franken; PB = Photo by Philip Brookstein; Copyright © Suanne C. Skidd. All Rights Reserved; PF = Phil Franks; Copyright © 1970 – 2003 Phil Franks, All Rights Reserved; PG = Philip Gould; PGR = Collection of Paul Grushkin; PL = Pilar Law; PR = Paul Ryan; PSi = Peter Simon; PSILO= reproduced by kind permission of Greg Poulos/ www.psilo.com/dead; PT = Peter Turnley; RAl = Robert Altman, www.altmanphoto.com; RAr = Richard Arridge; RC = Rob Cohn; RD = Ron Delaney; RED = Redferns; RET = Retna Pictures Ltd; REX = Rex Features; RF = Rex Foundation; RH = Rune Hellestad; RM = © Rod Mann; RMa = courtesy of Mr Robert Mallindine; RMcC = Richard McCaffrey; RMcG = Rosie McGee; RP = Richard Peschner; RR = Roger Ressmeyer; SB = Steve Brown; SBCS = Sunset Boulevard/Corbis Sygma; SFC = San Francisco Chronicle; SK = © Suki Coughlin, www.sukicoughlin.com/Dead; SM = Susana Millman, www.mamarazi.com; SS = ©B. Heinrich/Fotex-Shooting Star-CEA; SSch = Steve Schneider; SZ = Susila Ziegler; TC = Terry Cryer; TD = Tony Dwyer; TO = Tim Owen; TP = Getty Images/Timepix; TS = Ted Streshinsky; UI = urbanimage.tv photo agency; VMA = Vin Mag Archive; WC = Westminster Cathedral. BK = Bob Marks.

Picture credits

t = top, b = below, l = left, r = right, c = center, i = inset

Endpapers, DK; 2, C/BE; 3, DK/SB; 4–5, JAn; 7, JB; 9,HG; 10, C/BE; 11br, C/TC; 11bl, tr, HA; 12cr, CL; 12tl, C/AG; 12b, HA; 13t, C/AG; 13b, HA; 14cl, tl, CI; 14tr, bl, C/BE; 15b, C/BE; 15tr, HA; 15tl, AT; 16, HG; 19, BW; 20, BW; 21, BW; 22, BMe; 23, CBS; 24bl, C/AG; 24br, GDA; 24tr, RED; 25r, C/RR; 25bl, C/BE; 26 courtesy of William Kreutzmann; 27, AT; 28, EP; 29tl, GDA; 29tr, JB; 29b, RM; 30br, cr, t, C/AG; 31b, t, GA; 32b, C/TS; 32t, SM; 33, HA; 34bl, C/MB; 34t, MOA/PR; 34cr, RED/HG; 35tr, C/SBCS; 35cr (George Hunter/Michael Ferguson) private collection; 36bl, C/BE; 36cr, BW; 37t, GA; 37b, LL; 38, C/RR; 39all, MOA/PR; 40, GA; 43, BW; 44, GA; 45, GA; 46t, HG; 47br, t, C/TS; 48bc, DK; 48l, GA; 48tl (Wes Wilson) private collection; 49b, tl, tr, GA; 50bl, cr, GA; 50cl, RM; 51br, GA; 51t, RM; 52tl, DK; 52–53tr, RET; 53cr, PGR; 54bl, br, t, HG; 55, HG; 56tr, C/TS; 56l, (Linda Nimmer) PGR; 57r, MIJ; 57l, RMcG; 58bl, (Wes Wilson © 1987) BGA/BG23; 58r, C; 59tr, ED; 59cr, (Alton Kelley/Stanley Mouse) FD22; 60l, (Alton Kelley/Stanley Mouse) FD26; 60b, RED/HG; 61b, cr, tci, tr, GDA; 62cr, tr, GA; 62l, (Alton Kelley/Stanley Mouse) FD33; 63tr, MV; 63cl, clt, SB; 64t, SM; 65bl, cl, cli, GA; 65br, cr, t, LL; 66bl, t, GA; 67, DK; 68bcl, bl, lct, lcb, tl; 68–69t, GA; 69bcl, br, GA; 70bc, bl, ct, GA; 70l, Collection of Dennis King; 71cr, BW; 71l, (Michael Wood/Pyxis Studios) private collection; 72l, C/JA; 72tc, C/TS; 72br, GJ; 72tr, MOA/PR; 73, b, GA; 73tr, (Frank Melton) private collection; 74bl, br, t, GA; 75bl, RED; 75br, MOA; 76br, GA; 76bl, BW; 76cl, (Jim Blashfield) BGA/BG81; 77br, tl, tr, BW; 78tl, 78–79bl, GA; 80r, tri, GA; 80cl, BW; 81ci, cl, tr, GA; 82b, C/NPo; 82cl, SM; 82tl, (Gut) private collection; 83b, BCJ; 83t, C/TS; 84tl, LL; 84b, cr, SB; 85bl, Dennis McNally; 86br, cl, tl, tr, RMcG; 87bl, DK; 87br, cr, RED/MOA; 88, DK; 89tri, bc, br, ci, l, RMcG; 90bl, br, cl, GDA; 91cr, tl, tr, GDA; 92bc, GA; 92bl, BW; 93b, tr, BW; 94tl, GDA; 94b, 94–95t, RMcG; 95tr, RMcG; 96br, c, clt, clb, tl, RMcG; 97bl, LL; 97br, BW; 97t, private collection; 98bl, cl, PB; 99, DK; 100b, DK; 100tr, ED; 101tr, HA; 101clt, clb, tl, LM; 101cr, LL; 101bl, BW; 102b, RMcG; 102t, BW; 103cr, VM; 103tl, tr, BW; 104, DK; 105br, BO; 105bl, cl, RAL; 106, MOA; 109, BW; 110, RED; 111, DL; 112, DK/SB; 113tr, EP; 113b, tl, RAL; 114b, DK/SB; 114tr, EX; 115cl, HA; 115cb, VM; 116, PF; 117br, cr, t, PF; 118, PSi; 119, DK; 120, bl, AP; 120cl, (Daniel Clyne) private collection; 121, GDA/MZ; 122b, C/HD; 122t, DK; 123br, GA; 123bl, TP; 123cl, LM; 124, DK; 125cl, DK; 125tc, RAL; 125cr, tr, AT; 126b, C/HD; 126tl, DK; 126cr, (James Pierce) GDA; 127b, EP; 127t, KP; 128-129b, BK; 128, SM; 130t, JB; 130cl, PSILO; 130bc, bl, RMcG; 131bc, DK/SB; 131ci, t, RMcG; 132–133, RMcG; 134b, DK/SB; 134l, GA; 135c, EP; 135t, JAn; 135b, PSILO; 136tl, DK; 136cr, MAM; 137l, DK; 138bl, tr, GDA; 139cl, DK; 139tc, ES; 139cr, RA; 139tr, (Gary Grimshaw) PGR; 140br, DK; 140tr, MAM; 140bl, RED; 141, DK; 142br, cl, cr, tr, SZ; 142bl, MAM; 143, SZ; 144t, DK; 144bl, br, cr, MAM; 145cri, DK/SB; 145b, cr, MAM; 145tl, tr, BP; 145cl, r, JSu; 146bl,-147, bc, ct, DG; 146tl, private collection; 147br, PSILO; 148l, DK; 148cr, AT; 149bl, br, ci, cl, cr, TD; 150tl, DK; 150cr, GDA; 150b, PSILO; 151t, PSILO; 151b, BK; 152cri, tr, BT; 152b, BK; 153bl, cl, tr, BT; 153br, DK/SB; 153ti, PSILO; 154, BP; 155, b, c, tl, GDA; 155ti, PSILO; 156bl, JB; 156br, BPo; 156tli, PSILO; 156c, RMcG; 156l, private collection; 156–157t, SB; 157c, DK; 157tr, DK/SB; 157b, IWS; 157cl, tl, RMcG; 158, DK; 159b, SK; 159t, DK; 159cl, DK/SB; 159cr, ES; 160tr, DK/SB; 160cl, b, GDA; 161t, DK; 161br, DK/SB; 162cl, t, BPo; 162br, PSILO; 163t, BPo; 163bi, PSILO; 164bl, LL; 164–165c, BPo; 165t, DK; 165b, BPo; 166–167b, MAM; 167t, JAn; 168b, JAn; 168bl, br, SB; 168c, JSi; 169bl, br, tri, EP; 169t, JAn; 169t, SSch; 170c, DK; 170br, DK/SB; 170l, BPo; 171t, DK; 171bl, DK/SB; 172, DK; 173t, DG; 173br, tri, DK/SB; 174br, DK/SB; 174tr, JAn; 174c, (Gunther Kieser); 175bi, DK/SB; 175b, BK; 176, RMcC; 177t, DK; 177bc, br, EP; 178, DK; 179bl, tr, DK; 179cl, PSi; 180bl, c, tl, tr, DK/SB; 181t, DK; 181br, DK/SB; 182br, C/RR; 182tl, DK; 182brt, cr, cr, EP; 182c, courtesy of EP; 183b, EP; 183ct, tr, SB; 184bl, EP; 184br, courtesy of EP; 184, courtesy of JB t x4; 185c, l, DK; 186, TP; 189, JB; 190, EP; 191, JB; 192br, EP; 192t, TP; 193b, BM; 193t, DK; 194br, BM; 194c, cli, tr, EP; 195cr, JAn; 195bl, br, KP; 195t, JSi; 196–197, JAn; 198bl, ct, EP; 198cl/199b, RMcC; 199ci, BM; 199ct, EP; 199br, cr, RMcC; 200tc, DG; 200b, tl, EP; 201b, tri, DG; 201t, EP; 202bl, br, t, EP; 203cr, DK/SB; 203tl, EP; 204t, EP; 204bl, BPo; 205bi, BM; 205ct, tl, JAn; 205br, KP; 206li, BM; 206t, JAn; 206b, PSi; 207br, t, EP; 207bl, PSi; 208tl, DK; 208br, DK/SB; 208bl, PSILO; 209c, tc, AS; 209br, EP; 209tr, LL; 210, JAn; 211tc, DK; 211cl, PSILO; 212cr, BM; 212tl, JAn; 212cl, PSILO; 212b, SM; 213b, tc, tl, RMcC; 214t, LL; 214ci, MC; 215cl, DK; 215tr, EP; 215br, BPo; 216bl, BM; 216br, EP; 217, DK; 218b, EP; 218tl, tr, JAn; 219clb, crb, t, EP; 220cl, 221b, 221t, BPo; 220ci, PSILO; 221tr, BPo; 221c, PSILO; 222clt, RAr; 222b, bl, br1, br2, c, ct, cb, cl, tc, tl, IF; 223b, t, IF; 224–225t, JAn; 224tc, KP; 224bl, LFI; 224ci, PSILO; 224–225b, UI; 225tr, EP; 225br, BPo; 226, DK; 227bl, cr, EP; 227cl, RMcC; 228bci, br, cri, BM; 228cl, JAn; 228t, SSch; 229cr, EP; 229bl, Jan; 229c, private collection; 230b, C/RR; 230tr, ED/HG; 231bli, DK/SB; 231bl, br, c, cl, t, tr, EP; 232b, cl, JB; 232–233t, BPo; 233b, BM; 233cr, DK/SB; 234tl, tr, EP; 234b, DL; 235t, AS; 235bl, br, c, C/RR; 236bl, br, cl, cr, 237t, JB; 237tr, BM; 237b, JB; 237ci, PSILO; 238tl, DK/SB; 238tr, JB; 238bl, br, RMcC; 239bri, DK/SB; 239b, DL; 239cl, cr, RMcC; 240bri, main, JB; 241bl, cl, cr, C/RR; 241tr, DK; 241br, SM; 242bl, DK; 242tl, EP; 242cr, tr, JB; 242br, KP; 242crb, PSILO; 243b, C/RR; 243t, DK; 244, C/RR; 247, RAl; 248, BW; 249, JB; 250crb, C/NPr; 250bl, br, cl, tr, JB; 250c, crt, tc, PSILO; 251b, C/GB; 251t, JB; 251cr, GDA; 252bl, DKPL; 252c, cr, tl, tr, JB; 252br, MAM; 252cl, PSILO; 253bl, br, JB; 253bcr, cl, PSILO; 253tr, SFC; 254c, clt, clb, tl, JB; 254crt, DL; 254cb, cli, PSILO; 254–255l, SM; 255bri, DK; 255bc, JB; 255cr, JAn; 255ct, DL; 255br, tr, PSILO; 256tl, C; 256cr, tr, HA; 256bc, cl, PSILO; 257bl, br, cl, t, JB; 258, JB; 259cr, t, JB; 260cr, DK; 260tl, JB; 260bc, JAn; 260bl, clt, clb, PSILO; 261t, DK; 261b, DK; 262bl, C/LG; 262cr, t, tri, SM; 263tl, C/LG; 263tr, MC; 263br, clt, cli, cr, SM; 264br, C/NPr; 264cli, tc, ES; 264cl, PSILO; 264tl, SM; 265cl, DK; 265tl, tr, ES; 266ct, AS; 266bl, br, BM; 266cl, tr, EP; 266cb, PSILO; 267cl, cr, tl, BM; 267bc, PSILO; 268tl, tr, C/RR; 268cl, DK; 268bc, courtesy of KH; 269b, JB; 269tr, made by LL; 270bl, br, cr, t, JB; 271tr, BM; 271bl, JB; 271cl, tcl, ci, PSILO; 272br, tl, GN; 272cr, KP; 272cl, (Jim Pinkoski) PGR; 272tr, PSILO; 273bc, DK; 273t, GN; 273bl, br, PSILO; 274bl, t, JB; 274bc, PSILO; 275br, BM; 275bl, tr, JB; 275cri, cli, PSILO; 276t, BM; 276bl, C/RR; 276tr, (Michael Priest) GDA; 276cr, tli, PSILO; 277tl, BM; 277bc, C/RR; 277br, PSILO; 278bl, AP; 278crt, crb, C/LG; 278–29tl, courtesy of MF; 279br, JB; 279bri, cr, tr, LL; 279cl, button made by LL; 279tl, (DL/D. Sawyer); 280cr, tl, DK; 280bl, PSi; 281bl, br, cl, cr, tl, tr, DG; 282, KF; 283tci, tri, JR; 283 background, bl, clb, crt, crb, SM; 284bl, cb, cr, tr, EP; 284cti, crb, ES; 284bli, MC; 285br, EP; 285cbl, ES; 285t, MC; 286br, BM; 286tli, DK; 286bl, DK; 286c, cl, 287t, EP; 286cbi, ES; 287rct, tr, EP; 287ci, ES; 287cl, PSILO; 287bl, SM; 288bc, DKPL; 288r ,tl, SM; 289tl, DK; 289bl, br, c, ctr, crt, ES; 289crb, MC; 290b, cl, LL; 290crt, crb, tr, ES; 291bl, cl, EP; 291cr, JAn; 292br, C/BE; 292bl, ES; 292cl, tl, tr, MC; 292ci, SM; 293li, main, JB; 294bl, DG; 294cr, t, MC; 295bl, clb, PL; 295cr, RF; 295cb, RMcG; 295tr, SM; 296br, JAn; 296tl, LL; 296tr, MC; 296bl, PGR; 297bc, DK; 297cr, tc, EV; 297cl, tr, JAn; 298tl, DK; 298bc, JB; 298crt, crb, JAn; 299b, cl, JAn; 300bl, C/BE; 300cb, C/NPr; 300cr, C/PG; 301b, C/PG; 300cl, EV; 300tr, SM; 301tc, DK; 301tl, DK; 302tr, fanzines, DK; 302bl, ES; 303cti, EV; 303bl, br, tl, JAn; 303cr, SM; 304tl, tr, BM; 304c, courtesy of LL; 304bl, br, SM; 305bc, c, cr, tli, JAn; 305clt, tr, MC; 305bl, SM; 306bl, br, clt, clb, crt, crb, tl, tr, JAn; 307tr, tri, MC; 307br, tl, SM; 308tl, DK; 308ci, clt, EV; 308bl, br, tc, RC; 309tl, C/BE; 309cri, EV; 309ct, RC; 309br, RMcG; 310cl, ES; 310b, RC; 310t, SM; 310cr, (Gary Kroman) Les Kippel/*Relix* magazine; 311tr, BM; 311tl, GDA; 311b, RC; 312tl, DK; 312crt, tcr, EV; 312ct, tr, PSILO; 312bl, br, RMcG; 313, RC; 314ct, DK; 314br, c, RC; 315tr, BM; 315bl, C/Hulton-Deutsch Collection; 315br, DKPL; 315ci, cr, EV; 315tl, PSILO; 316cb, AS; 316bl, br, tr, DK; 316ct, tl, JR; 317tl, EV; 317r, JB; 317clt, cb, RMcG; 318tl, 319,bl, JB; 320bl, C/PG; 320br, t, JB; 321cl, DK; 321bl1, bl2 ,tr1, tr2, tr3, EV; 321br all, HU; 321bc, cr, RD; 322bl, C/RR; 322tr, JAn; 322br, RC; 323cl, trb, EV; 323bc, br, JB; 323trt, PSILO; 323tc, RC; 324bli, DK; 324tl, EV; 324br, JB; 324tr, RMcG; 325crt, tr, EV; 325ct, crb, JB; 325bl, br, tc, RMcG; 326br, RED; 326cl, t, SM; 327cl, tr, AS; 327br, DK; 327bl, JB; 327crt, PSILO; 327crb, SM; 328ct, tc, BM; 328bl, r, 329l, JB; 328cl, JR; 329r, DK; 330cl, tr, JB; 331b, c, crb, cri, ct, JB; 332main, tli, JB; 333tc, DK; 333cb, clb, cr, JB; 333clt, PSILO; 334bc, bl, cr, lc, 335t, JB; 335tr, DK; 335br, cb, cr, KP; 336b, tr, BM; 336cr, JB; 337bl, cl, JB; 337cr, tr, SM; 338, KF; 340, SM; 341, HG; 343, BW; 344bl, crb, BM; 344crt, tl, JB; 344br, LL; 345l, DK; 346br, ct, cl, SM; 347cl, DK; 347ct, cr, tr, JB; 348b, c, tl, tr, JB; 349br, cl, JB; 349ri, PL; 349t, SM; 350bl, JB; 350t, 351b, SM; 351ct, C/LG; 351br, JB; 351cr, DK/WC; 351cl, PL; 352t, DK; 352l, JB; 352br, JR; 353tr, DK; 353cl, JAn; 353bc, br, PL; 354cl, t, DK; 354tr, EV; 354br, cb, tr, JB; 355cr, tr, AS; 355c1, DK; 355c2, c3, c4, DK; 355tl, EV; 356tl, AS; 356cri, 357t, C/PG; 356bl, DKPL; 356c, EV; 356br, JB;

357cl, AS; 357c1, c2, cb, PL; 357br, PSILO; 357cr, TO; 358cl, BM; 358tr, KP; 358tl, SM; 359clt, tl, BM; 359cb, cr, JB; 360ct, C/Royalty-Free; 360tl, DK; 360cb1, EV; 360c, LL; 360cb2, PSILO; 361tri, GA; 361t main, JB; 361bl, LL; 361bc, PL; 362, JB; 363c, DK; 363t, EV; 364crt, crb, BM; 364cbi,EV; 364c, JB; 364bl, JR; 365cb, DK; 365c, tl, EV; 365tr, JB; 365cl1, cl2, PSILO; 366tl, C/RR; 366br, tc, JB; 366, rattle made by LL; 366bl, LL; 366tr, PL; 367cb, PL; 367cr, t, SM; 368cl, GN; 368b, JAn; 369tl, SM; 370bl, DK; 370tr, JAn; 371br, tl, DK; 372cr, C/S.I.N.; 372bl, tl, DK; 372br, PL; 373b, JB; 373cli, cri, PL; 373tc, SM; 374, JB; 375clt, C/OF; 375clb, C/PT; 375tr, JB; 375cri, PL; 375b, SM; 376l, C/NPr; 376–377t, JAn; 377bl, BM; 377br, DK; 377bc, JB; 377cr1, LL; 377cl, cr2, cr3, SM; 378cl, BM; 378br, DK; 378–379t, JB; 378cr, PL; 379cli, BM; 379bl, JB; 379cr, tr, SM; 380r, JR; 380l, SM; 381l, DK; 381br, GN; 381tr, SM; 382cl, DK; 382t, GDA; 383br, JR; 383bl, ci, SM; 383tr, SS; 384tr, DK; 384b, c, JR; 385b, BM; 385tl1, tl2, tl3, DK; 385cl, JB; 386b, PG; 386t, C/PG; 387br, C/BE; 387bl, JSi; 387tl, SM; 388t, DK; 389r all, DK; 389l, SM; 390b, C/HD; 390t, DK; 391bl, br, tr, AS; 392cl, CLG; 392br, DK; 392tr, SM; 393bl, tr, DK; 393tl, SM; 394t, JB; 394b, SM; 395c, C/NPr; 395bl, DG; 395tr, DK; 396tl, DK; 396bl, JB; 396br, SM; 397tl, DK; 397bl, DK/SB; 397br, JB; 397cri, PL; 397cl, clt, SM; 398, JB; 399bc, DK; 399tc, PL; 399br, tli, SM; 400cl, cr, EV; 400b, JAn; 401b, RMa; 401t, JAn; 402tl, DK; 402cr, MC; 403cri, t main, tri, JAn; 404br, cri, DH; 404tr, DK/SB; 404cl, JB; 405, REX; 405ci, SM; 406l, tr, BM; 406br, DK; 407, SM; 408br, BM; 408bl, JB; 408cri, LL; 408cli, PSILO; 409b, BM; 409ct, cl, tl, JB; 410, JB; 411bl, C/HD; 411br, tr, JB; 411ci, PL; 411bc, SM; 412b, DK; 412c, EV; 413tl, DK; 413tr, DK/SB; 413b, JB; 413c, SM; 414br, C/MM; 414tl, JB; 414c, PL; 414cli, SM; 415tl, AS; 415bl, C/MM; 415tr, JAn; 415br, PSILO; 416b, DK; 416tr1, tr2, EV; 416tl, TO; 417cl, DK; 417cr, EV; 417tr, JB; 417b, TO; 418bl, br, cl, JAn; 419c, cr, AS; 419br, DK; 419bl, JAn; 419cl, JR; 4211 all, DK; 421tr, GDA; 422–423bl, SM; 423cr, DK; 423br, EV; 424br, AS; 424bl, tl, 425b, SM; 425tr, GN; 425cri, JAn; 426b1, b2, b3, EV; 426t, SM; 427cl, EV; 427crt, PSILO; 427b, cr, SM; 428b, JAn; 429c, AS; 429bl, C/HD; 429ct, JAn; 430br, DK; 430bl, JB; 430tl, JAn; 430–431t, SM; 431bc, bl, AS; 432tl, DK; 432cl, 433b, JAn; 433tr1, tr2, EV; 433cr, JAn; 434t, JB; 434bl, br, SM; 435c, DKPL; 435clt, clb, EV; 435b, tr, SM; 436bcl, ci, AS; 436br, EV; 436bl, GN; 436–437t, JAn; 437ct, DK; 437br, GDA; 437cl, PSILO; 438b, cl, tl, SM; 439cbi, DK/SB; 439t, SM; 439cl, cli, SM; 440c, tr, JAn; 441tl, tr, JB; 441b, LL; 442bl, tr, EP; 442tl, JB; 442br, SM; 443tr, BM; 443bl, EP; 443br, tl, SM; 444–445, RED/MOA; 446, REX; 447ct, DK; 447b, GA; 448, JB; 450, JB; 451, JB; 452bc, br, cl, cr, DK; 452t, JB; 453cl, cr, DK; 453bl, c, EP; 454c, AS; 454bl, JB; 454cr, cri, tl, SM; 455tr, BM; 455bc, br, cr, DK; 455cl, JB; 456t, AS; 456b, cr, DK; 457bl, t, DK; 458cl, tl, DK; 458br, tl, JB; 459t, DK; 459bc, bl, JB; 460b, DK; 460cl, tl, JB; 461cr, tc, DK; 461cl, JB; 462bl, BM; 462cli, tl, tr, JB; 463all, DK; 464l, DK; 464r, SM; 465tr, DK; 465bl, br, tl, SM; 466c, t, BM; 466b, SM; 467b, JB; 467lt, lb, JAn; 468tc, tl, tr, JAn; 469b, JAn.

Background montages
Section 1: C/AG, HDC, TS, BE, RH
Section 2: all images GA
Section 3: BPo/BT/RP
Section 4: JAn/RMcC
Section 5: LL/SM
Section 6: JB
Section 7: JB/BM/SM

Additional Picture Credits (reissue)
The publisher would like to thank the following for their kind permission to reproduce their photographs:

468 Corbis: Erik Kabik / Retna Ltd. (tr). **Getty Images:** Erika Goldring (c); David McNew (cla); Jay West (bl). **469 Stanley Mouse**

All other images © Dorling Kindersley
For further information see: www.dkimages.com

Bibliography

Online Sources
www.accessplace.com/gdtc (GD timelines); www.accessplace.com/grateful.htm (Directory of GD sites); www.alembic.com; www.allmusic.com; arts.ucsc.edu/gdead/agdl (Annotated Grateful Dead lyrics); www.blairjackson.com; www.deadbase.com; www.deaddisc.com; www.deadlists.com; www.dead.net; www.diggers.org; www.geocities.com/weirheads/weirworks; www.jambands.com; www.philzone.com; www.pranksterweb.org; www.psilo.com/dead (Dead ephemera); www.ratdog.org; www.relix.com; www.rollingstone.com/reviews/cd; www.sfmuseum.org/hist1/rock.html (SF rock in the '60s); tcgdd.freeyellow.com/tcgdd.txt (Ihor W. Slabicky's site); www.thejerrysite.com

Print Sources
Adams & Sardiello, *Deadhead Social Science*, AltaMira Press, 2000
Bisbort & Puterbaugh, *Rhino's Psychedelic Trip*, Backbeat Books, 2000
Blakesberg, *Between the Dark and the Light*, Backbeat Books, 2000
Boyer, Clark, Kett, Salisbury, Sitkoff, Wolock, *The Enduring Vision—A History Of The American People—Vol 2*, DC Heath Co, 1996
Brightman, *Sweet Chaos*, Pocket Books, 1998
Brandelius, *Grateful Dead Family Album*, Warner Books, 1998
Constanten, *Between Rock & Hard Places*, Hulogosi, 1992
Crampton and Rees, *Q Rock Stars*, Dorling Kindersley, 1999
Dodd & Spaulding, *The Grateful Dead Reader*, Oxford University Press, 2000
Gans & Simon, *Playing in the Band*, St. Martin's Press, 2000
Gans, *Conversations with the Dead*, Citadel Press, 1991
Getz & Dwork, *Deadhead's Taping Compendiums, Vols. 1–3*, Owl Books, 1998, 1999, and 2000
Graham and Greenfield, *My Life Inside Rock and Out*, Doubleday, 1992
Greenfield, *Dark Star: An Oral Biography of Jerry Garcia*, Broadway Books, 1996
Grushkin, *The Art of Rock*, Cross River Press, 1987
Grushkin et al, *Grateful Dead: The Official Book of the Deadheads*, William Morrow, 1993
Harrison, *The Dead*, Celestial Arts, 1980
Harrison, *The Dead Book*, Links, 1973
Hayes, *Deadhead Forever*, Running Press, 2001
Henke (ed) with Puterbaugh, *I Want To Take You Higher—The Psychedelic Era 1965–1969*, Chronicle Books, 1997
Hunter, *A Box of Rain*, Viking, 1990
Jackson, *Garcia: An American Life*, Viking Penguin, 1999
McDonough, *San Francisco Rock 1965–1985*, Chronicle Books, 1986
McNally, *A Long Strange Trip*, Bantam Press, 2002
Perry, "From Eternity to Here" (*Rolling Stone* article)
Peters, *What a Long Strange Trip: The Stories Behind Every Grateful Dead Song 1965–1995*, Carlton Books, 1999
Rolling Stone eds., *Garcia*, Little, Brown and Company, 1996
Scott, Dolgushkin, Nixon, et al, *DeadBase X*, Deadbase, 1997
Sculatti and Seay, *San Francisco Nights—Psychedelic Music Trip*, St. Martin's Press, 1985
Scully & Dalton, *Living With the Dead*, Little, Brown and Company, 1995
Selvin, *Summer of Love*, Plume/Penguin, 1994
Shenk & Silberman, *Skeleton Key: A Dictionary for Deadheads*, Doubleday, 1994
Trager, *The American Book of the Dead*, Simon & Schuster, 1997
Wolfe, *The Electric Kool-Aid Acid Test*, Bantam Doubleday Dell, 1968
Wright (ed), *The New York Times Almanac 2002*, Penguin, 2001

Dark Star magazine, *Guitar Player, Melody Maker, New Musical Express, Record Collector, Relix, Rolling Stone, San Francisco Chronicle, The Golden Road, 20/20, Uncut, Zigzag.*

Topical references and current affairs were mainly sourced from DK's *Chronicle of America* and *Chronicle of the World.*

Acknowledgments

The publishers would like to acknowledge and thank the following, without whose enthusiasm, support, and encouragement this project would never have been completed:
Alan Sheckter; Alan Trist; Andrew Sclanders; Ann Kramer; Baron Wolman; Blair Jackson; Bob Minkin; Brian Goodman (Fat Tyre); Brigid Meier; British Library Newspaper Library; Bruce Polonsky; Cameron Sears; Carolyn Garcia (Mountain Girl); Chris Jones; Chuck Wills; Courtney Kisat; Craig Miller; Daniel Clark; David Gans; Dennis Barsotti; Dennis Larkins; Dennis McNally; Ed Perlstein; Eileen Law; Eric Schwartz, Lone Star Radio KNON 89.3FM, Dallas; Erik Van Ophuijsen; Gary Ombler; Gene Anthony; Greg Poulos at Psilo.com; Gregg Nixon; Hamza El-Din; Herb Greene; Ian Fry; Ihor W. Slabicky; James Swift; Jason Colton; Jay Blakesberg; Jim Anderson; John Rottet; Jon Sievert; Justin Kreutzmann; Ken Babbs; Ken Friedman; Ken Hunt; Kevin R. Papa; Lee Marshall; Les Kippel; Lisa Law; Mark Currie; Mary Ann Mayer; Michael Getz; Owsley Stanley; Peter Barsotti; Peter Golding and Louisa Pead; Peter Simon; Pilar Law; Richard McCaffrey; Rob Cohn; Robert Altman; Robert Minkin; Rosie McGee; Stephen Peters; Steven Bernstein; Steve Brown; Steve Silberman; Stuart Hirsch (Buzzyman); Susana Millman; Tom Constanten; Tom Salter; Toni Brown; Vicki Arkoff; Vintage Magazine; Wavy Gravy.

Dorling Kindersley would also like to thank the following, whose dedication to completing a vast undertaking on a surreal schedule cannot be underestimated:
Anita Ruddell; Bob Warner; Bryn Walls; Caroline Quiroga; Caroline Reid; Christine Heilman; Dave Almond; David Lloyd; Dean Scholey; Emily Wilkinson; Helen Grainge; Jake Woodward; Janet Gibbs; Jerry Udall; Jo Bull; Katie Dock; Kingsley Abbott; Konrad Chee; Louise Dick; Mabel Chan; Margaret McCormack; Mark Preston; Maria Gibbs; Michelle Crane; Nick Forro; Phil Gamble; Phil Hunt; Rob Damon; Sam Atkinson; Sarah Coltman; Scott Stickland; Sophie Cash; Steven Chan; Victoria Clark; Victoria Heyworth-Dunne; Wendy Penn.

Dennis McNally's personal thanks
I would like to thank Andrew Heritage, the book's Publisher, for the chance to work on this project; everyone on the team for being great, especially Vicky, Victoria, Chuck, David, Mabel, Phil G., Phil H., Michelle, Dean, Jerry, and Jake; Blair for being a priceless cohort; and, as always, Susana Millman, for being an artist. Also Jerry, for being an inspiration.

Stephen Peters' personal thanks
Thanks to my mother Dolores Peters; my partner Teresa Mason; my chum and colleague Vicki Arkoff for hooking me up; the great team at DK, including Jake Woodward, Andrew Heritage, and Victoria Heyworth-Dunne; and all the souls from California to Ohio and back who made the journey with me. This one's in memory of my father Don Peters and friend Marc Perkins, one of the kindest Deadheads the world has ever known—tell Jerry and the gang we said "hi."

Chuck Wills' personal thanks
My thanks to all who traveled the Golden Road before us, and left the signs we followed; to the dude who made me my first tape twenty-odd years ago and thus got me on the bus that brought me here; to Andrew Heritage, for keeping the faith; to Jake Woodward and the rest of the team that put this book together—true exemplars of "Misfit Power"; to the Poker/Pond Cottage Group, for so many years of friendship and support (sorry we couldn't fit in all of your "personal reflections," guys); and most of all to Rachel K, without whose encouragement, patience, and all-around kindness I would never have made it through.